The Square and the Tower

NIALL FERGUSON

The Square and the Tower

Networks, Hierarchies and the Struggle for Global Power

ALLEN LANE
an imprint of
PENGUIN BOOKS

ALLEN LANE

UK | USA | Canada | Ireland | Australia
India | New Zealand | South Africa

Allen Lane is part of the Penguin Random House group of companies
whose addresses can be found at global.penguinrandomhouse.com

First published 2017
003

Set in 10.5/14 pt Sabon LT Std
Typeset by Jouve (UK), Milton Keynes
Printed in Great Britain by Clays Ltd, St Ives plc

A CIP catalogue record for this book is available from the British Library

Hardback ISBN: 978–0–241–29046–0

Trade paperback ISBN: 978–0–241–29898–5

www.greenpenguin.co.uk

Penguin Random House is committed to a sustainable future for our business, our readers and our planet. This book is made from Forest Stewardship Council® certified paper.

'If I broke [my silence], the strength would depart from me; but while I held my peace, I held my foe in an invisible mesh.'

George MacDonald

Contents

PART III
Letters and Lodges

PART IV
The Restoration of Hierarchy

PART V
Knights of the Round Table

PART VI
Plagues and Pipers

PART VII
Own the Jungle

PART VIII
The Library of Babel

PART IX
Conclusion: Facing Cyberia

Illustrations

Plates

copyright © 2011 by Princeton University Press. Reprinted by permission of Princeton University Press)

12. George Washington as a Freemason (lithograph), American school, nineteenth century. (private collection/Bridgeman Images)
13. 'Le Gateau des Rois' (hand-coloured engraving), French school, nineteenth century. (private collection/The Stapleton Collection/ Bridgeman Images)
14. Angoulême. (Courtesy Emma Rothschild)
15. The Eastern Telegraph Co.'s network, 1894. (Copyright © The Porthcurno Collections Trust, by kind permission of the Telegraph Museum, Porthcurno)
16. 'The Anti-Chinese Wall' by Friedrich Gratz, from *Puck* (1882)
17. Europe in 1914: a German satirical map. (bpk-Bildagentur/Art Resource, NY)
18. First edition of John Buchan's *Greenmantle*.
19. Stalin as helmsman. (Universal History Archive/UIG/Bridgeman Images)
20. Isaiah Berlin and Anna Akhmatova, Leningrad, November 1945, by Leopold Plotek. (*Berlin and Akhmatova, Leningrad '45* (2005) (oil on canvas), 77 cm x 65 cm, copyright © Leopold Plotek)
21. Page from *First Military Conscription and What it Means to You!*
22. Steve Jobs and Bill Gates, 1991. (George Lange/Contour by Getty Images)
23. Stan Druckenmiller and George Soros, 1992. (Peter Morgan/ REUTERS)
24. The 9/11 plotter's network. (From Valdis E. Krebs, 'Mapping Networks of Terrorist Cells', *Connections*, 24, 3 (2002), 43–52. Copyright © 2002 by INSNA. Reprinted by permission)
25. graph of the global export 'product space'. (From the Center for International Development at Harvard University. Reprinted by permission)
26. 'Trumpworld'. (From Michael Hunger, 'Analyzing the BuzzFeed TrumpWorld Dataset with Neo4j' (19 January 2017))
27. Facebook headquarters and Trump Tower. (Jeff Hall Photography (top) and ErikN/123RF, LLC (bottom)

Preface: The Networked Historian

We live in a networked world, or so we are constantly told. The word 'network', which was scarcely used before the late nineteenth century, is now overused as both a verb and a noun. To the ambitious young insider, it is always worth going to the next party, no matter how late it is, for the sake of networking. Sleep may be appealing, but the fear of missing out is appalling. To the disgruntled old outsider, on the other hand, the word network has a different connotation. The suspicion grows that the world is controlled by powerful and exclusive networks: the bankers, the Establishment, the System, the Jews, the Freemasons, the Illuminati. Nearly all that is written in this vein is rubbish. Yet it seems unlikely that conspiracy theories would be so persistent if such networks did not exist at all.

The problem with conspiracy theorists is that, as aggrieved outsiders, they invariably misunderstand and misrepresent the way that networks operate. In particular, they tend to assume that elite networks covertly and easily control formal power structures. My research – as well as my own experience – suggests that this is not the case. On the contrary, informal networks usually have a highly ambivalent relationship to established institutions, and sometimes even a hostile one. Professional historians, by contrast, have until very recently tended to ignore, or at least to downplay, the role of networks. Even today, the majority of academic historians tend to study the kinds of institution that create and preserve archives, as if those that do not leave an orderly paper trail simply do not count. Again, my research and my experience have taught me to beware the tyranny of the archives. Often the biggest changes in history are the achievements of thinly documented, informally organized groups of people.

This book is about the uneven ebb and flow of history. It distinguishes the long epochs in which hierarchical structures dominated human life from the rarer but more dynamic eras when networks had the advantage, thanks in part to changes in technology. To put it simply: when hierarchy is the order of the day, you are only as powerful as your rung on the organizational ladder of a state, corporation or similar vertically ordered institution. When networks gain an advantage, you can be as powerful as your position in one or more horizontally structured social groups. As we shall see, this dichotomy between hierarchy and network is an over-simplification. Nevertheless, some personal disclosures may illustrate its usefulness as a starting point.

On the night in February 2016 when I wrote the first draft of this preface, I attended a book party. The host was the former mayor of New York. The author whose work we had gathered to celebrate was a *Wall Street Journal* columnist and former presidential speech-writer. I was there at the invitation of the editor-in-chief of Bloomberg News, whom I know because we attended the same Oxford college more than a quarter of a century ago. At the party, I greeted and briefly conversed with about ten other people, among them the president of the Council on Foreign Relations; the chief executive officer of Alcoa Inc., one of America's largest industrial companies; the editor of the *Journal*'s comment pages; a presenter on Fox News; a member of New York's Colony Club and her husband; and a young speech-writer who introduced himself by saying he had read one of my books (which is without fail the right way to strike up a conversation with a professor).

At one level, it is obvious why I was at that party. The fact that I have worked at a succession of well-known universities – Oxford, Cambridge, New York, Harvard and Stanford – automatically makes me part of multiple webs of college alumni. As a consequence of my work as a writer and professor, I have also joined a number of economic and political networks such as the World Economic Forum and the Bilderberg meetings. I am a member of three London clubs and one in New York. I presently belong to the boards of three corporate entities: one a global asset manager, one a British think tank, one a New York museum.

And yet, despite being relatively well networked, I have almost no power. An interesting feature of the party was that the former mayor took the opportunity, in his short speech of welcome, to hint (not very enthusiastically) that he was considering entering, as an independent candidate, the contest to choose the next US president. But as a British citizen I could not even vote in that election. Nor would an endorsement from me in any way have helped his or any other candidate's chances. For, as an academic, I am assumed by the overwhelming majority of Americans to be wholly detached from the real lives of ordinary people. Unlike my former colleagues at Oxford, I do not control undergraduate admissions. When I taught at Harvard, I could award good or mediocre grades to my students, but I had essentially no power to prevent even the weakest of them from graduating. I had just one among many senior faculty votes when it came to Ph.D. admissions; again, no power. I have a measure of power over the people who work for my advisory firm, but in the space of five years I have fired a grand total of one employee. I am a father of four, but my influence – never mind power – over three of these children is minimal. Even the youngest, who is five, is already learning how to defy my authority.

In short, I am just not a very hierarchical person. By choice, I am more of a networks guy. As an undergraduate, I enjoyed the lack of stratification in university life, particularly the multitude of haphazardly organized societies. I joined many and turned up, irregularly, to few. My two favourite experiences at Oxford were playing the double bass in a jazz quintet – an ensemble that to this day prides itself on not having a leader – and participating in the meetings of a small conservative discussion club called the Canning. I opted to become an academic because in my early twenties I strongly preferred freedom to money. Seeing my contemporaries and their fathers employed in traditional, vertical management structures, I shuddered. Observing the Oxford dons who taught me – fellows of a medieval corporate entity, citizens of an ancient republic of letters, sovereigns in their book-lined studies – I had an irresistible urge to follow in their leisurely, leathery footsteps. When academic life turned out to be rather less well remunerated than the women in my life seemed to expect, I strove to earn without submitting to the indignity of real employment. As a journalist, I preferred to be a freelance, at most a part-timer, preferably a columnist on a retainer. When I turned to broadcasting, I wrote and presented as an independent contractor, and later formed my own production company. Entrepreneurship has suited my love of freedom, though I would say that I have founded companies more to remain free than to become rich. The thing I enjoy most is writing books about subjects that interest me. The best projects – the history of the Rothschild banks, the career of Siegmund Warburg, the life of Henry Kissinger – have come to me through my network. Only very recently did I appreciate that they were also books *about* networks.

Some among my contemporaries pursued wealth; few achieved it without at least a period of indentured servitude, usually working for a bank. Others pursued power; they too rose through the party ranks and must marvel today at the indignities they once endured. There are humiliations in the early years of academic life, no doubt, but nothing to compare with being an intern at Goldman Sachs or a lowly campaign volunteer for the losing candidate of a party in opposition. To enter the hierarchy is to abase oneself, at least at first. Today, however, a few of my Oxford classmates sit atop powerful institutions as ministers or chief executives. Their decisions can directly affect the allocation of millions, if not billions, of dollars and sometimes even the fates of nations. The wife of an Oxford contemporary who entered politics once complained to him about his long working hours, lack of privacy, low salary and rare holidays – as well as the job insecurity inherent in democracy. 'But the fact that I would put up with all that,' he replied, 'just proves what a *wonderful* thing power is.'

But is it? Is it better today to be in a network, which gives you influence, than in a hierarchy, which gives you power? Which better describes your own position? All of us are necessarily members of more than one hierarchical structure. We are nearly all citizens of at least one state. A very large proportion of us are employees of at least one corporation (and a surprisingly large number of the world's corporations are still directly or indirectly state-controlled). Most people under the age of twenty in the developed world are now likely to be in one kind of educational institutional or another; whatever these institutions may claim, their structure is fundamentally hierarchical.

(True, the president of Harvard has very limited power over a tenured professor; but she and the hierarchy of deans beneath her have a great deal of power over everyone else from the brightest junior professor to the lowliest freshman.) A significant proportion of young men and women around the world – albeit a much lower one than in most of the last forty centuries – are engaged in military service, traditionally the most hierarchical of activities. If you 'report to' someone, even if it is only to a board of directors, then you are in a hierarchy. The more people report to you, the further you are from the bottom of the heap.

Yet most of us belong to more networks than hierarchies, and by that I do not just mean that we are on Facebook, Twitter or one of the other computer-based networks that have sprung up on the Internet in the past dozen years. We have networks of relatives (few families in the Western world today are hierarchical), of friends, of neighbours, of fellow enthusiasts. We are alumni of educational institutions. We are fans of football teams. We are members of clubs and societies, or supporters of charities. Even our participation in the activities of hierarchically structured institutions such as churches or political parties is more akin to networking than to working, because we are involved on a voluntary basis and not in the expectation of cash compensation.

The worlds of hierarchies and networks meet and interact. Inside any large corporation there are networks quite distinct from the official 'org. chart'. When a boss is accused by some employees of favouritism, the implication is that some informal relationships are taking precedence over the formal promotion process managed by 'Human Resources' on the fifth floor. When employees from different firms meet for alcoholic refreshments after work, they move from the vertical tower of the corporation to the horizontal square of the social network. Crucially, when a group of individuals meets, each one of whom has power in a different hierarchical structure, their networking can have profound consequences. In his Palliser novels, Anthony Trollope memorably captured the difference between formal power and informal influence when he depicted Victorian politicians publicly denouncing each other in the House of Commons and then privately exchanging confidences in the network of London clubs to which they all belonged. In this book, I want to show that such networks can be found in nearly all human history and that they are much more important than most history books lead their readers to believe.

In the past, as I mentioned already, historians were not especially good at reconstructing past networks. The neglect of networks was partly because traditional historical research relied heavily for its source material on the documents produced by hierarchical institutions such as states. Networks do keep records, but they are not so easy to find. As a very green graduate student, I remember arriving at the Hamburg State Archives and being directed towards a bewildering room full of *Findbücher* – the huge leather-bound volumes, handwritten in scarcely legible old German script, that constituted the archive's catalogue. These in turn led to the innumerable reports, minute books and correspondence produced by all the different 'deputations' of the Hanseatic city-state's somewhat antiquated bureaucracy. I vividly recall leafing through the books that corresponded to the period I was interested in and, to my horror, finding not a single page that was of the slightest interest. Imagine my intense relief, after a few weeks of abject misery, to be shown into the small, oak-panelled room that housed the private papers of the banker Max Warburg, whose son Eric I had met by sheer good luck at a tea party at the British consulate. Within a few hours, I realized that Warburg's correspondence with members of his own network offered more insight into the history of the German hyperinflation of the early 1920s (my chosen topic) than all the documents in the *Staatsarchiv* put together.

Yet for many years, like most historians, I was casual in the way that I thought and wrote about networks. In my mind's eye, there was a vague diagram that connected Warburg to other members of the German-Jewish business elite through various ties of kinship, business and 'elective affinity'. But it did not occur to me to think in a rigorous way about that network. I was content to think, lazily, of his social 'circles', a very imperfect term of art. And I am afraid I was not much more systematic when I came, a few years later, to write the history of the interlocked Rothschild banks. I focused too much on the complex genealogy of the family, with its far from unusual system of cousin-marriage, and too little on the wider network of agents and affiliated banks that was just as important in making the family the wealthiest in the nineteenth-century world. With hindsight, I should have paid more attention to those historians of the mid-twentieth century, such as Lewis Namier or Ronald Syme, who had pioneered prosopography (collective biography), not least as a way of downplaying the role of ideology as an historical actor in its own right. Yet their efforts had fallen short of formal network analysis. Moreover, they had been superseded by a generation of social(ist) historians who were intent on revealing rising and falling classes as the propellants of historical change. I had learned that Vilfredo Pareto's elites – from the 'notables' of revolutionary France to the *Honoratioren* of Wilhelmine Germany – generally mattered more than Karl Marx's classes in the historical process, but I had not learned how to analyse elite structures.

This book is an attempt to atone for those sins of omission. It tells the story of the interaction between networks and hierarchies from ancient times until the very recent past. It brings together theoretical insights from myriad disciplines, ranging from economics to sociology, from neuroscience to organizational behaviour. Its central thesis is that social networks have always been much more important in history than most historians, fixated as they have been on hierarchical organizations such as states, have allowed – but never more so than in two periods. The first 'networked era' followed the introduction of the printing press to Europe in the late fifteenth century and lasted until the end of the eighteenth century. The second – our own time – dates from the 1970s, though I argue that the technological revolution we associate with Silicon Valley was more a consequence than a cause of a crisis of hierarchical institutions. The intervening period, from the late 1790s until the late 1960s, saw the opposite trend: hierarchical institutions re-established their control and successfully shut down or co-opted networks. The zenith of hierarchically organized power was in fact the mid-twentieth century – the era of totalitarian regimes and total war.

I suspect I would not have arrived at this insight had I not embarked on writing a biography of one of the most adept networkers of modern times: Henry Kissinger. It was as I reached the halfway stage of that project – with volume I finished and volume II half researched – that an interesting hypothesis occurred to me. Did Kissinger owe his success, fame and notoriety not just to his powerful intellect and formidable will but also to his exceptional ability to build an eclectic network of relationships, not only to colleagues in the Nixon and Ford administrations, but also to people outside government: journalists, newspaper proprietors, foreign ambassadors and heads of state – even Hollywood producers? Much of this book synthesizes (I hope without over-simplifying) the research of other scholars, all of whom are duly acknowledged, but on the issue of Kissinger's network I offer an initial and, I think, original attempt to address that question.

A book is itself the product of a network. I would like to acknowledge, first of all, the director and fellows of the Hoover Institution, where this book was written, as well as that institution's overseers and donors. At a time when intellectual diversity is the form of diversity that seems to be least valued in universities, Hoover is a rare, if not unique, bastion of free inquiry and independent thought. I would also like to thank my former colleagues at Harvard, who continue to contribute to my thinking on my visits to the Belfer Center at the Kennedy School and the Center for European Studies, and my new colleagues at the Kissinger Center at the Paul H. Nitze School of Advanced International Studies, Johns Hopkins University, and at Schwarzman College, Tsinghua University in Beijing.

Invaluable research assistance was provided by Sarah Wallington and Alice Han, as well as Ravi Jacques. Manny Rincon-Cruz and Keoni Correa helped greatly to improve the quality of the network graphs and commentary. I received immensely insightful comments on related papers and presentations from (to name only those who committed their thoughts to paper) Graham Allison, Pierpaolo Barbieri, Joe Barillari, Tyler Goodspeed, Micki Kaufman, Paul Schmelzing and Emile Simpson. Early drafts were read by a number of friends, colleagues and experts whose advice I sought. Those who took the time to send me comments were Ruth Ahnert, Teresita Alvarez-Bjelland, Marc Andreessen, Yaneer Bar-Yam, Joe Barillari, Alastair Buchan, Melanie Conroy, Dan Edelstein, Chloe Edmondson, Alan Fournier, Auren Hoffman, Emmanuel Roman, Suzanne Sutherland, Elaine Treharne, Calder Walton and Caroline Winterer. I received invaluable comments on the concluding section of the book from William Burns, Henri de Castries, Mathias Döpfner, John Elkann, Evan Greenberg, John Micklethwait and Robert Rubin. For sharing their insights or giving me permission to cite their unpublished work, I would also like to thank Glenn Carroll, Peter Dolton, Paula Findlen, Francis Fukuyama, Jason Heppler, Matthew Jackson and Franziska Keller. For their help with the history of the Illuminati, I am indebted to Lorenza Castella, Reinhard Markner, Olaf Simons and Joe Wäges.

As usual, Andrew Wylie and his colleagues, notably James Pullen, have represented me and my work with great skill. And, once again, I have had the privilege of being edited by Simon Winder and Scott Moyers, amongst the most insightful editors working in the English-speaking world today. I should also not forget my copy-editor, Mark Handsley, my faithful Virginian proof-reader and friend, Jim Dickson, and my picture researcher, Fred Courtright.

Finally, my thanks to my children, Felix, Freya, Lachlan and Thomas, who have never complained when book-writing has taken precedence over time with them, and who remain a source of inspiration as well as pride and delight. My wife, Ayaan, has patiently tolerated my repetitive over-use of the words 'network' and 'hierarchy' in our conversations. She has taught me more than she knows about both forms of organization. I thank her, too, with love.

I dedicate this book to Campbell Ferguson, my much-missed father, whose name I hope and pray will be borne by his sixth grandchild by the time this book is published.

I

Introduction: Networks and Hierarchies

I

The Mystery of the Illuminati

Once upon a time, nearly two and a half centuries ago, there was a secret network that tried to change the world. Founded in Germany just two months before thirteen of Britain's American colonies declared their independence, the organization came to be known as the *Illuminatenorden* – the Order of the Illuminati. Its goals were lofty. Indeed, its founder had originally called it the *Bund der Perfektibilisten* (the League of the Perfectibles). As one member of the Order recalled its founder saying, it was intended to be:

> an association that, through the most subtle and secure methods, will have as its goal the victory of virtue and wisdom over stupidity and malice; an association that will make the most important discoveries in all fields of science, that will teach its members to become both noble and great, that will assure them of the certain prize of their complete perfection in this world, that will protect them from persecution, the fates and oppression, and that will bind the hands of despotism in all its forms.[1]

The Order's ultimate objective was to 'enlighten the understanding by the sun of reason, which will dispel the clouds of superstition and of prejudice'. 'My goal is to give reason the upper hand,' declared the Order's founder.[2] Its methods were, in one respect, educational. 'The sole intention of the league', according to its General Statutes (1781), was 'education, not by declamatory means, but by favouring and rewarding virtue'.[3] Yet the Illuminati were to operate as a strictly secret fraternity. Members adopted codenames, often of ancient Greek or Roman provenance: the founder himself was 'Brother Spartacus'. There were to be three ranks or grades of membership – Novice, Minerval* and Illuminated Minerval – but the lower ranks were to be given only the vaguest insights into the Order's goals and methods. Elaborate initiation rites were devised – among them an oath of secrecy, violation of which would be punished with the most gruesome death. Each isolated cell of initiates reported to a superior, whose real identity they did not know.

At first, the Illuminati were tiny in number. There were only a handful of founding members, most of them students.[4] Two years after its creation, the Order's total membership was just twenty-five. As late as December 1779, it was still only sixty. Within just a few years, however, membership had surged to more than 1,300.[5] In its early days, the Order had been confined to Ingolstadt, Eichstätt and Freising, with a few members in Munich.[6] By the early 1780s, the Illuminati network extended throughout much of Germany. Moreover, an impressive list of German princes had joined the Order: Ferdinand, prince of Brunswick-Lüneburg-Wolfenbüttel; Charles, prince of Hesse-Cassel; Ernest II, duke of Saxe-Coburg-Altenburg; and Charles August, grand duke of Saxe-Weimar-Eisenach;[7] as well as dozens of noblemen such as Franz Friedrich von Ditfurth, and the rising star of the Rhineland clergy, Carl Theodor von Dalberg.[8] Serving many of the most exalted Illuminati as advisers were other members of the Order.[9] Intellectuals, too, became Illuminati, notably the polymath Johann Wolfgang Goethe, the philosophers Johann Gottfried Herder and Friedrich Heinrich Jacobi, the translator Johann Joachim Christoph Bode, and the Swiss educationalist Johann Heinrich Pestalozzi.[10] Though he did not join, the dramatist Friedrich Schiller based the republican revolutionary character of Posa in his *Don Carlos* (1787) on a leading member of the Illuminati.[11] The influence of Illuminism has sometimes been detected in Wolfgang Amadeus Mozart's opera *The Magic Flute* (1791).[12]

Yet in June 1784 the Bavarian government issued the first of three edicts that effectively banned the Illuminati, condemning them as

* The allusion was to Minerva, the Roman name for the goddess of wisdom, Pallas Athene. The Illuminati's insignia consisted of an owl, the goddess's familiar, sitting on the pages of an open book.

'traitorous and hostile to religion'.[13] An investigative commission set about purging the academy and bureaucracy of members. Some fled Bavaria. Others lost their jobs or were exiled. At least two were imprisoned. The founder himself sought refuge in Gotha. For all intents and purposes, the Illuminati had ceased to function by the end of 1787. Nevertheless, their infamy long outlived them. King Frederick William II of Prussia was warned that the Illuminati remained a dangerously subversive force throughout Germany. In 1797 the eminent Scottish physicist John Robison published *Proofs of a Conspiracy against All the Religions and Governments of Europe, carried on in the Secret Meetings of the Free Masons, Illuminati, and Reading Societies*, in which he claimed that, 'through a course of fifty years, under the specious pretext of enlightening the world by the torch of philosophy, and of dispelling the clouds of civil and religious superstition', an 'association' had been 'exerting itself zealously and systematically, till it has become almost irresistible', with the goal of 'ROOTING OUT ALL THE RELIGIOUS ESTABLISHMENTS, AND OVERTURNING ALL THE EXISTING GOVERNMENTS OF EUROPE'. The culmination of the association's efforts, according to Robison, was nothing less than the French Revolution. In his *Memoirs Illustrating the History of Jacobinism*, also published in 1797, a former French Jesuit named Augustin de Barruel made the same allegation. 'Even to the most horrid deeds perpetrated during the French Revolution, everything was foreseen and resolved on, was combined and premeditated . . . the offspring of deep-thought villainy.' The Jacobins themselves, Barruel maintained, were the heirs of the Illuminati. These allegations – which won the praise of Edmund Burke[14] – quickly found their way to the United Sates, where they were adopted by, amongst others, Timothy Dwight, the president of Yale.[15] For much of the nineteenth and twentieth centuries, the Illuminati played an unintended role as *Ur*-conspirators in what Richard Hofstadter memorably called the 'paranoid style' in American politics, exponents of which invariably claimed to be defending the dispossessed against a 'vast, insidious, preternaturally effective international conspiratorial network designed to perpetrate acts of the most fiendish character'.[16] To give just two examples, the Illuminati featured in the anti-Communist John Birch Society's literature and in the Christian conservative Pat Robertson's book *New World Order* (1991).[17]

The myth of the Illuminati has persisted down to the present day. True, some of the writing inspired by the order has been avowed fiction, notably the *Illuminatus* trilogy published in the 1970s by Robert Shea and Robert Anton Wilson, Umberto Eco's novel *Foucault's Pendulum* (1988), the film *Lara Croft: Tomb Raider* (2001), and Dan Brown's thriller *Angels and Demons* (2000).[18] What is harder to explain is the widespread belief that the Illuminati really exist and are as powerful today as their founder intended them to be. There are, to be sure, a number of websites purporting to represent the Illuminati, but none is very professional-looking.[19] It has nevertheless been claimed that several US presidents have been members of the Illuminati, including not only John Adams and Thomas Jefferson[20] but also Barack Obama.[21] A fairly representative screed (the genre is enormous) describes the Illuminati as a 'super-rich Power Elite with an ambition to create a slave society':

> The Illuminati own all the International banks, the oil-businesses, the most powerful businesses of industry and trade, they infiltrate politics and education and they own most governments – or at the very least control them. They even own Hollywood and the Music Industry . . . [T]he Illuminati run the drug trade industry as well . . . The leading candidates for Presidency are carefully chosen from the occult bloodlines of the thirteen Illuminati families . . . The main goal is to create a One World Government, with them on top to rule the world into slavery and dictatorship . . . They want to create an 'outside threat,' a fake Alien Invasion, so that the countries of this world will be willing to unite as ONE.

The standard version of the conspiracy theory links the Illuminati to the Rothschild family, the Round Table, the Bilderberg Group and the Trilateral Commission – not forgetting the hedge fund manager, political donor and philanthropist George Soros.[22]

Such theories are believed, or at least taken seriously, by a remarkably large number of people.[23] Just over half (51 per cent) of 1,000 Americans surveyed in 2011 agreed with the statement that 'Much of what happens in the world today is decided by a small and secretive

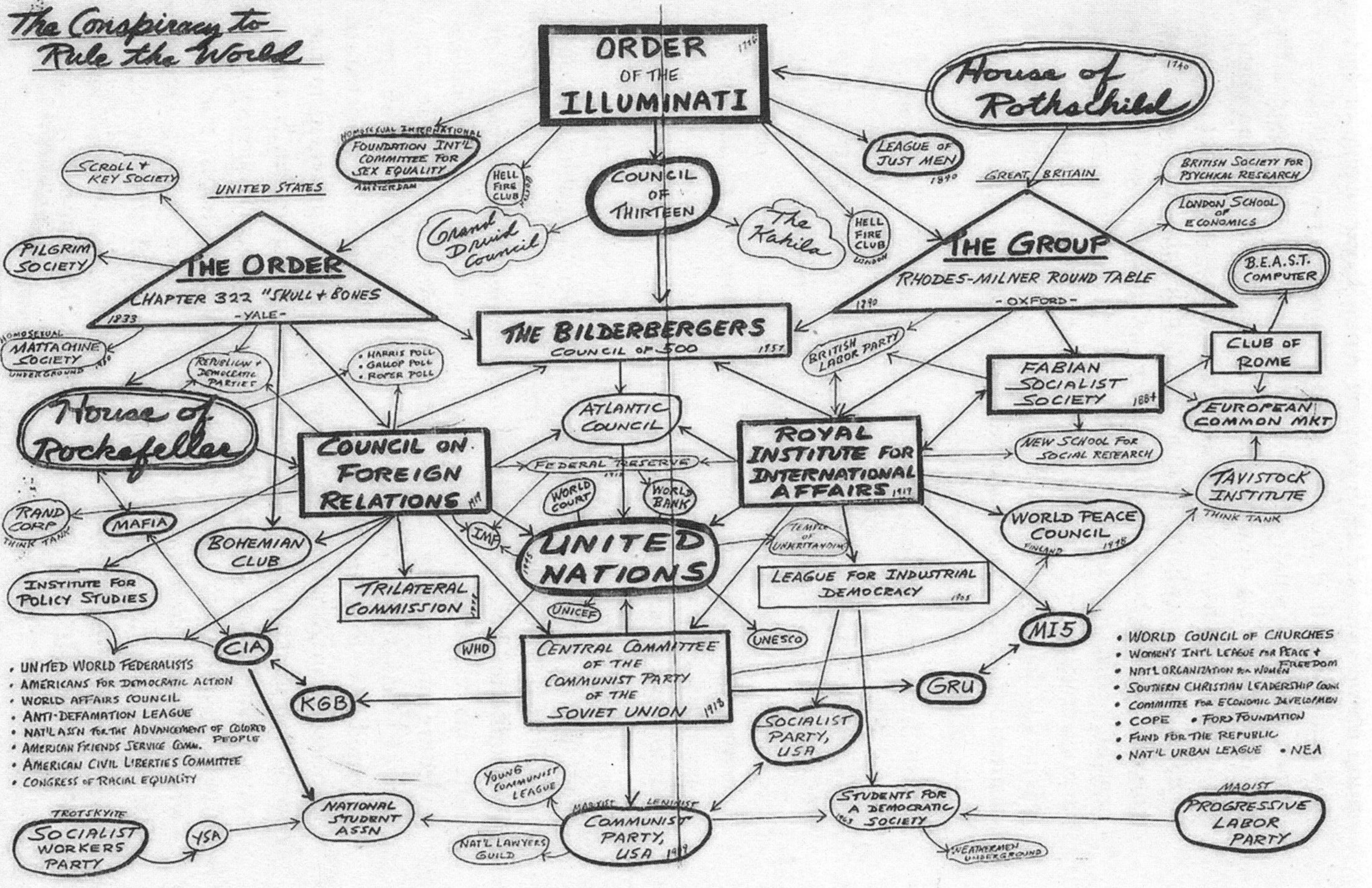

1. 'The Conspiracy to Rule the World'.

group of individuals.'[24] Fully a quarter of a larger sample of 1,935 Americans agreed that 'The current financial crisis was secretly orchestrated by a small group of Wall Street bankers to extend the power of the Federal Reserve and further their control of the world's economy.'[25] And nearly one in five (19 per cent) agreed that 'Billionaire George Soros is behind a hidden plot to destabilize the American government, take control of the media, and put the world under his control.'[26] Soros himself is routinely linked to the Illuminati by popular conspiracy theorists such as Alex Jones.[27] This may be lunatic, but it is lunacy that appeals to more than a fringe. The authors of a recent academic study of the prevalence of conspiracy theories concluded that:

> half of the American population agree with at least one conspiracy [theory] . . . Far from being an aberrant expression of some political extreme or a product of gross misinformation, a conspiratorial view of politics is a widespread tendency across the entire ideological spectrum . . . [M]any predominant belief systems in the United States, be they Christian narratives about God and Satan . . . or left-wing narratives about neoliberalism . . ., draw heavily upon the idea of unseen, intentional forces shaping contemporary events.[28]

Nor is this phenomenon peculiar to the United States. By the time of the Iraq War, significant proportions of the German public had come to believe that responsibility for the 9/11 attacks lay with 'highly interconnected but also decentred and deterritorialized networks of vested interests that are not necessarily the product of individual or collective intentionality . . .'[29] In Britain and Austria, too, large numbers of voters appear to believe in conspiracy theories – even ones invented by researchers.[30] Russian writers are especially attracted to theories of an American-led conspiracy,[31] though nowhere in the world can match the Muslim world, where 'conspiracism' has been rampant since 9/11.[32] Such beliefs can have tragic consequences. One American conspiracy theorist, Milton William Cooper, was shot while resisting arrest for tax evasion and firearms offences. He had based his resistance to authority on the belief that the federal government was controlled by the Illuminati.[33] To judge by global statistics on terrorism and its motivations, Muslim believers in an

American-Zionist plot against their religion are significantly more likely than American 'Truthers' to resort to violence.

The history of the Illuminati illustrates the central problem of writing about social networks, especially those that seek to remain secret. Because the subject attracts cranks, it is hard for professional historians to take it seriously. Even those who do must struggle with the problem that networks rarely maintain readily accessible archives. Bavarian archivists preserved records of the campaign against the Illuminati, including authentic documents seized from members of the Order, but it is only very recently that researchers have systematically – and very laboriously – edited the surviving correspondence and regulations of the Illuminati, which had ended in a variety of different locations, including the archives of Masonic lodges.[34] This kind of entry barrier explains why one eminent Oxford historian insisted he could write only 'about what has been believed and said about secret societies, not about secret societies themselves'.[35] Yet no case better illustrates the historical significance of networks than that of the Illuminati. In themselves, they were not an important movement. They certainly did not cause the French Revolution – or even much real trouble in Bavaria. But they became significant because their reputation went viral at a time when the political disruption precipitated by the Enlightenment – the achievement of a hugely influential network of intellectuals – was reaching its revolutionary culmination on both sides of the Atlantic.

This book attempts to find a middle way between mainstream historiography, which has tended to understate the role of networks, and the conspiracy theorists, who habitually exaggerate their role. It proposes a new historical narrative, in which major changes – dating back to the Age of Discovery and the Reformation, if not earlier – can be understood, in essence, as disruptive challenges posed to established hierarchies by networks. It also challenges the confident assumptions some commentators make today that there is something inherently benign in network disruption of hierarchical order. And it considers the experience of the nineteenth and twentieth centuries to identify ways in which the revolutionary energies transmitted by networks can be contained.

2

Our Networked Age

Networks, it seems, are everywhere today. In the first week of 2017, the *New York Times* ran 136 stories in which the word 'network' appeared. Just over a third of the stories were about television networks, twelve were about computer networks and ten about various kinds of political network, but there were also stories about transport networks, financial networks, terrorist networks, healthcare networks – not to mention social, educational, criminal, telephone, radio, electricity and intelligence networks. To read all this is to behold a world, as the cliché has it, 'where everything is connected'. Some networks link militants together, others connect medics, still others are between automated teller machines. There is a cancer network, a jihadi network, an orca network. Some networks – too often referred to as 'vast'[1] – are international, while others are regional; some are ethereal, others underground. There are networks of corruption, networks of tunnels, networks of espionage; there is even a tennis match-fixing network. Network attackers battle network defenders. And all of this is breathlessly covered by terrestrial, cable and satellite networks.

In *Bleak House* it was fog that was ubiquitous. Today it is networks that are, to borrow from Dickens, up the river and down the river. 'The alternative to networking is to fail,' we read in the *Harvard Business Review*.[2] 'A key reason why women lag behind in leadership,' the same journal asserts, 'is that they are less likely to have extensive networks to support and promote them as potential leaders.'[3] Another *HBR* article shows that 'mutual fund portfolio managers placed larger concentrated bets on companies to which they were connected through an education network', and that those investments performed better* than average.[4] However, not everyone would infer from this that the 'old boy' network is a benign force, worthy of emulation by old girls. In finance, some 'expert networks' have been revealed to be channels for insider trading or interest rate rigging.[5] Networks have also been blamed for the global financial crisis of 2008: specifically, the increasingly complex network that turned the world's banks into a global transmission and amplification system for losses on US subprime mortgages.[6] The world described by Sandra Navidi in *Superhubs* may seem glamorous to some. In her words, a 'select few' – she names just twenty individuals – 'preside over the most exclusive and powerful asset: a unique network of personal relationships that spans the globe'. These relationships are forged and maintained in an even smaller number of institutions: the Massachusetts Institute of Technology, Goldman Sachs, the World Economic Forum, three philanthropic entities, among them the Clinton Global Initiative, and the Four Seasons restaurant in New York.[7] Yet one of the core messages of Donald J. Trump's successful election campaign in 2016 was that these were the very 'global special interests' that stood behind the 'failed and corrupt political establishment' personified by Hillary Clinton, the candidate he defeated.[8]

No account of the 2016 US presidential election will be complete without a discussion of the roles played by media networks, from Fox News to Facebook to Twitter, the victorious candidate's network of choice.† One of many ironies of the election was that Trump's network-driven campaign directed so much of its fire at Clinton's elite network – a network to which Trump himself had once belonged, as the Clintons' presence at his third wedding attested. Just a few years before the election, an entity called 'The Trump Network' – set up in 2009 to sell products like vitamin supplements with Trump's endorsement – had gone bankrupt. Had Trump lost the election, he would have launched Trump TV as a television network. One of the

* The return was 21 per cent when both portfolio manager and chief executive went to the same university and took the same degree with some chronological overlap, compared with 13 per cent when there was no such connection.

† At the time of writing, Donald J. Trump has 33.8 million followers on Twitter. He himself follows just forty-five individuals or institutions.

many reasons why he did not lose was that Russia's intelligence network did its utmost to damage his rival's reputation, using the website WikiLeaks and the television network RT as its principal instruments. In the words of a partly unclassified report by the US intelligence agencies, 'the Russian President Vladimir Putin ordered an influence campaign in 2016' that was intended to 'denigrate Secretary Clinton, and harm her electability and potential presidency', reflecting the Kremlin's 'clear preference' for Trump. In July 2015, according to the report, 'Russian intelligence gained access to Democratic National Committee (DNC) networks and maintained that access until at least June 2016', systematically publishing the emails it obtained through WikiLeaks. At the same time, 'Russia's state-run propaganda machine – comprised of its domestic media apparatus, outlets targeting global audiences such as RT and Sputnik, and a network of quasi-government trolls – contributed to the influence campaign by serving as a platform for Kremlin messaging to Russian and international audiences.'[9]

Another reason Trump won, however, was that the Islamist terrorist network known as Islamic State carried out multiple attacks in the twelve months before the election, including two in the United States (in San Bernardino and Orlando). These attacks enhanced the appeal of Trump's pledges to 'expose', 'strip out' and 'remove one by one . . . the support networks for Radical Islam in this country', and 'totally dismantle Iran's global terror network'.[10]

We live, in short, in 'the network age'.[11] Joshua Ramo has called it 'the Age of Network Power'.[12] Adrienne Lafrance prefers 'the Age of Entanglement'.[13] Parag Khanna even proposes a new discipline – 'Connectography' – to map 'the Global Network Revolution'.[14] 'The network society', according to Manuel Castells, 'represents a qualitative change in the human experience.'[15] Networks are transforming the public sphere and with it democracy itself.[16] But for better or for worse? 'Current network technology . . . truly favours the citizens,' write Google's Jared Cohen and Eric Schmidt. 'Never before have so many people been connected through an instantly responsive network', with truly 'game-changing' implications for politics everywhere.[17] An alternative view is that global corporations such as Google are systematically achieving 'structural domination' by exploiting networks to erode national sovereignty and the collectivist politics that it makes possible.[18]

The same question can be asked of the effect of networks on the international system: for better or for worse? For Anne-Marie Slaughter, it makes sense to reconfigure global politics by combining the traditional 'chessboard' of inter-state diplomacy with the new 'web . . . of networks', exploiting the advantages of the latter (such as transparency, adaptability and scalability).[19] The stateswomen of the future, she argues, will be 'web actors wielding power and exercising leadership alongside governments' with 'strategies of connection'.[20] Parag Khanna looks forward with relish to a 'supply-chain world' in which global corporations, megacities, 'aerotropolises' and 'regional commonwealths' engage in an endless but essentially peaceful 'tug-of-war' for economic advantage that resembles 'a massive multiplayer game'.[21] Yet it seems doubtful – not only to Joshua Ramo, but also to his mentor Henry Kissinger – that such tendencies are likely to enhance global stability. 'The pervasiveness of networked communications in the social, financial, industrial, and military sectors,' Kissinger has written:

> has . . . revolutionized vulnerabilities. Outpacing most rules and regulations (and indeed the technical comprehension of many regulators), it has, in some respects, created the state of nature . . . the escape from which, according to Hobbes, provided the motivating force for creating a political order . . . [A]symmetry and a kind of congenital world disorder are built into relations between cyber powers both in diplomacy and in strategy . . . Absent articulation of some rules of international conduct, a crisis will arise from the inner dynamics of the system.[22]

If the 'first world cyberwar' has already begun, as some have claimed, then it is a war between networks.[23]

The most alarming prospect of all is that a single global network will ultimately render *Homo sapiens* redundant and then extinct. In *Homo Deus*, Yuval Harari argues that the age of large-scale 'mass cooperation networks' based on written language, money, culture and ideology – products of carbon-based human neural networks – is giving way to a new era of silicon-based computer networks based on algorithms. In that network, we shall quickly find ourselves about as important to the algorithms as animals currently are to us. Disconnection from the network will come to mean death for the individual, as the network will be maintaining our health around the clock. But connection will ultimately mean extinction for the species: 'The yardsticks that we ourselves have enshrined will condemn us to join the mammoths and Chinese river dolphins in oblivion.'[24] On the basis of Harari's bleak assessment of the human past, these would seem to be our just deserts.[25]

This book is about the past more than it is about the future; or, to be precise, it is a book that seeks to learn about the future mainly by studying the past, rather than engaging in flights of fancy or the casual projection forward of recent trends. There are those (not least in Silicon Valley) who doubt that history has much to teach them at a time of such rapid technological innovation.[26] Indeed, much of the debate I have just summarized presupposes that social networks are a new phenomenon and that there is something unprecedented about their present-day ubiquity. This is wrong. Even as we talk incessantly about them, the reality is that most of us have only a very limited understanding of how networks function, and almost no knowledge of where they came from. We largely overlook how widespread they are in the natural world, what a key role they have played in our evolution as a species, and how integral a part of the human past they have been. As a result, we tend to underestimate the importance of networks in the past, and to assume erroneously that history can have nothing to teach us on this subject.

To be sure, there have never been such large networks as we see in the world today. Nor have the flows of information – or, for that matter, disease – ever been so rapid. But scale and speed are not everything. We shall never make sense of the vast, swift networks of our own time – in particular, we shall have no inkling whether the network age will be joyously emancipatory or hideously anarchic – if we do not study the smaller, slower networks of the past. For these, too, were ubiquitous. And sometimes they were very powerful indeed.

3

Networks, Networks Everywhere

The natural world is to a bewildering extent made up of 'optimized, space-filling, branching networks', in the words of the physicist Geoffrey West, from the human circulatory system to a colony of ants, all of which have evolved to distribute energy and materials between macroscopic reservoirs and microscopic sites over an astonishing twenty-seven orders of magnitude. The animal circulatory, respiratory, renal, neural systems are all natural networks. So are plant vascular systems and the microtubial and mitochondrial networks inside cells.[1] The brain of the nematode worm *Caenorhabditis elegans* is the only neural network to have been comprehensively mapped, but more complex brains will in due course be given the same treatment.[2] From worms' brains to food chains (or 'food webs'), modern biology finds networks at all levels of life on earth.[3] The sequencing of the genome has revealed a 'gene regulatory network' in which 'nodes are genes and links are chains of reactions'.[4] The delta of a river is a network, too: your school atlas mapped those. Tumours form networks.

Some problems can only be resolved by network analysis. Scientists seeking to explain the massive algal blooms that afflicted the San Francisco Bay in 1999 had to map the network of marine life before they could identify the true cause. A similar mapping of neural networks was necessary to establish that the hippocampus is where the human memory resides.[5] The speed with which an infectious disease spreads has as much to do with the network structure of the exposed population as with the virulence of the disease itself, as an epidemic amongst teenagers in Rockdale County, Georgia, made clear twenty years ago.[6] The existence of a few highly connected hubs causes the

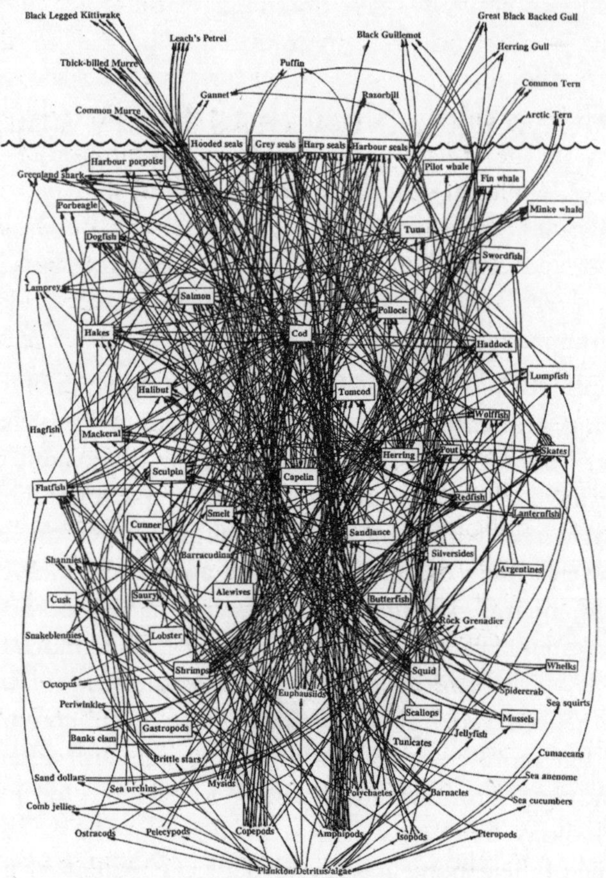

2. A partial food web for the 'Scotian Shelf' in the north-west Atlantic. Arrows go from the prey species to the predator species.

spread of the disease to increase exponentially after an initial phase of slow growth.[7] Put differently, if the 'basic reproduction number' (how many other people are newly infected by a typical infected individual) is above one, then a disease becomes endemic; if it is below one, it tends to die out. But that basic reproduction number is determined as much by the structure of the network it infects as by the innate infectiousness of the disease.[8] Network structures can also condition the speed and accuracy with which a disease is diagnosed.[9]

In prehistory, *Homo sapiens* evolved as a cooperative ape, with a unique ability to network – to communicate and to act collectively – that set us apart from all other animals. In the words of the evolutionary biologist Joseph Henrich, we are not simply bigger-brained, less hairy chimpanzees; the secret of our success as a species 'resides . . . in the *collective brains* of our communities'.[10] Unlike chimpanzees, we learn socially, by teaching and sharing. According to the evolutionary anthropologist Robin Dunbar, our larger brain, with its more developed neocortex, evolved to enable us to function in relatively large social groups of around 150 (compared with around fifty for chimpanzees).[11] Indeed, our species should really be known as *Homo dictyous* ('network man') because – to quote the sociologists Nicholas Christakis and James Fowler – 'our brains seem to have been built for social networks'.[12] The term coined by the ethnographer Edwin Hutchins was 'distributed cognition'. Our early ancestors were 'obligate collaborative foragers', who became interdependent on each other for food, shelter and warmth.[13] It is likely that the development of spoken language, as well as the associated advances in brain capacity and structure, was part of this same process, evolving out of ape-like practices such as grooming.[14] The same could also be said of practices such as art, dance and ritual.[15] In the words of the historians William H. McNeill and J. R. McNeill, the first 'worldwide web' in fact emerged around 12,000 years ago. Man, with his unrivalled neural network, was born *to* network.

Social networks, then, are the structures that human beings naturally form, beginning with knowledge itself and the various forms of representation we use to communicate it, as well of course as the family trees to which we all necessarily belong, even if only some of us possess detailed genealogical knowledge. Networks include the patterns of settlement, migration and miscegenation that have distributed our species across the world's surface, as well as the myriad cults and crazes we periodically produce with minimal premeditation and leadership. As we shall see, social networks come in all shapes and sizes, from exclusive secret societies to open-source movements. Some have a spontaneous, self-organizing character; others are more systematic and structured. All that has happened – beginning with the invention of written language – is that new technologies have facilitated our innate, ancient urge to network.

Yet there is a puzzle. For most of recorded history, hierarchies dominated networks in their scope and scale. Men and women were mostly organized into hierarchical structures, with power concentrated at the very top in the hands of a chief, lord, king or emperor. By contrast, the average individual's network was stunted in its scale. The typical peasant – and that word roughly describes what most human beings were for most of recorded history – was stuck in a tiny cluster called a family, inside a slightly larger cluster called a village, with almost no links to the wider world. This was how most human beings lived as recently as a hundred years ago. Even today, the inhabitants of Indian villages are, at best, connected in a 'social quilt . . . a union of small cliques where each clique is just large enough to sustain cooperation by all of its members and where the cliques are laced together'.[16] A key role in such isolated communities is played by the 'diffusion-central' individuals commonly known as gossips.[17]

So oppressive were traditional small-scale networks that some individuals preferred to retreat into complete isolation. Robert Burns's song 'Naebody' celebrates self-reliance as a kind of defiant disconnection:

I hae a wife o' my ain,
I'll partake wi' naebody;
I'll tak Cuckold frae nane,
I'll gie Cuckold to naebody.

I hae a penny to spend,
There, thanks to naebody;
I hae naething to lend,
I'll borrow frae naebody.

I am naebody's lord,
I'll be slave to naebody;
I hae a gude braid sword,
I'll take dunts frae naebody.

I'll be merry and free,
I'll be sad for naebody;
Naebody cares for me,
I care for naebody.

From the Lone Ranger to the High Plains Drifter, such insular individuals have been recurrent heroes of Western cinema. In the Coen brothers' film *Blood Simple* (1984), the narrator inhabits a world of unbridled, brutal individualism. 'Go ahead, complain,' he says, 'tell your problems to your neighbour, ask for help – and watch him fly. Now in Russia, they got it mapped out so that everyone pulls for everyone else – that's the theory, anyway. But what I know about is Texas. And down here . . . you're on your own.'[18]

Nevertheless, such rampant individualism is the exception, not the rule. As John Donne memorably put it in his 'Devotions upon Emergent Occasions':

> No man is an island, entire of itself; every man is a piece of the continent, a part of the main. If a clod be washed away by the sea, Europe is the less, as well as if a promontory were, as well as if a manor of thy friend's or of thine own were. Any man's death diminishes me, because I am involved in mankind; and therefore *never send to know for whom the bell tolls; it tolls for thee.*

Man is indeed a social animal and the misanthrope is shunned as well as shunning. The puzzle is why and how we natural networkers have for so long been in thrall to vertically structured and rigidly institutionalized hierarchies.

The word hierarchy derives from ancient Greek – ἱεραρχία (hierarchia), literally the 'rule of a high priest' – and was first used to describe the heavenly orders of angels and, more generally, to characterize a

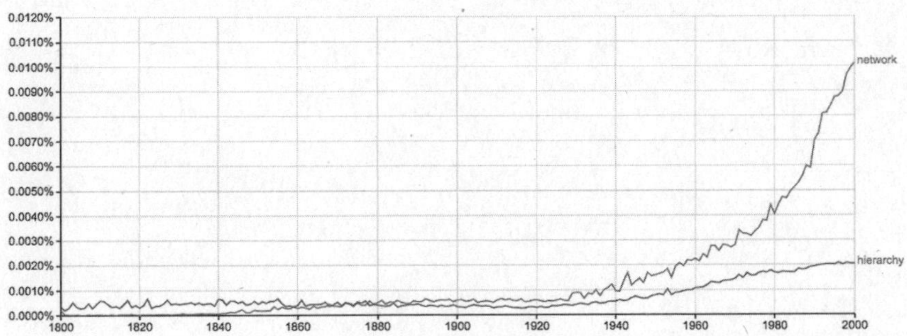

3. Google n-gram of the frequency of appearance of the words 'network' and 'hierarchy' in English-language publications between 1800 and 2000.

stratified order of spiritual or temporal governance. Up until the sixteenth century, by contrast, the word 'network' signified nothing more than a woven mesh made of interlaced thread. Occasionally, Shakespeare uses the words 'net' and 'web' metaphorically – Iago's plot against Othello is a 'net that shall enmesh them all' – but 'network' itself does not appear in any of his plays.[19] Scientists in the seventeenth and eighteenth centuries discerned that there were networks in nature – from spiders' webs to the human circulatory system of veins and arteries – but it was not until the nineteenth century that the term began to be used more metaphorically, by geographers and engineers to describe waterways and railways, and by writers to characterize the relations between people. The poet Coleridge (1817) spoke of a 'net-work of property', the historian Freeman (1876) of a 'network of feudal tenures'.[20] Even so, until around 1880, books published in English were more likely to contain the word 'hierarchy' than the word 'network' (see figure 3). It is possible retrospectively to subject the political and social relationships depicted in Anthony Trollope's 1869 novel *Phineas Finn* to network analysis,[21] but the word 'network' does not appear once in the text. Only in the later twentieth century did 'networks' begin to proliferate: first transport and electrical networks, then telephone and television networks, finally computer and online social networks. And not before 1980 was 'network' used as a verb to connote purposive, career-oriented socializing.

4
Why Hierarchies?

The tourist who visits Venice should reserve one afternoon for a trip to the lovely, listless island of Torcello. There, inside the Cattedrale di Santa Maria Assunta, is a perfect illustration of what we mean by hierarchy (see plate 1): an eleventh-century mosaic of the Last Judgement in five tiers, with Christ at the top and the fires of hell at the bottom.

This is roughly how most people think about hierarchies: as vertically structured organizations characterized by centralized and top-down command, control and communication. Historically, they begin with family-based clans and tribes, out of which (or against which) more complicated and stratified institutions evolved, with a formalized division and ranking of labour.[1] Amongst the varieties of hierarchy that proliferated in the pre-modern period were tightly regulated urban polities reliant on commerce and bigger, mostly monarchical, states based on agriculture; the centrally run cults known as churches; the armies and bureaucracies within states; the guilds that operated to control access to skilled occupations; the autonomous corporations that, from the early-modern period, sought to exploit economies of scope and scale by internalizing certain market transactions; academic corporations like universities; and the supersized transnational states known as empires.

The crucial incentive that favoured hierarchical order was that it made the exercise of power more efficient: centralized control in the hands of the 'big man' eliminated or at least reduced time-consuming arguments about what to do, which might at any time escalate into internecine conflict.[2] According to the philosopher Benoît Dubreuil, delegating judicial and penal power – the power to punish transgressors – to an individual or elite was the optimal solution for predominantly agrarian societies that required the majority of people simply to shut up and toil in the fields.[3] Peter Turchin prefers to emphasize the role of warfare, arguing that changes in military technology encouraged the spread of hierarchically organized states and armies.[4]

Moreover, absolutism could be a source of social cohesion. 'There's an invisible thread, like a spider's web, and it comes right out of his Imperial Majesty Alexander the Third's heart,' the Tsarist policeman Nikiforych explained to the young Maxim Gorky in around 1890. 'And there's another which goes through all the ministers, through His Excellency the Governor and down through the ranks until it reaches me and even the lowest soldier. Everything is linked and bound together by this thread . . . with its invisible power.'[5] Gorky lived to see Stalin turn that invisible thread into steel wires of social control beyond the wildest dreams of the tsars.

Yet the defect of autocracy is obvious, too. No individual, no matter how talented, has the capacity to contend with all the challenges of imperial governance, and almost none is able to resist the corrupting temptations of absolute power. Critiques of the hierarchical state have been both political and economic. Since the eighteenth century, the Western world has, albeit with some setbacks, taken a more positive view of democracy than ancient and Renaissance political theorists, or at least a more positive view of government limited by independent courts and some form of representative body. Apart from the inherent appeal of political freedom, more inclusive polities seem to be associated with more sustained economic development.[6] They are also better able to cope with complexity as populations grow and technologies advance. And they are less vulnerable to decapitation: when one man rules, his assassination can bring the entire hierarchical system crashing down. At the same time, economists since Adam Smith have argued that the spontaneous order of the free market is inherently better at allocating resources than a private monopolist or a too-powerful government.

In practice, of course, a large proportion of history's autocratic rulers left a considerable amount of power to the market, although they might regulate, tax and occasionally interrupt its operations.

That is why in the archetypal medieval or early-modern town – such as Siena in Tuscany – the tower representing secular power stands right next to, and indeed overshadows, the square where market transactions and other forms of public exchange took place (see plate 6). It would therefore be a mistake to follow Friedrich Hayek in conceiving of a simple dichotomy between the state and the market. This is not only because the government defines the legal framework within which the market works, but also because, as the late Max Boisot argued, markets and bureaucracies themselves are just ideal types of information-sharing networks, like clans or fiefdoms.[7]

Informal networks, however, are different. In such networks, according to the organizational sociologist Walter Powell, 'transactions occur neither through discrete exchanges nor by administrative fiat, but through networks of individuals engaged in reciprocal, preferential, mutually supportive actions . . . [that] involve neither the explicit criteria of the market, nor the familiar paternalism of the hierarchy'.[8] Students of corporate governance have long been aware of the role of networks of interlocking directorships in some economies. Japanese *keiretsu* groups are only one of many such business networks. Such arrangements recall Adam Smith's famous observation that 'People of the same trade seldom meet together, even for merriment and diversion, but the conversation ends in a conspiracy against the public, or in some contrivance to raise prices.'* Some scholars of politics, too, have become uneasily aware that networks occupy some intermediate terrain.[9] Are participants in a network surreptitiously trading, even if it is gifts rather than banknotes that are being exchanged?[10] Are networks just very loosely structured corporations?[11] Network theorists have been seeking answers to such questions for many years, though their work has frequently been overlooked – not least, until very recently, by historians.

* *The Wealth of Nations*, Book I, chapter 10. Translated literally, *keiretsu* means headless combine. It is the name given to a corporate structure in which a number of organizations link together, usually by taking small stakes in each other. Often the businesses concerned will be partners, e.g. in a supply chain.

5
From Seven Bridges to Six Degrees

The formal study of networks dates back to the mid-eighteenth century, the heyday of the East Prussian city of Königsberg, home of the philosopher Immanuel Kant. Among the sights of Königsberg were the seven bridges across the Pregel River that connected the two riverbanks to the two islands in the middle of the river, as well as linking the islands (see figure 4). It was a familiar conundrum to natives of the city that it was impossible to take a walk that crossed all seven bridges just once, without re-crossing any of them.* The problem attracted the attention of the great Swiss-born mathematician Leonhard Euler, who in 1735 invented network theory to demonstrate formally why such a walk was impossible. In the simplified graph (see figure 5), there are four 'nodes', representing the two main banks of the river and the smaller and larger islands, and seven 'edges', representing the bridges that connected them. Formally, Euler demonstrated that the possibility of a path that traverses each edge only once must depend on the *degree* of the nodes (the number of edges touching each node). The graph must have either two nodes with an odd number of edges or none. As the graph of the Königsberg bridges has four such nodes (one with five edges, the others with three), it cannot have a Eulerian path. A walk that crossed each bridge just once would be possible only if one edge – the bridge connecting the two islands – were removed; then only two nodes would have an odd-numbered

* Disappointingly, Kant's daily walk – so punctual that people were said to set their watches by it – did not include the seven bridges. According to the poet Heinrich Heine, he preferred to walk eight times up and down a tree-lined street, thereafter known as the Philosopher's Way.

degree. Since Euler's time, the basic units of graph theory – which he originally called 'the geometry of position' – have been nodes (or vertices) and edges (or links).

Nineteenth-century scientists applied this framework to everything from cartography to electrical circuits to isomers of organic components.[1] That there might also be *social* networks certainly occurred to some of the great political thinkers of that age, notably John Stuart Mill, Auguste Comte and Alexis de Tocqueville – the last of whom grasped that the rich associational life of the early United States was crucial to the working of American democracy. However, none attempted to formalize this insight. The study of social networks may therefore be said to date from 1900, when the schoolteacher and amateur social scientist Johannes Delitsch published a matrix that mapped the friendships of the fifty-three boys he had taught in his 1880–81 class.[2] Delitsch identified a close relationship between the boys' social affinities and their academic ranking – which in those days was the basis of classroom seating. Somewhat similar work was done three decades later in New York, where the idiosyncratic Austrian-born but anti-Freudian psychiatrist Jacob Moreno used sociograms to study the relationships between the 'delinquent' girls in a reformatory school in Hudson, NY. His research – published in 1933 as *Who Shall Survive?* – showed that the surge in the number of runaway girls in 1932 was explicable in terms of the runaways' positions in the school's social network of 'attractions and repulsions', which were both racial and sexual (see plate 2). Here, Moreno proclaimed, were 'the social forces which dominate mankind'. The book was, he believed, 'a new bible, the bible for social conduct, for human societies'.[3]

Thirty years later, the linguist and bibliographer Eugene Garfield devised a similar graphical technique to visualize the history of scientific fields by creating a 'historiograph' of citations. Citation indices and 'impact factors' have since become standard measures of academic achievement in science. They are also a way of mapping the process of scientific innovation – revealing, for example, the 'invisible colleges' implied by networks of citation, which look very different from the actual colleges that employ most scientists.[4] However, such metrics may simply show that scientists tend to cite the work of

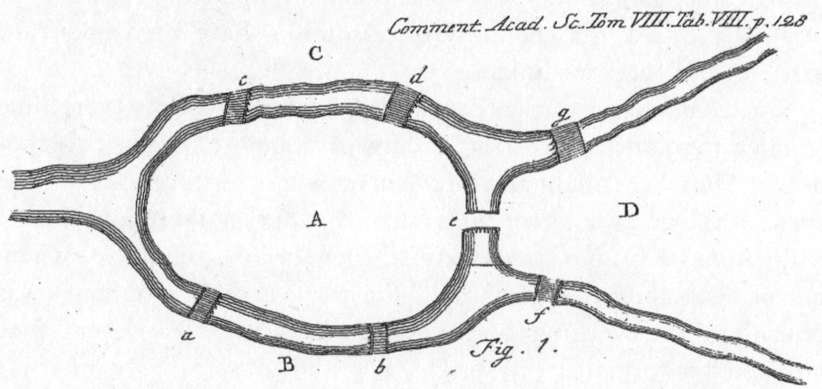

4. Euler's figure 1 from his *Solutio problematis ad geometriam situs pertinentis* (1741). Those wishing to test Euler's theorem literally cannot do so, as two of the seven original bridges did not survive the bombing of the city in the Second World War and two others were demolished after the city became Soviet-controlled Kaliningrad.

like-minded scientists. As the old adage says, birds of a feather flock together. What is true of citations is true more generally. The chances are that, when two nodes are linked to a third node, they will also be linked to each other, because (in the words of the economist James E. Rauch) 'two people who know me are more likely to know each other than are two randomly selected people'.[5] A triad, all three members of which are connected by positive sentiments, is said to be 'balanced' and exemplifies the idea that 'the friend of my friend is my friend'. Another triad, two members of which do not know each other, despite both knowing the third member, is sometimes called a 'forbidden triad'. (A variant, with two members that are amicable but one that is hostile, represents the uncomfortable case when 'the enemy of my friend is also my friend'.)[6]

'Homophily' – our tendency to gravitate towards people similar to us (also known as assortativity) – might therefore be regarded as the first law of social networks. Everett Rogers and Dilip Bhowmik were the first sociologists to suggest that homophily might be disadvantageous, in narrowing the range of an individual's milieu; there was, they suggested, an 'optimal heterophily'. Was homophily a kind of

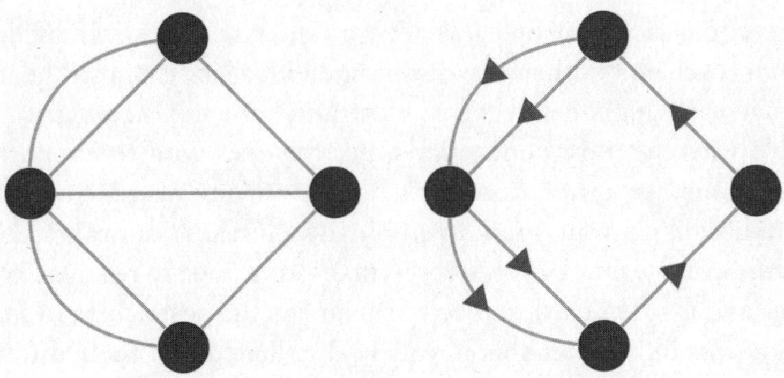

5. Simplified graph of Euler's Königsberg bridge problem. Only by removing the edge in the middle (the bridge linking the two islands in figure 4) can one solve the problem.

self-segregation? In the 1970s, Wayne Zachary plotted the friendship network between members of a university karate club. It clearly revealed two distinct clusters within the club. Homophily can be based on shared status (ascribed characteristics such as race, ethnicity, sex or age, and acquired characteristics such as religion, education, occupation or behaviour patterns) or shared values, in so far as those can be distinguished from acquired traits.[7] A familiar illustration is the tendency for American schoolchildren to self-segregate by race and ethnicity (see plate 3), though recent research suggests that this tendency varies significantly between racial groups.[8]

Can such graphs show us which individuals are important? It was not until the twentieth century that scholars and mathematicians formally defined importance as 'centrality'. The three most important measures of importance in formal network analysis are degree centrality, betweenness centrality and closeness centrality. Degree centrality – the number of edges radiating out from a specific node – captures what might be called sociability: the simple number of relationships an individual has to others. Formalized by the sociologist Linton Freeman in the late seventies, betweenness centrality measures the extent to which information passes through a particular node. Just as commuters, by individually seeking the shortest route to their destination, concentrate traffic in a few congested intersections, so too people in a network often rely on key individuals to connect them to otherwise distant individuals or groups. The individuals with high betweenness centrality are not necessarily the people with the most connections, but the ones with the important connections. (In other words, it's not how many people you know that matters; it's who you know.) Finally, closeness centrality measures the average number of 'steps' it takes for a node to reach all other nodes and is often used to discover who has the best access to information, assuming that this is widely distributed.[9] In their different ways, individuals in social networks with high degree centrality, betweenness centrality or closeness centrality act as 'hubs'.

The mid-twentieth century also saw important advances in how we understand a network's aggregate properties, which are often invisible from the perspective of any individual node. At the Massachusetts Institute of Technology, R. Duncan Luce and Albert Perry proposed the use of 'clustering' coefficients to measure how much a group of nodes are connected, with a clique being the extreme case in which each node is connected to all the others in the network. (Technically, the clustering coefficient is the proportion of social triads which are fully connected, meaning that each member of any trio is connected to the other two.) The 'density' of a network is a similar measure of interconnectedness.

The importance of such measures became apparent in 1967, when the social psychologist Stanley Milgram conducted a famous experiment. He sent out letters to randomly chosen residents of Wichita, Kansas, and Omaha, Nebraska. The recipients were asked to forward the letter directly to the intended final recipient – respectively, the wife of a Harvard divinity student and a stockbroker in Boston – if that person was known personally to them, or to forward it to someone they believed might know the final recipient, provided they knew that intermediary on a first-name basis; and also to send Milgram a 'tracer' postcard saying what they had done. In all, according to Milgram, forty-four of the 160 letters from Nebraska ultimately got through.[10] (A more recent study suggests it was just twenty-one.)[11] The completed chains allowed Milgram to calculate the number of intermediaries required to get the letter to its target: on average five.[12] This finding had been anticipated by the Hungarian author Frigyes

Karinthy, in whose story 'Láncszemek' ('Chains', published in 1929) a character bets his companions that he can link himself to any individual on earth they choose to name through no more than five acquaintances, only one of which he has to know personally. It was also borne out by separate experiments by other researchers, notably the political scientist Ithiel de Sola Pool and the mathematician Manfred Kochen.

A network that connects two nodes via five intermediaries has six edges. The phrase 'six degrees of separation' was not coined until John Guare's 1990 play of that title, but it therefore had a long prehistory. Like the concept of a 'small world' (made famous by the Disneyland ride devised in 1964), or the more technical concept of closeness, it neatly summed up the mid-twentieth century's growing sense of interconnectedness. There have since been numerous variations on the theme: six degrees of Marlon Brando, six degrees of Monica Lewinsky, six degrees of Kevin Bacon (which became a board-game), six degrees of Lois Weisberg (the mother of one of Malcolm Gladwell's friends) and the academic equivalent, six degrees of the mathematician Paul Erdös, himself a pioneer of network theory, as we have seen.[13] Recent research suggests the number is now closer to five than six, which suggests that technological change since the 1970s has perhaps been less transformative than is commonly supposed.[14] For the directors of Fortune 1000 companies, however, it is 4.6.[15] For Facebook users it was 3.74 in 2012,[16] and just 3.57 in 2016.[17]

6
Weak Ties and Viral Ideas

What makes this kind of finding so intriguing is that we tend to think of our networks of friends as relatively small clusters or cliques of similar, like-minded people, isolated from other groups whose members have different affinities with one another. The fact that we are all nevertheless just six degrees away from Monica Lewinsky is explained by what the Stanford sociologist Mark Granovetter called, paradoxically, 'the strength of weak ties'.[1] If all ties were like the strong, homophilic ones between us and our close friends, the world would necessarily be fragmented. But weaker ties – to the 'acquaintances' we do not so closely resemble – are the key to the 'small world' phenomenon. Granovetter's initial focus was on the way people looking for jobs were helped more by acquaintances than by their close friends, but a later insight was that, in a society with relatively few weak ties, 'new ideas will spread slowly, scientific endeavours will be handicapped, and subgroups separated by race, ethnicity, geography, or other characteristics will have difficulty reaching a *modus vivendi*'.[2] Weak ties, in other words, are the vital bridges between disparate clusters that would otherwise not be connected at all.[3]

Granovetter's was a sociological observation, based on interviews and similar data, and was subject to refinement on the basis of field studies. These revealed, for example, that strong ties matter more to the poor than weak ties, suggesting that the tightly knit networks of the proletarian world might tend to perpetuate poverty.[4] It was not until 1998 that the mathematicians Duncan Watts and Steven Strogatz demonstrated *why* a world characterized by homophilic clusters could simultaneously be a small world. Watts and Strogatz classified networks in terms of two relatively independent properties: the average closeness centrality of each node and the network's general clustering coefficient. Beginning with a circular lattice in which each node was connected only to its first- and second-nearest neighbours, they showed that the random addition of just a few extra edges sufficed drastically to increase the closeness of all nodes, without significantly increasing the overall clustering coefficient.[5] Watts had begun his work by studying the synchronized chirping of crickets, but the implications of his and Strogatz's findings for human populations were obvious. In Watts's words, 'the difference between a big- and a small-world graph can be a matter of only a few randomly required edges – a change that is effectively undetectable at the level of individual vertices . . . [T]he highly clustered nature of small-world graphs can lead to the intuition that a given disease is "far away" when, on the contrary, it is effectively very close.'[6]

For economists, too, advances in network science had important implications. Standard economics had imagined more or less undifferentiated markets populated by individual utility-maximizing agents with perfect information. The problem – resolved by the English economist Ronald Coase, who explained the importance of transaction costs* – was to explain why firms existed at all. (We are not all longshoremen, hired and paid by the day like Marlon Brando in *On the Waterfront*, because employing us regularly within firms can reduce the costs that arise when workers are hired on a daily basis.) But if markets were networks, with most people inhabiting more or less interconnected clusters, the economic world looked very different, not least because information flows were determined by the networks' structures.[7] Many exchanges are not just one-off transactions in which price is a matter of supply and demand. Credit is a function of trust, which in turn is higher within a cluster of similar

* Coase argued in 'The Problem of Social Cost' (1960, 15) that 'in order to carry out a market transaction it is necessary to discover who it is that one wishes to deal with, to inform people that one wishes to deal and on what terms, to conduct negotiations leading up to a bargain, to draw up the contract, to undertake the inspection needed to make sure that the terms of the contract are being observed, and so on'. Organizations like firms and indeed states exist to lower or eliminate such transaction costs with, for example, standardized long-term employment contracts. Larger units can do this more efficiently, hence 'economies of scale'.

people (e.g. an immigrant community). This has implications not only for employment markets, the case studied by Granovetter.[8] Closed networks of sellers can collude against the public and deter innovation. More open networks can promote innovation as new ideas reach the cluster thanks to the strength of weak ties.[9] Such observations prompted the question of how exactly networks are formed in the first place.[10]

In practice, it seems clear how networks form. From Avner Greif's eleventh-century Maghribi traders in the Mediterranean[11] to the modern entrepreneurs and managers studied by Ronald Burt, scholars have produced a rich literature on the role of business networks in generating social capital[12] and promoting – or discouraging – innovation. In Burt's terminology, competition between individuals and firms is structured by networks, with 'structural holes' – the gaps between clusters, where weak ties are lacking – as 'entrepreneurial opportunities for information access, timing, referrals, and control'.[13] Brokers – people who are able to 'bridge the holes' – are (or should be) 'rewarded for their integrative work' because their position makes them more likely to have creative ideas (or less likely to suffer from group-think). In innovative institutions, such brokers are always appreciated. However, in most contests between an innovator-broker and a network inclined towards 'closure' (i.e. insularity and homogeneity), the latter often prevails.[14] This insight applies as much to academic philosophers as to the employees of an American electronics company.[15]

An entire subfield of 'organizational behaviour' now occupies a foundational place in most master's programmes in business administration. Among its recent findings are that managers are more likely to be networkers than non-managers;[16] that a 'less hierarchical network may be better for producing solidarity and homogeneity in an organizational culture';[17] and that brokers are more likely to succeed in spanning structural holes if they 'fit culturally into their organizational group', while those who are 'structurally embedded' fare better when they are 'culturally distinct'. In sum, 'assimilated brokers' and 'integrated nonconformists' tend to do better than their peers.[18] Here, too, network theory offers insights that have utility beyond the typical corporate workplace satirized in Ricky Gervais's *The Office*.

After all, office networks are seldom very large. Yet network size matters because of Metcalfe's law – named after the Ethernet inventor, Robert Metfcalfe – which (in its original form) stated that the value of a telecommunications network was proportional to the square of the number of connected compatible communicating devices. This is in fact true of networks generally: put simply, the greater the number of nodes in a network, the more valuable the network to the nodes collectively. As we shall see, this implies spectacular returns to very large, open-access networks and, conversely, limited returns to secret and/or exclusive networks. Yet even in the largest networks there are nodes that act as brokers or hubs.

The phrase 'to go viral' has become a tiresome cliché, the holy grail of advertisers and marketers.[19] Nevertheless, network science offers the best way of understanding why some ideas can spread very rapidly. Ideas – and indeed emotional states and conditions such as obesity – can be transmitted through a social network, not unlike a contagious virus. However, ideas (or 'memes', to use the evolutionist's neologism) are generally less contagious than viruses. Biological and computer viruses typically carry out a 'broadcast search' across a network, as their goal is to spread themselves as far as possible, targeting every neighbour of every node they infect. We, by contrast, instinctively select the members of our network to whom we want to communicate an idea or from whom we are likely to accept one as credible.[20] An early contribution was the so-called 'two-step flow of communication model', associated with the sociologists Paul Lazarsfeld and Elihu Katz, who argued in the 1950s that ideas flowed from the media to the wider population via opinion 'leaders'.[21] Other late-twentieth-century researchers sought to measure the speed at which news, rumours or innovations moved. More recent research has shown that even emotional states can be transmitted through a network.[22] Though distinguishing between endogenous and exogenous network effects is far from easy,[23] the evidence of this kind of contagion is clear: 'Students with studious roommates become more studious. Diners sitting next to heavy eaters eat more food.'[24] However, according to Christakis and Fowler, we cannot transmit ideas and behaviours much beyond our friends' friends' friends (in other words, across just three degrees of separation). This is because the

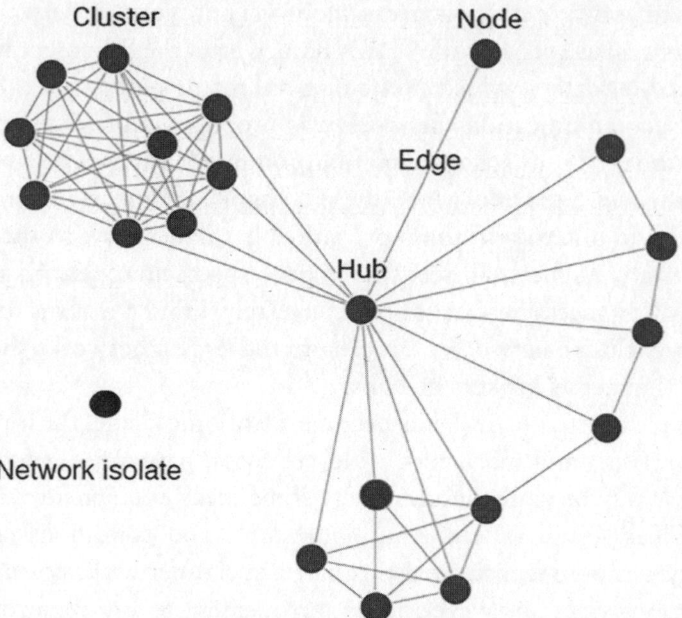

6. The foundational concepts of network theory. Each dot in the graph is a node, each line an edge. The dot labelled 'Hub' has the highest degree centrality and betweenness centrality. The nodes labelled 'Cluster' have a higher density or local clustering coefficient than other parts of the graph.

transmission and reception of an idea or behaviour requires a stronger connection than the relaying of a letter (in the case of Milgram's experiment) or the communication that a certain employment opportunity exists. Merely knowing people is not the same as being able to influence them to study more or over-eat. Imitation is indeed the sincerest form of flattery, even when it is unconscious.

The key point, as with disease epidemics, is that network structure can be as important as the idea itself in determining the speed and extent of diffusion.[25] In the process of going viral, a key role is played by nodes that are not merely hubs or brokers but 'gate-keepers' – people who decide whether or not to pass information to their part of the network.[26] Their decision will be based partly on how they think that information will reflect back on them. Acceptance of an idea, in turn, can require it to be transmitted by more than one or two sources. A complex cultural contagion, unlike a simple disease epidemic, first needs to attain a critical mass of early adopters with high degree centrality (relatively large numbers of influential friends).[27] In the words of Duncan Watts, the key to assessing the likelihood of a contagion-like cascade is 'to focus *not* on the stimulus itself but on the structure of the network the stimulus hits'.[28] This helps explain why, for every idea that goes viral, there are countless others that fizzle out in obscurity because they began with the wrong node, cluster or network.

7
Varieties of Network

If all social network structures were the same, we would inhabit a very different world. For example, a world in which nodes were randomly connected to one another – so that the numbers of edges per node were normally distributed along a bell curve – would have some 'small world' properties, but it would not be like our world.* That is because so many real-world networks follow Pareto-like distributions: that is, they have more nodes with a very large number of edges and more nodes with very few than would be the case in a random network. This is a version of what the sociologist Robert K. Merton called 'the Matthew effect', after the Gospel of St Matthew: 'For unto every one that hath shall be given, and he shall have abundance: but from him that hath not shall be taken away even that which he hath.'† In science, success breeds success: to him who already has prizes, more prizes shall be given. Something similar can be seen in 'the economics of superstars'.[1] In the same way, as many large networks expand, nodes gain new edges in proportion to the number that they already have (their degree or 'fitness'). There is, in short, 'preferential attachment'. We owe this insight to the physicists Albert-László Barabási and Réka Albert, who were the first to suggest that most real-world networks might follow a power law distribution or

* Random networks were first studied by the famously prolific and much cited mathematician Paul Erdös and Alfréd Rényi, one of his many co-authors. A random graph is constructed by placing *n* nodes on a plane, then joining pairs of them together at random until *m* edges are used. Nodes may be chosen more than once, or not at all.

† Matthew 25:28.

be 'scale-free'.* As such networks evolve, a few nodes will become hubs with many more edges than other nodes.[2] Examples of such networks abound, ranging from the directorships of Fortune 1000 companies to citations in physics journals and links to and from webpages.[3] In Barabási's words:

> [T]here is a hierarchy of hubs that keep those networks together, a heavily connected node closely followed by several less connected ones, trailed by dozens of even smaller nodes. No central node sits in the middle of the spider web, controlling and monitoring every link and node. There is no single node whose removal could break the web. A scale-free network is a web without a spider.[4]

In the extreme case (the winner-takes-all model), the fittest node gets all or nearly all the links. More often, there is a 'fit get rich' pattern whereby 'a heavily connected node [is] closely followed by several less connected ones, trailed by dozens of even smaller nodes'.[5] Other intermediate network structures can also be found: for example, the friendship networks of American adolescents are neither random nor scale-free.[6]

In a random network, as Erdös and Rényi showed long ago, each node within the network has approximately the same number of links to other nodes. The best real-world example is the US national highway network, in which each major city has roughly the same number of highways connecting it to others. An example of a scale-free network is the US air traffic network, in which a large number of small airports are connected to medium-sized airports, which in turn connect to a few huge and busy hubs. Other networks are more highly centralized without necessarily being scale-free. One way of

* Distributions that follow a power law are said to have 'fat tails', as the relative likelihood of very high degree and very low degree are higher than if links were formed at random. Technically, the term 'scale-free' refers to the fact 'that the relative frequency of nodes of degree d, compared to nodes of degree d', is the same as the relative frequency of nodes with degree kd compared to nodes of degree kd', when rescaling by an arbitrary factor $k > 0$.' In a scale-free network there is no typical node, and yet the 'scale' of difference between nodes appears the same everywhere. Put differently, the scale-free world is characterized by fractal geometry: the town is a large family, the city a large town, and the kingdom a large city.

understanding the tragedy that unfolds in Shakespeare's *Hamlet* is to depict the network of relationships between the characters, in which Hamlet and his stepfather Claudius have by far the highest degree centrality (i.e. number of edges: see figure 7).

Now consider all the ways in which a network can differ from the random version (see figure 8). A network could be highly deterministic and non-random, such as a crystal lattice or mesh, in which each node has the same number of edges as all the others (bottom left). A network could be modular – that is, it could be broken up into a number of separate clusters nonetheless tied together by a few bridging edges (bottom right). A network could also be heterogeneous, with each node differing greatly in terms of centrality, like the scale-free networks that characterize online communities (top left). Some networks are both hierarchical and modular, such as the complex genetic systems that regulate metabolism, which put certain sub-systems under the control of others (top right).[7]

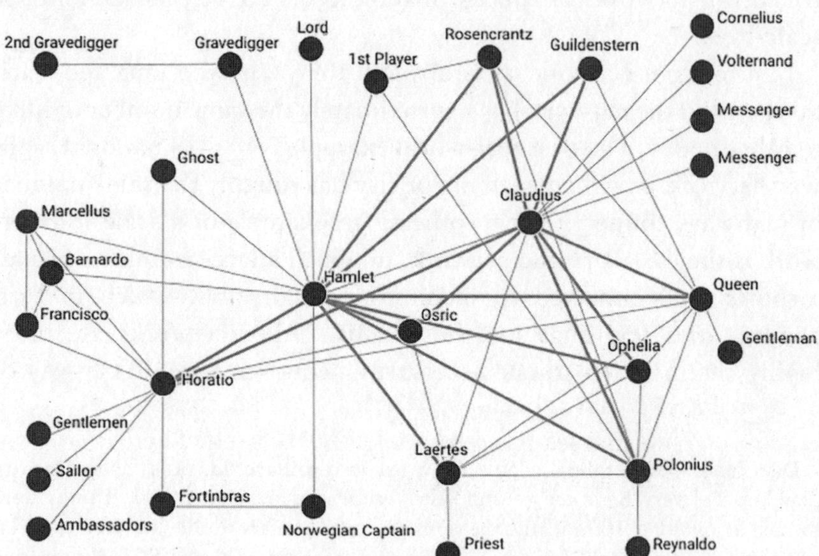

7. A simple (but tragic) network: Shakespeare's *Hamlet*. Hamlet leads in terms of degree centrality (sixteen, compared with Claudius's thirteen). The 'zone of death' in the play encompasses characters connected to both Hamlet and Claudius.

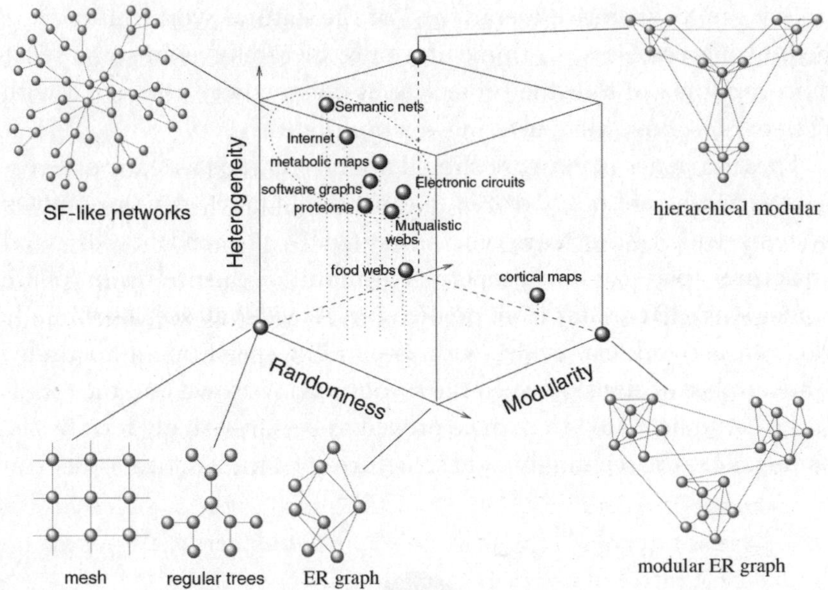

8. Varieties of network (SF: scale-free; ER: Erdös–Rényi, i.e. random).

We can now see clearly that, far from being the opposite of a network, a hierarchy is just a special kind of network. As figure 9 shows, edges in an idealized hierarchical network follow a regular pattern, like that of an upside-down tree (or the roots of a tree). To construct a hierarchical network, start with the top node, and add a certain number of subordinate nodes. To each subordinate node add the same number of subordinates again, and so on. The key is to always add nodes downwards, but never connect nodes laterally. Networks built in this way have special properties. For one, there are no cycles, that is, no path that leads from a node back to itself. There is only one path connecting any two nodes, which clarifies chains of command and communication. More importantly, the top node has the highest betweenness and closeness centrality – that is, the system is designed to maximize that node's ability both to access and to control information. As we shall see, few hierarchies achieve such a total control over information flows, though Stalin's Soviet Union came close. Most organizations are in practice only partially hierarchical, not unlike the 'cooperative hierarchies' of the natural world.[8] It may be helpful, nevertheless, to think of a pure hierarchy as in some sense 'anti-random', in that the promiscuous connectivity associated with networks – above all, clustering – is prohibited.

These varieties of network should not be regarded as static categories. Networks are rarely frozen in time. Large networks are complex systems which have 'emergent properties' – the tendency of novel structures, patterns and properties to manifest themselves in 'phase transitions' that are far from predictable. As we shall see, a seemingly random network can evolve with astounding speed into a hierarchy. The number of steps between the revolutionary crowd and the totalitarian state has more than once proved to be surprisingly few. By the same token, the seemingly rigid structures of a hierarchical order can

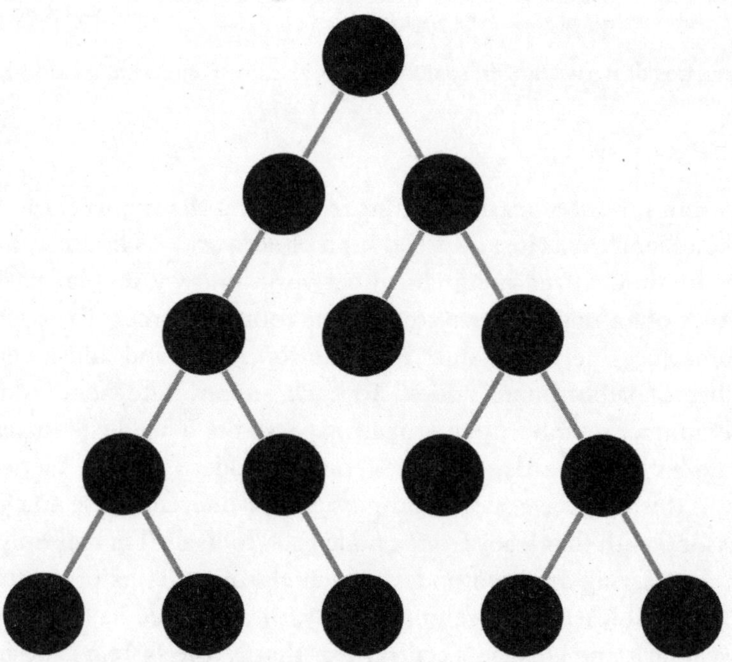

9. Hierarchy: a special kind of network. In the example shown here, the node at the top has the highest betweenness and closeness centrality. Other nodes can communicate with the majority of other nodes only through that one ruling hub.

disintegrate with astounding rapidity.[9] This comes as no shock to the student of networks. We know now that the random addition of a very small number of new edges can radically reduce the average separation between the nodes. It would not require too many additional edges in figure 9 to destroy the ruling node's near monopoly on communication. This helps explain why emperors and kings throughout history have fretted about conspiracies. Cabals, camarillas, cells, cliques, coteries: all such terms have sinister connotations in the context of a monarchical court. Hierarchs have long been uneasily aware that fraternizing amongst subordinates can be the prelude to a palace coup.

8
When Networks Meet

The final conceptual challenge – and the most important one for the historian – is to consider how different networks interact with one another. The political scientist John Padgett and his co-authors have proposed a biochemical analogy, arguing that organizational innovation and invention are both the results of interaction between networks, which takes three basic forms: 'transposition', 'refunctionality' and 'catalysis'.[1] In itself, a resilient social network will tend to resist change to its production rules and communication protocols. It is when a social network and its patterns are transposed from one context and refunctioned in another that innovation and even invention can occur.[2]

As we shall see, Padgett has used this insight to explain changes in the economic and social structure of Florence in the time of the Medici, when banking partnerships were incorporated into city politics. It clearly has a more general applicability, however. Networks are important not just as transmission mechanisms for new ideas, but as the sources of the new ideas themselves. Not all networks are likely to foster change; on the contrary, some dense and clustered networks have the tendency to resist it. But the point of contact between diverse networks may be the place to look for novelty.[3] The question is what the nature of that point of contact is. Networks can meet and fuse amicably, but they may also attack one another, as happened (in an example to be discussed below) when Soviet intelligence successfully penetrated the elite networks of Cambridge students in the 1930s. In such contests, the outcome will be determined by the relative strengths and weaknesses of the rival networks. How adaptable and resilient are they? How vulnerable to a disruptive contagion? How reliant on one or more 'superhubs', the destruction or capture of which would significantly reduce the stability of the whole network? Barabási and his colleagues simulated attacks on scale-free networks and found that they could withstand the loss of a significant fraction of nodes, and even of a single hub. But a targeted attack on multiple hubs could break the network up altogether.[4] Even more dramatically, a scale-free network could quite easily fall victim to a contagious node-killing virus.[5]

But why would one network attack another, as opposed to peaceably linking to it? The answer is that most attacks on social networks are not initiated by other networks but are ordered or at least encouraged by hierarchical entities. The Russian meddling in the 2016 US election is a case in point: according to US intelligence, as noted above, it was authorized by President Putin, one of the most unabashed autocrats in the world, but it was directed not just at the Democratic National Committee but at the whole complex of US media networks. This illustrates the fundamental difference between networks and hierarchies. Because of their relatively decentralized structure, because of the way they combine clusters and weak links, and because they can adapt and evolve, networks tend to be more creative than hierarchies. Historically, as we shall see, innovations have tended to come from networks more than from hierarchies. The problem is that networks are not easily directed 'towards a common objective . . . that requires concentration of resources in space and time within large organizations, like armies, bureaucracies, large factories, vertically organized corporations'.[6] Networks may be spontaneously creative but they are not strategic. The Second World War could not have been won by a network, even if superior networks (of atomic scientists or cryptographers) played an important part in the Allied victory. Not only that, but networks are as capable of creating and spreading bad ideas as good ideas. In cases of social contagion or 'cascades' of ideas, networks can spread panics as readily as they can communicate the wisdom of crowds – crazes for burning witches as easily as harmless manias for photographs of cats.

True, today's networks are better designed than the US electricity grid in the 1990s, which was so fragile that the failure of a single power line in western Oregon caused the tripping of hundreds more lines and generators. Yet we know that even a robust network can tip over into dysfunction as it grows and evolves: the normal congestion and delays at US airports are a case in point, as airlines compete to service hubs, but end up clogging them.[7] Quite aside from the Internet, there is little doubt that a targeted attack on US electrical and transport infrastructure would have devastatingly disruptive consequences. As Amy Zegart has said, the United States is simultaneously the most powerful and the most vulnerable actor in the cyberwar theatre. 'The cyber threats of tomorrow,' she has warned, 'could disable the cars that we drive, the airplanes that we fly, they could turn off power or water to cities across the country for days or weeks or longer, they could incapacitate our military or even turn our own weapons against us.'[8] And yet the United States 'seems unwilling to acknowledge the basic facts about new cyber-technologies or our cyber-vulnerabilities, let alone take the necessary measures to attribute, deter and defend against future attacks'.[9] The May 2017 epidemic, when the WannaCry 'ransomware' infected hundreds of thousands of computers in 150 countries, encrypting their hard drives and demanding payment in Bitcoin, exposed the vulnerability not only of European countries but also, ironically, of Russia, to criminal attacks.

The reality is that we find it very hard indeed to fathom the implications of the growth of networks in our own time. For every article extolling their positive effects in empowering the young and enlivening democracy – for example, in the Arab revolutions of 2010–12 – there is another warning of their negative effects in empowering dangerous forces – for example, political Islam. For every book prophesying a 'singularity' in which a 'global brain' or 'planetary superorganism' arises from the Internet,[10] there is another foreseeing collapse and extinction.[11] Anne-Marie Slaughter expects that 'the United States and other powers will gradually find the golden mean of network power: not too concentrated and not too distributed', and looks forward to the emergence of 'a flatter, faster, more flexible system, one that operates at the level of citizens as well as states'.[12] Writing before 9/11, Graham Allison was relatively confident that the United States would have an inbuilt advantage in a world of global networks.[13] Yet Joshua Ramo is far less optimistic. 'The simple, once-appealing idea that connection is liberation is wrong,' he writes. 'To connect now is to be encased in a powerful and dynamic tension.' The inability of old leaders to make sense of the Network Age is 'the reason [their] legitimacy . . . is failing, the reason our grand strategy is incoherent, the reason our age really is revolutionary'. In his eyes, 'the fundamental threat to American interests isn't China or Al Qaeda or Iran. It is the evolution of the network itself.'[14]

In one respect only does there seem to be consensus: few futurologists expect established hierarchies – in particular, traditional political elites, but also long-established corporations – to fare very well in the future.[15] Francis Fukuyama is unusual in arguing that hierarchy must ultimately prevail, in the sense that networks alone cannot provide a stable institutional framework for economic development or political order. Indeed, he argues, 'hierarchical organization . . . may be the *only* way in which a low-trust society can be organized'.[16] By contrast, the iconoclastic British political operative Dominic Cummings hypothesizes that the state of the future will need to function more like the human immune system or an ant colony than a traditional state – in other words, more like a network, with emergent properties and the capacity for self-organization, without plans or central coordination, relying instead on probabilistic experimentation, reinforcing success and discarding failure, achieving resilience partly through redundancy.[17] This may be to underestimate both the resilience of the old hierarchies and the vulnerabilities of the new networks – not to mention their capacity to fuse to form even newer power structures, with capabilities potentially greater even than those of the last century's totalitarian states.

9
Seven Insights

For the historian, then, the insights of network theory, in all its forms, have profound implications. I have tried to sum them up here under seven headings:

1. *No man is an island.* Conceived of as nodes in networks, individuals can be understood in terms of their relationships to other nodes: the edges that connect them. Not all nodes are equal. Located in a network, an individual can be assessed in terms not only of degree centrality (the number of her relationships), but also of betweenness centrality (the likelihood of her being a bridge between other nodes). (Other metrics include eigenvector centrality, which measures proximity to popular or prestigious nodes, though this will not feature in what follows.[1]) As we shall see, an important but neglected measure of an individual's historical importance is the extent to which that person was a network bridge. Sometimes, as in the case of the American Revolution, crucial roles turn out to have been played by people who were not leaders but connectors.
2. *Birds of a feather flock together.* Because of homophily, social networks can be understood partly in terms of like attracting like. However, it is not always self-evident which shared attribute or preference causes people to cluster together. Moreover, we must be clear about the nature of the network linkages. Are the links between nodes relationships of acquaintance or amity? Are we looking at a family tree or a circle of friends or a secret society? Does something other than knowledge – money, say, or some other resource – get

exchanged within the network? No network graph can do justice to the rich complexity of human interactions, but we sometimes know enough to differentiate between the directions of edges (e.g. A commands B, but not vice versa), their modes (e.g. A knows B but sleeps with C), and their weights (e.g. A occasionally meets B but sees C every day).

3. *Weak ties are strong.* It also matters how dense a network is, and how connected it is to other clusters, even if it is only through a few weak links. Is it a component of a larger network? Are there 'network isolates', nodes that are wholly 'off the grid' like Burns's misanthrope? Are there brokers seeking to exploit structural holes in the network? Does the network exhibit 'small world' properties – and, if so, how small is the world (i.e. how many degrees of separation are there between nodes)? How modular is the network's structure?
4. *Structure determines virality.* Many historians still tend to assume that the spread of an idea or an ideology is a function of its inherent content in relation to some vaguely specified context. We must now acknowledge, however, that some ideas go viral because of structural features of the network through which they spread. They are least likely to do so in a hierarchical, top-down network, where horizontal peer-to-peer links are prohibited.
5. *Networks never sleep.* Networks are not static, but dynamic. Whether they are random or scale-free, they are prone to phase transitions. They can evolve into complex adaptive systems with emergent properties. Very small changes – the addition of just a few edges – can radically alter the network's behaviour.
6. *Networks network.* When networks interact, the result can be innovation and invention. When a network disrupts an ossified hierarchy, it can overthrow it with breath-taking speed. But when a hierarchy attacks a fragile network, the result can be the network's collapse.
7. *The rich get richer.* Because of preferential attachment, most social networks are profoundly inegalitarian.

When we understand these core insights of network science, the history of mankind looks quite different: not so much 'one fucking thing after another', in the playwright Alan Bennett's droll phrase,[2] nor even one thing after another fucking, but billions of things linked to one another in myriad ways (including, but by no means only, sexual intercourse). Moreover, when set in its proper historical context, the present time appears less unnervingly unprecedented and more familiar. It is, as we shall see, the second era when superannuated hierarchical institutions have been challenged by novel networks, their impact magnified by new technology. On the basis of historical analogy, as will become clear, we should probably expect continued network-driven disruption of hierarchies that cannot reform themselves, but also the potential for some kind of restoration of hierarchical order when it becomes clear that the networks alone cannot avert a descent into anarchy.

10

The Illuminati Illuminated

With these insights of network theory in mind, we can now revisit the history (as opposed to the conspiracy theory) of the Illuminati. The founder of the Order was, in fact, an obscure South German academic named Adam Weishaupt. Born in 1748 – and so just twenty-eight years old when he founded it – Weishaupt was the orphan son of a professor of law at the University of Ingolstadt in central Bavaria. Thanks to the patronage of Baron Johann Adam Ickstatt, who had been appointed Rector by the Elector Maximilian III Joseph with a mandate to reform the Jesuit-dominated university, Weishaupt was able to follow in his father's footsteps. In 1773, he was appointed professor of canon law and, a year later, dean of the faculty of law.[1]

What induced the young professor three years later to establish a secret and in many ways revolutionary society? The answer is that, under Ickstatt's influence, Weishaupt had become an enthusiastic reader of works by the more radical philosophers of the French Enlightenment, notably Claude Adrien Helvétius, whose best-known book was *De l'esprit* (1758), and Paul-Henri Thiry, Baron d'Holbach, the pseudonymous author of *Le Système de la nature* (1770). As a boy, Weishaupt had been educated by Jesuits, an experience he had not enjoyed. The atheist tendencies of Helvétius and d'Holbach greatly excited him. Yet in conservative Bavaria, where the Roman Catholic clergy were already fomenting a 'counter-Enlightenment', such views were dangerous. A young man who had been given a chair formerly monopolized by the Jesuits, Weishaupt was under pressure. The idea of a secret society, which masked its true purposes even from its recruits, made sense. Weishaupt himself said he got the idea from a Protestant student named Ernst Christoph Henninger, who had told him about the student associations at Jena, Erfurt, Halle and Leipzig, where he had previously studied.[2] In other respects, paradoxically, the Illuminati were modelled on the Jesuits, a powerful and far from transparent network who had themselves been dissolved by Pope Clement XIV in 1773. Weishaupt's first sketch for 'A School of Humanity' envisaged that every member should keep a journal in which to record his thoughts and feelings, and should turn over a summary to his superiors; in return, there would be a library, healthcare, insurance and other benefits.[3] To call Weishaupt's thinking eclectic would be an understatement: his designs for the Order also included elements from the ancient Greek Eleusinian mysteries and Zoroastrianism (including use of the old Persian calendar). Another source of inspiration was the *Alumbrados*, a seventeenth-century spiritual movement in Spain.

Had the Illuminati remained faithful to Weishaupt's original blueprint, they would long ago have been forgotten, if they had ever been heard of at all. The key to their growth and later notoriety was their infiltration of German Masonic lodges. Though its roots lay in the brotherhoods of medieval stonemasons, by the eighteenth century Freemasonry was itself a rapidly growing network that, beginning in Scotland and England, offered male sociability exalted by mythology and ritual, uninhibited by the status difference between aristocracy and bourgeoisie.* It had spread rapidly throughout Germany, including the southern German states, despite efforts by the Roman Catholic Church to prohibit Catholics from becoming Masons.[4] It was the suggestion of Franz Xaver Zwackh, one of Weishaupt's pupils, to recruit Illuminati within German lodges, exploiting the mounting dissatisfaction of many Freemasons with their own movement.

The late 1770s were a time of ferment within German Freemasonry, with some purists objecting to the lack of secrecy and declining respect for the myth of its descent from the Knights Templar, as asserted by the 'Rite of Strict Observance'.[5] One of those dissatisfied with the seeming degeneration of the Masonic orders into vacuous dining clubs was Adolph Franz Friedrich Ludwig, Baron von Knigge, the Göttingen-educated son of a Hanoverian official, who had been a

* For a full discussion of Freemasonry, see chapter 2.

Freemason since 1772.[6] Knigge yearned for something more exclusive and uplifting than was on offer in the lodges he frequented in Cassel and Frankfurt, a wish he expressed to another aristocratic Freemason, the marchese Costanzo di Costanzo, in 1780. To Knigge's amazement, the marquess revealed that such an elite organization already existed, and that – under the name Diomedes – he was a member of it. An accurate characterization of the Illuminati after 1777 – when Weishaupt himself had been initiated into the Munich lodge 'Zur Behutsamkeit' – is that it was 'a clandestine network embedded within freemasonry . . . rather like a parasitic plant'.[7] A similar parasite was Rosicrucianism, a more esoteric movement than Illuminism, much written about in the early seventeenth century but given concrete form as 'the Golden and Rosy Cross' within a number of German Masonic lodges at around the same time.

The recruitment of Knigge was a turning point for two reasons. First, he was a far better-connected individual than Weishaupt. Second, he understood what like-minded aristocratic Freemasons craved.[8] Knigge – who took the name Philo after he joined the Illuminati – was startled to find how embryonic the organization was (as well as how backward Bavaria was when he visited it).[9] 'The Order does not yet exist,' Weishaupt candidly confessed, 'only in my mind . . . Would you forgive my little fraud?' Knigge not only forgave Weishaupt but enthusiastically seized the initiative, envisioning the Illuminati as an instrument for radically overhauling Freemasonry itself.[10] He radically revised and expanded the structure that Weishaupt had envisaged by subdividing the three ranks or classes of the Illuminati and adding a great deal of Masonic ritual. The preparatory Minerval class was divided in two: Minerval and *Illuminatus Minor*. The second Freemasonic class was also split in two: *Illuminatus major* or 'Scottish Novice', and *Illuminatus dirigens*, or 'Scottish Knight'. The third Mysteric class was further stratified into 'Lesser Mysteries' (with the rank of *presbyter* or *princeps*) and 'Greater Mysteries' (with the ranks of *magus* or 'docetist' and *rex* or 'philosophus'). From the Illuminati holding this last position were to be drawn the highest functionaries of the order: national inspectors, provincials, prefects and deans of the priests. These higher degrees would replace the original apex of Weishaupt's system, the 'Areopagites'.[11] At the same time as these elaborate 'degrees' were being devised, the organizational structure of the rapidly growing Order was becoming more elaborate, with numerous local 'Minerval 'churches' reporting to 'Prefectures', 'Provinces' and 'Inspections'.[12]

The first paradox of Illuminism, then, was that it was a network that craved an elaborate hierarchical structure, even as it inveighed against existing hierarchies. In his 1782 'Address to the newly promoted Illuminati dirigenti', Weishaupt set out his worldview. In the state of nature, man had been free, equal and happy; division into classes, private property, personal ambition and state formation had come later, as the 'great unholy mainsprings and causes of our misery'. Mankind had ceased to be 'one great family, a single empire' because of the 'desire of men to differentiate themselves from one another'. But Enlightenment, spread by the activities of secret societies, could overcome this stratification of society. And then 'princes and nations would disappear from the earth without any need for violence, the human race would become one family, and the world would become the habitation of rational beings'.[13] This was not easily reconciled with Knigge's successful campaign to recruit princely and noble Freemasons into the Order.[14]

The second paradox of Illuminism was its ambivalent relationship to Christianity. Knigge himself appears to have been a Deist (he admired Spinoza, though he also published sermons he had delivered). Weishaupt may have shared this inclination, but he took the view that only the elite of the Order – those with the title *rex* – should be explicit about their sympathy for d'Holbach. In some of Weishaupt's writings, Jesus Christ is portrayed as 'the liberator of his people and all human kind' and the prophet of 'the doctrine of reason', whose paramount goal had been 'to introduce general freedom and equality amongst men without any revolution'. The argument of Knigge's 'Lesson in the First Chamber' was that the priests of the Illuminati were the bearers of Christ's authentic and broadly egalitarian message, which had been distorted over the centuries.[15] Yet neither man actually believed that; it was all a 'pious fraud' (as Knigge privately admitted), to be revealed as such when an Illuminatus attained the highest degree. The ultimate goal of the Illuminati was therefore a pseudo-religious 'World Reformation' on the basis of Enlightenment ideals.[16]

It was on these rocks – both organizational and religious – that the

Illuminati foundered. Knigge complained about Weishaupt's 'Jesuitical character'. Two eminent Göttingen Illuminati, Johann Georg Heinrich Feder and Christoph Meiners, accused him of leaning towards the radical political theories of Jean-Jacques Rousseau. Another Illuminatus, Franz Carl von Eckartshausen, resigned when he became aware of Weishaupt's admiration of Helvétius and d'Holbach. As archivist to Charles Theodore, the Prince Elector Palatine who had inherited the Bavarian Electorate on the death of Max Joseph in 1777, Eckartshausen was in a position to press for the Order to be banned. In 1784, after protracted discussions in Weimar (some attended by Goethe), Knigge was forced to resign.[17] Weishaupt handed over the leadership to Count Johann Martin zu Stolberg-Rossla, who is believed to have dissolved the Order in April 1785, just a month after the second Bavarian edict against secret societies,[18] though there is some evidence of continued activity until mid-1787 and Johann Joachim Christoph Bode did not give up the idea of reviving it in Weimar until 1788.[19] Even had they not been prohibited, it seems clear, the Illuminati would almost certainly have liquidated themselves two years before the French Revolution began. Weishaupt himself spent the rest of his life under the protection of Ernest II, duke of Saxe-Gotha-Altenburg, first in Regensburg then in Gotha itself, churning out turgid works of self-justification such as *A Complete History of the Persecutions of the Illuminati in Bavaria* (1785), *A Picture of Illuminism* (1786) and *An Apology for the Illuminati* (1786). Though there were some continuities from the Illuminati to Karl Friedrich Bahrdt's German Union, these should not be overstated. As Knigge pointed out in his own work of self-defence, *Philo's endliche Erklärung* (1788), the Illuminati were from the outset a contradiction in terms: an organization in the service of the Enlightenment that shrouded itself in obfuscation.

For defenders of mainstream Freemasonry and opponents of the French Revolution, however, there were strong incentives to exaggerate the scale and the malignancy of the Illuminati. In their tracts of 1797, both John Robison and the abbé Barruel had to draw on some highly imaginative German sources to make their charges against the Illuminati – especially the claim that they had caused the French Revolution – seem credible. The nearest thing to an authentic link between the Illuminati and the Revolution is that Honoré Gabriel

Riqueti, comte de Mirabeau, met Jacob Mauvillon – who had become an Illuminatus at the instigation of Johann Joachim Christoph Bode – when Mirabeau visited Brunswick in the mid-1780s. But the notion that French Masonic lodges were the conduits through which revolutionary ideas reached Paris from Ingolstadt cannot withstand even casual scrutiny. The revolutionary ideas had, after all, originated in Paris. The true lines of communication ran from the salons of the French capital to Bavaria, through the libraries of enlightened officials such as Ickstatt, Weishaupt's mentor, not in the opposite direction. There was, as we shall see, an international network that connected philosophers and other scholars all over Europe and indeed extended across the Atlantic to North America. But it was primarily a network of publication, book-sharing and correspondence. Masonic lodges and secret societies played some part; salons, publishing houses and libraries were more important.

The Illuminati therefore need to be understood not as an omnipotent conspiracy, sustained by sinister means over more than two centuries, but as a revealing footnote to the history of the Enlightenment. As a network within much larger networks of Freemasonry and French philosophy, Weishaupt's Order exemplified an era when it was hazardous to express ideas that fundamentally challenged the religious and political status quo. Secrecy made sense. Yet secretiveness ultimately made it possible for the authorities to exaggerate the revolutionary threat posed by the Illuminati. The reality was that it was the wider network of Enlightenment that had the revolutionary potential, precisely because the ideas in question circulated quite freely in books and journals – and would have spread virally in Europe and America even if Adam Weishaupt had never lived.

Historians have struggled to write this history because, like so many networks, the Illuminati left behind not a single, orderly archive but scattered records: until the archives of the Masonic lodges became accessible, researchers were heavily reliant on memoirs and documents confiscated and published by the Order's foes. Amongst the materials said to have been in Franz Xaver Zwackh's possession were impressions of government seals to be used for counterfeiting, dissertations in defence of suicide, instructions for making poisonous gas and secret ink, a description of a special safe for the safeguarding of secret papers, and receipts for procuring abortions, along with a formula for making a tea that would induce an abortion. We now know that these were hardly representative of the Order's activities.[20] More typical were the meticulously recorded exchanges between Bode and the Thuringian Illuminati he recruited, which capture the essential tensions inherent in a secret society that aimed to advance Enlightenment, a hierarchical network that expected intimate self-revelation from novices, but offered them hocus-pocus in return.[21] Confronted with the might of the Bavarian state, as wielded by the Elector Charles Theodore, the Illuminati were easily crushed. Yet the Elector himself was living on borrowed time. Just ten years after his prohibition of secret societies, the armies of revolutionary France invaded the Palatinate, which Charles Theodore also ruled, and proceeded towards Bavaria. From 1799 until the eve of the Battle of Leipzig in 1813, Bavaria was a satellite of what became Napoleon's Empire. Meanwhile, in Gotha – where the remnants of Illuminism had found shelter – Duke Ernest's son and heir, Augustus, distinguished himself by his sycophancy to the French tyrant.

The Illuminati did not cause the French Revolution, much less Napoleon's rise – though they certainly benefited from it (all but Weishaupt were pardoned and some, notably Dalberg, became very powerful). Far from continuing their plot for world government down to the present, they ceased to operate in the 1780s and efforts to revive the order in the twentieth century were largely bogus.* Nevertheless, their story is an integral part of the complex historical process that led Europe from Enlightenment to Revolution to Empire – a process in which intellectual networks unquestionably played a decisive role.

Drawing on the best modern scholarship, this book seeks to rescue the history of networks from the clutches of the conspiracy theorists, and to show that historical change often can and should be understood in terms of precisely such network-based challenges to hierarchical orders.

* Leopold Engel revived the Illuminati in March 1901 along with Theodor Reuss, later an associate of the famous British occult master Aleister Crowley. During and after the Second World War, it was the turn of a Swiss economist named Felix Lazerus Pinkus and a baker named Hermann Joseph Metzger to resuscitate the name. Until the death of Annemarie Aeschbach, the Swiss village of Stein, in the Canton of Outer Appenzell, claimed to be the modern home of the Illuminati.

11

Emperors and Explorers

11

A Brief History of Hierarchy

In Sergio Leone's epic spaghetti western *The Good, the Bad and the Ugly*, Clint Eastwood and Eli Wallach are hunting for stolen Confederate gold. The treasure, they discover, is buried under a headstone in a huge Civil War cemetery. Unfortunately, they have no idea which headstone. Having earlier taken the precaution of emptying Wallach's revolver, Eastwood turns to him and utters the immortal lines: 'You see, in this world there's two kinds of people, my friend. Those with loaded guns. And those who dig. You dig.'

This is a modern example of an ancient truth. For most of history, life has been hierarchical. A few have enjoyed the privileges that come from monopolizing violence. Everyone else has dug.

Why did hierarchies precede networks in history? The obvious answer is that even the earliest group of prehistoric hominoids had a division of labour and a hierarchy of physical strength and intellectual capacity imposed upon it by nature. For that reason, primitive tribes were and are more like cooperative hierarchies than distributed networks.[1] Even 'obligate collaborative foragers' need leadership.[2] Someone needs to decide when to stop grooming and start hunting. Someone needs to divide up the kill and to ensure that the helpless young and old get their shares. And someone else needs to do the digging.

As they began to form larger groups and to engage in more complex forms of hunting and gathering, early humans developed the first conceptual frameworks – explanatory myths of gods with superhuman powers over nature – as well as the first mind-altering practices and substances.[3] They also learned the first rudimentary arts of war, producing remarkable quantities of basic weapons like axes, bows and arrows.[4] The early agricultural communities of the Neolithic Age (beginning around 10,200 BC) evidently had to devote significant resources to defend themselves against raiders (or to organize raids of their own). The stratification of society into masters and slaves, warriors and labourers, priests and supplicants, would seem to have begun early. With the evolution of symbolic writing out of cave painting, the first form of data storage external to the brain was born, and with it a new learned class.

In other words, although early political structures varied – some more autocratic, some more corporate – they had in common a fundamental social stratification. The power to punish transgressors was nearly always delegated to some individual or council of elders. The capacity to wage war successfully became the key attribute of a ruler. The state, it has been said, was a 'predictable outcome of human nature'.[5] So, too, was the arms race, as innovations in military technology – harder arrow-heads, horses as offensive vehicles – offered short-cuts to power and wealth.[6] And so was the advent of 'a new kind of hierarchy dominated by a "Big Man" who did not need to be physically strong, just rich enough to pay a small cabal of armed and trusted subordinates'.[7]

Hierarchy has many benefits, in economics as well as in governance. There were good reasons why the overwhelming majority of polities from the ancient world until the early modern period were hierarchical in structure. Like corporations in a later age, early states sought to exploit economies of scale and to reduce transaction costs, especially in the realm of military action. There were also good reasons why so many ambitious autocrats sought to enhance their legitimacy by identifying themselves with the gods. Hierarchy was easier for the helots to endure if it seemed to be divinely ordained. Yet rule by the Big Man had and still has chronic disadvantages, notably the misallocation of resources that normally occurs to satisfy the appetites of the Big Man, his offspring and his cronies. The recurrent and near-universal problem of ancient history was that the citizens of warring states generally ceded excessive powers to hereditary warrior elites, as well as to priestly elites whose function it was to inculcate religious doctrines and other legitimizing ideas. Wherever this happened, social networks were firmly subordinated to the prerogatives of the hierarchy. Literacy was a privilege. The lot of the ordinary man and woman was toil. They lived in their villages, each 'laterally insulated' (in Ernest Gellner's phrase) from all but their nearest neighbours – a state of insulation powerfully rendered as a kind of permanent mental fog in Kazuo Ishiguro's novel *The Buried Giant*.[8] Only the ruling elite was able to sustain network ties over distances: for example, the Egyptian pharaohs, whose networks in the fourteenth century BC extended from local Canaanite rulers to their counterparts in cities such as Babylon, Mitanni and Hattusa.[9] But even those elite networks were a source of danger to the hierarchical order: from the earliest historical records we read of conspiracies and plots, such as those against Alexander the Great – dark, malevolent clusters within the network.[10] This was not a world in which innovators were encouraged, but a world in which deviants were put to death. This was not a world where information flowed upwards or across, but one where it flowed downwards, if at all. Consequently, the archetypal ancient history was like that of the Third Dynasty of Ur (*c.* 2100–2000 BC) in southern Mesopotamia, which was capable of building a large-scale system of irrigation, but incapable of responding to the problem of salinization of the soil and collapsing crop yields.[11] (A similar fate later befell the Abassid Caliphate, which failed to maintain the irrigation infrastructure in what is now southern Iraq because of recurrent succession disputes, a common pathology of hereditary hierarchies.)[12]

There were, of course, experiments with more distributed political structures – the 'small world' of Athenian democracy,[13] the Roman Republic – but, significantly, these experiments did not endure. In his classic study *The Roman Revolution*, Ronald Syme argued that the Republic had in any case been run by a Roman aristocracy whose feuds had allowed Italy to descend into civil war. 'The policy and acts of the Roman People were guided by an oligarchy, its annals were written in an oligarchic spirit,' observed Syme, a New Zealander whom Oxford had made cynical. 'History arose from the inscribed record of consulates and triumphs of the *nobiles*, from the transmitted memory of the origins, alliances and feuds of their families.' Augustus came to power not just because he was talented, but because he understood the importance of having 'allies . . . a following'. It was by building his followers into a 'Caesarian party' that Augustus was able gradually to concentrate power in his own hands while nominally restoring the Republic. 'In certain respects,' wrote Syme, 'his Principate was a syndicate.' The 'old framework and categories' subsisted: like the Republic before it, Augustus's monarchy was the façade behind which oligarchy ruled.[14]

In Roman times, to be sure, there were also the Silk Roads – 'a network', in the words of Peter Frankopan, 'that fan[ned] out in every direction, routes along which pilgrims and warriors, nomads and merchants . . . travelled, goods and produce [were] bought and sold, and ideas exchanged, adapted and refined'.[15] However, that network was as conducive to the spread of disease as to commercial exchange, while the prosperous urban hubs along that road were always vulnerable to nomadic attack by the likes of the Xiongnu (Huns) and the Scythians.[16] The core lesson of classical political theory was that power should be hierarchically structured and that power naturally became concentrated in fewer hands the larger a political unit became. To a remarkable extent, the Roman and Qin-Han empires evolved in parallel ways, at least until the sixth century, not least because they faced similar challenges.[17] Once the costs of further territorial expansion began to exceed the benefits, the imperial system's *raison d'être* was the peace and order provided by its large army and bureaucracy, the costs of which it covered through a combination of taxation and currency debasement.

Why, then, did the empire at the western end of Eurasia not survive, whereas the one at the eastern end did? The classical answer is that Rome could not afford to withstand the increasing pressures of immigration – some would say invasion – by Germanic tribes. In addition, unlike the Chinese empire, Rome had to contend with the disruptive impact of a new religion, Christianity, a heretical Jewish sect that spread through the Roman world thanks to the efforts of Saul of Tarsus (the apostle Paul) after his conversion on the road to Damascus in around AD 31–6. Epidemics in the 160s and 251 created an opening for this religious network, because Christianity not only offered an explanation for the catastrophes, but also encouraged behaviours (such as charity and tending for the sick) that led to the disproportionate survival of believers.[18] The Roman Empire was a true hierarchy, with four main social orders – senatorial, equestrian, decurion and plebeian – but Christianity appears to have permeated every tier.[19] And Christianity was only the most successful of many religious manias that swept the Roman Empire: the cult of the north Syrian storm god Jupiter Dolichenus also spread from northern Syria to southern Scotland from the early second century AD, mainly because of its adoption by Roman army officers.[20] Migration, religion and contagion: by the fifth century, these network-borne threats – which nobody planned or commanded, but which spread virally – had crumbled the hierarchical structure of Roman imperial rule, leaving only vestiges of an old order to haunt the imaginations of Europeans for centuries to come. Beginning in the seventh century, a new monotheistic cult of submission – Islam – erupted from the deserts of Arabia, mutating between Mecca and Medina from just another prophet-led faith into a militant political ideology that imposed itself by the sword.

Though founded by charismatic prophets, the two great monotheistic movements were network-like in their viral spread. And yet, having thoroughly disrupted Roman rule, they ended up producing theocratic hierarchies in Byzantium and Baghdad. Western Christianity – sundered from Orthodoxy by the Great Schism of 1054 – came under its own form of hierarchical control with the ascendancy of the Roman Papacy and a stratified ecclesiastical system. Politically, however, Western Christendom remained more like a network: from the ruins of the Roman Empire in the West emerged a fractal geometry of states, most of them tiny, a few of them large; most of them hereditary monarchies, some of them in practice aristocracies, a handful of them city-states run by oligarchies. In theory, the Holy Roman Emperor had inherited power over most of these entities; in practice, after Pope Gregory VII's victory over the Emperor Henry IV in the Investiture Controversy, it was the Holy See that had the greater cross-border authority, controlling as it did the appointments of bishops and priests, and subjecting everywhere to its own canon law (a revival of the sixth-century Justinian Code). Temporal power was substantially decentralized in the system of heritable land titles and military or fiscal obligations known as feudalism. Here, too, authority was defined by law: civil (derived from Roman codes) on the Continent and in Scotland, common (based on precedent) in England.

By contrast, the lesson learned in China from the experience of warring kingdoms was that stability could be achieved only in a single, monolithic empire, with a culture (Confucianism) centred on filial piety (*xiao*). There was no religious authority superior to the emperor.[21] There was no law other than laws the emperor made.[22] Regional and local power was checked by an imperial bureaucracy recruited and ranked on the basis of merit and competence, with the system of civil service examinations offering upward mobility to young men on the basis of talent, not birth. In both the Western and the Chinese systems, however, the principal obstacle to stable state formation was the persistence of familial, clan or tribal networks.[23] Contests between such networks for control of the rents generated by government resulted in periodic civil wars, most of which are better characterized as dynastic duels.

For centuries, sages reflected on the seeming impossibility of having order without more or less absolute authority. They wrote their thoughts down on parchment or paper, using pens or brushes, in the certain knowledge that only a tiny minority of their fellow men would ever read them, and that their best hope for immortality was that their writings should be copied and preserved in one or more of the great libraries of the age. Yet the fate of the library of Alexandria – destroyed in a series of attacks that culminated in AD 391 – illustrated how fragile the data storage of the ancient world was. And the almost total lack of intellectual exchange between Europe and China in the ancient and medieval periods meant that the world was still very far from being a single network – except in one, lethal, respect.

12
The First Networked Age

The population of the entire Eurasian land mass was devastated in the fourteenth century by the Black Death, the bubonic plague caused by the flea-borne bacterium *Yersinia pestis*, which was transmitted along the Eurasian trade networks described above. So sparse were these networks – so few the ties between the clusters of settlement – that this highly infectious disease took four years to travel across Asia at a pace of less than a thousand kilometres per year.[1] But the impact was very different in Europe, where roughly half the population died (including perhaps three quarters of the population of Southern Europe), compared with Asia. For example, labour shortages appear to have been more severe in the far west, leading to significant gains in real wages, especially in England. The main institutional difference between the west and the east of Eurasia after 1500, however, was that networks in the west were relatively freer from hierarchical dominance than those in the east. No monolithic empire recurred in the west; multiple and often weak principalities prevailed, with the papacy and the loosely structured Holy Roman Empire as the sole remnants of Roman imperial power, while Byzantium considered itself to be the true heir of the emperors. In one former Roman province, England, the power of the monarch was so limited that from the twelfth century the merchants of the capital city were free to manage their own affairs through a self-governing corporation. In the Orient, the networks that mattered most were familial: the ties of clan. In a more individualistic Western Europe, it has been argued, other forms of association – brotherhoods in name rather than in fact – came to matter more.[2]

We should nevertheless be careful not to antedate the 'great divergence' of west from east, which remains the most striking feature of economic history between the late fifteenth century and the late twentieth.[3] Had its people remained confined to their own shores – or had the Mongol invaders of the thirteenth century got further west than the Hungarian plain – the history of Western Europe would have been altogether different. The persistence of familial networks in fourteenth-century Europe is well illustrated by the rise of the Medici family in Florence, who came to occupy a unique position as brokers within the network of elite Florentine families, exploiting the various structural holes in the system (see figure 10).[4] The rise of the Medici was partly a matter of strategic marriage (including even to members of such hostile families as the Strozzi, the Pazzi and the Pitti): here, as in most pre-modern societies, the most important network was the family tree.[5] However, in the

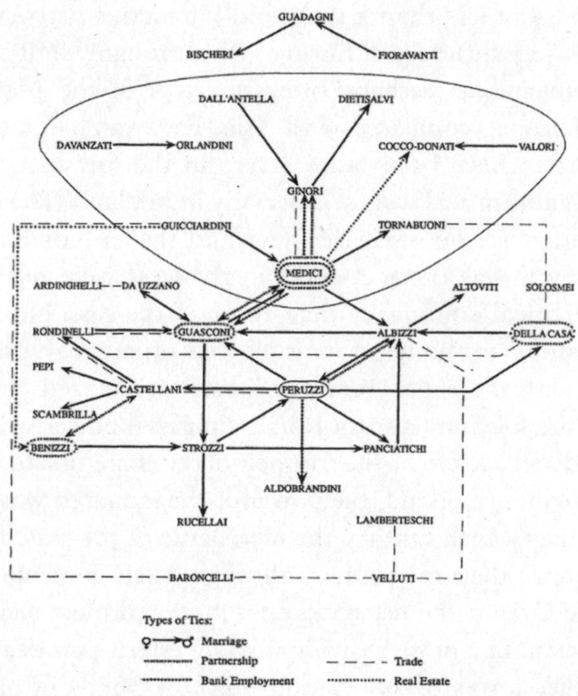

10. The Medici network: a fourteenth-century dynastic strategy that made one family dominant in Florence.

period after the Revolt of the Ciompi (1378–82), the elevation of bankers like the Medici into the Florentine political elite led to a significant economic innovation: the transposition of the domestic guild methods of the *Arte della Cambio* (bankers) to the international plane hitherto dominated by the *Arte della Calimala* (cloth merchants) and the emergence of the partnership as the basis of a new kind of financial capitalism.[6] With the advent of Medici rule in 1434, 'Renaissance man' was born, a polymath engaged simultaneously in finance, trade, politics, art and philosophy – 'part businessman, part politician, part patriarch, part intellectual aesthete'.[7]

13
The Art of the Renaissance Deal

Though less well known than the Medici, Benedetto Cotrugli is a perfect illustration of the ways that European networks were evolving in the Renaissance era – ways that created a new cosmopolitan class of interconnected individuals. Cotrugli's *Book of the Art of Trade* is, it is tempting to suggest, the fifteenth-century equivalent of Donald Trump's *Art of the Deal.* However, Cotrugli was no Trump. Amongst many pieces of wise advice, Cotrugli warns merchants against involving themselves in politics. 'It is not expedient,' he writes, 'for a merchant to have to do with the courts, nor above all to involve himself in politics or the civil administration, because these are perilous areas.'[1] Far from glorying in verbal vulgarity and ostentatious displays of wealth, Cotrugli was a highly educated humanist whose ideal merchant embodied the classical virtues of the commoner-citizen as they had been conceived by the ancient Greeks and Romans and rediscovered by Italian scholars in the Renaissance.

As a young man, Cotrugli had in fact attended the University of Bologna, but (as he ruefully observes) 'Destiny and ill-luck contrived it that right in the midst of the most pleasurable of philosophical studies, I was seized from studying and made to become a merchant, a trade I was obliged to follow, abandoning the sweet delights of study, to which I had been utterly dedicated . . .'[2] Returning to run the family business in Ragusa (present-day Dubrovnik), Cotrugli was disgusted by the low intellectual level of his new milieu. In the absence of any kind of formal business education, there was nothing more than an 'inadequate, ill-organized, arbitrary and threadbare' system of learning on the job, 'to the extent that my compassion was aroused and it pained me that this useful and necessary activity had fallen into the hands of such undisciplined and uncouth people, who carry on without moderation or orderliness, ignoring and perverting the law'.[3] In many ways, *The Art of Trade* was Cotrugli's attempt not just to raise the standard of business education but also to elevate the standing of business itself. Though it is best known to scholars as the earliest work to describe the system of double-entry book-keeping – more than thirty years before Luca Pacioli's better-known treatise *De computis et scripturis* (1494) – *The Art of Trade* is most remarkable for the breadth of its subject matter. Cotrugli offers much more than just practical advice on accounting. He offers an entire way of life. This is not a dry textbook but an exhortation to his fellow merchants to aspire to be Renaissance businessmen.

Cotrugli's book also gives the modern reader a fascinating glimpse of a vanished world. Born in Ragusa, Cotrugli and his brother Michele were importers of Catalan wool as well as dyes, paying in Balkan silver or, more commonly, bills of exchange. In the course of his business career, he spent time in Barcelona, Florence, Venice and, finally, Naples, where he lived from 1451 to 1469. This was truly a Mediterranean life; indeed, Cotrugli knew the sea well enough to write another book on the subject, *De navigatione*, which he dedicated to the Venetian Senate. He also served Ferdinand, king of Aragon, as ambassador to Ragusa and master of the Naples Mint. Life in the fifteenth century was precarious even for a successful merchant. In 1460 Cotrugli was accused of, and tried for, illegally exporting bullion, though he appears to have been acquitted. *The Art of Trade* was written in rural Sorbo Serpico while he was escaping an outbreak of plague in Naples. He was in his early fifties when he died in 1469.

Yet Cotrugli's was a life well lived. He might have missed the libraries of Bologna, but he took considerable pride in his commercial calling. Indeed, parts of *The Art of Trade* read as a defence of merchants against the charges – of usury, of greed, of avarice – frequently levelled at them by religious zealots at the time. Cotrugli declared himself 'astonished that exchange, being so useful, easy and entirely necessary to the conduct of human affairs, should be condemned by so many theologians'.[4] (At a time when usury was still illegal, he was careful to define usurers as 'those who, on the maturation of a debt, will not extend it without interest to borrowers unable to pay immediately'.)[5] In addition to promoting rigorous accounting, Cotrugli was an early believer in diversification as a way of managing and reducing risk. He imagines a Florentine merchant entering into various partnerships with merchants in Venice, Rome and Avignon, investing some of his capital in wool, some in silk. 'Having in a safe and orderly way put my hand to so many transactions,' he observes, 'I will gain nothing but advantage from them, because the left hand will help the right.'[6] And again: 'You must never risk too much on a single throw, by land or by sea: however rich you may be, at the most five hundred ducats a shipload, or a thousand for a large galley.'[7]

Cotrugli was a node in a burgeoning commercial network of credit and debt – hence his condemnation of 'those that keep only one column of accounts, that is how much is owing to themselves and not how much others are expecting from them', whom he calls 'the worst type of merchant, the basest and most iniquitous'.[8] 'A merchant,' writes Cotrugli, 'should be the most universal of men and one that *has the most to do, more than his fellows, with different types of men and social classes*' (my emphasis). Consequently, 'everything a man might know may be helpful to a merchant', including cosmography, geography, philosophy, astrology, theology and law. In short, *The Book of the Art of Trade* can also be read as a manifesto for a new society of networked polymaths.

14
Discoverers

The advances achieved in Italy and its environs show that, in terms of cultural and economic development, Europe was already diverging from the rest of the world before the end of the fifteenth century. However, the decisive breakthrough that prefigured the age of European world domination was not the Italian Renaissance so much as the Iberian age of exploration. Beginning in the reign of Henrique the Navigator (1415–60), sailors from Portugal began to venture further away from Europe – first southwards, following the West African coast, and then all the way across the Atlantic, Indian and finally the Pacific oceans. These extraordinarily ambitious and hazardous voyages created a network of new oceanic trade routes that would rapidly transform the global economy from a patchwork of regional markets into a single world market. Although royally sponsored, the explorers were themselves a social network, sharing knowledge of shipbuilding, navigation, geography and warfare. As so often in history, new technologies propelled these new networks into being, while at the same time the networks accelerated the pace of innovation. Better ships, better astrolabes, better maps and better guns all contributed to the breath-taking achievements of the age of exploration. So, too, did the transmission across the Atlantic of Eurasian diseases to which Native Americans had no resistance. These ensured that, in the New World more than in Asia, this was also an age of conquest.

Beginning in 1434, when Gil Eanes succeeded in passing Cape Bojador – the 'bulging cape' of what is now the northern coast of Western Sahara – sailors who had trained off the cliffs of Sagres incrementally increased the range of Portuguese navigation, venturing far from the sight of land. In the spring of 1488, Bartolomeu

Dias reached as far as Kwaaihoek, today's Eastern Cape, discovering the Cape of Good Hope on his way back to Portugal. A decade later, Vasco da Gama continued the journey on to Mozambique and – directed by a local pilot – across the Indian Ocean to Calicut (Kozhikode) in Kerala. In February 1500, Pedro Álvares Cabral set off in their wake but, sailing south-west to avoid the doldrums of the Gulf of Guinea, ended up reaching the coast of Brazil. Not content with its discovery, he proceeded to Calicut and from there – after a violent altercation with rival Muslim traders – sailed further south to Cochin (Kochi). Between 1502 and 1511 the Portuguese systematically established a network of fortified trading posts that included the island of Kilwa Kisiwani (Tanzania), Mombasa (Kenya), Kannur (Kerala), Goa and Malacca (Malaysia).[1] These were all places completely unknown to earlier generations of Europeans.

In August 1517 eight Portuguese ships arrived off the coast of Guangdong. The occasion deserves to be better remembered, for it was one of the first contacts between Europeans and the Chinese empire since the time of Marco Polo in the late thirteenth century.* The commander of the Portuguese flotilla was Fernão Peres de Andrade; also on board was the apothecary Tomé Pires, who was intended to be the Portuguese crown's emissary to the Ming court. Perhaps the reason why the expedition is largely forgotten is that nothing seemed to come of it. After trading at Tunmen (today Nei Lingding Island) in the Pearl River estuary, the Portuguese left again in September 1518. Eleven months later, three Portuguese ships returned, this time under the command of Simão de Andrade, the brother of Fernão. In January 1520 Tomé Pires set off northwards in the hope of securing an audience with the Zhengde emperor, but he was repeatedly put off and, with the death of the emperor on 19 April 1521, found himself held captive. At some point shortly after that, another Portuguese fleet, under Diogo Calvo, reached Tunmen. Chinese officials requested that he depart. When Calvo refused, fighting broke out. Not even the arrival of two additional ships from Malacca could avert a humiliating defeat at the hands of a Chinese fleet under

* The first merchants to reach China in this period were Jorge Álvares in 1514, and an Italian, Rafael Perestrello, in 1515–16.

the command of the Ming admiral Wang Hong. All but three Portuguese vessels were sunk. A year later, in August 1522, the Portuguese tried again when three ships arrived at Tunmen under Martim Coutinho. Though they brought with them a royal commission to make peace, fighting again broke out and two of the Portuguese ships were sunk. Captured Portuguese sailors were put in cangues (heavy wooden collars) and executed in September 1523. Tomé and other members of the original diplomatic mission were forced to write letters home conveying the Chinese authorities' demand that the Portuguese return Malacca to its rightful owner.

This, in short, was a non-event – a reminder that European overseas expansion was very far from a smooth and inexorable process. Indeed, it is easy to forget how very dangerous all the voyages described above were. On Vasco da Gama's first voyage to Calicut, he lost half his crew, including his own brother. Cabral set off with twelve ships in 1500; only five made it. Why, then, did the Portuguese run such large risks? The answer is that the rewards to be earned from establishing – and then monopolizing – a new route for trade with Asia were worth the risk. It is well known that European demand for Asian spices such as pepper, ginger, cloves, nutmeg and mace grew rapidly in the sixteenth century. The price differentials between Asian and European markets were initially enormous. Less well known is the extent to which the Portuguese were essentially muscling in on existing intra-Asian trade. Flowing into Ming China were not only pepper from Sumatra but also opium, gallnuts (for tannin, used in Chinese medicine as an astringent), saffron, coral, cloth, vermilion, quicksilver, blackwood, putchuck (pachak) for incense, frankincense and ivory. Flowing out of China were copper, saltpetre, lead, alum, tow, cables, ironwork, pitch, silk and silk stuffs (e.g. damasks, satin, brocade), porcelain, musk, silver, gold, seed pearls, gilded chests, gilt wood, salt dishes and painted fans.[2] There were other motives for sailing halfway around the world, to be sure. Asian medical knowledge was in some respects superior to European at this time; Tomé Pires evidently hoped to learn more about it. There was also the religious motive to spread Christianity, which grew more important with the arrival in Asia of the Jesuits, a Roman Catholic network founded by the Spanish soldier Ignacio de Loyola in the 1530s. Finally, there was the undoubted advantage to be derived from establishing diplomatic relations with the Chinese emperor. Nevertheless, without the commercial imperative, it seems doubtful that these other motives would have sufficed to propel men over such immense distances and through such hardships.

The Portuguese did not arrive with many products of their own to offer Asian consumers (though they did bring some slaves and gold from their West African outposts). That was not the point. Nor did they come as conquerors, intent on acquiring territory or new subjects for their king. What the Portuguese had was a series of technological advantages that made their bid to establish a new and superior trade network viable.[3] Their study of Arabic, Abyssinian and Indian texts meant that they could systematically teach the correct use of quadrants and astrolabes with texts like the *Regimento do Estrolabio & do Quadrante* (1493) and the *Almanach Perpetuum* (1496) of the Sephardic astronomer Abraão Zacuto, one of many Jews who had settled in Portugal after their expulsion from Spain in 1492. Portuguese craftsmen such as Agostinho de Goes Raposo, Francisco Gois and João Dias perfected the construction of nautical instruments. The Portuguese caravel – and its successors the great nau (1480) and the galleon (1510) – were also significantly better than other sailing ships of the time. Finally, with the Cantino Map of 1502, the Portuguese achieved a breakthrough in cartography: the first modern projection of the world's geography, with largely accurate depictions of the world's major continents aside from Australia and Antarctica (plate 7).

What happened when this extraordinarily innovative and dynamic network sought to establish a new 'node' in South China illustrates what can go wrong when a network encounters an entrenched, institutionalized hierarchy. The Chinese emperor ruled from on high. 'I reverently took on the mandate of Heaven and I rule the Chinese and the *yi*,' wrote the Yongle emperor to the ruler of Ayudyha in Thailand in 1419. 'In my rule, I embody Heaven and Earth's love and concern for the welfare of all things and I look on all equally, without distinguishing between one and the other.' The correct role of lesser potentates was 'to respect Heaven and serve the superior' by paying tribute.[4] The Yongle emperor had in fact favoured oceanic navigation.

It was in his reign that Admiral Zheng He led his treasure fleet as far as the East African coast.[5] However, the successors of Yongle had yielded to the preference of the imperial bureaucracy for autarky, so that overseas trade was formally prohibited. In the eyes of the Ming, the Portuguese intruders were *Fo-lang-chi* (from the Indian–Southeast Asian term 'ferengi', derived from the Arabic term for the 'Franks' of the Crusades). This was not a term of endearment. The Chinese regarded the foreigners as 'people with filthy hearts'. Rumours circulated that they roasted and ate children.

The Portuguese were not wrong that China presented a genuine economic opportunity. An illicit trade already flourished with both Siam and Malacca through Yueh-kang (near Zhangzhou in Fujian). While the mandarins of the imperial administration – scholar magistrates such as Qiu Dao-long and He Ao – might wish to minimize foreign intercourse, the eunuchs who dominated the imperial court had a hunger for exotic imports, as well as the foreign silver to be made from trade. Yet the Portuguese overplayed a weak hand. Simão de Andrade showed a crass disregard for local sensibilities. Without the consent of imperial officials, he built a fort at Tunmen, hanged a Portuguese sailor in violation of Chinese law, excluded non-Portuguese ships from the harbour and, when challenged, knocked a mandarin's hat off. His purchases of Chinese children as servants fuelled the suspicion that the *Fo-lang-chi* were indeed cannibals. The Chinese bureaucracy, for its part, treated Tomé Pires with haughty disdain. Having completed the long trek to Beijing, Pires and his companions were ordered to go and prostrate themselves before a wall of the Forbidden City on the 1st and 15th of every lunar month. Unbeknown to them, the Zhengde emperor was much too intent on his own debauchery to contemplate for a moment giving them the audience they desired.

Yet the biggest Portuguese mistake was to underestimate the tributary system. The essence of a hierarchical structure, it extended the Chinese emperor's influence far beyond the imperial frontier. The Portuguese now regarded the vital commercial hub of Malacca as theirs. This was not the view of the Raja of Bintang (Bentan), the son of the fugitive Malaccan king, Mahmud Shah. In Bejiing, his ambassador warned the Chinese authorities that the Portuguese were plotting 'to have the country for our own . . . that we were robbers', according to a letter by Christovão Vieyra, one of the Portuguese sailors later taken prisoner by the Chinese. This warning resonated with imperial officials: Mahmud Shah had been a reliable tributary.[6]

Why then did the Portuguese ultimately prevail, to the extent of establishing Macau as a part of their network in 1557 – an acquisition they proceeded to retain in their possession for more than 400 years? The answer is that two things changed. First, the Chinese prohibition on trade proved unenforceable. New men arrived from Portugal – Leonel de Sousa and Simão d'Almeida – who succeeded in establishing a foothold in the Guangdong trade. With the right incentives, officials such as Wang Po, the vice-commissioner for the Guangdong maritime defence circuit, could be turned from foes into business partners. Second, while the Chinese had won the early naval encounters, they had appreciated the superiority of Portuguese ships and cannon. Crucially, as compared with indigenous East Asian pirates, the Portuguese came to be regarded by Ming officials as the lesser evil. In June 1568, Tristam Vaz da Veiga helped the Chinese navy defend Macau against a fleet of about a hundred pirate ships.[7] After 1601, Portuguese and Chinese forces would fight together to repel new interlopers, from the Netherlands.

15
Pizarro and the Inca

As Portugal's maritime network spread eastwards, Spain's went west and south. Under the Treaty of Tordesillas (1494), Spain laid claim to the Americas aside from Brazil. There was another difference. Whereas Portuguese discoverers were mostly content to establish a network of fortified trading posts, their Spanish counterparts were willing to strike inland in their quest for gold and silver. A third difference was that whereas the Asian empires that the Portuguese encountered were able to withstand their incursions, making only minor territorial concessions, the American empires the Spaniards attacked collapsed with astonishing speed. This owed much more to the devastating effects of the infectious Eurasian diseases brought by the Spaniards across the Atlantic than to any technological advantage. In other respects, however, what happened when Francisco Pizarro and his 167 associates encountered the Inca Atahualpa at Cajamarca in November 1532 was similar to what had happened in Guangdong a decade earlier. In essence, a European network attacked a non-European hierarchy.

The *conquistadores* were a motley gang. They were tough, no doubt, as their long march southward had been as arduous as any Atlantic crossing. With their horses, guns (arquebuses) and steel swords, they were also better armed than the indigenous Mayan peoples of Peru, whose weapon of choice was a wooden club. Like the Portuguese discoverers, their primary motive was economic: they came not to trade but to plunder the plentiful gold and silver of the Inca empire. Pizarro's first expedition alone yielded 13,420 lb of 22.5 carat gold, worth $265m today, and 26,000 lb of silver ($7m). Like the Portuguese, the Spaniards brought Christian clergymen with them (six Dominican friars, of whom one survived). And, like the Portuguese, the Spaniards used violence to overcome resistance: including torture, mass rape, burnings and indiscriminate slaughter. Yet the most striking characteristic of the conquistadors was their propensity to quarrel, often bloodily, amongst themselves. The animus of Pizarro's brother Hernando against Diego de Almagro was just one of many feuds. It was not the strength of the Spanish invaders that doomed the Inca empire, but the empire's weakness.

As the architecture of Pachacamac, Cuzco and Machu Picchu shows to this day, the Inca emperors ruled over a substantial and sophisticated civilization, which they called *Tahuantinsuyo*. For a century, they had held sway over 14,000 square miles of Andean territory, with a population we now estimate at between 5 and 10 million. Their mountainous kingdom was held together by a network of roads, stairways and bridges, many of which can still be used.[1] Their agriculture, based on the cultivation of llama wool and maize, was efficient. Theirs was a relatively wealthy society, though they used gold and silver for ornamentation not money, preferring to use *quipucamayoc* (made of string and beads) for accounting and administrative purposes.[2] The ethos of Inca rule was cruelly hierarchical. A cult of sun worship went along with human sacrifice and draconian punishments. An aristocracy lived off the surplus generated by a helot class. True, this was not a civilization as sophisticated as China's: it lacked a written language, much less a literature or code of laws.[3] Still, it seems unlikely that, on their own, Pizarro and his men could have overcome the numerical odds against them, which at Cajamarca were roughly 240 to 1. Two weaknesses proved fatal. The first, and most important, was smallpox, which more than decimated the native population as it spread southwards, moving much faster than the Spaniards who had brought it to the New World. The second was division: at the time of the Spanish conquest, Atahualpa was waging a war of succession against his half-brother, Huáscar, over which of them was the rightful heir of the Inca Huayna Cápac. Pizarro had no difficulty in recruiting local auxiliaries.

But is 'conquest' the correct term to describe what followed? Certainly, Pizarro was able to humiliate, rob and ultimately murder Atahualpa, as well as to quell the revolt of Manco Inca in 1536, a sequence of events vividly depicted in Felipe Guaman Poma de Ayala's *Nueva Corónica y Buen Gobierno* (1600–1615). Yet the mixed Mayan–Hispanic name of the book's author tells its own story. Unlike in North America, where the indigenous population was smaller and the European settlers much more numerous, in South America fusion was the order of day. To give a single example, Francisco Pizarro took as a mistress the favourite sister of Atahualpa, who had been given to Francisco in marriage by her brother. After his death, she married a Spanish cavalier named Ampuero and left for Spain, taking her daughter, Francisca, who would later be legitimized by imperial decree. Francisca Pizarro Yupanqui then married her uncle, Hernando Pizarro, in Spain in October 1537. Pizarro also had a son, who was never legitimized, Francisco, by a wife of Atahualpa whom he had taken as a mistress. This was typical of the way the first generation of conquistadors established a new 'multicultural family web' designed to legitimize their own position atop the hierarchical systems they had taken over (figure 11). A more apt term than conquest might be 'co-mingling'. (The best-known chronicler of the Spanish conquest, Garcilaso de la Vega, was himself the son of a conquistador and an Inca princess, Palla Chimpu Ocllo.[4]) Similar strategies were pursued by other European settlers in the New World; for example, the French farmers and fur traders who established themselves in Kaskaskia, Illinois, in the 1700s.[5] The European 'conquerors' not only took over existing systems of administration and land management; they fused genetically with indigenous societies.[6]

Nevertheless, the enduring legacy of this approach in South America was not a culture that acknowledged the fact of genetic mingling,[7] but rather one that ranked people according to the 'purity of blood' (*limpieza de sangre*), a concept the Spaniards brought with them to the New World as a legacy of the expulsion of the Moors and the Jews. The *casta* classifications depicted in eighteenth-century paintings from New Spain begin with the more or less familiar – *De Español e Yndia nace mestizo* ('From a Spanish man and an Indian woman is born a mestizo'), *De Español y Negra sale Mulato* ('From a Spanish man and a black woman a mulatto is begotten') – but quickly become bizarre. Crossing a Spaniard with a mulatto woman, for example, was said to produce a *Morisco* (Moorish, a term that

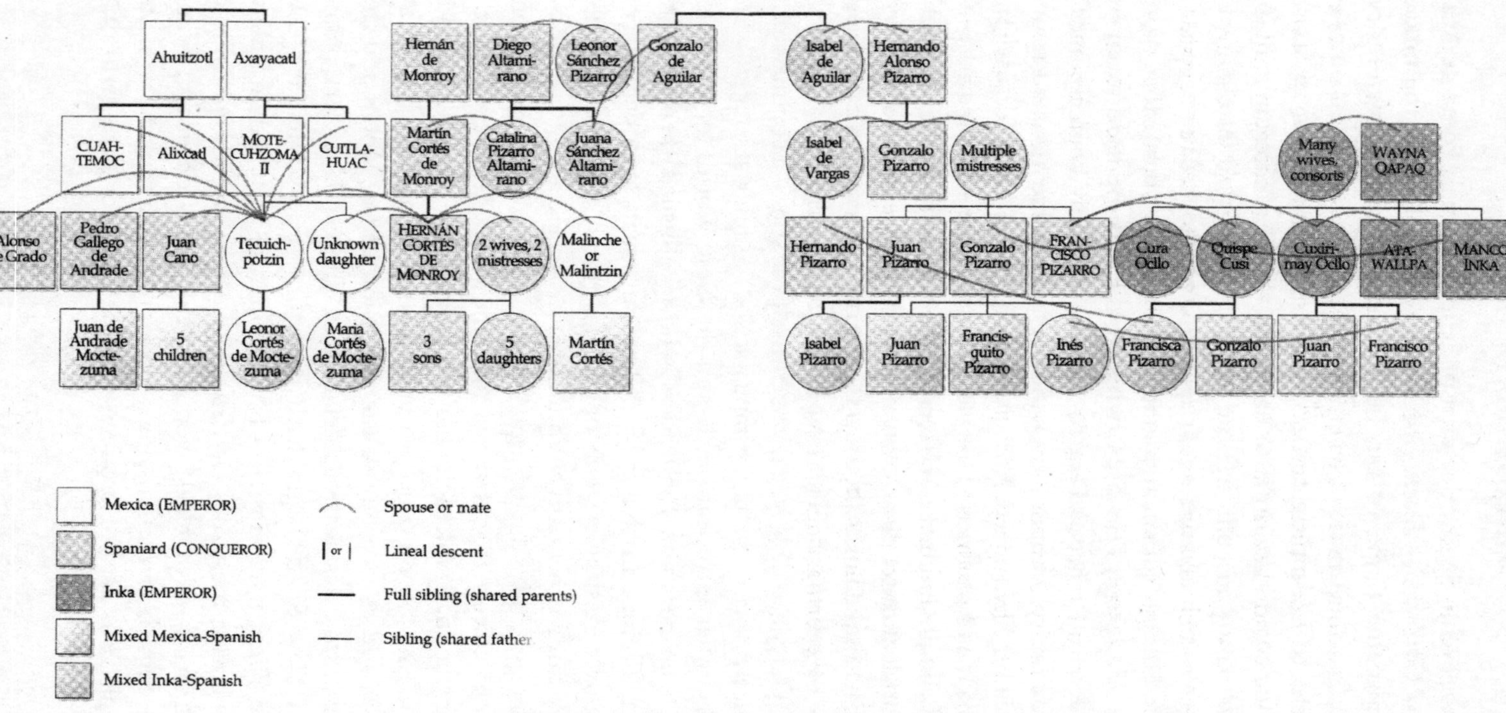

11. A network of 'conquest': the intermarriage of conquistadors and elite Aztec and Inca families.

had been applied in Spain to former Muslims who had converted to Christianity after the *reconquista*). Crossing a mulatto with an Indian produced a *Calpamulato*. Other variants in the series of sixteen paintings done in 1770 by the Mexican artist José Joaquín Magón included *Lobo* (literally 'wolf'), *Cambuja*, *Sambahiga*, *Cuarteron*, *Coyote* and *Albarazado*. There was even a category called *Tente en el Aire* ('Suspend in Mid-Air').[8] The number of different phenotypes in such classifications typically ranged between sixteen and twenty, though some early nineteenth-century sources list over 100. The *casta* system was of more than mere anthropological interest, though it did reflect a sincere attempt to apply contemporary theories of heredity. Although the possibility of 'purification' existed – a mestizo could, by marrying a pure Spaniard, produce a *Castiza*, who in turn could produce a Spaniard by marrying a Spaniard – the system as a whole implied (for it was never formally integrated into the colonial legal code) discrimination against those with little or no Hispanic ancestry. Thus was a new kind of hierarchy imposed on the cat's cradle of intermarriage that was Spanish America.

16
When Gutenberg Met Luther

The Iberian network of discoverers and conquerors was one of two networks that transformed the early modern world. In Central Europe, in the same period, a new technology helped to unleash the huge religious and political disruption we know as the Reformation, as well as to pave the way for the Scientific Revolution, the Enlightenment and much else that was antithetical to the Reformation's original intent. Printing had existed in China long before the fifteenth century, but no Chinese printer had ever been able to achieve what Johannes Gutenberg did, which was to create an entirely new economic sector. Gutenberg's first printing press was established in Mainz at some point between 1446 and 1450. The new movable type technology was rapidly diffused by skilled Germans in concentric circles around Mainz because it was economically preferable to have multiple local printers, rather than centralized production, due to the high cost of transporting printed matter. By 1467, Ulrich Hahn had established the first press in Rome. Six years later Heinrich Botel and Georg von Holz had opened a press in Barcelona. In 1475, Hans Wurster began printing in Modena. By 1496, Hans Pegnitzer and Meinard Ungat had established a press in Granada, a mere four years after Muhammad XII, the last of the Nasrid monarchs, surrendered the Alhambra to Ferdinand and Isabella. By 1500 roughly a fifth of Swiss, Danish, Dutch and German cities had adopted printing.[1] England lagged behind but finally caught up. In 1495 just eighteen book titles were produced in England. By 1545 there were fifteen printing establishments and the number of titles printed annually had risen to 119. By 1695 some seventy printing establishments produced 2,092 titles.

Without Gutenberg, Luther might well have become just another heretic whom the Church burned at the stake, like Jan Hus.[2] His original ninety-five theses, primarily a critique of corrupt practices such as the sale of indulgences, were originally sent as a letter to the Archbishop of Mainz on 31 October 1517. It is not wholly clear if Luther also nailed a copy of them to the door of All Saints' Church, Wittenberg, but it scarcely matters. That mode of publishing had been superseded. Within months, versions of the original Latin text had been printed in Basel, Leipzig and Nuremberg. By the time Luther was officially condemned as a heretic by the Edict of Worms in 1521, his writings were all over German-speaking Europe. Working with the artist Lucas Cranach and the goldsmith Christian Döring, Luther revolutionized not only Western Christianity but also communication itself. In the sixteenth century German printers produced almost 5,000 editions of Luther's works, to which can be added a further 3,000 if one includes other projects he was involved with, such as the Luther Bible. Of these 4,790 editions, almost 80 per cent were in German, as opposed to Latin, the international language of the clerical elite.[3] Printing was crucial to the Reformation's success. Cities with at least one printing press in 1500 were significantly more likely to adopt Protestantism than cities without printing, but it was cities with multiple competing printers that were most likely to turn Protestant.[4]

The printing press has justly been called 'a decisive point of no return in human history'.[5] The Reformation unleashed a wave of religious revolt against the authority of the Roman Catholic Church. As it spread from reform-minded clergymen and scholars to urban elites to illiterate peasants, it threw first Germany and then all of northwestern Europe into turmoil. In 1524 a full-blown peasants' revolt broke out. By 1531 there were sufficient Protestant princes to form an alliance (the Schmalkaldic League) against the Holy Roman Emperor, Charles V. Although defeated, the Protestants were powerful enough to preserve the Reformation in a patchwork of territories and, under the Peace of Augsburg (1555), to establish the crucial principle of *cuius regio, eius religio** (coined in 1582 by the German jurist Joachim

* This translates best as 'to each ruler, the religion he chooses'. The Treaty allowed the Holy Roman Empire's various princes to select either Lutheranism or Catholicism within the domains over which they ruled. The principal weakness of the

Stephani), which effectively left monarchs and princes to determine whether their subjects would be Lutherans or Roman Catholics. Religious conflict continued to simmer, however, and erupted again in the Thirty Years' War, a conflict that turned Central Europe into a charnel house.

It was only after prolonged and bloody conflict that the monarchies of Europe were able to re-impose control over the new Protestant sects, but that control could never be as complete as the Pope's had been. Censorship persisted, but it was patchy and even the most heterodox authors could find someone to print their works. Especially in north-western Europe – in England, Scotland and the Dutch Republic – it proved impossible to re-establish Roman Catholicism, even when Rome turned the technologies and networking strategy of the Reformation against it, in addition to the more traditional array of cruel tortures and punishments that had long been the Church's forte.

Why was Protestantism so resistant to repression? One answer to that question is that, as they proliferated throughout northern Europe, the Protestant sects developed impressively resilient network structures. Protestants suffered severe persecution in England during the reign of Mary I, trials and tribulations commemorated in works such John Foxe's *Acts and Monuments* ('Book of Martyrs'). Yet the 377 committed Protestants who wrote to Foxe, or received or were mentioned in Foxe's letters and related sources, can be seen to have constituted a strong network centred on a number of key 'hubs': martyrs such as John Bradford, John Careless, Nicholas Ridley and John Philpot.[6] The executions of no fewer than fourteen of the top twenty nodes (ranked by betweenness centrality)* certainly reduced the connectedness of the survivors, but it did not destroy the network because other figures with high betweenness centrality, including letter couriers and financial supporters such as Augustine Berner and William Punt, took over.[7] Few things better symbolized the sixteenth-century crisis of hierarchical order than the vain efforts of Henry VIII's

---

settlement was that it explicitly excluded other strains of Protestantism, e.g. Calvinism, from its provisions.

* A reminder: that is the measure of the extent to which a node serves to connect different sections of the network, i.e. acts as a hub.

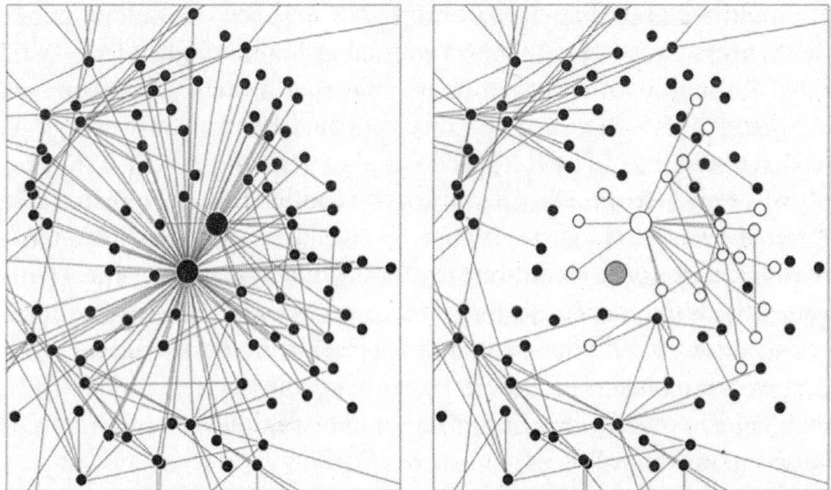

12. The English Protestant network immediately before (left) and after (right) John Bradford's execution on 1 July 1555. The death of Bradford (the large node coloured black on the left, grey on the right) cut off an entire subnetwork centred on his mother (the nodes coloured white on the right).

eldest daughter to undo the religious revolution her father had opportunistically embraced in order to divorce her mother.

It is now half a millennium since the Portuguese ships arrived off the coast of Guangdong, and since Luther nailed his theses to the door of All Saints' Church in Wittenberg. The world in 1517, as the great disruptions of European exploration and Reformation got under way, was a world of hierarchical orders. The Zhengde emperor and the Inca Huayna Capac were just two members of a global elite of despots. It was in 1517 that the Ottoman Sultan Selim I – Selim the Grim – conquered the Mamluk Sultanate – which stretched from the Arabian Peninsula to Syria, Palestine and Egypt itself. To the east, the Safavid Shah Ismail ruled over all of modern-day Iran and Azerbaijan, southern Dagestan, Armenia, Khorasan, eastern Anatolia and Mesopotamia. To the north, Charles I – heir of the Houses of Habsburg, Valois–Burgundy and Trastámara – ruled over the Spanish kingdoms of Aragon and Castile, as well as the Netherlands; within two years, as Charles V, he would also be elected Holy Roman Emperor in succession to his grandfather Maximilian I. In Rome, Leo X – the second son of Lorenzo de' Medici – was Pope. Francis I reigned in France, while Henry VIII ruled England with no less absolute power; at his whim, the kingdom adopted Luther's Reformation (albeit piecemeal and inconsistently). As we have seen, hierarchy is a special kind of network, in which the centrality of the ruling node is maximized. The social network that can be inferred from the Tudor State Papers, which contain letters from more than 20,000 people, illustrates this point. For Henry VIII's reign the person with the highest degree is Thomas Cromwell (the king's principal secretary, Lord Privy Seal, and Chancellor of the Exchequer) with 2,149 correspondents, followed by the king himself (1,134), and Cardinal Thomas Wolsey, his Lord Chancellor (682). However, in terms of betweenness centrality, the king came first.[8]

The striking feature of this hierarchical world was how similar the exercise of power was in all these empires and kingdoms, despite the fact that connections between the European and non-European worlds were tenuous if they existed at all. (Outside Europe, where the monarchs engaged in a perpetual tournament of war and dynastic diplomacy, there was no despots' network.) Selim the Grim was famously ruthless towards his grand viziers, executing so many that 'May you be a vizier of Selim's' became a Turkish curse. Henry VIII treated his ministers and wives with no less celebrated callousness, while Vasili III, Grand Prince of Moscow, was equally ready to mete out death sentences to powerful courtiers – and, like Henry, he divorced his first wife when she failed to produce an heir. In East Africa, the emperor of Ethiopia, Dawit II, made war on the Muslim Emirate of Adal in ways not so different from the conflicts between Christian and Muslim rulers that had long raged around the Mediterranean littoral. Historians today recognize a little over thirty empires, kingdoms and large duchies with extent and cohesion approximating to statehood in the world of 1517. In all of them – even the one republic, Venice – power was concentrated in the hands of a single individual, usually a man (Queen Joanna of Castile was the world's sole female ruler in that year). Some kings inherited their thrones by birth. Others were elected (though none was democratically elected). Some, like Jungjong of Joseon (Korea), ascended their thrones through violence. There were young kings (James V of Scotland was just five in 1517) and old ones (Sigismund I, king of Poland and grand duke of

Lithuania, lived to be eighty-one). A few titular rulers were weak, notably the Emperor Go-Kashiwabara in Japan, where real power lay in the hands of the shogun Ashikaga Yoshiki. The relative power of lesser landowners varied from place to place. Some kingdoms, like Ryukyu in the reign of Shō Shin, were peaceful. Others – notably Scotland – were strife-torn. However, the majority of early modern monarchs enjoyed a kind of untrammelled personal power – including the power of life and death over subjects – that today exists in only a handful of Central and East Asian states. Despite being separated by thousands of miles, successful Asian autocrats such as Krishnadevaraya, the Vijayanagara emperor – the most powerful Hindu ruler in early sixteenth-century India – comported themselves in ways strikingly similar to their contemporaries in Renaissance Europe, taking pride in their martial and judicial prowess, patronizing the arts and literature.

From the early 1500s, this world of hierarchy came under a dual assault from revolutionary networks. Harnessing their superior navigational technology and seeking new commercial opportunities, 'discoverers' and 'conquerors' from Western Europe sailed to other continents in increasing numbers, toppling – with the assistance of the pathogens that accompanied them – all the established rulers of the Americas and establishing a global network of fortified entrepôts that more slowly gnawed away at the sovereignty of Asian and African polities. At the same time, disseminated through the printing press as well as from pulpits, a religious virus that came to be known as Protestantism disrupted an ecclesiastical hierarchy that could trace its lineage back to St Peter. The consequences of the Reformation were at first felt in Europe, and they were terrible indeed.[9]

Religious wars recurrently wreaked havoc within and between kingdoms from 1524 until 1648. The authority of Rome having been successfully challenged, northern Europe witnessed an epidemic of religious innovation: Lutherans were soon challenged by Calvinists and Zwinglians, who rejected the Lutheran position that, in the ritual of holy communion, the consecrated elements of bread and wine are the true body and blood of Christ. Unlike earlier schisms within Christianity (the dispute over Arianism in the fourth century, the great division between Western and Eastern Christianity in 1054, the period of rival popes between 1378 and 1417), the divisions of the Reformation tended to multiply: its fissiparity was indeed one of its defining traits. The extreme case were the Anabaptists, who maintained that baptism should be a conscious and voluntary rite that children were too young to undergo. In February 1534 a group of Anabaptists led by Jan Bockelson (John of Leiden) and Jan Matthys seized power in the Westphalian town of Münster and founded what we might now call 'the Christian State': a radically egalitarian, iconoclastic and theocratic regime supposedly based on biblical literalism. Burning all books except the Bible, the Anabaptists proclaimed the 'New Jerusalem', legalized polygamy, and prepared to wage war on unbelievers in anticipation of Christ's Second Coming. By the mid-seventeenth century, in the period of the English Commonwealth, Protestant dissenters who rejected the Anglican 'middle way' between Lutheranism and Catholicism had formed numerous rival sects, notably Fifth Monarchists (named after the prophecy in the Book of Daniel that four ancient monarchies would precede the kingdom of Christ), Muggletonians (named after Lodowicke Muggleton, one of two London tailors who claimed to be the last prophets foretold in the Book of Revelation), Quakers (who 'trembled at the word of the Lord'), and Ranters (so named for their noisy and allegedly hedonistic worship).

Was the Reformation a disaster? By 1648, the date of the Peace of Westphalia (plate 9),* it had certainly been responsible for a shocking number of violent and often hideously cruel deaths. In the British Isles it ultimately caused a political revolution. This had begun, according to one innovative interpretation, as a result of machinations by the earl of Bedford and the Puritan (i.e. staunchly Protestant)

* The Peace of Westphalia is frequently cited as a moment when hierarchical structures were re-imposed on Europe after the upheaval of the Thirty Years' War. It consisted of three distinct treaties, one between the Dutch Republic and Spain, one between the Holy Roman Empire and France and their allies, and one between the Empire and Sweden and their allies. Though more than a hundred delegations participated in the negotiations in the neighbouring cities of Catholic Münster and partly Lutheran Osnabrück, the Peace of Westphalia is commonly said to have established a framework based on co-existing but competing sovereign states that agreed not to intervene in one another's domestic (i.e. religious) affairs. This principle had already been established at the Peace of Augsburg nearly a century before, but it was reaffirmed at Westphalia.

earl of Warwick, each of whom sought to constrain King Charles I for political as much as religious reasons. This aristocratic 'junto' aspired not so much to religious revolution, but to rendering the English king little more than a Venetian doge, subordinate to their oligarchy.[10] After 1642 tensions between 'court' and 'country' – and between England, Scotland and Ireland – escalated to the point of a civil war, which the king lost. After he was beheaded on 30 January 1649, England was declared to be a 'Commonwealth', a republic. True to the predictions of classic political theory, it did not last long: in 1653 the New Model Army dissolved the so-called Rump Parliament and named Oliver Cromwell as 'Lord Protector'. This institution, too, did not long survive; in May 1660, just two years after Cromwell's death, a new parliament declared that Charles II had in fact been king ever since his father's execution. Perhaps around 100,000 people in England and Wales had lost their lives in the Civil War. The mortality rates were probably higher in Scotland and much higher in Ireland. Indeed, the latter probably suffered more severe losses of population in relative terms than in the Great Famine of the 1840s, and certainly as much as Germany in the Thirty Years' War.

The wars and persecutions the Reformation unleashed were certainly very far from what Luther had intended. From the vantage point of the Roman Catholics whose Counter-Reformation at least kept Protestantism out of Southern Europe (and out of the empires of Spain and Portugal), the moral was very clear: challenges to Papal and episcopal hierarchy by a network calling itself the 'priesthood of all believers' led in short order to bloody anarchy. British aristocrats learned a different lesson. After James II's doomed attempt to restore Roman Catholicism, they concluded that the monarch's powers should permanently be constrained by parliaments that they dominated through networks of patronage,[11] and that religious 'enthusiasm' should as far as possible be restrained by an Anglican Church that kept to a *via media* between Puritanism and 'Popery'. There was much truth in both of these views. Yet they overlooked vital and equally unintended benefits of the disruption that Luther had unleashed.

III

Letters and Lodges

17
The Economic Consequences of the Reformation

The ultimate failure of the Counter-Reformation to defeat the 'Calvinist International'[1] had far-ranging economic and cultural consequences. Prior to the Reformation, there had been relatively little to distinguish the economic performance of north-western Europe from that of, say, the Chinese or Ottoman empires. After Luther's revolution, Protestant states began to show signs of greater economic dynamism. Why was this? One answer is that, despite Luther's desire to purify the Church, the Reformation led to a large-scale reallocation of resources from religious to secular activities. Two thirds of monasteries were closed in the Protestant territories of Germany, the lands and other assets mostly appropriated by secular rulers and sold to wealthy subjects, as also happened in England. A rising share of university students gave up thoughts of the monastic life, turning their attention to more worldly vocations. Church-building diminished; secular construction increased. As has been justly observed, the Reformation had wholly unintended consequences, in that it was 'a religious movement that contributed to Europe's secularization'.[2]

At the same time, the printing revolution that had made the Reformation possible was having its own unintended consequences. Between 1450 and 1500 the price of books fell by two thirds, and the price continued to fall thereafter. In 1383 it had cost the equivalent of 208 days' wages to pay a scribe to write a single missal (service book) for the bishop of Westminster. By the 1640s, thanks to printing, over 300,000 popular almanacs were sold annually in England, each roughly 45–50 pages long and costing just twopence, at a time when the daily wage for unskilled labour was 11½ pence. On average the real price of books in England fell by 90 per cent between the late

1400s and the late 1500s.[3] There was more than just a book boom. Between 1500 and 1600, cities where printing presses had been established in the late 1400s grew at least 20 per cent (and perhaps as much as 80 per cent) faster than similar cities that were not early adopters. The diffusion of printing accounted for between 18 and 80 per cent of urban growth between 1500 and 1600.[4] Dittmar goes so far as to argue that 'the welfare impact of the printed book was equivalent to 4 per cent of income by the 1540s and 10 per cent of income by the mid-1600s', significantly more than the welfare impact of the personal computer in our time, estimated at no more than 3 per cent of income in 2004.[5] The decline in the price of a PC between 1977 and 2004 followed a very similar trajectory to the decline in the price of a book between the 1490s and the 1630s. Yet the earlier, slower revolution in information technology appears to have had the larger economic impact. The best explanation for this difference is the role of printing in disseminating hitherto unavailable knowledge fundamental to the functioning of a modern economy. The first known printed mathematics text was the *Treviso Arithmetic* (1478). In 1494, Luca Pacioli's *Summa de arithmetica, geometria, proportioni et proportionalita* was published in Venice, extolling the benefits of double-entry book-keeping. Books on manufacturing technologies such as brewing and glass-blowing soon followed, ensuring the rapid spread of best practice.

Nor was this all. Prior to the Reformation, Europe's cultural life had been heavily centralized around Rome. After Luther's revolution, the network of European culture entirely changed. Based on data for the places of birth and death of European thinkers, we can trace the emergence of two overlapping networks: a 'winner-takes-all' regime, with massive centralization around Paris, and a 'fit-gets-richer' regime, where many sub-centres competed with each other in clusters throughout Central Europe and northern Italy.[6] After 1500 not all roads led to Rome (see plate 10).

18
Trading Ideas

While some slaughtered, others studied. Despite the upheavals unleashed by the Reformation – which could still precipitate a Scottish rebellion in support of the ousted Catholic Stuart dynasty as late as 1745 – European intellectual history in the seventeenth and eighteenth centuries was characterized by a succession of network-driven waves of innovation, of which the Scientific Revolution and the Enlightenment were the most important. In each case, the sharing of novel ideas within networks of scholars produced remarkable advances in natural science and philosophy. Rather like the spread of the technology of printing, there was a geographic pattern to the spread of science which can be reconstructed on the basis of the careers of individual scientists. In the sixteenth century, the main hub of the scientific network was Padua, which was at the centre of a cluster of other Italian university towns. There were ties from this cluster to nine other mainly south European cities, as well as to distant Oxford, Cambridge and London. Two German nodes – Wittenberg and Jena – were connected only to one another. In the course of the seventeenth century, Padua was joined by four other hubs of scientific activity: London, Leiden, Paris and Jena. Copenhagen became one of a number of new nodes on the geographical periphery.[1]

Correspondence networks allow us a deeper insight into the evolution of the Scientific Revolution. Ismaël Boulliau was a French astronomer and mathematician who was also interested in history, theology and classical studies. His correspondence was voluminous: 4,200 letters for the years 1632–93, plus another 800 to or from him that are not included in the *Collection Boulliau*. It was also extensive, extending far beyond France to Holland, Italy, Poland, Scandinavia and the Near East.[2] Comparable in scale was the correspondence of Henry Oldenburg, the first secretary of the Royal Society, who wrote or received 3,100 letters between 1641 and 1677. In addition to England, Oldenburg's network included France, Holland, Italy, the Near East and a number of English colonies.[3] In quantitative terms, it should be said, this was nothing new. The leading figures of the Renaissance and Reformation appear to have produced comparable numbers of letters: over three thousand survive from Erasmus, more than four thousand apiece from Luther and Calvin, and more than six thousand from Ignatius Loyola, the founder of the Society of Jesus. Substantially larger numbers of letters were produced by some merchants and aristocrats.[4] The difference was that, with the advent of institutions such as the Royal Society, scientific correspondence began to resemble a collective effort.

A good illustration of the way science spread through such networks was Antonie van Leeuwenhoek's research into the treatment of gout, which revealed the efficacy of a remedy first observed in the Dutch colony of Batavia (now part of Indonesia). Leeuwenhoek's report to the Royal Society disseminated the new knowledge not only to members of the Society but further afield. Correspondence to non-members of the Society – classic weak ties – gave them access to the intellectual cluster that had formed in and around London.[5] The Charter for the Royal Society was explicit in granting to its president, council and fellows, and their successors, the freedom 'to enjoy mutual intelligence and knowledge with all and *all manner of strangers and foreigners, whether private or collegiate, corporate or politic*, without any molestation, interruption, or disturbance whatsoever' (emphasis added).[6] The sole condition was that the sharing of intelligence must be to the benefit and interest of the Society. Beginning with Oldenburg, successive secretaries played a crucial role (albeit with varying degrees of success) in managing the Society's extensive correspondence. Under Edmond Halley, incoming letters (among them Leeuwenhoek's) were allowed to accumulate unread, but under his successor, the physicist James Jurin, the Society acted as a hub for an international network of scientifically minded scholars, including surgeons and physicians, professors, clergymen and apothecaries, a quarter of them based in Europe, and around 5 per cent in the North American colonies. In December 1723 Jurin read his 'Proposal for Joint Observations on the Weather', which argued for co-ordinated meteorological observations through a network of correspondents. His premise was that 'a true Theory of the Weather is not to be Attained by a knowledge of the Successive Alterations in any one certain place', but 'must needs require the joint Assistance of many Observers'.[7] In the succeeding months he received observations from Berlin, Leiden, Naples, Boston, Lunéville, Uppsala and St Petersburg.

By contrast, the Académie des sciences in Paris was originally the private property of the crown. When it met for the first time on 22 December 1666, it was in the king's library and had an official policy of secrecy. All discussion and deliberation was private, and non-members were barred from sessions.[8] Its members were thus effectively removed from the rapidly growing pan-European network that would produce the Scientific Revolution. The position was similar in much of Catholic Europe. It was not accidental that the Portuguese intellectuals who were able to join the wider scientific network were known as *estrangeirados*, meaning 'the foreign-ized ones'.[9] Fittingly, it was the emergence of a cosmopolitan scientific network that gave birth to network theory itself, with Euler's work on the Königsberg bridge problem (see Introduction). Born in Basel, where he studied under Johann Bernoulli, Euler had risen to fame after coming second in the Paris Academy Prize Problem competition at the age of just twenty. He was working at the Imperial Russian Academy of Sciences in St Petersburg when he solved the Königsberg puzzle, moving to Berlin at the invitation of Frederick the Great in 1741 (though the two men did not hit it off and Euler later returned to Russia).

It was not only mathematical theorems that were being traded in the eighteenth century. The networks created by transatlantic trade and migration were by this time growing exponentially, as European merchants and settlers exploited rapidly falling transportation costs and the availability of effectively free land in North America, as well as cheap slave labour in West Africa. The Atlantic economy of the eighteenth century has been described as 'a massive trading network in which not only everyone knew everyone but everyone had friends who had friends'.[10] It would be more accurate to think of multiple interconnected networks, with major ports as the hubs.[11] A good illustration is the way Scots traders came to play a dominant role in the island of Madeira's wine trade in the course of the eighteenth century. By 1768, a third of the forty-three foreign resident traders on the island were Scots, including five of the ten largest wine exporters. Though some of the wine merchants were related, most of the links in the network were between 'correspondents' and 'connections'. True, the relative looseness of these ties had its disadvantages, in that principals had the usual difficulties getting their agents to comply with instructions. Information flows were voluminous but often contaminated with idle gossip; transaction costs were high as traders constantly bargained with one another.[12] On the other hand, this network was dynamic and responsive to market shifts.[13]

One solution was to combine the benefits of networking with some element of hierarchical management. Formally, the directors of the East India Company (EIC) in London controlled a substantial part of the trade between India and western Europe. In reality, as the records of over 4,500 voyages by Company traders show, ship's captains often made illicit side trips, buying and selling on their own account.[14] By the late eighteenth century the number of ports in the resulting trade network was more than a hundred, ranging from open emporia such as Madras to regulated markets such as Canton (Guangzhou).[15] In effect, private trading provided the weak links that knitted together otherwise disconnected regional clusters.[16] This network had a life of its own that the Company's directors in London simply did not control. Indeed, that was one of the keys to the success of the EIC: it was more a network than a hierarchy. Significantly, its Dutch rival banned private trade by its employees. This may help explain why it ended up being superseded.[17] Only when the EIC's traders encountered very hierarchically ordered ports, such as Batticaloa – which the Sinhalese royal family monopolized – did its networking strategy fail.[18] When the EIC pulled out of intra-Asian trade to concentrate on its trade between Asia and Europe, the density of its maritime network proved crucial.[19] Only as the Company's business model shifted from trade to the taxation of Indians did it become more hierarchical in structure. Indeed, by the time of Robert Clive, the EIC was taking on the character of a colonial government with a substantial war-making capability.

For the type of ambitious, adventurous family that was once so

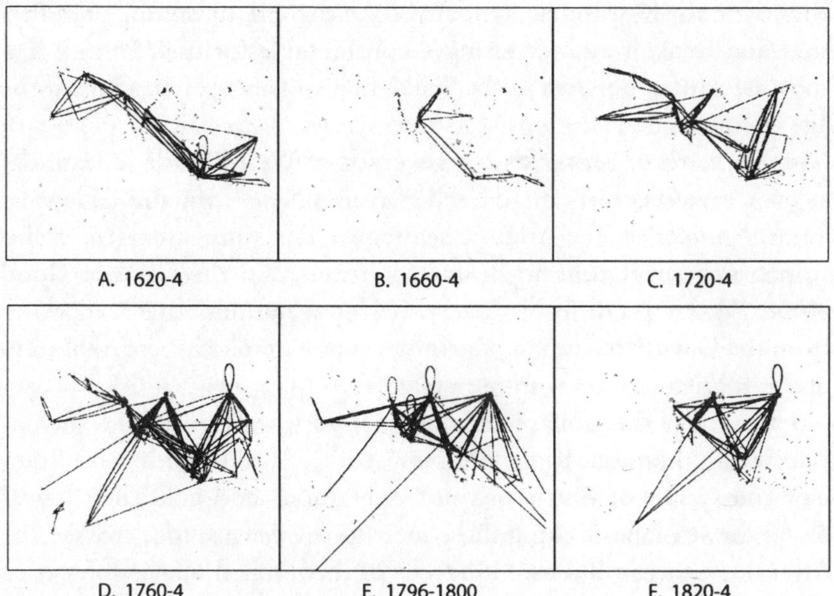

13. The trade network of the British East India Company, 1620–1824. Traders benefited from the EIC's infrastructure, but the Company benefited from traders' ability to build a network between multiple ports.

common in the Scottish Lowlands, this was a world of opportunity.[20] The Johnstones hailed from Westerhall in Dumfriesshire, what Daniel Defoe called 'a wild and mountainous Country, where nothing but what was desolate and dismal could be expected'. Of the eleven children of James and Barbara Johnstone who survived into adulthood, nearly all spent a substantial part of their lives outside Scotland. Four brothers, James, William, George and John, were eventually elected to the House of Commons; from 1768 until 1805 there was always at least one Johnstone in Parliament. The second son, Alexander, purchased a large sugar plantation in Grenada which he renamed 'Westerhall'. His younger brother, Sir William Johnstone Pultney, led the association of investors who in 1792 purchased the Genesee Tract, more than a million acres in western New York state. By the time of his death, he had also accumulated property in Dominica, Grenada, Tobago and Florida. The three youngest Johnstones – John, Patrick and Gideon – all spent time on the Indian subcontinent in the employ of the East India Company. John thrived, mastering both Persian and Bengali and amassing a considerable fortune. Patrick had the misfortune to perish in the 'black hole of Calcutta' in 1756, at the age of nineteen. The Johnstones also served in the British colonies in North America: George as the governor of West Florida, Alexander as an army officer in Canada and northern New York and Gideon as a naval officer on the Atlantic seaboard. The youngest of the Johnstones also spent time in Basra, Mauritius and the Cape of Good Hope. At one point in his career, he ran a business that sold water from the Ganges to Indian pilgrims.[21] (For a graphical representation of the Johnstones' network, see plate 11.)

The hubs of the global mercantile network were port cities such as Edinburgh, London, Kingston, New York, Cape Town, Basra, Bombay and Calcutta. But it was not only goods and gold that flowed along the sea-lanes linking these metropoles. Slaves, too, crossed the Atlantic in their millions. Hundreds of them toiled on the Johnstone plantation on Grenada; it was a Johnstone who lost the court case that ended the legal recognition of slavery in Scotland; it was a Johnstone (John) who owned Belinda, the last person recognized by Scotland's courts as legally enslaved. Yet ideas – including ideas of emancipation – also flowed through the commercial network of the eighteenth century. Margaret Johnstone was an ardent Jacobite who escaped from imprisonment in Edinburgh Castle, dying in exile in France. William Johnstone was a member of the Edinburgh club known as the Select Society, along with Adam Smith, David Hume and Adam Ferguson, who held his intellect in high esteem. William's son John subscribed to the Edinburgh Society for the Abolition of the African Slave Trade. His uncles James and John were also opponents of slavery; William took the other side. George flirted with support for the American Revolution and was sent to the colonies in 1778 as a member of the ill-fated peace commission. The Johnstones knew both Alexander Hamilton and his nemesis, Aaron Burr, who once paid a visit to Betty's home in Edinburgh.[22] The Johnstones were perhaps an extreme case of a globalized family. But even in Angoulême, a French provincial town north of Bordeaux, a surprisingly high proportion of inhabitants in the eighteenth century had travelled or lived outside France (plate 14).

19
Networks of Enlightenment

The printed word had made the Reformation possible, as well as propelling forward the Scientific Revolution. Perhaps paradoxically, the Enlightenment owed as much, if not more, to the old-fashioned written word. To be sure, the *philosophes* published, many of them prolifically. Yet some of their most important exchanges of ideas were by private letter. Indeed, it is the survival of so much of this correspondence – tens of thousands of letters exchanged between more than 6,000 authors – that enables modern scholars to reconstruct the Enlightenment network.

We are tempted to think of the Enlightenment as a cosmopolitan phenomenon, linking together *philosophes* and *literati* all over Europe, from Glasgow to St Petersburg. Yet the correspondence of leading eighteenth-century thinkers turns out, on close inspection, to be more nationally clustered.[1] Voltaire's network of more than 1,400 correspondents, for example, was 70 per cent French.[2] We know the provenance and destination of about 12 per cent of Voltaire's letters. Of these, more than half (57 per cent) were sent from or to Paris. To be sure, Voltaire exchanged letters with Jonathan Swift and Alexander Pope, but only a handful. His principal English correspondents were obscure figures: Sir Everard Fawkener, a silk merchant, and George Keate, a minor poet he met in Ferney.

Voltaire was one of a number of *lumière* 'hubs' – two others were Jean-Jacques Rousseau and the *Encyclopédie*'s editor, Jean-Baptiste le Rond d'Alembert – whose ego-networks were the major components of a wider network that contemporaries thought of as a *société littéraire ou savante*.[3] It was a network geographically centred on Paris. Twelve per cent of a sample of roughly 2,000 of its members died

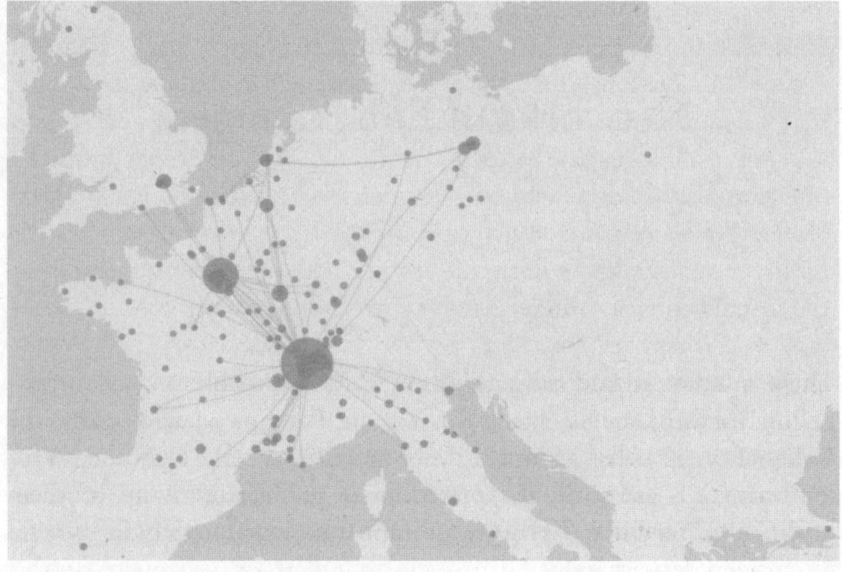

14. Voltaire's network of correspondents. This was more Francocentric than traditional views of the Enlightenment as an international movement might have led us to expect.

there, as did 23 per cent of those who contributed to the *Encyclopédie*.[4] It was also a socially rarefied network, which included eighteen princes and princesses, forty-five dukes and duchesses, 127 marquises and marquesses, 113 counts and countesses, and thirty-nine barons and baronesses.[5] Aristocrats made up around 0.5 per cent of the eighteenth-century French population, but around a fifth of the so-called 'republic of letters'. Moreover, for a network commonly associated with its critical view of the established order, this republic encompassed a strikingly large number of high royal officials.[6] Finally, though we tend to assume significant continuities between the Scientific Revolution and the Enlightenment, in reality there were few practising scientists in this network, though a great many were members of bodies such as the Académie française and the Académie royale des sciences. It was a republic of letters more than a republic of numbers, a network of essayists more than of experimenters.

Correspondence networks tell only a part of the story of the

Enlightenment, of course. Those who knew Voltaire, Rousseau or d'Alembert were as eager to meet them as to write to them. This was a 'republic of salons', too, hence the important brokerage role played by the *salonnières*, those women whose homes became centres for sociable exchange, and whose invitations were coveted by aspirant intellectuals.[7] Seldom invited were the lowly hacks of Paris's Grub Street. Yet there were 'weak ties' between the lofty network of the *lumières* and the lowly network of the gutter press: eight members of the so-called literary underground corresponded with Voltaire, Rousseau or d'Alembert'.[8]

Each nation found Enlightenment in its own fashion. As in Paris, so in Edinburgh, new free-thinking networks evolved in the interstices of the established institutions of crown and church. The Scottish capital was home to the Courts of Session, the High Court of Justiciary, the Exchequer, the minor Commissar and Admiralty Courts, the Faculty of Advocates, the Convention of Royal Burghs, the General Assembly of the Church of Scotland and Edinburgh University. From 1751, Adam Smith was a university professor (though in Glasgow rather than the capital). From 1752, David Hume was Keeper of the Advocates Library. As in France, so in Scotland, aristocratic patronage was another crucial source of material support for intellectual life. Between 1764 and 1766 Smith was tutor to the young duke of Buccleuch. The great thinkers of Edinburgh were, like their French counterparts, scarcely revolutionaries. Nor, on the other hand, were they reactionaries. Most deplored Jacobitism and embraced the Hanoverian order. (One of the proposed layouts for Edinburgh's New Town was in the shape of a Union Flag.)[9] Nevertheless, the intellectual action of the time was not in established institutions but in the Old Town's new and informal clubs: the Philosophical Society (founded in 1737 with the more cumbersome title of the Edinburgh Society for Improving Arts and Sciences and Particularly Natural Knowledge) and the Select Society (1754–62). And, just as the *dévots* of France deplored and sought to prosecute the *philosophes*, so Presbyterian traditionalists regarded the *literati* of Scotland as 'imps from hell'. Within just a few generations, the firebrand heirs of the sixteenth-century Calvinist revolution had become the custodians of a dour religious establishment, 'the Kirk'. John Home was publicly tried by the Presbyterian Synod of the Church of Scotland, and sentenced to be suspended from the ministry, for having written the play *Douglas* (1757).* Here, as everywhere in Protestant Europe, the printing press had proved itself a Pandora's box.

Like the French *lumières*, the Scottish *literati* thought globally but acted nationally, to judge by the correspondence of ten eminent Scots, including Hume and Smith (see figure 15).† Ten times as many letters went to or from Glasgow and Edinburgh as went to or from Paris. However, London mattered more than Glasgow: this was a British network, not a Scottish one. In any case, the Enlightenment was not a correspondence course; nor were its leading lights mere pen-pals. As tutor to the duke of Buccleuch, Adam Smith visited Paris, where he met (among other luminaries) d'Alembert, the physiocrat François Quesnay and Benjamin Franklin. The republic of letters was mobile. The great thinkers of the eighteenth century were also pioneering tourists.

For aspirant intellectuals born and raised an ocean away, indeed, there was no real alternative but to spend at least some time in Great Britain and France. Benjamin Franklin personified the colonial Enlightenment. Born the fifteenth child of a Puritan immigrant from Northamptonshire, Franklin was an autodidact and polymath, as much at home in the laboratory as in the library. In 1727, he formed the 'Junto', a club for men like himself to meet and exchange views. Two years later he began publishing the *Pennsylvania Gazette*. In 1731 he set up the first American subscription library. That was followed twelve years later by another new institution, the American Philosophical Society. In 1749, Franklin became the first president of the Academy, Charity School and College of Philadelphia. Yet, with a population of just 25,000, Philadelphia was no Edinburgh, much less Paris, which was more than twenty times larger. Prior to 1763, Franklin had no correspondents outside the American colonies. It

* The elders of the Kirk took exception to these un-Calvinistic lines: 'Hard is his fate; for he was not to blame! There is a destiny in this strange world. Which oft decrees an undeserved doom: Let schoolmen tell us why.'

† The others are Hugh Blair, Gilbert Elliot (Lord Minto), Adam Ferguson, Henry Home (Lord Kames), John Home, Allan Ramsay, Thomas Reid and William Robertson.

15. Parody on Raphael's *School of Athens* by James Scott, after Sir Joshua Reynolds (1751). The Enlightenment network was based on tourism as well as correspondence.

was only after his voyage to London that year that the share of non-Americans amongst his correspondents jumped from zero to nearly a quarter. Though he never corresponded with his near-contemporary Voltaire, Franklin's visits to Europe ensured that he became a fully integrated part of the Enlightenment network. He was elected a Fellow of the Royal Society, and also of the Royal Society of Arts, in 1756. In addition to multiple trips to London, Franklin visited both Edinburgh and Paris, as well as travelling in Ireland and Germany.[10] All this was before he had emerged as one of those rebellious colonists willing to contemplate independence from the mother country, severing the hierarchical ties that subordinated the American colonies to the sovereign 'king in parliament' in distant London. Ironically, for Franklin's generation of colonial intellectuals, London remained 'the capital of America', even if they grew to resent the political restraints it imposed on them.[11]

20

Networks of Revolution

In the great political revolutions of the late eighteenth century, as in the earlier religious and cultural revolutions, the role of networks was vital. Once again, a crucial role was played by the written and printed word. In books, in pamphlets, in newspapers, but also in countless handwritten letters, the arguments for radical political change were made, the criticisms of royal authority spelled out. In the eyes of 'men of letters', the pen frequently did appear to be mightier than the sword, and the writer – poet, playwright, novelist, polemicist – emerged as one of the heroes of the age, aided by the fearless publisher. Small wonder that taxes on the press became an object of rebellious ire.[1] Joined together in a veritable mesh of social networks, the scribblers and printers of the Western world seemed intent on writing their way out of hereditary rule. From Boston to Bordeaux, revolution was in large measure the achievement of networks of wordsmiths, the best of whom were also orators whose shouted words could rally the crowd in the square and incite them to storm the towers of the old regime.

And yet revolutions, to succeed, need fighters as well as writers. Moreover, revolutionary networks need to be resilient; they cannot simply fall apart when the hierarchical power clamps down. In this context, the case of Paul Revere has long been seen as significant. Henry Wadsworth Longfellow's poem is no longer memorized by schoolchildren, nor does anyone now remember Thomas Edison's *Midnight Ride of Paul Revere*, one of the first American movies, but the story remains a familiar one.[2] 'One if by land, and two if by sea' – the vital signal to Revere from the North Church steeple – is one of many phrases that still resonate:

A hurry of hoofs in a village-street,
A shape in the moonlight, a bulk in the dark,
And beneath from the pebbles, in passing, a spark
Struck out by a steed that flies fearless and fleet:
That was all! And yet, through the gloom and the light,
The fate of a nation was riding that night;
And the spark struck out by that steed, in his flight,
Kindled the land into flame with its heat.

Longfellow's kindling spark is a metaphor, of course, for a process of news transmission that we instinctively understand – or think we do:

So through the night rode Paul Revere;
And so through the night went his cry of alarm
To every Middlesex village and farm, –
A cry of defiance, and not of fear,
A voice in the darkness, a knock at the door,
And a word that shall echo forevermore!

Yet, as Malcolm Gladwell has noted, it is not immediately obvious why Revere was so successful in communicating the intelligence that regular troops were to be deployed to the towns north-west of Boston – Lexington and Concord – to arrest the colonial leaders John Hancock and Samuel Adams in the former and to seize the weapons of the colonial militia in the latter. Revere rode just thirteen miles, knocking on doors, and warning of the soldiers' approach at every town. But his news spread far further and faster than he could possibly have ridden, reaching Lincoln by 1 a.m., Sudbury by 3 a.m., and Andover – forty miles from Boston – by 5 a.m. This was achieved by no other technology than word of mouth. In his book on Revere's ride, David Hackett argued that Revere 'had an uncanny genius for being at the centre of events . . . [and] in mobilizing the acts of many others'.[3] Gladwell argues that, unlike William Dawes (who undertook a similar journey), Revere was able to cause a 'word of mouth epidemic' because of 'the Law of the Few'.[4] Revere was one of those rare types: a 'Connector', 'gregarious' and 'naturally and irrepressibly social'.[5] But he was also 'a Maven', an accumulator of knowledge, who not only had 'the biggest Rolodex in colonial Boston' but was also 'actively engaged in gathering information about the British'.[6]

This version of Paul Revere's ride is appealing but it is incomplete. It omits the fact that Revere's bona fides as a rebel messenger was already well established by April 1775. Not strictly a member of the literati but a skilled engraver as well as a silversmith, he had become notorious in New England for his exaggerated depiction of the Boston Massacre.[7] On 6 October 1774 it was Paul Revere who rode from Boston to Philadelphia to deliver to the Continental Congress the inflammatory Suffolk Resolves – which called for non-payment of taxes and a boycott of British goods in retaliation for the 'Intolerable Acts' and the Quebec Act.[8] On 13 December, Revere rode all the way to Portsmouth, New Hampshire, to warn that town's committee of correspondence that regular troops might shortly seize the arms and ammunition stored on New Castle Island, off Portsmouth Harbor.[9] Revere had already been to Concord on 8 April, warning – more than a week prematurely – that 'the regulars are coming up to Concord the next day, and if they come . . . there will be bloody work'.[10] On 16 April (as Revere himself later recalled) he rode to Lexington to tip off Hancock and Adams that trouble was afoot and that 'it was thought they were the objects' of the impending troop deployment.[11] In addition to William Dawes, there were other sources of intelligence about British movements, not least because citizens of Somerville, Cambridge and Menotomy heard the troops advancing, despite General Thomas Gage's best efforts.[12] Revere and Dawes were working together, not competing, and they also rode together – along with a third man, Dr Samuel Prescott – from Lexington to Concord, taking turns to knock on farmhouse doors.

Revere was captured in the vicinity of Lincoln.[13] He was the fourth illicit messenger the regulars had caught. Moreover, Revere was lucky to escape with his life. At one point a jumpy regular officer 'Clap'd his Pistol to [Revere's] head' and threatened to 'blow [his] brains out' if Revere did not answer his questions. Only the mounting chaos as shots began to be fired persuaded his captors to let Revere go, though without his horse.[14] Having walked gingerly back to Lexington, Revere was flummoxed to find Hancock and Adams still trying to decide what to do, three hours after he had told them the regulars were coming.[15] Had Revere not succeeded in getting back to Cambridge, and had he not survived the Revolutionary Wars to tell the tale (he lived to be eighty-three), it seems doubtful that his ride would have become so enduringly famous.

Paul Revere's network also repays closer scrutiny.[16] In fact, he was one of the two key brokers – or weak ties – between clusters that might otherwise have been too unconnected to have coalesced into a revolutionary movement. Colonial Massachusetts had been growing more socially stratified in the pre-revolutionary era. Boston was an increasingly hierarchical society, with significant gaps between the patrician 'Brahmin' elite, a middle class of artisans and farmers, and poor labourers and indentured servants. The close relationship between Revere, a mere artisan, and Dr Joseph Warren, a physician, was therefore vital. There were five Boston associations that were more or less sympathetic to the 'Whig' cause: the St Andrew's Lodge, the Masonic lodge that met at the Green Dragon Tavern; the Loyal Nine, which was the nucleus of the Sons of Liberty; the North End Caucus, which met at the Salutation Tavern; the Long Room Club in Dassett Alley; and the Boston Committee of Correspondence. A total of 137 men were in one or more of these groups, but the great majority (86 per cent) appeared only on a single list, while no one appeared on all five lists. Only Joseph Warren was in four groups; Paul Revere was in three, as were Samuel Adams and Benjamin Church. In terms of 'betweenness centrality', however, Warren and Revere were the key men (see figure 16).

Network analysis thus reveals that Paul Revere was one half of a duo that crossed the class divide in revolutionary Massachusetts between artisans and professionals. Yet that analysis, insightful though it is, cannot discern which of the associations Revere and Warren belonged to was or were the most important. One plausible conjecture is that Freemasonry was the key network of the American Revolution.

In *Freemasonry in the American Revolution*, published in 1924, Sydney Morse (himself a Mason) argued that Freemasonry 'brought together in secret and trustful conference the patriot leaders' in a 'fight for freedom'. According to Morse, it was Masons who sank the *Gaspee* in 1772, who organized the Boston Tea Party, and who

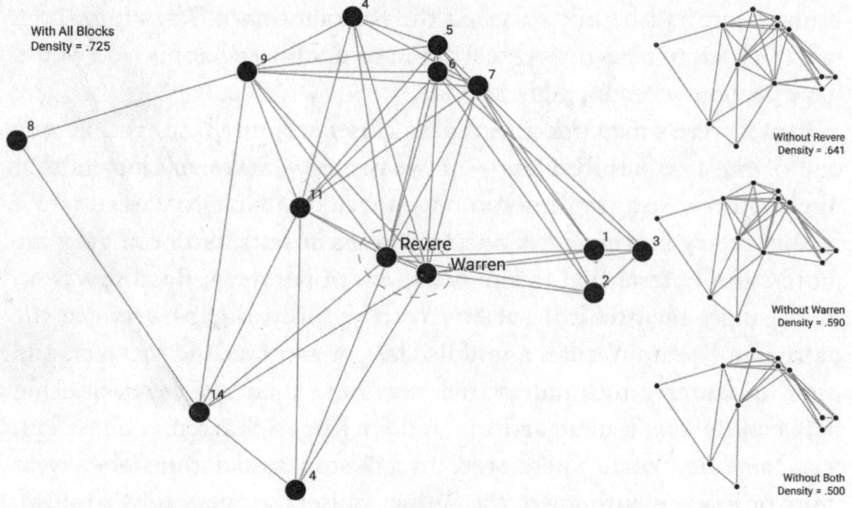

16. The revolutionary network in Boston, *c.* 1775. Note the betweenness centrality of Paul Revere and Joseph Warren. Removing either or both of them would significantly have reduced the density of the network. Individuals are grouped together into single nodes according to shared club memberships. Only Revere and Warren belonged to more than two.

dominated the institutions that led the revolution, including the Continental Congress.[17] Paul Revere was one of the names most frequently cited by Morse.[18] Though repeated in the 1930s by the French historian Bernard Faÿ, this claim was for a long time ignored by the leading historians of the American Revolution.[19] When Ronald E. Heaton researched the backgrounds of 241 'founding fathers', he found that only sixty-eight had been Masons.[20] Just eight of the fifty-six signers of the Declaration of Independence belonged to Masonic lodges.* For years the mainstream view was that it was 'doubtful whether

* They were: Benjamin Franklin, of the Tun Tavern Lodge at Philadelphia; John Hancock, of St Andrew's Lodge in Boston; Joseph Hewes, who was recorded as a Masonic visitor to Unanimity Lodge No. 7, Edenton, North Carolina, in December 1776; William Hooper, of Hanover Lodge, Masonborough, North Carolina; Robert Treat Payne, present at Grand Lodge at Roxbury, Massachusetts, in June 1759; Richard Stockton, charter Master of St John's Lodge, Princeton, Massachusetts, in

Freemasons *qua* Freemasons played a significant role in the American Revolution'.[21] But this conclusion itself seems doubtful. Apart from anything else, it assumes that all founding fathers were equal in their importance, whereas network analysis shows that Revere and Warren were the most important revolutionaries in Boston, the most important city in the revolution. It also understates the importance of Freemasonry as a revolutionary ideology. The evidence suggests that it was at least as important as secular political theories or religious doctrines in animating the men who made the revolution.[22]

Freemasonry furnished the Age of Reason with a powerful mythology, an international organizational structure and an elaborate ritual calculated to bind initiates together as metaphorical brothers. Like much else that transformed the eighteenth-century world, its origins were Scottish. European stonemasons had certainly organized themselves into lodges in the Middle Ages, and had (like other medieval crafts) distinguished between apprentices, journeymen and masters, but these organizations were not greatly formalized before the late fourteenth century. In 1598 the Scottish lodges were given a new set of regulations, known as the Schaw Statues after William Schaw, the Principal Master of Work to the Crown. It was not until the mid-seventeenth century, however, that Freemasonry evolved into something more than a loose network of guilds of skilled craftsmen, with lodges in Kilwinning and Edinburgh admitting 'speculative' or 'accepted' (i.e. non-practising) Masons. It was an Aberdonian, James Anderson, whose book *The Constitutions of the Free-Masons* (1723) provided the new era with an appropriately grandiose prehistory. In Anderson's narrative,* the Supreme Architect of the Universe had endowed Adam with the skills of masonry – geometry and the 'mechanical arts' – which he then passed on to his progeny, who in turn transmitted them to the Old Testament prophets. God's chosen people were 'good Masons before they possess'd the promis'd land',

1765; George Walton, of Solomon's Lodge No. 1, Savannah, Georgia; and William Whipple, of St John's Lodge, Portsmouth, New Hampshire.

* This narrative did not go unchallenged. For example, Andrew Michael Ramsay, another Scotsman, traced the origins of Freemasonry back to Palestine at the time of the Crusades.

and Moses was their 'Grand Master'. The supreme achievement of early Masons was Solomon's great temple in Jerusalem, built by Hiram Abif, 'the most accomplish'd Mason upon earth'.[23]

Like many successful networks, Freemasonry had a hierarchical element. All Masons belonged to local lodges, most of which were linked together under one or other of the grand lodges formed in the eighteenth century in London, Edinburgh, York, Dublin, and later on the Continent and the American colonies. Each lodge had a master, wardens and other officers. Prospective Masons had to be nominated for membership and approved unanimously, and, even before being initiated as 'entered apprentices' into the Masonic rituals and secrets, had to agree to be bound by the 'Charges' in Anderson's *Constitutions*. The initiation rites themselves were elaborate – and even more so for those promoted to the higher ranks of fellowcraft and master Mason – involving gestures, an oath and ceremonial garb. However, a striking feature of the 'Charges' was how undemanding they were. All Masons had to be 'good and true Men, free-born, and of mature and discreet Age, no Bondmen, no Women, no immoral or scandalous Men, but of good report'. No Mason could be 'a stupid Atheist, nor an irreligious Libertine'. Masons were equal as brothers within the lodge, although Masonry took 'no Honour from a Man that he had before', and those of a higher social station often held the most prestigious positions.[24] This mattered a good deal, as part of the appeal of the lodges was precisely that they allowed nobleman and bourgeois to mingle. On the other hand, Freemasons were not prohibited from participating in political rebellion. True, Anderson's *Constitutions* stipulated that 'a Mason is a peaceable Subject to the Civil Power, wherever he resides or works, and is never to be concern'd in Plots and Conspiracies against the Peace and Welfare of the Nation'. But involvement in rebellion was explicitly not a ground for expulsion from a lodge.[25]

Though Anderson himself was a Presbyterian minister, one inference that could be drawn from his very lax religious criteria was that Freemasonry was compatible with Deism. Indeed, some colonial lodges admitted Jews.[26] Not everyone was prepared to go this far in the direction of Enlightenment religious scepticism – hence the 1751 split between 'Ancients' and 'Moderns'. Ancients favoured the 1738 edition of Anderson's *Constitutions*, which obliged Masons to obey Christian precepts regardless of where they lived. Moderns, confusingly, preferred the earlier 1723 edition of the *Constitutions*, which exhorted Masons to conform to the religion of their homeland. This schism came to Massachusetts in 1761, some twenty-eight years after the grand lodge of St John's had been established as the first Masonic lodge in Boston. Whereas that lodge had been established under a warrant from London, the new 'Ancient' grand lodge of St Andrew derived its authority from Edinburgh. Though initially acrimonious, the split did not endure; the two lodges merged in 1792. However, at the time of the Revolution, it appears to have reflected a real social and political division, in that the St Andrew's lodge – founded by men who had been excluded from St John's as socially inferior – became a hotbed of sedition, especially after Joseph Warren became its master (and later the grand master of a new grand lodge for Boston Ancients).[27] The Green Dragon tavern, which the St Andrew's lodge purchased in 1764, became the headquarters of the revolutionary movement in Boston.[28] Indeed, the lodge's minute book for November and December 1773 hints at the involvement of so many members in the Boston Tea Party that meetings had to be adjourned due to low attendance.[29] When Warren – who was killed in the fighting of 1775 – was reinterred, his friend and fellow Mason Perez Morton praised him as a virtuous, 'matchless Patriot' in his public life and as a 'Pattern for Mankind' in his private affairs. Warren had fallen 'to the Cause of Virtue and Mankind', but it was as a Mason that he should be remembered. 'What a bright example he set [as grand master],' declared Morton, 'to live within Compass, and act upon the Square.' Of all the associations to which Warren had belonged, Morton said, 'on none did he place so high a Value' as Masonry. Indeed, Morton explicitly likened Warren's death 'by the Hands of Ruffians' to that of Hiram Abif, the builder of Solomon's temple (who, according to Masonic lore, was murdered when he refused to divulge the Master Masons' secret passwords).[30] Revere, too, was no rank-and-file Mason; in 1788 he became deputy grand master of the Massachusetts Grand Lodge.[31]

Conspiracy theorists and writers of pulp fiction have long been attracted to the idea that Freemasonry was the covert network behind the American Revolution. That may help explain the doubts of respectable historians. Certainly, we should not exaggerate the homogeneity of colonial Masonry. There were Loyalists in the Boston lodges, too, such as Benjamin Hallowell, the customs commissioner, and his brother Robert, both of whom belonged to St John's, and at least six members of the St Andrew's lodge. Yet the concentration of revolutionary leaders in St Andrew's simply cannot be overlooked. Its members included not only Warren and Revere, but also Isaiah Thomas, publisher of the *Massachusetts Spy* and *New England Almanac*, William Palfrey, secretary of the Sons of Liberty, and Thomas Crafts of the Loyal Nine.[32] The Ancients' grand lodge formed nineteen new lodges during the revolutionary war; St Andrew's alone accepted thirty new members in 1777, twenty-five in 1778, and forty-one over the succeeding two years. At a June 1782 dinner, the lodge entertained the Boston selectmen and the French consul at Faneuil Hall.[33] Thirteen years later, on 4 July 1795, it was Paul Revere, dressed in Masonic vestments, who laid the cornerstone of the Massachusetts State House. Revere urged his audience to 'live within the compass of Good Citizens' in order to show 'the World of Mankind . . . that we wish to stand upon a level with them, that when we part we may be admitted into the Temple where Reigns Silence and Peace'. Just days before, a minister had told Revere and his officers that Masons were 'the Sons of REASON, the DISCIPLES of WISDOM, and the BRETHREN of Humanity'.[34] This illustrates the harmony at this time between Masonry and at least some clergymen of the early republic. A good example of a minister-Mason was the Reverend William Bentley, a Congregational minister who lived in Salem. In 1800, Bentley visited Boston to attend the commemoration of George Washington's death, dining with his fellow Masons Revere and Isaiah Thomas.[35]

Just thirty years later, the atmosphere would be very different. One consequence of the 'Great Awakening' of religion in New England was an outbreak of fierce anti-Masonism, which led to a steep decline in new initiations by St Andrew's and its ilk.[36] Here we find another explanation for the later deprecation of the Masonic role in the American Revolution: it was simply not a feature of the republic's founding that nineteenth-century Americans wished to remember.

Yet the circumstantial evidence is compelling. Not only did Benjamin Franklin become grand master of his lodge in Philadelphia; he was also the publisher (in 1734) of the first American edition of Anderson's *Constitutions*. Not only did George Washington join Lodge No. 4 in Fredericksburg, Virginia, at the age of twenty; in 1783 he also became master of the newly formed Alexandria Lodge No. 22.

At his first presidential inauguration on 30 April 1789, Washington swore the oath of office on the Bible of the St John's Masonic Lodge No. 1 of New York. The oath was administered by Robert Livingston, the Chancellor of New York (the state's highest judicial office) and another Mason, indeed the first grand master of the Grand Lodge of New York. In 1794, Washington sat for the artist Joseph Williams, who painted him dressed in the full Masonic regalia the president had worn to level the cornerstone of the United States Capitol a year before.[37] George Washington's apron deserves to be as famous in the folklore of the American Revolution as Paul Revere's ride, for it seems doubtful that either man would have had the influence he enjoyed had it not been for his membership of the Masonic brotherhood. Later historians have cast doubt on the Masonic origins of iconography of the Great Seal of the United States, globally recognizable since its incorporation in the one-dollar bill in 1935.[38] Yet the all-seeing eye of Providence that crowns the unfinished pyramid on the obverse of the seal does closely resemble the eye that gazes out at us from Washington's apron in nineteenth-century lithographs of the first president in Masonic attire (see plate 12).

The scientific, philosophical and political revolutions of the eighteenth century were intertwined because the networks that transmitted them were intertwined. The makers of the American Revolution were men of many talents. Though on the periphery of the European networks that produced the scientific and philosophical revolutions of the era – despite self-consciously imitating the associational life of Great Britain with their Masonic lodges – the founding fathers proved to be politically the most innovative men of their age. In many ways, the constitution that emerged from their deliberations in the 1780s was intended to institutionalize an anti-hierarchical political order. Acutely aware of the fates that had befallen republican experiments in the ancient world and in early-modern Europe, the founders devised a system that both separated and devolved power, greatly circumscribing the executive authority of their elected president. In the first of *The Federalist Papers*, Alexander Hamilton clearly identified the principal danger the infant United States would face:

> [A] dangerous ambition more often lurks behind the specious mask of zeal for the rights of the people than under the forbidding appearance of zeal for the firmness and efficiency of government. History will teach us that the former has been found a much more certain road to the introduction of despotism than the latter, and that of those men who have overturned the liberties of republics, the greatest number have begun their career by paying an obsequious court to the people; commencing demagogues, and ending tyrants.[39]

It was a theme he returned to in 1795. 'It is only to consult the history of nations,' Hamilton wrote, 'to perceive, that every country, at all times, is cursed by the existence of men who, actuated by an irregular ambition, scruple nothing which they imagine will contribute to their own advancement and importance . . . in republics, fawning or turbulent demagogues, worshipping still the idol – power – wherever placed . . . and trafficking in the weaknesses, vices, frailties, or prejudices' of the people.[40]

That the American system worked so well astonished European visitors, not least those from France, where a republic created in 1792 had lasted precisely twelve years. The French social and political theorist Alexis de Tocqueville saw the vitality of American associational life, along with the decentralized nature of the federal system, as the keys to the success of the new democracy. It was indeed remarkable that such a system should have arisen in colonies populated by religious refugees from a country that had abandoned its republican experiment in 1660. As Tocqueville noted, 'whilst the hierarchy of rank [had] despotically classed the inhabitants of the mother-country', the American colonists had 'present[ed] the novel spectacle of a community homogeneous in all its parts'.[41] It was this peculiarly egalitarian character of colonial society that had made possible the uniquely dense network of civic associations which, Tocqueville argued, were the key to the success of the American experiment. The country he described in Book II, chapters 5 and 6, of his *Democracy in America* was, it might be said, the first networked polity. 'In no country in the world,' declared Tocqueville, 'has the principle of association been more successfully used or applied to a greater multitude of objects than in America':

> Besides the permanent associations which are established by law under the names of townships, cities, and counties, a vast number of others are formed and maintained by the agency of private individuals. The citizen of the United States is taught from infancy to rely upon his own exertions in order to resist the evils and the difficulties of life; he looks upon the social authority with an eye of mistrust and anxiety, and he claims its assistance only when he is unable to do without it . . . In the United States associations are established to promote the public safety, commerce, industry, morality, and religion. There is no end which the human will despairs of attaining through the combined power of individuals united into a society.[42]

Tocqueville saw America's political associations as an indispensable counterweight to the danger of tyranny that was inherent in modern democracy – if only the tyranny of the majority. However, the greatest strength of the American system, he argued, lay in its non-political associations:

> Americans of all ages, all conditions, all minds constantly unite. Not only do they have commercial and industrial associations in which all take part, but they also have a thousand other kinds: religious, moral, grave, futile, very general and very particular, immense and very small; Americans use associations to give fêtes, to found seminaries, to build inns, to raise churches, to distribute books, to send missionaries to the antipodes; in this manner they create hospitals, prisons, schools. Finally, if it is a question of bringing to light a truth or developing a sentiment with the support of a great example, they associate.[43]

The contrast with the political and social structures of his native France fascinated Tocqueville. Why had the revolution there – located as it was in one of the crucial hubs of the Enlightenment – produced results so disappointingly different?

IV

The Restoration of Hierarchy

21
The Red and the Black

In Stendhal's novel *Le Rouge et le Noir* (1830), Julien Sorel embarks on a clerical career, realizing that it is his best hope of advancement in the France of the restored Bourbon monarchy. The son of a carpenter, Sorel would have preferred the meritocratic system of 'career open to talent' that had characterized Napoleon Bonaparte's reign. Sorel comes to a bad end, less the victim of his philandering than of the rigid social hierarchy of the Restoration era. However, Stendhal is more forgiving of Sorel's impetuous nature than of Bourbon snobbery. 'There is only one true nobility left; namely, the title of Duke. Marquis is absurd, [but] at the word Duke one turns one's head,' reads one of the book's epigraphs (many of which Stendhal simply made up). 'Service! talent! merit! bah!' is another: 'Belong to a coterie.' And: 'The prefect riding along on his horse thought to himself, "Why should I not be a minister, head of the Cabinet, a duke? . . . I would have innovators put in chains."'[1]

The Bourbon bid to restore the hierarchies of the *ancien régime* proved unsustainable. In 1830 another French revolution toppled Charles X. Eighteen years later, a third revolution dealt the same fate to his Orleanist successor, Louis Philippe. Finally, in 1870, German invasion and another revolution overthrew Emperor Napoleon III, paving the way to the third and longest-lived of France's (to date) five republican constitutions. A large part of the fascination of this era in European history is precisely the precariousness of each new attempt to re-establish monarchical order. Yet the nineteenth century was a time when, slowly but surely, the revolutionary energies that had been unleashed by the printing press were contained in new structures of power. If not by bringing back the Bourbons, then how?

Network-based revolutions – the Reformation, the Scientific Revolution and the Enlightenment – had profoundly transformed Western civilization. Political revolutions, not only in the United States and France, but also all over the Americas and Europe, had promised a new democratic age based on the ideal of universal brotherhood prefigured by Freemasonry and ecstatically invoked in Schiller's 'Ode to Joy'. That promise was not fulfilled. To understand why the advantage shifted back from networks to hierarchies, we need once again to avoid imagining a false dichotomy between the two. Even the stifling stratification of 1820s France had its distinctive network architecture. As we have seen, most networks are hierarchical in some respects, if only because some nodes are more central than others, while hierarchies are just special kinds of network in which flows of information or resources are restricted to certain edges in order to maximize the centrality of the ruling node. That is precisely what frustrates Julien Sorel about Bourbon France: there are so few ways to ascend the social ladder that he is compelled to depend too heavily on a handful of patrons. Moreover, a central leitmotif of Stendhal's novel is what network theory calls the impossible triad. To win the heart of his aristocratic employer's daughter, Mathilde de Mole, Sorel feigns a preference for a widow, Madame de Fervaques. Though Sorel woos both women, they are incapable of colluding against him. When an earlier lover, Madame de Rênal, denounces him to Mathilde's father, he attempts to murder her. Imprisoned, he is visited separately by both Mathilde and Madame de Rênal. Writing in 1961, the literary critic René Girard coined the phrase 'mimetic desire': Mathilde only desires Sorel when she realizes that he is desired by another woman.

Networks are simpler in hierarchical orders, sometimes because those at the top consciously apply the principle of divide and rule, sometimes because in a hierarchical order only a small number of hubs really matter. As they sought to reassemble Europe's political order after the upheaval of the French Revolutionary and Napoleonic Wars, the statesmen who met at the Congress of Vienna created another kind of simple network: a 'pentarchy' of five great powers which, by its very nature, had a finite number of ways in which it could achieve equilibrium. Its success was based partly on this very simplicity. The balance of power, as we shall see, took it for granted that the majority of European states did not matter: equilibrium depended on the relations between Austria, Britain, France, Prussia and Russia, and only those five (see plate 13).

The nineteenth century's reassertion of hierarchical order did not nullify the intellectual, commercial and political networks that had been created in the previous three centuries. Those lived on. Indeed, religious life in the Protestant world grew more lively and fractious, thanks to a succession of 'awakenings' and 'revivals'. The Industrial Revolution – in many ways the most transformative of all revolutions – could quite easily be likened to the other revolutions of the eighteenth century as it, too, was the product of a network of innovators, some scientifically trained, others tinkering autodidacts. And, even if Freemasonry declined after 1800, its goal of expanding and institutionalizing the notion of brotherhood (beyond the narrow sense of male siblings) was shared by a host of new movements, not only the trades union movement but also many nationalist organizations, notably the German student fraternities. The difference was that royal, aristocratic and ecclesiastical hierarchies grew steadily better at co-opting all these networks, harnessing their creative energies, and bending them to their wills.

22
From Crowd to Tyranny

Not everyone realized as swiftly as Edmund Burke that the French Revolution would be a great deal bloodier than the American. By the time of the Terror the difference was undeniable. The attempt to replace Louis XVI with 'the will of the people' had unleashed internecine violence unlike anything seen in France since the St Bartholomew's Day Massacre of 1572 (plate 8). The revolutionary violence may be said to have begun on 21 April 1789, with a riot in the *faubourg* Saint-Antoine in which around 300 people demonstrating in support of the self-proclaimed National Assembly were killed by royal troops. Three months later, in a more famous clash, roughly a hundred people lost their lives when soldiers defending the Bastille opened fire. This time, the tables were turned when some of the defenders joined the revolutionary crowd. The decapitation of the garrison commander de Flesselles marked an important escalation, as did the public hanging and dismembering of the officials Foulon de Doué and his son-in-law, Bertier de Sauvigny, at the Place de Grève on 22 July (the former's head and the latter's heart were stuck on poles and paraded through the streets).

No sooner had the Parisian crowd taken up arms than a wave of unrest also swept the French countryside. Fearful of a plot by the nobility to reassert their power through mysterious 'brigands', peasants all over France resorted to violence that summer in what became known as *la grande peur* – the Great Fear. Initially it was feudal registers that were burned and chateau wine-cellars that were plundered, but in its scale and duration this was more than a traditional peasants' revolt or *jacquerie*. The contagious speed with which the Great Fear spread is especially striking and hard to explain, given the relatively poor communications of provincial France at that time – another illustration of the point that rumours can go viral without sophisticated information technology.[1] Compared with what was to come, the Great Fear was mild. Though many landowners were threatened and humiliated, there were only three murders: of a noble deputy to the Estates General and an official suspected of being a food monopolist (in Ballon, north of Le Mans), and of an officer in the marines (in Le Pouzin, north of Avignon). Yet the epidemic of chateau-burning was remarkable. In the space of less than two weeks, between 27 July and 9 August, nine chateaux were razed to the ground and eighty suffered damage just in the province of Dauphiné, in south-eastern France.[2]

It would be superfluous here to do more than list the major massacres that preceded the Terror of 1793–4: the women's march and attack on the royal palace at Versailles in October 1789, the National Guard's firing on the crowd at the Champ de Mars in July 1791, the September Massacres of 1792 (when *sans-culottes* stormed the prisons of Paris, murdering hundreds of the inmates), the war against counter-revolutionaries in the Vendée (1793–6), not forgetting the extremely bloody slave revolt on Saint-Domingue (Haiti). The point is that, unlike in Britain's American colonies – but as in most revolutions since – insurrection led inexorably to anarchy and thence to tyranny, much as predicted by classical political theory. Whereas the American colonists had evolved their own networks of civic association, out of which the American Revolution and the United States organically grew, the French crowd was quite differently structured. The Committee of Public Safety was itself an attempt to impose order on the disorderly bloodletting of the *canaille* – the mob.[3] Yet none of the expedients of the Jacobins or their successors in the Directory sufficed to stabilize either the capital or the country at large. Gruesome mass killings like the deliberate drownings of thousands of people in Nantes testified to a near total breakdown of social and political order, comparable in its character to the worst atrocities of the Arab revolutions in our own time. In the name of a false utopia, sadists ran amok.

The man who restored order to France (though he did the very opposite to the rest of Europe) possessed a preternatural energy.

Napoleon Bonaparte's ascent from Corsican obscurity to the command of the artillery of the revolutionary Army of Italy – a promotion he received at the height of the Terror – was of course made possible by the collapse of the aristocratic system that would have barred his way prior to 1789. Like Stendhal's Julien Sorel, Bonaparte was both a climber and a philanderer; unlike Sorel, he combined lack of scruples with the luck of good timing. Yet it was what the man did with time – with each waking minute – that was truly prodigious. In a time of chaos, it is the micro-manager who ascends – the man who instinctively takes every task upon himself. 'I'm extremely unhappy at the manner in which the loading of the sixteen pieces [of cannon] has been performed,' the newly promoted brigadier scrawled in one of 800 letters and despatches he wrote in the space of just nine months in 1796. 'I'm surprised that you are so tardy in the execution of orders,' he complained to his *chef de bataillon*. 'It's always necessary to tell you the same thing three times.' His vision ranged from grand strategy – it was at this time that he drafted his plan for an invasion of Italy – to minutiae (the imprisonment of a corporal who was absent without leave in Antibes or the precise location of drummer boys on the parade ground).[4]

Napoleon was what would now be termed a workaholic. He worked sixteen hours a day, every day. In April 1807 – a month of unusual tranquillity in his reign – he still managed to compose 443 letters. By this time, he was dictating all his correspondence except the love letters. 'The ideas go on fastest,' he once said, 'and then goodbye to the letters and the lines!' On one occasion, without reference to notes, he dictated to his interior minister no fewer than 517 articles setting out the regulations for a new military academy at Fontainebleau.[5] As a general rule, he would spend just ten minutes at the dinner table, except when he ate with his family on Sunday nights; then he might stay as long as half an hour. When he left the table, he leapt up 'as if he had received an electric shock'.[6] As one of his hard-pressed secretaries recalled, he would sleep 'in several short naps, broken at will during the night as in the day'.[7] He travelled with the same relentless vigour. In July 1807 he was driven by carriage from Tilsit in Prussia to Saint-Cloud, a 100-hour journey which, in his impatience, he refused to interrupt. He arrived in the early hours of the morning and immediately summoned his council of ministers.[8] Two years later he rode from Valladolid in Spain to Paris, 'simultaneously lashing the horse of his aide-de-camp and digging the spurs into his own'. It took him just six days to cover more than 600 miles.[9] On foot, too, he always was in a hurry, leaving others panting in his wake. Even when bathing or being shaved, he wasted no time: someone was always on hand to read the latest newspapers to him, including translations from the invariably hostile British press.[10] It was Napoleon's combination of indefatigable energy and attention to detail that brought the anarchy of the French Revolution to an end. The law was codified, the monetary system reformed, public credit restored. But alongside those enduring achievements were an infinity of tiny things: the number of servants that officers might take in the event of an invasion of England; the uniform that Irish rebels might wear if they joined the French cause; the need for Corporal Bernaudat of the thirteenth Line to drink less; the identity of the stagehand who had broken the arm of the singer Mademoiselle Aubry at the Paris Opéra.[11]

With his overweening self-belief, Napoleon set out to run not only France but all Europe as if it were one vast army that could be commanded – mastered by sheer force of will. In many respects, he was the last of the enlightened absolutists: a French Frederick the Great. Yet he was also the first of the modern dictators. Technologically there was little real difference between the armies Frederick and Napoleon commanded. Yet everything the latter did was on a larger scale* and at a faster speed. The two great military theorists of the age, Carl von Clausewitz and Antoine-Henri de Jomini, drew somewhat different lessons from Napoleon's success. For Clausewitz, Napoleon's genius lay in his ability to concentrate his forces rapidly at the enemy's centre of gravity (the *Schwerpunkt*) and to defeat him in a decisive battle, the *Hauptschlacht*. For Jomini, the key was his ability to exploit the advantages of superior interior lines of operation

* When Carl von Clausewitz first saw action as an ensign at the Battle of Valmy in 1792, 64,000 men on one side fought against 30,000 on the other, in a battle lasting one day. By 1813, when Clausewitz participated as a major-general at the Battle of Leipzig, 365,000 men fought 195,000 in a battle lasting three days.

(*lignes d'opérations*). Jomini thought Napoleon was applying universal principles of warfare.[12] Clausewitz saw that Napoleon's style of warfare was historically specific because of the way it tapped the popular nationalism that the French Revolution had unleashed.[13] In *War and Peace*, published forty-eight years after Napoleon's death in exile on the forlorn South Atlantic island of St Helena, Leo Tolstoy mocked his imperial pretensions. How could a single man by his command send hundreds of thousands of men from France to Russia, throwing the lives of countless others into turmoil? And yet Napoleon did just that. The problem was that, no matter how much he wrapped himself in the trappings of legitimate rule, appropriating Egyptian, Roman and Habsburg regalia and iconography, Napoleon could never achieve the one thing upon which hierarchical systems of rule ultimately depend (and insist upon): legitimacy.

23
Order Restored

> It is generally thought that our age possesses only the tendency, the pressure, towards dissolution. Its significance seems to lie in putting an end to the unifying, binding institutions which have remained since the Middle Ages ... From this same source comes the irresistible inclination towards the development of great democratic ideas and institutions, which of necessity causes the great changes which we are witnessing.

Leopold von Ranke's 1833 essay on the 'great powers' of Europe is a seminal work of nineteenth-century historiography. Whereas many of his contemporaries remained convinced that the revolutionary energies that had swept Europe from the German Reformation to the French Revolution were inexorable, Ranke saw that a new international order was taking shape that would check the seemingly universal tendency towards dissolution. This order was based on what he called a pentarchy of five great powers: Austria, Britain, France, Prussia and Russia. This order had begun to emerge in the course of the eighteenth century but had been wrecked by Napoleon's bid for mastery over Europe. However, with his defeat, the pentarchy could be completed:

> Far from merely satisfying itself with negations, our century has produced the most positive results. It has completed a great liberation, not in the sense of a dissolution, but in a constructive, unifying sense. Not only has it first of all created the great powers; it has renewed the principle of all states, religion and law; and revitalized the principle of each individual state ... In just this fact lies the characteristic of our age ... [With states and nations] the union of all depends on the

> independence of each . . . A decisive positive dominance of one over the other would lead to the others' ruin. A merging of them all would destroy the essence of each. Out of separate and independent development will emerge the true harmony.[1]

That a new and stable balance of power was created by the statesmen who met at the Congress of Vienna has been a truth almost universally acknowledged since Ranke's time. In his first book, *A World Restored*, Henry Kissinger argued that the period of relative peace enjoyed by Europe between 1815 and 1914 was due in large measure to the 'generally accepted legitimacy' of this five-power order.[2] In Kissinger's account, this was the achievement of two especially gifted diplomats: Prince Metternich, the Austrian foreign minister, and Lord Castlereagh, his British counterpart. Metternich's goal – a reconstructed legitimate order in which liberalism itself was illegitimate – differed fundamentally from Castlereagh's, which was essentially a scheme for a balance of power in which Britain played the part of 'balancer'.[3] A crucial reason for their success and Napoleon's failure was the latter's inability to recognize his own limits and to stabilize his own position following his marriage to the daughter of the Austrian emperor.[4] A major challenge to Metternich and Castlereagh was the emergence of Tsar Alexander I as a potential revolutionary, aspiring to be the 'arbiter of Europe' following Napoleon's defeat in Russia. The end result was a kind of tragic success. Ultimately, Britain could not commit itself to uphold a counter-revolutionary European order of the sort Metternich aspired to create, and which he encouraged the Tsar to believe was his own idea. Political crises in Spain, Naples and later Piedmont were, in Metternich's eyes, life-threatening menaces to the new order; to the British they seemed like little local difficulties, intervention in which might just as easily unbalance that same order.[5] At another congress, held at Troppau, Metternich was able to represent his doomed 'battle against nationalism and liberalism' as a European rather than an Austrian enterprise.[6] Castlereagh saw only too clearly that Russia would be equally willing to intervene on the side of nationalism if, as in the Balkans, it was directed against the Ottoman Empire. On 12 August 1822, Castlereagh, weary of the vitriol directed at him by Whigs and

Radicals and despairing at the intolerable weight on his shoulders, committed suicide, severing his own carotid artery with a penknife. All that remained after the Congress of Verona was 'the legitimizing principle' – at once counter-revolutionary and anti-French – as the basis for the 'Holy Alliance' between Austria, Prussia and Russia.[7]

Yet the idea of a balance of power did not die with Castlereagh. Although Britain's 'continental commitment' was intermittent over the ensuing century, it was sufficient – until 1914 – to prevent any one power on the Continent from challenging, as France had under Napoleon, the fundamental legitimacy of the pentarchical order. In essence, European stability was based on a balance between the four continental powers, which Britain preserved by occasional diplomatic or military interventions. In Kissinger's terms, Britain was the balancer. The result was a European order that endured until the end of the century. It was only the fall of Otto von Bismarck and the non-renewal of the Secret Reinsurance Treaty between Germany and Russia – 'perhaps the most important thread out of the fabric of Bismarck's system of overlapping alliances'[8] – that made the system rigid to the point of fragility and indeed combustibility.[9]

Subsequent research has of course modified this picture in numerous ways. Some argue that there had been a fundamental 'transformation' of international politics, as the old rules that had assumed conflict and competition gave way to new rules that aspired to concert and equilibrium.[10] Others insist that the old rancorous relations persisted; only 'narrow self-interest' averted large-scale war.[11] The critical point remains, however, that a new hierarchy was established at Vienna which set the 'great powers' – first the four victors of Waterloo, then (after 1818) the victors plus the defeated France – apart from the lesser states.[12] Thus Article VI of the Quadruple Alliance (November 1815) committed the four signatories to hold periodic meetings 'for the purpose of consulting upon their interests, or for the consideration of measures . . . which shall be considered the most salutary for the purposes and prosperity of Nations and the maintenance of the Peace of Europe'.[13] Spain might complain, Bavaria grumble, but there was not much more they could do. Castlereagh might warn against the great powers becoming 'a European Council for the management of the affairs of the world'. Friedrich

Gentz, Metternich's secretary, might fret that this new 'dictatorship' might become 'a source of abuse, injustice and vexation for the estates of the lesser rank' – a fear also shared by the young Lord John Russell. Gradually, however, the leaders of the great powers grew accustomed to exercising a collective hegemony.[14] As Gentz put it, looking back on 1815, the congress system had, in effect, united

> the sum total of states in a federation under the direction of the major powers . . . The second-, third-, and fourth-rate states submit in silence and without any previous stipulation to the decisions jointly taken by the preponderant powers; and Europe seems to form finally a great political family, united under the auspices of an areopagus of its own creation.[15]

Even if they were not unanimous on some issues – Castlereagh could not endorse Metternich's counter-revolutionary strategy – there was an implicit consensus that any future bid for hegemony by one of their number should be resisted and that a general war was to be avoided.[16] Of course, on closer inspection the system was always a more complex and evolving one than Ranke's pentarchy implied. The Ottoman Empire was more than just a passive object of great power policy; that was precisely what made the 'Eastern Question' (which was essentially about its future) so intractable.[17] The new states that were created in the nineteenth century – not only the German Reich (which significantly enlarged one of the big five) and the Kingdom of Italy, but also Belgium, Bulgaria, Greece, Romania and Serbia – changed the nature of the network in important ways. Yet there was no denying that something new had been established – and no denying that it worked. In the century between the Utrecht settlements (1713–15) and the Congress of Vienna, there had been thirty-three European wars involving some or all of the eleven acknowledged powers of the period (which included Spain, Sweden, Denmark, Holland and Saxony). For the 1815–1914 period, there were seventeen such wars, even if Spain and Sweden are still counted as powers. The probability of war participation by any power declined by roughly a third.[18] There were, in effect, world wars in the eighteenth century as there were in the twentieth – the Seven Years' War was a truly global conflict – but there was no world war in the nineteenth century.

Put differently, the international order was now clearly a hierarchical system, but with five hubs playing the dominant role. Those five nodes could link together in a variety of different combinations – could indeed quarrel amongst themselves – but never between 1815 and 1914 did they all go to war. Although the system was not so stable as to avoid war altogether, the conflicts between Waterloo and the Marne were far less destructive than the one that had gone before and the one what was to follow. Even the biggest European war of the nineteenth century – the Crimean War (1853–6), which pitted Britain and France against Russia – was an order of magnitude smaller than the Napoleonic Wars. Moreover, the great powers conferred with each other more often than they clashed. Between 1814 and 1907, there were seven congresses and nineteen conferences between the great powers.[19] Diplomacy, punctuated by small amounts of war, became the normal state of affairs, in marked contrast to the two decades before 1815, when the exact opposite had been the norm. As we shall see, no explanation of the origins of the First World War is complete if it fails to explain why this ceased to be the case in 1914.

24
The House of Saxe-Coburg-Gotha

The restoration of order to Europe after Napoleon required more than just a new diplomatic hierarchy that ranked five states above all the rest, however. Of comparable importance was the way that the institution of monarchy itself was re-legitimized. In this process, an often overlooked role was played by an old-fashioned kind of network, namely the intertwined genealogies of European royalty. One family in particular played a crucial role in reconciling the hereditary principle with the new ideals of constitutional government that so many nineteenth-century liberals embraced. Coburg was one of those petty German states that had been threatened with extinction when Napoleon swept away the Holy Roman Empire and created the Confederation of the Rhine. However, the sons of the dowager Duchess Augusta managed to steer a careful course between France and Russia and were duly rewarded when, under Russian pressure, the duchy was restored to her eldest son, Ernest, in 1807. With the exception of one daughter (Sophie, who married Count Mensdorff), all of Augusta's children either married royalty, achieved royal status in their own right or secured it for their children. One daughter married the brother of Alexander I of Russia; another the duke of Württemberg; a third married the duke of Kent, one of the brothers of George IV of Great Britain. But it was Augusta's youngest son, Leopold, who was the real founder of the Saxe-Coburg dynasty. Leopold suffered a severe setback when his first wife, Princess Charlotte, daughter of George IV, died in childbirth in November 1817, just eighteen months after their marriage. But his circumstances were transformed when, having previously toyed with the idea of accepting the throne of Greece, he accepted the title of 'King of the Belgians' in 1831. So frequently were thrones subsequently offered to members of his family that in 1843 Leopold was 'much amused' when 'a very rich and influential American from New York assur[ed] me that they stood in great need of a Governement [*sic*] which was able to grant protection to property, and that the feeling of many was for Monarchy instead of the misrule of mobs, as they had it, and that he wished very much some branch of the Coburg family might be disposed for such a place. *Qu'en dites-vous* [he asked his niece], is this not flattering?'[1] Leopold's niece was Queen Victoria.

As *The Times* noted in 1863, the history of the Saxe-Coburgs showed 'how much one success leads to another in Princely life'.[2] Augusta of Saxe-Coburg's grandchildren included not only both Queen Victoria and her husband, Albert, but also Ferdinand, who married the Queen of Portugal, and Leopold's son, namesake and heir to the Belgian throne. The Saxe-Coburgs were further linked by marriage to the Orléans family and the Habsburgs.* Moreover, Victoria and Albert's eldest child was not the only one to marry royally: all but one of their nine children did. Thus, besides Frederick William of Prussia, Queen Victoria's sons-in-law included Prince Christian of Schleswig-Holstein and Henry of Battenberg, whose brother Alexander became prince of Bulgaria, while her daughters-in-law included Princess Alexandra of Denmark and Princess Marie, daughter of Tsar Alexander II and sister of Tsar Alexander III. By the time the future Nicholas II arrived in London for his first visit to England, in 1893, a family reunion had come to resemble an international summit:

> We drew into Charing Cross. There we were met by: Uncle Bertie [the future Edward VII], Aunt Alix [Alexandra of Denmark], Georgie [the future George V], Louise, Victoria and Maud [his sisters, the last of whom would marry Prince Carl of Denmark, later Haakon VII of Norway] . . .
>
> Two hours later Apapa [Christian IX of Denmark], Amama and Uncle Valdemar [of Denmark] arrived. It is wonderful to have so many of our family gathered together . . .

* Leopold I married one of Louis Philippe's daughters, Leopold II married Marie Henriette, Archduchess of Austria, and his sister, Charlotte, married the ill-starred Archduke Maximilian, briefly Emperor of Mexico.

> At 4.30 I went to see Aunt Marie [wife of Alfred, duke of Saxe-Coburg] at Clarence House and had tea in the garden with her, Uncle Alfred, and Ducky [their daughter, Victoria Melita].[3]

When this last married Ernest Louis, heir to the Grand Duchy of Hesse-Darmstadt the following year (see figure 17), the guests included an emperor and empress, a future emperor and empress, a queen, a future king and queen, seven princes, ten princesses, two dukes, two duchesses and a marquess. They were all related.

To be sure, by the 1880s, the Coburgs had their enemies. In the wake of the abdication of Alexander of Battenberg as prince of Bulgaria,[4] it was possible for Herbert von Bismarck to mock the Coburg 'clan'. 'In the English Royal Family and its nearest collaterals,' he told the Tsar, 'there is a sort of worship of the undiluted family principle and Queen Victoria is regarded as a kind of absolute Chief of all branches of the Coburg clan. It is associated with codicils, which are shown to the obedient relation from afar. (Here the Tsar laughed heartily.)'[5] Yet the clan outlasted the power of the Bismarcks. In 1894, Queen Victoria was pleased to be addressed as 'Granny' by the future Tsar Nicholas II, after his betrothal to yet another of her granddaughters, Alix of Hesse.[6] With 'Willy' (her grandson William II of Germany) corresponding cheerfully with his cousins 'Nicky' and 'George',[7] it seemed for a time as if the vision that had inspired Leopold I had been realized: from Athens to Berlin, from Bucharest to Copenhagen, from Darmstadt to London, from Madrid to Oslo, from Stockholm to Sofia and even in St Petersburg, the Saxe-Coburgs ruled. When the future Edward VIII was born in 1894, Victoria urged that her great-grandson be christened Albert – as if to set the seal on the familial achievement:

> This will be the Coburg line, like formerly the Plantagenet, the Tudor (for Owen Tudor) the Stewart & the Brunswick for George the 1st – he being the gt. gd. son of James I & this wd. be the Coburg Dynasty – retaining the Brunswick & all the others preceding it, joining in it.[8]

17. The House of Saxe-Coburg-Gotha. Queen Victoria and members of her family at Coburg on 21 April 1894, assembled for the wedding of Princess Victoria Melita and Ernest Louis, Grand Duke of Hesse, two of her forty grandchildren. Sitting to the left of the Queen is her eldest daughter, Victoria, Dowager Empress of Germany; to the right sits her grandson Kaiser William II. Standing behind the Kaiser, with the beard and bowler hat, is Tsar Nicholas II of Russia, whose engagement to another of Victoria's grandchildren, Princess Alexandra (Alix) of Hesse (standing next to him), had just been announced. Behind the Tsar, to the left, is Queen Victoria's eldest son, the Prince of Wales, later King Edward VII. Among the figures in the back row is another of Queen Victoria's grandchildren, Princess Marie, who became Queen of Romania in 1914. Grandchildren not pictured here included the future queens of Greece, Norway and Spain. Photograph by Edward Uhlenhuth.

25
The House of Rothschild

The French polemicist who likened the Saxe-Coburgs to the Rothschilds in the 1840s[1] was closer to the mark than he knew. For these two south German dynasties had an almost symbiotic relationship with one another dating back to Leopold of Saxe-Coburg's engagement to Princess Charlotte in 1816.[2] The Saxe-Coburgs had, with skill and luck, risen to the top during and after the Napoleonic upheaval. From much humbler origins, the Rothschilds did the same. Between around 1810 and 1836, the five sons of Mayer Amschel Rothschild rose from the confines of the Frankfurt ghetto to attain a position of new and unequalled power in international finance. Despite numerous economic and political crises and the efforts of their competitors to match them, they still occupied that position when the youngest of them died in 1868; even after that, their dominance was only slowly eroded. So extraordinary did this achievement seem to contemporaries that they often sought to explain it in mystical terms. According to one account dating from the 1830s, the Rothschilds owed their fortune to the possession of a mysterious 'Hebrew talisman'. It was this that had enabled Nathan Rothschild, the founder of the London house, to become 'the leviathan of the money markets of Europe'.[3] Similar stories were being told in the Russian Pale of Jewish settlement as late as the 1890s.[4]

The Rothschilds' achievement was epoch-making. There had never been a larger concentration of financial capital than that accumulated by the Rothschild family by the middle decades of the nineteenth century. As early as 1828, their combined capital exceeded that of their nearest rivals, the Barings, by an order of magnitude. A narrowly economic explanation of their success would stress the innovations they introduced to the international market for government debt, and the ways their rapidly accumulated capital allowed them to expand into the markets for commercial bills, commodities, bullion and insurance. However, it is important also to understand the distinctive structure they gave their business, which was at once a strictly governed family partnership and a multinational – a single 'general joint concern' with affiliated 'houses' in Frankfurt, London, Vienna, Paris and Naples. The Rothschilds resisted centrifugal forces partly through intermarriage. After 1824, Rothschilds tended to marry Rothschilds. Of twenty-one marriages involving descendants of Mayer Amschel between 1824 and 1877, no fewer than fifteen were *between* his direct descendants. Although marriage between cousins was far from uncommon in the nineteenth century – especially amongst German-Jewish business dynasties – this was extraordinary. 'These Rothschilds harmonize with one another in the most remarkable fashion,' noted the poet Heinrich Heine. 'Strangely enough, they even choose marriage partners from among themselves and the strands of relationship between them form complicated knots which future historians will find difficult to unravel.'[5] Self-conscious references to 'our royal family' suggest that the Rothschilds themselves were aware of the parallel with the Saxe-Coburgs.[6]

Yet of equal importance to all this was the speed with which the Rothschilds built their network – not just of agents and associated lesser financiers around Europe, but of political 'friends in high places'. 'You know, dear Nathan,' wrote Salomon in October 1815, 'what father used to say about sticking to a man in government.'[7] And again: '[Y]ou remember father's principle that you have to be ready to try everything to get in with such a great government figure.'[8] Nor had Mayer Amschel left them in no doubt as to how such politicians could best be wooed: 'Our late father taught us that if a high-placed person enters into a [financial] partnership with a Jew, he belongs to the Jew [*gehört er dem Juden*].'[9] Among the most important Rothschild clients in this period were Karl Buderus, the Elector of Hesse-Cassel's senior finance official; Carl Theodor von Dalberg, the former Illuminatus who had been prince-primate of the Confederation of the Rhine from 1806 until 1814; Leopold of Saxe-Coburg, consort to Princess Charlotte and later King of the Belgians; John

Charles Herries, British commissary-in-chief in October 1811, later (briefly) Chancellor of the Exchequer and president of the Board of Trade; Charles William Stewart, third marquess of Londonderry, the brother of Lord Castlereagh; the duc d'Orléans, later Louis Philippe, king of France; the Austrian chancellor, Prince Metternich; and Prince Esterházy, the Austrian ambassador in London.

One of the crucial ways in which the Rothschilds endeared themselves to the political elite (as well as outdoing their business competitors) was by having an exceptional intelligence and communications network. In this period, postal services were slow and insecure: letters sent from Paris to Frankfurt usually took just forty-eight hours in 1814; but mail from London could take up to a week to reach Frankfurt, and the service from Paris to Berlin took nine days in 1817.[10] Compulsive correspondents as they were, the brothers soon dispensed with the post, relying instead on their own private couriers, including agents at Dover who were authorized to charter boats for Rothschild business.[11] It has long been believed that Nathan Rothschild was the first man in London to learn the news of Napoleon's defeat at Waterloo, thanks to the speed with which a Rothschild courier was able to relay the fifth and conclusive extraordinary bulletin (issued in Brussels during the night of 18/19 June) via Dunkirk and Deal to reach New Court roughly twenty-four hours later – at least thirty-six hours before Major Henry Percy delivered Wellington's official despatch to the Cabinet.[12] Doubt has recently been cast on this story, but the fact remains that Rothschild received the news early enough – even if it was on 21 June – to 'do well by the early information . . . of the victory'. A report of the battle's outcome was sent later that day by the London correspondent of the *Caledonian Mercury*, who cited as his source a 'good authority – one who has seen a letter from Ghent, received by Rosschild [*sic*], the great stockbroker whose information is invariably the best'.[13] By the mid-1820s, the Rothschilds were making regular use of private couriers: in December 1825 alone, the Paris house sent eighteen couriers to Calais (and hence to London), three to Saarbrücken, one to Brussels and one to Naples.[14] From 1824, carrier pigeons were also used, though the brothers do not seem to have relied on these as much as has sometimes been assumed.

The development of this network of swift and secure communication had a number of benefits. First, it allowed the Rothschilds to offer a first-class postal service to the European elite. While in London in 1822, the vicomte de Chateaubriand received 'an important despatch' from the duchess of Duras through her 'protégé Rothschild'.[15] By 1823, 'receiving news from Rothschild' was an integral part of the Countess Nesselrode's routine.[16] Perhaps the most eminent enthusiasts for the Rothschild postal service after 1840 were the young Queen Victoria and her consort, Prince Albert.[17] Second, their courier service also meant that the Rothschilds were in a position to provide a unique news service. Major political events as well as confidential information could be relayed from one city to another well ahead of official channels. In 1817, James offered to relay details of French diplomatic despatches from Paris to London so that they reached Nathan before the despatches themselves reached the French ambassador.[18] In 1818 a British diplomat bound for the Aix Congress was 'struck very much' by Nathan's 'correct information as to the details of our party and his knowledge of the persons likely to compose it, some of whose names I believe had not even transpired at the Foreign Office'.[19] When the duc de Berry (the third son of the French king, Charles X) was assassinated in February 1820, it was the Rothschilds who broke the story in Frankfurt and Vienna.[20] Likewise, when Princess Charlotte died in 1821, it was again the Rothschilds who spread the news to Paris.[21] As prime minister, George Canning disliked the fact that the Rothschilds constantly scooped British ambassadorial reports, but he could hardly afford to ignore such important items of Rothschild intelligence as the Turkish capitulation at Ackerman.[22] The Rothschilds also broke the news of the French revolution of July 1830 to Lord Aberdeen in London and Metternich in Bohemia.[23] It was not long before statesmen and diplomats began themselves to make use of the Rothschilds' network of communication, partly because it was quicker than the official courier systems used for relaying diplomatic correspondence, but also because messages of a non-binding nature could be sent from government to government indirectly via the brothers' own private correspondence.

Of course, if the Rothschilds had relied solely on their own five houses for intelligence, the system would have been very limited. But they soon developed a reach that extended far beyond their original European bases. As none of Mayer Amschel's grandsons wished (or was allowed) to establish a new 'house', this was done by building up a select group of salaried agents employed to take care of the bank's interests in other markets: principally Madrid, St Petersburg, Brussels and later New York, New Orleans, Havana, Mexico and San Francisco. The lines of communication with these agents formed a complex new intelligence and business network.[24] Men such as August Belmont in New York or Daniel Weisweiller in Madrid inevitably enjoyed considerable autonomy because of their remoteness and their greater local knowledge; however, they always remained Rothschild agents first and foremost and were not allowed to forget it. Nor was this network of formal influence all; of comparable importance was the larger but looser network of links to other banks, as well as to stockbrokers, central banks and financial newspapers.

Contemporaries were not slow to grasp that a new kind of financial power had emerged. In 1826 the French liberal Vincent Fournier-Verneuil made the first of many claims that the French government was the corrupt puppet of 'the aristocracy of finance, the most arid and least noble of all aristocracies', at whose head stood none other than 'M. le baron R . . .'[25] Two years later, the Radical MP Thomas Duncombe complained in the British House of Commons about:

> a new, and formidable power, till these days unknown in Europe: master of unbounded wealth, he boasts that he is the arbiter of peace and war, and that the credit of nations depends upon his nod; his correspondents are innumerable; his couriers outrun those of sovereign princes, and absolute sovereigns; ministers of state are in his pay. Paramount in the cabinets of continental Europe, he aspires to the domination of our own . . .[26]

In the mid-1830s an American magazine gave a similar assessment, though in less pejorative terms: 'The Rothschilds are the wonders of modern banking . . . holding a whole continent in the hollow of their hands . . . Not a cabinet moves without their advice.'[27] The English diarist Thomas Raikes noted at around the same time: 'The Rothschilds have become the metallic sovereigns of Europe. From their different establishments in Paris, London, Vienna, Frankfurt and Naples, they have obtained a control over the European exchange which no party ever before could accomplish, and they now seem to hold the strings of the public purse. No sovereign without their assistance now could raise a loan.'[28] An anonymous German cartoonist made essentially the same point (though more vividly) when he portrayed a grotesquely caricatured Jew – clearly a composite Rothschild – as *Die Generalpumpe* (a play on the double meaning of the German *pumpen*, to pump or to lend). Rothschild, the cartoon suggests, is a monstrous engine, pumping money around the world.[29]

A frequent charge in the 1820s was that the Rothschilds were politically aligned with the forces of reaction and restoration. According to one source, they had become 'la haute Trésorerie de la Sainte Alliance'.[30] Indeed, when the itinerant German Prince Pückler-Muskau first described Nathan in a letter to his wife, he introduced him as 'the chief ally of the Holy Alliance'.[31] Nathan was caricatured as the insurance broker to the 'Hollow Alliance', helping to prevent political fire in Europe.[32] In 1821 he even received a death threat because of 'his connexion with foreign powers, and particularly the assistance rendered to Austria, on account of the designs of that government against the liberties of Europe'.[33] As early as August 1820 the Bremen delegate to the German Confederation's Diet in Frankfurt noted that 'Austria needs the Rothschilds' help for her present demonstration against Naples, and Prussia would long ago have been finished with her constitution if the House of Rothschild had not made it possible for her to postpone the evil day.'[34] To the liberal writer Ludwig Börne, they were 'the nation's worst enemies. They have done more than any to undermine the foundations of freedom, and it is unquestionable that most of the peoples of Europe would by this time be in full possession of liberty if such men as Rothschild . . . did not lend the autocrats the support of their capital.'[35]

Yet such judgements exaggerated the extent of the Rothschilds' political allegiance to Metternich's vision of conservative restoration. As the Bremen delegate to Frankfurt rightly observed:

> This house has, through its enormous financial transactions and its banking and credit connections, actually achieved the position of a

> real Power; it has to such an extent acquired control of the general money market that it is in a position either to hinder or to promote, as it feels inclined, the movements and operations of potentates, and even of the greatest European Powers.[36]

The Rothschilds could, if the price was right, underwrite loans for Austria. But it could do the same for more liberal states, too. When the Austrian emperor remarked that Amschel Rothschild was 'richer than I am', he was not being wholly facetious.[37] In the twelfth canto of his *Don Juan*, Lord Byron asked 'Who hold the balance of the world? Who reign / O'er Congress, whether royalist or liberal?' and answered (with mocking punctuation): 'Jew Rothschild, and his fellow-Christian, Baring.' The bankers were 'the true lords of Europe'.[38] The crucial point is that Byron saw Rothschild as influential over both royalist and liberal regimes. In his essay 'Rothschild and the European States' (1841), Alexandre Weill made the point succinctly: while 'Rothschild had need of the states to become Rothschild', he now 'no longer needs the state, but the state still has want of him'.[39] A year later, the liberal historian Jules Michelet noted in his journal: 'M. Rothschild knows Europe prince by prince, and the bourse courtier by courtier. He has all their accounts in his head, that of the courtiers and that of the kings; he talks to them without even consulting his books. To one such he says: "Your account will go into the red if you appoint such a minister."'[40] Here was another respect in which hierarchical order had not so much been 'restored' as rearranged after 1815. The extended kinship group that was the House of Saxe-Coburg-Gotha might give the new order the legitimacy of royal genealogy. But it was the upstart House of Rothschild – with its new networks of credit and information – that underwrote European monarchism.

26
Industrial Networks

Before attaining these heights, Nathan Rothschild had begun his career in Britain humbly, buying manufactured cloth for export to the Continent. The records that survive from those early years provide a vivid picture of an economy in the early stages of the first industrial revolution. Between 1799, when he arrived in England for the first time, and 1811, when he formally established the firm of N. M. Rothschild in London, Rothschild travelled not only around Lancashire but also to Nottingham, Leeds, Stockport and even Glasgow in search of textiles to ship to customers in Germany. He did not confine himself to buying finished cloth. 'As soon as I got to Manchester,' he later told the MP Thomas Fowell Buxton, 'I laid out all my money, things were so cheap; and I made good profit. I soon found that there were three profits – the raw material, the dyeing, and the manufacturing. I said to the manufacturer, "I will supply you with material and dye, and you will supply me with manufactured goods." So I got three profits instead of one, and I could sell goods cheaper than anybody.'[1] With new spinning and weaving technology spreading rapidly throughout the north of England and central Scotland, and with numerous small manufacturers competing against one another, the opportunities for an aggressive intermediary were immense. As he explained in December 1802:

> On Tuesdays and Thursdays the weavers who live in the country twenty miles round Manchester bring here their goods, some twenty or thirty pieces, others more, others less, which they sell to the merchants here at two, three and six months credit. But as there are generally some of them in want of money and willing to sacrifice some profit to

> procure it, a person who goes with ready money may sometimes buy 15 or 20 per cent cheaper.[2]

Moreover, as his business expanded and he began to export to firms other than his father's, Rothschild began to offer not only low prices but also reasonable credit terms, telling the same buyer that he regarded his money as being 'as safe in your hands as if I had it in my Pocket'.[3] If the rewards were large, so were the risks. Prices and interest rates were highly volatile. Suppliers failed to deliver almost as often as buyers failed to pay. And, with the eruption of economic warfare between Britain and France following Napoleon's prohibition of all continental trade with Britain in 1806 and 1807, Rothschild had to resort to smuggling.

Like the intellectual and political revolutions of the nineteenth century, the Industrial Revolution was the product of networks. No ruler ordered it, though some government actions (notably the Acts discriminating against cloth imports from India) certainly advanced it. In addition to credit networks like the one to which Nathan Rothschild belonged, there were also capital networks, which allowed entrepreneurs and investors to pool information and resources, and technological networks, which enabled the exchange of productivity-enhancing innovations. James Watt could not have achieved his improvements to the steam engine without belonging to a network that also included Professor Joseph Black of Glasgow University and the members of the Lunar Society of Birmingham.[4] Most textile-manufacturing firms were small and relatively easy to finance, but capital intensive ventures such as joint-stock canal companies or insurance companies were heavily reliant on investor networks.[5] As in the pre-industrial age, international exports and imports were to a large extent managed by commercial networks. In all these networks, kinship, friendship and shared religion played a part. The same was true as the new technologies of manufacturing crossed the Atlantic to the United States.[6] As figure 18 shows, there was no direct link between Watt and Oliver Evans, the Philadelphia inventor who patented a superior high-pressure steam engine. There were in fact four degrees of separation between them.[7] But the urge to innovate – the 'improving mentality' – spread almost (according to one scholar) like a religious belief.[8] At each stage of the Industrial Revolution, networks played the crucial role, not only of disseminating new processes but, more importantly, of pooling brainpower and capital. Just as the development of increasingly efficient steam engines was the collective effort of a network, not of individual heroic inventors, so the later breakthroughs in aeronautics owed as much to key members of the American Society of Civil Engineers, the American Society of Mechanical Engineers and the American Association for the Advancement of Science as to the Wright brothers. In that 'small world', Octave Chanute, the author of *Progress in Flying Machines* (1894), was the most important connector – the Paul Revere of the first aircraft.[9]

The central puzzle of British history in the age of industrialization is why economic revolution was not associated with political revolution. To pose the question differently, why were the networks that arose in

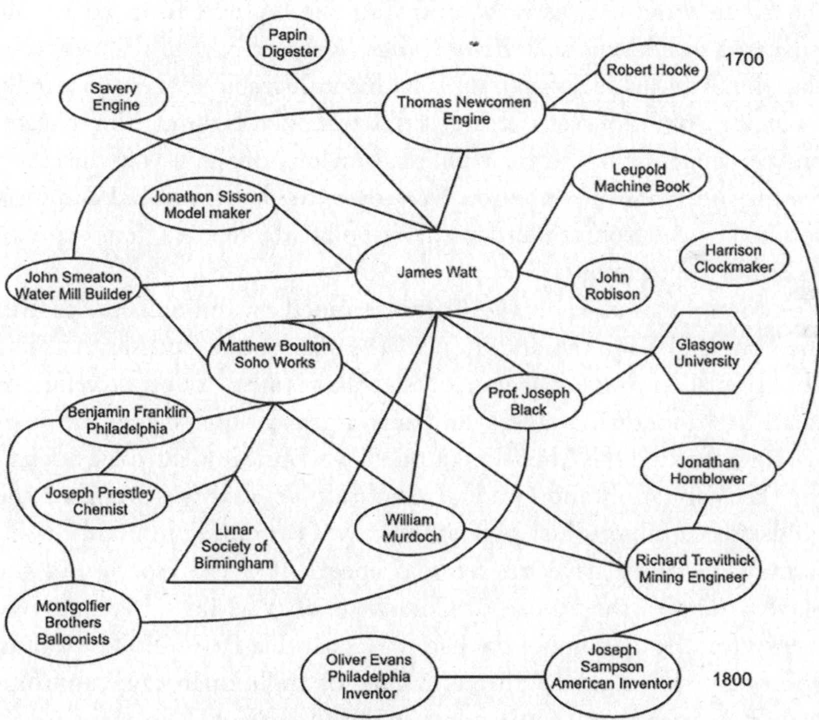

18. The 'steam network': James Watt, Matthew Boulton and the social network of steam engine technology, *c.* 1700–1800.

late eighteenth-century England and Scotland powerful enough to give birth to modern manufacturing, but not powerful enough to overthrow the United Kingdom's monarchical, aristocratic and ecclesiastical hierarchies? All over the European Continent in 1848, people who had signed petitions about one grievance or another were swept up in another wave of revolution – this time extending as far as Berlin and Vienna, and leading to Metternich's downfall.[10] There was nothing close to this in Britain. The celebrated Whig orator Henry Brougham founded a Society for the Diffusion of Useful Knowledge, not a society for the diffusion of republican ideas. Even the Chartists, as they organized their campaign for a broadening of the franchise, were orderly in their gatherings and harboured few revolutionary elements. Part of the explanation is that the politics of the eighteenth century did a great deal to inculcate in the 'lower orders' that as 'Britons' they had a patriotic stake in the existing social order.[11] The biggest riots of the Hanoverian era were the anti-Catholic Gordon Riots so vividly imagined in Dickens's *Barnaby Rudge*. Another part of the answer is that the British elite adapted itself with considerable skill to the rapidly changing conditions of the industrial era. Victoria and Albert were, on the whole, liberal in their political inclinations in a way that their relatives in Hanover were not. Moreover, the new financial elite personified by the Rothschilds was more politically flexible than many of its critics appreciated.

A good illustration of why Britain avoided revolution is the case of the campaigns for the abolition of the slave trade and slavery. The abolitionist movement began outside Parliament amongst religious minorities (notably Quakers) and new organizations such as the Society for Effecting the Abolition of the Slave Trade and later the Society for the Mitigation and Gradual Abolition of Slavery. It reached the House of Commons just as revolution was beginning in France. William Wilberforce gave his seminal speech 'On the Horrors of the Slave Trade' in the House of Commons on 12 May 1789, just one week after the opening of the Estates General in Paris. No fewer than 400,000 people signed petitions calling for abolition in 1792, approximately 12 per cent of the adult male population – in the case of Manchester, closer to half.[12] In 1816 the number of signatures on petitions objecting to the resumption of the French slave trade was

1,375,000.[13] The agitation was even larger in 1833, when Parliament received petitions with almost 1.5 million signatures, including one that was half a mile in length, signed by 350,000 women and sewn together by Thomas Fowell Buxton's daughter Priscilla.[14] The abolitionist movement was an authentic network-based phenomenon. Yet, unlike in the American colonies and France, this network never threatened to tip the country into revolution. One obvious reason for this was that the issue concerned the interests of people very far indeed from the British Isles: African slaves and West Indian planters. A second reason was that, though it dragged its feet in the 1790s, the political elite responded relatively swiftly to the extra-parliamentary pressure, abolishing the slave trade in 1807 and then emancipating nearly 800,000 slaves in British possessions in 1833. The third and final reason was that the West Indian planters were too small an interest group to exert a veto power.

Debate has long raged as to whether the British sugar producers of the Caribbean were already in crisis on the eve of abolition or were cut off in their economic prime, as historians have struggled to make sense of the speed with which Britain went from being the dominant player in the Atlantic slave trade to being its avowed and active opponent.[15] It is clear that, despite soaring consumption in England, sugar prices were in a sustained decline through the eighteenth century. They spiked significantly during the French Revolutionary and Napoleonic Wars – as the disruption of production caused by the slave revolt in Saint-Domingue was only partially offset by the increased output of plantations in Cuba, as well as Mauritius and India – but then fell again prior to 1807, and fell further with the coming of peace. By comparison, there was no downward trend in the average price of a slave. Yet the argument that these trends doomed the West Indian sugar plantations – that 'abolition was the direct result of [West Indian] distress'[16] – is not convincing. With rising demand for sugar all over Europe, the opportunities that kept slavery going in Cuba, not to mention Brazil, would also have existed for British plantations, but for abolition, which inevitably drove up labour costs. The real problem for the British planters was the rapid diversification of the UK economy, as cotton imports for manufacture and re-export rapidly overtook sugar imports in importance.

Already by the late 1820s, cotton goods accounted for half of British exports. As the capital city of the British textile industry, Manchester had more political influence in London than Jamaica had, and could easily turn a blind eye to the continuation of the slave trade and slavery in the South of the United States, from whence a rising share of Lancashire's raw cotton came. Appropriately enough, it was Nathan Rothschild – the former cotton trader turned banker – who funded the £15m government loan necessary to compensate the slave-owners after the 1833 Act.[17] Indeed, Nathan dined with Thomas Fowell Buxton immediately after the legislation freeing the slaves had been passed.[18] Later, Nathan's sons would play a leading role in the campaign for Jewish emancipation in Britain; Queen Victoria would elevate his grandson Nathaniel to the House of Lords.

Britain in 1815 was an exceptionally unequal society. Landed wealth was heavily concentrated in the hands of a hereditary aristocracy – more so than in most European countries, including *ancien régime* France. The tax system was exceptionally regressive, with most revenue coming from taxes on consumption and most expenditure going to the army, the navy, and the wealthy holders of office and government bonds. Yet none of the extra-parliamentary movements of the early nineteenth century – not abolitionism, nor the movement for electoral reform that followed it – ever seriously threatened the established order. This was because, unlike its French counterpart, the British hierarchy knew when to bend with the wind. Abolitionists saw the accession of the youthful Queen Victoria in 1837 as an opportunity for reform, not an obstacle to it, and the young monarch was soon under pressure to endorse their campaign. She left the task to the Prince Consort, who made his first public speech, just three months after his marriage, at a meeting for the Society for the Extinction of the Slave Trade and for the Civilization of Africa. 'I deeply regret,' Prince Albert said, 'that the benevolent and persevering exertions of England to abolish that atrocious traffic in human beings (at once the desolation of Africa and the blackest stain upon civilized Europe) have not as yet led to any satisfactory conclusion. But I sincerely trust that this great country will not relax in its efforts until it has finally, and for ever, put an end to a state of things so repugnant to the spirit of Christianity, and the best feelings of our nature.'[19]

27
From Pentarchy to Hegemony

In the years after 1815 the chaos that had been unleashed in the 1790s was brought under control. France's networked anarchy was tamed by the imposition of a new hierarchical order under Napoleon. The French revolutionary challenge to the other European states was finally overcome by the imposition of a new 'concert' under the collective supervision of the five great powers, among them a restored French monarchy. Throughout the nineteenth century, monarchy remained the predominant political form in the world. Inside each European state, it was not only the legitimacy of the hereditary principle that was restored; it was also a new model of social stratification in which a cosmopolitan royal elite entered into a symbiotic relationship with a new plutocratic elite (and more venerable national aristocracies sneered ungratefully at both). 'Restoration' in that sense was an imperfect description and those (notably the Bourbons in France) who attempted an unqualified return to the *ancien régime* did not last long.

The clock could not be turned back. Nor could it be stopped from going forward. The Industrial Revolution increased both incomes and populations. For the first time in history, the cities of north-western Europe grew larger than those of east Asia. The new technologies of manufacturing proved to have uses besides the more efficient production of clothing. Warfare, too, began to be industrialized with ironclad ships and more lethal guns. National economies fell increasingly under the sway of large industrial corporations, whose owners and managers, along with the bankers who financed them, began to constitute a new social and political elite, albeit one intimately connected to the old regime. The map of the world by

1900 was an imperial jigsaw, with eleven Western empires controlling disproportionate shares (58 per cent, in all) of the earth's territory, not to mention its population (57 per cent) and economic output (74 per cent).[1] Even the United States acquired overseas colonies.

This was assuredly not the future for which Paul Revere had ridden to Lexington. The redcoats had won. By the eve of the First World War, Great Britain – a kingdom with a population of 45.6 million and a land surface of just over 120,000 square miles – ruled over more than 375 million people and 11 million square miles. Perhaps the most remarkable thing about this vast empire was how lightly it was garrisoned. In 1898 there were 99,000 regular soldiers stationed in Britain, 75,000 in India and 41,000 elsewhere in the Empire. The navy required another 100,000 men, and the Indian native army was 148,000 strong. These represented tiny fractions of the total imperial population. It was governed lightly, too. Between 1858 and 1947 there were seldom more than 1,000 members of the 'covenanted' Indian Civil Service (ICS), compared with a total population which, by the end of British rule, exceeded 400 million. Nor was this skeletal staffing unique to India. The entire administrative elite of the African colonial service, spread over a dozen colonies with a population of around 43 million, numbered just over 1,200.[2] How was this possible? How was the largest empire in world history simultaneously – in the derogatory phrase coined by the German socialist Ferdinand Lassalle in 1862 – a night-watchman state?

V

Knights of the Round Table

28
An Imperial Life

In John Buchan's novel *The Thirty-Nine Steps*, a sinister organization known as the Black Stone is plotting to steal Britain's plans for 'the disposition of the British Home Fleet on mobilization'. Only after a string of murders and one of the most elaborate chases in popular fiction is the plot foiled by Buchan's indefatigably patriotic hero, Richard Hannay. After Rudyard Kipling, Buchan was the writer who best captured the ethos of early twentieth-century British imperialism.[1] Like so much of his writing, *The Thirty-Nine Steps* arranges the world into a hierarchy of racial types, with bright but muscular Scotsmen at the top, rugged South Africans next, insufficiently military Americans next, sexually suspect Germans in the middle, Jews beneath Germans, and more or less everyone else at the bottom.* Yet, as nearly always in Buchan's fiction, the real protagonists in *The Thirty-Nine Steps* are not individuals but networks: secret societies such as the Black Stone, and noble bands of imperial gentlemen engaged in improvised counter-espionage – in this case, a Scotsman returned from Rhodesia, an American freelance and a naïve landowning politician.

Born in Perth in 1875, the son of a minister of the Presbyterian Free Church of Scotland, and raised in Kirkcaldy, Buchan ascended the kind of career ladder that the United Kingdom and its Empire had offered ambitious Scotsmen since the time of James Boswell. After attending Hutcheson's Grammar School in Glasgow, he read Literae

* Edmund Ironside, the soldier who was said to be the basis for the character Richard Hannay, 'professed special dislike of the Irish, Jews, Latins, and "lesser races", that is, most of mankind'.

Humaniores (the degree course in ancient Greek and Roman literature, also known as 'Greats') at Brasenose, Oxford, where he was a scholar, took a first, and won the presidency of the Oxford Union, the prestigious debating society that continues to prepare future prime ministers for parliamentary strife. Between 1901 and 1903 – during and after the Boer War – he served as political private secretary to Lord Milner, the high commissioner for South Africa. In 1907 he married well: Susan Grosvenor, a cousin of the duke of Westminster. Not content with being a prolific author, Buchan read law and was called to the bar. He became a partner in the publishing house of Thomas Nelson & Sons as well as, for a time, the editor of *The Spectator*. During the First World War, spared or denied the front line because of ill-health, he directed the new Department of Information, and after the war sat in the House of Commons for eight years as a Unionist member for the Scottish universities. Throughout all this, he wrote indefatigably: a thriller a year on average plus a multi-volume history of the Great War. His apotheosis came in 1935, when he was ennobled (as Lord Tweedsmuir of Elsfield) and appointed governor-general of Canada.[2]

In sum, Buchan rose through the imperial hierarchy, ascending academically, socially, professionally, politically and then officially – if not quite as high as he had aimed (Viceroy of India or at least a Cabinet position). Yet his career cannot be understood apart from the network to which he belonged: the 'Kindergarten' or 'Round Table' associated with Milner. This is another of those historical networks that has become notorious, thanks in large measure to the writings of the influential Georgetown historian Carroll Quigley,* who called it 'a secret society that was, for more than fifty years, . . . one of the most important forces in the formulation and execution of British imperial and foreign policy'.[3] The aim of this society, according to Quigley, was 'to unite the world, and above all the English-speaking

* Quigley's course on the development of civilizations was very popular at the School of Foreign Service at Georgetown, where he taught from 1941 until 1972. (Amongst his students was the young Bill Clinton.) It is not clear quite why he became so obsessed with Milner's network. However, his Boston-Irish background doubtless instilled in him a visceral dislike of British imperialism.

world, in a federal structure around Britain' and its methods were 'secret political and economic influence behind the scenes and . . . the control of journalistic, educational, and propaganda agencies'.[4] Writing in the late 1940s, Quigley acknowledged that the Round Table had 'been able to conceal its existence quite successfully, and many of its most influential members, satisfied to possess the reality rather than the appearance of power, are unknown even to close students of British history'. Nevertheless:

> It plotted the Jameson Raid of 1895; it caused the Boer War of 1899–1902; it set up and controls the Rhodes Trust; it created the Union of South Africa in 1906–1910; it established the South African periodical *The State* in 1908; it founded the British Empire periodical *The Round Table* in 1910, and this remains the mouthpiece of the Group; it has been the most powerful single influence in All Souls, Balliol, and New Colleges at Oxford for more than a generation; it has controlled *The Times* for more than fifty years, with the exception of the three years 1919–1922; it publicized the idea of and the name 'British Commonwealth of Nations' in the period 1908–1918; it was the chief influence in Lloyd George's war administration in 1917–1919 and dominated the British delegation to the Peace Conference of 1919; it had a great deal to do with the formation and management of the League of Nations and of the system of mandates; it founded the Royal Institute of International Affairs in 1919 and still controls it; it was one of the chief influences on British policy toward Ireland, Palestine, and India in the period 1917–1945; it was a very important influence on the policy of appeasement of Germany during the years 1920–1940; and it controlled and still controls, to a very considerable extent, the sources and writing of the history of British Imperial and Foreign Policy since the Boer War.[5]

Whatever the truth of these remarkable claims, the last of them is certainly no longer applicable. It is now therefore possible for scholars to write openly and dispassionately about the Round Table, though conspiracy theorists will doubtless continue to repeat Quigley's allegations.

29
Empire

Even if the Round Table did not run the world, it was undeniably the case that a very small number of British men ran quite a lot of the world. To repeat: how was this possible?

A part of the answer to that question was the way the British absorbed into their empire existing structures of local power. In Tanganyika, for example, Sir Donald Cameron strove to reinforce the links from 'the peasant . . . up to his Headman, the Headman to the Sub-Chief, the Sub-Chief to the Chief, and the Chief to the District Office'. In West Africa, Lord Kimberley thought it better to 'have nothing to do with the "educated natives" as a body. I would treat with the hereditary chiefs only.' 'All Orientals think extra highly of a Lord,' insisted George Lloyd, before taking up his duties as the newly ennobled high commissioner in Egypt. The whole purpose of the Empire, argued Frederick Lugard, the architect of Britain's West African empire, was 'to maintain traditional rulerships as a fortress of societal security in a changing world . . . The really important category was status.'[1] Lugard invented an entire theory of 'indirect rule', according to which British dominance could be maintained at minimal cost by delegating all local power to existing elites, retaining only the essentials of central authority (in particular the purse strings) in British hands. In his book *The Dual Mandate in British Tropical Africa* (1922), Lugard defined indirect rule as the 'systematic use of the customary institutions of the people as agencies of local rule'.[2] Atop all these traditional status hierarchies the British added their own imperial meta-hierarchy. Protocol in India was strictly governed by the 'warrant of precedence', which in 1881 consisted of no fewer than seventy-seven separate ranks. Throughout the Empire, officials thirsted after membership of the Most Distinguished Order of St Michael and St George, whether as CMG ('Call Me God'), KCMG ('Kindly Call Me God') or, reserved for the very top tier of governors, GCMG ('God Calls Me God'). There was, declared Lord Curzon, 'an insatiable appetite [among] the British-speaking community all the world over for titles and precedence'. He might have added decorations, for ribbons and medals were almost as much desired. For all his worldly success, John Buchan was tortured by his meagre haul of such 'gongs'.

Yet the British Empire would not have reached such a vast extent, nor have lasted for as long as it did, by relying on hierarchy – not to mention snobbery – alone. Revolutionary networks did not evaporate in the nineteenth century. On the contrary, with the spread of Karl Marx's doctrine amongst intellectuals and workers, there was born one of the biggest networks of the modern era: the socialist network. Other revolutionary movements, ranging from anarchism to feminism to radical nationalism, also flourished in the later nineteenth century. Yet the hierarchical structures of the era – the empires and nation-states – were able quite easily to dominate these networks, even when they resorted to terrorism. This was because the new communication technologies created by the Industrial Revolution – the railway, the steamship, the telegraph and later the telephone, as well as national postal services and newspapers – not only created much larger networks than the socialists could, even when they succeeded in knitting together the myriad forms of labour organization that proliferated in the industrial economies,[3] but also lent themselves well to centralized control.

It is obvious that steam power and electrical cables accelerated communication. In the days of sail it had taken between four and six weeks to cross the Atlantic; with the introduction of steamships that was reduced to two weeks in the mid-1830s and just ten days in the 1880s. Between the 1850s and the 1890s, the journey time from England to Cape Town was cut from forty-two to nineteen days. Moreover, steamships got bigger as well as faster: in the same period, average gross tonnage roughly doubled. Not only did it therefore take much less time to cross the oceans from metropolis to empire; it also cost a great deal less. The cost of shipping a bushel of wheat from New York to Liverpool was halved between 1830 and 1880 and halved again between 1880 and 1914. Even greater wonders were worked by the telegraph. After 1866 it was possible to relay information across the Atlantic at the rate of eight words a minute.

The tendency for control to become centralized is less immediately obvious. The British railway network had been constructed after 1826 with only minimal state intervention, but the railways the British built throughout their Empire, though they too were constructed by private-sector companies, depended on generous government subsidies, which effectively guaranteed that they would pay dividends. The first line in India, linking Bombay to Thane twenty-one miles away, was formally opened in 1853; within less than fifty years, track covering nearly 25,000 miles had been laid. This network was from its very inception strategic as well as economic in purpose. The same was true of the telegraph, which was sufficiently developed in India by 1857 to play a decisive part in suppressing the rebellion of that year, which began as a mutiny by native soldiers. (One mutineer, on his way to execution, identified the telegraph as 'the accursed string that strangles me'.) However, the crucial breakthrough in the centralization of communication was the construction of durable undersea cables. Significantly, it was an imperial product – a form of rubber from Malaya called gutta-percha – that made this possible, allowing the first cross-Channel cable to be laid in 1851 and the first transatlantic cable to follow fifteen years later. When the first successful telegraph line was laid across the Atlantic, it was plainly the dawn of a new era. That the cable ran from Ireland to Newfoundland made it clear which power was most likely to dominate the age of the telegraph. By 1880 there were altogether 97,568 miles of cable across the world's oceans, linking Britain to India, Canada, Australia, Africa and Australia. Now a message could be relayed from Bombay to London at the cost of four shillings a word in the space of as many minutes. In the words of Charles Bright, an apostle of the new technology, the telegraph was 'the world's system of electrical nerves'. As one eminent imperial commentator put it, the Victorian revolution in global communications achieved 'the annihilation of distance'. It also made possible long-distance annihilation. 'Time itself is telegraphed out of existence,' proclaimed the *Daily Telegraph*.[4] So too were rebels who dared to challenge the imperial world order.

Yet for all the strategic advantages of the global cable network that grew so rapidly in the second half of the nineteenth century, its ownership remained largely in private hands. It was not Queen Victoria who realized the dream of transatlantic telegrams, but a risk-loving Scotsman named John Plender. Born in the Vale of Leven, Plender made his first fortune trading cotton in Glasgow and Manchester, and it was his experience as a trader – constantly awaiting news from across the sea – that persuaded him to invest first in the English and Irish Magnetic Telegraph Company and then in the Atlantic Telegraph Company. The second investment turned sour when the company's painstakingly laid 1858 cable was blown – the fault of the unqualified 'chief electrician', who sought to improve the clarity of transmission by increasing the voltage by a factor of more than three. Plender tried again in 1865, merging the Atlantic Telegraph Co. into a new Telegraph Construction and Maintenance Company. Disaster struck a second time when the better-insulated but much heavier cable snapped and sank to the ocean floor halfway across the Atlantic. Undaunted, Plender and his partner, the English railway engineer Daniel Gooch, established a new company, the Anglo-American Telegraph Company Ltd, to take over the venture and, at the third attempt, the job was done. Gooch – who himself supervised the laying of the successful cable from the mighty *Great Eastern*, the biggest steamship of its day – described the jubilation with which he and the crew were greeted when they reached Heart's Content, Newfoundland:

> There . . . was the wildest excitement I had ever witnessed. All seemed mad with joy, jumping into the water and shouting as though they wished the sound to be heard at Washington. As soon as the cable touched the land a signal from the shore was made, and all the ships in the harbour fired a salute. I do not know how many guns were fired, but the noise was something tremendous, and the smoke soon hid the ships from our view. The reverberations of the sound of the guns amongst the hills round the bay was very grand . . . As soon as it [the cable] reached . . . the wooden house now used as a telegraph office . . . another wild scene of excitement took place. The old cable hands seemed as though they could eat the end; one man actually put it in his mouth and sucked it.[5]

Two days later, Gooch saw some of his crew reading the telegraphed *Times* leader celebrating their achievement. 'One of them after doing so said to the other, "I say, Bill, we be benefactors to our race." "Yes," says Bill, "we be", and he strutted along with his back straight and his head at least two inches higher.'[6]

Whereas in 1868 the British government nationalized the domestic telegraph network, there was no attempt to do the same to the transatlantic cables. Pender did not waste time. In 1869 he founded the Falmouth, Gibraltar and Malta Telegraph Company, the British–Indian Submarine Telegraph Company and the China Submarine Telegraph. Within just a few years, London was connected by telegraph to Malta, Alexandria, Bombay, Singapore and Hong Kong. By 1872, two other Pender companies had connected Bombay to Adelaide via Singapore. Having merged the core elements of his burgeoning cable empire to form the Eastern Telegraph Company, Pender continued relentlessly to expand, connecting Lisbon to Pernambuco in Brazil in 1874, and in the 1880s extending his reach to Africa. In all, he founded thirty-two telegraph companies, most of them ending up as subsidiaries of the Eastern Telegraph Company. At the time of his death in 1896, Pender controlled companies that owned one third of the entire global telegraph system (plate 15).

Inventors experimented. Businessmen invested and competed. Governments took a strategic interest. And international bodies – such as the International Telegraph Union established in 1865 – regulated or at least harmonized.[7] But what ultimately emerged was a privately owned duopoly in international telegraphy: after 1910, when it acquired Anglo-American, the US company Western Union controlled transatlantic traffic, while the Eastern Telegraph ran the rest of the world. The hub of the entire system was London, but the government there did not need directly to own the network, any more than it needed directly to rule the princely states of India. A Liberal and later Liberal Unionist MP from the 1860s, KCMG in 1888 and GCMG in 1892, Pender could be relied upon as a fully integrated member of that status-obsessed British political elite so scathingly portrayed in Trollope's *The Way We Live Now*.

The sequence of events that led from Pender's bold entrepreneurship to the creation of a global telegraph network was characteristic of nineteenth-century imperialism. A somewhat similar process had led to the development of the rubber plantations of Malaya, the source of the gutta-percha without which the oceanic cable network would have been technically impossible. It was a wayward overseas adventurer, Henry Wickham, who – having failed at trading and planting – acquired seeds of the rubber tree *Hevea brasiliensis* from Brazil and sent them to London. However, his efforts were subsidized by Sir Clements Markham, secretary of the Royal Geographical Society, and the real work of research and development was done at the Royal Botanical Gardens in Kew (where Charles Darwin's friend Joseph Hooker was director) and its counterparts in Ceylon and Singapore. Finally, the investment in large-scale plantations in south-east Asia, especially the Malay States, was left to private capital. The Malayan colonial authorities became involved only when prices collapsed after the First World War.[8]

A key reason for the British Empire's scale and durability, then, was the relatively light touch of the central authority. Though its theory was hierarchical – indeed, like John Buchan, Victorian racial theorists ranked mankind according to inherited levels of intelligence – its practice was to delegate considerable power to local rulers and private networks. Unlike Napoleon's short-lived European empire, the British Empire was not run by a micro-managing genius, but by a club of gentlemanly amateurs, whose seemingly effortless superiority depended on the unsung strivings of local agents and native collaborators. Nearly every aspect of British expansion was managed in this way, from finance[9] to missionary work.[10] The 'head office' was in London, but the 'man on the spot' enjoyed considerable autonomy, as long as he showed no signs of 'going native'. In some cases, British influence spread with almost no central direction. A case in point is the spread of the monitorial system of primary education in Latin America, a region where informal imperialism was the rule. This teaching system, which had been developed by Joseph Lancaster and Andrew Bell for use in England and British India, was brought to South America in the nineteenth century by a combination of Hispanic-American politicians who had encountered it in London and James Thomson, the travelling representative of the British and Foreign School Society and the British and Foreign Bible Society, as well as the Spanish Real Sociedad Económica de Amigos del País.[11]

Yet the economic trend of the later nineteenth century was unmistakably towards increasing returns to scale. In almost every industrial sector, there was a pronounced tendency towards concentration. Firms grew fewer; a handful grew vast. With a few notable exceptions like the Rothschilds' banking partnership, the biggest firms ceased to be owned and managed by the founders' families. On the banks of the River Clyde, as all over the industrial world, joint-stock companies became the dominant form of large-scale enterprise.[12] Andrew Carnegie, a Scottish immigrant to the United States, was an industrial Bonaparte whose eponymous steel company was one of the behemoths of the American gilded age. 'The price which society pays for the law of competition,' he explained in an essay published in 1889:

> like the price it pays for cheap comforts and luxuries, is . . . great; but the advantages of this law are also greater still, for it is to this law that we owe our wonderful material development, which brings improved conditions in its train. But, whether the law be benign or not, we must say of it, as we say of the change in the conditions of men . . . It is here; we cannot evade it; no substitutes for it have been found; and while the law may be sometimes hard for the individual, it is best for the race, because it insures the survival of the fittest in every department. We accept and welcome therefore, as conditions to which we must accommodate ourselves, great inequality of environment, the concentration of business, industrial and commercial, in the hands of a few, and the law of competition between these, as being not only beneficial, but essential for the future progress of the race . . . A condition of affairs under which the best interests of the race are promoted . . . inevitably gives wealth to the few.[13]

But Carnegie was not out to found a dynasty; indeed, he despised inherited wealth and gave almost his entire fortune away. His Carnegie Steel Company, itself the result of a merger in 1892, was absorbed into the vast (though not monopolistic) United States Steel Corporation nine years later. The concentration of capital was not confined to the realms of telegraphy and steel. The international financial system grew to resemble a scale-free network, with a vast amount of financial wealth concentrated in a handful of financial centres, of which London was *primus inter pares*.[14] The same was true of news.

At first sight, the world was awash with countless local newspapers; on closer inspection, the supply of national and international news came to be dominated by a cartel of three European news agencies – Reuters, Havas and Wolff's Telegraphisches Bureau – whose reports the vast majority of papers simply reprinted.[15]

By the later nineteenth century, even the academic world showed signs of centralization. The loose international network of the Scientific Revolution was transformed with the dramatic growth in importance of the German universities.[16] German education seemed to mimic the Prussian army in the rigidity of its hierarchical structure. In the *Gymnasien*, the elite high schools, boys sat in class according to their position in the academic ranking.[17] At the great universities – Göttingen, Heidelberg, Jena, Marburg, Tübingen – professors were martinets, tyrannizing their graduate students. In terms of increasing the quality and quantity of published research in fields ranging from classical literature to organic chemistry, the system worked. Though the German Empire lagged behind its British counterpart in terms of square miles of overseas territory, in science and then in industry it forged ahead.

The British elite was relatively open. Aristocrats invested in railways, joined bank boards, married their sons to Jewish or American 'new money'. A contrasting feature of life in the German Reich was that economic modernity seemed to have been grafted onto a pre-industrial social structure, in which the Prussian *Junker* class still appeared to retain the upper hand. Studies of rural communities in Central and Eastern Europe in the nineteenth century remind us that, for a very large proportion of the European population, modernity was a distant prospect, even in 1850 – and the further east one travelled, the further back in time one also went. German communities outside the Reich inhabited a world that Londoners were likely to encounter only in the fairy tales of the Brothers Grimm.* In the Austrian Gail valley,

* Jacob and Wilhelm Grimm's 1812 collection of traditional German stories for children, *Kinder- und Hausmärchen*, proved to be one of the most successful publications of the nineteenth century. The brothers were serious scholars of folklore, having studied at Marburg under the eminent jurist Karl von Savigny. They were typical of their generation in combining romanticism, liberalism and nationalism. Indeed, Jacob was elected to the National Assembly at the time of the 1848 Revolutions.

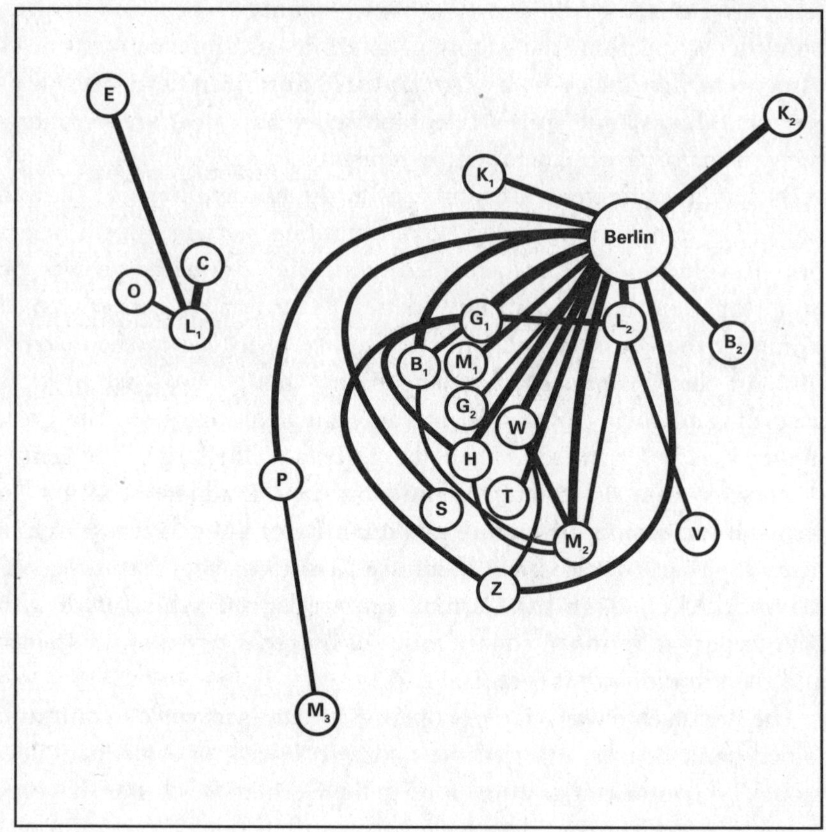

19. Nineteenth-century networks of scientific practice: the ascendancy of the German universities. The diagram is based on the places where the leading scientists of the century worked.
B_1 Bonn, B_2 Breslau, C Cambridge, E Edinburgh, G_1 Göttingen, G_2 Giessen, H Hiedelberg, K_1 Kiel, K_2 Königsberg, L_1 London, L_2 Leipzig, M_1 Marburg, M_2 Munich, M_3 Montpellier, O Oxford, P Paris, S Strasbourg, T Tübingen, V Vienna, W Würzburg, Z Zurich.

patterns of 'structural endogamy' dominated marriage decisions and genealogy as they had since the sixteenth century.[18] On the landed estate of Pinkenhof, in the Russian Baltic province of Livonia, multiple families lived together in wooden farmstead dwellings under a designated head who directed their work in the fields.[19] Yet the reality was that industrialization and democratization – introduced for most Germans with the foundation of the Reich in 1871 – posed fundamental challenges to the old order. In Theodor Fontane's novel *Der Stechlin*, published in 1899, the local glass factory at Globsow symbolizes the impending collapse of the old rural order in the Mark of Brandenburg. As the old Junker Dubslav von Stechlin laments:

> They . . . send [the stills that they manufacture] to other factories and right away they start distilling all kinds of dreadful things in these green balloons: hydrochloric acid; sulphuric acid; smoking nitric acid . . . And each drop burns a hole, whether in linen, or in cloth, or in leather; in everything; everything is burnt and scorched. And when I think that my Globsowers are playing a part, and quite happily supplying the tools for the great general world conflagration [*Generalweltanbrennung*] – ah, *meine Herren*, that gives me pain.[20]

The networks of notables – *Honoratioren* – whose families had dominated local power structures for generations[21] – came under sustained attacks not only from new national political parties, but also from growing bureaucracies at the national, regional and local level. The great sociologist Max Weber (whose struggle to excel as the ideal type of Teutonic professor led to nervous collapse) understood this advance as a rationalization of the political process and a 'demystification' of the world. But he also discerned the power that demagogues would be able to exert in a political landscape increasingly denuded of traditional networks.

30
Taiping

As the European empires extended their iron, steel and rubber-coated networks over land and under sea, the surviving imperial dynasties of the Oriental world – in particular, the Ottoman and the Qing – grappled with the dilemma of how far to imitate their ways. The structure of power in the Qing Empire was very different from those of Western empires. Local power continued to be dominated by kinship networks, as for many centuries.[1] However, as we saw in chapter 11, imperial officials were selected on the basis of a meritocratic competitive examination, the effect of which was to insulate officials from loyalties other than the all-important one to the emperor.[2]

With justice, Qing China has been called a 'bureaucratic monarchy', governed by 'men whose careers [were] measured by prestige and power, mobility and security, within a hierarchical order'.[3] The nightmare of each successive dynasty was the kind of network-driven rebellion that periodically arose in the provinces. Indeed, there was a tradition among Confucian officials to imagine a recurrent threat from a nebulous 'White Lotus Society', a group of lay Buddhists that traced its origins back to the famous monk Huiyuan in AD 402. Throughout the Yuan, Ming and Qing eras, there was a tendency to identify any kind of unorthodoxy as either White Lotus Teachings, 'heretical teachings' (*xiejiao*) or 'Christianity' (*tianzhujiao*).[4] Just as revolutionary France had been swept by a 'great fear' in 1789, so in China – just two decades before – a 'soul-stealing' panic had swept the Empire, with villagers accusing not only beggars and itinerant monks but also officials and even the emperor of magically seizing human souls.[5] The Qianlong emperor succeeded in turning the panic to his advantage, reasserting his authority over the imperial bureaucracy. Yet the soul-stealing mania revealed a grave weakness in the system: that its bureaucratic capacity was thinly spread by European standards, and that its legitimacy was open to question. In the nineteenth century, the system was strong enough to extend Qing rule northwards and westwards, far beyond the core historic territory of the Ming and their predecessors,[6] but too weak to resist European, and especially British, encroachments beginning in the 1840s – and only just strong enough to survive an internal crisis that wholly eclipsed the White Lotus and soul-stealing episodes: the Taiping Rebellion.

Europe in the nineteenth century was relatively peaceful, as we have seen. China was not. By any measure, the civil war that swept the Qing Empire between 1850 and 1865 was the biggest conflict of the nineteenth century, directly or indirectly causing the deaths of between 20 million and 70 million people, roughly decimating the Chinese population. This was vastly more destructive than even the War of the Triple Alliance (1864–70) between Paraguay, Argentina, Brazil and Uruguay, or the American Civil War (1861–5), respectively the century's second- and third-largest conflicts. Hundreds of Chinese cities were destroyed. Massacres of civilians and mass executions of prisoners became the norm. Epidemics (especially of cholera) and famine followed hard on the heels of battles. The significance of the Taiping for the history of networks is threefold. First, the rebellion arose from a cult that initially attracted adherents only from marginal groups, but then spread virally through substantial parts of the heartland of Han China. Secondly, external (again, mostly British) influences both precipitated the conflict and then acted to defeat the insurgents. Third, the devastating effect of the civil war led to a veritable Chinese exodus – an emigration almost as large as the contemporaneous outflow of people from the poorer parts of Europe. This in turn stimulated a less violent but in some ways more consequential populist revolt within the United States and elsewhere. Such were the unintended consequences of greater connectedness.

The revolt began in Guangxi province, far to the south of the Qing capital, in early 1851, when a 10,000-strong rebel army routed government troops in the town of Jintian (present-day Guiping). At first, a key role was played by the Zhuang ethnic minority, who constituted as much as a quarter of the Taiping army. From Guangxi, the rebels swept to Nanjing, which Hong Xiuquan, the self-styled 'Heavenly King', made his capital. By 1853 they controlled the entire Yangzi valley. The leaders of the movement were outsiders. Hong was a member of the Hakka ('guest people') community, a Han subgroup that inhabited southern China, farming marginal land. He had failed the civil service exam four times at the provincial level. Yang Xiuqing was a firewood merchant from Guangxi.

It is possible to tell the story of the Taiping as a popular revolt against an alien dynasty, personified by the Xian Feng emperor (r. 1850–61) and the Dowager Empress Cixi (1835–1908). Because of their refusal to wear their hair in the Manchu queue (shaved at the front, braided at the back), the Taiping rebels were nicknamed 'Long-hairs' (*Chángmáo*). They chose as their headquarters Nanjing, because it had once been the Ming capital. Their goals were in some ways revolutionary, calling for 'property in common' and equality for women (including the abolition of foot binding). Yet it is hard to believe the Taiping movement would have been so successful had it not been for the external influences that were simultaneously working to weaken Qing rule. The first was the East India Company's aggressive export of opium to China. The second was the weaponry the Europeans were equally ready to sell. The sheer ruthlessness of British policy could only be justified with difficulty. 'Uninvited, and by methods not always of the gentlest,' conceded Lord Elgin, 'we have broken down the barriers behind which these ancient nations sought to conceal from the world without the mysteries, perhaps also, in the case of China at least, the rags and rottenness of their waning civilizations.'[7]

Somewhat more respectful of Chinese tradition were the Protestant missionaries – men like Robert Morrison of the London Missionary Society, who had arrived in Canton (Guangzhou) in 1807, and William Milne, the co-translator of the first Chinese Bible, published in 1833. Yet the missionaries' influence was just as disruptive as the sellers of narcotics and armaments. Having been introduced to Christianity by Milne, Hong Xiuquan succumbed to religious delusions following an exam-induced nervous breakdown. Convinced that he was the younger brother of Jesus Christ, he conceived of his movement as a 'Society of God Worshippers' and styled himself the ruler of the 'Heavenly Kingdom of Great Peace' (*Taiping Tianguo*). Hong's partner, Yang Xiuqing, claimed to be the voice of God. Another Taiping leader, Hong Rengan, had been baptized a Lutheran by the Swedish missionary Theodore Hamberg, one of a number of missionaries who published an account of the rebellion. The American Baptist missionary Issachar Jacox Roberts became an adviser to both Hong Xiuquan and Hong Rengan. Another sympathetic missionary was Charles Taylor of the American Southern Methodist Episcopal Mission.[8]

In short, the Taiping movement was a mutant form of Christianity, which adopted not only some of the language of Christianity but also some Christian practices, notably baptism and iconoclasm. What the missionaries had not foreseen was how readily their Oriental flock would embrace the most militant elements in their religion, as if consciously intending to re-enact the Thirty Years' War in China. A banner in the Taiping throne room was unequivocal: 'The order came from God to kill the enemy and to unite all the mountains and rivers into one kingdom.' Nothing so clearly vindicated the decision of the Yongzheng emperor in 1724 to expel the previous wave of Christians, mostly Jesuits who had arrived in the seventeenth century. Viewed from afar, the Taiping could easily be mistaken for a revolution similar to the ones Europe had witnessed in 1848. On closer inspection, it was much more like an earlier war of religion. Hong Xiuquan was in some ways a much more successful Chinese version of Jan of Leiden, the Anabaptist.

It is easy to forget how close the Taiping came to making their kingdom a reality. In 1860, Taiping forces captured Hangzhou and Suzhou. Their failure to capture Shanghai and their subsequent retreat to Nanjing were due in no small part to yet more foreign intervention. In August 1860, Shanghai was defended by a force of Qing imperial troops and Western officers under the command of the American Frederick Townsend Ward. After Ward's death, the 'Ever Victorious Army' was led to a succession of victories by the British officer Charles 'Chinese' Gordon. Not until August 1871 was the last Taiping army, led by Li Fuzhong, completely wiped out. This outcome was in some ways analogous to the defeat of the Confederacy by the United States in the American Civil War. In both cases, British statesmen seriously contemplated some kind of intervention on the side of rebellion, if only a recognition of the rebels as belligerents. In both cases, they opted to back the status quo. In the American case this was a decision based partly on the manifest economic superiority of the North. In the Chinese case, it reflected the view that, after winning the Second Opium War (1856–60) and humiliating the imperial government in Beijing, Britain had an interest in shoring up the Qing Empire as a weak structure that could be relied on to accept informal economic subordination. Lord Palmerston's denunciation of the Taiping as 'Revolters not only against the Emperor, but against all laws human and Divine' was not based on any great respect for the Qing dynasty, but on the recognition that even waning hierarchies had their uses, and were on balance preferable to revolutionary networks.

31
'The Chinese Must Go'

Because they largely remained in private hands, the imperialist travel and communication networks of the late nineteenth century were relatively open. In the 1860s and 1870s access to the ocean liner and the telegraph office was rationed by price and nothing more – and, thanks to technological advances, the prices of both travel and communication were falling steadily. Access to news from abroad, meanwhile, was available to anyone who could read a newspaper – or hear one read aloud. This mattered a great deal because it meant that, all over the world, people living in misery had options unavailable to their ancestors. They could hear of better places. And they could get to them.

Poverty alone is seldom enough to drive mass emigrations. What is needed is political upheaval at home and the prospect of a more stable habitat within affordable reach. The period between around 1840 and 1940 presented roughly 150 million people living at the two extremities of the Eurasian landmass – Europe and China – with both. Revolutions, wars and the attendant miseries coincided with a steep decline in transport costs. The result was an exodus – or, to be precise, three exoduses, each of comparable magnitudes. The well-known mass migration (55–8 million people) was from Europe to the Americas, principally to the United States. The less familiar were the great outflows of Chinese and Indians to south-east Asia, the Indian Ocean rim and Australasia (48–52 million), and of Russians and others to Manchuria, Siberia and Central Asia (46–51 million).[1] One historical puzzle is why there was not a larger flow of Chinese to the United States. Though the Pacific Ocean is much wider than the Atlantic, the passage from Shanghai to San Francisco was not impossibly expensive, and the economic opportunities in booming California were numerous and financially enticing. There was nothing to stop Chinese migrant clusters performing the same role as Irish and Italian clusters on the East Coast, attracting more and more people to cross the sea to the promised land. The answer to the puzzle is politics. For had it not been for a populist backlash against Chinese immigration to the United States, the flow across the Pacific would surely have been larger – and the Chinese-American population today commensurately larger, too.

Few today recall the name of Denis Kearney, the leader of the Workingmen's Party of California and author of the slogan 'The Chinese Must Go!' Himself an Irish immigrant to the United States, Kearney was part of a movement of nativist parties and 'Anti-Coolie' clubs that sought to end Chinese immigration into the United States. The report of the Joint Special Committee to Investigate Chinese Immigration in 1877 gives a flavour of the times. 'The Pacific coast must in time become either Mongolian or American' was the committee's view. The Chinese brought with them the habits of despotic government, a tendency to lie in court, a weakness for tax evasion and 'insufficient brainspace . . . to furnish [the] motive power for self-government'. Moreover, Chinese women were 'bought and sold for prostitution and treated worse than dogs', while the Chinese were 'cruel and indifferent to their sick'. Giving such inferior beings citizenship, the committee's report declared, 'would practically destroy republican institutions on the Pacific coast'.[2]

The realities were, it scarcely needs to be said, very different. According to the 'Six Companies' of Chinese in San Francisco – corporate bodies that represented the Chinese population of the city – there was compelling evidence that Chinese immigration was a boon to California. Not only did the Chinese provide labour for the state's fast-developing railroads and farms; they also tended to improve the neighbourhoods where they settled. Moreover, there was no evidence of a disproportionate Chinese role in gambling and prostitution, while statistics showed that the Irish were more of a charge on the city's hospital and almshouse than the Chinese.[3] Nevertheless, a powerful coalition of 'laboring men and artisans', small businessmen and 'Grangers' (who aimed to shift the burden of taxation onto big business and the rich) rallied to Kearney's cause. As one shrewd contemporary observer noted, part of his appeal was that he was attacking not just the Chinese but also the big steamship and railroad companies who profited from employing them, not to mention the corrupt two-party establishment that ran San Francisco politics:

> Neither Democrats nor Republicans had done, nor seemed likely to do, anything to remove these evils or to improve the lot of the people. They were only seeking (so men thought) places or the chance of jobs for themselves, and could always be bought by a powerful corporation. Working men must help themselves; there must be new methods and a new departure ... The old parties, though both denouncing Chinese immigration in every convention they held, and professing to legislate against it, had failed to check it ... Everything, in short, was ripe for a demagogue. Fate was kind to the Californians in sending them a demagogue of a mean type, noisy and confident, but with neither political foresight nor constructive talent.[4]

Kearney may have lacked foresight and 'constructive talent', but there is no gainsaying what he and his ilk were able to achieve. Beginning in 1875, with the Page Law prohibiting the immigration of Asian women for 'lewd or immoral purposes', American legislators scarcely rested until Chinese immigration to the United States had been altogether stopped. The Chinese Exclusion Act of 1882 suspended immigration of Chinese for ten years, introduced 'certificates of registration' for departing workers (effectively re-entry permits), required Chinese officials to vet travellers from Asia, and for the first time in US history created an offence of illegal immigration, with the possibility of deportation as a part of the penalty. The Foran Act (1885) banned 'alien contract labor', which meant the practice whereby American corporations hired Chinese 'coolies' and paid for their passage to the United States. Legislation passed in 1888 banned all Chinese from travel to the United States except 'teachers, students, merchants, or travelers for pleasure'. In all, between 1875 and 1924, more than a dozen pieces of legislation served to restrict and finally to end altogether Chinese immigration.[5]

The lesson of this episode is very clear. Just as global networks of communication and transportation had made the mass migrations of the late nineteenth century possible,[6] so political networks of populism and nativism sprang into life to resist them. For all his coarseness and bombast, Denis Kearney and his allies effectively sealed the US border along the Pacific Coast of the United States; indeed, one cartoon of the time depicted them building a wall across the San Francisco harbour (plate 16). In the 1850s and 1860s, as many as 40 per cent of all Chinese emigrants had travelled beyond Asia, though the numbers arriving in the United States had in fact been relatively small. (Between 1870 and 1880, 138,941 Chinese immigrants came, just 4.3 per cent of the total, a share dwarfed by the vast European exodus across the Atlantic in the same period.)[7] What exclusion did was to ensure that Chinese immigration would not grow further, as it surely would have, but dwindled and then ceased.

The European empires, led by the British, had made globalization a reality by the late nineteenth century. With distance 'annihilated' by the new technologies of steam transportation and the telegraph, international movements of goods, people, capital and information reached unprecedented volumes. Yet the networks that came into existence in the age of empire – in particular, the networks of migration that created with such speed a 'Little Italy' and a 'Chinatown' in so many cities around the world – had unforeseen effects on indigenous politics. We give the generic name 'populism' to the backlash against free trade, free migration and international capital that was such a striking feature of American and European politics. But each country, and indeed each region, had its own distinctive populist flavours. If the Chinese were resented on the West Coast in the 1870s, the Irish were the objects of Eastern scorn, while German and French populists alike directed their fire against the Jews migrating westwards from Eastern Europe. By the 1890s and 1900s, with the surge of Jewish emigration from the Russian Pale to the United States, anti-Semitism spread across the Atlantic. Paradoxically, opponents of immigration simultaneously disparaged the poverty of the newcomers and exaggerated the power of their supposed leaders. The Chinese in San Francisco were simultaneously bestially indigent and monopolists of the laundry business. The Jews in New York were at once verminous and the string-pulling masters of the global financial system. Few images better illustrate the growing belief in an all-powerful

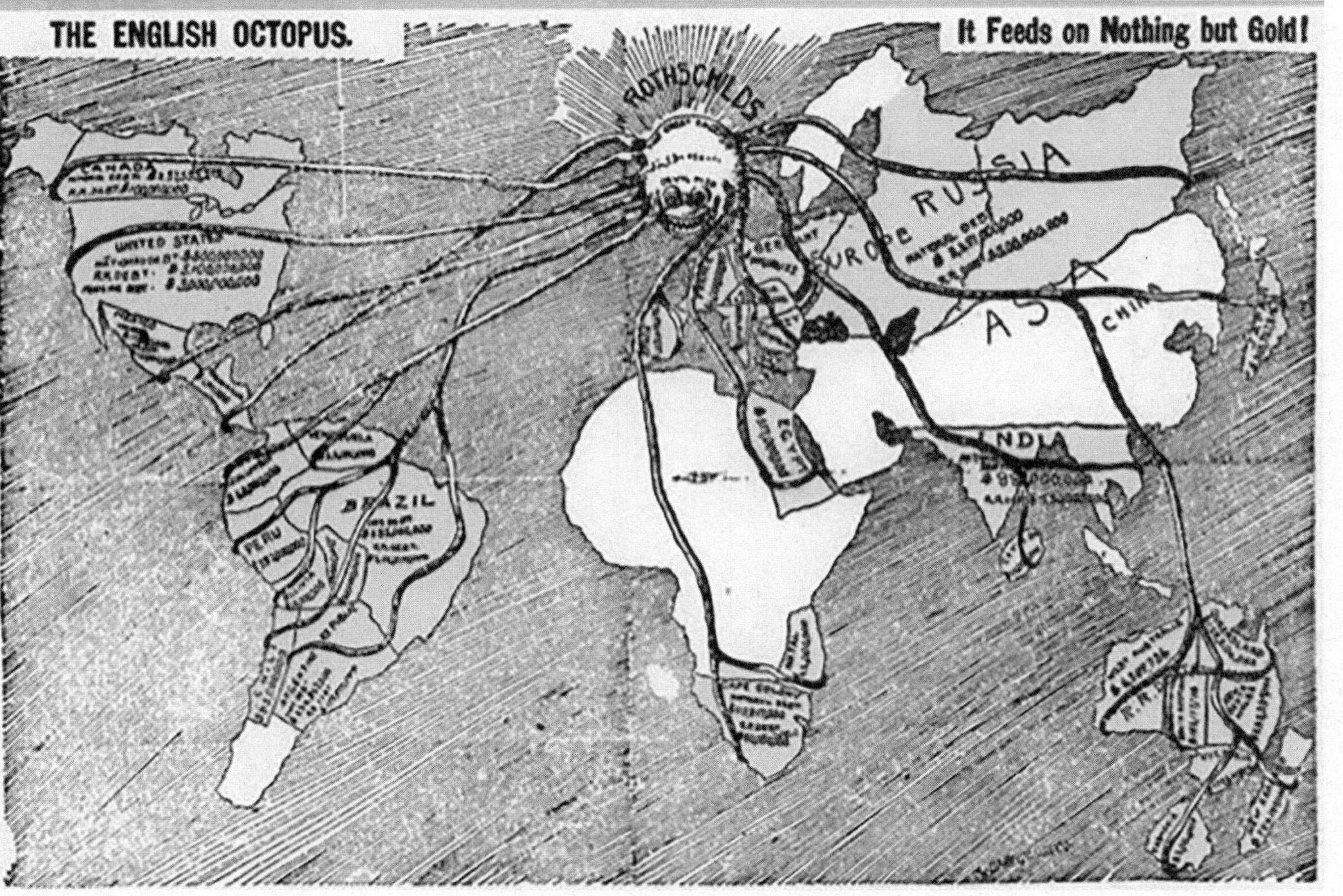

20. 'The English Octopus: It Feeds on Nothing but Gold!' Anti-Rothschild cartoon, 1894.

network of Jewish finance than the cartoon 'The English Octopus', published in the 1894 populist pamphlet *Coin's Financial School*, written by William H. Harvey, a critic of the gold standard and adviser to the populist firebrand and three-time unsuccessful Democratic presidential candidate, William Jennings Bryan. Here was the imperial network, reimagined in a way that would ultimately fire more than just the imaginations of anti-Semites (see figure 20).

32
The Union of South Africa

It is a common misapprehension to think that the populist backlash of the late nineteenth century had something to do with the origins of the First World War. The two are in fact almost wholly unrelated. The catalyst for populist movements on both sides of the Atlantic was the financial crisis of 1873. In terms of electoral success, the populist era was largely at an end by the middle of the 1890s. By that time, the various populist policies and preoccupations – protectionism, immigration restriction, bimetallism, anti-Semitism – had been absorbed wholly or partially by established political parties (most obviously, the Democrats in the United States and the Conservatives in Germany). The populists in their original form had not been imperialists – on the contrary, they had regarded empire as a project of the cosmopolitan elites they disdained, and correctly identified the intimate links between imperialism, free trade, free migration, free capital movement and the gold standard. The populists' problem was not their diagnosis: in a globalized, networked world, inequality really was increasing because immigrant labour was eroding the wages of native-born workers, while the profits of the great concentrations of industrial and financial capital were flowing to a tiny elite. The problem was that the populists' remedies seemed insufficient: like the tariffs imposed on imports, the exclusion of Chinese migrants had a barely perceptible impact on the lives of working Americans. Meanwhile, criticisms of the gold standard lost much of their force as huge new gold discoveries – notably in South Africa – eased the deflationary pressures that had been propelling populism by driving down agricultural and other prices. By the turn of the century, the initiative had passed from populists to progressives, or Social Democrats as they were known in Europe, where organized labour was much more susceptible to the theories of Karl Marx and his disciples. The progressives' remedies – which included higher direct taxation, state pensions, increased regulation of the labour market, weakening of private monopolies and public ownership of utilities – were ultimately more compelling and politically marketable than the populists' had been.

For all the world's elites, the sustained advance of the political left was more disquieting than the populist wave had been. Especially alarming were the extreme utopian sects that flourished at the *fin de siècle*: not only Marxists but also anarchists and nationalists who, from Cork to Calcutta, from Sarajevo to Saigon, threatened the very integrity of the empires themselves. Yet metropolitan intellectuals of the age of empire believed they had a solution. Some spoke of 'liberal imperialism', others of 'social imperialism', but the notion was widespread at the turn of the century that the empires could aspire to something loftier than the exploitation of the impoverished periphery. If they could only address the needs of the labouring classes of the imperial core, then the various subversive menaces would fade.

Alfred Milner was an unlikely imperial redeemer. The son of an Anglo-German academic who had taught English at the University of Tübingen, Milner was shaped above all by Balliol College, Oxford, where he read Greats under Benjamin Jowett and befriended the economic historian Arnold Toynbee. His academic prospects were brilliant, but he opted for London, trying his hand at the law, journalism and politics, until finding his métier as a mandarin, first as private secretary to the Liberal Unionist George Goschen, then as under-secretary of finance in Egypt, then as chairman of the Board of Inland Revenue, a post he held for five years. Herbert Asquith later summed Milner up as 'an Expansionist, up to a point a Protectionist, with a strain in social and industrial matters of semi-Socialist sentiment'.[1] This was astute. Yet, by a considerable irony, Milner became after 1897 an agent of one of the most ruthless capitalists in British imperial history, Cecil Rhodes, a man who drew no clear distinction between the advance of his own business empire and the British Empire in Africa, and who was prone to flights of fancy as to how best to advance the interests of both. According to Quigley, in 1891

Rhodes formed a 'Junta of Three' along with the journalist William T. Stead and the courtier Reginald Brett, later Viscount Esher. This triumvirate was to run 'The Society of the Elect', which would be assisted by an 'Association of Helpers'.[2] Such schemes were of a piece with Rhodes's draft will, which instructed Nathaniel Rothschild – the first member of the family to be elevated to the peerage – to establish in Rhodes's memory an imperialist version of the Jesuit Order.*[3]

Milner was appointed High Commissioner of South Africa in 1897, in the wake of the crisis that followed the abortive 'Jameson Raid' against the Afrikaner republic in the Transvaal. In Quigley's account, the staff of eighteen men that Milner recruited – his so-called 'Kindergarten' – became the core of one of the most powerful networks of the twentieth century.[4]

The reality was less thrilling. The initial members of Milner's staff were Robert Brand, Lionel Curtis, John Dove, Patrick Duncan, Richard Feetham, Lionel Hichens, J. F. (Peter) Perry and Geoffrey Robinson (later Dawson). They were joined after 1905 by Philip Kerr, later marquess of Lothian, and Dougal Malcolm. Other members included Leo Amery, Herbert Baker, John Buchan, George Craik, William Marris, James Meston, Basil Williams and Hugh Wyndham, later fourth Baron Leconfield.[5] Milner recruited Perry and Robinson from the Colonial Office, where they had previously worked with him; Perry recruited Brand; Duncan had been Milner's private secretary at the Inland Revenue. Many of the rest came as a result of Oxford connections. Indeed, Brand, Curtis, Dove, Feetham, Hichens, Kerr, Malcolm, Williams and Wyndham had all attended New College, Milner's *alma mater*. Working, socializing and living together – after 1906 at Moot House in Parktown, Johannesburg, a building designed by Herbert Baker – the group resembled nothing more sinister than the junior fellows of an Oxford college on an extended reading holiday.[6] It was Milner's critics in the Cape

* Rhodes told Rothschild that his estate should be used to found an elite society dedicated to advancing the interests of the British Empire. 'In considering question suggested take Constitution Jesuits if obtainable,' Rhodes scribbled, 'and insert English Empire for Roman Catholic Religion.' The ultimate result was the Oxford Rhodes Scholarships.

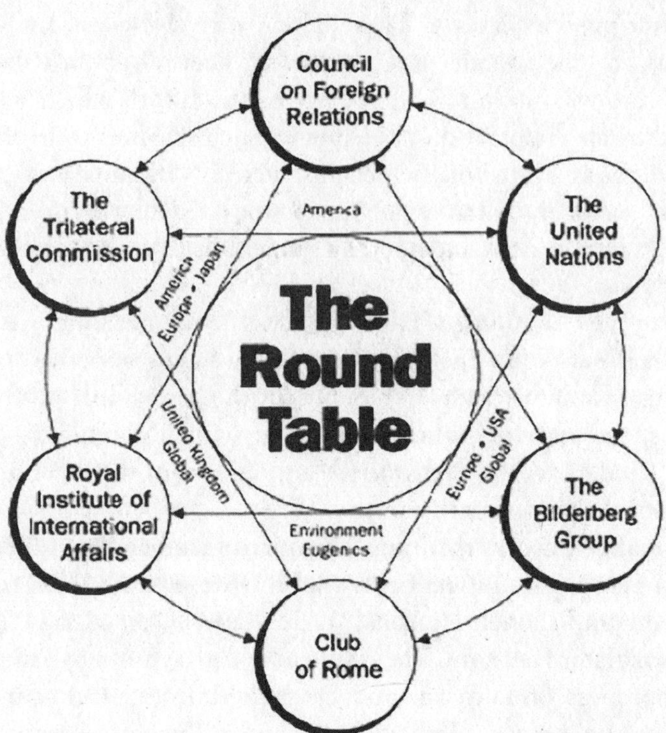

21. The myth of Lord Milner's network. This exaggerated view of Milner's influence was greatly encouraged by the Georgetown historian Carroll Quigley. The choice of a six-cornered star is not accidental, as the hexagram's religious associations (e.g. as the Star of David or Seal of Solomon) add the vital ingredient of mystique to the conspiracy theory.

parliament who accused him of 'setting up a sort of kindergarten . . . to govern the country'.[7] Though that name stuck, its members preferred the more romantic 'round table', which became the title of their journal after most had returned to London.

For a group of academically inclined civil servants, Milner's circle were remarkably ready to resort to force in pursuit of their objectives. The evidence is persuasive that it was Milner who forced the pace towards war after his arrival in South Africa. As early as February 1898, he had concluded that 'there is no way out of the political troubles . . . except reform in the Transvaal or war'.[8] In a letter of

1899, he set out his aims as follows: 'The *ultimate* end is a self-governing white Community, supported by *well-treated* and *justly governed* black labour from Cape Town to Zambezi. There must be one flag, the Union Jack, but under it equality of races and languages.'[9] On closer inspection, what Milner aspired to was to overwhelm the Afrikaners with immigration from the UK and its white Dominions. ('If, ten years hence,' he wrote in 1900, 'there are three men of British race to two of Dutch, the country will be safe and prosperous. If there are three of Dutch to two of British, we shall have perpetual difficulty.')[10] Milner's promises of good treatment and just government for the black population in fact implied subjugation. In his diary for 1901, Curtis remarked that 'it would be a blessed thing if the negro, like the Red Indian, tended to die out before us'. Dove regarded the 'almost brutal contempt and dislike of most white men' for blacks as a 'healthy sign. It marks the determination of the white South African not to allow his race to become mongrel.'[11] On one occasion, Milner himself defined his goal as being to make South Africa 'a white man's country . . . not a country full of poor whites, but one in which a largely increased white population can live in decency and comfort'.[12]

We can see now the extent to which Milner's regime laid the foundations of what would ultimately become the odious system of apartheid. That was not how Milner thought of it. In his eyes, the subordination of black Africans was the least controversial of his goals. The prize was a dilution of Afrikaner power and 'the establishment in South Africa [as he put it in 1904] of a great and civilized and progressive community, one from Cape Town to the Zambezi, independent in the management of its own affairs, but still remaining, from its own firm desire, a member of the great community of free nations gathered together under the British flag. That has been the object of all my efforts.' A united, British-dominated South Africa would in turn contribute to 'the great idea of Imperial Unity . . . a group of states, all independent in their local concerns, but all united for the defence of their own common interests and the development of a common civilization'.[13] Having defeated the Boers in a vicious war, herding their women and children into lethal concentration camps, Milner and his young men worked indefatigably to realize his vision. They created an Intercolonial Council, which linked the Transvaal and Orange River Colony; they amalgamated the railways; they created a customs union; they organized Closer Union societies in each colony; they extolled the benefits of a South African Union in publications like *The State*; they wrote the first drafts of what ultimately became the constitution of the Union of South Africa in 1910.[14]

Yet, as one leading historian of the British Empire has rightly observed, the Milnerite vision of a British-run South Africa was an 'imperial fantasy'.[15] Milner's dictatorial style could not prevent a revival of Afrikaner politics under the leadership of Louis Botha and Jan Smuts.[16] There was no way of making large-scale English settlement work; given the abundance of cheap African labour, there was already a 'poor whites' problem even before the Boer War.[17] The inner contradictions of the 'Empire project' were laid bare when, at the Randlords' request, Milner brought in 50,000 Chinese 'coolies' to work in the goldmines. This unleashed a storm of protest against 'Chinese slavery' in both South Africa and Britain. Indeed, the issue became a stick with which the Liberals successfully beat the Unionists in the 1906 election, and it ensured Milner's demise.[18] His successor, Lord Selborne, accepted that union under Smuts's leadership was the only viable way forward, not least as a way of minimizing Liberal interference from London. Modern South Africa had been forged, but not as the new Canada or Australia of Milner's imaginings.

In most history, success is over-represented, for the victors outwrite the losers. In the history of networks, the opposite often applies. Successful networks evade public attention; unsuccessful ones attract it, and it is their notoriety, rather than their achievement, that leads to their over-representation. This was true of the Illuminati in the late eighteenth-century Germany. It was also true of Milner's Kindergarten and Round Table. The French Radical politician Joseph Caillaux accused Milner's circle of plotting 'the restoration of the tottering power of the caste to which they belong and the strengthening of the supremacy of Great Britain in the world'. Wilfrid Laurier, the Canadian prime minister, complained that Canada was being 'governed by a junta sitting in London, known as the "Round Table"'. Even the 'People's Chancellor', Lloyd George, spoke of 'a very powerful combination – in its own way perhaps the most powerful in the country'.[19] But none of this is evidence of the Kindergarten's power; rather the reverse. Even common-or-garden imperialists had their doubts about Milner. The Conservative *National Review* denounced a 'clique which encourages every centrifugal force in the British Empire'. The equally right-wing *Morning Post* was no more friendly to what it called 'a phalanx or palace-guard of idealists, who could be trusted by a sort of spiritual perversion to take a line injurious to British interests on every question'. The Liberal prime minister, Sir Henry Campbell-Bannerman, was nearer the mark when he referred half mockingly to a *religio Milneriana*. Quigley and his American heirs made the mistake of taking literally the lofty ambitions of Milner and his circle and taking seriously the condemnation of their critics, omitting only to notice that one of the latter's principal criticisms was of Milner's near total failure.

33
Apostles

The universities of Oxford and Cambridge are very much alike – to the tourist, all but indistinguishable. Their ancient rivalry can seem to outsiders to be based firmly on the narcissism of small differences. Oxford calls its second term 'Hilary', while Cambridge says 'Lent'. Oxford undergraduates have tutorials; their counterparts at Cambridge, supervisions. Oxonians punt standing inside the punt, with the 'box' pointing forwards; Cantabrigians stand on the 'till' of their differently designed vessels. Such trivial differences are innumerable. Yet there have often been profound philosophical differences between the two universities. Never, surely, was the intellectual distance between Isis and Cam greater than in the years before and after the First World War. While Milner's network of Oxford men envisioned a muscular, martial, imperial and heterosexual future, their counterparts at Cambridge aspired to almost the precise opposite. The network that evolved there in and around the Cambridge 'Apostles' was effete, pacifist, liberal and homosexual.

The 'Conversazione Society' had been founded in 1820 by students at St John's College, though its institutional home would quickly become Trinity, much the largest and wealthiest of all the Oxbridge colleges. The Society's founding fathers included the poet Alfred Tennyson and Oscar Browning,[1] as well as the 'moral philosopher' Henry Sidgwick and Frederick Denison Maurice, a theologian and founder of the movement of Christian Socialism.[2] In some respects, the Society had its roots in Cambridge's 'intellectual aristocracy' (in Noel Annan's later phrase): surnames such as Keynes, Strachey and Trevelyan appeared to confer automatic membership.[3] In other respects, with its elaborate system of election and its somewhat silly rituals, it was just another all-male fraternity of the sort that could also be found at Harvard, Princeton and Yale in the same era. Yet two things set the Conversazione Society apart. No comparable society of the era was so intellectually exclusive. 'Apostles' were chosen primarily on the basis of their philosophical aptitude. And in no other society did the sense of superiority give rise to such a strong sense of alienation from the established order – ultimately in nearly all its aspects. 'Is it monomania,' one Apostle asked another in the early 1900s, 'this colossal moral superiority that we feel?'[4] The Society was 'real', the Apostles liked to joke, the rest of the world 'phenomenal'. When the philosopher J. Ellis McTaggart married late in life, he quipped that he was merely taking a 'phenomenal wife'. They were, in a word, insufferable.

In total, there were around 255 Apostles between 1820 and 1914. So exalted were the criteria for membership that in some years there were no new elections at all. Between 1909 and 1912, for example, there was only one.[5] Potential recruits were known as 'embryos' and were sized up at a succession of famously awkward afternoon teas. On the rare occasions that an undergraduate was thought worthy, he was 'born' into the Society, which entailed swearing the inevitable blood-curdling oath of secrecy. Thereafter he was expected to attend its weekly meetings each Saturday evening during term time, at which members, speaking from the 'hearthrug', read papers with titles such as 'Beauty' or 'Ethics in Relation to Conduct', and put (traditionally unrelated) questions to a vote. 'Brother' was the correct form of address when Apostle spoke unto Apostle. Also in attendance, and sharing the mandatory anchovies on toast ('whales'), were so-called 'Angels' – former members who had resigned ('taken wings') on graduating. The possibility of intense, Hellenistic friendships between members of different generations were one of the things the Apostles prided themselves on.[6] Angels who had remained in Cambridge as academics – the philosophers Bertrand Russell and A. N. Whitehead, for example – regularly attended meetings.

The politics of the nineteenth-century Apostles was not so different from that of their Oxford contemporaries. In 1864, they were said to be 'Tory in politics, Evangelical in religion'.[7] Indeed a number became Conservative Members of Parliament. Roughly 14 per cent of

Apostles became MPs or civil servants; between a quarter and a third went into the law.[8] Nor was the Society's later anti-imperialism much in evidence before 1900. Its leading lights vied with one another for senior positions in the Indian Civil Service, which were awarded on the basis of a harrowing examination.[9] The Apostles were split on the issue of Irish Home Rule, much like the British elite as a whole.[10] Yet already in its early years – partly because of its secretiveness – the Society had a reputation for radicalism. As early as 1830, Richard Chevenix Trench had to refute the claim that the Apostles were a 'secret Society established for the purpose of overthrowing all established Governments'.[11] That subversive spirit grew more pronounced after 1900 with the advent of a new generation centred on the philosopher G. E. Moore, the Socrates of the new century.

It was not that Moore was political; on the contrary, he encouraged his disciples to regard politics with contempt.[12] Moore's passion was for private virtues. The watchwords of his *Principia Ethica*, published in 1903, were sensibility, personal relations, the liberation of the emotions, the creative instincts and ruthless honesty about oneself.[13] These ideas – which found literary articulation in the novels of another Apostle, E. M. Forster – enthralled three brilliant young men: Lytton Strachey, Leonard Woolf and John Maynard Keynes, who on 28 February 1903 became Apostle No. 243.[14] Strachey was the eighth of ten children of General Sir Richard Strachey, who had served in India, and his second wife, a Scot named Jane Maria Grant. With his diminutive frame and high-pitched voice, he was as unmilitary a son as ever a general sired. The less flamboyant, habitually doleful Woolf was the third of the ten children of Sidney Woolf, a Jewish barrister. Keynes was a true aristocrat in the Cambridge sense: his father, a don, yearned only for his elder son to win every mathematical prize the university had to offer. However, it was not maths young Maynard truly cared for. It was men.

Strachey and Keynes were not merely gay; they were militantly homosexual, regarding their sexual preference as superior to commonplace heterosexuality and indulging in misogynistic sniping when any woman entered their exalted social circle. It was an apostolic tradition dating back to Browning, of whom the *Dictionary of National Biography* ventured to write that when 'in Rome he assisted young Italians, as he had young Englishmen, towards the openings they desired'. By 1903 this culture was beyond a joke. Strachey and Keynes fought over the pulchritudinous but ultimately vacuous Arthur Hobhouse, securing his 'birth' as an Apostle for primarily aesthetic reasons. They bragged about their dedication to 'the Higher Sodomy', which did not exclude encounters with members of the lower classes when the opportunity arose. By 1909 their public displays of attention were attracting adverse attention.[15] To judge by the early correspondence between Rupert Brooke and James Strachey, the Conversazione Society was now primarily concerned with sexual rather than intellectual intercourse.[16] The Apostles of the previous generation, in Sidgwick's words, had believed in 'the pursuit of truth with absolute devotion and unreserve by a group of intimate friends'.[17] Keynes and Strachey simply pursued their intimate friends.

Not all Apostles were gay, to be sure. But a rising proportion were. And even those (like Woolf) who were not nevertheless subscribed to the somewhat solipsistic ideals of the gay 'brothers'. The older generation, Desmond MacCarthy argued in a paper read to the Society in December 1900, had been in thrall to the old institutions: 'the family, the state, laws of honour, etc.' But these had 'failed to produce convincing proofs of their authority' to the younger generation. They took 'everything more *personally*'.[18] 'Only connect' was the new categorical imperative, and would be the key phrase in Forster's finest novel, *Howard's End* (1921). Certainly, the rarefied network of the Conversazione Society was as intoxicating as the bureaucratic hierarchies of Whitehall were a bore. Having won his place in the Indian Civil Service, Keynes quickly grew 'sick' of it. 'Now the novelty has worn off,' he complained:

> I am bored nine tenths of the time and rather unreasonably irritated the other tenth whenever I can't have my own way. It's maddening to have thirty people who can reduce you to impotence when you're quite certain you're right. Then the preoccupation, which seems characteristic of officials, to save their own skin, is fatal.[19]

Yet it was hypocritical of Keynes to condemn his ICS colleagues for 'dread[ing] taking responsibility'. Looking back on his 'early beliefs' in 1938, Keynes went further:

> We entirely repudiated a personal liability on us to obey general rules. We claimed the right to judge every individual case on its merits, and the wisdom to do so successfully. This was a very important part of our faith, violently and aggressively held, and for the outer world it was our most obvious and dangerous characteristic. We repudiated entirely customary morals, conventions and traditional wisdom. We were, that is to say, in the strict sense of the term, immoralists. The consequences of being found out had, of course, to be considered for what they were worth. But we recognized no moral obligation on us, no inner sanction, to conform or obey.[20]

Writing a year later, Forster captured the perilous implication of Moore's philosophy when taken to these extremes: 'If I had to choose between betraying my country and betraying my friend, I hope I should have the guts to betray my country . . . Love and loyalty to an individual can run counter to the claims of a State. When they do – down with the State, say I.'[21]

Even before the moment of truth in 1914, some members of the Society had tired of all this. Rupert Brooke might be Adonis-like, but he was not gay and he was soon spotted in the company of female Fabians.[22] Having been 'born', the Viennese-born philosopher Ludwig Wittgenstein took one look at the Apostles and fled, resigning after a single meeting. Although Strachey persuaded him to withdraw the resignation, he did not attend meetings.[23] With the outbreak of war, the spell was shattered. The majority of Apostles did not enlist. By contrast, Brooke enthusiastically joined up and – on a French hospital ship off Skyros on St George's Day, 1915 – died one of the most famous deaths in English history.[24] Matters came to a head with the introduction of conscription. Keynes, working at the Treasury, did not require an exemption, but he formally sought one on the ground of conscientious objection. 'I work for a government I despise for ends I think criminal,' he bitterly complained to Duncan Grant.[25] Privately, Keynes used his influence and resources to support other Apostles who declared themselves to be conscientious objectors, notably James Strachey and Gerald Shove,[26] but it was not enough for Lytton Strachey, who one night in February 1916 left a jingoistic newspaper cutting on Keynes's dinner plate with the simple covering note: 'Dear Maynard, Why are you still at the Treasury?'[27]

It was not only the Apostles' network that the war disrupted. Overlapping with it at numerous points – Forster, Keynes, Strachey and Woolf, to name just four of the ten[28] – was another intellectually kindred network, the Bloomsbury Group. Unlike the Conversazione Society, Bloomsbury admitted women – notably the Stephen sisters, Vanessa and Virginia – and indeed came to revolve around married couples: Vanessa and Clive Bell (at 46 Gordon Square) and Virginia and Leonard Woolf (who in 1915 moved to Richmond). The effect of the war was to drive a central component of Bloomsbury – predominantly the writers and artists – out of London, to the large farmhouse at Charleston in Sussex to which Vanessa Bell and Duncan Grant moved in 1916. New analysis of the Bloosmbury network by Peter Dolton makes clear that Lytton Strachey had the highest degree and betweenness centrality in both 1905 and 1925. In the later period, Duncan Grant, Maynard Keynes and Virginia Woolf were second, third and fourth after Strachey.[29] Yet the striking feature of Bloomsbury was not how much its members liked walking on the South Downs. As with the Apostles, it was once again sexual relationships that defined the network. Grant slept not only with Keynes, Lytton Strachey, Adrian Stephen and Vanessa Bell, but also with David Garnett. Vanessa Bell slept not only with Grant but also with Roger Fry and sometimes even her own husband, Clive. Keynes slept with Grant, Garnett, Strachey and, eventually, the Russian ballerina Lydia Lopokova. The complications of Bloomsbury love lives were endless. Garnett felt unrequited love for Vanessa Bell. Ottoline Morrell had the same problem with Virginia Woolf; Dora Carrington with Lytton Strachey; Lytton Strachey with Mark Gertler; and Mark Gertler with Dora Carrington. As Dolton puts it: 'Vanessa Bell was married to Clive Bell but lived with Duncan Grant. Leonard Woolf was married to Virginia Woolf, and Harold Nicolson was married to Vita Sackville-West but it was Vita and Virginia who fell in love with each other.'[30]

In *Howard's End* the brilliant Margaret tries to explain Bloomsbury principles to her rather pedestrian husband, Henry. 'Only connect! That was the whole of her sermon. Only connect the prose

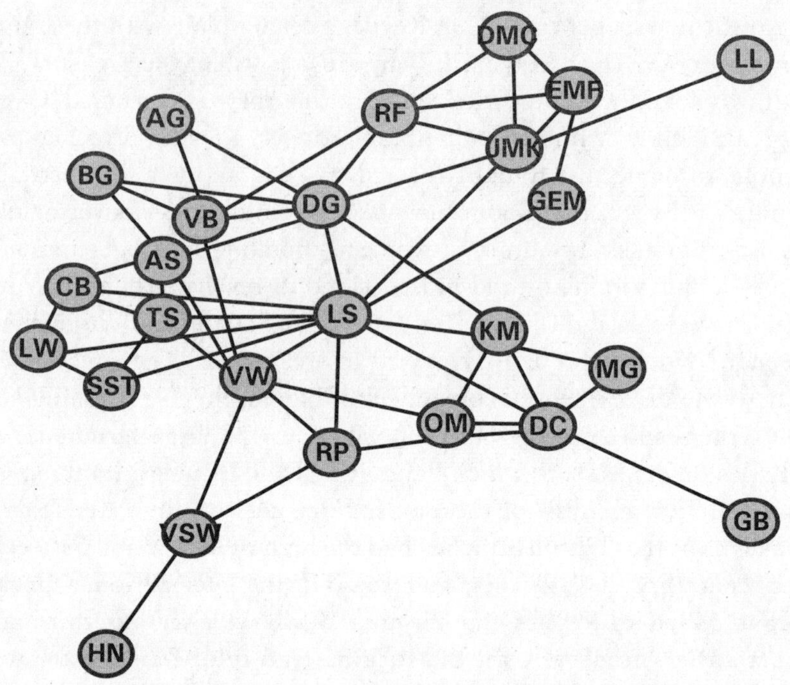

22. The Bloomsbury Group in around 1925. At the core of the network: Clive Bell (CB), Vanessa Bell (VB), E. M. Forster (EMF), Roger Fry (RF), David 'Bunny' Garnett (BG), Duncan Grant (DG), John Maynard Keynes (JMK), Desmond McCarthy (DMC), Lytton Strachey (LS), Leonard Woolf (LW), Virginia Woolf (VW). The 'outer group': Thoby Stephen (TS), Saxon Sydney-Turner (SST), Adrian Stephen (AS), Gerald Brenan (GB), Dora Carrington (DC), Angelica Garnett (AG), Ottoline Morrell (OM), Ralph Partridge (RP), Harold Nicolson (HN), Vita Sackville-West (VSW), Mark Gertler (MG), Katherine Mansfield (KM), Lydia Lopokova (LL) and G. E. Moore (GEM).

and the passion, and both will be exalted, and human love will be seen at its height. Live in fragments no longer. Only connect, and the beast and the monk, robbed of the isolation that is life to either, will die.' But, as Forster says, 'she failed'. For Henry's motto is not 'Only connect' but 'Concentrate'. And he tells her flatly: 'I've no intention of frittering away my strength on that kind of thing.'[31] When one reflects on the sexual couplings of the Bloomsbury Group, one sees his point.

34
Armageddon

The failure of Milner's Kindergarten in South Africa had revealed the limits of British imperial expansion. The fracturing of the Apostles and Bloomsbury showed that Cambridge, if not Oxford, had lost all sympathy with the project of empire itself. And yet in 1914 Britons – to say nothing of their imperial subjects – went to war in response to the challenge posed by the growing economic power and geopolitical ambition of the German Reich. Britain's ultimate victory in that war owed much to the unity between the English-speaking peoples that Milner and his acolytes had urged. Australia, Canada, New Zealand and indeed South Africa all made significant economic and military contributions to the British war effort between 1914 and 1918, as did the Empire as a whole and India in particular.[1] The lamentations of Bloomsbury became audible only after the war's end, with the publication of two devastating polemics: Strachey's *Eminent Victorians* and Keynes's *Economic Consequences of the Peace*.

There is no need here to re-enter the overcrowded courtroom that is the historiography of the First World War.[2] Like the lawyers in Dickens's *Bleak House*, the historians continue picking over the dusty documents (in a case that has sometimes deserved the Dickensian name *Germany v Germany*). Yet there will be no final verdict in this case, for the century-long search for 'war guilt' is a futile one. A general European war broke out in 1914 for the simple reason that the order established at Vienna in 1815 broke down. The correct historical question to ask is why that happened, not whose fault it was.

By the early 1900s, Ranke's pentarchy of five great powers had evolved into five great empires, each extracting modest rents from the international networks of trade, migration, investment and information described above. For a time after the Crimean War it had seemed that a *modus vivendi* had arisen between the old hierarchies of hereditary rule and the new networks of globalization. The governments that ran the great European empires were to a remarkable extent nightwatchman states, making only minimal demands on the market economies with which they co-existed. They might insist on controlling some postal, telegraph and rail services, in addition to the armies and navies, but they left much else in private hands. In the great European cities, royal and imperial hierarchies lived in close social proximity to the new elites of credit, of commerce and of comment: indeed, earls married the daughters of Jewish bankers. Optimists, from Andrew Carnegie to Norman Angell, felt sure that the emperors would not be so foolish as to jeopardize all this.[3]

This proved to be a delusion. According to Henry Kissinger's classic account, the pentarchy ceased to be stable because 'with Germany unified and France a fixed adversary, the system lost its flexibility'.[4] After 1871 the system depended on the virtuoso diplomat Bismarck to keep it in equilibrium. The key stratagem was the Secret Reinsurance Treaty that Bismarck signed with the Russian foreign minister, Nikolay Girs, in June 1887, whereby Germany and Russia each agreed to observe neutrality should the other be involved in a war with a third country, unless Germany attacked France or Russia attacked Austria–Hungary. This committed Germany to neutrality if Russia sought to assert control over the Black Sea Straits, but the real point was to discourage the Russians from seeking a mutual defence treaty with France, which was exactly what happened after Bismarck's fall from power led to the non-renewal of the Secret Reinsurance Treaty. 'Paradoxically,' in Kissinger's words, 'it was precisely that ambiguity which [had] preserved the flexibility of the European equilibrium. And its abandonment . . . started a sequence of increasing confrontations, culminating in World War I.'[5] After Bismarck had gone, Kissinger argued, the great-power system 'aggravated' rather than 'buffered' disputes. Over time, 'political leaders lost control over their own tactics' and 'in the end, the military planning ran away with diplomacy'.[6] From 1890 onwards, in other words, there was a significant probability of a conflict that would pit Germany and Austria–Hungary against France and Russia. The surprising thing is not that such a war happened in 1914, but that it did not happen sooner.

Although unfashionable amongst historians, Kissinger's approach finds considerable support amongst political scientists and network theorists. Certainly, the sharp increase in the number of militarized disputes after 1890 supports his argument that there was some kind of change around that time.[7] So, too, does an elegant paper by the mathematician Tibor Antal and the physicists Paul Krapivsky and Sidney Redner, who show that – in terms of network theory – the evolution of the great-power system after 1890 was, paradoxically, in the direction of 'social balance': two roughly equal alliances emerged. Balance in this case was 'a natural outcome', but not a good one if neither side was deterred by the other (see figure 23).[8]

There are of course alternative interpretations. One hypothesis is that the system failed because the great powers allowed lesser powers in the Balkans to drag them into a conflict.[9] It was the complex of

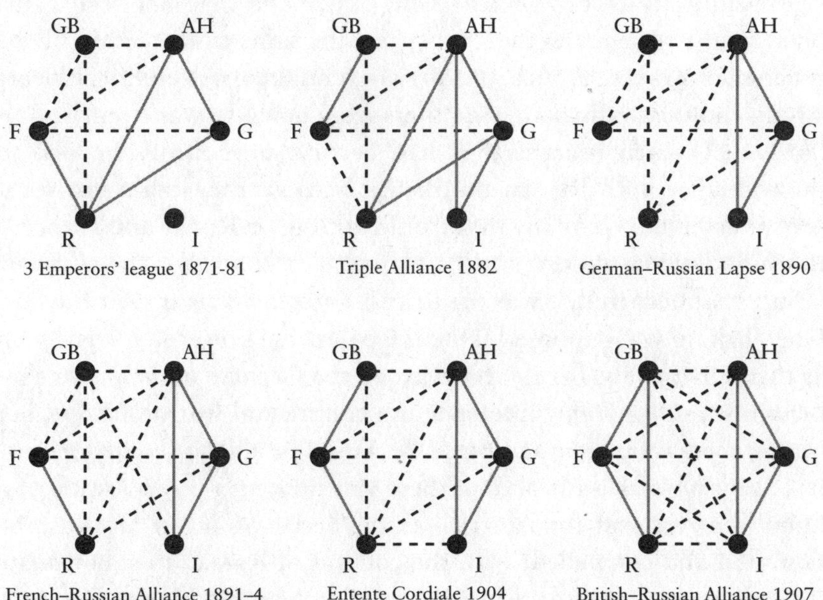

23. Evolution of the major relationship changes between the protagonists of the First World War, 1872–1907. GB = Great Britain, AH = Austria–Hungary, G = Germany, I = Italy, R = Russia, F = France.

lesser alliances that destabilized the system.[10] Yet it is simply not plausible that it was their ties to Romania or Japan, much less Spain or Portugal, that led the great powers to Armageddon in 1914.[11] Lesser countries mattered only because they raised the probability of a great-power conflict. Austro-Hungarian annexation of Bosnia in 1908 and the Serbian-sponsored assassination of the heir to the Austro-Hungarian throne six years later created a unique conjuncture because – unlike in previous crises over Morocco or previous Balkan wars – three of the great powers saw war as the sole alternative to a crushing diplomatic blow.[12] The view in Vienna and Berlin was not unreasonable: Russia appeared intent on exploiting the Bosnian crisis with a view to the permanent weakening, if not dismemberment, of Austria–Hungary.[13] Given that the next in line to the Habsburg throne had been the victim of what looked suspiciously like an act of state-sponsored terrorism, the Austrians were well within their 'Metternichian' rights to demand satisfaction from Serbia. The notorious Austrian ultimatum to Belgrade was not significantly different from the kind of demand that had been made on second-tier states in the 1820s.* At the same time, neither of the other two powers, France and Britain, could conceive of arguments strong enough to dissuade the others from going to war over the Balkans: the French because they had become uncritically wedded to their alliance with Russia, the British because they could not see a way of deterring Germany that would not egg on Russia and France.[14] If any individual deserves to be blamed personally for the systemic failure that occurred, it was the British Foreign Secretary, Sir Edward Grey. Britain was supposed to be the balancing power in a crisis such as this. On 29 July 1914, Grey warned the German ambassador that Britain would probably intervene if a continental war broke out, but that, if mediation were accepted, 'he would be able to secure for Austria every possible satisfaction; there was no longer any question of a humiliating retreat for Austria, as the Serbs would in any case be punished and compelled, with the consent of Russia, to subordinate themselves to Austria's wishes'.[15] Two days later he told the Germans

* It was no more unreasonable or unwarranted than the demand made by the United States to the Afghan regime after the 9/11 attacks.

1. Mural in the Cattedrale di Santa Maria Assunta, on the island of Torcello, Venice. 'Hierarchy' is from ἱεραρχία (*hierarchia*), 'rule of a high priest'.

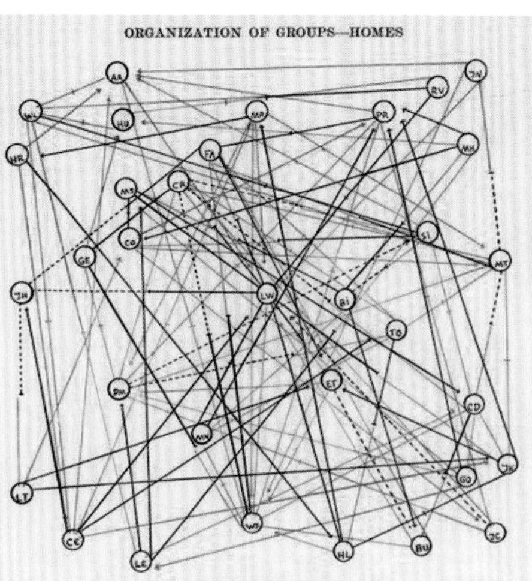

ORGANIZATION OF GROUPS—HOMES

STRUCTURE OF A COTTAGE FAMILY—C12

Criterion: Living in proximity, sharing the same house; 5 choices; no limit placed on rejections.

33 girls. *Unchosen* 1; *Unchosen and Rejected* 4; *Mutual Pairs* 31; *Mutual Rejections* 7; *Incompatible Pairs* 21; *Chains* 2; *Triangles* 2; *Stars* (of attraction) 4; *Stars* (of rejection) 1.

Classification: Introverted Group Organization; Inward Aggressive. Special Feature—Out of 33 individuals there are 31 who are either rejected or who reject some member of the group; only two are free from this pattern of aggression. It is interesting that this cottage is one of the two colored houses within the community, which is overwhelmingly white. The girls project most of their attractions as well as rejections upon the girls of their own race, producing an excess of love as well as of hate within a small social area.

Note for the Group Psychotherapist: Start a sociodrama and break the group into two opposing camps, the one unit consisting of individuals who indicate self preference, the other consisting of individuals who indicate self rejection. The problem to be explored will be whether self preference means here love for one's own race and self rejection hostility against one's own race.

2. One of Jacob Moreno's 'sociograms' of a residential cottage at the New York Training School for Girls in Hudson, NY. Note his commentary on this case, one of the two 'colored' houses in the institution.

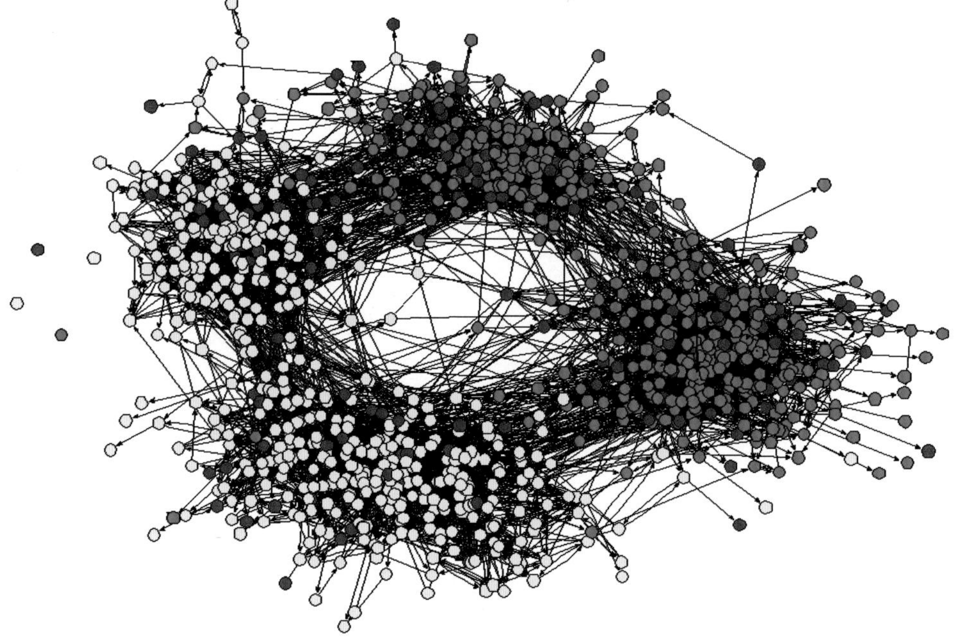

3. Homophily in action: the network of the friendships in a high school, from the National Longitudinal Survey of Adolescent to Adult Health ('Add Health'). Two nodes are connected if one student named the other student as a friend. Note the clustering of the two large groups (yellow and green nodes) but the more random distribution of the third group. Note also the 'network isolates' – nodes with no edges, i.e. pupils with no friends.

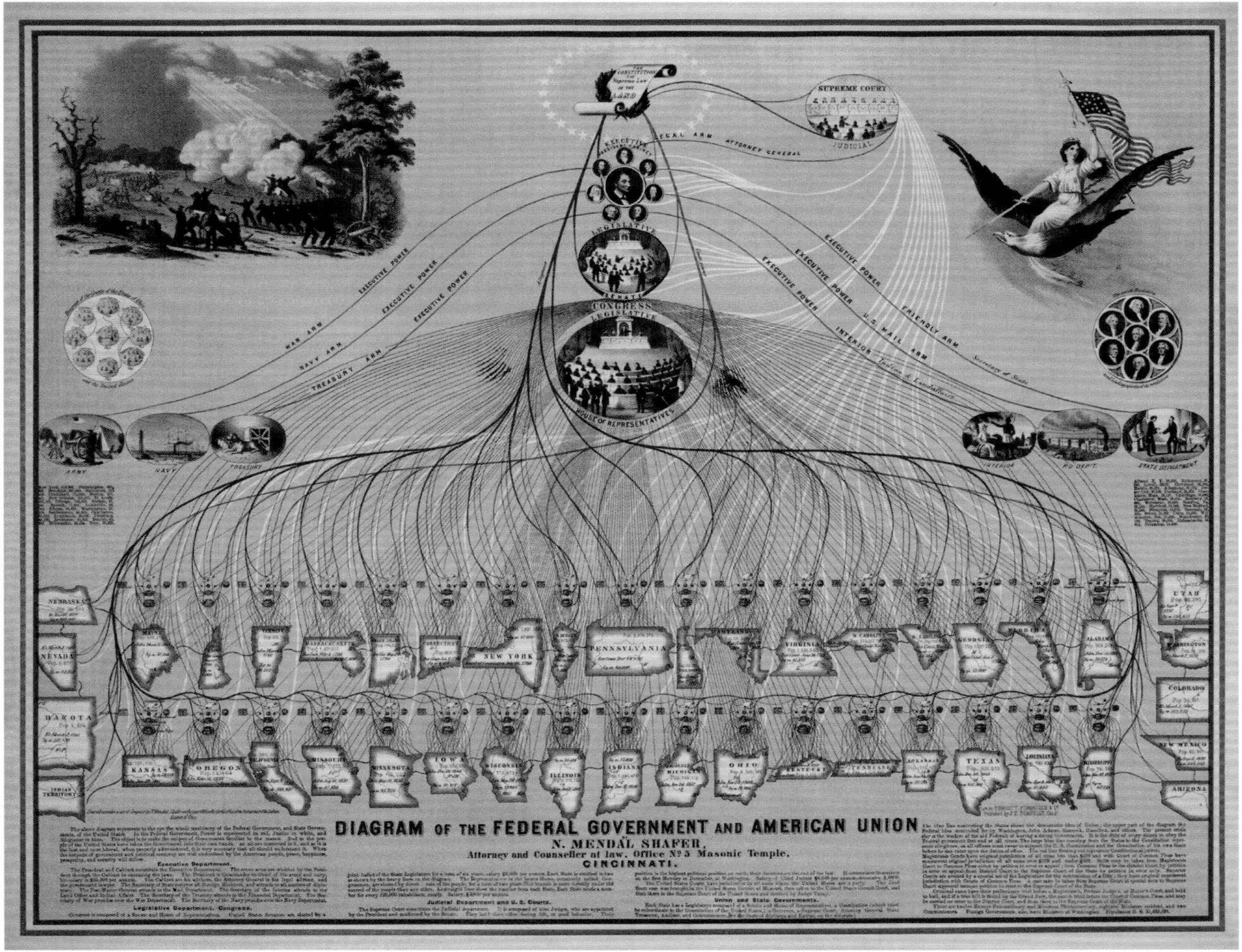

4. The United States federal government as a hierarchy, 1862.

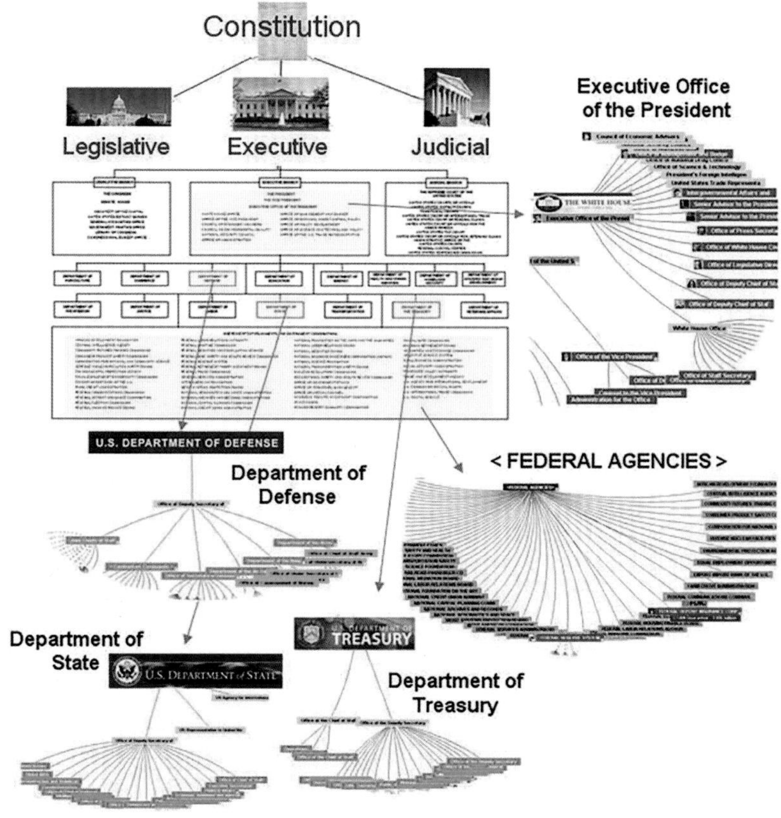

5. The United States federal government as a hierarchy, *c.* 2010.

6. (*below*) The square and the tower: Piazza del Campo in Siena, in the shadow of the Torre del Mangia of the Palazzo Pubblico.

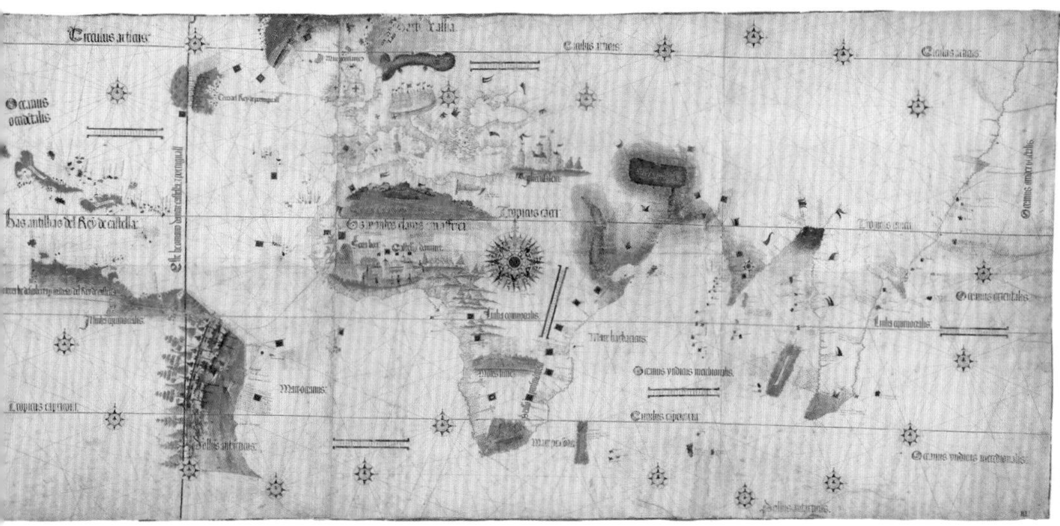

7. The Cantino planisphere (1502). In 1515–17, using the world's best maps and astrolabes, Fernão Peres de Andrade sailed 6,777 miles from Lisbon to Guangdong.

8. The Reformation as great disruption: the St Bartholomew's Day massacre of Huguenots (Protestants), Paris, 1572.

9. (*above*) The restoration of hierarchy? Gerard ter Borch, *Ratification of the Treaty of Münster, May 15, 1648.*

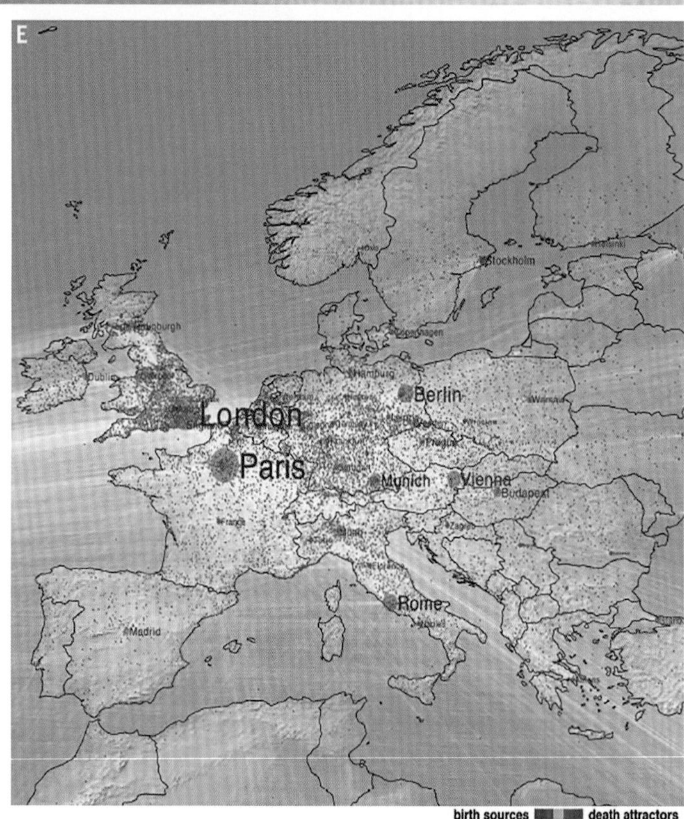

10. (*right*) 37,062 European locations, mapped on the basis of the birth and death data of 120,211 notable individuals from 1069 BCE to 2012 CE. The size of nodes represents their importance.

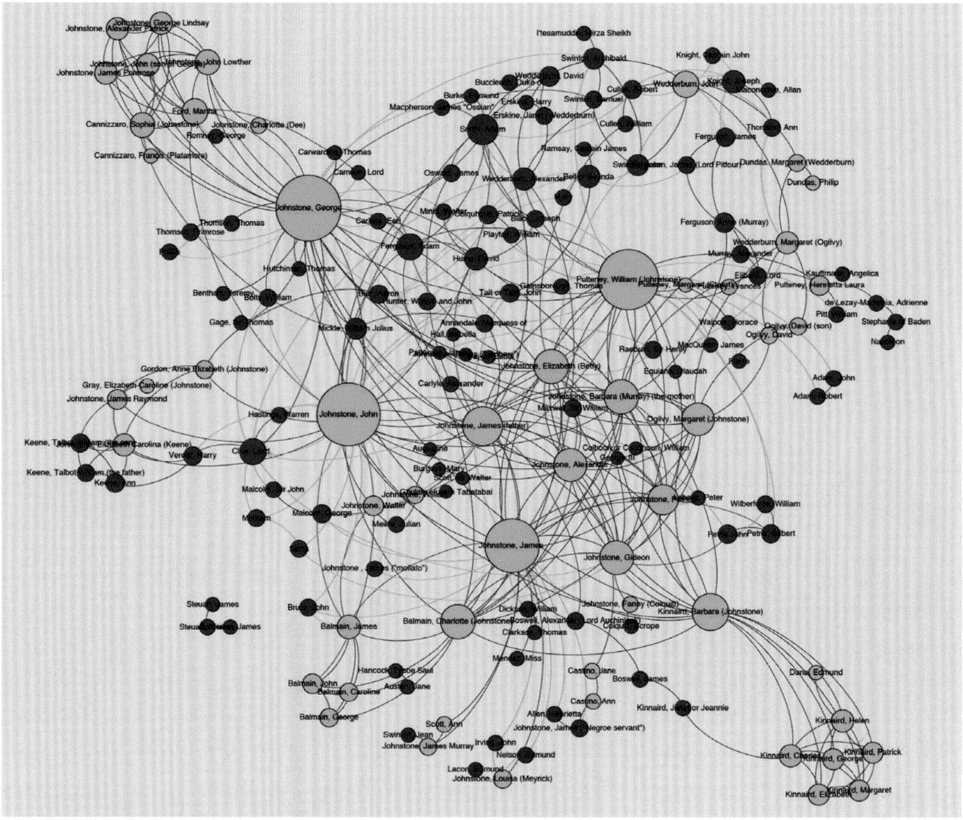

11. (*above*) An eighteenth-century network: the Johnstones are depicted as blue nodes, while their acquaintances (including both friends and rivals) are red. Family links are in purple, professional ones in green. Personal relationships are drawn in red, casual acquaintances are in blue, and relations between slaves and owners are drawn in yellow. Individuals are sized according to how interconnected they were.

12. (*left*) George Washington, Founding Father and Freemason.

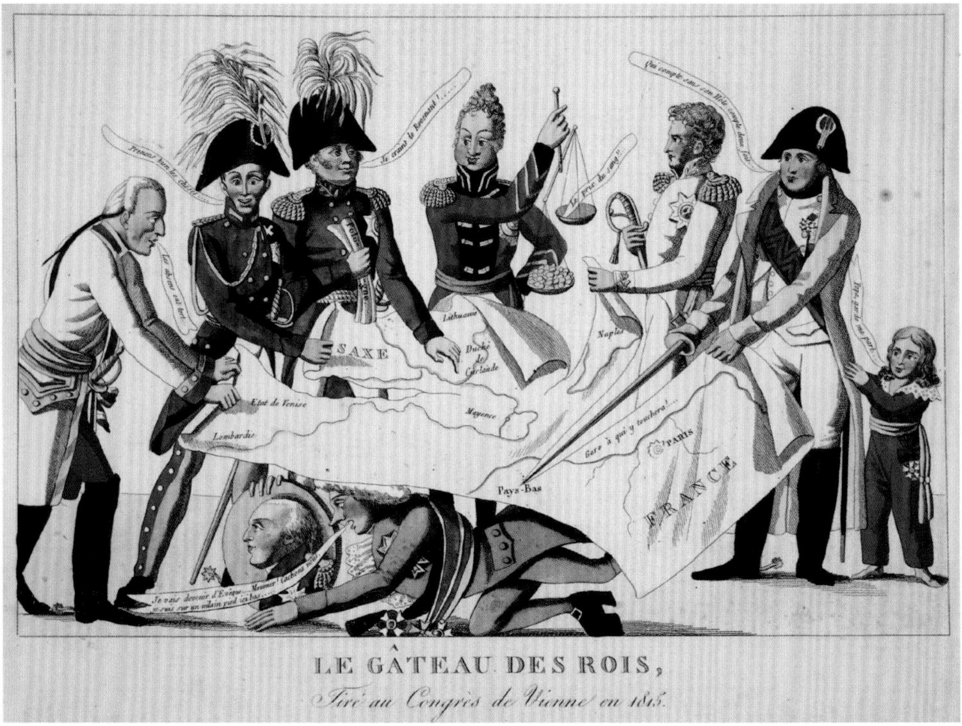

LE GÂTEAU DES ROIS,

Tiré au Congrès de Vienne en 1815.

13. The Congress of Vienna: but the 'cake of kings' could only be cut up with the help of the Rothschilds' financial network.

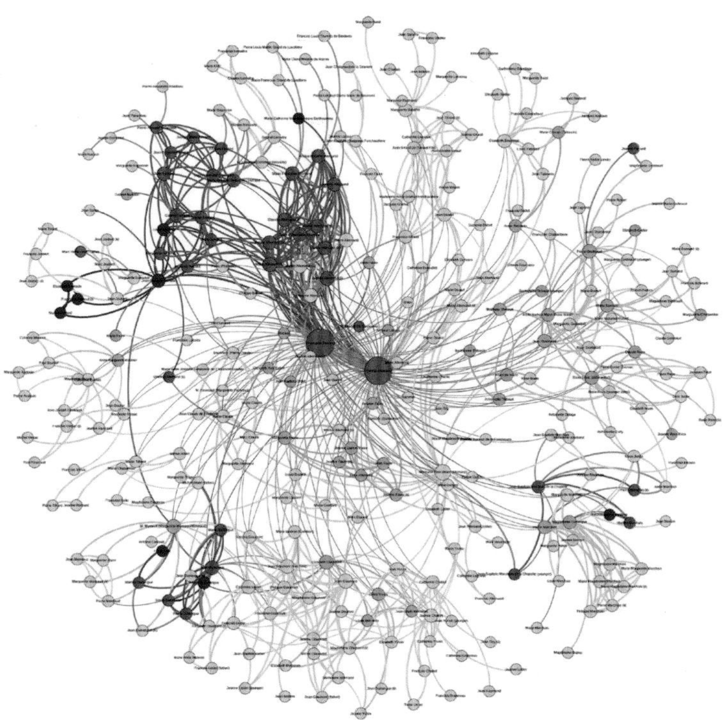

14. Angoulême: a French provincial network of the eighteenth century. Individuals who had travelled outside France are coloured dark red.

that, if they came up with a reasonable proposal, he would support it and would tell France and Russia that, if they did not accept it, Britain would have 'nothing more to do with the consequences'.[16] But by this time it was too late because the Germans had received the news of the Russian general mobilization, after which the time for diplomacy was over. We can imagine a more effective Foreign Secretary – a Castlereagh, perhaps – sending those messages a week earlier, and averting the conflagration. The truth was that Grey was privately too committed to France and Russia to play this part.

So effective was the imperial system of command, control and communication by 1914 that when the emperors (or rather their ministers) resolved to go to war over two arcane issues – the sovereignty of Bosnia–Herzegovina and the neutrality of Belgium – they were able, over more than four years, to mobilize in excess of 70 million men as soldiers or sailors. In France and Germany around a fifth of the pre-war population – close to 80 per cent of adult males – ended up in uniform. The triumph of hierarchy over networks was symbolized by the complete failure of the Second International of socialist parties to prevent the First World War. When the leaders of European socialism met in Brussels at the end of July 1914, they could do little more than admit their own impotence. The Viennese satirist Karl Kraus's observation that 1914 was made possible by the co-existence of thrones and telephones was perceptive.[17] Empowered by technology, the monarchs of Europe were able to march their young male subjects off to Armageddon merely by sending them telegrams. And the many commentators – Keynes amongst them – who thought this war would not last long sorely underestimated the imperial state's ability to sustain industrialized slaughter.

In a global war against the British Empire, the German Reich was at a severe disadvantage, symbolized by the ease with which, in the early hours of 5 August 1914, a British cable ship cut through the five underwater cables that ran from Emden to Vigo, Tenerife, the Azores and the United States. Thereafter, the Germans' telegrams to their embassy in Washington, DC, had to be sent on the US transatlantic cables from Sweden or Denmark, both of which ran through the Eastern Telegraph Company's relay station at Porthcurno in Cornwall, where they were intercepted and sent to the Admiralty's Room

49 to be deciphered. As we have seen, Britain dominated the international communications networks: not only the telegraph but also monetary and financial systems, of which London was the undisputed hub, as well as (though to a lesser extent) the merchant marine. In terms of naval power, too, Germany had failed to close the gap. There were therefore only a small number of ways in which the Germans could hope to win the First World War: by decisively defeating the British, French and Russian armies on land, by disrupting their imports through submarine attacks at sea, or by disrupting their empires by fomenting revolutions within them – in effect activating anti-imperialist networks to disrupt the hierarchical structures of empire. As we shall see, they came close to succeeding in all three respects. But the boldest of their ploys was the plot romanticized in John Buchan's *Greenmantle*, the sequel to *The Thirty-Nine Steps*.

'There is a jehad [*sic*] preparing,' Sir Walter Bullivant, the head of British intelligence, tells Hannay at the beginning of *Greenmantle*. 'The East is waiting for a revelation. It has been promised one. Some star – man, prophecy, or trinket – is coming out of the West. The Germans know, and that is the card with which they are going to astonish the world.'[18] To the modern reader, the idea of a German-orchestrated call to Muslims to rise up in holy war against the British Empire seems far-fetched. It comes as something of a surprise to discover that Buchan based *Greenmantle* on real events.

VI

Plagues and Pipers

35
Greenmantle

In the story of the *Pied Piper of Hamelin*, an exotically dressed rat catcher is hired by a town to lure away the rats that infest the town by playing on his magical pipe. The rats follow the piper's music and are led away to the nearby River Weser, where they drown. However, when the townspeople refuse to pay the piper in full, he performs the same trick with their children, whom he leads away into a cave. All but three are never seen again. The story dates from the thirteenth century and may well be based on real events, though it is not entirely clear what it was that caused the loss of so many children. One plausible hypothesis is that the story is about an outbreak of bubonic plague, which was known to be spread by rats, though there is no mention of rats in the original version of the story; they were a late sixteenth-century addition.

The twentieth century was also a time of plagues – and of pipers. As is well known, the final phase of the First World War coincided with a global pandemic, as a lethal version of the influenza virus swept the world, killing tens of millions of people, particularly the young.* It was not the only plague of the years between 1917 and 1923. A mutant strain of Marxism developed by the Russian

* Unusually, this particular strain of flu was most deadly for people aged between around twenty and forty. An estimated 675,000 Americans died of influenza during the pandemic, ten times as many as died in the world war. Of the US soldiers who died in Europe, half were victims of influenza. The mass mobilization of young men that followed US entry into the war undoubtedly contributed to the rapid spread of the disease, which attacked the lungs and essentially caused victims to drown in their own blood. The first American cases were in an army camp in Kansas in early 1918. By June it had reached India, Australia and New Zealand. Two months later,

Bolsheviks also swept across the Eurasian land mass. New and extreme forms of nationalism produced virulent fascist movements in nearly every European country. So contagious were these ideologies that even fortunate Englishmen in the sequestered courts of Cambridge could be infected. There was an economic plague, too: the plague of hyperinflation, which wrought havoc not only in Germany but also in Austria, Poland and Russia. In the face of these plagues, people turned to pied pipers: men who offered charismatic leadership and drastic solutions. Like the people of medieval Hamelin, however, those who empowered such pipers paid with the lives of their children.

The world before all this had been a world of empires. The conflict that broke out between the European empires in the summer of 1914 was, as we have seen, the result of a breakdown of the international order that had emerged after the Napoleonic Wars, which had elevated a five-node network of great powers above all the other states. To reduce the causes of the war to their bare essentials, Britain failed to play the part of balancer as two rival combinations – Russia plus France and Germany plus Austria–Hungary – went to war over an assassination carried out by Serbian terrorists in the newly acquired and seemingly trivial Habsburg territory of Bosnia–Herzegovina. When it became clear that Germany's planned offensive against France necessitated the violation of Belgian neutrality, Britain intervened on the other side, not so much to uphold the 1839 treaty that had made Belgium neutral, as to prevent a German victory over France and Russia. In military terms, the Germans might have had the capacity to win a continental war, despite the weakness of their allies. They certainly succeeded in inflicting astonishing casualties on the French army in the first six months of the war – far more than sufficed to produce a French collapse in 1870 and 1940. Yet Britain's unmatched resources in terms of finance, manufacturing, shipping and manpower were enough to keep the war going in Western Europe despite the relentless attrition of French fighting capacity – to keep it going, but not to end it. The war itself was contagious. The

a second wave struck all but simultaneously in Boston, Massachusetts, Brest in France and Freetown in Sierra Leone.

vast overseas possessions of the combatant empires ensured its rapid globalization. Other states joined in, too. Before 1914 was over, Montenegro, Japan and the Ottoman Empire entered the war. In May 1915 Italy belatedly chose the Entente side; Bulgaria joined the Central Powers (Germany and Austria–Hungary). Portugal and Romania took up arms with the Entente in the course of 1916. In 1917 the United States was only one of twelve new combatants: the others were Bolivia, Brazil, China, Cuba, Ecuador, Greece, Liberia, Panama, Peru, Siam (now Thailand) and Uruguay. All were aligned against the Central Powers.[1] In the final year of the war, their example was followed by Costa Rica, Guatemala, Haiti, Honduras and Nicaragua. In Europe, only Spain, Switzerland and the Scandinavian countries stayed neutral (see plate 17).

Even before the military stalemate on the Western Front had become apparent, the German government had begun experimenting with what would prove to be the decisive, war-winning weapon. The idea was to destabilize the other side's empires by unleashing an ideological 'virus'. With help from their Ottoman allies, the Germans sought to spark a jihad throughout the British Empire, as well as the French.[2] The plot of John Buchan's *Greenmantle* – which can strike the modern reader as one of his most far-fetched – was therefore based on real events.[3] The Germans were right that something like this would work. Yet their first attempt at triggering a revolution failed. The critical point is that only some of the revolutionary ideas of 1914–1918 went viral, in the sense that they spread fast enough and far enough to destabilize and topple an imperial hierarchy. The call to jihad did not undermine British or French rule in those parts of the Muslim world that they controlled, but the British counterattack in the form of sponsorship of Arab nationalism did indeed undermine the Ottoman Empire, just as the German campaign to spread Bolshevism destroyed the Russian Empire – before sweeping westwards to destroy the German Empire itself. To understand why the first of these initiatives failed while the second succeeded and the third succeeded then backfired, we need to remember that network structures are as important as viruses in determining the speed and extent of a contagion.[4]

Outlandish ideas stand a better chance of success if they come with royal approval. The German Kaiser, William II, had an Orientalist streak that strongly inclined him to romanticize Islam. A visit to the Near East in 1898 so impressed him that he imagined himself as 'Hajji Wilhelm', confiding in his cousin Tsar Nicholas II that he had felt 'profoundly ashamed before the Moslems and that if I had come there without any Religion at all I certainly would have turned Mahommetan!'[5] This kind of Islamophilia was fashionable amongst German scholars, too, notably Carl Heinrich Becker.[6] In addition, there were strategic reasons to draw the Ottoman Empire into the German sphere of influence. Though not a member of Ranke's pentarchy, the 'Sublime Porte'* was in practice an integral part of the network of European great powers. Indeed, its future had been the central issue of nineteenth-century diplomacy: the so-called 'Eastern Question'. 'Either the German flag will fly over the fortifications of the Bosphorus,' William declared in 1913, 'or I shall suffer the same sad fate as the great exile on the island of St Helena' (an allusion to his hero, Napoleon).[7] There appeared to be economic opportunities in Turkey, too, hence the German scheme for a railway linking Berlin to Baghdad, construction of which was well under way (though in some financial and technical difficulties) by the summer of 1914.[8]

For William, however, it was the notion of Islam as an ally that was especially alluring. Encouraged by Max von Oppenheim – the *Legationsrat* at the German consulate in Cairo – William became fascinated by the idea that the Muslim subjects of the British Empire could be turned against it by a summons to jihad.[9] Indeed, this was the Kaiser's first thought on learning that Britain would not remain neutral in the war that was breaking out on the Continent. Incensed by the prospect of the 'encirclement of Germany', William scribbled down what amounted to the plot of *Greenmantle*. 'Our consuls in Turkey and India, agents etc., must fire the whole Mohammedan world to fierce rebellion against this hated lying, conscienceless nation of shopkeepers; for if we are to be bled to death, England shall at least lose

* Contemporary European diplomats often referred to the Ottoman government as the 'Sublime Porte', a French translation of the Turkish *Bâbıâli* ('High Gate', or 'Gate of the Eminent'), the name of the gate in Istanbul that led to the buildings housing the principal departments of government, including the foreign ministry.

India.'[10] The idea was taken up in August by Helmuth von Moltke, the chief of the general staff, who issued a memorandum on the need to 'awaken the fanaticism of Islam' in the Muslim populations of the empires fighting on the other side. In October 1914, Oppenheim responded with a 136-page top-secret 'Memorandum on the Revolutionizing of the Islamic Territories of Our Enemies', in which he described Islam as 'one of our most important weapons'. He envisaged religious revolts in India and Egypt, as well as the Russian Caucasus.[11] Becker chimed in with a pamphlet entitled *Deutschland und der Islam.*

This idea was much less fantastic than it appears in hindsight. True, it was by no means a foregone conclusion that the Ottoman Empire would join the Central Powers.[12] Indeed, Hans Freiherr von Wangenheim, the German ambassador, and General Liman von Sanders, the head of the German military mission there, were rather dubious about the benefits of an Ottoman alliance. But the 'Young Turks' – who had been in control of the Empire since the forced restoration of constitutional government by Sultan Abdul Hamid II in 1908 – had good reasons for allying themselves with Berlin. The Young Turk leaders, Ismail Enver and Mehmed Taalat, argued that the Entente powers – Britain, France and Russia – were the ones with the lethal designs on Ottoman territory, whereas the Germans and Austrians were honest brokers who might countenance the restoration of at least some of the possessions lost since the 1870s.[13] With the Kaiser's encouragement, an alliance was hastily concluded on 2 August.[14] Moreover, Enver and his colleagues were fully persuaded that religious sentiment could be exploited as a source of Ottoman power. They saw it as the crucial bond between Turks and Arabs.[15] They also saw it as legitimizing their genocidal campaign against Christians within the Empire, particularly the Armenians. As Wangenheim reported in mid-August, 'the revolutionizing of the Islamic world desired by His Majesty is prepared and has been for some time. These measures have been undertaken under strict secrecy.'[16] His only concern was that any massacres of Armenians would be blamed on the Germans. [17]

On 14 November 1914, at Istanbul's Fatih Mosque, Urgüplü Hayri Bey, the Seykh-ul-Islam of the Ottoman Empire, presented Sultan Mehmed Reshad V with the Sword of the Prophet in a ceremony that formally unleashed the jihad against the Entente.[18] With an 'immense crowd' outside the mosque, a fatwa was read aloud which took the form of a series of questions:

> The Moslem subjects of Russia, of France, of England, and of all the countries that side with them in their land and sea attacks dealt against the Caliphate for the purpose of annihilating Islam, must these subjects, too, take part in the Holy War against the respective governments from which they depend?
>
> Yes.
>
> The Moslems who in the present war are under England, France, Russia, Serbia, Montenegro, and those who give aid to these countries by waging war against Germany and Austria, allies of Turkey, do they deserve to be punished by the wrath of God as being the cause of harm and damage to the Caliphate and to Islam?
>
> Yes.[19]

This was, to be sure, an unusual kind of jihad, since it applied only to infidels living in specific European empires, and not to those in Germany and Austria. It also involved attacking Muslims who were fighting on behalf of the Entente.[20] Belgian citizens were legitimate targets, but not Americans living in Turkey.[21] On the other hand, there is no gainsaying the effort that the Ottoman authorities put into disseminating the call to arms.[22] Moreover, the German Foreign Office's Intelligence Office for the Orient had been able to recruit an impressive number of Muslim collaborators, including the Tunisian cleric Salih al-Sharif al-Tunisia and the Egyptian scholar 'Abd al-'Aziz Shawish.[23]

From the vantage point of Max von Oppenheim, the prospects for global jihad were dazzlingly bright. A real-life Buchan villain, Oppenheim was the grandson of the Jewish banker Simon Oppenheim. Having made his name as a travel writer and amateur archaeologist,* he had successfully parlayed his knowledge of the Muslim world into a glamorous double life: in Berlin he was the Kaiser's favourite

* It was Oppenheim who discovered and excavated the immensely rich site at Tell Halaf in north-eastern Syria, the location of the ancient Aramaean city-state of Guzana or Gozan.

intellectual, while in Cairo he relished the pleasures of the exotic East, including his own harem. Bemoaning 'the stage of degradation to which the world of Islam has arrived', Oppenheim inveighed against the Entente empires in a 1915 pamphlet that was evidently intended for widespread distribution. In India, Egypt and Sudan, 'hundreds of millions of Muslims' had fallen 'into the grasp of the enemies of God, the infidel English'. The people of the Maghreb had been subjugated by the French, those 'enemies of God and his Apostle'. Muslims in the Crimea, the Caucasus and Central Asia toiled under the Tsarist knout. The Italians oppressed the Senussi, a Sufi order and tribe in Tripoli.[24] The time had come for all these Muslims to fight back. Oppenheim and his collaborators churned out numerous pamphlets in this vein in multiple languages.[25]

Nor were the Germans content with writing propaganda. In 1915, dressed as a Bedouin, Oppenheim set out from Damascus to spread his message in rural Syria, going as far as the Sinai Peninsula and the environs of Medina.[26] His protégé Carl Prüfer sought to whip up anti-British sentiment in Egypt. Major Friedrich Klein was despatched to southern Iraq to meet the Shi'a mujtahids of Karbala and Najaf. Consul Wilhelm Wassmuss made similar efforts in Iran.[27] Edgar Pröbster, the German consul in the Moroccan city of Fes, was sent by submarine to convince the sheikh of the Senussi to take up arms against the Entente and, in a second expedition, to achieve the same feat with the Moroccan Hiba and Suss tribes. There were even German missions to Sudan and the Horn of Africa.[28] Most ambitious of all was the expedition to Afghanistan led by Oskar Ritter von Niedermayer, a Bavarian artillery officer who had travelled widely in the East, and Werner Otto von Hentig, a diplomat who had served in Beijing, Constantinople and Tehran. Their goal was to persuade the Afghan king, Amir Habibullah, to declare full independence from British influence and enter the war on the side of the Central Powers.[29] Accompanied by a party of Turks led by Captain Kazim Orbay, three Indian revolutionaries and several Pashtun tribesmen, Niedermayer and Hentig arrived in Kabul on 7 September 1915. The final component of the German strategy was a sustained effort to win over Muslim prisoners-of-war from the Entente armies, who were gathered together in a special camp called Halbmondlager (Camp

Crescent) in Wünsdorf – the site of the first mosque in Germany, an elaborate wooden structure modelled on the Dome of the Rock in Jerusalem.[30] Leaflets like the one written by an Algerian deserter named Lieutenant Boukabouya were also dropped on trenches known to be manned by French colonial troops. German soldiers were trained to shout across no-man's-land in Arabic: 'Why are you fighting us? We are your brothers, we are Muslims like you.'[31]

Nor were these efforts doomed to fail. True, Wangenheim suspected that the Sultan-Caliph's appeal would 'coax only a few Moslems from behind the warm stove'.[32] But Oppenheim's schemes cannot be dismissed as mere 'fantasy'.[33] As a tool for mobilizing the diverse groups within the Ottoman Empire, the call for jihad was in many ways a success. 'Should our enemies wish to soil our land with their filthy feet,' Enver wrote to Nakibzade Talib Bey of Basra on 10 August 1914, 'I am convinced that Islamic and Ottoman honour and strength will destroy them.'[34] That proved to be true. The ill-starred British invasion at Gallipoli might conceivably have succeeded if the Ottoman Empire had still been the 'sick man of Europe'. Religion was certainly one of the sources of Turkish morale in that bloody campaign. The call to jihad also elicited a strong positive response from the Shi'ite tribes of the mid-Euphrates – the al-Fatla, the Bani Hasan, the Bani Huchaym and the Khaza'il – as well as those tribes in the lower Euphrates dominated by the Muntafiq confederation. On 19 November 1914, the Grand Mujtahid Muhammad Kadhin Yazdi wrote to Sheikh Khaz'al of Muhammara, explicitly urging him to 'make every effort to repel the Infidels'.[35]

Yet the fact remains that the German vision of a generalized Muslim revolt against the Entente failed to materialize. Why was this? A part of the answer was a mixture of German incompetence and effective British and French counter-espionage. The explorer Leo Frobenius only barely avoided capture on his way to Eritrea and was deported back to Europe by the Italian authorities.[36] Alois Musil, an Austrian Orientalist sent to woo the feuding Arab leaders Ibn Saud and Ibn Rashid, not only failed to do so, but wholly misread their intentions.[37] In Iran, Wassmuss's code book fell into British hands, along with a box containing 'thousands of violently inflammatory pamphlets printed in English, Urdu, Hindu, Punjabi and Sikh, and addressed to the Indian Army', with a 'special appeal to the Mohammedans in that army, urging them to join in a Holy War against the infidel English'.[38]

However, there was a more profound problem. The reality was that the call to jihad simply did not resonate very far beyond the core Ottoman provinces.[39] For example, having leased Abadan to the Anglo-Persian Oil Company, Sheikh Khaz'al opted to ignore the Grand Mujtahid's appeal to Muslim unity and threw in his lot with the British. Although some French officials initially worried that their North African subjects might be influenced by German propaganda, it soon became obvious that they were just as ready to believe – in the words of Lieutenant Si Brahim, addressing North African soldiers at Arles – that 'in taking up arms for our country' they were 'defending the interests of their faith, the honour of their homes, and the integrity of the lands of Islam'.[40] In Libya, the Senussi were eventually prevailed upon to take up arms, but only in return for money, and they soon melted away when they encountered effective British resistance. In Afghanistan, the German mission was kept waiting for weeks, after which the Amir summoned a Loya Jirga of tribal leaders, which voted to remain neutral in the war.[41] As for India, the British had no difficulty in persuading leading Muslims – notably the Aga Khan, the Nawab Bahadur of Dacca and the Council of the All-India Muslim League – to denounce the call to jihad as a cynical German ploy.[42]

In short, the 'pan-Islamism' that had been touted before the war by men like Oppenheim proved to be a desert mirage. No amount of pamphlets could activate a network that simply did not exist outside the imaginations of Orientalists. Like Oppenheim, whom she in some ways resembled, the British traveller Gertrude Bell called Islam 'the electric current by which the transmission of sentiment is effected', and argued that 'its potency is increased by the fact that there is little or no sense of territorial nationality to counterbalance it'. More experienced colonial administrators were sceptical. 'As a factor in British policy,' argued Ronald Storrs, the Oriental secretary to the British consul-general in Egypt, 'the doctrine of the caliphate – of pan-Islamic theocracy – was mainly the creation of the India Office.'[43] Even that did an injustice to the India 'hands'. In a memorandum written in June 1916, T. W. Holderness – the under-secretary at the India Office – argued that 'both from the past history of Mohammedanism and from the events of the present war . . . pan-Islamism as a motive force can easily be overrated'. Holderness astutely put his finger on the Muslim world's 'want of cohesion and its sectarian divisions and animosities', arguing that, on the whole, Muslims were 'inspired by nationality rather than by creed'.[44] That turned out to be true in the all-important region of the Hejaz, the location of the Islamic holy places of Mecca and Medina.

The Germans had sought to whip up the Muslim subjects of all three of their enemies' empires into a religious insurrection. This failed, and nowhere more so than in Mecca itself. The British pursued a more limited objective, which was to persuade the Arab subjects of the Ottoman Empire to defect. This worked. Even before the war began, Hussein bin Ali, the sixty-year-old Sharif of Mecca, had sent his second son, Abdullah, to convey to the British that he might consider rebelling against his Ottoman overlords. A social conservative, Hussein deeply distrusted the Young Turks in Istanbul, with their modernizing schemes. Indeed, he suspected them of plotting to depose him and end his Hashemite family's suzerainty over the Hejaz.[45] On 24 September 1914, the Secretary of State for War, Lord Kitchener, sent a secret letter via Storrs in Cairo to Abdullah to ask Hussein if 'he, his father and Arabs of the Hejaz would be with us or against us', should Turkey join the Central Powers. The letter concluded with a bold hint: 'It may be that an Arab of true race will assume the Caliphate at Mecca or Medina and so good may come with the help of God out of all evil that is now occurring.'[46]

What Kitchener probably had in mind was to establish Hussein in the same kind of subordinate relationship to the British Empire that had become familiar in south Asia and sub-Saharan Africa in the nineteenth century. That was not what Hussein envisaged. Ottoman rule over the Arabs was far from defunct,[47] but the alternative to it was not British rule but Arab independence. This was the option under discussion when Faisal, Hussein's elder son, met secretly with representatives of the Arab nationalist secret military society al-Ahd and the civilian al-Fatat movement. The Ottoman offer was essentially obedience or deposition. The Arabists offered more: if Hussein could persuade the British to accept the vast independent Arab state defined in their Damascus Protocol (which included not only the whole Arabian peninsula but also Mesopotamia and much of Syria), then they would join his revolt against the Sultan and make him 'king of the Arabs' when the war was over.[48] The momentous decision of Sir Henry McMahon, the High Commissioner in Egypt, to make this deal with Hussein – albeit after a protracted wrangle about the precise borders of the 'Arab Khalifate' – was in part a response to the German–Ottoman call for jihad, as well as to the panic induced by successive British defeats at Gallipoli and Kut al-Amara.[49] In the words of Gilbert Clayton, director of intelligence at the Cairo Residency, 'If we succeed in this we shall have robbed the Germans and Turks of Arab support, and shall have precluded all possibility of their being able to raise against us, and against the French and Italians, a genuine Jehad, engineered from the Holy Places of Islam . . . I think rather too much stress has been laid on what I may call the "positive" advantages of an alliance with the Arabs, and that the very great "negative" advantages of denying them to the Germans and Turks have been rather overlooked.'[50] The British agreement with the Hashemites, along with the separate agreements with France regarding Mesopotamia and Syria* and with the Zionist movement to create a Jewish national home in Palestine, laid a new political foundation for the region that we now know as the 'Middle East'.[51] It would endure for a century.

The Arab Revolt that began on 5 June 1916 beat the Germans at their own game and turned the tide of the war against the Ottomans.[52] But to understand why Britain succeeded (with French support) where the Germans and Ottomans had failed, we need to appreciate more than merely the military successes made famous by

* McMahon accepted the boundaries proposed by Hussein with the following exclusions: he ruled out Cilicia (today in south-eastern Turkey) and those 'portions of Syria lying to the west of the districts of Damascus, Homs, Hama and Aleppo' in which France had declared its interest, and upheld British claims to the provinces of Baghdad and Basra in Mesopotamia. The Anglo-French designs on Syria and Mesopotamia were incorporated in the notorious May 1916 agreement between Sir Mark Sykes and François Georges-Picot, which envisaged the complete post-war partition of the Ottoman Empire.

T. E. Lawrence, the most avid British proponent of Arab independence.[53] We need also to appreciate that Lawrence was working with an active network – that of the Arab nationalists – while Oppenheim and his confederates were trying to activate a largely dormant and disconnected one: the *Ummah* of all Muslims. The fatal mistake that the Germans made was to underestimate the extent to which Arab consciousness had undermined the formal structures of Ottoman rule even before the outbreak of war.[54] Oppenheim had flattered himself that he knew the Muslim world, but he had completely misread the intentions of the Hashemites. To have proclaimed a global holy war without first securing the holy places was an elementary blunder worthy of one of Buchan's caricature Teutons; just as it took a Buchanesque hero to 'live in the dress of Arabs, and to imitate their mental foundation' as Lawrence was able to.

36
The Plague

All but one of the German plots to win the First World War by subterfuge failed. The 'German–Hindu Plot' to send arms to Indian nationalists was a flop, as was the German-funded invasion of India from Siam. The German consignment of 25,000 captured Russian rifles to Ireland could not make a revolution of the doomed Easter Rising. Most hopeless of all was the ham-fisted bid to bring Mexico into the war by proposing the reconquest of New Mexico, Texas and Arizona, details of which were intercepted by British intelligence and relayed to the United States because, as we have seen, German transatlantic telegrams had to pass through a British relay station. Yet the one German plot that worked proved to be so successful that it very nearly revolutionized the whole world. This was the plot to send the Bolshevik leader Vladimir Ilyich Lenin, then living in exile in Switzerland, back to Russia, in the wake of the February 1917 Revolution that overthrew Tsar Nicholas II.

Having been alerted to the potential of Lenin's doctrine of 'revolutionary defeatism' by two professional revolutionaries named Alexander Helphand ('Parvus') and Alexander Kesküla, the German government supplied Lenin not only with a railway ticket from Zurich to Petrograd – via Frankfurt, Berlin, Sassnitz and Stockholm – but also with lavish funds to subvert the new provisional government.* Instead of having Lenin and his nineteen associates arrested on arrival, as they richly deserved to be, the new Russian provisional

* It has been estimated that 50 million gold marks ($12m) were channelled to Lenin and his associates, much of it laundered through a Russian import business run by a woman named Evgeniya Sumenson. Adjusting on the basis of unskilled wage inflation, that is equivalent to around $800m today.

government dithered. The Bolsheviks set to work, buying a centrally located new headquarters (the former residence of the ballerina Mathilde Kshesinskaya, a noted royal courtesan) and a private printing press, and literally handing out banknotes to get people to join their demonstrations. To an extent that most accounts still underrate, the Bolshevik Revolution was a German-financed operation, though it was greatly facilitated by the incompetence of the Russian liberals.[1] Lenin's goose should have been cooked after the failure of the first Bolshevik coup attempt in early July and his exposure as a German agent in the newspaper *Zhivoe Slovo*, which led to formal charges of treason against him and ten other Bolshevik leaders. But Alexander Kerensky, the Socialist Revolutionary minister of justice who took control of the provisional government on 7 July, lacked the killer instinct. Convinced by a wholly unreliable intermediary that the new commander-in-chief, General Lavr Kornilov, was planning a military coup, Kerensky relieved him of his post and allowed the provisional executive committee (Ispolkom) of the Petrograd soviet (workers' council) to give the Bolsheviks what amounted to an amnesty. Leon Trotsky, a gifted Menshevik journalist who had thrown in his lot with Lenin, was released from jail. In the second week of October, once he was sure the treason charges against him had been dropped, Lenin returned from Finland, where he had fled after the July Days. Thereafter, they and their confederates' plotting to overthrow the provisional government and hand 'all power to the soviets' was scarcely concealed. In the early hours of 25 October 1917, following a half-baked attempt by Kerensky to crack down on them once again, the Bolsheviks staged a coup d'état of their own. Each side tried to cut the phone lines of the other side, but it was the number of armed supporters that decided the issue. The provisional government had the Women's Death Battalion on its side, but the Bolsheviks had more men and the added advantage of the guns of the Peter and Paul Fortress, which they trained on the Winter Palace.[2]

It is now well known that fewer people were killed in the October Revolution than were killed in the shooting of Sergei Eisenstein's tenth-anniversary film about it.* Yet it would be wrong to underplay the significance of the original event. The first astonishing thing about the Bolshevik Revolution is the speed with which it spread. Bolshevik slogans and placards began to appear in the Russian northern army as early as 18 April. As the provisional government geared up for an offensive into Galicia, officers reported the first outbreaks of *shkurnyi bol'shevizm* ('skin Bolshevism', adopted by men who wanted to save their own skins). The commander of the Twelfth Army complained of 'the strengthened agitation of the Bolsheviks, who have woven themselves into a firm nest' – a revealing image.[3] Reinforcements from Petrograd arrived at the front line with Bolshevik banners bearing the slogan 'Down with the war and the provisional government!'[4] A single deserter, named A. Y. Semashko, was able to recruit 500 men in the First Machine Gun Regiment to the Bolshevik cause.[5] Though the epidemic was momentarily checked by the fiasco of the July Days, Kerensky's arrest of Kornilov re-established the Bolsheviks' credibility in the lower ranks. The Fifth Army was hit by a wave of desertions. Bolshevik 'commissars' seized control of its telegraph equipment. To army intelligence officers, it seemed as if a 'Bolshevik wave' was sweeping away all discipline.[6] By the end of September, support for Lenin's party had surged sufficiently in Russia's major cities to give it control of the Moscow and Petrograd soviets. It was also strong in the Kronstadt naval base and the Baltic Fleet. Only amongst the vast peasantry and the Cossacks did the Bolsheviks lack backers – which helps explain the rapid descent of Russia into an urban–rural civil war in the course of 1918.† Essentially, the Bolshevik virus travelled by train and telegraph, and literate soldiers, sailors and workers were most susceptible to it. The catch for the Germans was that, like mustard gas blown the wrong way by a changing wind, the Bolshevik plague could infect their soldiers, sailors and workers, too. When it became clear – as it did in the

* There was in fact much more serious fighting in Moscow, including fierce close-quarter combat within the Kremlin.

† In the elections to the Constituent Assembly on 12 November 1917, the Socialist Revolutionaries won 40 per cent of the 41 million votes cast, to the Bolsheviks' 24 per cent. The peasants regarded the SRs as their party.

summer of 1918 – that even total Russian collapse could not avert the defeat of the Central Powers, Soviet-style governments were also proclaimed in Budapest, Munich and Hamburg. The red flag was even raised above Glasgow City Chambers. Exhilarated, Lenin dreamed of a 'Union of Soviet Republics of Europe and Asia'. Trotsky extravagantly declared that 'the road to Paris and London lies via the towns of Afghanistan, the Punjab and Bengal'.[7] Even distant Seattle and Buenos Aires were rocked by strikes. This was a proletarian pandemic.

The second astonishing thing was how ruthlessly the Bolsheviks turned their revolutionary network into a new hierarchical system, in many respects much harsher than the old Tsarist regime. The Bolshevik Party grew exponentially in size after 1917, but even as it expanded it grew more centralized – an outcome Lenin had anticipated in his pre-war tract *What is to be Done?* Setbacks in 1918 legitimized Lenin's urge to play the part of Robespierre, assuming dictatorial powers in the spirit of 'the Revolution endangered'. On 17 July 1918 the deposed Tsar and his family were shot dead in the basement of the house where they were being held captive in Yekaterinburg. Four days later, there was a mass execution of 428 Socialist Revolutionaries in Yaroslavl.[8] The only way to ensure that peasants handed over their grain to feed the Red Army, Lenin insisted, was to order exemplary executions of so-called 'kulaks', the supposedly rapacious capitalist peasants whom it suited the Bolsheviks to demonize. 'How can you make a revolution without firing squads?' Lenin asked.[9] 'If we can't shoot a White Guard saboteur, what sort of great revolution is it? Nothing but talk and a bowl of mush.' Convinced that the Bolsheviks would not 'come out the victors' if they did not employ 'the harshest kind of revolutionary terror', he called explicitly for 'mass terror against the kulaks, priests and White Guards'. 'Black marketeers' were to be 'shot on the spot'. On 10 August 1918 he sent a telegram to Bolshevik leaders in Penza that speaks volumes:

> The kulak uprising in [your] five districts must be crushed without pity . . . An example must be made. 1) Hang (and I mean hang so that *the people can see*) *not less than 100* known kulaks, rich men, bloodsuckers. 2) Publish their names. 3) Take *all* their grain. 4) Identify

> hostages . . . Do this so that for hundreds of miles around the people see, tremble, know and cry: they are killing and will go on killing the bloodsucking kulaks . . . P.S. Find tougher people.[10]

Kulaks, Lenin declared, were 'blood-suckers, spiders, leeches and vampires'. Things only got worse after the unsuccessful assassination attempt against Lenin on 30 August by a Socialist Revolutionary named Fanny Kaplan.

At the heart of the new tyranny was the 'All-Russian Extraordinary Commission for Combating Counter-Revolution and Sabotage' – the Cheka for short. Under Felix Dzerzhinsky the Bolsheviks created a new kind of political police that had no compunction about simply executing suspects. 'The Cheka', as one of its founders explained, 'is not an investigating commission, a court, or a tribunal. It is a fighting organ on the internal front of the civil war . . . It does not judge, it strikes. It does not pardon, it destroys all who are caught on the other side of the barricade.'[11] The Bolshevik newspaper *Krasnaya Gazeta* declared: 'Without mercy, without sparing, we will kill our enemies in scores of hundreds. Let them be thousands, let them drown themselves in their own blood. For the blood of Lenin . . . let there be floods of blood of the bourgeoisie – more blood, as much as possible.'[12] Dzerzhinsky was happy to oblige. On 23 September 1919, to give just one example, sixty-seven alleged counter-revolutionaries were summarily shot. At the top of the list was Nikolai Shchepkin, a liberal member of the Duma (parliament) that had been set up after 1905. The announcement of their execution was couched in the most vehement language, accusing Shchepkin and his alleged confederates of 'hiding like bloodthirsty spiders [and] put[ting] their webs everywhere from the Red Army to schools and universities'.[13] Between 1918 and 1920, as many as 300,000 such political executions were carried out.[14] These included not just members of rival parties, but also fellow Bolsheviks who were so rash as to challenge the new dictatorship of the party leadership. By 1920 there were already more than a hundred *kontsentratsionnye lageri* for the 'rehabilitation' of 'unreliable elements'. Their locations were carefully chosen to expose prisoners to the harshest possible conditions – places like the former monastery of Kholmogory, in the icy wastes beside the White Sea. Thus was the Gulag born.

Iosif Vissarionovich Dzhugashvili – Stalin ('man of steel'), to his fellow revolutionaries – was not the intended heir to Lenin as leader (*vozhd'*) of the Soviet system. He lacked the charisma and flair of other leading Bolsheviks. When Lenin made Stalin 'general secretary' of the Central Committee in April 1922, however, he gravely underestimated his skill as a bureaucrat. As the only person with positions on all three of the most powerful Party institutions – the politburo, orgburo and secretariat – and, as the apparatchik with by far the largest staff, Stalin set about establishing his control by a combination of administrative rigour and personal deviousness. He quickly established his loyalists in the localities and, crucially, in the secret police. He developed the list of senior functionaries known as the *nomenklatura* so that (as he told the Twelfth Party Congress in April 1923) 'people who occupy these positions are capable of implementing directives, comprehending those directives, accepting those directives as their own and bringing them to life'.[15] The business directorate gave him power over much more than just officials' expenses; its 'secret department', hidden behind steel doors, became an agency for intra-party denunciations and investigations. And the government phone system – the *vertutshka* – and telegram cipher unit gave him control over communications, including the power to eavesdrop on others.

Like Lenin, Stalin was the product of a clandestine revolutionary network. He had suffered his share of hardships as a young conspirator against the Tsarist regime. It was a distinctive feature of the twentieth-century dictators that, perhaps because of their own roots underground, they saw conspiracies against themselves everywhere. The alleged spies and saboteurs convicted in show trials like the Shakhty Trial (1928), the Industrial Party Trial (1930) and the Metro-Vickers Trial (1933) were victims of only the most spectacular of innumerable pseudo-legal and extra-legal procedures. By defining the slightest grumble as treason or counter-revolution, the Stalinist system was in a position to send whole armies of Soviet citizens to the Gulag. Files now available in the Russian State Archives show just how the system worked. Berna Klauda was a little old lady from Leningrad; she could scarcely have looked less like a subversive element. In 1937, however, she was sentenced to ten years in the Perm Gulag for expressing anti-government sentiments.[16] 'Anti-Soviet

Agitation' was the least of the political crimes for which one could be convicted. More serious was 'Counter-revolutionary Activity'; worse still, 'Counter-revolutionary Terrorist Activity' and, worst of all, 'Trotskyist Terrorist Activity'. In fact, the overwhelming majority of people convicted for such offences were guilty – if they were guilty of anything at all – of trivial misdemeanours: a word out of turn to a superior, an overheard joke about Stalin, a complaint about some aspect of the all-pervasive system, at worst some petty economic infraction like 'speculation' (buying and reselling goods). Only a tiny fraction of political prisoners were genuinely opposed to the regime – revealingly, little more than 1 per cent of camp inmates in 1938 had higher education; a third were illiterate. By 1937 there were quotas for arrests just as there were quotas for steel production. Crimes were simply made up to fit the punishments. Prisoners became mere outputs, referred to by the NKVD* as 'Accounts' (male prisoners) and 'Books' (pregnant female prisoners). At the height of the Gulag system, there were 476 camp systems scattered all over the Soviet Union, each composed of hundreds of individual camps. All told, around 18 million men, women and children passed through the Gulag under Stalin's rule. Taking into account the six or seven million Soviet citizens who were sent into exile, the share of the population who experienced some kind of penal servitude under Stalin approached 15 per cent.[17]

No one was safe. Lenin had first introduced the practice of 'purging' the party periodically, to get rid of 'idlers, hooligans, adventurers, drunkards and thieves'.[18] Stalin, who compulsively mistrusted his fellow Communists, went much further. Few groups were more ruthlessly persecuted in the 1930s than those Old Bolsheviks who had been Stalin's own comrades in the decisive days of revolution and civil war. Senior Party functionaries lived in a state of perpetual insecurity, never knowing when they might fall victim to Stalin's paranoia. Those who had been most loyal to the Party were as likely to be arrested and imprisoned as the most notorious criminal. Loyal

* *Narodnyi Kommissariat Vnutrennikh Del*, the People's Commissariat for Internal Affairs. The Cheka had been renamed the GPU in 1922, then OGPU (1923). In 1934 it became the NKVD.

Leninists were charged with being 'wreckers' loyal to the imperialist powers or 'Trotskyites' in league with Stalin's disgraced and exiled arch-rival (whom he finally succeeded in having murdered in 1940). What had begun as a crackdown on corrupt or inefficient officials in 1933 escalated after the murder of the Leningrad Party boss, Sergei Kirov, in December 1934 into a bloody and self-perpetuating purge. One after another, the men and women who had been in the vanguard of the Revolution were arrested, tortured and interrogated until they were induced to confess to some 'crime' and to denounce yet more of their comrades, and then shot. Between January 1935 and June 1941, there were just under 20 million arrests and at least 7 million executions in the Soviet Union. In 1937–8 alone, the quota for 'enemies of the people' to be executed was set at 356,105, though the actual number who lost their lives was more than twice that.[19] Of the 394 members of the Executive Committee of the Communist International in January 1936, 223 had fallen victim to the Terror by April 1938, as had forty-one of the sixty-eight German Communist leaders who had fled to the Soviet Union after 1933.

At the height of Stalin's Terror, 'public welfare' meant total private insecurity. Literally no one could feel safe – least of all the men who ran the NKVD. Genrikh Yagoda was shot as a Trotskyite in 1938; Nikolai Yezhov, his successor, was shot as a British spy in 1940; Lavrenti Beria was shot shortly after Stalin's own death. Those who survived this life 'beneath the gun' were not necessarily the conformists. They were merely lucky. Among those arrested were fifty-three members of the Leningrad Society for the Deaf and Dumb. The charges against this alleged 'fascist organization' was that they had conspired with the German secret service to blow up Stalin and other Politburo members with a home-made bomb during the Revolution Day parade in Red Square. Thirty-four of them were shot; the rest were sent to the camps for ten or more years. What had in fact happened was that the chairman of the Society had informed on some members who had been selling trinkets on local trains to make ends meet. This denunciation led to the NKVD's involvement. The chairman himself was subsequently implicated in the alleged conspiracy and shot. The following year the NKVD decided that the original investigation itself was suspect. The local police were then arrested.[20]

By the late 1930s, Stalin had turned the Soviet Union into a vast slave camp, with himself as commandant. It was possible for him to sit on the balcony of his Sochi dacha and dictate an order that would immediately be sent as a telegram to Moscow, where it would be turned into a formal edict, which would then be distributed down the pyramidal hierarchy of the Soviet Communist Party and, if necessary, to Communist parties abroad. Local officials did not dare ignore such an order for fear that their failure to carry it out would subsequently be discovered, leading inevitably to investigation, prosecution, conviction and quite possibly execution.[21] Stalin's power consisted of three distinct elements: total control of the party bureaucracy, total control of the means of communication – with the Kremlin telephone network as the central hub – and total control of a secret police staffed by men who themselves lived in fear. No Oriental despot had wielded such complete personal power over an empire, because no previous hierarchy had been able to make participation in unofficial networks – even suspected participation – so terrifyingly dangerous.

37
The Leader Principle

Fascism, too, began as a network, especially in Germany, where popular support for Hitler grew exponentially during the Depression. Most fascist regimes, beginning with Benito Mussolini's in Italy, started out by royal or aristocratic appointment and then swiftly centralized power. National Socialism was different. No other fascist parties came close to achieving the electoral success of the National Socialists. In terms of votes, fascism was a disproportionately German phenomenon; add together all the individual votes cast in Europe for fascist or other extreme nationalist parties between 1930 and 1935, and a staggering 96 per cent were cast by German-speakers.[1] In the wake of the hyperinflation of 1923, many voters had drifted away from the middle-class parties of the centre-right and centre-left, disillusioned with the horse-trading between business and labour that seemed to dominate Weimar politics. There was a proliferation of splinter parties and special interest groups, a slow process of fission that was the prelude to the political explosion of 1930, when the Nazi share of the vote leapt to seven times what it had been in 1928. The growth of party membership had a similar exponential quality. In 1928, the NSDAP had 96,918 members. By January 1933 membership had increased eightfold to 849,009 and it grew by a factor of nearly three in the following two years, as opportunists rushed to join the winning party. It continued to grow until the very end of the Third Reich, from 2.5 million in 1935 to 5.3 million in 1939, 7.1 million in 1941, 7.3 million in 1943, and more than 8 million in May 1945. Readership of the party newspaper, the *Völkische Beobachter*, followed a similar trajectory. Having reached 330,000 by 1933, it exceeded 1 million by 1940 and sold about 1.7 million copies a day in 1944.[2]

Contrary to the old claims that it was the party of the countryside, or of the north, or of the middle class, the NSDAP attracted support right across Germany and right across the social spectrum. Analysis at the level of the main electoral districts misses this point and exaggerates the differences between regions. More recent research based on the smallest electoral unit (the *Kreis*) has revealed the extraordinary breadth of the Nazi vote.[3] There is an almost fractal quality to the picture that emerges, with each electoral district somewhat resembling the national map, and hotspots of support (Oldenburg in Lower Saxony, Upper and Middle Franconia in Bavaria, the northern parts of Baden, the eastern region of East Prussia) scattered all over the country. It is true that places with relatively high Nazi votes were more likely to be in central, northern and eastern parts, and those with relatively low Nazi votes were more likely to be in the south and west.[4] But the most important point is that the Nazis were able to achieve some electoral success in nearly any kind of local political milieu, covering the German electoral spectrum in a way not seen before or since. The Nazi vote did not vary proportionately with the unemployment rate or the share of workers in the population. As many as two fifths of Nazi voters in some districts were working class, to the consternation of the Communist leadership. The only significant constraint on the growth of the Nazi vote was the comparatively greater resilience of the Catholic Centre party compared with parties hitherto supported by German Protestants.[5]

In short, National Socialism was a movement and Hitler, its charismatic leader, can be said to have gone viral between 1930 and 1933. To many observers, it seemed like a religious awakening. As one *Sturmabteilung* sergeant explained: 'Our opponents . . . committed a fundamental error when equating us as a party with the Economic Party, the Democrats or the Marxist parties. All these parties were only interest groups, they lacked soul, spiritual ties. Adolf Hitler emerged as the bearer of a new political religion.'[6] The Nazis developed a self-conscious liturgy, with 9 November (the date of the 1918 Revolution and the failed 1923 Beer Hall putsch) as a Day of Mourning, complete with fires, wreaths, altars, blood-stained relics and even a Nazi book of martyrs. Initiates into the elite *Schutzstaffel* (SS) had to incant a catechism with lines like 'We believe in God, we believe in Germany which He created . . . and in the Führer . . . whom He has sent us.'[7] It was not just that Christ was more or less overtly supplanted by Hitler in the iconography and liturgy of 'the brown cult'. As the SS magazine *Das Schwarze Korps* argued, the very ethical foundation of Christianity had to go too: 'The abstruse doctrine of Original Sin . . . indeed the whole notion of sin as set forth by the Church . . . is something intolerable to Nordic man, since it is incompatible with the "heroic" ideology of our blood.'[8] The Nazis' opponents also recognized the pseudo-religious character of the movement. As the Catholic exile Eric Voegelin put it, Nazism was 'an ideology akin to Christian heresies of redemption in the here and now . . . fused with post-Enlightenment doctrines of social transformation'. The journalist Konrad Heiden called Hitler 'a pure fragment of the modern mass soul' whose speeches always ended 'in overjoyed redemption'. An anonymous Social Democrat called the Nazi regime a 'counter-church'.[9] Yet Nazism was not literally religious: the institutional seedbed from which it sprouted was the existing network of secular associational life in Germany. The denser the associational life in a town, the faster the Nazi party grew.[10]

Like a church and like the Bolshevik party before it, the Nazi party became more hierarchical as it grew. Since *Mein Kampf*, Hitler had believed firmly in the *Führerprinzip* – the leader principle – and his followers learned to 'work towards the Führer'. At the apex of the Third Reich stood Hitler himself. Then came an elite of trusted lieutenants: men such as Martin Bormann, Joseph Goebbels and Heinrich Himmler. Subordinate to the national leaders were the *Gauleiter*, or regional leaders, responsible for territories coinciding with the German states, the *Kreisleiter*, responsible for whole cities or metropolitan areas, and the *Ortsgruppenleiter* and *Stützpunktleiter*, the local leaders. Even further down the scale were the *Zellenleiter* (cell leaders) and *Blockleiter*, the neighbourhood leaders. As of 1936, there existed thirty-three *Gaue*, 772 *Kreise*, and 21,041 *Ortsgruppen* and *Stützpunkten*. By 1943, partly as a result of the expansion of the Reich, the numbers had increased to forty-three *Gaue*, 869 *Kreise*, 26,103 *Ortsgruppen*, 106,168 *Zellen*, and nearly 600,000 neighbourhood groups.[11] Yet it would be wrong to think of Hitler's Germany as simply a party pyramid in the way that Stalin's Soviet

Union was. Where Stalin favoured obsessive-compulsive control, Hitler preferred a more chaotic style of government, in which the old hierarchy of the Reich government competed with the new hierarchy of the party and, later, the even newer hierarchy of the Security Service (*Sicherheitsdienst*). Historians have sometimes represented the system as one of 'polycratic chaos', whereby ambiguous orders and overlapping jurisdictions gave rise to a 'cumulative radicalization', as rival individuals and agencies competed to carry out what they took to be the Führer's wishes. The result was a mixture of inefficiency, egregious corruption and escalating violence against all groups deemed to lie outside the 'ethnic community' – the *Volksgemeinschaft* – especially the Jews.

38
The Fall of the Golden International

There was nothing original about Hitler's anti-Semitism. Nazism flourished especially readily in small towns with a tradition of violent anti-Semitism that could be traced back to the fourteenth century.[1] More recently, as we have seen, populists on both the left and the right had regularly directed their fire at the supposedly excessive power of Jewish finance throughout the nineteenth century, and not only in Germany. Racial theories about Jewish inferiority or nefariousness were prevalent on both sides of the Atlantic long before 1933. The novelty was the ruthlessness with which Hitler pursued his hatred of the Jews to the ultimate, bitter end of genocide.[2] Long before mass murder was even discussed as a possibility within the Nazi leadership, however, the regime had revealed a paradox. Despite the repeated claims of its propaganda that Germany had suffered from the depredations of a 'golden international' of Jewish bankers, who were allied in some obscure way with the 'Jewish Bolshevism' of the Communist International,[3] the Nazi regime was able to disempower and expropriate the German-Jewish elite with the utmost ease. The giant spider that the Nazis appropriated from the American populists of the 1890s looked menacing on the front page of *Der Stürmer*, sucking the lifeblood from helpless German workers ensnared in its web (see figure 24). But Hitler was able to crush it under his heel. One of the triumphs of Nazi propaganda was to keep ordinary Germans believing in a powerful Jewish conspiracy, capable of starting a world war,[4] while constantly confronting them with the reality of Jewish weakness.

It was not a conspiracy theory to argue that Jews played a leading role in the German economy from the 1830s until the 1930s. They

24. *Die Ausgesaugten* ('The Sucked Dry'). A National Socialist cartoon depicts a giant Jewish spider, sucking the German people dry. Published on the front page of *Der Stürmer*, No. 8, February 1930.

did. In the exclusive world of private banking, names such as Warburg, Arnhold, Friedländer-Fulds, Simon and Weinberg were among the most distinguished. Of the joint-stock banks, Deutsche Bank and Dresdner Bank were directed by Oskar Wassermann and Herbert Gutman, respectively, while the Berliner Handels-Gesellschaft was dominated by Carl Fürstenberg until his death in 1933. The Darmstädter und Nationalbank (Danat-Bank), which went bankrupt in 1931, was run throughout the 1920s by Jakob Goldschmidt. Nor was Jewish influence confined to finance. Two of the leading department stores in Germany bore the Jewish names Wertheim and Tietz.[5] The leading electrical engineering company, Allgemeine Elektricitäts-Gesellschaft, had been founded by Emil Rathenau. There were many less well-known wealthy German Jews. Before the First World War, at a time when the share of Jews in the German population was less than 1 per cent, Jews accounted for more than a fifth of Prussian millionaires.[6] Moreover, Jews were over-represented in German corporate governance. In 1914 about 16 per cent of German public companies' board members were of Jewish background, rising to a quarter at the centre of the corporate network, where individuals had three or more board positions. More than two thirds of the large German corporations had at least one Jewish director.[7] The same argument can be made about the cerebral heights of German academic and cultural life, where Jews were just as prominent, if not more so. The glaring exception was in political life, where they continued to play a minimal role. As Hugo Valentin pointed out in 1936:

> In the twenty Cabinets that held office from [1818 to 1933], there were altogether two Jewish Ministers . . . and four of Jewish descent . . . out of about 250 Ministers . . . Out of about 250 higher officials in the Ministries of the Reich, including Secretaries of State and members of Government boards, there were before Hitler's victory at most fifteen Jews or men of Jewish birth. The number of Jewish Secretaries of State in the administration between 1918 and 1933 was just two. Out of about 300 higher officials in the Prussian Ministries some ten were Jews or of Jewish birth. Out of Prussia's twelve *Oberpräsidente*, thirty-five *Regierungspräsidente*, and over four hundred *Landräte* . . . there was not a single Jew . . . Of all Government officials in Germany [in 1925] 0.16 per cent were Jews; of the higher officials 0.29 per cent; of the intermediate and lower officials 0.17 per cent.[8]

Why were Jews so prominent in German economic life? Was it merely because they were better educated, on average? Was their measurable centrality in the dense German corporate network of interlocking directorships simply a function of their over-representation in banking, which in turn led to their holding multiple board positions? Or was there a special advantage to belonging to a community that was anchored in religion and tradition, leading to higher levels of trust and 'social embeddedness'? In a fascinating analysis of the German corporate network in the early twentieth century, Paul Windolf argues that:

> Both Jewish and non-Jewish managers were integrated into this institution of cooperative capitalism ('Germany Inc.'). Jewish members did not create a network of their own that was separate from the overarching corporate network. Instead, Jewish and non-Jewish members had contact with one another through their seats on the supervisory boards of big firms. Both groups were integrated into this network . . . Even though there was a clear tendency for homophily, Jews had, on average, more contacts to non-Jews than to their own group members.[9]

We are compelled by the data to fall back on more intangible explanations, such as genetics, or the educational benefits of Jewish family life, or some kind of Weberian 'Jewish ethic' even more aligned with the spirit of capitalism than the Protestant ethic. Yet these arguments, too, seem problematic, not least because Jews in Weimar Germany were less and less likely to marry other Jews. For Germany as a whole, the percentage of Jews marrying outside their own faith rose from 7 per cent in 1902 to 28 per cent by 1933. It reached a peak of more than a third in 1915.[10] (The comparable percentages for the United States were roughly 20 per cent in the 1950s and 52 per cent in 1990.)[11] Though Hamburg and Munich saw the highest rates of intermarriage, the figures were also well above average in Berlin, Cologne, and the Saxon cities of Dresden and Leipzig, as well as Breslau in Silesia.[12] When Arthur Ruppin gathered data for other European cities, he found only Trieste had a higher rate of intermarriage. Though relatively high, the rates in Leningrad, Budapest, Amsterdam and Vienna lagged behind those in the major German cities.[13] Of 164,000 Jews who remained in Germany in 1939, 15,000 were partners in mixed marriages.[14] When the Nazis came to define the children of mixed marriages as *Mischlinge*, they estimated there were nearly 300,000 of them, though the real figure lay between 60,000 and 125,000.[15] Few minorities subjected to persecution have ever been as socially – and indeed sexually – assimilated as the German Jews were in 1933.

Although at times after Hitler came to power some German Jews felt themselves to be enmeshed in a network of persecution, in reality they were the victims of multiple, hierarchically structured but at times competing bureaucratic agencies.[16] It began with the boycott of

Jewish businesses, instigated by the Nazi Enterprise Cells Organization (*Nationalsozialistische Betriebszellenorganisation*), the League of Middle-Class Employees and Artisans (*Kampfbund für den gewerblichen Mittlestand*) and sections of the SA.[17] At this early stage, to avoid economic disruption, bigger businesses such as the Tietz department stores were spared.[18] The process of 'Aryanization' of Jewish firms also proceeded slowly at first.[19] The experience of the Hamburg banker Max Warburg illustrated the predicament of the elite to which he belonged. They had thought they were a fully integrated part of the German business elite. When the Gentile members of that elite acquiesced in their exclusion, there was nothing they could do. At Warburg's last meeting as a director of the Hamburg–Amerika shipping line – a business established by another Jew, Albert Ballin – there was an embarrassing silence, whereupon Warburg ironically gave a speech on behalf of the board thanking himself for his years of service and wishing himself 'a *calm old age*, good luck and many blessings' to his family.[20] It was not until after the pogroms of 11 November 1938 that the process of expropriation got under way in earnest, with Hermann Göring's formal ban on all Jewish business activity in the Reich.[21] German Jews permitted to emigrate found themselves systematically fleeced by the authorities of nearly all their property before receiving their exit visas.[22] From 1 January 1939 all Jews were required to add the name 'Israel' (for males) or 'Sara' (for females) to their first names if their own names did not appear in the official list of 'typically Jewish' names issued by the Interior Ministry. The Jews were increasingly at the mercy of the Gestapo, who began the process of gathering them together in so-called *Judenhaüser*.[23]

Seven months before the outbreak of war, on 30 January 1939, Hitler made it horribly clear what would be the fate of the Jews, in a speech before the Reichstag that set out clearly the theory on which his anti-Semitism was based:

> For hundreds of years Germany was good enough to receive these elements, although they possessed nothing except infectious political and physical diseases. What they possess today, they have by a very large extent gained at the cost of the less astute German nation by the most reprehensible manipulations.

> Today we are merely paying this people what it deserves . . . [T]he German nation was, thanks to the inflation instigated and carried through by Jews, deprived of the entire savings which it had accumulated in years of honest work . . . We are resolved to prevent the settlement in our country of a strange people which was capable of snatching for itself all the leading positions in the land, and to oust it . . . German culture, as its name alone shows, is German and not Jewish, and therefore its management and care will be entrusted to members of our own nation . . .
>
> The world has sufficient space for settlements, but we must once and for all get rid of the opinion that the Jewish race was only created by God for the purpose of being in a certain percentage a parasite living on the body and the productive work of other nations. The Jewish race will have to adapt itself to sound constructive activity as other nations do, or sooner or later it will succumb to a crisis of an inconceivable magnitude.
>
> One thing I should like to say on this day which may be memorable for others as well as for us Germans: In the course of my life I have very often been a prophet, and have usually been ridiculed for it. During the time of my struggle for power it was in the first instance the Jewish race which only received my prophecies with laughter when I said that I would one day take over the leadership of the State, and with it that of the whole nation, and that I would then among many other things settle the Jewish problem. Their laughter was uproarious, but I think that for some time now they have been laughing on the other side of their faces. Today I will once more be a prophet: If the international Jewish financiers in and outside Europe should succeed in plunging the nations once more into a world war, then the result will not be the Bolshevization of the earth, and thus the victory of Jewry, but the annihilation of the Jewish race in Europe![24]

The Rothschilds had not long before been the richest family in the world and remained the most famous of Jewish dynasties – famous enough to have an entire film devoted to them by Joseph Goebbels's Propaganda Ministry. Yet the power the Nazis attributed to them proved frail indeed. In Germany (where the bank had long ago ceased to have a branch), their foundations were Aryanized.[25] The private property of the few family members still resident in Germany was expropriated, including the historic house in the Bockenheimer Landstrasse that had been the first real estate purchased by a Rothschild, following the emancipation of the Jews more than a century before. Immediately following annexation of Austria in 1938, Louis von Rothschild – the head of the Vienna house – was arrested and taken to the Gestapo headquarters at the Hotel Metropol. SS men were seen looting artworks from his palatial residence almost immediately after his arrest.[26] The firm of S. M. von Rothschild was put under state administration and later sold to the German bank Merck, Finck & Co. It proved more difficult to seize the huge Rothschild-founded Witkowitz ironworks, as it was in Czech territory and ownership had been transferred to the British Alliance Assurance company, but that obstacle was swept aside after the partition of Czechoslovakia in 1939, which brought the works under direct German rule.[27] As Hitler's legions conquered continental Europe one state at a time, the fake legality of peacetime expropriation gave way to unbridled looting. One Rothschild art collection after another was seized; one chateau after another commandeered. It was Alfred Rosenberg – the pre-eminent Nazi racial theorist – who took the lead in tracking down and plundering these collections, arguing that 'the Rothschilds are an enemy Jewish family and all their machinations to save their possessions should leave us cold'.[28] True, only two members of the family perished as a direct result of the Nazi policy of genocide, but that was because the majority had been able to flee beyond the reach of the Nazi empire: to England, to Canada, to the United States.

After all that had been written about the web of Jewish power, the only networks that really mattered were the ones that enabled emigration, and those were often simple family ties. The Rothschilds had those aplenty. For more modestly circumstanced families, a single well-situated relative could suffice. In the case of the Fürth schoolteacher Louis Kissinger, it was his wife's aunt, living in Westchester County, New York, who gave his sons Heinz (later Henry) and Walter the chance of life in the United States; the alternative would have been death in Germany, as it was for more than a dozen of their relatives who could not or would not get out. With immigration to the United States strictly limited by a quota system, only those German

Jews with relatives willing to vouch for them financially stood a chance.[29] For less fortunate families, the only hope of survival was the comfort of strangers – as well the comfort of friends of friends. According to her detailed memoir of life in wartime Berlin, Erna Segel and her children approached a total of twenty strangers seeking their help. On three occasions, strangers actually took the initiative in offering assistance. By contrast, of seventeen old acquaintances the family sought help from, only three were willing to provide them with shelter for more than one night. However, the old acquaintances did act as brokers, introducing them to people willing to provide longer-term accommodation. Of twelve contacts that led to long-lasting assistance, six were brokered by old acquaintances.[30] Sadly, the Segels were exceptional. Fewer than one in ten of the 214,000 German Jews still in the Reich at the outbreak of the war survived. Far more typical was the case described in Hans Fallada's 1947 novel *Jeder stirbt für sich allein* (literally, 'Everyone Dies for Himself Alone'), of a Jewish widow who is protected by one of the residents of her apartment block, an anti-Nazi judge, but persecuted by a family of ardent Nazis whose brutality ultimately drives her to suicide.

Fallada's novel (his last) repays reading for the penetrating insights it provides into life under totalitarianism. The book is based on the true story of Otto Hampel, an unpolitical, unsophisticated working man who sought to resist the Nazi regime following the death of his son during the invasion of France. Hampel's idea was that if he left handwritten postcards denouncing the regime lying in carefully selected buildings and mailboxes around Berlin, the effect would be to catalyse popular disaffection. For over a year, Hampel and his wife, Elise, wrote hundreds of these postcards, with simple messages such as: 'Mother! The Führer has murdered my son. Mother! The Führer will murder your sons, too, he will not stop till he has brought sorrow to every home in the world.' However, so fearful were the people who found the postcards that nearly all were immediately handed in to the authorities, enabling the Gestapo eventually to track down and arrest their authors. The Hampels were tried in the People's Court and sentenced to death by the odious Nazi judge Roland Freisler.[31] As a writer whom the regime distrusted, but who nevertheless remained in Germany throughout the Nazi period, Fallada

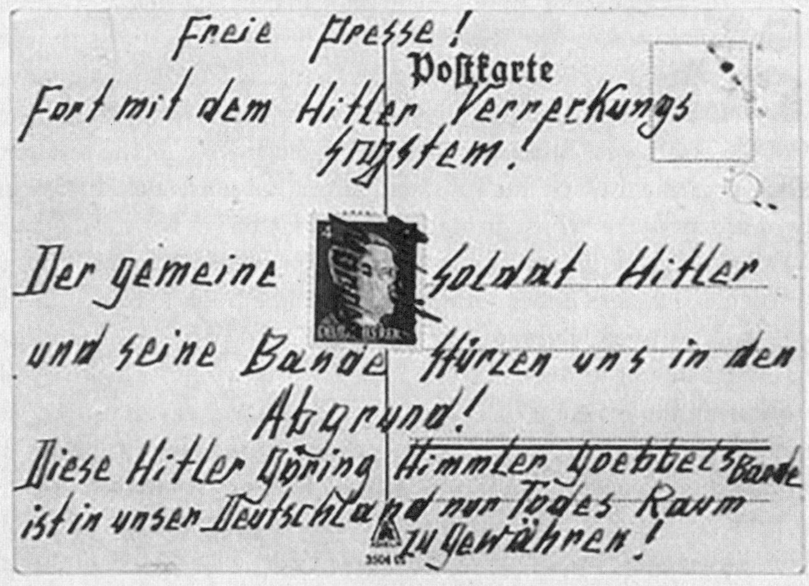

Freie Presse!
Postkarte
Fort mit dem Hitler Verreckungs
system!

Der gemeine Soldat Hitler
und seine Bande stürzen uns in den
Abgrund!
Diese Hitler Göring Himmler Goebbels Bande
ist in unsern Deutschland nur Todes Raum
zu gewähren!

25. Alone in Berlin: Otto Hampel and his wife, Elise, executed on 8 April 1943, for 'undermining military morale' (*Wehrkraftzersetzung*) and 'preparing for high treason'. Their crime was to write postcards like the one above, which reads: 'Free Press! Away with the Hitler system of ruination! The common soldier Hitler and his gang are hurling us into the abyss. The only thing to allow this Hitler Goering Himmler Goebbels gang in our Germany is dying space' (a pun on the Nazis' *Lebensraum*).

unforgettably conveys the way Nazi rule had isolated individuals, making trust even between neighbours extremely hazardous, and rendering impossible the Hampels' attempt to spread opposition virally. The secret of totalitarian success was, in other words, to delegitimize, paralyse or kill outright nearly all social networks outside the hierarchical institutions of party and state, and especially networks that aspired to independent political action. *Alone in Berlin* – the title of the most recent English translation of the novel – neatly encapsulates the atomization that made the Third Reich so resilient, even after it became obvious that Hitler was leading Germany to catastrophic defeat.

39
The Ring of Five

So repulsive were both the totalitarian regimes – Hitler's and Stalin's – that it remains difficult to fathom why anyone living in a free society would have been attracted to either of them. But people were. Even more remarkable, some of the most exclusive networks in England allowed themselves to be penetrated by agents of fascism and communism. As is well known, some sections of the British aristocracy were attracted to Hitler and certainly favoured a policy of appeasing rather than confronting him. According to Duff Cooper, the duke of Westminster 'inveighed against the Jews and . . . said that after all Hitler knew that we were his best friends'.[1] The marquess of Lothian, who had cut his teeth in Lord Milner's South African 'Kindergarten', was another aristocrat who sympathized with the Nazi regime, as was the Anglo-German earl of Athlone (who had renounced the German title of Prince of Teck during the war), to say nothing of the shipping heiress Nancy Cunard and the Mitford sisters Unity and Diana, the former of whom described Hitler as the 'greatest man of all time' and the latter of whom was married to the British Fascist leader, Sir Oswald Mosley, in a private ceremony in Goebbels's drawing room.[2] In February 1935, Lothian told readers of *The Times* that Hitler had personally assured him 'that what Germany wants is equality, not war; that she is prepared absolutely to renounce war'. Hitler's concern was not Western Europe, in any case, but the Soviet Union. 'He regards Communism as essentially a militant religion,' explained Lothian. If it were one day to 'try to repeat the military triumphs of Islam', would 'Germany than be regarded as the potential enemy or as the bulwark of Europe'?[3] Oxford – and especially All Souls College – had more than its fair share of such appeasers. Yet nothing that happened there could compare with the grim fate of the most exclusive and iconoclastic of Cambridge networks, which was to be infiltrated by the KGB.*

In the history of networks, few episodes are more instructive than that of the Cambridge Spies: the 'Magnificent Five', as they were known to their controllers in Moscow Centre, or the 'Homintern' as they were wittily nicknamed by Maurice Bowra, the dean of Wadham, Oxford. All five of them belonged to a network that prided itself on its exclusivity. Yet this elite network allowed itself to be so thoroughly penetrated by Russian intelligence that for more than a decade five of its members were the Soviet foreign intelligence service's most valuable assets, betraying countless secrets – and Western agents – to Stalin.

We have already seen in the previous chapter how the members of the Conversazione Society had become estranged from Victorian values both sexually and politically after around 1900. By the time of the First World War, a significant proportion of Apostles agreed with E. M. Forster's position that friendship came before loyalty to King and Country. A new generation took this estrangement a step further: from conscientious objection to treason. Anthony Blunt was 'born' into the Society in 1928. He, in turn, was Guy Burgess's sponsor four years later. Both were Trinity men. Both were academically brilliant. And both were gay. (Though Burgess was as flamboyant as Blunt was staid, it has been claimed that they were lovers for a time.)[4] However, the historically significant fact about Blunt and Burgess is that they were Communists who willingly offered their services to Stalin.

To be sure, the Apostles were not themselves a communist or even socialist organization. Marxism was all around in 1930s Cambridge, in a variety of explicitly political student bodies – notably the Cambridge University Socialist Society, which had been thoroughly penetrated by the Communist Party of Great Britain – and with the encouragement of Marxist dons such as the Pembroke economist Maurice Dobb. But the

* The NKVD was renamed NKGB in February 1941, then changed back to NKVD in July 1941, then reverted to NKGB in 1943. After the war, the agency was successively named MGB (1946), MVD (1953) and, finally, KGB (1954). For the avoidance of confusion, it will be referred to throughout this section as the KGB.

Apostles were more than merely representative of the spirit of the age. Of thirty-one Apostles 'born' between 1927 and 1939, no fewer than fifteen were Marxists, among them John Cornford, James Klugmann, Leo Long, Michael Straight and Alister Watson.[5] The subjects of Saturday evening talks reflected this politicization: one of Burgess's, on 28 January 1933, was 'Is the Past a Signpost?'[6] Burgess was an activist in more ways than one. As an undergraduate, he helped organize a strike by the Trinity dining staff and another by Cambridge bus drivers. The 'Angels' of the previous generation can hardly have been unaware of what was happening to their once so unpolitical Society. If they protested, however, no record survives.

Not all the Cambridge spies were Apostles, of course. It was Burgess's dream to organize a 'ring of five', in imitation of anti-Nazi Communist cells that were said to be active in Nazi Germany.[7] The Soviets knew better than to recruit five agents from a single organization. Nevertheless, they were willing to recruit from the wider network to which Blunt and Burgess belonged. The Soviet agents Willi Münzenberg and Ernst Henri had already begun 'talent-spotting' in Cambridge in the early 1930s, but it was an agent named Arnold Deutsch* who realized Burgess's vision.[8] Deutsch (whose KGB codename was OTTO) began not with an Apostle but with Kim Philby, a Trinity man but academically not first class. Born in India and named after the hero of Kipling's greatest book, *Kim*, Philby was the son of a former member of the Indian Civil Service who had become an adviser to King Ibn Sa'ud of Saudi Arabia, where he had 'gone native' by converting to Islam. Perhaps the Soviets saw the possibility of another conversion. After Cambridge, at the suggestion of Maurice Dobb, he had gone to Vienna to work for the Communist-backed International Workers Relief Organization. There he had met and married Litzi Friedmann, the first of four wives. Friedmann introduced him to Deutsch, who recruited him and gave him the codename SÖHNCHEN ('Sonny').[9] Philby then nominated his Cambridge friend Donald Maclean, who became WAISE ('Orphan'). Also in

* A Czech Jew who had a brilliant academic career, Deutsch was able to establish himself in London without attracting suspicion as he was the cousin of the founder of the Odeon cinema chain.

Deutsch's rapidly growing espionage network was Maclean's friend James Klugmann (MER), though he was too well known as a Communist to do much more than spy on the other spies. Burgess somehow guessed that Maclean was working for the Soviets; according to one account Deutsch had to recruit Burgess to keep him quiet. The insatiably promiscuous Burgess was given the codename MÄDCHEN ('Girl').[10] Burgess then recruited his fellow Apostle Blunt (unimaginatively codenamed TONY), who was now teaching at Trinity.[11] Blunt in turn recruited Michael Straight (NIGEL), an American who was also an Apostle and president-elect of the Union.[12] Blunt also nominated his student John Cairncross, a Trinity undergraduate of Scottish extraction, who became MOLIÈRE (a bizarre choice, as Cairncross had published scholarly articles about the French playwright).[13] Yet another recruit – more or less simultaneously to the Apostles and KGB – was Leo Long, whom Blunt ran as a sub-agent.[14] Finally, Alister Watson was added to the KGB payroll. The attentive reader will have noted that there were more than five Cambridge spies. There were at least nine.

Deutsch's strategy was that all members of the 'ring of five' should disavow Marxism and seek positions in or close to government institutions. A remarkable feature of the case of the Cambridge spies is how readily their disavowals were believed. In 1937, Philby posed as a fascist sympathizer covering the Nationalist side of the Spanish Civil War, first as a freelance then for *The Times*.[15] We now know he had been sent to Spain as part of a Soviet plot to assassinate Franco.[16] Maclean was told to abandon his plans to write a Marxist dissertation and instead to apply for the Foreign Office. He was accepted in 1935, despite admitting that he had 'not entirely shaken off' his Communist views.[17] Cairncross had been a Communist since his time at the Sorbonne, before he even went up to Cambridge. The Foreign Office accepted him, too, without cavil. In 1934, Burgess had travelled to Berlin and Moscow, where he had met Osip Pyatnitsky, head of the Communist International's International Liaison Department.[18] However, following Deutsch's orders, Burgess pretended to give up Communism and embrace conservatism, seeking a job at Conservative Central Office and ending up as personal assistant to the Tory MP John 'Jack' Macnamara, who shared his sexual proclivities. It was in this capacity that Burgess helped recruit Tom Wylie, private secretary to the permanent under-secretary of war, Sir Herbert Cready.[19] From late 1936, Burgess was employed as a producer of current affairs broadcasts by the BBC; his greatest feat was to get the KGB operative Ernest Henri to deliver a talk in favour of an Allied second front.[20] On 11 January 1939 Burgess joined Section D (for 'Destruction' or, more accurately, 'Dirty Tricks') of the Secret Intelligence Service (SIS, also known as MI6), though officially he was at the Ministry of Information's Foreign Division Directorate.[21] Michael Straight was told to leave Cambridge and go back to the United States, feigning grief at the death of his friend and fellow Apostle John Cornford in the Spanish Civil War. He was hired as a speechwriter for President Franklin D. Roosevelt and held posts in the Department of the Interior and the State Department.

Why did they do it? The naïve answer is that they were all men of principle, appalled by the rise of fascism, disillusioned by the policy of appeasement, who saw Stalin as the only credible counterweight to Hitler. Yet not one of them had second thoughts on 23 August 1939, when the Ribbentrop–Molotov Pact was announced. (Only the Oxford-educated Welshman Goronwy Rees, whom Burgess had added to Deutsch's list, drew the correct conclusion.) On the contrary, the Cambridge spies were especially active in the period when Hitler and Stalin were on the same side – and, of course, the other side from Great Britain. After serving as the *Times* correspondent in France in 1940, Philby was turned down by the Code and Cypher School at Bletchley Park, but thanks to Burgess was offered a job at Section D, SIS. When Section D was folded into the new Special Operations Executive (SOE), Burgess was dropped but Philby stayed on as an instructor, from which position he continued to supply Moscow with assessments of UK policy. Later he was moved to SIS Section V. Klugmann was also at SOE (in the Yugoslavian section). John Cairncross was at Bletchley Park. Having at first been rejected by the Intelligence Corps because of his pre-war Communist leanings, Blunt wormed his way into MI5 (Britain's Security Service), thanks to the support of his friend Victor Rothschild – also an Apostle, as well as a Trinity man and a peer of the realm – who accepted Blunt's feeble claim that he was interested in Marxism only in so far as it concerned art history.[22] Blunt soon began handing over MI5 documents as well as intelligence on the German order of battle, which he received from Leo Long, now working at the War Office's MI14 section. Late in 1940 Blunt recruited Burgess to SIS, though it was decided not to make him an SIS officer.[23]

The scale of the Cambridge spies' contribution to the Soviet war effort was staggering. In 1941 London was easily the KGB's most productive residency, supplying close to 9,000 classified documents. Between 1941 and 1945, Blunt alone provided Moscow Centre with 1,771 documents.[24] On 26 May, eleven days before the Allied invasion of Normandy, he provided the Soviets with the entire deception plan devised as part of OVERLORD (D-Day), as well (it seems likely) as the monthly reviews of British anti-Axis intelligence operations that went to Churchill.[25] Philby (now codenamed STANLEY) also passed on to his handlers the 'source-books' listing all SIS agents and sought to satisfy Moscow's thirst for evidence that London was plotting a separate peace with the Germans.[26] Burgess told the Russians details of Roosevelt's and Churchill's talks at Casablanca in January 1943, including their decision to postpone an invasion of France until 1944, as well as relaying intelligence about Allied plans for post-war Poland. In the first six months of 1945 he supplied no fewer than 289 'top secret' Foreign Office documents.[27] After the end of the war and the British general election, Burgess was appointed personal assistant to the young Labour politician Hector McNeil, the minister of state in the Foreign Office, a position that gave him access to even higher-level material, notably the policy papers prepared for the four Allied powers' Moscow Conference. All of it was handed over to his Soviet handlers. So successful were the Cambridge spies that for a time – with a rich irony – their Soviet masters ceased to trust them, convincing themselves with typically Stalinist paranoia that the entire Cambridge operation must be a brilliant double-cross.[28]

Why was it so easy for the Soviets to penetrate British intelligence? The simple answer is that there was a chronic lack of counterespionage. As Soviet spymasters knew well, Britain's pre-war vetting checks for the civil service were inadequate to detect people who purposefully distanced themselves from outward forms of communism, as the Ring of Five did. There was a counter-espionage department, SIS's Section V, but when Victor Rothschild pushed to involve Anthony Blunt in it, the result was worse than having no counter-espionage.[29] The senescent head of MI5, Sir Vernon Kell, insisted as late as 1939 that Soviet activity in the UK was 'non-existent, in terms of both intelligence and political subversion'.[30] Roger Hollis – later (1956–65) director-general of MI5 – was critical of SIS's failure to monitor the Soviet threat, with good reason: in 1944 (incredibly) Philby succeeded in being made head of a new Section IX dedicated to Soviet and Communist counter-espionage.[31] But Hollis was so blind to his own service's sins of omission and commission that for a time he himself was suspected of being the 'Fifth Man' (as was Rothschild). Even in December 1946, A4 – the department tasked with surveillance of Soviet diplomatic personnel – had just fifteen members, and no car.[32] Yet, as Philby himself later observed, he and his fellow traitors were also protected by 'the genuine mental block which stubbornly created the belief that respected members of the Establishment could not do such things'.[33] In that sense, it was the wider network – the 'old boy' network of elite schools and Oxbridge – that had been penetrated.

Beginning in 1945, the evidence began to mount up that would ultimately lead to the Cambridge spies' exposure. The defection in Ottawa in September 1945 of Igor Gouzenko, a cipher clerk for Soviet military intelligence, began the process of revelation. He disclosed that the Soviets had penetrated multiple Canadian institutions and had even obtained samples of the uranium used in the American atomic bombs thanks to Alan Nunn May, a physicist who had been a contemporary of Maclean's at Trinity Hall.[34]At SIS's Section IX, Philby was in a position to keep the spycatcher Jane Archer off the scent after she was moved over from MI5. When another Soviet operative – Konstantin Volkov, a KGB officer in Istanbul – attempted to defect, with the clear intention of exposing Burgess and Maclean – Philby intervened, ensuring that Volkov was intercepted and whisked back to Moscow. Philby also tipped off May that he had been rumbled.[35] Oblivious to this systematic sabotage, SIS promoted Philby once again – this time to become the agency's representative in what was now the most important capital city in the world: Washington, DC. Even more bizarrely, Maclean was appointed head of the Foreign Office's American desk. This promotion came after he had suffered a complete nervous breakdown while serving as counsellor and head of chancery at the embassy in Cairo, where he and his drinking companion, Philip Toynbee, had smashed up the apartment of two girls working for the US embassy, tearing their underclothes to shreds in an inebriated frenzy. No one in London had an inkling that Maclean's increasingly erratic behaviour was the result of intensifying stress, following two unsuccessful attempts to sever his ties to Moscow. No one paid any attention when, in a drunken condition, he described himself as 'the English [Alger] Hiss', the US State Department's best-known Communist mole.[36]

Yet Burgess remains the most baffling case. Even if he had not been a Soviet spy, his drunkenness, drug abuse and disorderliness – not to mention delinquent sexual antics – ought to have got him fired. Instead, he kept being given new jobs: with the Foreign Office Information Research Department in 1947, with the Far Eastern Department and then, in August 1950, with the Washington Embassy, as second secretary. It was at around this time that Burgess's friend Guy Liddell, the deputy director-general of MI5, confidently maintained that he was 'not the sort of person who would deliberately pass confidential information to unauthorized parties'. In reality, the Five were arguably at the height of their value to the Soviets at the outbreak of the Korean War. Burgess was living with Philby in Washington, acting as his courier to Valeri Makayev in New York. From his position in the Defence Divisions of the Treasury, Cairncross was meanwhile giving Moscow details of the British atomic bomb programme.[37] Philby had the gall to propose to Liddell that he could combine SIS and SS (MI5) representation in Washington.[38] This, however, was a defensive ploy. He knew the net was slowly tightening. In addition to new intelligence from defectors, the Americans were painstakingly extracting more and more information from the Soviet intelligence messages intercepted and decrypted by their Venona programme. Realizing that Maclean was the spy identified as HOMER in the decrypts, Philby tipped him off via Burgess, who was being sent back to London after yet another bout of scandalous misconduct. Burgess also informed Blunt.[39] At midnight on Friday,

25 May 1951, in an exfiltration operation masterminded by Yuri Modin, their London case officer, Maclean and Burgess fled from Maclean's house in Tatsfield to Southampton, where they boarded the pleasure boat *Falaise* to Saint-Malo – a service that did not require passports – proceeding by train from Rennes to Paris to Berne, where they were issued with false passports by the Soviet embassy. In Zurich the two men boarded a plane bound for Stockholm via Prague, but at the Czech capital they changed planes and flew to Moscow. Two of the five birds had flown simply because MI5's counterespionage department lacked the resources to maintain surveillance at weekends.[40]

MI5 (not to mention the FBI and CIA) now had Philby in their sights. He was recalled from Washington (at American insistence) and officially retired. He was interviewed, then interrogated, but held up and was encouraged to do so by his defenders in SIS. In 1955, on the basis of US intelligence, he was accused of being the Third Man in the New York *Sunday News* and then in the House of Commons. Yet he was protected by the government of Anthony Eden, as well as by Nicholas Elliott within MI6 and by James Angleton at CIA. Brazenly, Philby held a press conference in his mother's living room, telling the press: 'The last time I spoke to a Communist, knowing he was one, was in 1934.'[41] Incredibly, his former colleagues mostly believed it – despite fresh circumstantial evidence from the Venona programme that he was the Soviet agent STANLEY, as well as testimony from the KGB defector Anatoli Golitsyn and from Flora Solomon, whom Philby had tried to recruit to the Soviet side before the war. Even Philby's second wife, Aileen, now suspected him. (According to one of their friends, she blurted out over dinner one night: 'I know you're the Third Man!') His systematic mental cruelty and her alcoholism led to her death in December 1957.[42] Yet he was allowed to move to Beirut, where he worked as a journalist and an informal source for MI6. Unabashed, he seized the first opportunity to resume working for the Soviets. When MI6 finally exposed Philby on the basis of new information obtained in 1961–2, he 'confessed' to Elliott, claiming that he had broken off contact with the Russians in 1946. He was effectively allowed to escape to Moscow in January 1963.[43]

Perhaps the greatest mystery of all about the Cambridge spies –

even more mysterious than their going so long undetected – is that they had few illusions about the regime they were serving. In Moscow, Burgess continued with his customary behaviour, drinking, chain-smoking and making a mess, periodically yelling 'I *hate* Russia' at the concealed microphones in his apartment. His verdict on Moscow was 'like Glasgow on a Saturday night in Victorian times'.[44] Philby wrote a KGB-sponsored pro-Soviet memoir, had an affair with Melinda Maclean, attempted suicide in 1970, and married his fourth wife, a Russian. When he received the Order of Lenin, he compared it to a knighthood – 'one of the better ones'[45] – but it rankled with him that he was never more than a mere 'agent' within the KGB. Burgess died in August 1963 of liver failure. Maclean also drank himself to death. Philby's liver somehow kept going until 1988. The others declined the option of flight to the workers' paradise. 'I know perfectly well how your people live,' Blunt told Modin after Burgess and Maclean had fled, 'and I can assure you that it would be very hard, almost unbearable, for me to do likewise.'[46] After Michael Straight admitted that Blunt had recruited him when he was an undergraduate at Trinity, Blunt confessed to MI5 in 1964 – though he was not publicly unmasked until November 1979. (In his memoirs, not made public until 2009, Blunt said he regretted ever working for Soviet intelligence, calling it the 'biggest mistake of my life'.) Finally, Cairncross was exposed by documents in his hand that Blunt had failed to remove from Burgess's flat, but the evidence against him was not sufficient for arrest, so he was discreetly retired and allowed to pursue an academic career in the United States. In 1964 he confessed to MI5 that he had spied for the Soviets, but declined to return to the UK, accepting a job at the UN World Food and Agriculture Organization in Rome. In 1970 he received an assurance of immunity from prosecution. Not until 1982 was he confirmed as the 'Fifth Man'. Not until 1990 was this made public, after years of often wild speculation had wrongly accused at least ten other Cambridge graduates with intelligence connections, including Hollis and Rothschild.[47] Thus none of the Cambridge spies was ever tried or convicted, much less imprisoned – unlike George Blake, a Soviet spy without the right kind of Establishment connections, who was sentenced to forty-two years for his crimes.

40
Brief Encounter

'Only connect' – as opposed to 'only defect' – had once been the Apostles' watchword. But even the briefest connection could be fatal, or close to fatal, in Stalin's Soviet Union, which the Cambridge spies had so loyally served. One November night in Leningrad, just months after the end of the war, the Oxford philosopher Isaiah Berlin met the Russian poet Anna Akhmatova. For both of them, it was an unforgettable encounter, a kind of intellectual and spiritual communion, as devoid of political content as it was chaste. Yet the meeting very nearly destroyed Akhmatova's life. It would be difficult to find a more perfect illustration of totalitarianism, the ultimate hierarchical system, than this. Two intellectuals could not discuss literature in a private apartment without Stalin himself taking a personal and malignant interest in the event and using it as evidence to justify further persecution.

Akhmatova had long lived under a cloud of suspicion. Born Anna Andreevna Gorenko, she was already an established poet before the Revolution. Her first husband, the romantic nationalist writer Nikolay Gumilev, had been executed for anti-Soviet activity in 1921.[1] The cloud darkened following the reception of her fourth book of poetry, *Anno Domino MCMXXI*. One critic referred to the 'contradictory' or 'double' image' of her heroine: 'half "harlot" burning with passion, half "nun" able to pray to God for forgiveness'. Another wrote that all Russia was divided between Mayakovskys and Akhmatovas, damningly implying that she was the conservative to Vladimir Mayakovsky's revolutionary.[2] Her work ceased to be published after 1925.[3] Ten years later, her son, Lev Gumilev, and third husband, Nikolai Punin, were both arrested. On the advice of a friend, the writer Boris

Pasternak, she wrote a desperate, direct appeal to Stalin, begging for the release of 'the only two people who are close to me'. Miraculously, Stalin granted her plea, scrawling on her letter an order that the two men be released.[4] However, Gumilev was arrested again in March 1938 and sentenced to ten years in the Arctic labour camp at Norilsk, the world's northernmost settlement.[5] Though Akhmatova was briefly rehabilitated in 1939, the backlash against the publication of a selection of her poems (*From Six Books*, 1940) was swift: the head of the Leningrad Party, Andrei Zhdanov, ordered the seizure of the book, condemning 'this lechery of Akhmatova's'.[6] It was during this period, between 1935 and 1940, that the poet wrote most of her cycle of poems about the Terror, 'Requiem', which searingly articulates the agony of the millions who lost loved ones to Stalin's heartless tyranny.[7]

That there should be a strong emotional connection between Akhmatova and the brilliant young English philosopher is not so surprising. Though educated at St Paul's and Corpus Christi College, Oxford, Berlin had been born in Riga to a prosperous Jewish family in 1909 and, as a precocious child, had witnessed the Russian Revolution. However, the Berlins had opted to leave the Soviet Union in 1920 and a year later settled in London. Though immersed in philosophy as a young academic, Berlin never lost touch with his Russian roots. His linguistic skills led to a temporary posting as first secretary at the British embassy in Moscow in the summer of 1945. It was on a visit to Leningrad, escorted by Brenda Tripp of the British Council, that Berlin made Akhmatova's acquaintance, at a second-hand bookshop owned by Gennady Rakhlin.[8] On 14 November 1945 she invited him to her apartment in Fontanny Dom, the once magnificent palace of the Sheremetevs on the Fontanka canal. This first meeting was somewhat farcically cut short. However, Berlin paid a second nocturnal visit to Akhmatova at some point before his return to Moscow on the twentieth. It was after midnight, when they were alone, that the transformative connection occurred. He told her of her long-lost friends who, like his family, had fled the Revolution: the composer Artur Lurié, the poet Georgy Adamovich, the mosaicist Boris Anrep, the society beauty Salome Andronikova. She described her childhood by the Black Sea, her marriages, her love for the poet Osip

Mandelstam (who had died in the Gulag in 1938), then recited some cantos from Byron's *Don Juan* (in unintelligible English) followed by a selection of her poems, including the still unfinished 'Poem without a Hero' and 'Requiem', which she read from a manuscript. Their literary discussions – of Chekhov, Tolstoy, Dostoevsky, Kafka, Pushkin, Alexander Blok, Marina Tsvetaeva, Pasternak and a host of other lesser poets – went on until late the next morning and made an indelible impression on them both. They touched on music, too. Nothing could illustrate better how completely the Soviet regime had destroyed the literary and artistic networks of pre-1920s Europe than that Akhmatova – like Pasternak, whom Berlin also met – knew scarcely anything about the more recent work of writers and artists she had previously known, and still less about the work of newcomers. To be a poet in Stalin's Russia was to be a network isolate. For his part, Berlin had been amazed to find that Akhmatova still existed: 'It was as if I had suddenly been invited to meet Miss Christina Rossetti,' he later wrote.[9] He was only her second foreign visitor since the First World War. Had she left Russia before Stalin's rise, she would have not have been out of place in Bloomsbury. As she confessed to Berlin, she was 'apt to fall in love easily'. She shared with Bloomsbury an excessive interest in 'the personalities and acts of others . . . compounded of sharp insight into the moral centre of both characters and situations . . . together with a dogmatic obstinacy in attributing motives and intentions'. Her whole life, Berlin reflected, was 'one uninterrupted indictment of Russian reality'. But she 'would not move: she was ready to die in her own country, no matter what horrors were in store; she would never abandon it', even although 'Leningrad after the War was for her nothing but a vast cemetery, the graveyard of her friends: it was like the aftermath of a forest fire – the few charred trees made the desolation still more desolate.'

The two met again, briefly, on 5 January 1946, before Berlin's departure from Russia. He was not wholly surprised when she gave him, inscribed in a volume of her earlier work, 'the poem that was later to form the second in the cycle entitled Cinque . . . [which] in its first version, had been directly inspired by our earlier meeting'. The meeting had been no less moving for him. It had, he later wrote, 'affected me profoundly and permanently changed my outlook'. He thought her regal, her poetry 'a work of genius'. Their encounter had, he later said, given him back his 'homeland'. It may well have been the stimulus that diverted him away from philosophy and into the history of political thought, where he went on to do his best work in defence of individual freedom and against historical determinism. 'It had been no normal love affair', as one commentator has written. 'There was no physical contact. This must be one of the purest encounters between two human personalities on record. Two extraordinary minds seem for a moment to have engaged perfectly together to drive each other up to ever greater heights of mutual love and understanding. Indeed, it may stand as a kind of *ne plus ultra*, the very Platonic idea of human communication.'[10] In fact, as Pasternak wrote to Berlin the following year, Akhmatova developed something of an infatuation with Berlin: '[H]er every third [word] was – you. And so dramatically and mysteriously! At night, for example, in a taxi on the way back from some evening or reception, inspired and weary, and slightly in the clouds (*or* intoxicated) in French: *Notre ami* (that's you) *a dit, ou a promis*, etc. etc.'[11] 'Cinque' was certainly inspired by Berlin.[12] Some have also inferred that she saw in Berlin the hero who had been so conspicuous by his absence in 'Requiem',[13] though the 'third and last' dedication of Akhmatova's masterpiece – 'Poem without A Hero' – may not have been written with Berlin alone in mind:

> Enough, I've frozen in fear too long,
> So now I'll summon Bach's Chaconne,
> And with it a man will come to me.
> It's not for him to be my espoused,
> But what we together will bring about
> Will trouble the Twentieth Century.
> I received him by mistake
> As one touched by a hidden fate
> And, with him, the worst of all drew near.
> Along the Fontanka Canal he'll walk,
> Arriving late through night and fog,
> He'll drink my wine to greet the New Year.
> And he'll remember Epiphany Eve,

The maple, the wedding candles' beams,
And the poem in its mortal flight.
But not the first lilacs of the spring,
Nor love's sweet prayers, nor yet a ring –
It's doom he'll come bearing me that night.[14]

As the final line suggests, the consequences for Akhmatova of her meetings with this 'guest from the future' (a phrase from her poem 'The Year 1913') were disastrous. It was hardly surprising, given her track record and Berlin's official status – made more conspicuous by the unexpected and incongruous appearance of the prime minister's raffish son Randolph Churchill outside Akhmatova's apartment on the occasion of Berlin's first visit.[15] Stalin may never have uttered the words 'So our nun has been receiving British spies', but the supposition would not have been unreasonable in the fraught post-war atmosphere.[16] Within days, the secret police had clumsily installed microphones in the ceiling of Akhmatova's home. They forced a Polish woman who was translating her work to give them details of Berlin's visits.[17] Her peril only worsened the following April, when Akhmatova accepted an invitation to give a poetry reading in the House of Unions in Moscow. The ecstatic reception of the audience, repeated in Leningrad four months later, alarmed her, and with good reason.[18] Surveillance of her and her friends intensified. Stalin once again intervened, this time not to save her but to engage in literary criticism, observing that one could count Akhmatova's good post-revolutionary poems 'on the fingers of one hand'.[19] On 14 August the Central Committee issued a resolution 'on the magazines *Zvezda* and *Leningrad*' that attacked their editors for printing 'ideologically harmful' works by Akhmatova and the satirist Mikhail Zoshchenko. Both authors were then vituperatively denounced at a meeting of the Leningrad writers' union by Akhmatova's old nemesis Zhdanov, who had been prompted to act by Georgi Alexandrov, the head of the agit-prop department of the Central Committee, who had in turn been prompted to act by a denunciation by an employee of his department.[20] The terms of Zhdanov's attack were revealing:

> [Akhmatova's work] is the poetry of a spoilt woman-aristocrat, frenziedly vacillating between boudoir and chapel . . . It would be hard to

> say whether she is a nun or a fallen woman; better perhaps say she is a bit of each, her desires and her prayers intertwined . . . This mood of solitude and hopelessness, which is foreign to the spirit of Soviet literature, runs through the whole of Akhmatova's work . . . Akhmatova's work is a matter of the distant past; it is foreign to Soviet life and cannot be tolerated in the pages of our journals . . . These works can sow nothing but gloom, low spirits, pessimism, a desire to escape the vital problems of social life and activity into a narrow little world of personal experiences.[21]

In the totalitarian state, even personal experiences were off-limits.

Akhmatova was publicly humiliated but – to Berlin's relief – was not arrested and her modest pension and food ration were only temporarily suspended.[22] However, there could be no further communication between them. Berlin therefore was not informed that her son, Lev – released from the Gulag to fight as an anti-aircraft gunner in the 'Great Patriotic War' – had been arrested once again in 1949 and sentenced to a further ten years in a camp in Kazakhstan. Nor did he hear of her third husband Punin's re-arrest and subsequent death in the Gulag.* In 1954, in the slight thaw that followed Stalin's death, a party of British students, including the young Harry Shukman, saw her at the Leningrad House of Writers. Akhmatova believed Berlin had sent them, but in reality he knew nothing of the visit.[23] When the *New Republic* published a sensationalized account of Berlin's encounter with Akhmatova, he was beside himself with fury.[24] He would have been still more incensed if he had known that the author, Michael Straight, was one of the Cambridge students Anthony Blunt had persuaded to spy for the Soviets. Three years later, in August 1956, when Berlin returned to Russia, Akhmatova told him, through Pasternak, that she did not want to meet him in case her son – newly released – should suffer, though (somewhat illogically) they spoke once on the telephone. It did not help matters that Berlin

* Berlin's Uncle Leo, a Soviet citizen, was also arrested in 1952, rounded up and accused of belonging to a British spy ring. Under torture, he confessed that he was indeed a British spy. After a year in jail, he was released after Stalin's death, but suffered a heart attack shortly afterwards when he passed one of his tormentors in the street.

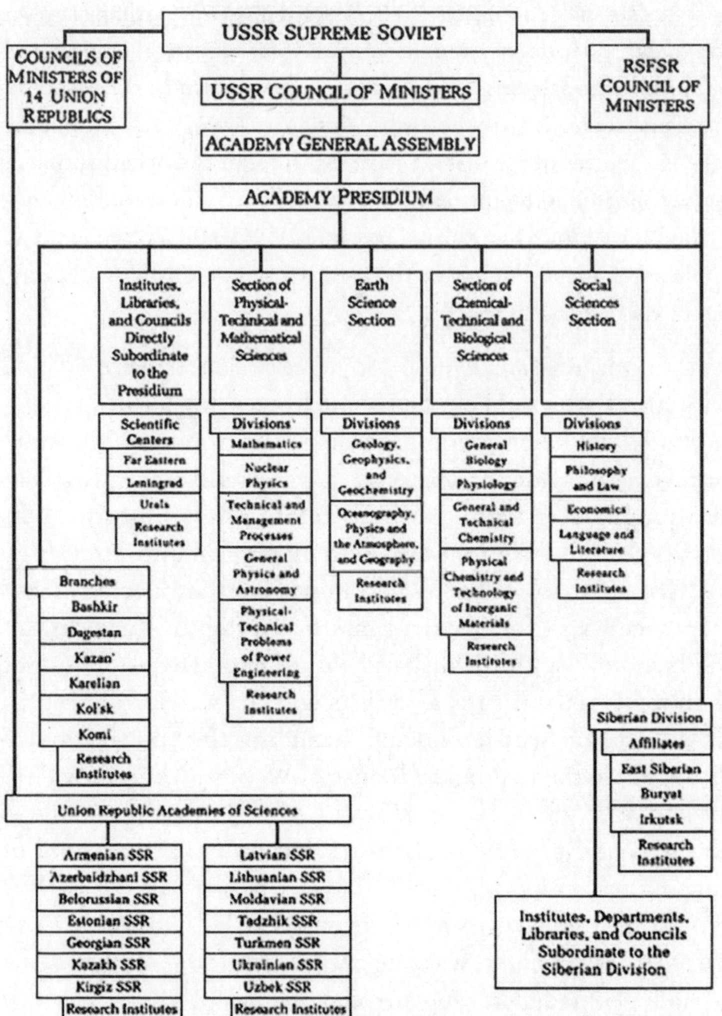

26. The Soviet organization of science under Stalin ('Research System of the USSR Academy of Sciences of the Union Republics').

had only recently got married, which evidently came as a blow to the inveterate romantic poet.[25] Her visit to Oxford nine years later, where she received an honorary degree, was filled with pathos. She earnestly assured Berlin that, because it had angered Stalin so much, their meeting had 'started the Cold War and thereby changed the history of mankind'. Berlin, no lover of confrontation, did not argue with the now elderly and half-broken woman.[26] To his credit, he had throughout been faithful to the original spirit of both the Conversazione and Bloomsbury, despite never having belonged to those networks, even as a loathsome coterie of his Cambridge contemporaries had betrayed it.

41
Ella in Reform School

The mid-twentieth century was the zenith of hierarchy. Although the First World War had ended with the collapse of no fewer than four of the great dynastic empires – the Romanov, Habsburg, Hohenzollern and Ottoman – they were replaced with astonishing swiftness by new and stronger 'empire states' that combined the extent of empire with an insistence on ethno-linguistic homogeneity and autocracy. Not only did the 1930s and 1940s witness the rise of the most centrally controlled states of all time (Stalin's Soviet Union, Hitler's Third Reich and Mao Zedong's People's Republic); in response to the Depression and the approach of another global conflict, the major democratic states also grew more centralized in their administrative structures. Between 1939 and 1945 the complex of conflicts that we call the Second World War led to an unprecedented mobilization of young men. All over the Eurasian landmass, North America and Australasia, men from their teens to their thirties received instructions to present themselves for induction into the armed services. More than 110 million people, nearly all men, served in military forces of the combatant states. By the end of the war, a quarter of the British workforce was in uniform, 18 per cent of the American workforce and 16 per cent of the Soviet workforce. Huge proportions of these vast armies never returned home. Total military deaths in the Second World War II were around 30 million (though the civilian death count was even higher). Roughly one in four German servicemen lost their lives; the mortality rate in the Red Army was almost as high. Thus did the pied pipers of Europe lead a generation of boys to their deaths.

Yet armies were only the biggest of the mid-century's organizational pyramids. Hierarchies also predominated in the economic, social and cultural spheres. Central planners ruled, whether they worked for governments or big business, whether their mission was to destroy or to produce. In the United States, Alfred Sloan's General Motors defined the 'M-form' corporation, which swiftly became the template for business organization throughout the developed world (see figure 27).

In the wake of the Second World War, the international system was also reconfigured hierarchically. Notionally, all nation-states enjoyed equal representation in the United Nations. In practice, two heavily armed alliance systems swiftly emerged, with the United States and the Soviet Union as the dominant members. With them on the UN Security Council sat three other victors of the war: Britain, China and (implausibly) France, which had been one of the Axis powers' earliest conquests. Though the Cold War would swiftly render the Security Council a place of stalemate – 'a room without a view', as a Venezuelan diplomat memorably called it – in principle the template of Vienna had been applied and a new pentarchy of five great powers created.

To the men who fought in the world wars, it doubtless seemed natural to carry over into civilian life at least some of the modes of operation they had learned while in uniform. However, the

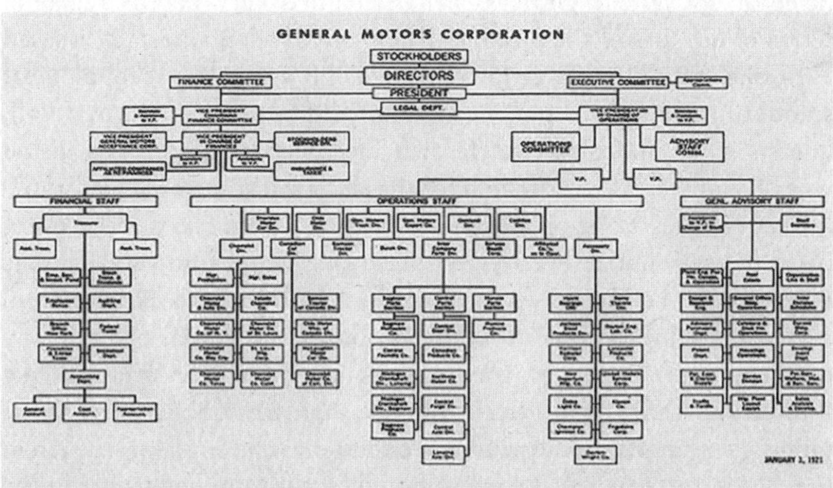

27. Alfred Sloan's 'Organization Study' for General Motors (1921).

experience of large-scale conventional warfare is not a sufficient explanation for the top-down structures of so many mid-century organizations. There was also a technological conjuncture that favoured control from above. The Viennese satirist Karl Kraus had been right: the communication technology of the mid-twentieth century overwhelmingly benefited hierarchies. Though the telephone and radio certainly created vast new networks, they were networks with a hub-and-spoke structure that were relatively easy to cut, tap or control. Like newsprint, cinema and television, radio was not a true network technology, because it generally involved one-way communication from the content provider to the listener. Those who used wireless technology to converse were generally viewed as cranks ('radio hams'); the technology was never successfully commercialized. With good reason, Joseph Goebbels described radio as 'the spiritual weapon of the totalitarian state'. Stalin might have added that the telephone was God's gift to eavesdroppers.

It is important to note that these technologies also lent themselves to social control in freer societies. In the United States – where transcontinental telephony was launched on 25 January 1915[1] – the telephone system swiftly came under the authority of a national monopoly in the form of Theodore Vail's AT&T.[2] Although the US network (known as the 'Bell System', after the Edinburgh-born inventor Alexander Graham Bell) remained very decentralized in terms of use (in 1935 less than 1.5 per cent of telephone calls crossed even one state line), in terms of ownership as well as technological standardization it was a single system.[3] 'Competition,' declared Vail, 'means *strife*, industrial warfare; it means contention.'[4] His vision was of 'a universal wire system for the electrical transmission of intelligence (written or personal communication), from every one in every place to every one in every other place, a system as universal and as extensive as the highway system of the country which extends from every man's door to ever other man's door'.[5] Vail was as open to government surveillance of the network as he was hostile to any innovation that came from outside his monopoly.[6] Telephone tapping – a simple matter with any circuit-switched system – began in the 1890s and was ruled constitutional by the Supreme Court in the case of the Seattle bootlegger Roy Olmstead, who had been convicted on evidence from a tapped phone line. Precedents existed. In 1865 the US Postal Service had been authorized to seize obscene materials, which could of course only be discovered by opening private mail. US military intelligence had reached an arrangement with Western Union to intercept suspect telegrams in the 1920s, though in 1929 the Secretary of State, Henry L. Stimson, declined to read intercepted Japanese military cables on the impeccably outmoded grounds that, as he put it, 'Gentlemen do not read each other's mail.' Pearl Harbor and all that followed swept such scruples into oblivion. The National Security Agency, established in 1952, conducted large-scale sweeps of US telegraph traffic in an effort to catch Soviet spies. Meanwhile, the Federal Bureau of Investigation under J. Edgar Hoover was unrestrained in its bugging of telephone lines. On 19 October 1963, for example, the attorney general, Robert F. Kennedy, authorized the FBI to begin wiretapping the home and office lines of the Rev. Martin Luther King, Jr., a programme of surveillance that continued until June 1966.[7]

Radio was not quite so centralized, thanks in part to Herbert Hoover's resistance to federal control of the airwaves during his time as commerce secretary. The Radio Act of 1927 gave the Federal Radio Commission (FRC) the power to divide up the spectrum and to decide which applicants would receive licences to run stations at specific wavelengths, power levels, locations and hours.[8] Seven years later, a new Federal Communications Commission took over this role. Henceforth, licences were granted for three years at a time to broadcasters who could persuade the FCC that their station would serve 'public convenience, interest, or necessity', criteria that were never applied to newspapers. As a consequence, free speech on air was severely circumscribed by both regulators and (because of the importance of advertising as a source of revenue) commercial interests.[9]

Though many intellectuals feared that the United States was developing totalitarian tendencies in the early Cold War era, there was of course a profound difference between American life and Soviet life. White American citizens enjoyed the full range of civil and political rights guaranteed by the Constitution and could challenge the intrusions of government in the courts if they chose. For many black

Americans, however, the benefits of life in the USA relative to life in the USSR were less self-evident, a point often made, albeit hypocritically, by Soviet propaganda. A corollary of the social conformism of the late 1940s, 1950s and early 1960s was institutionalized racial discrimination. Then, as now, African-Americans were significantly more likely to fall foul of the penal system. A single example may suffice to illustrate the point. On 10 April 1933, Westchester County's judge George W. Smyth sentenced a fifteen-year-old 'colored' girl named Ella Fitzgerald to the New York State Training School for Girls in Hudson, NY, because she was 'ungovernable and [would] not obey the just and lawful commands of her mother'. It was not a happy institution. When Jacob Moreno devised the first 'sociograms' in 1933, it was to help explain a spate of runaways from the school (see Introduction). In the 1930s, even network theory served the panopticon.* Happily, Fitzgerald escaped to Manhattan and a stellar singing career. Her Russian counterparts were more brutally treated.

American society was justly famed in the nineteenth century for the richness of its associational life. Indeed, as we have seen, Alexis de Tocqueville had seen this as one of the foundations of the country's success as a democracy. Yet the very ease with which social networks could form in the United States created a vulnerability that was ruthlessly exploited by a foreign network imported into the country during the great influx of migrants from southern Italy that occurred in the late nineteenth century and early twentieth: the Mafia. This process was glamorized in Mario Puzo's novel *The Godfather* and the films based on it. The film was not wholly fictional, to be sure.† There were indeed 'Five Families' who controlled much of the gambling, loan-sharking, protection rackets and (during Prohibition) bootlegging in the New York metropolitan area. Their origins

* Devised by the English Utilitarian theorist Jeremy Bentham in the late eighteenth century, the panopticon was a prison or asylum in which all inmates could be observed by a single watchman without their being able to tell whether or not they were being watched.

† Having seen the film, Sammy 'the Bull' Gravano said: 'I left the movie stunned . . . I mean I floated out of the theater. Maybe it was fiction, but for me, then, that was our life. It was incredible. I remember talking to a multitude of guys, made guys, who felt exactly the same way.'

were in the south Italian immigrant communities such as Little Italy on Manhattan's Lower East Side and East Harlem. The fictional character of Vito Corleone was based partly on Frank Costello (born Francesco Castiglia) of the Luciano/Genovese family and partly on Carlo Gambino of the Gambino family. The singer Johnny Fontane was clearly Frank Sinatra. The Jewish gangsters were also based on real people: the brutal Las Vegas casino operator Moe Greene on Benjamin 'Bugsy' Siegel and the more cerebral Hyman Roth on Meyer Lansky. Nor did Puzo greatly exaggerate the extent of the Mafia's influence in the United States. Before the Second World War, Lansky and Siegel had set up the 'The Commission' with Salvatore 'Lucky' Luciano in an attempt to impose some kind of central governance not just on the Five Families of New York but on organized crime throughout America. Luciano's reign had effectively ended in 1936, when he was arrested and successfully prosecuted by special prosecutor (later governor) Thomas E. Dewey for running a prostitution racket. However, his place was soon taken by Costello. There is no question, too, that by the 1950s the various Mafia families were deeply involved in legitimate business – ranging from entertainment to casinos in pre-revolutionary Cuba – as well as in organized labour and politics. For example, John F. Kennedy's campaign may have called on Mafia assistance to defeat Richard Nixon in 1960, and Kennedy certainly shared a mistress, Judith Campbell Exner, with the Chicago gangster Sam Giancana. Between August 1960 and April 1961 the CIA even sought to assassinate Fidel Castro using Mafia hit-men. (It does not seem likely, however, that the Mafia were responsible for the assassination of Kennedy, a conspiracy theory that has proved remarkably resistant to both official inquiry and scholarly scrutiny. Mercifully, Puzo resisted the temptation to include it in his novel.)

Yet there has been a tendency to exaggerate the organizational sophistication of the Mafia, precisely because so little reliable documentation exists about its operations aside from testimony from the minority of Mafiosi who violated *omertà* (roughly 'manliness'), the code of silence that forbids initiates, on pain of death, from betraying their comrades to the authorities. It was Joseph Valachi who revealed that initiates preferred to speak not of the Mafia but of *Cosa*

Nostra – 'our thing' – when he testified before the Permanent Subcommittee on Investigations of the Senate Committee on Government Operations in 1963. Twenty-one years later, the Italo-Brazilian informant Tommaso Buscetta described to American prosecutors the hierarchical structure of a typical Mafia family: at the top a boss (*capofamiglia* or *rappresentante*), below him a *capo bastone* or *sotto capo*, and advising the boss one or more advisers (*consigliere*). The lower ranks were organized into groups (*decina*) of about ten 'soldiers' (*soldati*, *operai* or *picciotti*), each led by a *capodecina*. Testifying after his arrest in 1996, Giovanni Brusca – the Sicilian mafioso nicknamed *Il Porco*, who had murdered the anti-Mafia prosecutor Giovanni Falcone in 1992 – described his own initiation rites in 1976. Invited to a 'banquet' at a country house, he had been confronted by several mafiosi sitting around a table on which were laid a gun, a dagger and a piece of paper bearing the image of a saint. After Brusca had affirmed his commitment to a life of crime, the most senior mafioso pricked his finger with a needle and told him to smear his blood on the image of the saint, which he then set alight: 'If you betray Cosa Nostra,' they told him, 'your flesh will burn like this saint.' Such stories are fascinating, no doubt, but how much credence should they be given? One possibility is that these structures and rituals were in fact of relatively recent origin, if they existed at all.

Mafia was originally a culture or way of life that arose out of peculiarities of Sicilian history. The word derives from the adjective *mafiusu* (swagger or bravado), the etymology of which (perhaps Arabic, a remnant of Muslim rule) has long been inconclusively debated. The word was given currency in 1865 by an obscure play *I mafiusi di la Vicaria* ('The Mafiosi of the Vicaria') and was first used officially by the Tuscan aristocrat Count Filippo Gualterio two years later. But the preferred term favoured by Sicilians was in fact 'the Honoured Society' (*Onorata Società*). The historian Diego Gambetta has characterized this society as, in essence, a 'cartel of private protection firms'.[10] It arose in the later nineteenth century following Sicily's integration into the Kingdom of Italy – in effect, a Piedmontese empire – at a time when there was next to no police force and landowners relied on private armies to protect their property and produce. It then evolved into a general system of contract enforcement, with homicide as the sanction for breaches. Similar 'societies' arose elsewhere in southern Italy: Camorra, operating in the region of Campania, 'Ndrangheta in Calabria, Sacra Corona Unita in Apulia. The enduring poverty of these regions makes clear that such organizations are not optimal bases for social order. Yet to call them 'organizations' may be misleading. In his *Lettere Meridionali*, published in the mid-1870s, the Neapolitan historian and politician Pasquale Villari declared: 'The Mafia has no written statutes, it is not a secret society, hardly an association. It is formed by spontaneous generation.'[11] So shadowy was the Mafia in Sicily that it proved relatively easy to get rid of it during the period of Fascist rule when Cesare Mori was the 'Iron Prefect' of Palermo (1925–9).[12]

It has sometimes been claimed that, after the fall of Sicily to the Allies in the summer of 1943, the Allied Military Government (AMG) somehow conspired with the Mafia to bring about a restoration of its old power on the island, with 'Lucky' Luciano playing a mediating role. Such assertions are groundless. The reality was that Allied officers produced highly insightful assessments of a culture of criminality as they encountered it, re-emerging from wherever it had hidden itself during Mussolini's reign. In October 1943, for example, the American vice-consul in Palermo, Capt. W. E. Scotten, argued that the Mafia was not a centrally organized entity but something more akin to a network, bound together by a code of honour and secrecy. 'Mafia can scarcely be described as formal organization with a recognized hierarchy of leaders,' wrote Scotten:

> What organization it has is more horizontal in character than vertical. It is an association of criminals, the common bond of which is their mutual interest in frustrating interference from the authorities. It is a conspiracy against the forces of law which takes form essentially in the conspiracy of silence known as *omertà*, a code imposed on its victims as well as the general public, who are thus forced to become involuntary accomplices. Mafia is, in a sense, more than a[n] association; it is also a social system, a way of life, a profession. Thus the difficulty, from the police standpoint, lies in the peculiar nature of Mafia itself. If it had a formal organization, progressive removal of its leaders from the top down would cause its collapse.[13]

As the occupying forces struggled to cope with the immense administrative problems of running post-Fascist, post-conflict Sicily, officials like Scotten confronted a painful reality: they lacked the resources to get rid of this strange and violent culture. Indeed, in some measure they had to live with it in order to restore any kind of order to the island. The British writer Norman Lewis formed similar impressions.[14]

This was the Mafia that operated in American cities from the 1920s until the 1960s. Despite the newspapers' enthusiastic coverage of 'Murder Inc.', the families portrayed in *The Godfather* were closer in practice to their Sicilian origins, in the sense that their rackets were relatively decentralized. There was no *capo de tutti capi*. As soon as the families attempted any such formalization of their system, they were done for, just as Scotten understood. The era portrayed in *The Godfather* was in that sense a time of hubris, when organized crime attempted simultaneously to become more organized and less criminal. When the Racketeer Influenced and Corrupt Organizations Act (RICO Act) became law in 1970, the American Mafia was demolished with striking ease. In the course of the 1980s, twenty-three bosses from around the country were convicted, along with thirteen underbosses and forty-three captains. The network had made the fatal mistake of becoming the hierarchy depicted in the movies.

Even as illegal networks flourished and penetrated the American political elite, perfectly legal ones were the object of harassment by the authorities. When black Americans began their campaign for equal civil rights, they faced shocking levels of both legal and extra-legal oppression. The civil rights movement had its origins in black churches, black colleges and the Southern chapters of the National Association for the Advancement of Colored People, which had been founded in 1909.[15] It was precisely these deep institutional roots that made the movement so hard to stop: these were networks maintained and renewed each Sunday. As Martin Luther King put it, 'The invitational periods at the mass meetings, when we asked for volunteers, were much like those invitational periods that occur every Sunday morning in Negro churches, when the pastor projects the call to those present to join the church. By twenties and thirties and forties, people came forward to join our army.'[16] The bugging of his home phone was just a tiny part of the sustained campaign to disrupt and defeat the civil rights movement. Yet that campaign ultimately failed. By contrast, white Americans in this period struggled to organize protests, as the case of the 1957 property tax demonstrations in Los Angeles County illustrates. Though there was widespread outrage at the higher taxes assessed that year, the opposition campaign petered out because the LA suburbs lacked the kind of social networks and leadership that had emerged from the black churches of the South.[17]

Americans had not lost their urge to network, to be sure. Indeed, the mid-century saw the rise of one of the most successful social networks in American history: the self-help network for drunks, Alcoholics Anonymous. Founded in Akron, Ohio, in 1935 by a New York stockbroker named William Wilson ('Bill W.') and an Akron doctor, Robert Smith ('Dr Bob'), AA offered alcoholics a twelve-step path back to sobriety, but its real strength lay in the therapeutic network effects of regular meetings at which experiences of addiction were confessed and shared.[18] Though not as intellectually significant as Isaiah Berlin's meeting with Anna Akhmatova, Wilson's earlier meeting with Ebby Thacher, another chronic drinker, was the first edge in what would ultimately become a global network.* 'My thoughts began to race,' Wilson recalled, 'as I envisioned a chain reaction among alcoholics, one carrying this message and these principles to the next.'[19] A striking feature of AA was and remains its quasi-religious and wholly unpolitical character. (It was in fact an outgrowth of the Christian evangelical Oxford Group.) Had anyone informed J. Edgar Hoover that alcoholism was somehow linked to communism, however, AA meetings would no doubt swiftly have been placed under surveillance. In reality, the earliest AA groups were inclined to exclude people who – aside from their alcoholism – were not socially respectable, including (as Wilson ironically put it) 'beggars, tramps, asylum inmates, prisoners, queers, plain crackpots, and fallen women'. It was not until 1949 that the organization resolved to admit any person, regardless of other factors, who professed a 'desire to stop drinking'.[20]

The pathologies of the totalitarian states, like the much milder

* Today, there are approximately 115,000 registered AA groups with more than 2 million members in over 150 countries.

authoritarian traits that developed in democracies of the same era, were certainly an inducement to abuse alcohol. It was not only the Cambridge spies who drank like fish. Trapped in intolerant hierarchical chains of command, afraid to join social networks that might be construed as subversive, the average mid-century man sought solace in bottles. In Soviet Russia the drug of choice was vodka. In Nazi Germany, where alcohol production was sacrificed to rearmament, more exotic drugs were favoured, such as Pervitin (methamphetamine) and Eudokal (a morphine derivative).[21] In the United States after prohibition, spirits were consumed in volumes that today seem astonishing. The generations of the world wars also smoked tobacco with suicidal frequency. Nevertheless, the comforts afforded by such stimulants were fleeting. In Aldous Huxley's *Brave New World* (1932), even narcotics are controlled by the Fordist World State, along with everything else, from eugenics to euthanasia; the fate of the nonconformist Bernard Marx is banishment. In Orwell's *Nineteen Eighty-Four* (1949) there is not the slightest chance that Winston Smith will successfully defy Big Brother's rule over Airstrip One; his fate is to be tortured and brainwashed. A remarkable number of the literary heroes of the mid-century were thus crushed, from Joseph Heller's John Yossarian to Alexander Solzhenytsin's Ivan Denisovich to John le Carré's Alec Leamas – memorably portrayed as a boozer by the alcoholic actor Richard Burton. Fittingly, what had begun as a wave of man-made ideological plagues ended with a pandemic of self-induced liver and lung malfunctions.

VII

Own the Jungle

42
The Long Peace

The great, hierarchically ordered empires that waged the Cold War against each other left little space for networks to form amongst their citizens, unless their character was wholly unpolitical. However, the further one travelled from the imperial metropole, the less total was the control of the central planner. The Third World War was not fought with nuclear missiles in the stratosphere, but with semi-automatic weapons in the jungles of what became known as the Third World. Here, far beyond the reach of rail, road, telegraph and telephone networks, the superpowers were deprived of the command, control and communications on which they depended. The exposure of their limitations in far-flung, impoverished countries worked dialectically to produce a crisis of their own domestic political structures. The 1970s and 1980s witnessed a resurgence of networks and a breakdown of hierarchies, culminating in the rapid disintegration of the Soviet Union and its empire in Eastern Europe. The fact that this same period saw the birth of the Internet raises the tempting possibility that technology had once again tilted the balance of power, this time to the detriment of the totalitarian state and its authoritarian offshoots. As we shall see, however, the historical process was not quite so neat. Rather than being a cause of the late twentieth-century crisis, the Internet appears to have been a consequence of the breakdown of hierarchical power.

Historians of the Cold War have long debated why it stayed cold – why, in other words, the United States and the Soviet Union did not go to war with each other as the United Kingdom and the German Reich had twice. The commonplace answer is that the advent of nuclear weapons had raised the stakes so high that statesmen in

Washington and Moscow were more risk-averse than their counterparts in London and Berlin had been in 1914 and 1939. Another approach is to argue that the networks of alliance were more stable after 1945 than they had ever been before. Both superpowers constructed large, dense and relatively stable networks of allies that combined mutual defence commitments with commercial integration. Between 1816 and 1950, the number of alliances per country had been on average just over 2.5. By contrast, in the period from 1951 until 2003 the average was more than four times larger (10.5).[1] A further elaboration points to the growth of trade in reducing conflict.[2] Interestingly, the growth of security alliances for strategic purposes seems to have prefigured the growth of trade within them.[3] Such network effects doubtless played some part. However, the defining characteristic of nearly all agreements – military and economic – in the Cold War era was their hierarchical structure. Even if the great powers of the UN Security Council could never agree, other clusters of power were possible: the original six signatories of the 1957 Treaty of Rome, for example, or the original members of the 'group of seven', which began in 1974 as an informal meeting of the financial officials of the world's five largest economies: the United States, the United Kingdom, West Germany, Japan and France.

Yet the idea of the Cold War as a 'long peace' makes sense only if we confine our attention to such developed countries. If we consider the world as a whole, the period from the 1950s until the 1980s was anything but peaceful in Africa, Asia and Latin America. Civil wars were endemic in those regions of the world, and very often they escalated precisely because warring groups received military assistance from the superpowers and therefore acted as their proxies.[4] The Cold War was also a time of revolutions and coups as the European overseas empires disintegrated. It was the perception that such political crises were contagious that gave rise to the idea of a 'domino effect'.[5] As President Dwight Eisenhower put it, following the French defeat at Dien Bien Phu at the hands of the Vietminh in Indo-China: 'You have a row of dominos set up. You knock over the first one . . . What will happen to the last one is the certainty that it will go over very quickly.' If the alliances of the Cold War created hub-and-spoke networks, the domino effect threatened the outer nodes of those networks with contagion. Keeping dominoes from falling called for a particular set of military skills that would come to be known as 'counter-insurgency', but is perhaps more vividly described by the name of one of its precursors: 'jungle warfare'.

43
The General

In his novel *The General* (1936), C. S. Forester painted a lurid portrait of an archetypal British general of the First World War generation – the personification of the mid-twentieth-century era of rigid hierarchy. His personality was:

> noticeable [even] in his selection of his subordinates, and so through them to the holders of the lesser commands. The men who were wanted were men without fear of responsibility, men of ceaseless energy and of iron will, who could be relied upon to carry out their part in a plan of battle as far as flesh and blood – their own and their men's – would permit. Men without imagination were necessary to execute a military policy devoid of imagination, devised by a man without imagination. Anything resembling freakishness or originality was suspect in view of the plan of campaign. Every General desired as subordinates officers who would meticulously obey orders undaunted by difficulties or losses or fears for the future; every General knew what would be expected of him (and approved of it) and took care to have under him Generals of whom he could expect the same. When brute force was to be systematically applied only men who could fit into the system without allowance having to be made for them were wanted.[1]

It would be hard to find a better description of a hierarchical regime than that. By the 1940s, however, the British Army had learned through bitter experience that a different, more dynamic kind of leadership was needed. They had seen, in the course of two world wars, that the exceptional effectiveness of the German army depended not on the rigid implementation of battle plans but rather on decentralization of decision-making and flexibility amid the fog of war.[2] In 1940, for example, freely roaming German Panzers had exploited wireless communication and the French road network to drive deep behind the enemy's front line, which then collapsed in confusion. The more inaccessible the battlefield, the more important it was to free officers (including the non-commissioned variety) from the constraints of centralized command and control. No campaigns had made that more abundantly clear than those waged in Asia against the Japanese. In the battle for Burma, a new kind of British general had emerged – the very antithesis of Forester's iron-willed, unimaginative Blimp. In the jungle, 'freakishness and originality' were at a premium.

Born in 1912, the son of an Assam tea-planter, Walter Colyear Walker had been much too young to witness the slaughter of the Somme and Ypres. All his life, Walker was pugnacious to a fault. At school in England, he took the view that bullying was best countered with 'a straight left to the nose or an uppercut to the jaw'. At Sandhurst he chafed at drill and thirsted to fire his rifle rather than just clean it. As an officer in the 1/8 Gurkhas, he served with distinction in operations against the Faqir of Ipi* in Waziristan, where he became an expert in ambush techniques. In 1944 Walker took over command of the 4/8 Gurkhas, whom – after two months of retraining – he transformed into a formidable fighting force, earning himself a DSO. The British were learning a new kind of warfare. 'Experience shows,' read the so-called *Jungle Book* manual of 1943, 'that command must be decentralised so that junior leaders will be confronted with situations in which they must make decisions and act without delay on their own responsibility . . .'[3] This was Walker's gospel. After the war, as a general staff officer in Kuala Lumpur, he was given the task of training what became known as 'Ferret Force', a mixture of British, Gurkha, Chinese and indigenous Dyak troops. In 1948–9, as Communist terrorists plunged Malaya into a state of emergency, Walker commanded the Far East Land Forces Training Centre, establishing what later

* The Faqir of Ipi, known to his followers as 'Haji Sahib' (Respected Pilgrim), had declared jihad against the British after a colonial judge had ruled against the marriage of an underage girl whose family claimed she had been abducted and forcibly converted to Islam. The Faqir succeeded in uniting the Muslim tribes of Waziristan in a sustained campaign of violence against British rule.

became the Jungle Warfare School at Kota Tinggi.[4] The doctrine that emerged from the school was enshrined in 'The Conduct of Anti-Terrorist Operations in Malaya', which effectively became the British Army's counter-insurgency manual.[5] The key insight was that the ultimate goal of military action should be to ensure that 'guerrilla attacks did not disrupt the process of legitimate political rule'.[6] What that meant in practice was the merciless extirpation of the Communists on the basis of coordinated intelligence-gathering (by both police and military forces), aggressive small-unit patrolling and meticulously planned ambushes.[7] In 1958 Walker was responsible for Operation Tiger, in which 99 Gurkha Brigade eliminated the last Communists operating in the state of Johore. 'My Special Branch man,' Walker later declared, 'had guaranteed the CTs [Communist terrorists] would come and after 28 days they came and were killed in the swamp.' Men who could patiently lie in wait in sweltering heat for as long as four weeks were a priceless asset, in Walker's eyes. He was incandescent when he was informed of a plan afoot in London to cut the Gurkhas from their official strength of more than 10,000 to 4,000.[8] 'Malaya is the last bulwark against Communism in this part of the world,' he argued, deploying the domino analogy: 'If Malaya falls, the situation in South-East Asia becomes irretrievable.'[9]

It was in the dense jungles of Borneo – the world's third-largest island – that Walker would prove his point. With no railways, almost no roads, and precious few landing strips, Borneo was a place where decentralized decision-making was the only sort possible. Having been somewhat arbitrarily divided between the British and Dutch empires, the island had a large internal frontier between the British territories of Sarawak, Brunei and North Borneo, and Indonesian (formerly Dutch) Borneo, known as Kalimantan. The British plan for a graceful exit was to merge Sarawak, Brunei and North Borneo with Malaya and Singapore to form a Federation of Malaysia. Before this could be carried out, however, there was an Indonesian-backed revolt against the planned merger in Brunei and, in April 1963, the beginning of what became known as the *Konfrontasi* (Confrontation), as Indonesian troops crossed the border into eastern Sarawak and obliterated the police station at Tebedu, near Kuching.

President Sukarno of Indonesia dreamed of building a Greater

28. General Sir Walter Walker, hero of the Borneo *Konfrontasi*, pioneer of counter-insurgency. His maxim was 'Own the jungle.'

Indonesia including, at the very least, all of Borneo. Walter Walker's job as commander (and later director of operations) of British Forces, Borneo, was to dispel that dream at minimal cost. On his way to his new command, Walker wrote a directive based on his experience in the Malayan Emergency, laying out what he called the 'Six Ingredients of Success':

> unified operations; timely and accurate information, which means a first-class intelligence machine; speed, mobility and flexibility; security of our bases, wherever they were and whatever they might be (airfield, patrol base, etc.); . . . domination of the jungle [and] . . . winning the hearts and minds of the people, and especially indigenous people.[10]

This was a manifesto for networked warfare – the antithesis of the rigid, hierarchical mode of operation of the old British Army. A favourite Walker word was 'Jointmanship'. One key lesson he had learned in Malaya was the importance of 'unity – between the armed forces themselves, between the armed forces and the police, and between the security forces as a whole and the civil administration' and 'joint planning and joint operations at all times and at all levels'.[11] Army, Air Force and Navy headquarters were brought together and compelled to work closely with the civilian authorities and police.[12] Walker likened the new command structure to 'a triumvirate – civilian, policeman, soldier – all under the single direction of a "military" Director of Operations', whose job it was 'to make sure that the system operates as two pairs of scissors, neither subordinate to the other, but each making it possible for the other to succeed'.[13] Communications were also as integrated as the radio technology of the time permitted.[14]

On the ground, Walker's emphasis was on 'complete mobility and flexibility'.[15] In forward areas, at least two thirds of any garrison were 'always out in an offensive role, dominating the jungle and ambushing tracks by day and night, so that the enemy never knew where we were, and was always liable to be contacted and savaged'. The key, as he memorably put it, was to *own* the jungle:

> Results could not be achieved merely by attacking and shooting the enemy and then returning to base. He had to be played at his own game, by living out in the jungle for weeks on end, by winning the hearts and minds of the people and by planting our own agents in villages known to be unfriendly. In these conditions, your base must be carried on your back, and that base consists of a featherweight plastic sheet, a sockful of rice and a pocketful of ammunition. The jungle has got to belong to you; you must own it; you must control and dominate it.[16]

Three especially effective innovations were Walker's use of border scouts, special forces and helicopters. The men from the border areas were crucial. In the words of J. P. Cross, the officer entrusted with their training, 'If the border peoples could stay put by being made to feel they were taking an active and positive part in their own defence and that government was behind them Confrontation would probably fail. Border Scouts were, therefore, essential for victory.'[17] Walker's vision was of 'the Scouts out in front roaming like a screen, being the eyes and ears of the Conventional Forces, with a sting. This entail[ed] getting them to merge in with the background, taking off their status-symbol jungle boots and going without their morale-raising rifle, so as to appear like a farmer, fisherman, trader, wood-cutter, etc.' Cross trained his men not only to blend in, but also to memorize any trace they encountered of hostile activity and to track the enemy 'using jitter tactics against him, fading into the background, shadowing him and picking off stragglers, leaving signs so that those following can readily understand what goes on'.[18] Working closely with the border scouts were around seventy men from 22 SAS Regiment, whose role was to 'live among the people, earning their trust and assisting with medical and other issues', while at the same time 'spotting incursions'.[19] Finally, Walker made full use of the helicopters at his disposal (never more than eighty) to move heavier weapons rapidly from one hotspot to another, giving the impression that there was artillery in every forward base.[20]

Few people today remember the defeat of the *Konfrontasi* in darkest Borneo. That is because it was so complete. As Walker put it, 'To dominate and own the jungle over 1,000 miles, to a depth of 100 miles, against this enemy, and smash him every time he attempted an incursion, was no mean achievement on the part of the 13 battalions concerned.'[21] Casualties were limited: British and Commonwealth troops suffered 114 killed and 181 wounded, compared with confirmed Indonesian casualties of 590 killed, 222 wounded and 771 captured. The significance of these low figures lies in the contrast between what happened in Borneo and what was happening simultaneously 700 miles to the north, in Vietnam, where American forces were in the early stages of what would prove to be a disastrously costly and ultimately unsuccessful effort to preserve the independence of South Vietnam. As Walker noted in an article published in 1969, his aim in Borneo had been 'to prevent the conflict from escalating into open war, similar to that in South Vietnam today'. He had done it by winning not only 'the opening rounds of the jungle battle' but also the 'psychological battle in the kampongs and villages of the up-country tribal peoples'.[22] Above all, he had done it by owning the jungle, because:

> an army that travels secretly, mostly in small groups, making rendezvous only at the precise moment of battle, cannot be ambushed. That

> is the way the Viet Cong usually travels. It is the way our soldiers learned to move: and they did it better than the enemy. They out-guerrilla-ed the guerrilla in every department of the game through sheer good training, based on operational experience.[23]

As we shall see (in chapter 50), it took the US military fully a generation to learn this art of networked warfare – though they would end up waging it in concrete jungles, rather than in the tropical rainforests once owned by Walter Walker.

44
The Crisis of Complexity

'What should they know of England, who only England know?' Kipling had memorably asked in 'The English Flag'. For imperial warriors like Walter Walker, who scarcely knew England at all, the problem was different. Walker knew the jungle. The country he returned to in 1965, when he was appointed Deputy Chief of Staff, Allied Forces Central Europe, was *terra incognita*. Postings in Paris, Brunssum in the Netherlands, and finally Kolsås in Norway were anticlimactic and bureaucratic. As commander-in-chief of Allied Forces Northern Europe (from 1969 until his retirement in 1972), Walker saw his role as being to warn of an impending Soviet *Konfrontasi* in Scandinavia. (He later published two books on the subject, unambiguously titled *The Bear at the Back Door* and *The Next Domino*.) This did not endear him to the politicians in London, who by this time had discovered the benefits of détente with the Soviets, not the least of which was the excuse it gave them for more defence spending cuts.

The general in C. S. Forester's novel spent his retirement pathetically playing bridge in a bath-chair. Walter Walker was not the kind of old soldier who fades away, however. In July 1974 he wrote a letter to the *Daily Telegraph* in which he warned darkly of 'the Communist Trojan horse in our midst, with its fellow travellers wriggling their maggoty way inside its belly' and called for 'dynamic, invigorating, uplifting leadership . . . above party politics' to 'save' the country. In his view, the Irish Republican Army – then wreaking havoc with car bombs and assassinations on the British mainland – was a Communist front organization. 'Northern Ireland should now be declared a proper operational area, or even war zone,' he argued, 'in which would-be murderers caught carrying or using arms would be subject to summary trial and execution.' Asked by the *Evening News* if the Army should take over the country, Walker replied: 'Perhaps the country might choose rule by the gun in preference to anarchy.' Claiming the support of Admiral of the Fleet Sir Varyl Begg and Marshal of the RAF Sir John Slessor, Walker set up an 'anti-chaos' organization, known at first as Unison and later as Civil Assistance, the stated aim of which was to create a force of 'trustworthy, loyal, levelheaded men' to maintain essential services in case of a general strike. Suspecting the prime minister, Harold Wilson, of being himself a Communist – the Fourth and Fifth Man had yet to be named, after all – Walker was one of many conservatives attracted by Enoch Powell's combination of opposition to both immigration and European integration. Unhesitatingly, Walker took the side of the Rhodesian leader Ian Smith, made six visits to South Africa's apartheid regime, and condemned homosexuals for 'us[ing] the main sewer of the human body as a playground'. (In *Who's Who* he listed his own recreations as 'normal'.)[1]

It was all much too easy to mock. Walker's home in Somerset became 'Lambrook-les-Deux-Églises' (an allusion to the former French president Charles de Gaulle's rural retreat, Colombey-les-Deux-Églises). It did not help that one of Walker's avowed supporters was the comedian Michael Bentine, formerly of *The Goon Show*, now hosting a children's show called *Potty Time* on Thames Television. In the television series *The Fall and Rise of Reginald Perrin* (1976–9), the character of Reggie's brother Jimmy (Maj. James Anderson, ret.) was a cruelly funny parody of Walker's type:

> REGGIE: Who are you going to fight against when this balloon of yours goes up?
>
> JIMMY: Forces of anarchy. Wreckers of law and order. Communists, Maoists, Trotskyists, neo-Trotskyists, crypto-Trotskyists, union leaders, Communist union leaders, atheists, agnostics, long-haired weirdos, short-haired weirdos, vandals, hooligans, football supporters, namby-pamby probation officers, rapists, papists, papist rapists, foreign surgeons – headshrinkers, who ought to be locked

up – Wedgwood Benn, keg bitter, punk rock, glue-sniffers, 'Play For Today', squatters, Clive Jenkins, Roy Jenkins, Up Jenkins, up everybody's, Chinese restaurants – why do you think Windsor Castle is ringed with Chinese restaurants?

REGGIE: Is that all?

JIMMY: Yes.

REGGIE: I see. You realize the sort of people you're going to attract, don't you, Jimmy? Thugs, bully-boys, psychopaths, sacked policemen, security guards, sacked security guards, racialists, Paki-bashers, queer-bashers, Chink-bashers, basher-bashers, anybody-bashers, rear Admirals, queer admirals, Vice Admirals, fascists, neo-fascists, crypto-fascists, loyalists, neo-loyalists, crypto-loyalists.

JIMMY: You really think so? I thought support might be difficult.

Thus did the master of jungle warfare end up as fodder for the writers of sitcoms. The real Walker faded away more tragically, the victim of two bungled hip operations that left him disabled.

Yet, for all their absurdities, the likes of Walter Walker were correct that *something* was rotten in the state of England, even if it was not the Communist plot of their febrile imaginings, much less the social and sexual liberation they so deplored. Britain in the mid-1970s was indeed a mess. The inflation rate was one of the highest in the developed world. Industrial unrest was rife. The same frivolous cynicism that made television comedy so good at that time also made daily life in the United Kingdom rather bad. The problem was not 'forces of anarchy'. It was the breakdown of the centralized British state that had been built in the era of the world wars.

For the majority of Britain's civilian elite – not only the civil servants in Whitehall but also the Oxford and Cambridge dons and the titled members of 'the great and the good' – the lesson of the two victories of 1918 and 1945 had seemed clear: centralized planning worked. In the post-war period, every bureaucrat, it seemed, had a plan that could be designed and run from the political centre and merely implemented in the localities.[2] From housing to healthcare, from school milk to Scottish hydro-electricity, everything called for planning. The self-confidence of the technocrats at that time is nicely exemplified by MONIAC (the Monetary National Income Analogue Computer), a hydraulic device designed by the New Zealand-born Bill Phillips that was supposed to simulate the effects of Keynesian economic policy on the UK economy. Not until the 1970s did it begin to become apparent that, in peacetime, even the best-laid plans were liable to descend into a quagmire of stagflation and corruption. High-modernist planning wreaked all kinds of havoc in its heyday, from the collectivization of Soviet agriculture to the building of Brasilia and the compulsory *ujamaa* villages in Tanzania. Yet it could always survive such catastrophes, if only because their effect was to kill off any kind of opposition. It was in its decrepitude that the planned system could be challenged.[3]

29. William Phillips with MONIAC (the Monetary National Income Analogue Computer), a hydraulic model of the UK economy built in England in 1949.

The problem for the planners was that a hierarchical system that had been well-suited to the activity of total war – an activity characterized by monopsony, as the state is the sole buyer, and standardization, as destruction is much simpler than production – was wholly unsuited to a consumer society. Those who had fought in the world wars had been promised prosperity as well as victory. In practice, that could be achieved only if millions of households were freed to make billions of choices, to which hundreds of thousands of firms could respond. The result was rising complexity, in which 'lateral interactions become much more important, boundaries between sub-systems within [any] organization . . . more fluid'.[4] As the physicist Yaneer Bar-Yam has argued, 'a group of individuals whose collective behaviour is controlled by a single individual cannot behave in a more complex way than the individual who is exercising the control'. The five-year plan might have worked in Stalin's Soviet Union, where the individual was little more than a cog in a system of collectivized agriculture, heavy industrial production, total warfare and penal slavery. It was bound to break down in Harold Wilson's Britain. As a general principle, once the 'complexity of demands upon collective human systems have . . . become larger than an individual human being . . . the hierarchy is no longer able to impose the necessary correlations/coordination on individuals. Instead, interactions and mechanisms characteristic of networks in complex systems like the brain are necessary.'[5]

The transition to a more networked world manifested itself in myriad ways in the 1970s. The driver was not so much technological as organizational. Friedrich Hayek was one of the first to rediscover Adam Smith's old insight that the spontaneous order of the market was bound to be superior to 'any that could have been achieved by deliberate organization'. As Hayek observed, 'To maintain that we must deliberately plan modern society because it has become so complex is therefore paradoxical, and the result of a complete misunderstanding . . . The fact is, rather, that we can preserve an order of such complexity . . . only indirectly by enforcing and improving the rules conductive to the formation of a spontaneous order.'[6] Others found this out for themselves the hard way. At the Ford Motor Company, senior executives began to notice that the volume of information they had to handle was overwhelming, while assembly lines had become so tightly optimized that small changes in the design of a car required protracted interruptions of production. They had 'got too good'.[7] Vertically integrated conglomerates found themselves under pressure to break up in what economic historians have called the 'second market revolution'[8] because they could not compete with more nimble rivals that outsourced their supply chains.[9] The shift away from hierarchy was accelerated by the growing awareness of Western political elites that prosperity would also be furthered by increasing international trade. Mid-century dreams of autarky yielded to a glad, confident era in which comparative advantage could once again be exploited. The term 'globalization' – defined as 'making worldwide in scope or application' – made its first appearance in the Merriam–Webster dictionary in 1951.[10] In 1983 Theodore Levitt published his seminal essay on 'The Globalization of Markets' in the *Harvard Business Review*.[11]

Yet it was not wholly true that the national plan was giving way to the global market. As Walter Powell pointed out in an illuminating 1990 article, the growth of business networks at both the national and international level represented something more than simply the triumph of markets over the hierarchical corporation. 'In markets,' he argued, 'the standard strategy is to drive the hardest possible bargain on the immediate exchange. In networks, the preferred option is often creating indebtedness and reliance over the long haul':[12]

> In network modes of resource allocation, transactions occur neither through discrete exchanges nor by administrative fiat, but through networks of individuals engaged in reciprocal, preferential, mutually supportive actions. Networks can be complex: they involve neither the explicit criteria of the market, nor the familiar paternalism of the hierarchy. A basic assumption of network relationships is that one party is dependent on resources controlled by another, and that there are gains to be had by the pooling of resources. In essence, the parties to a network agree to forgo the right to pursue their own interests at the expense of others.[13]

This has its obvious advantages and is certainly a more flexible arrangement than a hierarchy. But it also implies a measure of collusion between the network members against new entrants.[14] This insight had important implications for attempts to adapt the public sector to the new environment of the 1970s. It was obvious enough that the centralized hierarchy personified by the omniscient yet incompetent 'man from Whitehall' no longer worked. It was less clear how market forces were to be introduced into the natural or imposed monopolies that had been created in the halcyon days of 'nationalization'. Beginning in Augusto Pinochet's Chile and Margaret Thatcher's Britain, the term of art was 'privatization'. In practice, however, hierarchies tended to be replaced by networks of the well-connected rather than truly competitive markets.[15] It was probably always a delusion that 'market forces' could somehow be brought to bear on such intractable institutions as the National Health Service or British Rail. The reality was that grandiose plans gave way to networks united by bonds of trust and gift-giving.[16] The results were generally better, in the sense that the various privatized utilities became more efficient, but the 'quangos' and 'magic circles' in charge of them could never hope to enjoy popular legitimacy.

45
Henry Kissinger's Network of Power

Nothing better illustrates the simultaneous efficacy but illegitimacy of the emergent networked order than the career of Henry Kissinger. A refugee from Nazi Germany who found his métier as a scholar of history, philosophy and geopolitics while serving in the US Army, Kissinger was one of many Harvard professors who were drawn into government during the Cold War. His appointment as Richard Nixon's national security adviser in December 1968 nevertheless came as a surprise to many people (not least Kissinger himself), because for most of the previous decade he had been so closely identified with Nelson Rockefeller, Nixon's patrician rival within the Republican Party. From his sick-bed, the former President Eisenhower expressed his scepticism about the appointment. 'But Kissinger is a professor,' he exclaimed when he heard of Nixon's choice. 'You ask professors to study things, but you never put them in charge of anything.'[1] This was to underestimate the professor in question.

Kissinger arrived in the White House with an already well-developed intolerance – which the new president shared – of bureaucracy. (This allergy had begun in the Army, where he had most enjoyed the rank-less but powerful role of counter-intelligence agent, and continued throughout his time at Harvard, where his instinct was to establish new institutions rather than bow to the senior faculty and deans.) 'The spirit of policy and that of bureaucracy are diametrically opposed,' he had written in his doctoral dissertation. 'The essence of policy is its contingency; its success depends on the correctness of an estimate which is in part conjectural. The essence of bureaucracy is its quest for safety; its success is calculability . . . The attempt to conduct policy bureaucratically leads to a quest for calculability which tends to become a prisoner of events.'[2] Throughout the 1950s and 1960s, Kissinger complained of the tendency of each president to be 'confronted with *faits accomplis* by the bureaucracy which he can ratify or modify but which preclude a real consideration of alternatives'.[3] In a 1966 article entitled 'Domestic Structure and Foreign Policy', Kissinger observed that the government bureaucracy made 'a deliberate effort to reduce the relevant elements of a problem to a standard of average performance'. This became a problem when 'what [the bureaucracy] defines as routine does not address the most significant range of issues or when its prescribed mode of action proves irrelevant to the problem'. At the same time, there was a tendency for inter-departmental 'bureaucratic contests' to become the only means of generating decisions, or for the various elements of the bureaucracy to make 'a series of nonaggression pacts with each other and thus reduce the decision-maker to a benevolent constitutional monarch'. What most people did not understand about presidential speeches on foreign policy, Kissinger argued, is that they were usually intended to 'settle an internal debate in Washington'.[4] In the spring of 1968, just months before being offered the job of national security adviser, Kissinger went so far as to argue that there was 'no such thing as an American foreign policy'; only 'a series of moves that have produced a certain result' that they 'may not have been planned to produce' and to which 'research and intelligence organizations, either foreign or national, attempt to give a rationality and consistency . . . which it simply does not have'. The 'highest level in which people can still think' in a government department, he argued, was 'the middle level of the bureaucracy – that of the assistant secretary and his immediate advisers . . . Above that, the day to day operation of the machine absorbs most of the energy.' Under these circumstances, 'decisions do not get made until they appear as an administrative issue'.[5]

The best illustration of Kissinger's argument was the abject failure of US strategy in Vietnam. There was, he wrote after several visits to South Vietnam, 'no such thing . . . as a Vietnam policy; there is a series of programs of individual agencies concerned with Vietnam. These programs are reconciled or not, as the case may be, if there is a conflict between the operating agencies.' There were three problems with this. First, the system worked only when there were two opposing agencies, one on either side of an issue; it went awry when a small, dedicated, unopposed group got to work. Second, there could be no planning because no one had time for it. ('Planning involves conjectures about the future and hypothetical cases. They are so busy with actual cases that they are reluctant to take on theoretical ones.') Third, policy-makers were plagued by a 'congenital insecurity' because they lacked the expertise of their advisers; they therefore sought refuge in 'a quest for administrative consensus'. All this had disastrous results the moment the United States sought to negotiate an end to the conflict with the formidably intransigent North Vietnamese. There was always a temptation in Washington not to make a decision at all but simply to see, after a negotiation had begun, 'what the other side had to offer'.

> Therefore, in periods of preliminary diplomacy, our position is very rigid and tough, but this changes rapidly when a negotiator has been appointed because he acts as spokesman for the other side. It is not his problem to worry about the overall picture. He worries about the success of the negotiations, and you make the negotiations succeed by taking very seriously into account what the other side has to say.[6]

'Pragmatism and bureaucracy', as Kissinger put it, had 'combine[d] to produce a diplomatic style marked by rigidity in advance of formal negotiations and excessive reliance on tactical considerations once negotiations start.'[7]

It was this critique of bureaucracy that led Kissinger and a group of like-minded colleagues at Harvard to advise the new president-elect against appointing a powerful chief of staff, empowered to control access to the president. A successful chief executive, they argued, needed to mix 'elements of hierarchy and diffused access'. It would be much better to appoint a key strategic adviser with the broadest possible range of responsibilities.[8] Did Kissinger have himself in mind when making this recommendation? Probably not; at the time of writing, the most he could hope for was deputy secretary if Nixon offered Rockefeller the Department of Defense. Nevertheless, the role of chief strategist was one he very soon found himself playing in all but name, albeit with a mandate strictly confined to foreign policy.

Most writers who have studied his subsequent career in Washington have tended to explain the rapid growth of Kissinger's influence, for better or for worse, in terms of his close relationship to Nixon or his talent for the very bureaucratic infighting he had condemned as an academic. However, this is to overlook the most distinctive feature of Kissinger's mode of operation. While those around him continued to be bound by the rules of the hierarchical bureaucracy that employed them, Kissinger from the outset devoted considerable energy to building a network that extended horizontally in all directions beyond the Washington Beltway: to the press and even the entertainment industry inside the United States and, perhaps more importantly, to key foreign governments through a variety of 'back channels'. Kissinger brought to this task an innate capacity to make emotional as well as intellectual connections even with the most aloof of interlocutors, a skill he had honed long before his appointment by Nixon.

As we have seen (in chapter 40), a characteristic feature of the Soviet system, which endured long after Stalin's death, was the systematic destruction of private networks and the isolation of individuals. Anna Akhmatova's handful of encounters with Isaiah Berlin cost her dearly. Even in the late 1960s, when Soviet citizens encountered Americans – which of course they very rarely did – they had to be on their guard. The Pugwash conferences of scientists were a rare exception. Today, having been awarded the Nobel Peace Prize in 1995, Pugwash is almost synonymous with disarmament and conflict resolution through so-called 'track two diplomacy'.[9] During the Cold War, however, the conferences had a more ambiguous character, since the Soviet academics who attended had to be approved in advance by the Central Committee of the Communist Party and sometimes even by the Politburo.[10] In that sense, as the physicist Victor Weisskopf put it, 'through Pugwash we [American scientists] had a rather direct line of communication with Soviet government'.[11] A less positive verdict was that the conferences 'serve[d] as sounding boards for anti-American and pro-Soviet propaganda'.[12]

When Kissinger attended his first Pugwash conference in Stowe, Vermont, in 1961, he experienced both propaganda and meaningful exchange. At first the Soviet delegates stuck to the Party line, but Kissinger managed to disarm at least some of them with his trademark mordant humour. Just before they left for the airport, the Russian historian Vladimir Khvostov and the physicist Igor Tamm approached him and asked a series of officially inspired questions about US policy towards Berlin. Would a United Nations guarantee of American rights in West Berlin be acceptable? Kissinger replied that the US 'would not agree to a status which could be changed every year by a majority in the General Assembly. Tamm asked how about a guarantee for five years. I said that was too short. He then asked how about ten years. I replied that if this kept up I would suggest one hundred and fifty years and perhaps we could meet in the middle. He laughed and said we understood each other.' *Homo sovieticus* liked this sort of repartee.[13] At moments such as these, Pugwash was an almost unique network running through the Iron Curtain.

Five years later, at the Pugwash conference in the Polish resort of Sopot, Kissinger was startled by the violence of Soviet invective against China. 'China was no longer Communist but Fascist,' the Soviet mathematician Stanislav Emelyanov told him during a boat trip to Gdańsk harbour. 'The Red Guards reminded him of nothing so much as the Hitler Youth. The U.S. and the U.S.S.R. had a common interest in preventing Chinese expansion.' Candidly, Emelyanov admitted he had not seen the Soviet government so confused since the aftermath of Khrushchev's de-Stalinization speech.[14] It was through Pugwash that Kissinger received an invitation to go from Poland to Prague, where he met Antonín Šnejdárek, the former head of Czech intelligence operations in Germany who was now director of the country's Institute of International Politics and Economics. The two men met again in Vienna at the annual meeting of the London-based Institute for Strategic Studies. The Czech frankly warned Kissinger that the Soviets had no sincere intention of helping the Americans extricate themselves from Vietnam. Indeed, he said, the crisis in South-East Asia might end up being 'a convenient pretext [for Moscow] to tighten control over Eastern Europe'. (Little did Kissinger realize it, but his frank discussions with Šnejdárek were themselves an intimation of the coming Prague Spring, a political thaw that the Czech already suspected would be unacceptable to the Kremlin.)[15]

The most revelatory of all these encounters came in January 1967, when Kissinger returned to Prague. Again Šnejdárek warned that

Moscow 'was becoming increasingly sensitive about the growing freedom of movement of the East European countries and especially the Czech effort to reduce their economic dependence on Moscow'. But now he startled Kissinger with a question that Kissinger had to admit 'had never occurred to me': if he thought a 'U.S.–Chinese deal was in the making'. Sensing the American's surprise, Šnejdárek explained:

> The Soviets took the Chinese attack on them [a key feature of Mao's Cultural Revolution] extremely seriously. They could not easily reconcile themselves to the end of Socialist unity and even less to the challenge to their position as the chief interpreters of Leninism. The extent of their attempt to influence internal Chinese developments is therefore not always grasped. They supported the party apparatus against Mao . . .

The Maoists, in turn, were now desperate 'to expel the Soviets physically from China. Nothing less than a complete rupture with the Soviet Union will enable them to feel secure.' True, the Cultural Revolution looked like an ideological rift, with the Chinese as the more radical Marxists. But:

> [w]hatever Mao's ideological fervor, the human material available to him will force him in a nationalist direction – assuming he is still in charge of his movement. Despite their wild talk, the Maoists might turn out to be more flexible toward the U.S. than their opponents. They will have to shut off China in any event to reconstitute governmental authority and a form of non-aggression treaty with the United States might fit this design very well. Of course they hate the U.S. too; but . . . no Communist can forget the Hitler–Stalin pact.

From a Czech point of view, such a 'Johnson–Mao pact' was an alarming scenario because 'if the United States settled with China it would step up the [Soviet] pressure in Europe'. Fearful of isolation, the Soviets would clamp down on what Šnejdárek obliquely called 'the prospects of East European national development'. Kissinger was amazed; yet his Czech host's fear of 'a U.S.–Mao deal' seemed 'genuine and deep'.[16] Scholars have long speculated as to which American strategist conceived of the opening to China that would so transform the geopolitical landscape in 1972. But it was not Americans who thought of it first. It was the strategic thinkers of the Soviet bloc who foresaw the new world conjured up by the Sino-Soviet split, and they did so more than four years before Nixon's historic visit to China.

Beginning in January 1969, Kissinger set about applying some of the lessons he had learned as an academic and public intellectual: in particular, the lesson that informal networks could provide diplomatic channels superior to foreign ministries and embassies. As a prelude to writing the second volume of his life, I have attempted to map Kissinger's network on the basis of all the published memoirs that relate to his period in government. This provides a preliminary plot of his and others' networks as they were remembered by Kissinger himself and his contemporaries in government. The graphs below depict Richard Nixon's and Henry Kissinger's ego networks, based on their memoirs; the Nixon and Ford administrations' ego network, based on all members' memoirs; and the Nixon and Ford administrations' directed network, depicting how prominently members figure in each other's memoirs.[17] In the first three graphs (figures 30–32), relative importance is represented by both the proximity to the central 'ego' node (which in the third case is the combined identities of all members who wrote memoirs) and the area of the node. In the fourth graph (figure 33), we can see who mentioned whom and how often they did so in terms of mutual proximity, edge width and arrow direction.

This exercise represents a starting point for a more thorough exploration. It is inherently a study in retrospection and representation: in essence, we see here the relative importance of individuals in the Nixon and Ford years as members of the two administrations remembered their relationships and – just as important, especially in a period riven by the Watergate scandal – wished them to be remembered. No doubt a somewhat different picture will emerge from graphs based on different sources.* Nevertheless, these graphs serve

* For example, in 'Quantifying Kissinger,' a dissertation under way at the City University of New York, Micki Kaufman is attempting a network analysis of the National Security Archive's Kissinger Correspondence, a collection of more than 18,000 documents. She shows, among other things, how Kissinger's network

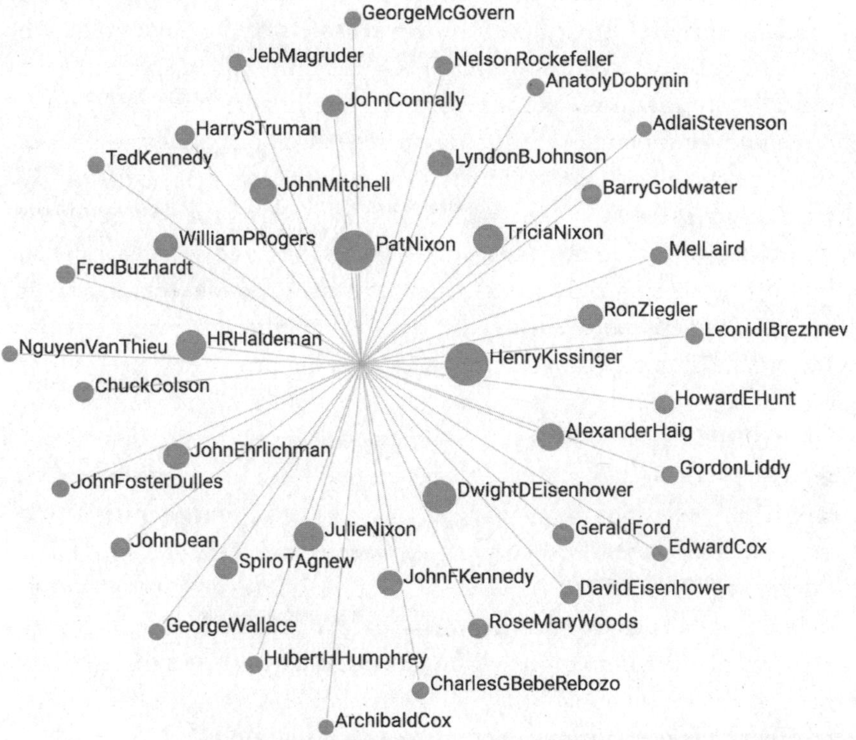

30. Richard Nixon's ego network, based on his memoirs.

to illustrate some of the methodological benefits to the historian of social network analysis.

Firstly, we have here a valuable corrective to any assumptions we might be tempted to make about who 'mattered' in the Nixon–Ford era. Kissinger abounds – as important to Nixon as his wife, and the second most important member of the two administrations, outranking Ford, who became president. Next in terms of

expanded after his appointment as secretary of state, but also that his personal networks – as distinct from established bureaucratic channels – facilitated his management of key geopolitical events of the era such as the Arab–Israeli War of 1973, the Vietnam War, the opening to China, military action in Cambodia and diplomatic efforts to resolve the Rhodesian Bush War.

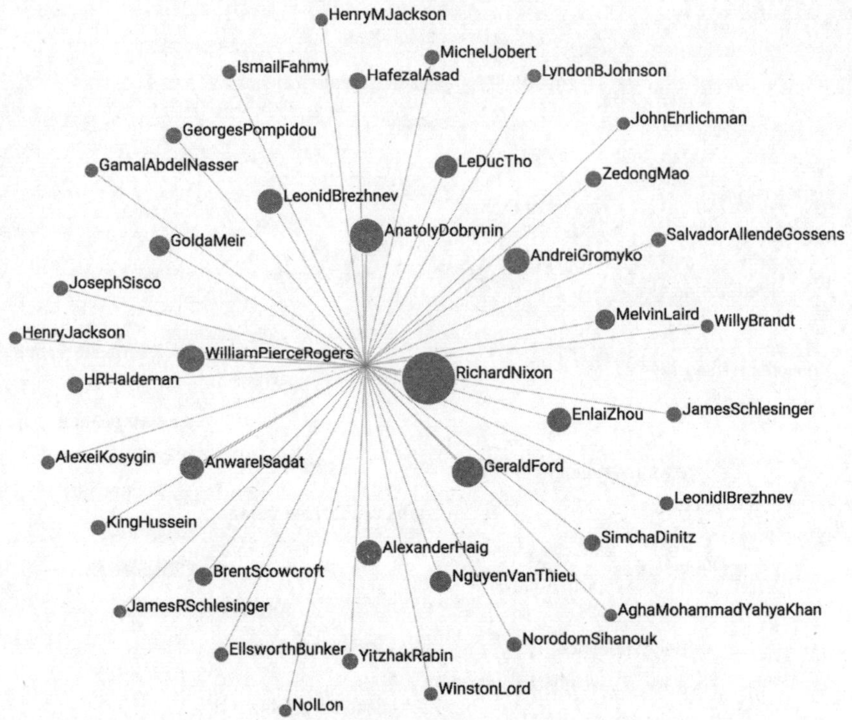

31. Henry Kissinger's ego network, based on his memoirs.

betweenness centrality (see figure 33) came Nixon's Chief of staff, H. R. Haldeman, followed by Ford and White House counsel John Dean. Also ranked highly on this basis were John Ehrlichman (assistant to the president for domestic affairs), Treasury Secretary John Connally, future president George H. W. Bush and Alexander Haig (Kissinger's assistant, then deputy, and Haldeman's successor after Watergate).

It is striking, too, how large the dead loomed in the minds of the memoir-writers. After Nixon and Kissinger, Lyndon Johnson (who died in January 1973) was the thrid most frequently mentioned figure in all the memoirs combined, and John F. Kennedy was seventh (figure 32). Former presidents Dwight Eisenhower (died March 1969), Franklin D. Roosevelt and Harry S. Truman (died December 1972)

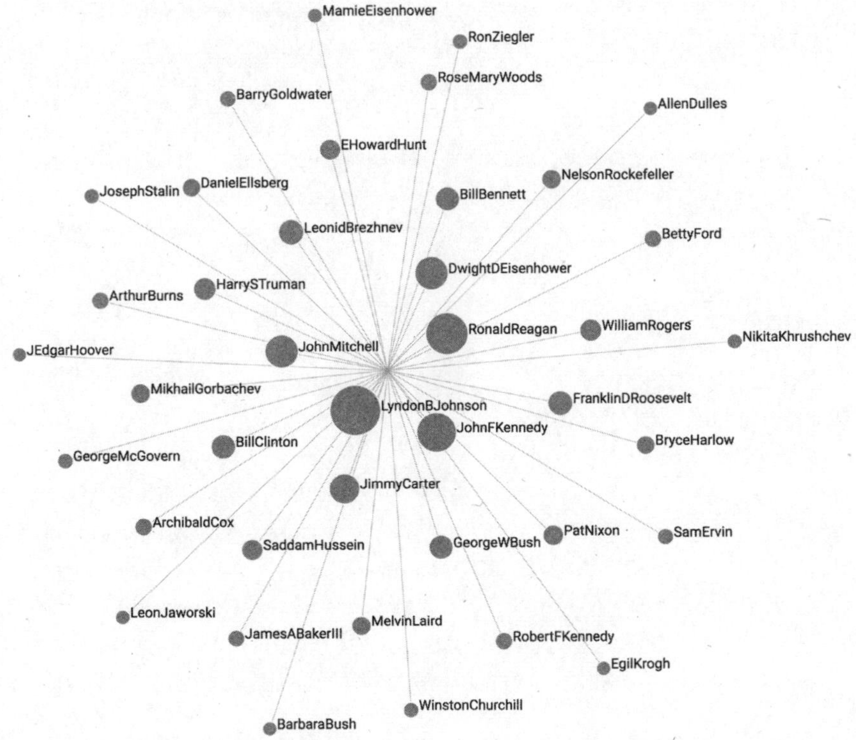

32. The Nixon and Ford administrations' ego network, based on all members' memoirs.

were the tenth, sixteenth and twenty-first most frequently mentioned individuals. Churchill was fifty-third, stalin fifty-fourth. It is perhaps reassuring to the historian to find that the writers of autobiographies so often look back on the periods before they served in government, if only to refer to the dominant personalities of their youths.

Thirdly, we see the difference between 'the world according to Nixon' and 'the world according to Kissinger'. Nixon's inner circle (figure 30) was that of a man whose experience of the presidency was to a remarkable extent confined within the walls of the White House. Aside from his wife and daughters, he refers most often in his memoir to Kissinger, Eisenhower (whose vice-president he was), Haldeman, Erlichman and Haig. Kissinger, by contrast, mentions key foreign

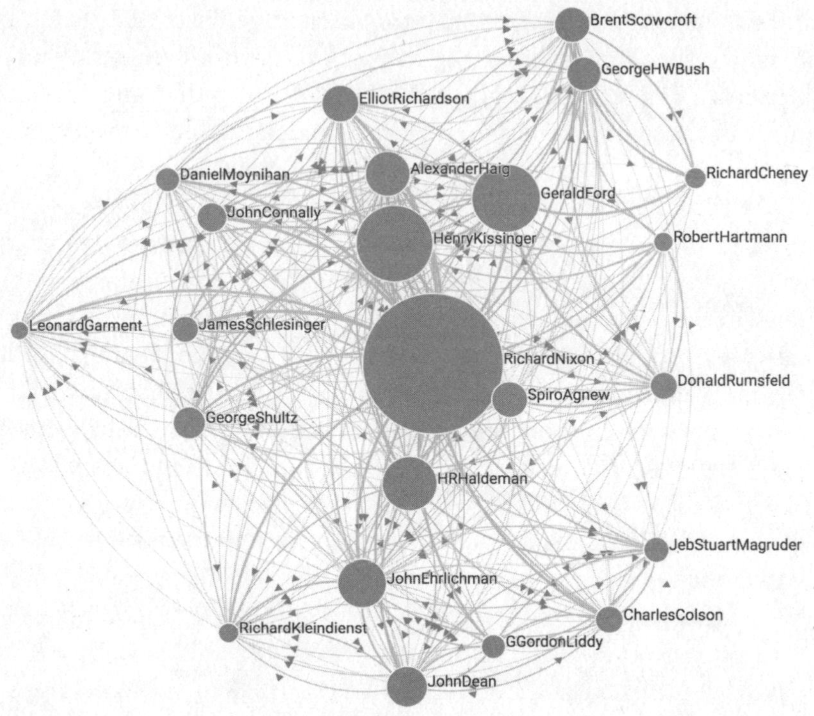

33. The Nixon and Ford administrations' directed network, depicting direction and frequency of members' references to each other in their memoirs.

leaders almost as much as the presidents he served, and more often than the secretary of state who preceded him in that office, William Rogers (figure 31). The more striking thing is which foreign leaders loom largest in Kissinger's memoirs: the Soviets (their ambassador in Washington, Anatoly Dobrynin, their foreign minister, Andrei Gromyko, and their premier, Leonid Brezhnev) came first, followed by Zhou Enlai, the Chinese premier, and Anwar Sadat, the Egyptian president. Apart from Brezhnev and Dobrynin, only one other foreigner was amongst the forty individuals most frequently mentioned by Nixon: Nguyen Van Thieu, the South Vietnamese president. By contrast, only sixteen of Kissinger's top forty were Americans. Of course, we would expect the national security adviser and secretary of state to spend more time than the president with foreigners: that is the nature of the job. Yet it is difficult to believe that any previous holder of those offices had been quite as indefatigable a traveller and negotiator.

While in office, Kissinger appeared on the cover of *Time* magazine no fewer than fifteen times. He was, according to one of the magazine's profiles of him, published in 1974, 'the world's indispensable man . . . the right man in the right place at the right time' – though one who stood accused by his critics of paying more 'attention to principals than principles'.[18] The hypothesis must be that Kissinger's influence and reputation were products not only of his intellect and industriousness, but also of his preternatural connectedness. Shuttle diplomacy was a part of this. So was schmoozing journalists, at which Kissinger excelled, though he scarcely mentioned them in his memoirs, despite the closeness of his friendships to the Alsop brothers, Stewart and Joseph, and the columnist Tom Braden. As *Time* put it, Kissinger 'carefully preserved the ritual required of a subordinate who takes orders from a Commander in Chief', even as Nixon's presidency was falling apart. The 'formal and correct rather than personal' relationship with Nixon remained institutionally vital until his final resignation. As *Time* noted, Kissinger had 'a finely tuned sense of hierarchy'.[19] But what mattered much more were all the other relationships in a network – including an 'old boy network' of former participants in Kissinger's summer seminars at Harvard – that spanned the globe. 'He always looks for the guy who can deliver,' an unnamed aide told *Time*. 'A lot of doors open for him,' said a 'Washington friend and admirer'. The network was the precondition for his 'chain reaction' diplomacy – a phrase used by the Israeli deputy premier, Yigal Allon. That was what justified the claim that Kissinger 'probably [had] more impact than any other person in the world'.[20]

The weakening of hierarchy and strengthening of networks that characterized the 1970s had many benefits. From Kissinger's point of view, these trends significantly reduced the risk of a Third World War: that, after all, was the central rationale of more frequent dialogue with the Soviet Union (as well as the beginning of communication with the People's Republic of China). Contemporaries often summarized Kissinger's foreign policy as 'détente'. He preferred to speak of 'interdependence'. A 'new international system' had replaced 'the structure of the immediate postwar years', he declared in London in December 1973: one based on 'the paradox of growing mutual dependence and burgeoning national and regional identities'.[21] 'The energy crisis,' he suggested three months later, was one of 'the birth pains of global interdependence'.[22] By April 1974, 'The Challenge of Interdependence' had become a speech title; by 1975 interdependence was 'becoming the central fact of our diplomacy'. 'If we do not get a recognition of our interdependence,' Kissinger warned in October 1974, 'the Western civilization that we now have is almost certain to disintegrate.'[23] Academics at his alma mater such as Richard Cooper and Joseph Nye obliged by writing books on the subject.[24] Interdependence found institutional expression with the first meeting of the Trilateral Commission* at the Rockefeller estate in Pocantico Hills in 1972 and the first meeting of the 'Group of Six' (Britain, France, Italy, Japan, the United States and West Germany) at Rambouillet in 1975. The *New York Times* chose to mark the Bicentennial of the Declaration of Independence with an editorial entitled 'Interdependence Day'.[25] It was a concept enthusiastically adopted by President Jimmy Carter and his national security adviser, Zbigniew Brzezinski.

Yet there were costs as well as benefits to inhabiting a more interdependent world. As Brzezinski argued in his book *Between Two Ages*, the new 'global city' being created by the 'technetronic age' was 'a nervous, agitated, tense, and fragmented web of interdependent relations'.[26] This was true in more ways than one. During the first half of the Cold War, the superpowers had been able to control information flows by manufacturing or sponsoring propaganda and

* Under the original plan for the Trilateral Commission, the executive committee would comprise thirty-four delegates: fourteen from the EEC, nine from Japan, nine from the United States, and two from Canada. This was a remarkable act of self-effacement on the Americans' part, as the US economy was still substantially larger than the EEC's at this time.

classifying or censoring anything deemed harmful. Sensation surrounded every spy scandal and defection; yet in most cases all that happened was that classified information was passed from one national security state to the other. This, too, changed in the 1970s. Leaked official documents began to reach the public in the West through the free press – beginning in 1971 with the so-called 'Pentagon papers' given by Daniel Ellsberg to *The New York Times* – and (to a much smaller extent) in the Soviet bloc through *samizdat* literature, notably Alexander Solzhenitsyn's *Gulag Archipelago*. Leaks to the media in turn fuelled the dramatic escalation of social protest on university campuses and inner cities that made the early 1970s seem so febrile compared with the sedate quarter-century after 1945. Altogether close to 400 different groups were involved in some form of protest in the United States between the 1960s and the 1980s: what had begun with the campaign for African-American civil rights soon encompassed campaigns for women's rights, Native American rights, gay and lesbian rights, and campaigns against the Vietnam War, nuclear weapons, poverty and industrial pollution.[27] Like most members of the generation who fought in the Second World War, Nixon and Kissinger had little patience with these groups; indeed, Kissinger likened the student radicals he encountered at Harvard in the late 1960s to the German students who had attended the Nuremberg Rallies in the early 1930s.[28] Nevertheless, in the small hours of 9 May 1970, Nixon ventured out of the White House to confront a group of student protesters who were camped out at the Lincoln Memorial. It was an uncharacteristic attempt at connection by a man notorious for his reclusiveness and misanthropy. As he told them:

> I was sorry they had missed it [his press conference the previous day] because I had tried to explain . . . that my goals in Vietnam were the same as theirs – to stop the killing, to end the war, to bring peace. Our goal was not to get into Cambodia by what we were doing, but to get out of Vietnam.
>
> There seemed to be no – they did not respond. I hoped that their hatred of the war, which I could well understand, would not turn into a bitter hatred of our whole system, our country and everything that it stood for.

> I said, I know you, that probably most of you think I'm an SOB. But I want you to know that I understand just how you feel.[29]

Perhaps Nixon did understand how the protesters felt. But, as they subsequently made clear to the reporters who swiftly descended on them, they did not remotely understand how he felt, or care to.

Long before Nixon fell victim to the exposure of his own skulduggery by the *Washington Post* – as well as to the consequences of his own vulnerability as a network isolate, with too few friends in the institutions that might conceivably have saved him – Kissinger had understood that networks were more powerful than the hierarchies of the federal government. The protesting students he knew well enough not to waste time on. But he did tour the country in the Ford years giving speeches to Midwestern audiences in an effort to explain his strategic concept to the wider public – though with only limited success. In some ways, his most remarkable feat was to isolate himself from the one component of the Nixon network that would have been fatal to him: that part which plotted the Watergate break-in. It took a networker of genius to know exactly which nodes to avoid connecting to. Kissinger's power, still based on a network that crossed not only borders but also professional boundaries, endured long after he left government in 1977, institutionalized in the advisory firm Kissinger Associates, maintained by almost incessant flying, meeting, mingling, dining. By contrast, the executive branch after Nixon saw its power significantly curtailed by congressional scrutiny and greatly emboldened newspapers. No future national security adviser or secretary of state, no matter how talented, would ever be able to match what Kissinger had achieved.

46
Into the Valley

Why did hierarchical power structures plunge into crisis in the 1970s? It might be assumed that, as Brzezinski believed, the answer to this question is technological. It is certainly true that the seventies were the decade of genesis for both the personal computer and the Internet. However, the crisis of hierarchical power predated the spread of electronic networking in the United States. Indeed, the causation was the other way around: it was precisely the relaxation of central control that made the American information technology revolution possible.

To all the world's states, it is now clear, the new informational, commercial and social networks of the Internet Age pose a profound challenge, but the scale of that challenge only gradually became apparent. To begin with, the creation of network technologies was intended to enhance the national security state. The task assigned to the RAND* researcher Paul Baran in 1964 was to develop a communication system that would survive a Soviet nuclear attack. Baran suggested three possible structures for such a system. It could either be 'centralized', with one central hub and multiple spokes, 'decentralized', with multiple components linked loosely together by a number of weak ties, or 'distributed', like a lattice or mesh. In theory, the last option was the most resilient, in that it could withstand the

* Originally set up by the commander of the US Army Air Force in October 1945 to research into the weapons of the future, the RAND Corporation ('research and development') was spun off from the Douglas Aircraft Company three years later as a non-profit entity funded jointly by government and the private sector. It was as chief strategist at RAND that Hermann Kahn wrote his classic book *On Thermonuclear War* (1960).

destruction of numerous nodes, and that was indeed Baran's preferred model for what became the Advanced Research Projects Agency Network (ARPANET).[1] In practice, paradoxically, such a structure could have been maintained only through centralized planning. As Melvin Conway pointed out in 1968 – in a seminal paper entitled 'How Do Committees Invent?' – there was a kind of law about the way systems of communication were designed: 'Organizations which design systems (in the broad sense used here) are constrained to produce designs which are copies of the communication structures of these organizations.'[2] Just as Kissinger had seen at first hand the dysfunction of the government bureaucracy when confronted with major strategic challenges, Conway – a systems analyst with experience of government defence contracts – had observed that:

> The structures of large systems tend to disintegrate during development, qualitatively more so than with small systems. This observation is strikingly evident when applied to the large military information systems of the last dozen years . . . some of the most complex objects devised by the mind of man . . .
>
> Why do large systems disintegrate? The process seems to occur in three steps . . .
>
> – First, the realization by the initial designers that the system will be large, together with certain pressures in their organization, make irresistible the temptation to assign too many people to a design effort.
>
> – Second, application of the conventional wisdom of management to a large design organization causes its communication structure to disintegrate.
>
> – Third, the homomorphism insures that the structure of the system will reflect the disintegration which has occurred in the design organization.[3]

It therefore mattered greatly that what became the Internet was *not* designed in that way, but rather arose more or less spontaneously and organically, with academics and private sector computer engineers rather than military planners taking the lead.

On 29 October 1969 computer spoke unto computer for the first time when an incomplete message was sent via Arpanet between the

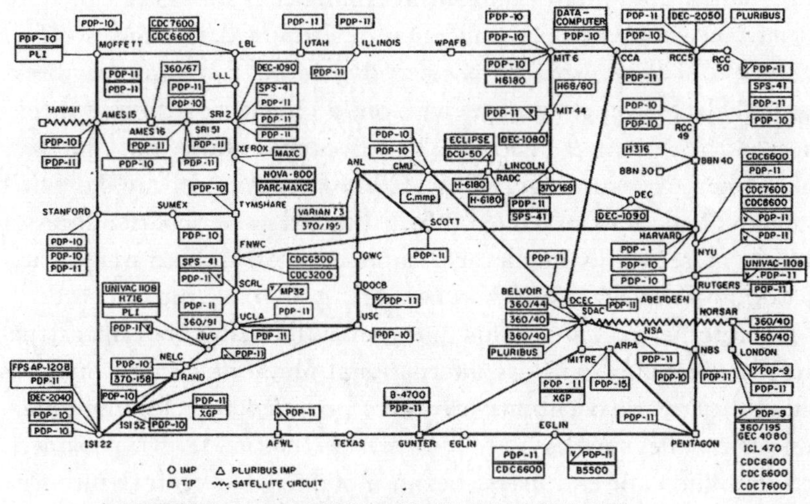

34. Network design for Arpanet, 1969.

Stanford Research Institute and the University of California Los Angeles.[4] Two years later, the number of nodes in the network had passed forty, connecting both universities and private companies. Similar networks sprang up elsewhere (Hepnet, Span, Telenet and others) so that by 1974 the challenge had become to link these networks together in a single 'inter-network'. The 1970s were a time of hectic but highly decentralized innovation, each new advance contributing to the integration process: the Unix operating system that would later inspire Linux and FreeBSD, the idea of email with names and addresses separated by the @ symbol, the first email program (MSG) with 'reply' and 'forward' options, the first modem. And of course these advances coincided with the seemingly unstoppable exponential growth of computer processing power according to Moore's 'Law'.* The most important development, however, was the

* It was Gordon E. Moore, one of the co-founders of Intel, who observed in 1965 that the number of transistors per square inch on an integrated circuits chip had been doubling every year. He predicted that this rate would be sustained, though in

stipulation by Vinton (Vint) Cerf and Robert Kahn that the network of networks should have no central control and should not be optimized for any particular application or form of data packet.[5] Their TCP/IP software protocol envisaged that all computer networks should be able to communicate with one another, regardless of differences in their internal structure. This became a reality on 1 January 1983, when Arpanet switched to TCP/IP.[6] A year later came the first Domain Name Servers (DNS), which allowed numerical IP addresses to have more readily memorable names. By 1987, there were nearly 30,000 hosts on what was now being referred to as 'the Internet'.

The Internet was not planned; it grew. The vast global infrastructure we use today, with its international fibre-optic trunk lines, its national network backbone providers provided by telecommunications companies such as AT&T, its myriad Internet service providers, and its billions of end users, began modestly. No central authority designed it, which explains why it avoided the pitfalls of Conway's Law. No permission was or is needed to add a new spur or subtract an old one.[7] There is no central depository where the overall structure of the Internet is recorded. It cannot in fact be mapped. Brinton and Chiang define the three fundamental concepts that underlie the Internet as:

- packet switching, in which resources are shared instead of dedicated
- distributed hierarchy, in which control is spread across different segments of the network geographically, and
- modularization, in which tasks are divided into different functional layers and managed separately.[8]

We users take for granted the extent to which the Internet empowers us, seamlessly routing the packets of information we wish to send or receive along the shortest paths, using feedback messages to gauge

1975 he modified his prediction, suggesting that after 1980 it would double every two years. There is no space here for a more detailed account of the advances in computing power that accompanied the growth of the Internet; suffice to say that Moore's Law has roughly held ever since.

network conditions and avoid congestion.[9] Such a complex system simply could not have been designed by a single agency.

The 'World Wide Web' that evolved in the 1980s as the Internet's principal form of traffic did so in a similar way.[10] It began with an academic, Tim Berners-Lee, working at the European Organization for Nuclear Research (CERN), who devised a program called ENQUIRE to help particle physicists manage their research. In March 1989, Berners-Lee published a proposal for a global version of the program, which he at first wanted to call 'Mesh', before the name 'World Wide Web' occurred to him. It was Berners-Lee who devised the now universal tools of web communication: HyperText Markup Language (HTML), Hypertext Transfer Protocol (HTTP) and Uniform Resource Locator (URL). Within a few years this open-source computer code allowed the rapid proliferation of user-friendly web browsers such as Mosaic and Netscape Navigator. Like the Internet on which it ran, the World Wide Web was the product of organic growth, not central control. It is a network in which the nodes are user-created web pages and the edges are hyperlinks that allow us to navigate from one page to another, usually only in one direction (i.e. the destination page does not necessarily have a hyperlink leading back to the page where you began).[11] Like the Internet, it is the work of many hands: cookies, plug-ins, sessions and scripts were all patches devised to manage the system's growing complexity. And, like the Internet, the World Wide Web is unknowably large, as none of the search engines that enable us to explore the web can come close to archiving all web pages – though we do know that its structural core is a giant densely interconnected component of mutually reachable nodes.[12]

In his farewell address to the nation in 1960, Eisenhower had warned of the excessive power of the 'military-industrial complex'. He need not have worried. Had it been so very powerful, it would surely have prevented or at least stunted the exponential growth of the Internet and the World Wide Web. Perhaps the most striking feature of the United States in the 1970s was simply that such decentralized innovation was possible, despite all the economic, social and political troubles we associate with that period. The young men drawn to 'Silicon Valley' – as the Santa Clara Valley was first nicknamed in 1971 – took the anti-authoritarian attitudes of their generation with them. When Congress passed the Communications Decency Act of 1996 – its first attempt to regulate Internet communications by imposing fines for the publication online of obscene language – it was appropriate that the Valley's response was written (as an email) by the former Grateful Dead lyricist John Perry Barlow.[13] His 'Declaration of the Independence of Cyberspace' was addressed to the 'Governments of the Industrial World, you weary giants of flesh and steel':

> I come from Cyberspace, the new home of Mind. On behalf of the future, I ask you of the past to leave us alone. You are not welcome among us. You have no sovereignty where we gather.
>
> We have no elected government, nor are we likely to have one, so I address you with no greater authority than that with which liberty itself always speaks. I declare the global social space we are building to be naturally independent of the tyrannies you seek to impose on us. You have no moral right to rule us nor do you possess any methods of enforcement we have true reason to fear . . .
>
> Cyberspace does not lie within your borders. Do not think that you can build it, as though it were a public construction project. You cannot. It is an act of nature and it grows itself through our collective actions . . .
>
> Cyberspace consists of transactions, relationships, and thought itself, arrayed like a standing wave in the web of our communications . . . We are creating a world that all may enter without privilege or prejudice accorded by race, economic power, military force, or station of birth.
>
> We are creating a world where anyone, anywhere may express his or her beliefs, no matter how singular, without fear of being coerced into silence or conformity.
>
> Your legal concepts of property, expression, identity, movement, and context do not apply to us . . . [Your] increasingly hostile and colonial measures place us in the same position as those previous lovers of freedom and self-determination who had to reject the authorities of distant, uninformed powers.[14]

Despite the more febrile visions of the student radicals of the 1970s, there would be no revolution in the United States. As Barlow's famous email made clear, the Internet *was* the revolution. Or so it seemed. The Electronic Frontier Foundation established by Barlow and other cyber-libertarians won its first major victory in 1997 when the Supreme Court struck down the Communications Decency Act as a violation of the First Amendment.[15] The US government was minimally involved in the work of the Internet Engineering Task Force, which was seen by its creators as the only government the Internet needed. In the words of David D. Clark, the Internet's chief protocol architect: 'We reject kings, presidents, and voting. We believe in: rough consensus and running code.'[16] In that bright and hopeful morning, few computer scientists or software engineers paused to ask what exactly they would do if the Internet became a crime scene.

Yet it was already obvious that, like the Garden of Eden, the Utopia of Cyberspace had its serpent and its sinners: malicious game-players who invaded 'multiple user dungeons' to commit virtual rape against other players' avatars, closely followed by real-world criminals, who readily seized the opportunities presented for fraud almost as soon as money began to change hands online.[17] Nor did Cyberspace keep out the government for long. In January 1998 Jon Postel, the first director of the Internet Assigned Numbers Authority (IANA), emailed eight of the twelve operators of the Internet's regional root name-servers, instructing them to change the root zone server to the IANA's, rather than that of Network Solutions, Inc., the original DNS registry set up by the Defense Information Systems Agency (DISA) in September 1991. Within a matter of days, the Department of Commerce's National Telecommunications and Information Administration issued a 'Proposal to Improve Technical Management of Internet Names and Addresses'.[18] A new not-for-profit corporation called the Internet Corporation for Assigned Names and Numbers (ICANN) was set up with a globally and functionally representative board of directors to manage the IANA, but under contract to – and under the oversight of – the Department of Commerce. What had begun as the Arpanet could not easily depart from the jurisdiction of its begetter: Uncle Sam himself. In that sense, Barlow's Declaration of Independence was a dead letter within two years of its appearance.

47
The Fall of the Soviet Empire

The Institute of Cybernetics was located on the outskirts of Kiev. It was there, beginning in 1972, that Viktor Glushkov tried to design the Soviet Internet – or, to give his project its full name, 'The All-State Automated System for the Gathering and Processing of Information for the Accounting, Planning and Governance of the National Economy, USSR'. Here in Communist-controlled Ukraine was something of the spirit that animated Silicon Valley. Glushkov and his colleagues imagined a land called 'Cybertonia', which would be governed by a council of robots, with a saxophone-playing robot as the supreme leader. Glushkov knew that, to be acceptable in the Kremlin, his Automated System would have to map onto the three-level pyramidal structure of the Soviet planned economy. Inevitably, there would have to be a central computer hub in Moscow, which would connect to as many as 200 mid-level nodes in major Soviet cities, which would in turn link to 20,000 computer terminals distributed across key production sites. However, while Moscow would have control over who was given access to the network, Glushkov envisaged that any authorized user would be able to contact any other user across the network without direct permission from the mother node.

Could such a Soviet Internet have worked? It seems doubtful. In any case, the experiment was never attempted – not because the members of the Politburo in Moscow detected the potential threat to their authority that Glushkov's proposal represented, but simply because the minister of finance, Vasily Garbuzov, killed it on the ground of cost.[1]

Knowing all we now know about the value-subtracting pathologies of the Soviet economy by the 1970s, we struggle to remember that the consensus view in Washington was that communism might ultimately prevail over capitalism. In the 1961 edition of his best-selling textbook, the economist Paul Samuelson had predicted that the Soviet economy would overtake the US economy at some point between 1984 and 1997. 'The Soviet economy,' he could still assert in the book's 1989 edition, 'is proof that, contrary to what many sceptics had earlier believed, a socialist command economy can function and even thrive.' As a later NSA report acknowledged, 'no official estimates even mentioned that the collapse of Communism was a distinct possibility until the coup of 1989'.[2] Yet it was obvious to any attentive visitor to the Soviet Union that something was amiss with the planned economy. Consumer goods were of dismal quality and in chronically short supply. In antiquated factories, pilfering, alcohol abuse and absenteeism were rife. It is hard to believe that any amount of computing power would have saved such a fundamentally flawed system.

For the majority of Soviet citizens, the resulting mood of demoralization did not translate into political activity – just into fatalism and yet more black humour. However, for those parts of Eastern Europe that had come under direct or indirect Soviet rule only as a result of the Second World War, it was a different matter. Encouraged by the commitments the Soviet leaders had (insincerely) made to uphold human rights in the Helsinki final accords, dissidents began tentatively to organize themselves. For the first time since the 1930s, people living under Communist rule found they could form networks without automatically risking their own lives and those of their families. Nowhere did independent voluntary associations grow faster than in Poland. The challenge was to build a network of networks – a kind of political Internet – that would allow the secular liberals of the universities to join forces with Roman Catholic and working class opponents of the regime.[3] Between 1969 and 1977, the opposition network grew in size by around 40 per cent with the addition of six new groups, including the Free Trade Unions group (WZZ), as well as in density as the civil, liberal, Catholic, nationalist and radical groups grew more closely connected. By 1980, stimulated by the heady experience of Pope John Paul II's visit the previous year, the network had grown again, with the new trade union Solidarity becoming the dominant hub.[4] To be sure, the imposition of martial law in December 1981 disrupted the network, as numerous key nodes were arrested or fled abroad. Yet General Wojciech Jaruzelski was no Stalin. When the government agreed to talks with Solidarity in February 1989, the network reconstituted itself and grew with breath-taking speed.

Revolutions, as we have seen, are networked phenomena. With every day that passed in 1989 without a crackdown, the resolve of the East European regimes weakened and the number of their citizens willing to risk overt protest went up. In Budapest in May the Hungarian Communists decided to open their border with Austria. Seizing

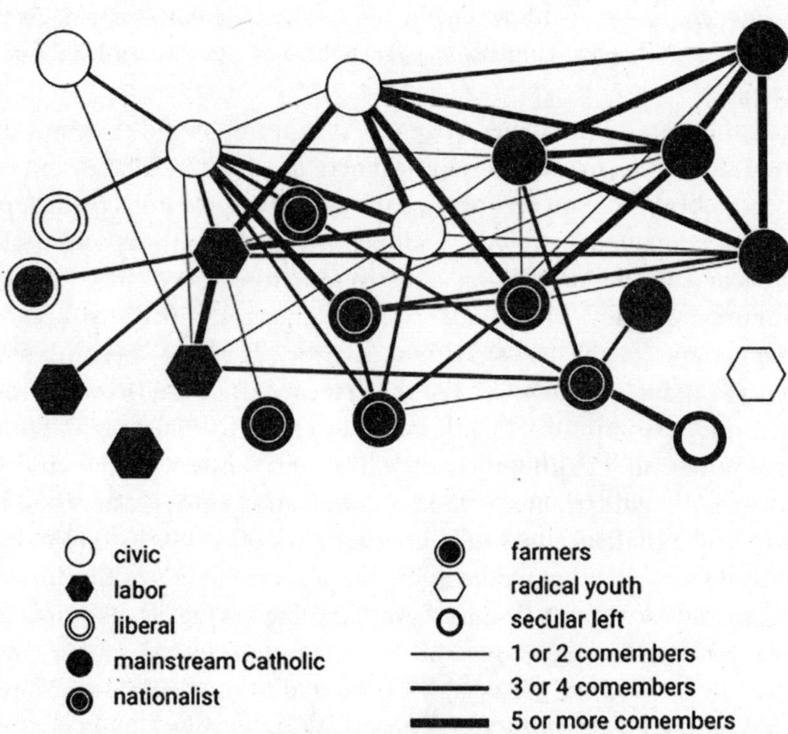

35. Networks of Polish opposition, 1980–81. The success of the free trade union Solidarity (the black hexagon at centre-left) was based partly on its connectedness to multiple other political associations.

the opportunity, around 15,000 East Germans set off via Czechoslovakia to 'holiday' in Hungary on what was in reality a one-way trip to the West. In June, Solidarity won the Polish elections and set about forming a democratic government. In September the Hungarian Communists followed the Polish example by agreeing to free elections. The following month, as Erich Honecker honed his plans to celebrate the German Democratic Republic's fortieth anniversary, hundreds, then thousands, then tens of thousands, then hundreds of thousands of people poured onto the streets in Leipzig, first chanting 'Wir sind das Volk' (We are the People), then amending that to 'Wir sind ein Volk' (We are One People). Here, too, localized networks of opposition – some church-based – quickly linked up, though the left- and right-wing components of the revolution were much less connected than in Poland.[5] On 9 November 1989 bemused reporters in East Berlin were informed that 'the decision [had been] taken to make it possible for all citizens to leave the country through the official border crossing points . . . to take effect at once', news that prompted a flood of East Berliners to the border checkpoints. Lacking clear orders, guards opted not to resist. By midnight all the checkpoints had been forced to open. The dominoes were falling, but this time in the opposite direction from the one Eisenhower had feared – and they continued to fall for the better part of two years. After the abortive Moscow coup of August 1991, the Soviet Union itself broke apart, leaving a rump Russian Federation shorn of the Baltic states, Ukraine and Belarus, the three big Caucasian republics and the five 'stans' of Central Asia. In the same timeframe, Yugoslavia disintegrated, with multi-ethnic Bosnia–Herzegovina all but torn apart. Only in Beijing did Communist rulers stick to the script of 1956 and 1968, sending tanks to crush popular protests in Beijing in June 1989.

This vast Eurasian chain reaction was not only the work of networks of political opposition; it was also propelled by television networks. In the first phase of the East German revolution, participation in protests was undoubtedly fuelled by West German television coverage, which most GDR citizens could see on their own TV screens. Only in one benighted 'valley of the clueless' (*Tal der Ahnungslosen*) – the south-eastern area around Dresden and the north-eastern part of the country near Greifswald – were people unable to receive the Western channels.[6]

Equally dangerous to the Soviet system, however, were the Western networks of finance that had been growing exponentially throughout the 1980s as a result of capital market liberalization and the introduction of computer technology. It was not a coincidence that the East European regimes (with the exception of Romania) entered their death throes only a few years after they had begun to borrow heavily from Western banks. For it was these banks that were among the first institutions to begin systematically and on a large scale exploiting the new information technologies being created in Silicon Valley. This development is sometimes forgotten about in histories of the 1980s, which tend to give disproportionate credit for the collapse of communism to a handful of heroic leaders: Gorbachev, Reagan, Thatcher, the Pope. These individuals mattered, no doubt, but they were more likely to achieve their goals when they were aligned with the rapidly growing network of international finance. The most important hub of that network was not Washington, or London, much less Rome. It was a small ski resort in the Swiss canton of Graubünden: Davos.

48
The Triumph of Davos Man

When John Perry Barlow emailed his 'Declaration of the Independence of Cyberspace' to the network in his online address book, it was appropriate that his physical location was Davos. As a participant in the World Economic Forum, Barlow was simultaneously networking both electronically and socially. The WEF was founded in 1971 by a bespectacled Harvard-trained German academic named Klaus Schwab with the idea that a regular conference of international business leaders could realize his vision of 'corporations as stakeholders in global society, together with government and civil society'.[1] The result has been described as 'a name-dropper's paradise', populated not only by the chief executives of multinationals and selected politicians, but also by 'central bankers, industrial chiefs, hedge-fund titans, gloomy forecasters, astrophysicists, monks, rabbis, tech wizards, museum curators, university presidents, financial bloggers [and] virtuous heirs': 'Davos is like Congress, the Factory, the Mormon Tabernacle, the Bohemian Grove, the "best dinner party in the world," the financial system, Facebook, Burning Man, boot camp, high school, Los Angeles, Quogue. Davos is an onion, a layer cake, a Russian doll.' Thanks to Schwab, Davos now truly deserves the name Thomas Mann once gave the mountain that towers above it: *der Zauberberg*, the Magic Mountain. Thanks to Davos, Schwab can now plausibly claim (in lineal succession to Kissinger) to be 'the most [or perhaps best] connected man on the planet'.[2]

Those who mock the World Economic Forum underestimate the power of networks. Few speeches in the history of the Forum have had a more profound historical importance than the one given in January 1992 by a recently released political prisoner from the opposite end of the earth. 'Our interdependence,' he told the conference delegates, as Schwab listened attentively and approvingly, 'demands that we all combine to launch a global offensive for development, prosperity and human survival.' It was, the speaker argued, 'necessary that a massive transfer of resources takes place from North to South' – but not 'as an act of charity or as an attempt to improve the lives of the "have-nots" by impoverishing the "haves"'. He then proceeded to list four steps his own country ought to take:

> [to] deal with . . . the debt problem, the issue of the continuous decline in the price of commodities that the poorer countries export, and access to markets for their manufactured goods.
>
> [to] ensure the growth of [our] economy . . . [which] will require a rapid and sustained growth in terms of capital formation or fixed investment, drawing on both domestic and external sources to finance this investment.
>
> [to establish] a public sector perhaps no different from such countries as Germany, France and Italy.
>
> [to] offer very good prospects for the investors present in this room, both South African and international.[3]

The speaker was Nelson Mandela and the gist of what he said was as clear as it was startling: for the sake of attracting foreign capital to the country he was poised to take over, the leading figure of the African National Congress would ditch one of the key commitments of its 1955 Freedom Charter: the nationalization of South Africa's key industries.[4]

Though a member of the South African Communist Party at the time of his imprisonment in 1962, Mandela was no ordinary communist. 'We must make a thorough study of all revolutions, including the ones that failed,' he had once written in his diary, referring to books by the Israeli leader Menachem Begin and the Boer guerrilla Deneys Reitz, as well as by Che Guevara and Mao Zedong. The revolutionary theory of the armed wing of the ANC (Umkontho we Sizwe), established in 1961, was Fidel Castro's more than Lenin's.[5] During his long years as a prisoner on Robben Island, Mandela changed his philosophy in many respects, but he clung to the idea of nationalizing the commanding heights of the economy. When in 1990 the British ambassador, Robin Renwick, tried to talk him out of nationalization, Mandela replied: 'It was your idea' – a reference to Clause Four of the British Labour Party's constitution, which committed the party to 'the common ownership of the means of production, distribution and exchange, and the best obtainable system of popular administration and control of each industry or service'.[6]

Why did Mandela abandon this last vestige of his socialism just two years later? He himself acknowledged the influence of his trip to Davos. As he later put it: 'I came home to say: "Chaps, we have to choose. We either keep nationalization and get no investment, or we modify our own attitude and get investment."'[7] Later, in 2000, he recalled how, as he 'moved around the world and heard the opinions of leading business people and economists about how to grow an economy', he was 'persuaded and convinced about the free market'.[8] However, other explanations have been put forward. For those to the left of him in the ANC, such as Ronnie Kasrils, 'the decision against nationalization was a "Faustian bargain" with the white world that sold out the South African poor'.[9] The journalist Anthony Monteiro has claimed that Mandela had in fact 'entered into secret talks with the white regime before being released', and had agreed at that early stage to abandon nationalization.[10]A kinder way of making a similar point is to say that Mandela (and Thabo Mbeki, who would later succeed him as president) paid heed to South African business leaders, notably Harry Oppenheimer, to whom the white anti-apartheid leader Helen Suzman introduced them.[11] An alternative theory is that it was in fact pressure from the International Monetary Fund that led to the change of policy: 'for a loan of $850 million . . . South Africa committed itself to austerity, liberalization, and privatization'.[12] According to Naomi Klein, the ANC was 'fed a steady diet of neo-liberal ideas' not only by the IMF but also by 'foreign business schools, investment banks, economic policy think tanks and the World Bank', not to mention 'the lawyers, economists and social workers who made up the rapidly expanding "transition" industry'.[13] In other accounts, it was Margaret Thatcher and the US secretary of state, James Baker, who turned Mandela away from his socialist principles. (Of nationalization, Baker is said to have remarked to Mandela: 'That's all old hat now.')[14]

36. Nelson Mandela with Klaus Schwab at Davos in January 1992, when Mandela dropped nationalization of the economy from the ANC programme.

Mandela's trip to Davos came at a decisive moment in South African history. Mandela had been released in February 1990. Within six months, the SACP had been legalized and the ANC's armed struggle had been suspended. However, by the end of 1991 South Africa was still a long way from having a democratically elected government. The multi-party negotiating process that ultimately produced a democratic constitution did not come until 1993; the first free elections not until April 1994. Many observers still believed that civil war was a more likely outcome of the end of apartheid than free elections. Yet it was not Western politicians or plutocrats who convinced Mandela to shift his position on nationalization. In the words of the future minister of labour Tito Mboweni (who accompanied Mandela to

Davos), it was in fact the Chinese and Vietnamese delegates to the WEF. 'We are currently striving to privatize state enterprises and invite private enterprise into our economies,' they told Mandela. 'We are Communist Party governments, and you are a leader of a national liberation movement. Why are you talking about nationalization?'[15] This makes sense. Why would Mandela be inclined to heed the advice of the Dutch minister of industry, another Davos delegate who advised him against increasing state ownership? He had just spent nearly thirty years as a captive of Dutch-speaking Afrikaners.[16] The network to which he had belonged throughout that time was one of the most successful of the twentieth century: the international network of Communists. What made Davos crucial was the integration of that older network into the new capitalist international devised by Klaus Schwab – an integration made possible by the Chinese and Vietnamese governments' embrace of market-based economic reforms.

49
Breaking the Bank of England

There is a serious flaw with narratives that represent the collapse of communism, the decline of socialism and the rise of globalization as a sinister conspiracy by capitalist multinationals and multilateral agencies against the liberation movements of the Third World. The flaw is that the network of global finance had nothing so politically coherent as 'shock doctrine'. It was as likely to direct its speculative efforts against a British Conservative government as against South African socialist revolutionaries – if there was money to be made. Nothing illustrates this point better than the events that unfolded in London just eight months after Nelson Mandela's renunciation of nationalization at Davos. Absent from the World Economic Forum that year – he did not begin attending regularly until 1995 – was the hedge fund manager George Soros. Though well on the way to becoming one of the wealthiest men in the world, the self-styled 'speculator' was still a relatively obscure figure. In September 1992, however, Soros shot to fame as the man who 'broke the Bank of England' – and with it the European Exchange Rate Mechanism (ERM).[1]

It was not only socialism that was at risk as global financial markets grew larger and more integrated in the 1980s and 1990s. The combination of deregulation (especially the abolition of exchange and capital controls) and computerization (especially the creation of faster information and transaction flows across borders) meant that any political enterprise predicated on hierarchical control was vulnerable.

The idea of pan-European unity, like the idea of universal working-class fraternity, had its roots in the nineteenth century. After the grim experiences of the mid-twentieth century, however, it had evolved from a utopian dream into a practical programme of economic integration.[2] It began with the creation of a 'Community' to regulate the production and pricing of coal and steel in six European states: West Germany, France, Italy, Belgium, the Netherlands and Luxembourg. The Treaty of Rome of 1957 then created a European Economic Community, with a reduction of customs duties and the establishment of a customs union between these countries. Trade between them had been growing rapidly before the formation of this EEC and continued to grow thereafter – as did world trade generally. In other respects, however, economic integration proceeded slowly. In agriculture, the development of an integrated market was positively hindered by the persistence of national subsidies until a Common Agricultural Policy superseded these. In manufacturing, too, national governments continued to resist pan-European competition by subsidizing politically sensitive sectors or by imposing non-tariff barriers. Such practices were less frequently adopted in the case of services, but only because services were less easily traded across national boundaries than goods. The exception to this rule was financial services, one of which – the sale of long-term corporate and public-sector bonds to relatively wealthy investors – became integrated in a quite novel way in the course of the 1960s.[3]

The rise of the so-called 'Eurobond' market was an early step in the direction of financial globalization.[4] But the birth of the Eurobond was also a major breakthrough in the history of European integration – though one largely unforeseen by the statesmen and technocrats who have been portrayed as the 'saints' or 'founding fathers' of the European Union's formative years.[5] It was the spontaneous result of innovation by private-sector actors, with some help from Britain's permissive monetary authorities. Within a few short years, the genesis and growth of this market transformed the European capital market, forging entirely new institutional links and networks across national borders, and it was bankers, not politicians, who made the running. In some measure, no doubt, their prime motive was the profit motive. Yet the architects of the Eurobond market regarded it not only as a way of making money, but also as a potent device for advancing Europe's political integration. In particular, they appreciated that European capital market integration could reinforce the case for British membership of the EEC. The French feared they would end up having to prop up sterling if Britain joined the EEC, since membership was expected to worsen the UK's already weak balance of payments; this was a key reason for both President Charles de Gaulle's vetoes of British membership in 1963 and 1967. The counterargument developed by the pioneers of the Eurobond market was that the French could not exclude Britain indefinitely if London re-established itself as Europe's financial centre for transactions in currencies other than sterling.[6]

No sooner had Britain successfully joined the EEC than bankers such as Siegmund Warburg – one of the key architects of the Eurobond market – began to discuss the possibility of monetary integration, beginning with the creation of a unit of account (he suggested the name 'Euro moneta') based on a basket of different national currencies.[7] Britain's post-war economic performance had been punctuated by recurrent sterling crises. Those who favoured the integration of Europe for the purposes of trade and financial services regarded the frequent need for currency realignments as more than just an inconvenience. Fluctuations in exchange rates seemed like just another barrier on the high road to European unity.

The idea of European monetary union was itself the product of a network of mostly Dutch, French and German thinkers.* Yet there is a certain irony that a network of intellectuals – some academic economists, some bureaucrats – could devise such a supremely hierarchical project as the creation of a single central bank for the heterogeneous nation states that had formed the EEC. An important explanation for that is the peculiarly tight-knit structure of the French governing elite: nearly all trained at the *grandes écoles* (mainly the École Polytechnique and École Nationale d'Administration) and employed by the *grands corps* (Inspection des Finances, Conseil d'État, Cour des Comptes, Corps des Mines). Those who chose to work in the private sector remained closely connected in a dense network of friendship, intermarriage, and membership of clubs such as Le Siècle and

* Graphic visualizations of 'the Founding Fathers Network' will be published in the forthcoming volume entitled *The Founding Fathers of the Euro: Individuals and Ideas in the History of European Monetary Union*, edited by Kenneth Dyson and Ivo Maes.

Masonic lodges, many of them dating back to before the French Revolution. Since the 1970s, between a third and a half of all government ministers, regardless of party affiliation, had been members of Le Siècle, with a peak of 72 per cent in Édouard Balladur's government (1993–5). The system known as *pantouflage* ensured a constant, 'revolving door' circulation of civil servants in and out of banking and industry. The top forty firms, in turn, were connected by a dense system of interlocking directorships, with a majority of directors serving on more than one other board.[8] To these so-called *énarques*, the idea of a single European currency was irresistibly appealing – not least because they saw the creation of a European central bank as a way of containing institutionally the growing economic predominance of Germany. This was the fundamental rationale behind the Treaty of Maastricht. From the German vantage point, monetary union was the price that had to be paid for French acceptance of German reunification: the proof, as the German Chancellor, Helmut Kohl, said repeatedly, that Germany's leaders now put Europe first, and Germany second.

Of course, Britain, too, had its governing elite. In the 1960s the journalists Henry Fairlie and Anthony Sampson had popularized the disdainful name that the historian A. J. P. Taylor had given it: 'The Establishment'. Nevertheless, despite being bound together by old school ties and Oxbridge scarves, the British ruling class was a good deal more heterogeneous than its French counterpart. Nothing better illustrated this than the Thatcher governments of the 1980s: not only was the prime minister a woman from provincial Lincolnshire (albeit one with an Oxford degree); there were enough ministers in her cabinet with Jewish backgrounds to inspire jokes about 'Old Estonians'. To Siegmund Warburg, whose merchant bank, S. G. Warburg (along with the older house of N. M. Rothschild), was a seedbed for some of the brightest Thatcherites, it was obvious that, as he put it in 1972, 'an economic and monetary union cannot be envisaged without a political union. I think it was Bismarck who always talked about "das primat der politik ueber die wirtschaft"* and this is as true today as it was in his age.'[9] The Conservatives had been the ones who, in the 1980s, had

* 'the primacy of politics over the economy'.

liberalized the City of London and ushered in a revival of British capitalism. They favoured Europe's commercial integration – indeed, they were the architects of the trade-liberalizing Single European Act of 1986. However, they were far from united in their support of monetary union. Even the transitional ERM ran counter to Thatcher's adage that governments could not 'buck the market'.* Alongside such economic objections there was a political one. Neither Labour nor Conservative politicians wanted to join a system requiring them to subordinate their macroeconomic policy to the German central bank. Although the Second World War had ended thirty-four years before Thatcher had moved into 10 Downing Street, the memory of 'the war' lingered on. The Conservative minister Nicholas Ridley was forced to resign in July 1990 for saying out loud what many privately thought: that the project for monetary union was 'a German racket designed to take over the whole of Europe'. The *Spectator* illustrated the interview in which this line appeared with a cartoon of Ridley daubing a Hitler moustache on a portrait of Kohl.

Nevertheless, by the mid-1980s, both the governor of the Bank of England and the Confederation of British Industry (CBI) were pressing Britain to join the ERM. Indeed, Nigel Lawson, the Chancellor of the Exchequer, was widely believed to be 'shadowing' the deutschmark, tacitly pursuing an exchange rate target. In June 1989, when Lawson and Geoffrey Howe, Thatcher's Foreign Secretary, both threatened to resign if Britain did not join the ERM, she finally acceded in principle, though she delayed acting until October 1990. By that point, the ERM advocates were so eager to move ahead, lest Thatcher change her mind, that there was no serious consideration of the central exchange rate at which Britain would enter the ERM, a rate some 'Euro-sceptics' saw as over-valued (2.95 deutschmarks to the pound). This concession by Thatcher did not suffice to save her. On 28 November 1990, she was replaced by her Chancellor, John Major, following an internal Conservative coup led by the pro-Europeans.

* In a speech on 'The Principles of Thatcherism', delivered in Seoul, on 3 September 1992, Thatcher expressed her view succinctly: 'If by artificially controlling the exchange rates between countries you try to buck the market, you will soon find that the market bucks you – and hard.'

Major and his supporters had underestimated the determination of their European counterparts to press on with monetary – and indeed political – union. They now proposed renaming the entity itself a 'European Union' by drawing up and signing a new foundational treaty. 'During the negotiations of the Maastricht Treaty,' the British Chancellor, Norman Lamont, later recalled with evident horror, 'for the first time I heard European politicians openly and enthusiastically arguing for the creation of a European state.'[10] Major was no more enthused. 'I did not want to see a single currency,' he later wrote. 'Nor did I like the political implications of monetary union.'[11] Major decided that Britain should sign Maastricht – otherwise he would alienate not only continental Europe but also the pro-European faction within his own Conservative Party – but that to appease the Euro-sceptics he would insist on 'opt-outs' for Britain from the single currency and the proposed Social Chapter.[12] The political stakes were high. Major had to face a general election in April 1992. The other Maastricht negotiators understood this, but they were still dismayed when he and Lamont produced, as the latter put it, 'a long, detailed and precise document in full legal form that specified all the articles of the treaty that would not apply to the UK, and bolted the door on any alternative interpretations'.[13] Lamont and Major simply refused to negotiate: either the other nations would accept the British opt-outs or Britain would not sign. This toughness played well at home. The *Daily Telegraph*'s headline proclaimed: 'Tory [Conservative] MPs cheer Major's success at Maastricht.'[14] The new treaty was signed on 7 February 1992. The French had got their promise of a single currency; they could live without British membership – as well as without the Danes, who also secured an opt-out – provided the new, enlarged Germany was locked in. Major scraped a narrow (and widely unexpected) victory in the British election just two months later.

The ERM was thus a halfway house between freely floating exchange rates and a single currency that not all of the participating countries would join when it was launched seven years hence. Meanwhile it was up to the twelve national central banks to keep their respective currencies within agreed trading ranges or bands. By August 1992, however, the predicament of several ERM members awakened doubts about whether they could do so. By this time, the economic consequences of German reunification were beginning to make themselves felt. To give East Germans a one-time reunification gift, their 'East marks' had been converted into much stronger West German deutschmarks at a one-to-one ratio. The effect was to increase East German purchasing power and the German money supply at a stroke, while at the same time rendering most of East German industry hopelessly uncompetitive.[15] There had to be massive investments in the East to bring its industrial infrastructure up to Western standards, as well as large unemployment payments and other transfers from West to East. The result was a surge in investment and government spending, much of it financed by borrowing. That in turn drove up German prices and wages.

The threat of German inflation threw into bold relief the conflict between the Bundesbank's domestic and European roles. One role – its statutory responsibility – was as the protector of the deutschmark's purchasing power; the other was as *de facto* anchor of the ERM. Legally bound to counteract German inflation, the Bundesbank responded to the reunification boom by raising the key interest rates at which it lent to German banks. From a pre-unification nadir of 2.5 per cent, the discount rate rose in measured steps to a peak of 8.75 per cent in August 1992. The Bundesbank was distinctly less concerned about its other role as the ERM's anchor. This was bad news for the other ERM members. By 1990 most of them, including the UK, France and Italy, had eliminated all restrictions on financial flows across their borders. Unless they also raised interest rates, mobile capital would move to Germany in search of higher returns. The problem was that the United Kingdom, France and Italy were not enjoying an expansion comparable to Germany's. On the contrary, their economies were slowing down and unemployment was rising. Indeed, Britain had suffered a recession in 1991.

The catalyst for a crisis was provided on 2 June 1992, when, in a referendum, Danish voters unexpectedly rejected the Maastricht Treaty.[16] On 1 July, President François Mitterrand announced that a French referendum would be held on 20 September.[17] If the French also rejected Maastricht, the new treaty would be dead.[18] Opinion polls soon indicated that this might indeed happen.[19] This political uncertainty was bad news for Britain. John Major might have opted out of the single currency, but he had invested a great deal of political capital in Maastricht. Moreover, he had been Chancellor when Britain had opted into the ERM. The last thing he wanted was for doubt to be cast on his commitment to that currency peg. Both he and Lamont gave speeches denying any conceivable possibility of devaluation.[20] To their dismay, they received little support for their position in Frankfurt. On four occasions in the summer of 1992, Bundesbank officials made disparaging remarks about other ERM currencies that were quoted in the press.[21] On 10 June the Bundesbank president, Helmut Schlesinger, gave an interview in which he openly spoke of a possible realignment of ERM currencies before the final move to monetary union.[22] Major and Lamont protested to Chancellor Kohl, but to no avail.[23] On 16 July, at a summer reception in 10 Downing Street, and later at a dinner hosted by the *Sunday Times*, Major, in a mixture of 'wishful thinking and bravado', asserted that in five or ten years' time, 'sterling would be among the world's strongest currencies – stronger perhaps than the Deutschmark'.[24] The very next day, the Bundesbank raised its discount rate – a legitimate step to curb German inflation – but at the same time ('incredibly', as Lamont put it) a Bundesbank spokesperson stated that 'market forces might eventually force weaker currencies toward devaluation'.[25] On 26 August, standing on the steps of the Treasury building in Whitehall, Lamont sought to remove any 'scintilla of doubt about the pound' by pledging to 'do whatever is necessary' to maintain sterling's position on or above its ERM floor of DM2.778.[26] That afternoon, Ian Plenderleith, the Bank of England director responsible for the money markets, invited senior officials of the big four high street banks to Threadneedle Street to unveil a plan to shore up sterling by borrowing more than £7.25bn in foreign currencies, mainly deutschmarks (a plan announced publicly eight days later).[27] Later the same day, Lamont read to his dismay that a member of the Bundesbank's board believed there was 'potential for realignment within the ERM'.[28] Four days later, Reuters got hold of an advance copy of a speech by a Bundesbank official which stated that an ERM realignment had been suppressed for years for 'prestige reasons', implying that it could not be deferred for much longer.[29]

To British politicians, steeped in the folk memories of the 1940s, it was obvious who the enemy was: the Germans.[30] In the first week of September, Lamont played host at a meeting of the European finance ministers in Bath. Perhaps encouraged by the quintessentially English location, he decided to put Schlesinger under maximum pressure. Schlesinger became so furious with Lamont's 'whining' that he threatened to walk out and had to be physically restrained from doing so by Theo Waigel, the German finance minister.[31] 'Never in the history of the Bundesbank has there been as much pressure on us as you are now exerting,' Schlesinger complained at one point.[32] ('Well,' Lamont reflected sardonically, 'perhaps he had not lived life very fully.')[33] At the end of the meeting, as the ministers were departing, Schlesinger retaliated by presenting Lamont's wife with a presentation case containing thirty silver deutschmarks. ('I have to confess,' Lamont later recalled, 'that unkind phrases about thirty pieces of silver reverberated in my mind.')[34] The war of words continued the following week, as Schlesinger flatly contradicted Lamont's suggestion that a German rate cut was imminent.[35] On 15 September the Bundesbank president gave an interview to the German financial paper *Handelsblatt* in which he did 'not rule out the possibility that, even after the realignment and the cut in German interest rates, one or two currencies could come under pressure before the referendum in France'.[36] The comment – published only as indirect speech because Schlesinger insisted on approving direct quotes – was soon posted on the Internet. Major insisted that Schlesinger be summoned from the dinner table to disavow the report, but the only result was an official Bundesbank statement that the text had not been 'authorized'.[37]

In blaming the Germans, however, Lamont had the wrong enemy. By 10 September the Germans had in fact come to terms with the need for a general realignment within the ERM, combined with a German interest rate cut. But this message did not reach the British government, mainly (it would seem) because the French finance minister, Jean-Claude Trichet, was determined to avoid such a realignment so soon before the French referendum on Maastricht. The most that seemed to be on offer was for Britain to devalue along with Italy, an option Major rejected, though when the Italians went ahead alone it only increased the pressure on sterling.[38] Yet it was not just ERM currencies that were under pressure that summer. On 8 September, Finland floated its currency, which immediately sank 14 per cent. The next day the Swedish central bank raised its overnight rate to 75 per cent to fend off devaluation. It later raised the rate to 500 per cent before finally giving up.[39] With US short-term interest rates at their lowest levels for thirty years, the dollar was also sliding relative to the high-yielding deutschmark. But the senior White House official who commented on the situation was closer to the truth than his Downing Street counterparts: 'We are in a hopeless position,' he said, 'at the mercy of the markets.'[40] This was the real point: it was not what Schlesinger said that mattered; it was how the markets reacted to his words. 'This generation at the Bank had never seen anything like it,' one Bank of England official remarked. 'It was as if an avalanche was coming at us.'[41]

After the crisis, the British media latched on to the idea that one man had broken the Bank of England: George Soros. But this was to miss the point almost as much as Major and Lamont when they blamed another man, Helmut Schlesinger.* Financial crises are not caused by individuals. They are caused by herds – as Soros understood. Born in Hungary, a refugee from Nazism and a graduate of the London School of Economics, Soros had built his Quantum Fund and other associated funds from about $5m in 1969 to about $5bn in 1992 by placing large financial bets with commensurate payoffs. Soros knew full well that a system of fixed exchange rates would come under strain if there were significant and persistent differences in the economic performance of the member states. But he also knew that, if his Quantum Fund and other associated hedge funds bet heavily enough against a currency, they could cause it to weaken regardless of the economic 'fundamentals'. Proudly unorthodox in his approach to economics, Soros believed that 'reflexivity' played a central role in financial markets. As he put it in a talk at the Massachusetts Institute of Technology in 1994, 'Reflexivity is, in effect, a two-way feedback mechanism in which reality helps shape the

* Major complained bitterly that the Bundesbank later fought speculators against the franc 'in a way they had not done in the case of sterling'. It provided not only massive currency intervention but also 'a joint Franco-German declaration that exchange rate changes were not justified' – something the United Kingdom had pleaded for but never received. As the *Economist* correctly pointed out, however, by any relevant financial measure the franc was not as vulnerable to devaluation as the pound. Indeed, it was undervalued even more than the pound was overvalued.

participants' thinking and the participants' thinking helps shape reality.'[42]

The crucial point was that Soros alone could not bring this about. 'Most of the time I am a trend follower,' he once observed, 'but all the time I am aware that I am a member of a herd and I am on the lookout for inflection points . . . Most of the time the trend prevails; only occasionally are the errors corrected. It is only on those occasions that one should go against the trend . . . [to be] ahead of the curve.'[43] As we have seen, Quantum's assets under management were around $5bn in 1992. The international reserves of the Bank of England were $44bn – nearly nine times greater – to which could be added the reserves of any other ERM members' central banks that chose to intervene on the British side. If Soros had taken on the Bank of England single-handedly, he would have lost. On the other hand, the Federal Reserve estimated that daily turnover on the world's foreign exchange markets had increased from $58bn in 1986 to $167bn in 1992.[44] In the words of the *Economist*, 'The British Treasury's seemingly comfortable reserves were as nothing compared with the speculators' firepower.'[45] The key to the Soros trade was thus to get a critical mass of investors to put on the same trade that he had in mind. That was not hard because Soros was already part of a network of like-minded investors.

It was in fact Robert Johnson of Bankers Trust who helped Soros and his partner Stan Druckenmiller devise the trade.[46] As Johnson explained, the critical point was the fact that the ERM currencies were being maintained within relatively narrow bands: whatever happened, the values of the currencies could not possibly rise far against the mark, so if speculators sold the pound short* and lost, they would not lose much. If they bet and won, they stood to gain a great deal: Johnson estimated that the depreciation could be as much as 20 per cent.[47] That was an argument for maximum commitment.

* To short a currency, you borrow that currency through a broker, sell it at its current price, and are credited with the money for selling it. If the exchange rate subsequently falls, you then buy the same amount of the currency at the new, lower price and return it to the broker. The difference between the higher price that you were credited with for selling the currency and the lower price that you pay for buying it is your profit. However, if the currency rises in value, you have to buy the amount you borrowed at the new higher price to return it to the broker, so you lose money.

Druckenmiller was certainly persuaded that the pound would be devalued, but he was hesitant about how much to bet. 'Well, if you love it so much . . .' said Soros snidely. He told Druckenmiller to 'go for the jugular' – to borrow as much as they could to short the pound.[48] After all, as Soros put it, the 'risk–reward relationship [was] extremely favourable', so why hold back?[49] With mounting excitement, he and Druckenmiller began borrowing as many pounds as they could get their hands on to place the biggest bet of their careers. But the key point was, as Johnson recalled, that they were not betting alone: 'I walked out of there with absolutely no question that we were going to go after this thing [and] *I knew other people in the banks and counterparties would imitate us.*'[50]

As Schlesinger's 'unauthorized' remarks from the previous Tuesday afternoon became public on Wednesday, 16 September, short selling of the pound escalated. Waiting anxiously to talk to the prime minister, Lamont lamented that 'we were losing hundreds of millions of dollars every few minutes'. The Bank of England vainly tried to staunch the outflow.[51] At 11 a.m., it announced that the minimum lending rate would be raised to 12 per cent. A little over three hours later, the rate was raised to 15 per cent, but with effect from the next day. Such desperate measures only egged Soros on.[52] And when Lamont announced that he would borrow an additional $15bn to defend sterling, Soros was 'amused because that was about how much we wanted to sell'.[53] He never got to that point, though; his position had reached approximately $10bn by the time the markets closed. That evening, while theatre-goers (amongst them this author) enjoyed Verdi's *The Force of Destiny* at the English National Opera, Lamont called an impromptu conference in the Treasury's central courtyard to announce that the UK was 'suspending' its participation in the ERM.[54] Despite its earlier official devaluation within the ERM, the lira was also driven out altogether on the same day.[55]

That George Soros is a hub in a large and powerful network has often been claimed by conspiracy theorists. According to one breathless account, he 'is the visible side of a vast and nasty secret network of private financial interests, controlled by the leading aristocratic and royal families of Europe, centred in the British· House of Windsor . . . and built upon the wreckage of the British Empire after World War

II'. This network allegedly extends from the Queen and the Rothschilds all the way down to 'indicted metals and commodity speculator and fugitive Marc Rich of Zug, Switzerland and Tel Aviv, secretive Israeli arms and commodity dealer Shaul Eisenberg, and "Dirty Rafi" Eytan'.[56] This is nonsense. The real network Soros belongs to – the 'larger and more intricate economic web' he alluded to in an interview – is a network of hedge funds seeking to make money in similar ways.[57] As Druckenmiller recalled, 'We really went after this thing and kept going and going and going like the Energizer bunny . . . So anybody with a brain is going to ask his dealer, "What the hell is going on?" And I know people talk. It's Quantum.' In some cases – notably Louis Bacon – Soros and Druckenmiller shared information over the phone. Other hedge fund managers who were in the trade included Bruce Kovner of Caxton and Paul Tudor Jones. Telepathy was not needed.

Magnifying the scale of the short selling were the efforts of the banks who were lending the hedge funds money.[58] Duncan Balsbaugh was running the fixed-income trading desk for Morgan Stanley in London. As he later recalled, Soros's request for funding meant that he 'was recruited to help plot an assault on an elderly woman – the Old Lady of Threadneedle Street, aka the Bank of England'. Soros 'warehoused' nearly all his holdings of European bonds as collateral for the cash he was borrowing to short the pound on the spot market. In addition to funding him, in Balsbaugh's words, 'We shadowed Soros.' There was, he recalled, 'cavalry behind (and often frontrunning) Quantum's pound sales – hedge funds such as Tudor, Bacon and Kovner, not to mention a leveraged legion of banks . . . all pounding the pound'.[59] Other banks that followed the hedge funds' lead included Citicorp, J. P. Morgan, Chemical Banking, Bankers Trust, Chase Manhattan, First Chicago and BankAmerica.[60] The Old Lady stood no chance. It was financial gang rape.

The sharp 15 per cent depreciation of the pound that followed the British capitulation on 'Black Wednesday' made Soros a vast amount of money.* In an interview with the *Times* journalist Anatole

* Soros's bet did not become public knowledge until 24 October, when the *Daily Mail* ran an article under the headline, 'I Made a Billion as the Pound Crashed'.

Kaletsky, he acknowledged – 'with an embarrassed wince that could not entirely hide some mischievous self-satisfaction' – that his four funds had made around $1bn from shorting the pound; his profits from a variety of ancillary positions such as interest rate futures and shorting the Italian lira were another $1bn.[61] Later, Soros claimed that the demise of sterling would 'have unfolded more or less the same way even if I had never been born'.[62] True, of the total loss of British reserves – $27bn dollars – he could notionally be held responsible for $10bn.[63] But the reality was that it was the collective effort of Soros's network that broke the peg. As Soros told Kaletsky, he had been the 'biggest single factor in the market', but not the whole market. He had led the trend.[64] It could just as easily have happened without him 'because had I not taken the position, somebody else would have taken [it]'.[65]

Soros's network had won. Who had lost? In 1997 the UK Treasury estimated the cost of Black Wednesday at £3.4bn, though eight years later the figure was revised downwards to £3.3bn. The Bank of England's trading losses in August and September were estimated at £800m, but the main loss to taxpayers arose because the devaluation might otherwise have made them a profit.[66] More lasting was the damage to the Bank's reputation, even if it was just the latest hierarchical organization brought low by what the American journalist Tom Friedman dubbed 'the electronic herd'. On the other hand, breaking the peg to the deutschmark brought relief to the UK economy. Short-term interest rates were swiftly lowered so that by January 1993 they were below 6 per cent, a welcome respite to a nation heavily exposed to adjustable-rate mortgages. The economy recovered.[67] The disaster was not economic but political: the government's agonizing over whether or not to join the ERM in the first place, its adamant declarations through the summer of 1992 that it would defend the pound to the last, and its final, abject capitulation on 16 September – all this permanently damaged the Conservatives' reputation for economic competence.[68] The Major government's standing

---

Accompanying the *Mail's* story was a photograph of Soros, smiling and holding a drink in his hand. The ensuing mayhem on the doorstep of his London residence persuaded Soros to tell his version of events to Anatole Kaletsky.

in the opinion polls never recovered and on 1 May 1997 – despite four years of buoyant growth – the Tories slumped to defeat at the hands of a rejuvenated Labour Party, led by Tony Blair, who had followed Nelson Mandela's example by abandoning 'the common ownership of the means of production' as a core policy goal.

As for the project of European integration, a surprising thing occurred. Some American economists deduced from the debacle of the ERM that to proceed even further – towards full monetary union – would be a recipe for economic disaster and perhaps even European conflict. This was not the view of George Soros. 'The only escape,' he argued:

> is to have no exchange-rate system at all, but a single currency in Europe, as in the U.S. It would put speculators like me out of business, but I would be delighted to make that sacrifice . . . I expect a period of tremendous turbulence in eastern Europe and this turmoil outside the gates will create the momentum for European union. Nationalism in the east is now so strong that only a united Europe can counteract it. Unless Europe holds together, war will engulf most of the former Soviet Union.

Asked about the Germans' devotion to their deutschmarks, he replied: 'If Maastricht is ratified, maybe I will even bet against the Bundesbank.'[69] The *Economist* also drew the conclusion that the ERM crisis was an argument for rather than against monetary union.[70] Thus did the victor of the 1992 crisis draw precisely the wrong conclusion from it. The leaders of continental Europe would indeed plough relentlessly ahead with monetary union, so that by the beginning of 1999 the euro – a single European currency managed by an authentically federal European Central Bank – was a reality. In doing so, they revealed their indestructible faith in the power of hierarchical structures even in an age of exponential network growth. In 1992 George Soros had owned the jungle, but the jungle had owned the politicians. In the years after 1999, the only thing that would change was that the jungle would grow vastly larger, denser and more intolerant of antiquated pyramid builders.

VIII

The Library of Babel

50
9/11/2001

The twenty-first century increasingly looks like the fulfilment of Jorge Luis Borges's short story 'The Library of Babel'. In it, he imagines a library containing not only all the books ever written, but all the books that ever could be written. With an infinity of information at their disposal, men swing swiftly from euphoria to madness. Some are seized by a 'hygienic, ascetic furore' to 'eliminate useless works', leading to the 'senseless perdition of millions of books'. Others seek the one book that is 'the formula and perfect compendium of all the rest' – or they seek the librarian who has read that book and is therefore 'analogous to a god'. In some parts of the vast library, men 'prostrate themselves before books and kiss their pages in a barbarous manner, but they do not know how to decipher a single letter'. In other parts, 'epidemics, heretical conflicts, peregrinations which inevitably degenerate into banditry, have decimated the population'.[1] The twenty-first-century world often seems like a vast realization of Borges's vision.

The defining event of this century's first years was an attack on the financial and transport networks of the United States by an Islamist gang that is best understood as an anti-social network. Although acting in the name of Al-Qaeda, the 9/11 plotters were only weakly connected to the wider network of political Islam, which helps explain why they were able to escape detection.

There was an evil genius to what the attackers of 11 September 2001 did. In essence, they targeted the main hubs of America's increasingly networked society, exploiting security vulnerabilities that allowed them to smuggle primitive weapons (box-cutters) onto four passenger planes bound for New York and Washington, respectively the central nodes of the US financial and political systems. By hijacking the planes, taking over the controls, and then flying them straight at the World Trade Center and the Pentagon, the Al-Qaeda operatives achieved the greatest coup in the history of terrorism. Not only did they generate an atmosphere of fear in the United States that persisted for many months; more importantly, they precipitated an asymmetrical response by the administration of President George W. Bush that almost certainly did more over the succeeding years to strengthen than to weaken the cause of Salafist Islam.

Both the air transport and financial systems seemed perfect targets for such attacks. Each had grown significantly more complex in the recent past. Each played a crucial role in the process of globalization which, by 2001, was widely regarded by leftists as well as Islamists as a new incarnation of American imperialism.[2] The attackers also had good reason to hope that by damaging such important nodes while at the same time generating public panic, they might create a cascade of disruption that would spread to other networks.[3]

The attackers themselves formed a network. Working on his own in the immediate aftermath of the attacks, using software called InFlow designed to analyse corporate networks, a Cleveland consultant named Vladis Krebs showed that Mohamed Atta was the crucial node in the 9/11 network (see plate 24). It was Atta who was in touch with sixteen of the nineteen hijackers as well as with fifteen other people connected with them. Of all the people in the network, Atta had the highest betweenness centrality, as well the highest activity (the number of times he contacted others) and closeness (his ability to connect directly to others without a go-between). However, Nawaf Alhazmi, one of the American Flight 77 hijackers, was second only to Atta in terms of betweenness centrality, suggesting that he may have been one of the planners of the operation. And if Atta had somehow been arrested before 9/11, Marwan Al-Shehhi could easily have taken over his leadership role.[4] As Krebs observed, however, the distinctive feature of the 9/11 network was its lack of social links to the wider world. A tightly knit group, many of whom had trained together in Afghanistan, the plotters were almost wholly without the weak ties that characterize normal social networks. Moreover, the plotters did not have much to do with one another after they reached the United States:

theirs was a sparse network, with communication kept to the barest minimum. In that sense, it truly was an anti-social network – all but invisible, as covert networks must be if they are to avoid detection.[5]

To Krebs, it was obvious in hindsight what was going on. Could it have been spotted beforehand, however? 'To win this fight against terrorism,' Krebs wrote, 'it appears that the good guys have to build a better information and knowledge sharing network than the bad guys.'[6] Such a network was supposed to exist in 2001, in the form of an Army project called Able Danger, which sought to map Al-Qaeda by 'identifying linkages and patterns in large volumes of data'. The problem was that because of the 'Kevin Bacon' problem – the fact that there are now fewer than six degrees of separation between everyone in the United States – the numbers of people identified as potential terrorists ran into the hundreds of thousands, if not millions.[7] Some of the network graphs that Able Danger produced were twenty feet long and almost wholly unintelligible because the print was so small.[8] Krebs himself concluded that there would be no substitute for human intelligence in the war on terrorism; the alternative would be to drown in big data.[9]

In the wake of the 9/11 attacks, as panic slowly subsided, some network specialists began to argue that Al-Qaeda was in fact relatively weak. Precisely its covert, anti-social character meant that it could not easily recruit and train new people.[10] It was all very well to say that the strength of Al-Qaeda lay partly in its decentralization,[11] but if Osama bin Laden could not order a second major attack on the United States, what was the use of such a network structure?[12] And if, following the American invasion of Afghanistan and the overthrow of the Taliban regime, the Al-Qaeda leadership was isolated somewhere in Pakistan, all that was needed was to track it down and decapitate the organization.[13] Some scholars drew analogies with covert criminal networks, such as the Caviar network, a cannabis- and cocaine-trafficking gang in the Montreal of the 1990s, though they noted the greater centralization of the criminal networks compared with the terrorist network.[14] A more important difference was that criminal gangs were not united by a common ideology in the way that the members of Al-Qaeda clearly were. Although not visibly connected to the wider Salafist network, all the 9/11 attackers belonged to it intellectually and were willing to die for their religious faith. There was, in other words, a much larger jihadist network, within which Al-Qaeda was a very weakly connected component. That wider network consisted of men who, as mujahedeen, had met and bonded during the Soviet–Afghan war; the South-East Asian members of Jemaah Islamiyah; and supporters in Arab communities in Europe and the Middle East.[15] What Western leaders found so baffling was that their retaliatory 'war on terror' required a narrow focus on only those Islamists who themselves engaged in violence. This overlooked the fact that the small networks of active terrorists were embedded in much larger networks of people who sympathized with the terrorists without engaging in violence themselves.[16] Young men do not become terrorists on a whim. They need sustained exposure to extremist preaching as well as entanglement in a network of Salafist activity.[17]

When a distributed network attacks a hierarchy, the hierarchy reacts in the ways that come naturally to it. In the immediate aftermath of 9/11, President George W. Bush and the key members of his administration with responsibility for national security made a series of

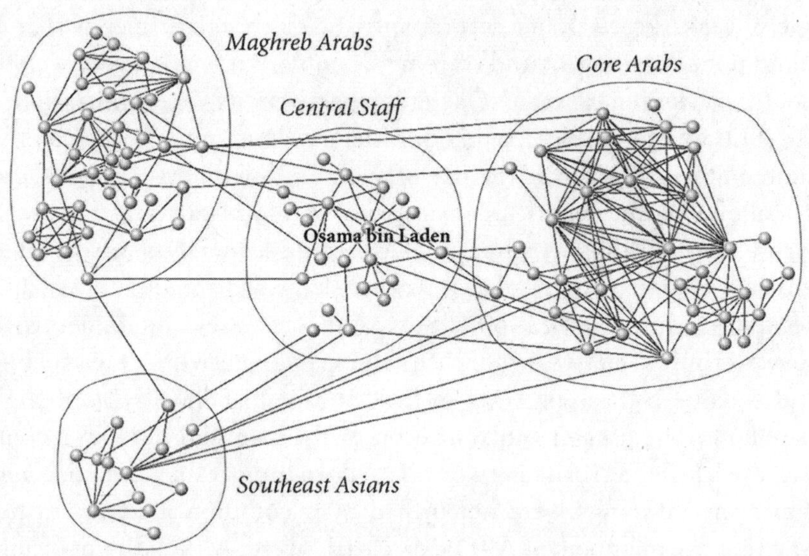

37. The global Salafi network, *c.* 2004: a rough sketch.

decisions that could scarcely have been better calculated to make the Islamist network grow. Correctly, the president urged that a plan be improvised to overthrow the regime in Afghanistan for harbouring Al-Qaeda. Wrongly, the president was persuaded by the vice president, Dick Cheney, and the secretary of defense, Donald Rumsfeld, that the attacks had created a pretext for a second military intervention, this time to overthrow Saddam Hussein in Iraq,* despite the fact that evidence for a causal link between Iraq and the 9/11 attacks was all but non-existent. At the same time, to combat future attacks on the United States, Bush created a new Department of Homeland Security. Writing in the *Los Angeles Times* as early as August 2002, before it was even clear that Iraq was to be invaded, John Arquilla presciently pointed out the flaws in this approach:

> [I]n a netwar, like the one we find ourselves in now, strategic bombing means little, and most networks don't rely on one – or even several – great leaders to sustain and guide them ... [Creating] a Cabinet-level Department of Homeland Security ... is a second major misstep. A hierarchy is a clumsy tool to use against a nimble network: It takes networks to fight networks, much as in previous wars it has taken tanks to fight tanks ... The kind of network we need can't be formed or sustained through coercive comments about being 'with us' or 'against us'.[18]

This was perhaps too pessimistic about what the national-security state would achieve. Of 109 known jihadist-linked plots to use violence against the US homeland between January 1993 and February 2016, just thirteen were carried out, thanks to a combination of surveillance and informants.[19] Nevertheless, in one respect Arquilla was right. In late 2001, Al-Qaeda had looked like an old-fashioned secret society that was forced to operate as an anti-social network, capable of only occasional if spectacular acts of violence. After the American-led invasion of Iraq, however, its affiliate in Iraq evolved into a much larger and more effective network as it exploited the chaos that followed the overthrow of Saddam's brutal hierarchy to whip up sectarian conflict. The result was

* On the very same day as the attacks, Rumsfeld argued that 'the U.S. response should consider a wide range of options and possibilities. The secretary said his instinct was to hit Saddam Hussein at the same time—not only Bin Ladin [*sic*].'

a bloody insurgency that was easily foreseeable by anyone familiar with Iraq's history. (Something very similar had befallen the British occupiers in 1920.) It took the American military several frustrating years belatedly to learn lessons that Walter Walker and his contemporaries had learned long before in the jungles of South-East Asia.

John Nagl was a US army officer who, as a Rhodes Scholar, had written a doctoral thesis comparing the conflicts in Malaya and Vietnam, arguing that while the British had adapted to the exigencies of jungle warfare, the Americans had not.[20] He was one of the authors of what became the Army's *Counterinsurgency Field Manual* (FM 3-24), under the direction of two visionary generals who had come to understand the urgent need for such a handbook: Lieutenant General David Petraeus and Lieutenant General James Mattis. Work began on FM 3-24 in October 2005, after Petraeus returned from his second tour of duty in Iraq. It was released in December of the following year.[21] The manual's most striking feature was its repeated discussion of the networked character of an insurgency. For example, the authors were at pains to distinguish between insurgencies with a 'formal and hierarchical structure' and those with a 'networked structure'. Each model had its strengths and weaknesses, but a networked insurgency tended 'to heal, adapt, and learn rapidly' as well as being hard to persuade to accept a negotiated settlement 'because no single person or small group is in charge'.[22] To a striking extent, FM 3-24 set out to educate the US military about network theory, explaining concepts such as network density, degree centrality and betweenness.[23] In the first edition, there was even an appendix entitled 'Social Network Analysis'.[24]

FM 3-24 owed more than a small debt to the work of an Australian army colonel named David Kilcullen, who had been seconded to the Pentagon in 2004. Kilcullen's Twenty-Eight Articles – 'Fundamentals of Company-Level Counterinsurgency' – argued that 'to build trusted networks' was 'the true meaning of the phrase "hearts and minds"':

> Over time, if you successfully build networks of trust, these will grow like roots into the population, displacing the enemy's networks, bringing him out into the open to fight you, and seizing the initiative. These networks include local allies, community leaders, local security forces,

NGOs and other friendly or neutral nonstate actors in your area, and the media ... Actions that help build trusted networks serve your cause. Actions – even killing high-profile targets – that undermine trust or disrupt your networks help the enemy.[25]

A key insight was that the global jihad the United States and its allies were fighting was based on a pre-existing social network of 'marriage relationships, money flows, alumni relationships, and sponsorship links'. Terrorism was 'merely one of the shared activities that the network engages in, while the core is the patronage network'.[26] At the same time, however, because of the growing importance of organized violence, the global jihad was already acquiring state-like characteristics:

[I]n a globalized insurgency, the insurgents' parallel hierarchy is a *virtual state*: it controls no territory or population but exercises control over distributed systems that, taken together, represent many elements of traditional state power. It is also a *pseudo-state*: a false state, a governing entity that acts like a state but is not one in terms of legal or political legitimacy. Moreover, it is not a single hierarchy but a federated network of linked systems that functions as an 'insurgent state' and competes with world governments.[27]

Amongst the tactics recommended by Kilcullen to defeat this nascent state were 'co-opting neutral or friendly women' because of their importance in insurgents' support networks; launching high-frequency 'counternetwork' intelligence operations, which 'can generate a lethal momentum that causes insurgency networks to collapse catastrophically'; 'asphyxiat[ing] the network by cutting the insurgents off from the people'; and interdicting the vulnerable links in the insurgent network.[28] This became the basis of Petraeus's 'Anaconda Strategy' of encircling and choking the Al Qaeda in Iraq network.[29]

The US Army learned its lesson well, if late in the day. During the decisive phase of the US 'surge' in Iraq in 2007, General Stanley McChrystal summed up what had been learned in Iraq. 'To confront [the Al-Qaeda in Iraq leader Abu Musab al-]Zarqawi's spreading network, [we] had to replicate its dispersion, flexibility, and speed. Over time, "It takes a network to defeat a network" became a mantra across the command and an eight-word summary of our core

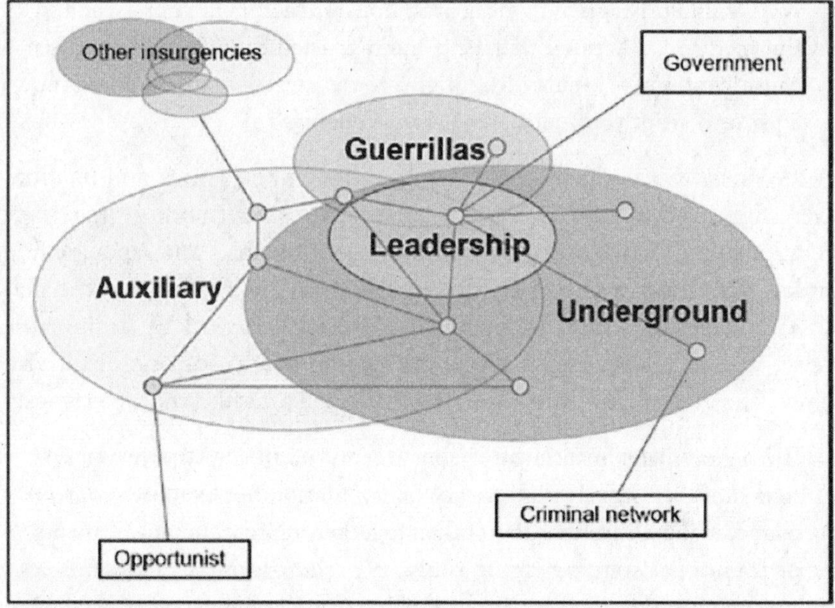

38. Networked insurgencies: diagram from the *Army Counterinsurgency Manual* (2014 edition).

operational concept.'[30] Thus did American soldiers work out how to own the concrete jungles of post-Saddam Iraq. In Afghanistan, too, a similarly painful learning process was happening. Emile Simpson's experience as a Gurkha officer convinced him that, while conventional two-way wars might still occur, the general tendency was towards multi-player conflicts, in which the Clausewitzian ideal of a decisive victory on the battlefield was unattainable. Victory in such conflicts amounted to the achievement of political stability.[31] So political was counter-insurgency as an activity that there might be cases where securing some level of consent from an insurgent network would be preferable to destroying it.

51
9/15/2008

In many ways, the effects of 9/11 were much less disruptive of the American financial and political system than Al-Qaeda had hoped. True, there was interruption of the payments system, a one-week closure of the New York Stock Exchange, a sharp drop in stock prices and a jump in financial volatility. The suspension of air transport also slowed down cheque-clearing and other non-electronic forms of transaction. However, the economic impact of the attacks was limited as major institutions were remarkably well prepared for such an eventuality and the Federal Reserve stepped in unhesitatingly to maintain market liquidity. Within a matter of weeks, the financial crisis was over.[1] The total cost of the attacks in terms of property damage, cleaning up, and earnings losses has been estimated at between $33bn and $36bn.[2] It was the Bush administration's decision to invade Iraq – which the Al-Qaeda leadership cannot possibly have foreseen – that increased these costs by anything up to two orders of magnitude, if one accepts the highest estimates of the costs of the 'war on terror'.[3] By contrast, what bin Laden seems to have aimed at was more of a chain reaction, in which the initial shock of the attacks would have a cascading effect through the US economic system. The fact that this did not happen suggested that the American capitalist network had more resilience than the jihadists had expected.

Network outages were a familiar concept by 2001. In 1996 there had been a major power blackout in the western United States when the failure of a single power line in Oregon had tripped hundreds of lines and generators, interrupting service to 7.5 million people. The following year, Toyota's entire manufacturing operation had ground to a halt after a fire had destroyed the factory of the sole supplier of a crucial brake component, jeopardizing the operations of around 200 other suppliers.[4] Just months before 9/11, on 18 July 2001, a fire in a railway tunnel in Baltimore caused a widespread slowdown in Internet speeds because it burned through fibre optic cables belonging to a number of major Internet Service Providers. Something similar happened in September 2003, when the entire Italian power grid (except that on the island of Sardinia) crashed after a tree fell on a high-tension line between Italy and Switzerland. An even bigger cascade occurred in November 2006, when the failure of a single power cable in north-west Germany caused outages as far away as Portugal.[5] The financial system, it seemed, was a more resilient network than the European electricity grid, if not the Internet itself.

This proved to be an illusion. The bankruptcy of Lehman Brothers on 15 September 2008 unleashed one of the biggest financial crises in history and came closer than any event since the Wall Street stock market crash of 1929 to causing a global outage of the international credit system. Moreover, the macroeconomic costs of the global financial crisis were certainly larger than those of the war on terror, especially if one imagines the output that would have been created had the world economy continued uninterruptedly along its trend path. (Plausible estimates for the US alone range from $5.7tn to $13tn, compared with a maximum estimate of the cost of the war on terror of $4tn.)[6] In short, 9/15 greatly exceeded the disruption caused seven years earlier by 9/11.

The causes of the financial crisis can be summarized under six headings. Major banks became dangerously undercapitalized, exploiting regulatory loopholes to increase their leverage ratios. Markets were flooded with asset-backed securities such as collateralized debt obligations that rating agencies egregiously mispriced. The Federal Reserve allowed monetary policy to be too loose between 2002 and 2004. Politicians created economically foolish incentives for poor Americans to become home-owners. Derivatives such as credit default swaps were sold on a massive scale, on the basis of unrealistic risk models. Finally, flows of capital from emerging markets, especially China, to the United States helped to inflate the American real estate bubble.[7] The crisis may be said to have begun when that bubble burst: declining house prices and mounting defaults on subprime mortgages were producing signs of financial distress already in late

2006. Yet it was the Lehman bankruptcy – at 1.45 a.m. on Monday, 15 September – that turned distress into global panic. The parent company's filing was followed by around eighty insolvency proceedings involving subsidiaries in eighteen foreign countries. In the main bankruptcy proceeding, about 66,000 claims – exceeding $873bn – were filed against Lehman. It was 'the largest, most complex, multi-faceted and far-reaching bankruptcy case ever filed in the United States'.[8] Incredibly, however, staff economists at the Federal Reserve saw no reason to anticipate a recession. 'I don't think we've seen a significant change in the basic outlook,' reported the Fed chief economist David J. Stockton to the Federal Open Markets Committee (FOMC) on 16 September, 'and certainly the story behind our forecast is . . . that we're still expecting a very gradual pickup in GDP growth over the next year.' Events would make a mockery of this and similar statements.[9] Only a few people in the room appreciated at this early stage the true nature of the Fed's position. In the revealing words of Eric S. Rosengren of the Boston Fed:

> I think it's too soon to know whether what we did with Lehman is right. Given that the Treasury didn't want to put money in, what happened was that we had no choice. But we took a calculated bet. If we have a run on the money market funds or if the . . . repo market shuts down, that bet may not look nearly so good. I think we did the right thing given the constraints that we had. I hope we get through this week . . . we shouldn't be in a position where we're betting the economy on one or two institutions.[10]

It was not until 29 October that Ben Bernanke, the Federal Reserve chairman, made his first allusion to the possibility that they were in a crisis analogous with that of the 1930s.[11] And only in mid-December did another member of the FOMC go so far as to suggest explicitly 'that we could have default rates greater than those of the Great Depression'.[12]

What the Fed had failed to understand was that, although Lehman's chief executive, Dick Fuld, was something of a network isolate on Wall Street, unloved by his peers (including the Treasury secretary, Henry Paulson, formerly CEO of Goldman Sachs), the bank itself was a crucial hub in an international financial network that had grown far larger and denser than ever before in the space of twenty years, thanks to the combination of globalization and the Internet. One of the few central bankers to appreciate the importance of this structural change was Andrew Haldane of the Bank of England, who argued that a complex adaptive system had been created that tended to amplify cyclical fluctuations.[13] Haldane's insight drew on the work of John Holland and others on complex systems which, unlike merely complicated systems, have the tendency to change in unpredictable ways. These 'emergent properties' were the thing missing from the Fed economists' model.[14] Quite simply, standard macroeconomics omitted network structure. No one had quite noticed that the global financial network had become connected enough for distress to cascade rapidly from one institution to many, but sparse enough for many institutions to be poorly diversified and inadequately insured against the failure of a counterparty.[15]

With delusional boasts about the 'great moderation' it had achieved

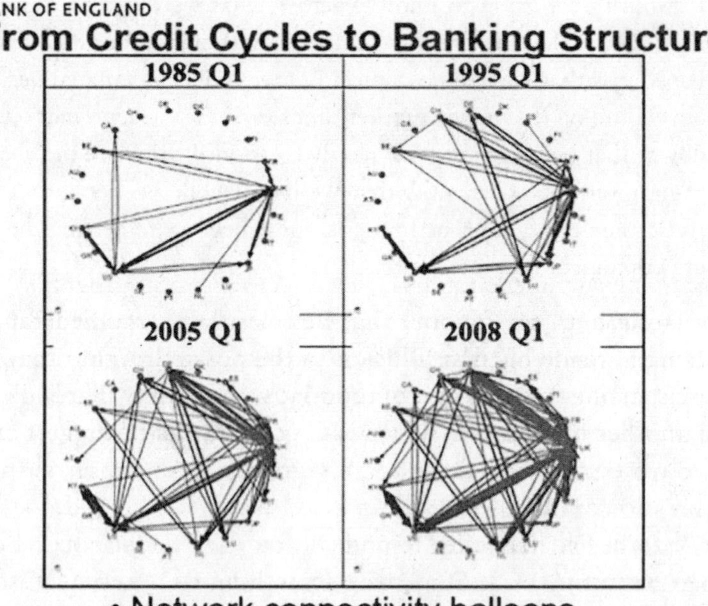

39. Network connectivity balloons in the international financial system, from a 2011 presentation by Andrew Haldane.

just a few years before disaster struck, the Federal Reserve had been one of the architects of the global financial crisis. To the credit of Chairman Bernanke, however, the speed with which he applied the lessons of the Great Depression ensured that the economic consequences were much less severe than in the 1930s. By purchasing all kinds of assets in the first phase of 'quantitative easing', and then large quantities of government bonds in the second and third phases, the Fed helped to contain the crisis. This was a triumph for the hierarchical system of monetary governance, an acknowledgement that, left to itself, the international finance network would not have repaired itself. Yet the main reason there was no second Great Depression was that, having let Lehman fail, the US Treasury stepped in to prevent further major financial bankruptcies. The bailouts of firms such as the insurance giant AIG and the other big banks, which received more than $400bn under the Troubled Asset Relief Program, were crucial in halting the chain reaction of insolvency that had begun on 9/15. That these same firms continued to pay their senior employees seven-figure bonuses prompted widespread criticism.[16] The public should not have been surprised. For the financial system was a network in more ways than one.

The US business elite has long been a tightly knit group with banks as the principal source of linkages between different sectors of the economy, including the realm of politics.[17] A good illustration of how the American system works is the career of Vernon Jordan, Jr, an urbane African-American lawyer who made his reputation as a civil rights lawyer in Georgia in the final years of segregation. In 1972 Jordan was invited to join the board of Celanese, a diversified manufacturer, whose chairman, John W. Brooks, then nominated him to join the board of Bankers Trust of New York. Through another Bankers Trust director, William M. Ellinghaus, Jordan was recruited to the board of the department store J. C. Penney in 1973. A year later, he joined the Xerox board, where he served with Archie R. McCardell, the president of Xerox, and Howard L. Clark, the chief executive of American Express, whose board McCardell was also on. Endorsed by both McCardell and Clark, Jordan joined the American Express board in 1977. In 1980 he joined the board of the tobacco company R. J. Reynolds and the following year he left his position at the National Urban League to join the Washington office of the Dallas law firm Akin Gump Strauss Hauer & Feld.[18] Jordan's close friendship with Bill Clinton, whom he first met through the NUL in 1973, became politically momentous after Clinton was elected president in 1992, as Jordan became his 'Quicker Fixer-Upper' in a succession of scandals, notably the Monica Lewinsky affair. In 1999 Jordan left Akin Gump Strauss to join the New York branch of Lazard, the investment bank and asset manager.[19]

By comparison, Timothy Geithner's career followed a different path. His mother, Deborah Moore, was a *Mayflower* descendant. He studied at Dartmouth College. Before entering government service, he worked at Kissinger Associates. As president of the Federal Reserve Bank of New York, however, Geithner became socially as well as professionally connected with members of the financial elite. For example, through shared memberships of non-profit institutions such as the Economic Club of New York or the Council on Foreign Relations, Geithner had personal connections to senior executives or directors of around twenty-one financial firms. According to one econometric study, these connections were valuable, in that the companies with links to Geithner saw their stock prices jump when it was announced on 21 November 2008 that he would be Barack Obama's Treasury secretary.[20] This is not to imply any impropriety – merely that propinquity to power is perceived to matter, especially in a time of crisis. Having played a key role at the Fed in the initial phase of the crisis, Geithner took the helm at the Treasury at a time when the economy had not yet reached its nadir. Investors would have been naïve if they had attached no importance whatever to perceived differences in political connectedness between financial firms. Dick Fuld's downfall had happened precisely because he was a relatively isolated node in the network.

52
The Administrative State

The financial crisis revealed another peculiarity of the financial system. On paper, banks were the most highly regulated entities in the financial system. Yet the numerous agencies charged with regulating them and their activities had somehow failed to anticipate the possibility of their falling like dominoes in a liquidity crisis. One explanation for this is that the federal government had degenerated into what has been called an 'administrative' or 'managerial' state, hierarchical and bureaucratic in its mode of operation, dedicated to generating ever more complicated regulation that had precisely the opposite effect of that intended.

The birth of the administrative state can be traced back to the early 1970s when Congress began chartering new regulatory agencies such as the Environmental Protection Agency and the Consumer Product Safety Commission. The US Code of Federal Regulations (CFR) was about 23,000 pages in length in 1950. It grew by about 21,000 pages between 1951 and 1970, 62,000 between 1971 and 1990 and another 40,000 pages between 1991 and 2010.[1] Under George W. Bush, Congress expanded federal regulation of primary and secondary schooling (the No Child Left Behind Act of 2001), election finance (the McCain–Feingold Campaign Reform Act of 2002), corporate governance (the Sarbanes–Oxley Act of 2002) and energy conservation (the Energy Independence and Security Act of 2007). However, no administration has generated more voluminous legislation and regulation than President Obama's in his first term.[2] The history of his presidency can be told concisely as a series of pledges to increase employment ('the stimulus'), reduce the risk of financial crisis and provide universal health insurance, each of which produced a major expansion of the administrative state. The Wall Street Reform and Consumer Protection Act (Dodd–Frank) ran to 848 pages and created two new agencies, the Financial Stability Oversight Council and the Consumer Financial Protection Bureau.[3] The Patient Protection and Affordable Care Act (ACA, for short) totalled 961 pages (along with the Health Care and Education Reconciliation Act) and created the Independent Payment Advisory Board. Even more cumbersome was the legislation that was drafted to enact the Trans Pacific Partnership, a trade agreement between twelve Pacific-rim countries. This was over 5,554 pages long, contained more than two million words and, when printed out, stood nearly three feet high.

Moreover, both Obamacare and Dodd–Frank spawned great shoals of regulation. After the ACA was passed, government agencies produced more than a hundred final regulations spelling out how the new laws were to be implemented. Dodd–Frank specifically instructed regulators to create more than 400 new rules. According to one estimate, the act could increase financial industry regulatory restrictions by nearly a third if this process is ever completed.[4] To get some idea of the scale of the regulation epidemic, assume that each of the 10,535 pages of healthcare regulations in the Federal Register contains 1,100 words. That adds up to more than 11 million words. By way of comparison, Magna Carta was a single sheet of parchment with fewer than 4,000 words. The original draft of the US Constitution was only slightly longer (4,543 words, to be precise). And the Declaration of Independence consists of just 1,458 words.

What are the forces responsible for the rise of the administrative state? Why did Washington degenerate into a version of the hypertrophic bureaucratic state once imagined by Franz Kafka? The simple answer might be that it is all the fault of lawyers and bureaucrats, but such people have been around for a long time, as readers of Dickens well know. A rather more plausible answer might be that this is the price we pay today for the failures of the past. Perhaps what killed representative government and the rule of law in so many countries in the twentieth century was inattention to detail. Perhaps 'terrible simplifiers' like Hitler triumphed precisely because instruments like the constitution of the Weimar Republic – though far from short, at 181 articles and around 10,000 words – did not explicitly prohibit men from Austria with toothbrush moustaches, a criminal record and genocidal tendencies from becoming chancellor. However, a better explanation may be the fundamental deterioration of standards in both legislation and governance that we see in nearly every democracy, regardless of their different twentieth-century histories.* The torrent of verbiage comes about because professional politicians are more concerned with spin than substance, the media never cease to howl for 'something' to be done after every mishap, the lobbyists ensure that the small print protects the vested interests they serve, and the lawyers profit from the whole sorry mess.[5] The consequences should worry us more than they do, for they extend far beyond unreadably tedious statutes. First, there is the advantage conferred on the corporate insiders, who alone can afford the huge 'compliance' departments that are necessary to navigate the sea of circumlocution. Second, there is the risk of systemic instability, which grows with every increase in overall complexity. Anyone who thinks the global financial system has been made more stable by legislation like Dodd–Frank is an optimist. The very opposite may well be true, as new regulation may have reduced the authorities' ability to cope with the problem of contagion (e.g. a run on uninsured short-term liabilities).[6] Meanwhile, as Francis Fukuyama has argued, the very legitimacy of democratic politics is being corroded because 'interest groups . . . are able to effectively buy politicians with campaign contributions and lobbying', a process that he dubs 'repatrimonialization'.[7] Political institutions are at once sclerotic yet seemingly unreformable: the electoral college, the primary system, the arcane rules of the Senate, and so on. The courts are too much involved in both policy-making and administration. Yet no one has a coherent plan to fix any of this.[8]

Complexity is not cheap; on the contrary, it is very expensive indeed. The administrative state has found an easy solution to the problem of increasing the volume of public 'goods' without making commensurate increases to taxation, and that is to finance current

* A century ago, according to Andrew Haldane, the Bank of England issued one speech a year. In 2016 alone, it issued eighty speeches, sixty-two working papers, close to 200 consultation documents, just under 100 blogs and over 100 statistical releases – in total, over 600 publications and around 9,000 pages.

government consumption through borrowing. At the same time, while very nearly doubling the federal debt, the Obama administration used its regulatory powers to raise money in new ways: more than $100bn in 'settlements' of investigations into bank mortgage practices, for example, and $20bn from the BP Horizon oil-spill compensation programme. (It also intervened in the 'managed bankruptcies' of General Motors and Chrysler on behalf of political allies.)[9] Yet all these expedients of the administrative state impose burdens on the private sector that ultimately reduce the rate of growth and job creation.[10] Intergenerational inequity in public finance, hypertrophic growth of regulation, deterioration in the rule of law and corrosion of educational institutions – taken together, these lead to a 'great degeneration' of both economic performance and (as we shall see) social cohesion.[11] In short, the administrative state represents the last iteration of political hierarchy: a system that spews out rules, generates complexity, and undermines both prosperity and stability.

53
Web 2.0

Even as the administrative state typed and filed its way towards the ultimate crisis of hierarchical order, the networked world was passing through a dramatic phase transition. Information technology professionals referred to it as 'Web 2.0' – the title of a conference hosted by the pioneering Internet publisher Tim O'Reilly in 2004. O'Reilly's ideal was to preserve the 'open source' form of the early World Wide Web. Wikipedia, with its collectively authored encyclopaedia entries, retained this ethos. So, too, did any website that relied on user-generated content. According to O'Reilly, innovations such as RSS and the API had the effect of 'syndicating data outwards, not controlling what happens when it gets to the other end of the connection . . . [–] a reflection of . . . the end-to-end principle'.[1] All software should therefore be in a state of 'perpetual beta', not only open source but open to re-engineering by users.[2] The gold standard was Linux: a 'world-class operating system' formed 'out of part-time hacking by several thousand developers', in the words of a libertarian programmer, Eric Raymond, author of the open-source manifesto, *The Cathedral and the Bazaar*.[3] In the 'bazaar', a large, global group of volunteer coders worked collaboratively to identify and fix bugs, thus steadily improving the software.[4] Raymond formulated Linus's Law, named after Linus Torvalds, the lead developer (but never owner) of Linux, which states: 'Given a large enough beta-tester and co-developer base, almost every problem will be characterized quickly and the fix obvious to someone.' (More colloquially: 'Given enough eyeballs, all bugs are shallow.')[5] In the hacker's virtual commune, 'the only available measure of competitive success is reputation among one's peers', and there is no tragedy of the commons* because, with open-source software, 'the grass grows taller when it's grazed upon'.[6] Raymond confidently predicted that the open-source movement would 'essentially [have] won its point about software within three to five years (that is, by 2003–2005)'.[7] He was to be disappointed.

After the innovation and creative anarchy come commercialization and regulation. That, at any rate, was the pattern in previous technological revolutions.[8] In the case of the Internet, however, the commercialization has happened; the regulation hardly at all. The open-source dream died with the rise of monopolies and duopolies that successfully fended off the interference of the administrative state. Microsoft and Apple established something close to a software duopoly, the former carving out a huge share of the personal computing market. Founded in the first phase of the network revolution, in 1975 and 1976, the two responded differently to the opportunities presented by the Internet. Microsoft sought to bundle its Windows operating system with its own web browser, Internet Explorer, a strategy that very nearly led to the company's break-up.† Though his operating system was in many ways superior to Bill Gates's, Apple's Steve Jobs preferred to compete by diversifying the hardware that Apple sold, adding to the original Mac desktop computer a music player (iPod, 2001), laptop (Macbook, 2006), smartphone (iPhone, 2007), tablet (iPad, 2010) and watch (Apple Watch, 2014). Jobs's genius was to combine alluring product design with a closed system of software and digital content released exclusively through the Apple Store and iTunes Store.

The second phase of the IT revolution came twenty years after the

* The allusion is to the ecologist Garrett Hardin's 1968 essay 'The Tragedy of the Commons', which made an argument for global population control by citing the example of the village of peasants who, enjoying unrestricted access to their common land, soon render it an infertile waste through over-grazing. The idea in fact originated with the Victorian economist William Forster Lloyd.

† On 3 April 2000, Judge Thomas Penfield Jackson ruled that Microsoft had committed monopolization, attempted monopolization and tying, in violation of the Sherman Antitrust Act. On 7 June 2000 the court ordered a breakup of Microsoft. However, the DC Circuit Court of Appeals overturned Judge Jackson's rulings and the company reached a settlement with the Department of Justice that left it intact.

wave of innovation that produced MS-DOS and Mac OS. The most important new companies founded in the mid-1990s were Amazon, eBay and Google. The first was an online bookseller founded in Seattle. The second – originally called 'Auction Web' – was an online auction market in San Jose. The third, named after the number googol (1×10^{100}), was an online search tool set up in a garage in Menlo Park. Each founder was in some sense an outsider: Jeff Bezos, the son of a Texan teenage mother, adopted by his Cuban stepfather; Pierre Omidyar, born in Paris to Iranian immigrants; Sergey Brin, the Moscow-born son of Jews who had emigrated from the Soviet Union in 1979. Only Larry Page started as an insider to computer science: both his parents taught in the field. Yet all these men gravitated to the West Coast of the United States, where Stanford University and Silicon Valley had together established themselves as the global hub of IT innovation. Did they set out to become billionaires? Probably not. The success of their companies came as a surprise. (Page and Brin came close to selling Google to Excite for $750,000 in 1999.) Having weathered the dot.com stock bust of that year, however, all three companies very rapidly acquired eye-popping valuations. Google's initial public offering (IPO) on 19 August 2004 gave it a market capitalization of more than $23bn. The explanation for this dramatic increase in value was simple. In 2000 Google began selling advertisements associated with search keywords, on the basis of a combination of price bids and 'click-throughs'. By 2011 this was the source of 96 per cent of the company's revenue. The huge inflow of revenue from advertisers then enabled Google to expand in multiple directions, launching an email service (Gmail, 2004), an operating system (Android, 2007) and a web browser (Chrome, 2008), and acquiring a string of other companies, beginning with Keyhole, which became Google Earth, followed by Urchin, which became Google Analytics, and Grand Central, which became Google Voice. YouTube was added in 2006, Motorola Mobility in 2012 (though it was later sold) and DeepMind in 2014. Google's original mission statement was 'to organize the world's information and make it universally accessible and useful'. Its unofficial slogan was 'Don't be evil.' A more accurate description of its mode of operation after 1999 was 'make a fortune from advertising and invest it adventurously'.

The discrepancy between ideal and reality was even more marked in the case of the most successful social networking company to emerge from the third wave of innovation in the mid-2000s. It should have been 'sixdegrees' that won; its owners had the original patent describing an online social network service based on email invitations and a database of connected members. However, Reid Hoffman of Friendster and LinkedIn and Mark Pincus of Tribe.net bought the patent (for $700,000) to make sure no one could monopolize social networking.[9] They did not fully reckon with Mark Zuckerberg.

The Harvard undergraduate has never been short of idealistic rhetoric. The mission statement for Facebook recruits, known (in homage to Chairman Mao) as the 'Little Red Book', states: 'Facebook was not originally created to be a company. It was built to accomplish a social mission – to make the world more open and connected.'[10] In 2004, in an interview with the *Harvard Crimson*, just five days after the launch of Thefacebook, Zuckerberg explicitly said he had not created the site with the intention of making money. 'I'm not going to sell anybody's e-mail address,' he said. 'The last hundred years have been defined by the mass media,' he declared in 2007. 'In the next hundred years, information won't be just pushed out to people. It will be shared among millions of connections people have.'[11]

So why did Facebook defeat the other contenders for the social networking crown? First, Zuckerberg leveraged the Harvard brand. The first users gave their real names and real email addresses, as there is no incentive to create an alias if you are at Harvard. It was through the Harvard alumni network that Zuckerberg was introduced to Don Graham of the Washington Post Company, who offered to invest in the company and went on to serve on its board.[12] Second, Zuckerberg overruled those who mistakenly thought the site would lose its appeal if opened up to people not in college, and later pushed to make it accessible to non-English speakers though a translation tool.[13] Third, he was quick to see the potential for add-ons such as photo-tagging, alerts to users when tagged, and the much more complex concept of a News Feed based on sharing information about friends' activities.[14] Fourth, unlike MySpace, Facebook allowed users to build apps within Facebook, a decision that proved hugely popular as Facebook-based games such as Farmville proliferated.[15] This was open source with a twist: the new policy allowed users to sell their own sponsored ads.[16]

Zuckerberg's pursuit of advertising revenue very nearly backfired with the introduction of Beacon, which gave companies access to the platform.[17] It was Sheryl Sandberg's job to make the transition to an advertising revenue model a success; this, after all had been her principal role at Google between 2001 and 2008, when she became Facebook's chief operating officer. The crucial difference was that 'Whereas Google . . . helped people find the things they had already decided they wanted to buy, Facebook would help them decide what they wanted', by enabling advertisers to deliver targeted messages to users, tailored to meet the preferences they had already revealed through their activity on Facebook.[18] At first, monetization was poor when measured by 'cost per mille' (the cost for every thousand showings of an ad).[19] Once ads were seamlessly inserted into users' News Feeds on the Facebook mobile phone app, however, the company was on the path to vast profits.[20] The *deus ex machina* that made Zuckerberg a billionaire was the largely unforeseen explosion of mobile-phone usage, propelled by Apple's innovative and addictive iPhone.

Facebook did not invent social networks. As we have seen, they are as old as *Homo sapiens* as a species. What Facebook did, by creating a service that was free to the user and unconstrained by geography or language, was to create the largest ever social network. At the time of writing, Facebook has 1.17 billion active daily users, and 1.79 billion users who log in at least once a month. These figures do not include Facebook's photo-sharing and messaging app Instagram.[21] In the United States, penetration is as high as 82 per cent of adults who use the Internet between the ages of 18 and 29, 79 per cent of those aged 30 to 49, 64 per cent of the 50–64 age group and 48 per cent of those aged 65 and older. If there are six degrees of separation for humanity as a whole, for Facebook users the average figure is now 3.57.[22] Not surprisingly, the Facebook network exhibits geographically based clustering, as most people's friendship circle has a significant local component.[23] Yet in a number of striking ways Facebook conquers distance. Mere proximity to other users is not the best predictor of one's likelihood to join Facebook; 'conversion' is a function of one's position in multiple existing social networks.[24] Users are characterized by homophily: birds of a feather, in terms of shared interests as well as personality types, flock together as always, and there may be a feedback loop that causes similar users to grow more interconnected through Facebook usage.[25] Immigrant communities to the United States can also be identified as distinct components of the network;[26] interestingly, there is significant variation in Facebook usage between ethnic groups.[27] In Europe, despite mounting concern about the resurgence of nationalism, Facebook has measurably increased integration: each summer, as Europeans travel to other European countries on holiday, the number of cross-country Facebook friendships goes up. The percentage of new friendships within Europe that are international has risen from below 2 per cent in January 2009 to above 4 per cent in August 2016.[28] Also striking is the capacity of the Facebook network to spread ideas, 'memes' and even emotions contagiously and across network clusters through weak ties.[29]

Like anything that is very popular, Facebook has its detractors. 'Facebook sells the attention of users to advertisers all over the world,' the journalist Jonathan Tepper wrote, shortly before deleting his account, 'and Facebook knows almost everything about their lives, their families and their friends . . . It is also a platform built on exhibitionism and voyeurism, where users edit themselves to exhibit a more flattering side and they quietly spy on their friends.' Far from increasing friendship, Tepper argued, it actually cheapens and displaces genuine friendship.[30] Certainly, the economics of Facebook are a far cry from its utopian ideology. It has been likened to a sharecropping economy, 'which provides the many with the tools for production, but concentrates the rewards into the hands of the few'.[31] Put more crudely, on Facebook 'the user is the product'.

Facebook promised to create an interconnected world of netizens. But its structure was profoundly inegalitarian. Facebook has 15,724 employees and close to 2 billion users, but only the tiniest fractions of these groups actually own Facebook stock. Zuckerberg himself owns just over 28 per cent of the company's B-shares. His co-founders Dustin Moskovitz, Eduardo Saverin and Chris Hughes together own just under 13 per cent. Early investors Sean Parker and Peter Thiel own 6.5 per cent in total. And two other early investors – Accel Partners,

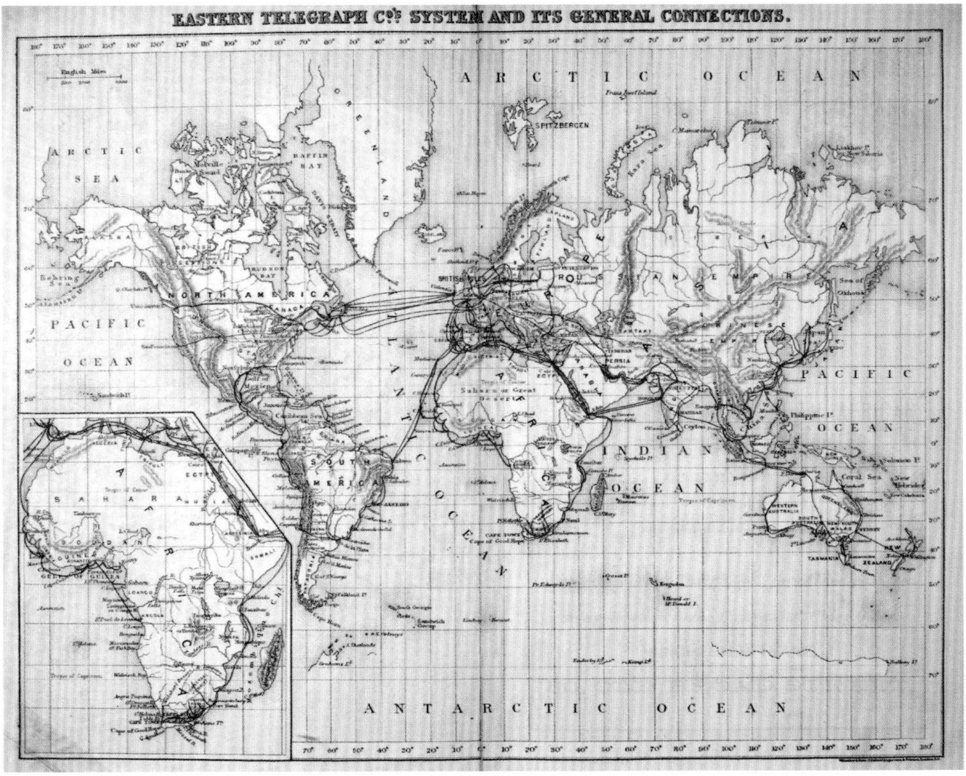

EASTERN TELEGRAPH Co's SYSTEM AND ITS GENERAL CONNECTIONS.

15. The Eastern Telegraph Co.'s network, 1894.

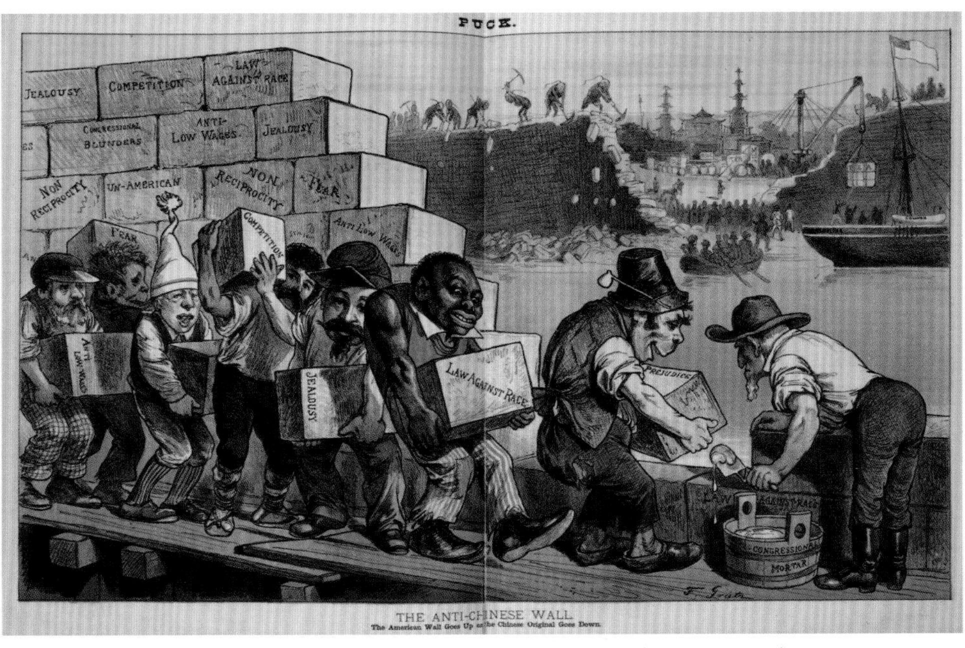

16. *The Anti-Chinese Wall* by Friedrich Graetz, from *Puck* (1882). Uncle Sam using 'Congressional Mortar' and bricks carried by Irish, African-American and other workers to construct a wall against Chinese immigrants. The bricks are labelled 'Prejudice', 'Law against Race', 'Jealousy', etc.

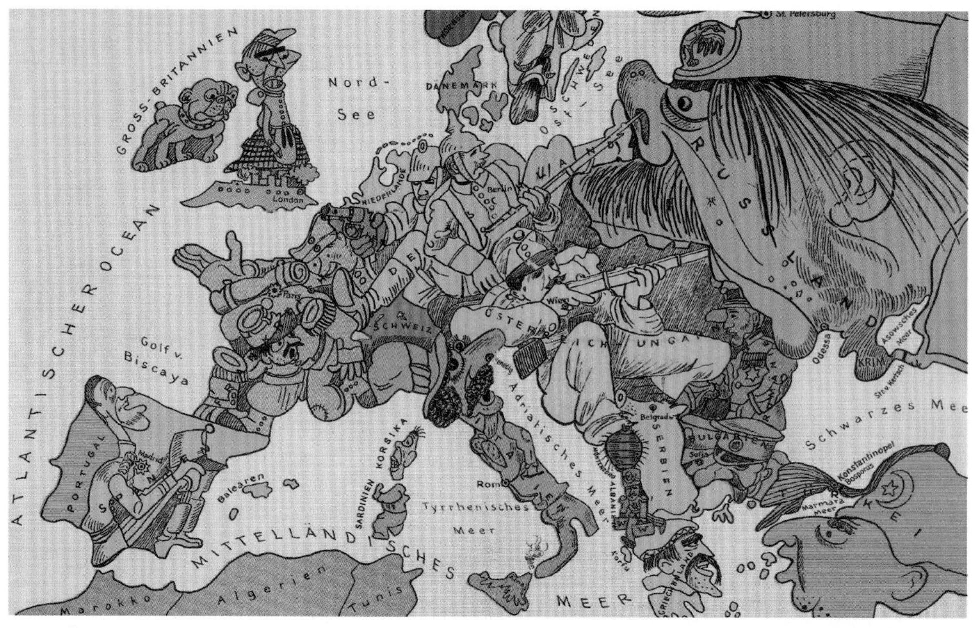

17. (*above*) Europe in 1914: a German satirical map.

18. (*right*) First edition of John Buchan's *Greenmantle*.

19. Stalin as helmsman: the supreme hierarch of the totalitarian age.

20. Isaiah Berlin and Anna Akhmatova, Leningrad, November 1945, by Leopold Plotek.

21. *The Second World War, or How to get young men to do what you tell them.*

22. (*below*) The cool and the uncool: Steve Jobs and Bill Gates in 1991.

23. Leaders of the electronic herd: Stan Druckenmiller and George Soros, 1992.

24. (*below*) The 9/11 plotters' network, as visualized by Vladis Krebs in 2002.

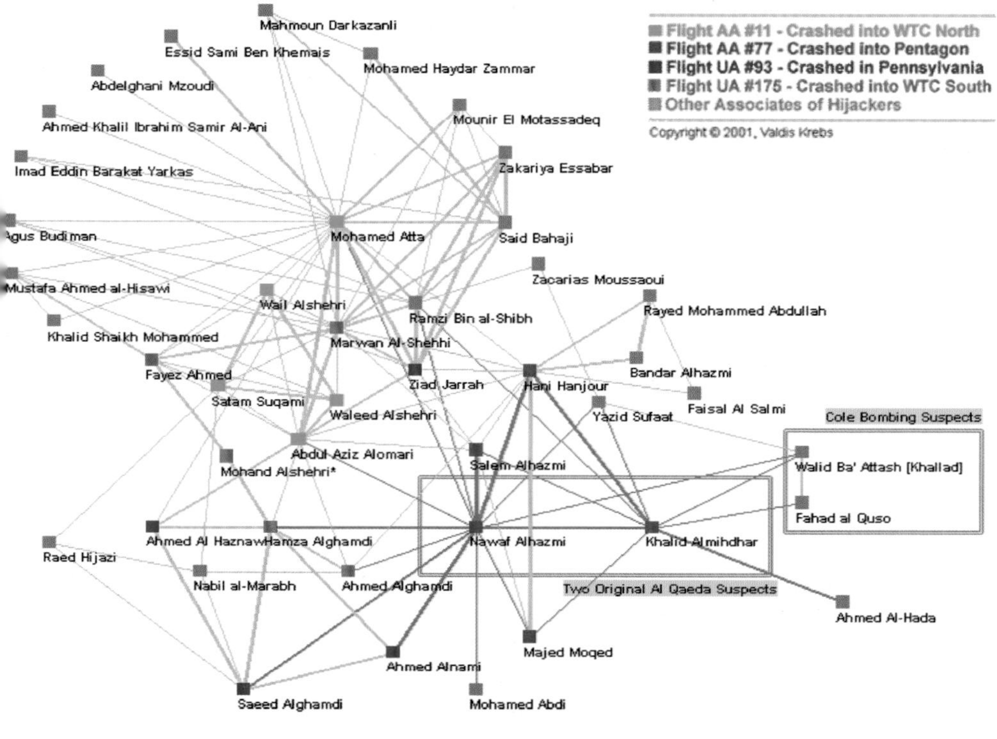

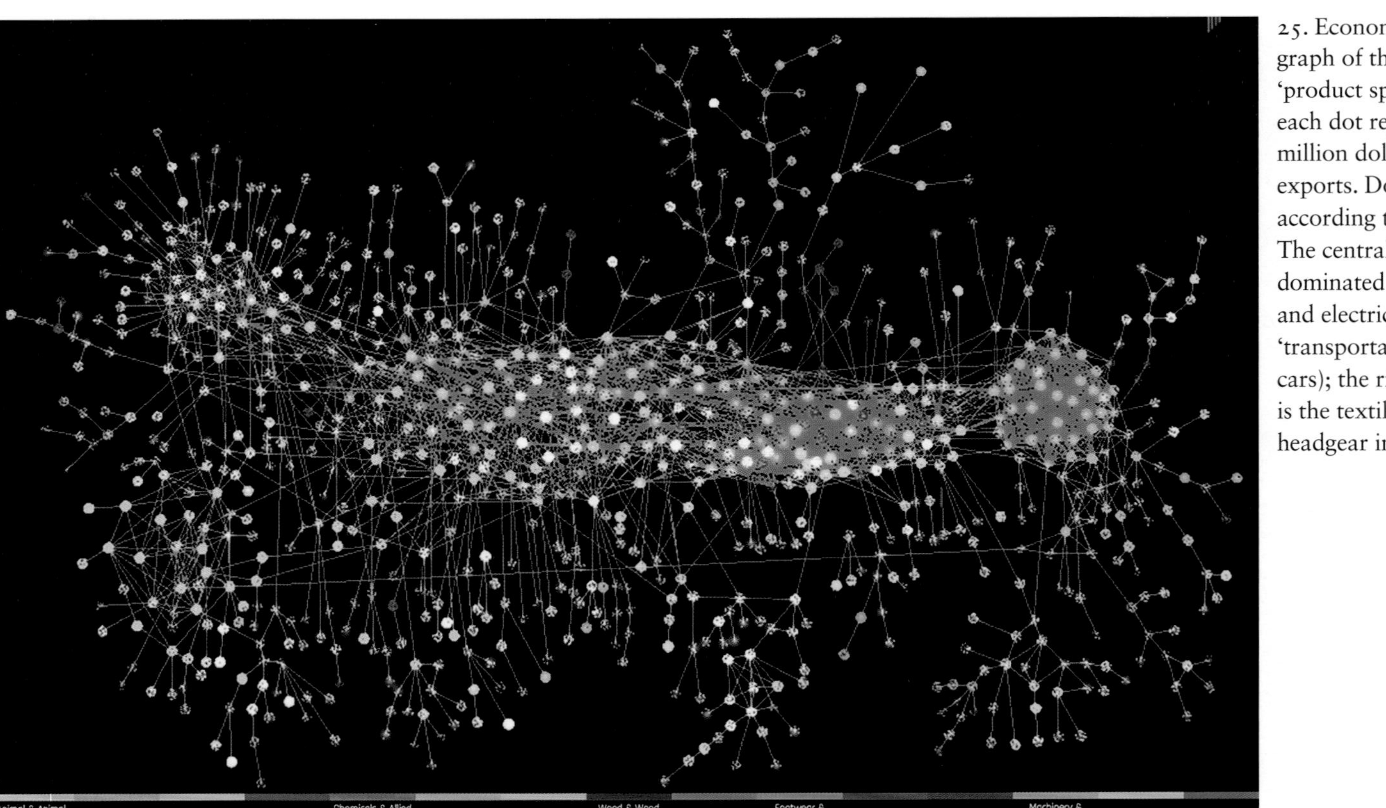

25. Economic complexity: graph of the global export 'product space', in which each dot represents 100 million dollars' worth of exports. Dots are coloured according to product type. The central component is dominated by 'machinery and electrical' and 'transportation' (including cars); the right-hand cluster is the textile, footwear and headgear industry.

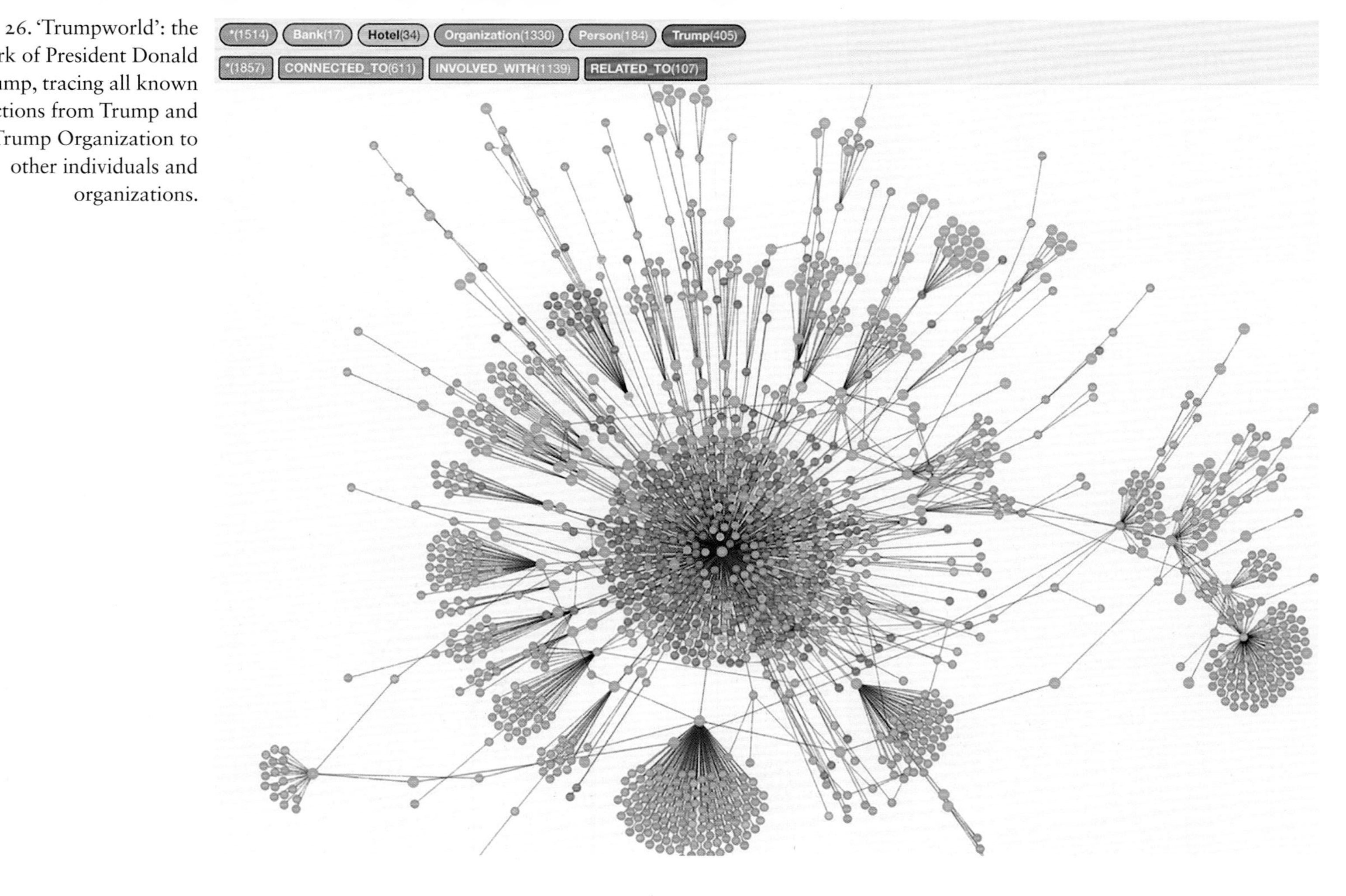

26. 'Trumpworld': the network of President Donald J. Trump, tracing all known connections from Trump and the Trump Organization to other individuals and organizations.

27. Facebook headquarters (*above*) and Trump Tower (*left*).

the Silicon Valley venture fund, and the Russian Internet company Digital Sky Technologies – own, respectively, 10 and 5.4 per cent. Only five other entities – three Silicon Valley venture firms, Microsoft and Goldman Sachs – own more than 1 per cent.[32] In the words of Antonio García Martínez, 'Anyone who claims the valley is meritocratic is someone who has profited vastly from it via nonmeritocratic means like happenstance, membership in a privileged cohort or some concealed act of absolute skulduggery.'[33] The global social network, in other words, is itself owned by an exclusive network of Silicon Valley insiders.

The social consequences of the post-open-source trend towards duopolies (Microsoft and Apple) and near monopolies (Facebook, Amazon and Google) were as predictable as they appear paradoxical. The world is connected as never before, as the cheerleaders of these companies never tire of saying. Yet the world is (in some respects) unequal as it has not been for a century. Six of the eight richest men in the world are Bill Gates (with personal wealth estimated at $76bn), Carlos Slim ($50bn), Jeff Bezos ($45bn), Mark Zuckerberg ($45bn), Larry Ellison ($44bn) and Michael Bloomberg ($40bn). Their fortunes have been built on, respectively, software, telecoms, online retail, social networking, enterprise software and business data.[34] The reason they have become so wealthy is not that they are the world's entrepreneurial 'superstars', but that each has established something close to a monopoly. As in the case of Facebook, more than a billion people use Microsoft Windows, YouTube and Android – not forgetting the messaging application WhatsApp, acquired by Facebook in 2014. These near-monopolies seem capable of generating huge rents to the principal equity-holders for the foreseeable future.[35] To give a single example: Google and Facebook are predicted to increase their combined share of all digital advertising in 2017 to 60 per cent. Google has 78 per cent of US search advertising. Facebook has nearly two fifths of online display advertising.[36] This dominance translates into giant revenues. Facebook is expected to make $16bn from display advertising in 2017. The business is valued today at around $500bn, including a vast cash pile, which equips Zuckerberg to acquire any potential competitor at an early stage (such as Instagram, which today has 600 million users, and

WhatsApp, which has more than a billion).[37] Moreover, dominance of advertising has another benefit. In 25,000 random Google searches, advertisements for Google products appeared in the most prominent slot more than 90 per cent of the time.[38]

It is an amazing state of affairs when one considers the functions these companies perform. Google is essentially a vast global library. It is where we go to look things up. Amazon is a vast global bazaar, where more and more of us go to shop. And Facebook is a vast global club. The various networking functions these companies perform are not new; it is just that technology has made the networks both enormous and very fast. The more interesting difference, however, is that in the past libraries and social clubs did not make money from advertising: they were non-profits, funded out of donations or subscriptions or taxes. The truly revolutionary fact is that our global library and our global club are both festooned with billboards, and the more we tell them about ourselves, the more effective the advertising becomes, sending us off to Bezos's bazaar with increasing frequency. Not for nothing is the investor's acronym for Facebook, Amazon, Netflix (the online movie company) and Google 'FANG'. Thanks to the 'fit-get-richer' effect that causes the global information technology to be scale-free – that is, dominated by a few super-connected hubs – the returns to these businesses do not diminish.[39]

It is not only in its unabashed pursuit of market dominance that Facebook's practice seems at odds with its propaganda. Zuckerberg's evolution from dorm-room hacker to Chairman Zuck was remarkably swift. 'In a lot of ways,' he said in 2008, 'Facebook is more like a government than a traditional company. We have this large community of people, and more than other technology companies we're really setting policies.'[40] The Little Red Book owed more than just its title to Mao; its tone was self-consciously that of a revolutionary vanguard: 'The quick shall inherit the earth.' 'Greatness and comfort rarely coexist.' And: 'Changing how people communicate will always change the world.'[41] After 2008, posters on the office walls began to echo totalitarian propaganda 'PROCEED AND BE BOLD! GET IN OVER YOUR HEAD! MAKE AN IMPACT!'[42] It has been said that Zuckerberg 'wants to rule not only Facebook, but in some sense the evolving communications infrastructure of the planet'.[43]

There has even been speculation that he might consider running for president of the United States.[44] Yet the mind-set of Facebook's founder seems at once more global and less democratic than might be expected from the holder of that office. As one ex-employee remarked, recalling how many employees chose to wear blue Facebook T-shirts to work, 'Brownshirts became Blueshirts, and we were all part of the new social media *Sturmabteilung*.'[45] That is surely the wrong analogy, as Zuckerberg seems sincere about his vision of an interconnected 'global community'. In February 2017 he published an essay arguing that his company's role should be to promote 'meaningful' local communities, to enhance 'safety' (by filtering out hate-inspiring content), to promote diversity of ideas, and to foster civic engagement – even at the global level. 'As the largest global community,' he wrote, 'Facebook can explore examples of how community governance might work at scale.'[46]

The real question is how far this vision of global community is a realistic one – and how far the unintended consequences of Facebook and its ilk lead in quite the opposite direction.[47]

54
Coming Apart

The world by 2010 was on the brink of two revolutions, each driven to a significant extent by the effects of information technology. The first was a revolution of rising expectations in the developing world. The second was a revolution of falling expectations in the developed world. The former was the result of falling inequality in the world as a whole. The latter was the result of increasing inequality within a number of important countries, notably the United States. It would be wrong to ascribe all the change to technology, just it would be wrong to ascribe it all to globalization, as the two processes cannot meaningfully be separated. A more accurate analysis would be that the rapid growth of a global super-network was the main driver of the revolution, as it was this phenomenon – a synthesis of technological change and global integration – that simultaneously made the world as a whole more 'flat' and yet caused American society (in Charles Murray's phrase) to 'come apart'.

According to a widely cited study by the anti-poverty charity Oxfam, the richest 1 per cent of people now have more wealth than the rest of the world combined. In 2015, according to Oxfam, just sixty-two individuals had the same wealth as 3.6 billion people – the 'bottom half' of humanity. And, since the turn of the century, that bottom half has received just 1 per cent of the total increase in global wealth, while 50 per cent of that increase has gone to the top 1 per cent.[1] Crédit Suisse arrives at similar figures: the bank estimates that the share of global wealth in the hands of the top 1 per cent reached 50 per cent in 2015. Around 35 million millionaires now own 45 per cent of all the world's wealth; 123,800 people have more than $50m apiece, 44,900 more than $100m, and 4,500 more than $500m.[2] Just under half of all millionaires live in the United States, where the cumulative gain in real income for the top 0.01 per cent since 1980 has been 542 per cent (based on calculations by the economists Emmanuel Saez and Thomas Piketty). For every American in the 90th percentile and below, real income has fallen slightly in the same period.[3] Median US household income in 1999 was $57,909 (in 2015 dollars). In 2015 it was $56,516.[4] Here is the ultimate hierarchy in the world today: a hierarchy of wealth and income shaped like a building with a very broad base and an enormously tall and thin steeple.

There are three important caveats, however. First, based on data from the US Survey of Consumer Finance, the increases in the shares of the top 1 per cent and the top 0.1 per cent in both wealth and income have not been quite as large as Piketty and Saez have claimed.[5] Second, the number of individuals in the Forbes 400 list who made it onto that list by dint of inherited wealth has declined steadily in our time: from 159 in 1985 to just eighteen in 2009.[6] Turnover at the very top has never been higher. Third, the growth of the global middle class – what Marxists preferred to call the bourgeoisie – is as profound a social change as the accumulation of wealth by the 1 per cent. Between 2000 and 2015, the Chinese middle class grew by 38 million; using the same definition, the American middle class also grew, by 13 million. Worldwide, the middle class has grown in size by 178 million, a 31 per cent increase since 2000.[7] According to one estimate, the Gini coefficient of global inequality declined from 69 in 2003 to 65 in 2013, and will decline further to 61 in 2035.[8] In short, the evidence is compelling that global income distribution has become significantly less unequal since 1970, and that this trend is likely to continue.[9] The biggest driver has been the *embourgeoisement* of China, but that is only around a fifth of the global story.[10]

The conventional interpretation is that globalization has reduced global inequality, in the sense that the very rapid growth of China and other emerging economies would not have been possible without the increased trade flows and capital flows that occurred after the 1970s. The increase in international migration in the same timeframe probably also helped to reduce inequality, by moving people from less productive to more productive economies. However, it is inconceivable that there would have been so much trade, cross-border investment and migration without the technological innovations discussed above, just as the technological leaps forward would have been fewer and further apart without cheap Asian-made components and global supply chains. It was the vastly greater increase in international information flows that made the more efficient global reallocation of capital and labour possible. The crucial point is that, for the majority of people in the world, there has been a significant improvement in relative as well as absolute terms in the past thirty or forty years. If revolutions in the developing world are to be explained, then the explanation should probably include the effect of rising expectations.

Yet globalization had quite different implications for income and wealth distribution *within* many countries. It used to be thought that this point was illustrated by the so-called 'elephant chart' devised by Branko Milanovic and Christoph Lakner, which depicted the working class and middle class in developed economies as the losers of globalization.* In fact, the elephant in the room leaves the room altogether if one adjusts for changes in country size and omits Japan, the former Soviet Union and China from the data.[11] Nevertheless, something did go wrong for the American working class and middle class, and perhaps also the middle class in some European countries.[12] Asian competition certainly did destroy a significant number of US manufacturing jobs.[13] Those people in the United States who did badly during and after the financial crisis are highly susceptible to pessimism about their futures, despite the largely unnoticed success of welfare programmes in mitigating the effects of the 'great recession' on lower income earners. Nearly two fifths of Americans surveyed by the McKinsey Global Institute in 2016 agreed strongly with one of the following two statements: 'My financial position is worse off than it was five years ago' and/or 'My financial position is worse than my parents' when they were my age.' Such people were

* The chart plotted the growth in average per capita household income for each percentile of the global income distribution, and purported to show that groups between the 10th and 70th percentile, along with those in the last percentile, had done significantly better between 1998 and 2008 than those between the 70th and 100th percentile. The line was supposed to resemble an elephant, with a curved back, a low neck and an erect trunk.

more likely to be pessimistic about their own and their children's financial futures. And those who were pessimistic were much more likely to blame immigration, foreign goods and 'cheap foreign labour' for, respectively, 'ruining the culture and cohesiveness of our society', 'leading to domestic job losses' and 'creating unfair competition to domestic businesses'.[14]

Such pessimism is rooted in more than just stagnating real incomes. Social mobility may or may not have declined in the United States.[15] But something is clearly amiss. All over the developed world, mortality rates are declining and lifespans are lengthening, but not in (non-Hispanic) white America, and especially not amongst those middle-aged white Americans whose education did not extend beyond secondary school. For this group, aged between forty-five and fifty-four, the mortality rate from poisonings (mostly drug overdoses) rose more than fourfold between 1999 and 2013, from 14 to 58 per 100,000, while mortality from chronic liver diseases and cirrhosis rose by 50 per cent, and the decline in mortality from heart disease stopped. If the white mortality rate had continued to fall at its pre-1999 rate of decline of 1.8 per cent per year, nearly half a million deaths would have been avoided in the period 1999–2013. One in three non-Hispanic whites aged between forty-five and fifty-four reports chronic joint pain, one in five reports neck pain and one in seven reports sciatica.[16] These trends, which continued through 2015, cannot be explained in simple economic terms: income profiles for similarly situated non-white Americans are no better, but they have not suffered these increases in ill-health and mortality. The best explanation available is that '*cumulative disadvantage* over life, in the labor market, in marriage and child outcomes, and in health, is triggered by progressively worsening labor market opportunities'.[17] Presumably, it is the most miserable middle-aged white Americans who drug or drink themselves into early graves. The non-suicidal merely exit the workforce, opting instead for Social Security Disability benefits, which helps explain why prime-age male labour force participation has declined more steeply in the United States than elsewhere.[18] Seen in this light, the political upheaval that was to come in the United States in 2016 was a revolution of *falling* expectations.

Perhaps the right way to understand the relationship between networks and inequality is to see that, in the words of the authors of a ground-breaking paper on the subject, 'inequality in social networks is reinforced by markets in case of complements, but lowered in the case of substitutes'.[19] When economic liberalization came to working-class networks in Bombay, the network and the market were substitutes, in the sense that the market crowded out the network by offering new options to poorly connected individuals. The result was reduced inequality. But when fishermen in Kerala acquired mobile phones, the networks and the market complemented each other, as better-connected fishermen were more able to take advantage of market opportunities. In that case, the result was greater inequality.[20] This framework applies globally, too. Globalization brought the market to the workers and peasants of China, who had hitherto been disconnected from the world and trapped in the rigid hierarchy established by Mao. This reduced inequality. But in the United States networks and markets were complementary, as the best-connected Americans collected most of the profits of globalization – a point acknowledged in a 2017 World Bank report.[21] There may be reasons to doubt the evidence from the US General Social Survey of a dramatic shrinkage in traditional social networks, which some have attributed to the rise of electronic networks and the mobile devices that encourage their use.[22] In fact, there is no convincing evidence that increased Internet use leads to less local social engagement; the opposite may even be true.[23] Nevertheless, it would be hard to deny that a distinctive feature of the past two or three decades has been an increase in social and political polarization. Salient features of this process have been a marked contraction of Americans' core discussion networks, which contain fewer non-family members than in the past,[24] and a withering of traditional networking institutions, such as those centred on churches and local voluntary associations.[25]

55
Tweeting the Revolution

As the case of the Kerala fisherman shows, the critical variable that made the social changes of the early twenty-first century so explosive was the exponential growth of mobile telephony. Innovations in mobile phones were a godsend to traditional telecommunications companies such as AT&T and Verizon (formerly Bell Atlantic and NYNEX) and their equivalents around the world.[1] Although there was competition between phone manufacturers (thanks in large measure to Google's creation of Android as a rival to Apple's iOS), there was only limited competition between network providers, so that subscriptions remained relatively high. Public demand kept them high. As figure 40 shows, societies as economically different as the United States, China and Egypt already had very high rates of mobile-phone ownership in 2010, and although Egypt lagged behind in terms of smartphone adoption, the use of phones for social networking and sharing political news was more advanced there.[2] With mobile phones, and even more with smartphones, social networks could be online all the time.

If Facebook initially satisfied the human need to gossip, it was Twitter – founded in March 2006 – that satisfied the more specific need to exchange news, often (though not always) political. By 2012, more than 100 million users were posting 340 million 'tweets' a day. But would the revolution be tweeted? Reflecting on the failure of the Iranian 'green' revolution of 2009, Malcolm Gladwell thought not. In his view, social media were no substitute for old-fashioned networks of activists of the sort that had overthrown communism in eastern Europe.[3] At Google, Eric Schmidt and Jared Cohen begged to differ. In a prescient article published in November 2010, they argued that

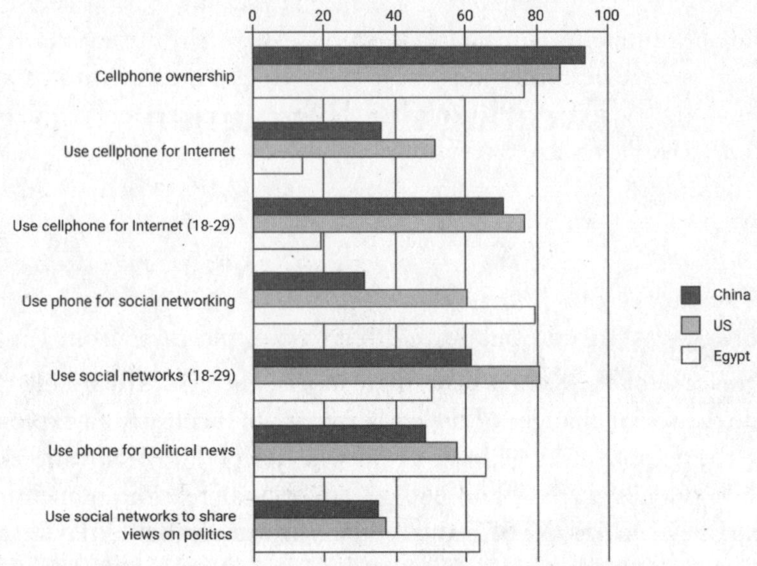

40. Use of mobile phones and social networks in China, the United States and Egypt, 2010.

governments would 'be caught off-guard when large numbers of their citizens, armed with virtually nothing but cell phones, take part in mini-rebellions that challenge their authority'.[4] The 'real action' in what they called 'the interconnected estate' could be found in 'cramped offices in Cairo' as well as 'on the streets of Tehran. From these locations and others, activists and technology geeks are rallying political "flash mobs" that shake repressive governments, building new tools to skirt firewalls and censors, reporting and tweeting the new online journalism, and writing a bill of human rights for the Internet age.'[5] Google beat Gladwell – perhaps not surprisingly, as evidence in support of the Schmidt–Cohen thesis had been accumulating for years, with mobile phones and social media playing important roles in political crises in countries as diverse as Moldova, the Philippines, Spain and even the Chinese province of Xinjiang.[6]

The financial crisis and the recessions that it caused eroded the legitimacy of governments all over the world. However, it was not in the United States or even in Europe that the true vulnerability of the established hierarchical order to these new forces was first exposed.

The revolutionary events that swept the Middle East and North Africa beginning in Tunisia in December 2010 – the misnamed 'Arab Spring' – were certainly facilitated by various kinds of information technology, even if it was probably the television channel Al Jazeera rather than Facebook or Twitter that transmitted the news of the revolutions to the majority of Arabs. As had happened in Europe after 1917, revolution spread like an epidemic, exploiting existing networks. 'This is a virus and is not part of our heritage or the culture of the Yemeni people,' the President of Yemen told reporters before he was driven from power. 'It's a virus that came from Tunisia to Egypt. And to some regions, the scent of the fever is like influenza. As soon as you sit with someone who is infected, you'll be infected.'[7] Monitoring Twitter hashtags became a way of anticipating demonstrations during the revolutionary events that swept Hosni Mubarak from power in Egypt.[8] In a similar way, the revolutionaries in Kiev who in 2014 overthrew the Ukrainian president, Viktor Yanukovych, used social networks to organize their protests in the Maidan and to disseminate their critique of Yanukovych and his cronies. From Taksim Gezi Park in Istanbul to the streets of São Paulo, protests swept the world. No matter what the object of the protesters' ire, their methods followed the Schmidt–Cohen playbook.[9] The Spanish philosopher Manuel Castells hastened to celebrate the revolutionary power of the 'network society', which created popular movements so large that it was simply impossible to 'round up the usual suspects'.[10] The inference drawn by some was that, under such pressures, more and more corrupt authoritarian states would be forced to become transparent and responsive 'smart governments', harnessing technology to make themselves more efficient and accountable. Eventually, every state would end up like Estonia, the pioneer of e-democracy.[11]

Yet it was naïve to assume that we were witnessing the dawn of a new era of free and equal netizens, all empowered by technology to speak truth to power. The Internet had its origins in the military-industrial complex, as we have seen. It was always highly probable that national security would take precedence over citizens' empowerment when it came to exploiting the potential of the social network to serve the government. The 9/11 attacks and the US government's travails in Iraq created a clear incentive for both the Bush administration and its successor. Stan McChrystal had learned in Iraq that in counter-insurgency it took a network to defeat a network.[12] The same applied to counter-terrorism. Al-Qaeda was understood by intelligence analysts to be a 'network of networks', with around seven regional or national franchises.[13] This network was 'adaptive, complex, and resilient' – and intent on inflicting further destruction and terror on the American 'homeland'.[14] American politicians had strong incentives to take revenge on the organization by decapitating and dismantling it, not only to prevent future attacks, but also as a show of strength. Beginning in 2007, the National Security Agency sought to apply the McChrystal principle on a global scale.

The hierarchical state's attempt to co-opt the private-sector owners of the networks hosted by the Internet was predictable. So, too, was

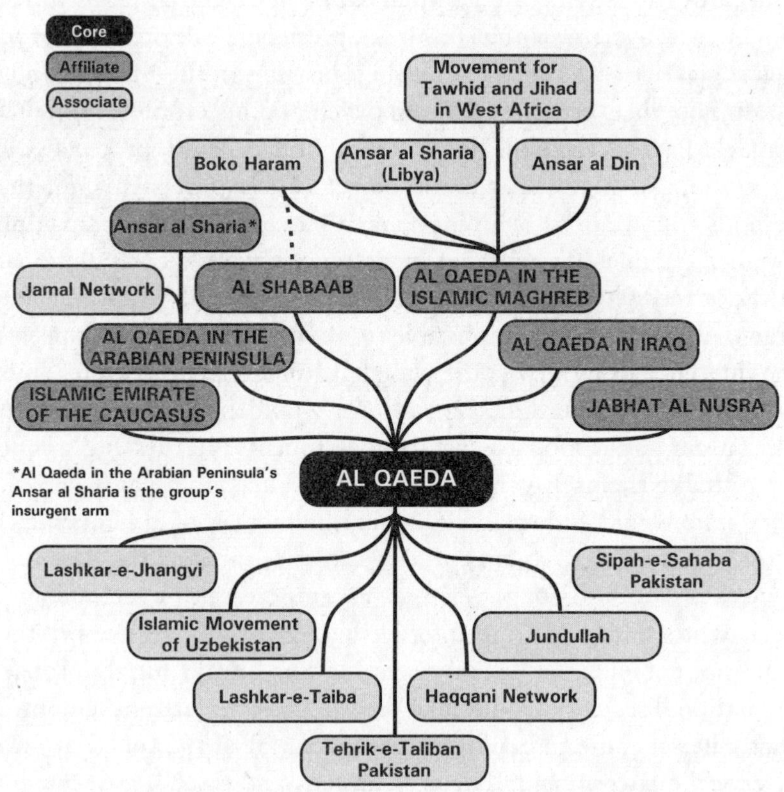

41. The Al-Qaeda network through American eyes, *c.* 2012.

the attempt's exposure. Beginning in 2007, the Special Source Operations (SSO) division of the NSA began requesting online communications from at least nine major US companies as part of a big-data surveillance programme codenamed 'PRISM'. The work of interception was in fact done by the FBI's Data Intercept Technology Unit, taking advantage of the fact that a large proportion of the Internet's physical infrastructure is located in the United States. Under the Protect America Act and section 702 of the Foreign Intelligence Surveillance Court Amendments Act of 2008, this was legal and the companies had little option but to comply. Formally, the surveillance was supposed to be of foreign nationals who might constitute a threat to US security, but any American citizen in communication with such a person was liable to be caught in the NSA's dragnet, provided at least one of the parties in an email exchange, Skype call, file transfer or Facebook exchange was on foreign soil. Participants in the PRISM programme included Facebook, YouTube, AOL, Skype and Apple, but the bulk of the information was gathered from Yahoo, Google and Microsoft. In 2012, the total number of user-data requests Facebook received from all government agencies was between 9,000 and 10,000 and they concerned roughly twice that number of user accounts. A parallel programme, MUSCULAR, directly tapped the unencrypted data inside the Google and Yahoo private 'clouds'. Also complicit in NSA surveillance were the telephone companies AT&T and Verizon.[15]

In the eyes of the 'national security state' (in practice a rather introverted network of bureaucrats),[16] PRISM was a logical response to a networked threat, not different in kind from wiretapping in the 1960s and 1970s or the CIA's routine espionage against both hostile and friendly governments. However, it was foolish to imagine that such a massive government intrusion would go undetected in the age of networks and could not, in turn, be retaliated against using the same tools. Already in December 2006 a website called WikiLeaks had begun publishing classified documents online, mostly relating to the conduct (or, as its founder Julian Assange saw it, misconduct) of the wars in Afghanistan and Iraq. As the principal target of the early leaks was the Bush administration, liberal newspapers such as the *Guardian* did not hesitate to promote WikiLeaks as a legitimate source. Among the 'whistle-blowers' who supplied WikiLeaks with documents was the US Army's Private Bradley (later Chelsea) Manning. In June 2013 an even bigger breach occurred when an NSA contractor, Edward Snowden, began releasing a huge hoard of documents, including details of PRISM, to the *Guardian* and *Washington Post*. Attempts by the UK Government Communications Headquarters (GCHQ) to destroy hard drives at the *Guardian*'s offices were futile and only added to the sensation. It appeared that Daniel Ellsberg's feat in leaking the Pentagon Papers had been eclipsed. Liberals gloated at the exposure of the NSA and dismissed claims that PRISM-based intelligence had prevented terrorist attacks. Yet there was intense embarrassment that such popular companies as Yahoo, Google and Microsoft – not to mention Facebook – were in cahoots with the dreaded 'national security state', and that the entire operation had continued unabated despite the election of the liberals' darling, Barack Obama, as president. Under Obama, the NSA collected not only the metadata of phone calls by 120 million Verizon subscribers, but also – under PRISM – the content of email, voice, text and video chats of an unknown number of Americans. Between April 2011 and March 2012, according to an internal NSA audit leaked by Snowden, there were 2,776 breaches of the rules supposed to govern surveillance of citizens.[17] It was all very well for Mark Zuckerberg to complain that he had been 'so confused and frustrated by the repeated reports of the behavior of the U.S. government' and to declare self-righteously: 'When our engineers work tirelessly to improve security, we imagine we're protecting you against criminals, not our own government.'[18] But he could hardly have known nothing about what was going on.

It did not help the Obama administration that Snowden's revelations coincided with a humiliating exposure of its failure to use technology effectively in a programme designed to benefit American citizens. As the 2008 election had made clear, politicians and voters remained the captives of a post-war vocabulary in which the former pledged not only to provide additional public goods but also to 'create jobs' without significantly increasing the cost of government in terms of taxation. President Obama's popularity declined fastest when the inability of the federal government to fulfil this pledge

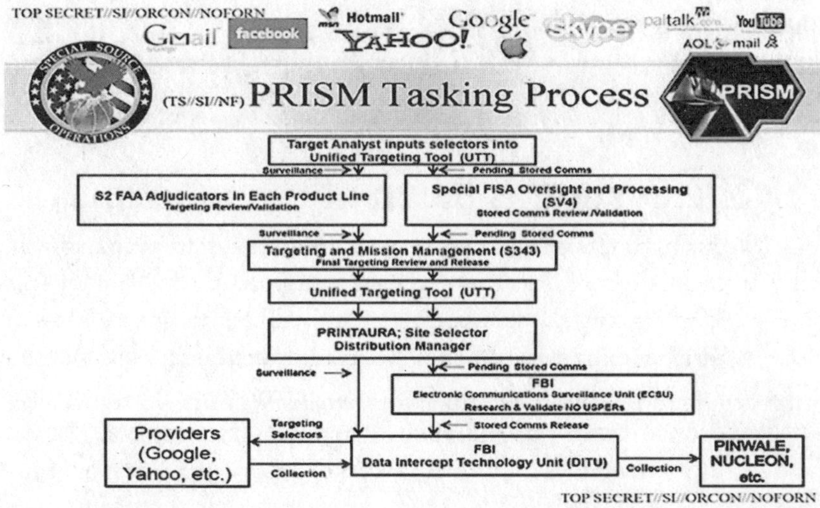

42. Classified slide published by WikiLeaks describing the National Security Agency's PRISM surveillance programme. Note the hierarchical structure of the diagram.

efficiently was most clearly exposed. The shortcomings of the website www.HealthCare.gov in many ways epitomized the fundamental problem: in the age of FANG, consumers expect basic functionality from websites. It was said to have cost between two and four times as much money to create the broken website than to build the original iPhone. The *Daily Show*'s host, Jon Stewart, spoke for hundreds of thousands of frustrated users when he taunted the secretary for health and human services, Kathleen Sebelius: 'I'm going to try and download every movie ever made, and you're going to try to sign up for Obamacare, and we'll see which happens first.'[19]

These calamities presented the technology companies with a choice. Should they distance themselves from the Washington hierarchy? This was the approach taken by Apple's CEO, Tim Cook, when he refused to comply with an FBI request and a court order to unlock the iPhone belonging to the terrorists Syed Rizwan Farook and Tashfeen Malik, who had murdered fourteen people in San Bernardino in December 2015. The alternative approach was taken by Google, which simultaneously affirmed its commitment 'to promote

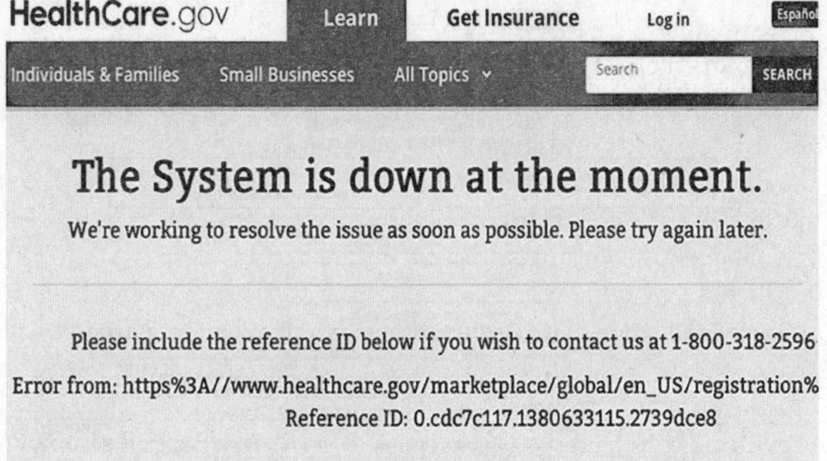

43. Big government has a small problem: the crash of HealthCare.gov in 2013.

free expression online and protect privacy',[20] while at the same time getting closer to the executive branch than any other technology company. Google employees and employees of associated entities visited the White House 427 times during the Obama presidency. Senior Google executives met the president at least twenty-one times. In 2016 alone, the company spent $15.4m on lobbying.[21]

There was a further problem with the NSA's strategy. Quite possibly, its surveillance programme did help prevent further Al-Qaeda attacks. The evidence furnished by Snowden is insufficient to conclude that PRISM was useless. Yet the damage done to the United States' reputation – especially in the eyes of its allies – surely outweighed whatever benefits there were. It was in the wake of the Snowden leaks that the United States yielded to foreign pressure to end the Department of Commerce's oversight of ICANN, which is now under the supervision of a 'global multi-stakeholder community'.[22] In any case, networks can adapt more quickly than hierarchies. As some analysts foresaw, the jihadists adapted to a top-down counter-terrorism strategy by mutating from the relatively closed network of Al-Qaeda into something better described as a 'swarm'.[23] What no one foresaw in the first flush of the 'global war on terror' was that the most ardent opponents of the Western vision of modernity might learn how to use the technologies of Silicon Valley to advance their cause.

The execution of Osama bin Laden in May 2011 was celebrated by the Obama administration as a major breakthrough. In reality, it merely confirmed Al-Qaeda's obsolescence. By this time, the organization's leadership had lost the initiative to its affiliate in Iraq, which had switched from direct attacks on US targets to targeting Shi'ite Iraqis, and made a virtue of its 'savagery' (*tawahoush*).[24] The US military had, to be sure, inflicted massive damage on Zarqawi's network during the 'Surge'. However, before that work could be completed, the Obama administration terminated the US military presence in Iraq. This was the first of a series of disastrous blunders. The administration propped up the Shi'ite-dominated government of the prime minister, Nouri al-Maliki, even as it fanned the flames of Sunni resentment. The president unhesitatingly fired McChrystal over indiscreet comments by a subordinate that ended up in *Rolling Stone* magazine. When asked about a new grouping called Islamic State of Iraq and al-Sham (ISIS), Obama dismissed it as a 'jayvee' (junior varsity) version of Al-Qaeda. Finally, in refusing to intervene effectively as Syria descended into civil war, Obama created a further vacuum into which ISIS could expand.[25]

ISIS was fundamentally different from Al-Qaeda in four respects. Its ideology was based on the claim of its leader, Abu Bakr al-Baghdadi, to have re-established the Caliphate on 29 June 2014. The language of al-Baghdadi's online proclamation in some ways echoed the call to jihad issued by the Ottoman regime in the early phase of the First World War a hundred years before. 'It is not permissible,' it declared, 'for anyone who believes in Allah to sleep without considering as his leader whoever conquers them by the sword until he becomes khalīfah and is called Amīrul-Mu'minīn [the leader of the believers].' This was a call to arms addressed to all Muslims:

> So rush O Muslims and gather around your khalīfah, so that you may return as you once were for ages, kings of the earth and knights of war. Come so that you may be honoured and esteemed, living as masters with dignity. Know that we fight over a religion that Allah

> promised to support. We fight for an ummah to which Allah has given honour, esteem, and leadership, promising it . . . empowerment and strength on the earth. Come O Muslims to your honour, to your victory. By Allah, if you disbelieve in democracy, secularism, nationalism, as well as all the other garbage and ideas from the West, and rush to your religion and creed, then by Allah, you will own the earth, and the East and West will submit to you. This is the promise of Allah to you . . .
>
> We – by Allah – do not find any sharʿī [legal] excuse for you justifying your holding back from supporting this state . . . if you forsake the State or wage war against it, you will not harm it. You will only harm yourselves . . .
>
> O soldiers of the Islamic State, Allah (the Exalted) ordered us [to wage] jihad and promised us . . . victory . . . And if anyone wants to break the ranks, split his head with bullets and empty its insides [*sc.* contents], whoever he may be . . .[26]

Unlike in 1914, however, there were no infidel allies to be spared as part of a calculated regional strategy. For ISIS, the ultimate goal was the apocalypse: its ambition was not conventional victory but to fulfil the prophecy of an Islamist Armageddon at Dabiq.

Secondly, ISIS practised what it preached with a ferocious literalism. In the words of Graeme Wood, its ideology constituted 'a sincere, carefully considered commitment to returning civilization to a seventh-century legal environment, and ultimately to bringing about the apocalypse'. The reality, Wood wrote in March 2015, was 'that the Islamic State is Islamic. Very Islamic . . . *No one has tried harder to implement strict Sharia by violence. This is what it looks like*' – namely, enslavements, amputations, beheadings, stonings and crucifixions.[27] Thirdly, ISIS was an open-source network, systematically disseminating not only its ideology but also the most hideous displays of exemplary violence through tens of thousands of Twitter accounts linking to one another as well as to Facebook and YouTube.[28] In some ways, its media operation became its greatest source of resilience in the face of a sustained campaign to assassinate its leadership.[29] Finally, ISIS was quite differently organized from Al-Qaeda. In the Middle East, it aspired to become an authentic, territorial state, effacing the borders of the century-old Sykes–Picot agreement.[30] In the wider band of Muslim-majority countries from North Africa to South Asia, it created a confederation of affiliates. In the West, it sought to build a new and much looser network of jihadists, luring up to 15,000 of the most ardent to come to Mosul and Raqqa,[31] but encouraging others to carry out crude, indiscriminate attacks in Western cities. Sheikh Abu Muhammad al-Adnani's call on Muslims in Western countries to find an infidel and 'smash his head with a rock' sums up the primitive mode of operation on the ground.[32] But graphs of the pro-ISIS network online revealed a great deal of sophistication in the ether.[33] A cluster of 'media mujahedeen' using multiple accounts constantly reconfigured itself like a swarm of bees or flock of birds in order to evade account closures.[34] Somewhat surprisingly, analysis of the betweenness centrality of nodes in the ISIS network has revealed the key role played by women in the organization.[35]

The Obama administration's response to ISIS was to try to decapitate it, as it had decapitated Al-Qaeda. No one wished to consider the possibility that the enemy they now confronted was an 'acephalous' or leaderless network, that could no more easily be killed than the many-headed hydra of ancient Greek mythology.[36] At the same time, the president went out of his way to dismiss ISIS's ideology, insisting repeatedly that it had 'nothing to do with Islam'. Convinced that to acknowledge the literalism of the group's reading of the Koran would be to legitimize 'Islamophobia', Obama instructed officials not to refer to Islam at all and instead to focus on 'combating violent extremism'. Only with the utmost reluctance did he agree to order air strikes against ISIS strongholds following the outcry over the sadistic executions of American and British hostages in 2014.[37]

As a result of these mistakes, the world now finds itself in the grip of an epidemic of Islamist terror. Of the last sixteen years, the worst year for terrorism was 2014, with ninety-three countries experiencing attacks and close to 33,000 people killed. The second worst was 2015, with over 29,000 deaths. In that year, four radical Islamic groups were responsible for three quarters of all deaths from terrorism: Islamic State, Boko Haram, the Taliban and al-Qaeda.[38] ISIS carried out over a hundred attacks a month.[39] Although

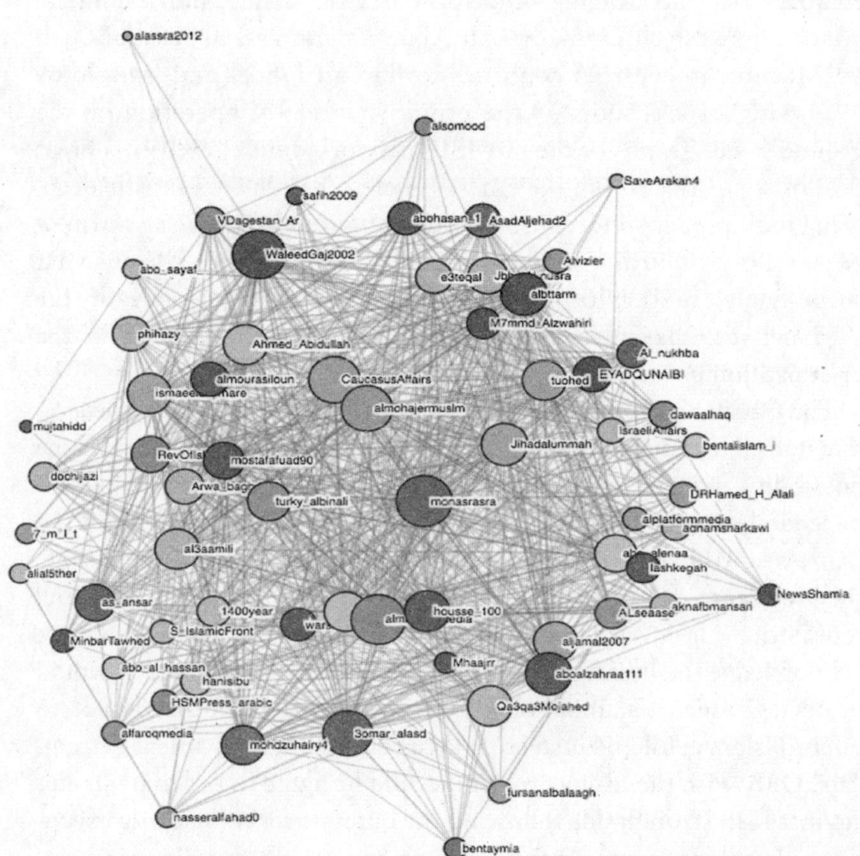

44. The sixty-six 'most important jihadi and support sites for jihad and the mujahideen on Twitter', as recommended by jihadist blogger Ahmad 'Abdallah in February 2013. The network density of the graph is approximately 0.2, meaning that around 20 per cent of all the connections that could exist in theory actually do exist. This was the delivery system for the gruesome videos released by ISIS in 2014.

Muslim-majority countries suffer the most from jihadist violence, the West is increasingly under attack. There were sixty-four ISIS-affiliated attacks in Western countries in 2015, including the massacres in Paris (130 killed) and Orlando (49 killed).[40] In a single week, as this chapter was being written, there were attacks in Antwerp, London and Paris. Only the constant vigilance of Western security services has stopped many more people from being killed in the past dozen years. In 2014/15, there were more terrorism-related arrests in the UK than in any year since 2000.[41] In all, there have been 135 British terrorism-related cases since 1998, resulting in 264 convictions, and the frequency of terrorism offences has roughly doubled since 2010.[42] Yet even this intensified effort cannot hope to pre-empt every jihadist.

The problem is that the ISIS network defies conventional counter-terrorist tactics. Contrary to popular belief, this is not because its relies on 'lone wolves', who by their very nature are hard to detect. The Paris attacks of November 2015 were a well-planned operation involving around eighteen people in addition to the nine attackers.[43] In any case, hardly anyone becomes a jihadist all on their own, just by surfing the Internet. Jihad is always preceded by *dawa* – the process of non-violent but toxic radicalization that turns the petty criminal into a zealot.[44] The network of *dawa* takes many different forms. In the UK, a key role has been played by the organization known as Al Muhajiroun (The Emigrants). But there are many less visible organizations – Islamic centres with shadowy imams – busily spreading the mind-poison.[45] Surveys of British Muslims' attitudes appear at first sight to be reassuring. Altogether 90 per cent of those surveyed by Policy Exchange in 2016 condemned terrorism. Fewer than one in ten regarded Islamophobia as a 'big problem', and only 7 per cent said they did not feel a strong sense of belonging to the UK. However, nearly half of respondents said they did not want to fully integrate with non-Muslims in all aspects of life, preferring some separation with respect to 'schooling and laws'. Asked whether they would support the introduction of sharia law, 43 per cent said 'Yes.' Two fifths said they favoured gender-segregated education. A clear majority of those surveyed in the south of the country supported making the hijab or niqab part of school uniform for girls. And one in ten of the whole sample opposed the prohibition of tutoring that 'promotes extreme views or is deemed incompatible with fundamental British values'. Most alarming of all, nearly a third (31 per cent) of those surveyed said they believed that the American government was responsible for the 9/11 attacks. More people blamed 'the Jews' for 9/11 (7 per cent) than said it was the work of al-Qaeda (4 per cent).[46]

No serious student of Islamism believes that such attitudes are consequences of social deprivation that can be changed through job creation or more generous welfare provision.[47] Nor does anyone involved in the online fight against ISIS imagine that pressurizing Twitter to delete pro-ISIS accounts will achieve more than a limited amount.[48] Much jihadist chatter has already relocated to Telegram, justpaste.it and Vkontake, the Russian social network.[49] After 7/7, the UK government's anti-terrorism strategy CONTEST was designed actively to 'Prevent' people from becoming terrorists or supporting terrorism. The Counter-Terrorism and Security Act 2015 even placed a duty on the police, prisons, local authorities, schools and universities to 'prevent people being drawn into terrorism'. As Home Secretary, Theresa May vowed 'systematically [to] confront and challenge extremist ideology'.[50] For this she was denounced by the Muslim Council of Britain, Hizb ut-Tahrir, CAGE and the Islamic Human Rights Commission, aided and abetted by fellow-travellers at the National Union of Teachers.[51] But the reality is that Prevent has not done enough. The problem is that it is very hard to stop a network like this one from flourishing when it can operate even in jails. Figures published in February by the Ministry of Justice showed the number of Muslims in prison (for all types of offences) had more than doubled to 12,255 between 2004 and 2014. One in seven inmates in England and Wales is Muslim.[52]

This problem is not going away, as the predicament of France illustrates. At least 8 per cent of the population is Muslim, which is roughly what the Pew Research Center expects it will be in Britain by 2030.[53] The French authorities estimate that they have 11,400 radical Islamists, far more than they can keep under surveillance. According to Farhad Khosrokhavar, Muslims make up as much as 70–80 per cent of inmates in prisons located on French urban peripheries, and 40 per cent of all French prisoners aged from eighteen to twenty-four.[54] According to official data, 27 per cent of the French prison population observed Ramadan in 2013.[55] Rising migration to Europe from North Africa, the Middle East and South Asia – in particular, the arrival of more than a million asylum-seekers and economic migrants in Germany in 2015 – will not help matters either. Large majorities of people from the source countries favour sharia law: for example, 84 per cent of Pakistanis and 91 per cent of Iraqis. Amongst those sharia supporters, three quarters of Pakistanis and more than two fifths of Iraqis support the death penalty for apostasy.[56] Even if, as seems likely, Islamic State is defeated in Iraq and Syria, its network in cyberspace and in the West will live on, a toxic milieu where the memes of *dawa* can breed, converting one loser after another to the cause of murderous martyrdom.

56
11/9/2016

Most people do not go online to participate in flash mobs or watch beheadings. They gossip, they shop, they share pictures, they share jokes, and they watch short video clips – of soccer goals, of cute cats, of sex. All those neural pathways produced by evolution make us irresistibly susceptible to the cascading stimuli of tweets and pokes from our electronic cluster of friends. The networks cater to our solipsism (selfies), our short attention spans (140 characters), and our seemingly insatiable appetite for news about celebrities made famous by reality television. It is this that gives modern democracy its distinctive quality. What can focus our attention, even briefly, on the tiresome question of how we are to be governed or, at least, by whom? When we speak of 'populism' today,[1] we sometimes mean nothing more than a politics that is audible as well as intelligible to the man in the street – or, to be precise, the man and woman slumped on their sofa, their attention skipping fitfully from flat-screen TV to laptop to smartphone to tablet and back to television, or the man and woman at work, sitting in front of desktop PCs but mostly exchanging suggestive personal messages on their smartphones.

Many people in developed countries are now online every waking hour of their lives. More than two fifths of Americans say they check their email, text and social media accounts constantly.[2] In the four years to May 2016, smartphone penetration in the UK leapt from 52 to 81 per cent of the adult population. Nine out of ten Britons aged between eighteen and forty-four now possess a smartphone. They check these devices compulsively, whether at home, at work, or between the two. More than two thirds use their smartphones even while dining with their families. Only when they sleep do they put the devices aside and even then it is hard to part with them. Over half of British smartphone owners check their phones within thirty minutes of turning out the lights at night, a quarter of them five minutes before, and one in ten immediately before. That same proportion of people reach for their phones as soon as they wake up, while a third check them within five minutes of waking and half within a quarter of an hour.[3] Americans are no less hooked. Already in 2009, the average American had mobile-phone contact on 195 days of the year, text-messaging contact 125 days a year, email contact 72 days a year, instant messaging contact 55 days a year and contact via social networking websites 39 days a year.[4] By 2012 Americans were checking their mobile phones 150 times a day. By 2016, they were spending an average of five hours a day on their phones. No theory of the populist revolt that swept Europe and the United States in the years after 2008 is complete if it fails to include this astounding transformation of the public sphere, which may legitimately be described as an all-out invasion of the private sphere.

No doubt the significant jumps in support for populists of both the left and the right were due partly to the revolution of falling economic expectations described above.[5] No doubt a cultural backlash against multiculturalism was complementing the revolt against the economics of globalization.[6] Yet, as Renee DiResta has argued, the digital crowd of the 2010s was fundamentally different from the crowd of the 1930s that had so fascinated and appalled Elias Canetti:

1. The crowd always wants to grow – and always can, unfettered by physical limitations.
2. Within the crowd there is equality – but higher levels of deception, suspicion, and manipulation.
3. The crowd loves density – and digital identities can be more closely packed.
4. The crowd needs a direction – and clickbait makes directions cheap to manufacture.[7]

Those who had pinned their hopes on the 'wisdom' of crowds, fondly imagining a benign 'crowd-sourced' politics, were in for a rude awakening. 'In the presence of social influence,' as two scholars of networks have observed, 'people's actions become dependent on one another, shattering the fundamental assumption behind the wisdom of crowds. When crowds follow their interdependence, they can be leveraged to spread information to the masses, even if it's incorrect.'[8]

Viewed from the vantage point of 2017, the US presidential election of 2008 seems to have happened in the distant past. John McCain, the defeated Republican candidate, had just 4,492 Twitter followers and 625,000 Facebook friends. He admitted that he had no email account and did not use the Internet.[9] He was overwhelmed not only by a financial crisis for which his own party was bound to be blamed, but also by the first socially networked campaign. Barack Obama had four times as many Facebook friends as McCain and twenty-six times as many Twitter followers. His website (www.barackobama.com) was the work of Chris Hughes, a co-founder of Facebook, and proved to be a vital engine not just for messaging but also for fundraising. Liberal elites on both coasts gloated over McCain's defeat: an elderly, white veteran with years of experience in Washington laid low by a young, cool, African-American 'community organizer' and one-term senator. Only a few noted two disquieting features of the contest. First, homophily in social networks seemed to result in polarization when politics became the topic of discussion, with individuals' views becoming more extreme in the 'echo chamber' of shared bias.[10] Second – though this was not formally demonstrated until the 2010 mid-term elections to Congress – Facebook was a highly effective tool for political mobilization, especially when used to target local non-digital networks.[11]

The implications were not lost on Dominic Cummings, the architect of the 'Vote Leave' victory in the 2016 referendum on British membership of the European Union. Almost uniquely in the British political class, Cummings had long been interested not only in history, which he had studied at Oxford, but also in complexity and networks. With only a limited budget (£10m) and limited time (ten months), Cummings had to fight not only 'decision makers at the apex of centralized hierarchies', who nearly all opposed 'Brexit', but also the undisciplined politicians on his own side. The odds were stacked against Leave. Amongst the keys to its narrow victory, Cummings argued, were 'nearly a billion targeted digital adverts', experimental polling, a data science team of 'extremely smart physicists' and a 'baseball bat marked "Turkey/NHS/£350 million"' – an allusion to the largely untruthful slogans that 'experiments had shown were most effective' in persuading people to vote Leave. For Cummings, Brexit was not a victory for the populist right at all, as his campaign had deliberately combined right-wing and left-elements (the threat of more Muslim immigrants if Turkey joined the EU, the promise of more money for the National Health Service if Britain left). As David Goodhart had pointed out years before, opposition to immigration and support for the welfare state were in fact complementary positions.[12] Rather, Cummings argued, Brexit was a victory for the 'healthy and effective system' of 'the English common law[, which] allows constant and rapid error-correction' over 'unhealthy and ineffective systems like the EU and modern Whitehall departments . . . [which] are extremely centralised and hierarchical', and therefore incapable of effective problem-solving.[13] Brexit, in short, was a victory for a network – and network science – over the hierarchy of the British establishment. While David Cameron and George Osborne had conducted a conventional campaign, concentrating all their fire on the economic risks of leaving the EU, Cummings had used his 'Voter Intention Collection System' (VICS) and Facebook to communicate the viral message that it was worth paying some economic price to 'take back control'. As Cummings recalled, 'We ran many different versions of ads, tested them, dropped the less effective and reinforced the most effective in a constant iterative process.'[14] It has been suggested that these techniques were made available to Cummings by the American hedge fund manager Robert Mercer's data analytics firm, Cambridge Analytica.[15]

Brexit was a dress rehearsal for the US presidential election of 2016. As in Britain, so in the United States, the political establishment took it for granted that the old ways would suffice. Despite the expenditure of hundreds of millions of dollars on conventional advertising, the campaigns of Jeb Bush and Hillary Clinton struggled to establish any connection with large sections of their parties' supporters. In the early months of 2016, it was a disreputable New York real estate magnate and a cantankerous Vermont socialist who connected. Once again, relatively unstructured networks challenged old-fashioned hierarchies: not merely the established parties that political scientists said 'decided' such contests, but also the dynasties – Bush and Clinton – that had been so politically dominant since the 1980s. Significantly, both Donald Trump and Bernie Sanders campaigned as outsiders, expressing hostility to the Washington hierarchy and articulating ideologies – nativism, protectionism and socialism – long considered beyond the pale of American democracy. With Sanders thwarted by a system of 'super-delegates' designed to maximize elite control of the Democratic party, the stage was set for a cathartic confrontation between Clinton – the personification of the established political hierarchy – and Trump, whom the establishment 'took literally, but not seriously', in Salena Zito's inspired formulation.[16] The reason why the necessary number of voters took him seriously but not literally was that Trump's scale-free network, based on a combination of self-organization and viral marketing, beat Clinton's hierarchically organized but over-complicated campaign. It was not that the Clinton campaign lacked networks. It suffered almost from a surfeit of them. There was a 'network of donors, friends, allies, and advisers' – a 'monster fund-raising network' – dating back to her husband's heyday. There was 'Ready for Hillary', which 'built grassroots enthusiasm . . . [and] gave Clinton a network across the states'.[17] There was also a 'vast network of unpaid advisers and professional skeptics', policy wonks with degrees from Yale Law School, busily churning out bullet points of minimal electoral value.[18] Yet Clinton's campaign manager, Robby Mook, shut down 'Ready for Hillary' and axed locally based state directors. Although the senior political operatives sent to plug gaps in the states were nicknamed 'ubers', this exaggerated the overall effectiveness of the campaign.[19] Lost in all the complexity was the simple reality that the candidate was connecting with key voters far less effectively than her most dangerous rival.

That social media played a crucial role in the 2016 election seems clear, even if television remained more important for the average voter.[20] Roughly half of Americans used Facebook and other social media sites to get news on the subject, with usage especially high amongst voters under fifty.[21] And around one third of social media users commented, discussed or posted on the subject of politics, despite a widespread view that social media discussions were less civil than those in other venues.[22] The crucial point, however, was that in the final phase of the election (after the party conventions) one candidate had a significantly greater presence on social media than the other. Trump had 32 per cent more Twitter followers than Clinton and 87 per cent more supporters on Facebook.[23] A few days before the election Trump had 12 million Facebook 'Likes', 4 million more than Clinton.[24] Trump also dominated Clinton by the more important Facebook measure of 'interest' – and he did so in every single state. (People in Mississippi were nearly twelve times more interested in Trump than in Clinton, but even in New York people found him three times more interesting than her.) The crucial swing states in the Midwest all signalled their intentions clearly through Facebook. Twitter data told a similar story. From 11 to 31 May 2016, Trump's posts on Twitter were retweeted almost 6,000 times on average while Clinton's tweets were retweeted only 1,500 times.[25] The Trump campaign also made effective use of YouTube – for example, for its final campaign attack ad directed against the global elite: Clinton, Soros, Goldman Sachs.[26] Above all, the Trump campaign, like the British

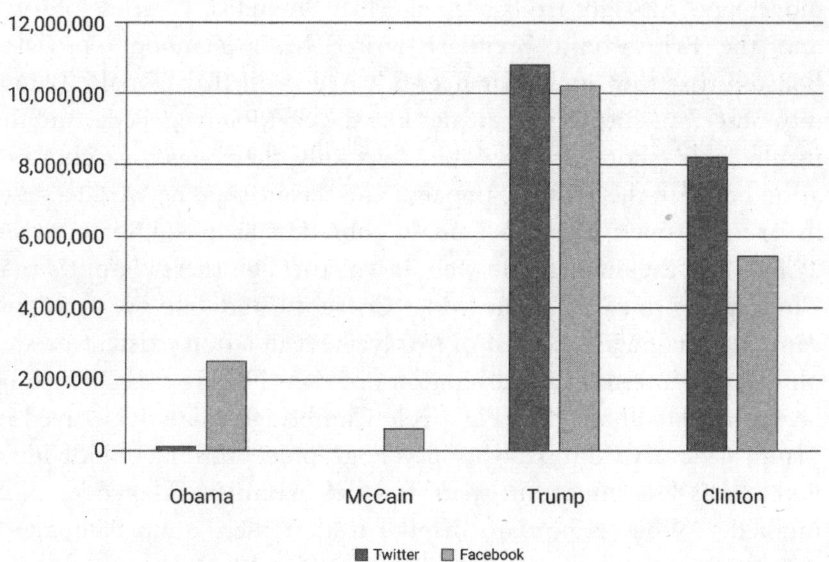

45. Social media followers of the leading candidates in two presidential elections, 2008 and 2016.

Vote Leave campaign, made full use of Facebook's ad-testing capability, trying tens of thousands of variants to establish what worked best on the voters being targeted.[27]

This was a richly ironic state of affairs, as from an early stage Silicon Valley had aligned itself with Clinton. Google employees gave $1.3m to her campaign, compared with just $26,000 to Trump's. Eric Schmidt's start-up Groundwork provided data support for Clinton's campaign.[28] Mark Zuckerberg faced an internal revolt when Trump posted his call for 'a total and complete shutdown of Muslims entering the United States' on Facebook, and the technology blog Gizmodo alleged that Facebook was manipulating trending topics to limit Trump's prominence.[29] Zuckerberg himself made no secret of his personal disdain for Trump's views.[30] Yet the networks he and Schmidt had done so much to build were now being used to promote ideas both men and their co-workers found abhorrent, as well as to help the Trump campaign raise money.[31] And even if Google and Facebook had somehow been able to ban Trump, they would merely have diverted more traffic to other networks, such as the anonymous message boards of 4Chan and 8Chan, the birthplace of the 'alt-right' movement. Alt-right trolls such as Matt Braynard, Charles Johnson and the British-born Breitbart writer Milo Yiannopoulos later boasted that they and their network had propelled Donald Trump into office by 'shitposting' memes like the cartoon frog, Pepe, and the insult 'cuck' (short for cuckold).[32] Certainly, there was close coordination between the Trump campaign and the alt-right network: a team in Trump Tower used TheDonald subreddit as a conduit between 4Chan and the mainstream web. It was through these channels that Clinton was smeared as the 'Most Corrupt Candidate Ever' and her campaign manager accused of involvement in a non-existent paedophile ring centred on a Washington pizzeria.[33] There continues to be heated debate about how big a role Cambridge Analytica played in Trump's victory.[34] Probably its 'psychographic' profiling of individual voters was less important than its chief executive, Alexander Nix, implied.[35] What is hard to dispute is that the Trump campaign's involvement with the alt-right brought anti-Semitism back into American politics in a way not seen since the 1930s.[36] That, however, was not why Trump won.

Perhaps the most painful aspect of the 2016 election for the masters of Silicon Valley was the way their networks were used to disseminate untrue stories – the 'fake news' that Trump repeatedly complained about, even while spreading myriad untruths of his own. In September, Facebook relayed the bogus story that Trump had been endorsed by the Pope.[37] In November, Google inadvertently gave top placement to a false claim that Trump had won the popular vote.[38] This also helped Trump. Of the known fake news stories that appeared in the three months before the election, the anti-Trump stories were shared on Facebook 8 million times; the anti-Clinton stories 30 million times.[39] Nearly a quarter of the links tweeted by a sample of 140,000 Michigan-based users during the ten days prior to 11 November were to fake news stories.[40]

The 2016 election was one of the closest in American history – and closer than the Brexit referendum result, too. If fewer than 39,000 voters in three swing states (Michigan, Pennsylvania and Wisconsin) had cast their ballots for Clinton rather than Trump, she would have won the Electoral College as well as the popular vote. Historians will debate endlessly which of an infinite number of variables was the decisive one, as if all other things would have remained equal if just one variable had been changed. Nevertheless, there is a compelling case to be made that, without harnessing social networks through online platforms, Donald Trump could never have become president of the United States. In a pre-Internet campaign, certainly, he would have struggled to match Clinton, as he lacked the financial resources for an old-style war of attrition through television advertising. It might be said that social networks allowed him to campaign far more efficiently, chaotic though his organization appeared to be, but that would be to overlook the crucial point. An electoral map of the United States shows that Trump won 'Trumpland' – the counties that voted for him account for 85 per cent of the US land surface – while Clinton won what might be called the Hillary Archipelago. Her support was heavily concentrated in the major metropolitan areas of the two coasts, whereas his was spread across the heartland of provincial cities, towns and rural communities. This suggests a paradox: Clinton ought to have had an advantage in a networked election, in that her supporters were more densely concentrated, as well as younger.

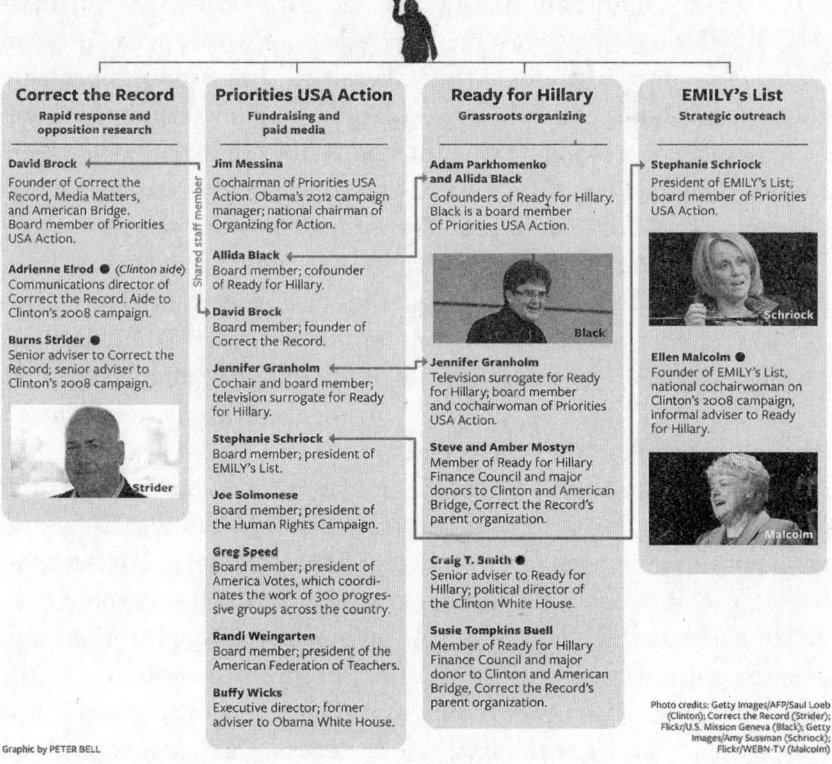

46. The 2016 Clinton campaign: a failed hierarchical structure.

There was a similar paradox in the case of Brexit: victory was delivered to the anti-EU campaign by older voters, predominantly located in the English and Welsh 'shires', not in the big cities. If social networks were the key to the politics of populism, why were groups less likely to be on Facebook – such as elderly country-dwellers – more likely to vote populist?[41] There is an explanation. Social media were undoubtedly used more effectively by Cummings and his counterpart in the Trump campaign, Stephen K. Bannon, than by their opponents. But the populist campaigns would not have been successful if the memes they disseminated had not been spread further in the non-electronic forums where ordinary people meet, and where friendships are real rather than (as on Facebook) fake: pubs and bars. And this, in turn, would not have happened if those memes had not resonated.

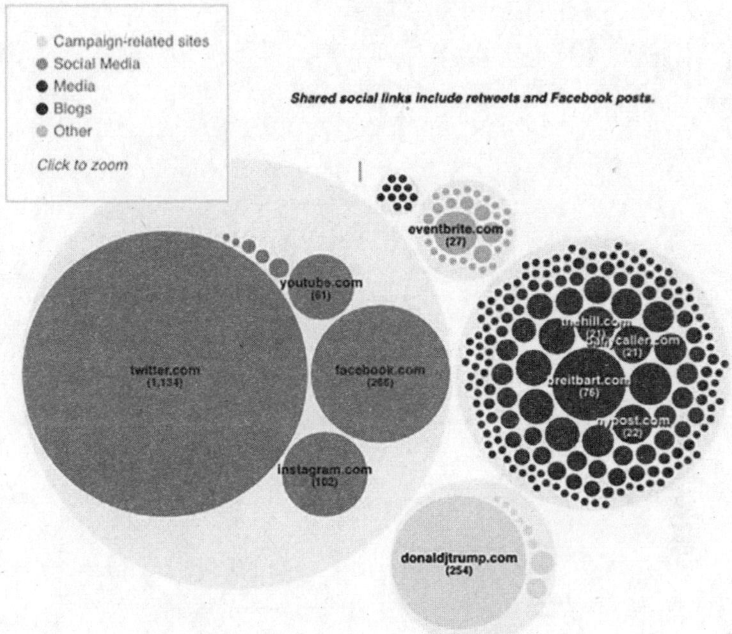

47. Donald Trump's online social network, 2016.

In the Library of Babel that is the Internet, much that one reads cannot be trusted. That is why the deepest social networks remain local and soci*able*. The political contests of 2016 were thus decided not in the Library of Babel but in the English-Speaking Hostelry. The Internet proposed; the saloon bars disposed.

But what had they wrought?

IX

Conclusion: Facing Cyberia

57
Metropolis

Fritz Lang's silent 1927 cinema classic *Metropolis* depicts the downfall of a hierarchical order at the hands of an insurgent network. Metropolis is a city of towering skyscrapers. At the top, in palatial penthouses, lives a wealthy elite led by the autocrat Joh Fredersen. Down below, in subterranean factories, the proletariat toils. After he witnesses an industrial accident, Fredersen's playboy son is awakened to the squalor and danger of working-class life. The upshot is a violent revolution and a self-inflicted if inadvertent disaster: when the workers smash the power generators, their own living quarters are flooded because the water pumps fail.

Metropolis is perhaps best remembered for the iconic female robot that becomes the doppelgänger of the heroine, Maria. Lang said the film was inspired by his first visit to New York. To his eyes, the skyscrapers of Manhattan were the perfect architectural expression of a chronically unequal society. Contemporaries, notably the right-wing media magnate Alfred Hugenberg, detected a Communist subtext (though Lang's wife, who co-wrote the screenplay, was a radical German nationalist and later joined the Nazi Party). Viewed today, however, *Metropolis* clearly transcends the political ideologies of the mid-twentieth century. With its multiple religious allusions, culminating in an act of redemption, *Metropolis* is modernity mythologized. The obvious question it poses is as relevant today as it was then: how can an urbanized, technologically advanced society avoid disaster when its social consequences are profoundly inegalitarian?

Yet there is an even more profound question in the subtext of Lang's film: who ultimately wins, the hierarchy or the network? For the greatest threat to the hierarchical social order of *Metropolis* is posed not by subterranean flooding, but by a clandestine conspiracy among the workers. Nothing infuriates Fredersen more than the realization that this conspiracy could be hatched in the catacombs beneath the city without his knowledge.

In today's terms, the hierarchy is not a single city but the nation-state itself, the vertically structured super-polity that evolved out of the republics and monarchies of early modern Europe. Though not the most populous nation in the world, the United States is certainly the world's most powerful state, whatever the vagaries of its political system. Its nearest rival, the People's Republic of China, is usually seen as a profoundly different kind of state, for while the United States has two major parties, the People's Republic has one, and only one. The US government is founded on the separation of powers, not least the independence of its judiciary; the PRC subordinates all other institutions, including the courts, to the dictates of the Communist Party. Yet both states are republics, with roughly comparable vertical structures of administration and not wholly dissimilar concentrations of power in the hands of the central government relative to state and local authorities. Economically, the two systems are certainly converging, with China looking ever more to market mechanisms, while the US federal government in recent years has steadily increased the statutory and regulatory power of public agencies over producers and consumers. And, to an extent that disturbs libertarians on both left and right, the US government exerts control and practises surveillance over its citizens in ways that are functionally closer to contemporary China than to the America of the Founding Fathers. In these respects, 'Chimerica' is no chimera. Once these economies seemed like opposites, with one doing the exporting, the other the importing, one doing the saving, the other the consuming.[1] Since the financial crisis, however, there has been a certain convergence. Today the real estate bubble, the excessive leverage, the shadow banks – not to mention the technology 'unicorns' – are almost as likely to be encountered in China as in America. In Chimerica 1.0, opposites attracted. In Chimerica 2.0, the odd couple have become uncannily alike, as often happens in a marriage.

Sitting alongside the United States and the People's Republic in the hierarchy of nation-states are the French Republic, the Russian Federation and the United Kingdom of Great Britain and Northern

Ireland. These are the five permanent members of the United Nations Security Council and they are thereby set above all the other 188 members of the UN – an institution where all nations are equal, but some are more equal than others. However, that is clearly not a sufficient description of today's world order. In terms of military capability, there is another somewhat larger elite of nuclear powers to which, in addition to the 'P5', also belong India, Israel, Pakistan and North Korea. Iran aspires to join them. In terms of economic power, the hierarchy is different again: the Group of Seven countries (Canada, France, Germany, Italy, Japan, the United Kingdom and the United States) were once considered the dominant economies in the world, but today that club is relatively less dominant as a result of the rise of the 'BRICS' (Brazil, Russia, India, China and South Africa), the biggest of the so-called 'emerging markets'. The Group of 20 was formed in 1999 to bring most of the world's big economies together, but with the Europeans over-represented (as the EU is a member in its own right, along with the four biggest EU member-states).

Yet to think of the world only in such terms is to overlook its profound transformation by the proliferation of informal networks in the past forty years. Picture, instead, a network graph based on economic complexity and interdependence, which delineates the relative sophistication of all the world's economies in terms of technological advancement as well as their connectedness through trade and cross-border investment. Such a graph would have a strongly hierarchical architecture because of the power-law-like distribution of economic resources and capabilities in the world, and the significant variation in economic openness between countries. Yet it would also unmistakably be a network, with most nodes connected to the rest of the world by more than one or two edges.[2]

The key question is how far this network of economic complexity now poses a threat to the hierarchical world order of nation-states comparable to the threat that networks of political complexity have recently posed to established domestic-political hierarchies – notably in 2011 in the Middle East, in 2014 in Ukraine, in 2015 in Brazil, and in 2016 in Britain and America. To put the question more simply: can a networked world have order? As we have seen, some say that it can.[3] In the light of historical experience, I very much doubt it.

58
Network Outage

According to folklore, Mahatma Gandhi was once asked by a reporter what he thought of Western civilization. He replied that he thought it would be a good idea. The same might be said about world order. In his book of that title, Henry Kissinger argues that the world is in a parlous condition verging on international anarchy. Four competing visions of world order – the European, the Islamic, the Chinese and the American – are each in varying stages of metamorphosis, if not decay. Consequently, there is no real legitimacy to any of these visions. The emergent properties of this new world disorder are the formation of regional blocs and the danger that friction between them might escalate into some kind of large-scale conflict, comparable in its origins and potential destructiveness with the First World War. 'Is the world moving toward regional blocs that perform the role of states in the Westphalian* system?' Kissinger asks. 'If so, will balance follow, or will this reduce the number of key players to so few that rigidity becomes inevitable and the perils of the early twentieth century return, with inflexibly constructed blocs attempting to face one another down?'[1] His answer to this question is laden with foreboding:

> [What we have to fear is] not so much a major war between states . . . as an evolution into spheres of influence identified with particular domestic structures and forms of governance – for example, the Westphalian model as against the radical Islamist version. At its edges each sphere would be tempted to test its strength against other entities of

* See the footnote above on p. 88.

> orders deemed illegitimate ... In time the tensions of this process would degenerate into maneuvers for status or advantage on a continental scale or even worldwide. A struggle between regions could be even more destructive than the struggle between nations has been.[2]

This is a theory similar to some of those we have already encountered about the origins of war in 1914. An unstable network of power has emerged that has the potential to 'go critical' even in response to a minor perturbation.

Contrary to those who claim (on the basis of a misreading of statistics of conflict) that the world is steadily becoming more peaceful and that 'wars between states ... are all but obsolete',[3] Kissinger argues that the contemporary global constellation of forces is in fact highly flammable. First, whereas 'the international economic system has become global ... the political structure of the world has remained based on the nation-state'.* Second, we are acquiescing in the proliferation of nuclear weapons far beyond the Cold War 'club', thus 'multiply[ing] the possibilities of nuclear confrontation'. Finally, we also have the new realm of cyberspace, which Kissinger likens to Hobbes's 'state of nature', in which 'asymmetry and a kind of congenital world disorder are built into relations between ... powers'.[4] Here and in recent interviews, Kissinger has outlined four scenarios which he regards as the most likely catalysts for a large-scale conflagration:

1. a deterioration in Sino-American relations, whereby the two countries tumble into the so-called 'Thucydides Trap'† that history appears to set for every incumbent power and the rising power that challenges it;[5]
2. a breakdown of relations between Russia and the West, based on mutual incomprehension and made possible by:

* This was a tension laid bare in the 2008 financial crisis, when (as the Governor of the Bank of England, Mervyn King, wittily remarked) international banks were 'global in life, but national in death'.

† The allusion is to the argument of Thucydides' *History of the Peloponnesian War*, which presents the fifth century BC war between the Athenian empire and Sparta as in some sense inevitable because of the 'growth in the power of Athens, and the alarm which this inspired in Lacedaemon [Sparta]'.

3. a collapse of European hard power, due to the inability of modern European leaders to accept that diplomacy without the credible threat of force is just hot air; and/or
4. an escalation of conflict in the Middle East due to the Obama administration's readiness in the eyes of the Arab states and Israel to hand hegemony in the region to a still revolutionary Iran.

One or a combination of these threats, in the absence of a coherent American strategy, threatens to turn mere disorder into large-scale conflict.[6]

Kissinger's warning cannot be lightly dismissed. The world today frequently resembles a giant network on the verge of a cataclysmic outage. In a typical week in early 2017, the president of the United States tweeted that his own intelligence agencies were illegally leaking classified information to *The New York Times* about his campaign's communications with the Russian government, but insisted that the story was 'fake news'. Meanwhile, having interfered in the US presidential election via WikiLeaks and an online army of trolls and bots (what might be called the LED Army), the Kremlin deployed a new cruise missile in breach of the 1987 Intermediate-Range Nuclear Forces Treaty, and sent the spy ship *Viktor Leonov* to reconnoitre the US submarine base at New London, Connecticut. On the other side of the Atlantic, French and German politicians alike fretted about Russian meddling in their impending elections. However, despite all this, the big story in Europe that week was the disgrace of the 27-year-old YouTube star Felix 'PewDiePie' Kjellberg, whose flirtation with anti-Semitism led to the cancellation of deals he had made with Google and Disney.*

Meanwhile, the self-styled Islamic State published an online guide to propaganda, explaining to its supporters how to use the news

* Shortly before this crisis, PewDiPie's YouTube channel had over 50 million subscribers. Though born in Sweden, PewDiePie lives in Brighton with his Italian girlfriend, but refers to his followers as 'Bros', a term borrowed from African-American rap music. He is not to be confused with Milo Yiannopoulos, though both men dye their hair blond.

industry's hunger for 'clicks' to launch pro-ISIS 'media projectiles'. A report on ISIS-run schools in Iraq and Syria revealed that pupils were being asked to calculate the number of Shi'ite Muslims or 'unbelievers' that could be killed by a suicide bomber. As if to help them find the answer, an ISIS terrorist blew himself up inside a crowded Sufi shrine in Sehwan, Pakistan, killing at least seventy-five people. In the same week, the Chinese government was reported to be relaxing its censorship of social media, but only because unfiltered blogposts would make it easier for the authorities to monitor dissent. In Seoul, the heir to the Samsung Electronics empire was arrested on suspicion of bribery, the latest casualty of the corruption scandal that toppled the South Korean President, Park Geun-hye, and her mysterious friend Choi Soon-sil, daughter of the founder of the Church of Eternal Life. Finally, at Kuala Lumpur's international airport, a female assassin splashed lethal VX nerve agent onto the face of Kim Jong-nam, the half-brother of the North Korean dictator, Kim Jong Un. Her T-shirt bore the universal webchat acronym 'LOL'.[7]

Laughing out loud seems like the wrong response. Globalization is in crisis. Populism is on the march. Authoritarian states are ascendant. Technology meanwhile marches inexorably ahead, threatening to render most human beings redundant or immortal or both. How do we make sense of all this? In pursuit of answers, many commentators resort to crude historical analogies. To some, Donald Trump is Hitler, about to proclaim an American dictatorship.[8] To others, Trump is Nixon, on the verge of being impeached.[9] But it is neither 1933 nor 1973 all over again. Easily centralized technology made totalitarian government possible in the 1930s. Forty years later, it had already got much harder for a democratically elected president to violate the law with impunity. Nevertheless, the media in the 1970s still consisted of a few television networks, newspapers and press agencies. And in more than half the world those organs were centrally controlled. It is impossible to comprehend the world today without understanding how much it has changed as a result of new information technology. This has become a truism. The crucial question is *how* has it changed? The answer is that technology has enormously empowered networks of all kinds relative to traditional hierarchical power structures – but that the consequences of that change will be determined by the structures, emergent properties and interactions of these networks.

As we have seen, the global impact of the Internet has few analogues in history better than the impact of printing on sixteenth-century Europe. The personal computer and smartphone have empowered networks as much as the pamphlet and the book did in Luther's time. Indeed, the trajectories for the production and price of PCs in the United States between 1977 and 2004 are remarkably similar to the trajectories for the production and price of printed books in England from 1490 to 1630 (see figure 48).[10] In the era of the Reformation and thereafter, connectivity was enhanced exponentially by rising literacy, so that a growing share of the population was able to access printed literature of all kinds, rather than having to rely on orators and preachers to convey new ideas to them.

There are three major differences between our networked age and the era that followed the advent of European printing. First, and most obviously, our networking revolution is much faster and more geographically extensive than the wave of revolutions unleashed by the German printing press. In a far shorter space of time than it took for 84 per cent of the world's adults to become literate, a remarkably large proportion of humanity has gained access to the Internet. As recently as 1998 only around 2 per cent of the world's population were online. Today the proportion is two in five. The pace of change is roughly an order of magnitude faster than in the post-Gutenberg

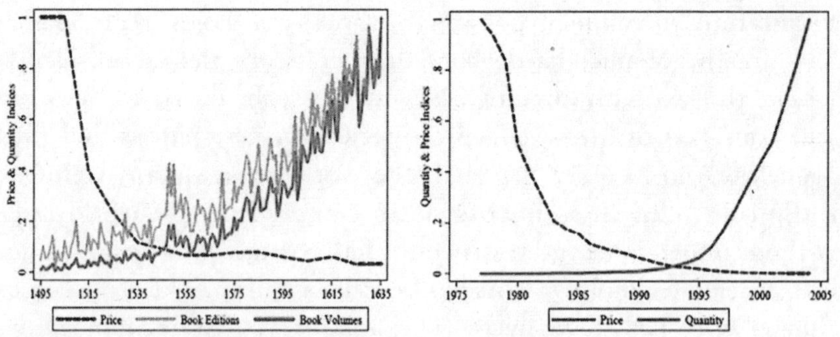

48. Prices and quantities of books and PCs, 1490s–1630s and 1977–2004, respectively.

period: what took centuries after 1490 took just decades after 1990. As we have seen, Google started life in a garage in Menlo Park in 1998. Today it has the capacity to process over 4.2 billion search requests every day. In 2005 YouTube was a start-up in a room above a pizzeria in San Mateo. Today it allows people to watch 8.8 billion videos a day. Facebook was dreamt up at Harvard just over a decade ago. Today it has close to 2 billion users who log on at least once a month.[11] And a hundred times that number of emails are sent every day. The world is indeed connected as never before. The rate of growth of the global network may be slowing, in terms of the numbers of new Internet users and smartphone owners added each year, but it shows no sign of stopping. In other respects – for example, the transitions from text to image and video, and from keyboard to microphone interface – it is speeding up. Literacy will ultimately cease to be a barrier to connectedness.

Nor is this technological revolution confined to developed countries. In terms of connectivity, if little else, the world's poor are catching up fast. Amongst the poorest 20 per cent of households in the world, roughly seven out of ten have mobile phones. The Indian telecom company Bharti Airtel has a customer base as large as the US population. Indeed, the number of Internet users in India now exceeds that in America. It took eight years for all Kenyan households to have mobile phones. It took just four years for Safaricom's pioneering M-Pesa payment system to reach 80 per cent of households.[12] Even impoverished and chaotic Somalia went from 5 to 50 per cent mobile-phone penetration inside five years.[13] Giving the world's poor mobile telephony is proving easier than providing them with clean water – an argument, perhaps, for leaving the provision of clean water to the private sector rather than weak, corrupt governments.[14]

Secondly, the distributional consequences of our revolution are quite different from those of the early-modern revolution. Fifteenth-century Europe was not an ideal place to enforce intellectual property rights, which in those days existed only when technologies could be secretively monopolized by a guild. The printing press created no billionaires: Gutenberg was not Gates (by 1456 he was effectively bankrupt). Moreover, only a sub-set of the media made possible by the printing press – newspapers and magazines – sought to make money from advertising, whereas the most important ones made possible by the Internet do. Nevertheless, few people foresaw that the giant networks made possible by the Internet, despite their propaganda about the democratization of knowledge, would be so profoundly inegalitarian. A generation mostly removed from conflict – the baby-boomers – had failed to learn the lesson that it is not unregulated networks that reduce inequality but wars, revolutions, hyperinflations and other forms of expropriation.[15]

To be sure, innovation has driven down the costs of information technology. Globally, the costs of computing and digital storage fell at annual rates of 33 and 38 per cent per annum between 1992 and 2012.[16] However, contrary to the hopes of those who envisioned a big bazaar of crowd-sourced applications, the Internet has evolved into a vast scale-free network, complete with hyper-connected super-hubs.[17] Oligopolies have developed in the realms of both hardware and software, as well as service provision and wireless networks. The nexus between the seemingly indestructible AT&T and the reinvented Apple illustrates an old truth: corporations will pursue monopoly, duopoly or oligopoly if they are left free to do so. Even those corporations committed to an 'open architecture' web – such as Amazon, Facebook and Google – seek monopolistic power in their segments: respectively, e-commerce, social networks and search.[18] Poor governance and regulation explain huge differentials in cellular service and Internet costs between countries.[19] They also explain why a small number of countries dominate the information and communications technology industry (though it is striking that the United States ranks seventh – some way behind Ireland, South Korea, Japan and the UK – in terms of the relative importance of ICT to its economy as whole).[20]

These dynamics explain why the ownership of the world's electronic network is so concentrated. At the time of writing, Google (or rather the renamed parent company, Alphabet Inc.) is worth $660bn by market capitalization. Around 16 per cent of its shares, worth around $106bn, are owned by its founders, Larry Page and Sergey Brin. The market capitalization of Facebook is approaching $441bn; 28 per cent of the shares, worth $123bn, are owned by its founder, Mark Zuckerberg. Despite their appearance as great levellers, social networks are thus 'inherently unfair and exclusionary'. Because of preferential attachment – the tendency for well-connected hubs to get even better connected – the ultimate 'social network truism' does indeed come from the book of St Matthew (see Introduction).[21] Unlike in the past, there are now two kinds of people in the world: those who own and run the networks, and those who merely use them. The commercial masters of cyberspace may still pay lip service to a flat world of netizens, but in practice companies such as Google are hierarchically organized, even if their 'org. charts' are quite different from that of General Motors in Alfred Sloan's day.

In traditional societies, the advent of market forces disrupts often hereditary networks, and as a result promotes social mobility and

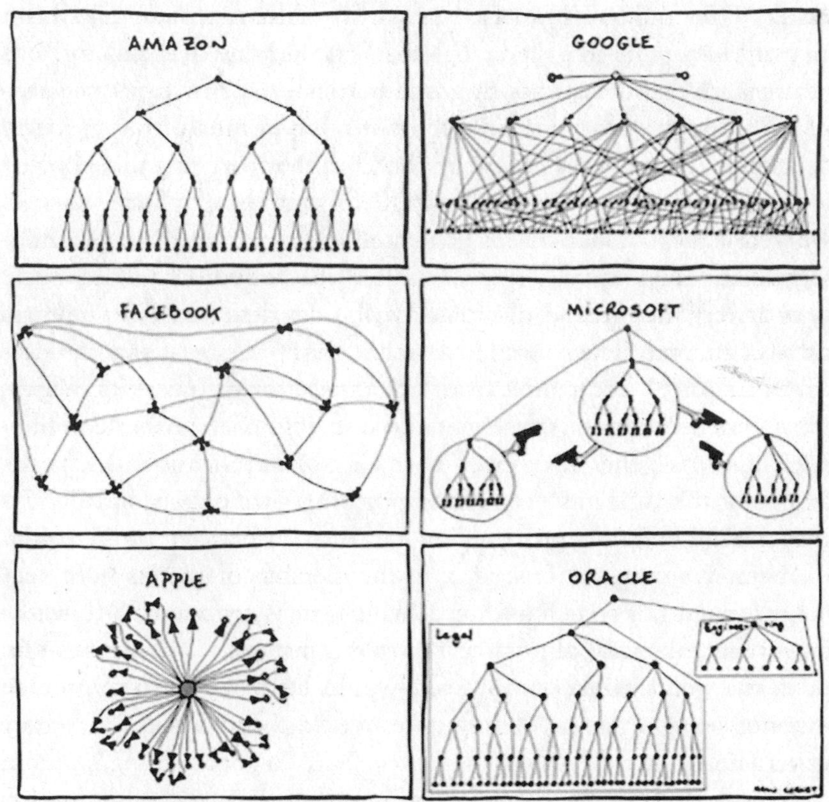

49. Satirical network diagrams of the principal US technology companies.

reduces inequality. Meritocracy prevails. But when networks and markets are aligned, as in our time, inequality explodes as the returns on the network flow overwhelmingly to the insiders who own it. Granted, the young and very wealthy people who own the modern networks tend to have somewhat left-wing political views. (Peter Thiel is the rare exception: a libertarian who was willing to sup with the populists in 2016.) However, few of them would welcome Scandinavian rates of personal income tax, much less an egalitarian revolution. The masters of the Internet would seem to relish being rich almost as much as the wolves of pre-crisis Wall Street a decade ago, though their consumption is less conspicuous than their pangs of conscience are. It is hard to imagine an investment banker following the example of Sam Altman of Y Combinator, who set off on a pilgrimage to Middle America as if doing penance for the 2016 election result.[22] Yet the San Francisco to which Altman returns remains a city of *Metropolis*-like inequality, not least because of the distortions that ensure that decent housing is ludicrously expensive. (Ownership of real property is second only to ownership of intellectual property as a determinant of wealth inequality, but the most valuable housing is not accidentally located nearest to the geographical clusters where the most valuable IP is generated.) And all that the big technology companies seem willing to offer the millions of truck- and taxi-drivers they intend to replace with driverless cars is some form of basic income. The sole consolation is that the largest shareholders of the FANG companies are US institutional investors which, insofar as they are the managers of the savings of the American middle class, have therefore given that class a significant stake in the profits of the ICT industry. An important qualification, however, is that foreign investors probably own at least 14 per cent of the equity of major US corporations, and, in the case of companies with very large foreign sales (such as Apple, which earns around two thirds of its revenue abroad), almost certainly much more.[23] No serious student of capital markets, however, would attribute to these foreign investors even a shred of influence over the companies' corporate governance.

Thirdly, and finally, the printing press had the effect of disrupting religious life in Western Christendom before it disrupted anything else. By contrast, the Internet began by disrupting commerce; only very recently did it begin to disrupt politics and it has really disrupted only one religion, namely Islam. As we have seen, networks were the key to what happened in American politics in 2016. There was the grassroots network of support that the Trump campaign built – and that built itself – on the platforms of Facebook, Twitter and Breitbart. These were the 'forgotten' men and women who turned out on 8 November to defeat the 'global special interests' and 'failed and corrupt political establishment' that Trump's opponent was alleged to personify. A role was also played by the jihadist network, as the ISIS-affiliated terror attacks during the election year lent credibility to Trump's pledges to 'strip out the support networks for radical Islam in this country' and to ban Muslim immigration.

As a very wealthy man who could nevertheless play the role of demagogue with aplomb, Trump himself embodied a central paradox of the age. He was at once a minor oligarch and a major brand. 'No American president,' it has been said, 'has taken office with a giant network of businesses, investments, and corporate connections like that amassed by Donald J. Trump', with known business links to 1,500 people and organizations.[24] At the same time, Trump's campaign succeeded where his opponents failed in harnessing the networks of Silicon Valley, to the dismay of the people who owned and thought they also controlled the networks. Their agony in the weeks after the election was palpable. Google at first sought to woo the new administration, only to denounce its executive orders limiting travel and migration to the United States from certain Muslim-majority countries.[25] Mark Zuckerberg absented himself from a meeting with the new president attended by other technology CEOs. Presumably it was some comfort to him that the Women's March against Trump also organized itself through Facebook.[26] It is hard to believe that there will not eventually be some kind of clash between the Trump administration and the big ICT companies, especially if the administration overturns its predecessor's decision in 2015 that the Federal Communications Commission should regulate the Internet as a public utility just like the old railroad or telephone network. There seems an obvious conflict of interest between telecom and cable companies and bandwidth-greedy platforms and content providers such as Netflix over the issue of 'net neutrality' (the principle that all bits of data should be treated alike, regardless of their content or value).[27] Anti-trust action against the FANG companies may be Trump's next move.

Yet in two respects there is a clear similarity between our time and the revolutionary period that followed the advent of printing. Like the printing press, modern information technology is transforming not only the market – most recently, by facilitating the sharing (i.e. short-term rentals) of cars and apartments – but also the public sphere. Never before have so many people been connected together in an instantly responsive network through which 'memes'* can spread even more rapidly than natural viruses.[28] But the notion that taking the whole world online would create a utopia of netizens, all equal in cyberspace, was always a fantasy – as much a delusion as Martin Luther's vision of a 'priesthood of all believers'. The reality is that the global network has become a transmission mechanism for all kinds of manias and panics, just as the combination of printing and literacy for a time increased the prevalence of millenarian sects and witch crazes. The cruelties of ISIS seem less idiosyncratic when compared with those of some governments and sects in the sixteenth and seventeenth centuries.[29] Rising levels of political violence also seem conceivable in the United States and perhaps in parts of Europe.[30] Secondly, as in the period during and after the Reformation, our time is seeing an erosion of territorial sovereignty.[31] In the sixteenth and seventeenth centuries, Europe was plunged into a series of religious wars because the principle formulated at the Peace of Augsburg (1555) – *cuius regio, eius religio* – was honoured mainly in the breach. In the twenty-first century, we see a similar phenomenon of escalating intervention in the domestic affairs of sovereign states.

There was, after all, a third network involved in the US election of

* For example, in September 2009, the following pro-Obamacare meme was copied by hundreds of thousands of Facebook users, some of whom (around 1 in 10) introduced slight mutations to the wording: 'No one should die because they cannot afford health care and no one should go broke because they get sick. If you agree please post this as your status for the rest of the day.'

2016, and that was Russia's intelligence network. At the time of writing, it is clear that the Russian government did its utmost to maximize the damage to Hillary Clinton's reputation stemming from her and her campaign's sloppy email security, using WikiLeaks as the conduit through which stolen documents were passed to the American media.[32] To visit the WikiLeaks website is to enter the trophy room of this operation. Here is the 'Hillary Clinton Email Archive', there are 'The Podesta Emails'. Not all the leaked documents are American, to be sure. But you will look in vain for leaks calculated to embarrass the Russian government. Julian Assange may still skulk in the Ecuadorean embassy in London, but the reality is that he lives, an honoured guest of President Vladimir Putin, in the strange land of Cyberia – the twilight zone inhabited by Russia's online operatives.

Russian hackers and trolls pose a threat to American democracy similar to the one that Jesuit priests posed to the English Reformation: a threat from within sponsored from without. 'We're at a tipping point', according to Admiral Michael S. Rogers, head of the NSA and US Cyber Command.[33] Cyber activities are now at the top of the director of national intelligence's list of threats. And WikiLeaks is only a small part of the challenge. The Pentagon alone reports more than 10 million attempts at intrusion each day.[34] Of course, most of what the media call 'cyber-attacks' are merely attempts at espionage. To grasp the full potential of cyber warfare, one must imagine an attack that could shut down a substantial part of the US power grid. Such a scenario is not far-fetched. Something similar was done in December 2015 to the Ukrainian electricity system, which was infected by a form of computer malware called BlackEnergy.

Computer scientists have understood the disruptive potential of cyber warfare since the earliest days of the Internet. At first it was adolescent hackers who caused mayhem: geeks like Robert Tappan Morris, who almost crashed the World Wide Web in November 1988 by releasing a highly infectious software worm,[35] or 'Mafia Boy', the Canadian fifteen-year-old who shut down the Yahoo website in February 2000. Blaster, Brain, Melissa, Iloveyou, Slammer, Sobig – the names of the early viruses betrayed their authors' youth.[36] It is still the case that many cyber-attacks are carried out by non-state actors:

teenage vandals, criminals, 'hacktivists' or terrorist organizations. (The 21 October 2016 attack launched against the domain name service provider Dynamic Network Services Inc., which used Chinese-manufactured webcams as 'bots', was almost certainly a case of vandalism.)[37] However, the most striking development of 2016 was the rise of Cyberia.

As the country that built the Internet, the United States was bound to lead in cyber-warfare, too. It began to do so as early as the first Reagan administration.[38] During the 2003 Iraq invasion, US spies penetrated Iraqi networks and sent messages urging generals to surrender.[39] Seven years later it was the United States and Israel that unleashed the Stuxnet virus against Iran's nuclear enrichment facilities.[40] The problem is not just that two can play at that game. The problem is that no one knows how many people can play at any number of cyber games. In recent years, the United States has found itself under cyber-attack from Iran, North Korea and China. However, these attacks were directed against companies (notably Sony Pictures), not the US government. The Russians were the first to wage war directly against the US government, seeking to compensate for their relative economic and military decline by exploiting the 'wide asymmetrical possibilities' that the Internet offers for 'reducing the fighting potential of the enemy'.[41] They learned the ropes in attacks on Estonia, Georgia and Ukraine. In 2017, however, the Kremlin launched a sustained assault on the American political system, using as proxies not only WikiLeaks but also the Romanian blogger 'Guccifer 2.0'.[42]

Let us leave aside the question of whether or not the Russian interference – as opposed to the fake news discussed in the previous chapter – decided the election in favour of Trump; suffice to say it helped him, though both fake and real news damaging to Clinton could presumably have been disseminated without Russia's involvement. Let us also leave aside the as yet unresolved questions of how many members of the Trump campaign were complicit in the Russian operation, and how much they knew.[43] The critical point is that Moscow was undeterred. For specialists in national security, this is only one of many features of cyberwar that are perplexing. Accustomed to the elegant theories of 'mutually assured destruction' that evolved during the Cold War, they are struggling to develop a doctrine for an entirely different form of conflict, in which there are countless potential attackers, many of them hard to identify, and multiple gradations of destructiveness. As the deputy secretary of defence, William Lynn, observed in 2010, 'Whereas a missile comes with a return address, a computer virus generally does not.' For Joseph Nye of Harvard's Kennedy School, deterrence may be salvageable, but that may be true only if the United States is prepared to make an example of an aggressor. The three other options Nye proposes are to ramp up cyber security, to try to 'entangle' potential aggressors in trade and other relationships (so as to raise the cost of cyber-attacks to them), and to establish global taboos against cyber akin to the ones that have (mostly) discouraged the use of biological and chemical weapons.[44] This analysis is not very comforting. Given the sheer number of cyber aggressors, defence seems doomed to lag behind offence, in an inversion of conventional military logic. And the Russians have proved themselves to be indifferent to both entanglement and taboos, even if China may be more amenable to Nye's approach. Indeed, the Russian government seems willing to enter into partnerships with organized criminals in pursuit of its objectives.[45]

How frightened should we be of Cyberia? For Anne-Marie Slaughter, our hyper-networked world is, on balance, a benign place and the 'United States . . . will gradually find the golden mean of network power.'[46] True, there are all kinds of networked threats ('terrorism . . . drug, arms, and human trafficking . . . climate change and declining biodiversity . . . water wars and food insecurity . . . corruption, money laundering, and tax evasion . . . pandemic disease'), but if America's leaders can only 'think in terms of translating chessboard alliances into hubs of connectedness and capability', all should come right. The key, she argues, is to convert hierarchies into networks, turning NATO into 'the hub of a network of security partnerships and a centre for consultation on international security issues', and reforming the United Nations Security Council, the International Monetary Fund and the World Bank by opening them up to 'newer actors'.[47] The institutions of world order established after the Second World War need to metamorphose into 'hubs of a flatter, faster, more flexible system, one that operates at the level of citizens as well as states', incorporating 'good web actors, corporate, civic, and public'. One example she gives is the Global Covenant of Mayors for Climate and Energy, which connects more than 7,100 cities around the world.[48] Another is the Open Government Partnership launched by the Obama administration in 2011, which now includes seventy countries committed to 'transparency, civic participation, and accountability'.[49] Ian Klaus, formerly Slaughter's colleague at the State Department, sees potential in a network of global cities.[50]

Can the 'good actors' join together in a new kind of geopolitical network, pitting their 'webcraft' against the bad actors? Joshua Cooper Ramo is doubtful. He agrees with Slaughter that 'the fundamental threat to American interests isn't China or Al Qaeda or Iran. It is the evolution of the network itself.' However, he is less sanguine about how easily the threat can be combated. Cyber defence lags ten years behind cyber-attack, not least because of a new version of the impossible trinity: 'Systems can be fast, open, or secure, but only two of these three at a time.'[51] The threat to world order can be summed up as 'very fast networks x artificial intelligence x black boxes x the New Caste x compression of time x everyday objects x weapons'.[52] In *The Seventh Sense*, Ramo argues for the erection of real and virtual 'gates' to shut out the Russians, the online criminals, the teenage net vandals and other malefactors. Yet Ramo himself quotes the three rules of computer security devised by the NSA cryptographer Robert Morris Sr.: 'RULE ONE: Do not own a computer. RULE TWO: Do not power it on. RULE THREE: Do not use it.'[53] If we all continue to ignore those new categorical imperatives – and especially our leaders, most of whom have not even enabled two-factor authentication on their email accounts – how will any gates keep out the likes of Assange and Guccifer?

An intellectual arms race is now under way to devise a viable doctrine of cyber security. It seems unlikely that those steeped in the traditional thinking of national security will win it. Perhaps the realistic goal is not to deter attacks or retaliate against them but to regulate all the various networks on which our society depends so that they are resilient – or, better still, 'anti-fragile', a term coined by Nassim Taleb to describe a system that grows stronger under attack.[54] Those, like Taleb, who inhabit the world of financial risk management, saw in 2008 just how fragile the international fina network was: the failure of a single investment bank nearly broug the whole system of global credit tumbling down. The rest of us hav now caught up with the bankers and traders – we are all now as interconnected as they were a decade ago. Like the financial network, our social, commercial and infrastructural networks are under constant attack from fools and knaves, and there is very little indeed that we can do to deter them. The best we can do is to design and build our networks so that they can withstand the ravages of Cyberia. That means resisting the temptation to build complexity when (as in the case of financial regulation) simplicity is a better option.[55] Above all, it means understanding the structures of the networks we create.

When half the nodes of a random graph the size of most real-world networks are removed, the network is destroyed. But when the same procedure is carried out against a scale-free model of a similar size, 'the giant connected component resists even after removing more than 80 per cent of the nodes, and the average distance within it [between nodes] is practically the same as at the beginning'.[56] That is a vitally important insight for those whose task is to design networks that can be anti-fragile in the face of a deliberate, targeted attack.

59
FANG, BAT and EU

In March 2017 the House of Commons Home Affairs Committee, led by its chair, Yvette Cooper, attacked Google, Facebook and Twitter for not doing enough to censor the Internet on their behalf. Cooper complained that Facebook had failed to take down a page with the title 'Ban Islam'. As she put it: 'We need you to do more and to have more social responsibility to protect people.'[1] In the same week, the German justice minister, Heiko Maas, unveiled a draft law that would impose fines of up to €50 million on social networks that fail to delete 'hate speech' or 'fake news'. In his words: 'Too little illegal content is being deleted and it's not being deleted sufficiently quickly.'[2]

One can argue for and against censorship of odious content. One can marvel that companies and government agencies would spend money on online advertising so indiscriminately that their carefully crafted slogans end up on jihadist websites. However, arguing that Google and Facebook should do the censoring is not just an abdication of responsibility; it is evidence of unusual naivety. As if these two companies were not already mighty enough, European politicians apparently want to give them the power to limit their citizens' free expression.

There are three essential points to understand about the IT revolution. The first is that it was almost entirely a US-based achievement, albeit with contributions from computer scientists who flocked to Silicon Valley from all over the world, and Asian manufacturers who drove down the costs of hardware. Secondly, the most important of the US tech companies are now extraordinarily dominant. Thirdly, as we have seen, this dominance translates into huge amounts of money. Confronted with this American network revolution, the rest of the world had two options: capitulate and regulate, or exclude and compete. The Europeans chose the former. You will look in vain for a European search engine, a European online retailer, a European social network. The biggest EU-based Internet company is Spotify, the Stockholm-based music and video streaming company founded in 2006.[3] The FANG has been sunk deep into the EU, and all the European Commission can do now is to harass the US giants with antitrust charges, backdated tax bills, and tighter rules on privacy and data protection, not to mention employment rights.[4] To be sure, the Europeans led the way in establishing that American companies could not operate in their territory independently of national or European law. It was a Frenchman, Marc Knobel, who established that Yahoo could not advertise Nazi memorabilia on its auction sites, not least because the server through which French users accessed the site was located in Europe (in Stockholm), but also because Yahoo was not (as it claimed) incapable of distinguishing French from other users.[5] A number of European countries – not only France but also Britain and Germany – have passed laws that require Internet Service Providers to block proscribed content (such as paedophile pornography) from being viewed by their citizens. Yet the European political elites now effectively rely on US companies such as Facebook to carry out censorship on their behalf, seemingly oblivious to the risk that Facebook's 'community standards' may end up being stricter than European law.[6]

The Chinese, by contrast, opted to compete. This was not the response predicted by Americans, who assumed that Beijing would simply try to 'control the Internet' – an endeavour President Bill Clinton famously likened to 'trying to nail Jell-O to the wall'.[7] 'The Internet is a porous web,' wrote one American academic in 2003, 'and if people in China . . . want to get information from sites in Silicon Valley, even the most omnipotent of governments will be hard pressed to stop them.'[8] This was not quite right. Certainly, there has been censorship. Since 2012, when Lu Wei was put in charge of the Central Leading Group for Cyberspace Affairs, China has increased the effectiveness of its Great Firewall, which blocks access to tens of thousands of Western websites, as well as its Golden Shield, which carries out online surveillance, and its Great Cannon, which can be used to attack hostile websites. Microblogs and social networks such as Sina Weibo are policed aggressively, with prison sentences for those convicted of posting false or subversive information online. In September 2016, to give just one example of how the authorities operate, Netease was forced by the government to close down all of its online forums, except for those on real estate and home.[9] Although a good deal of online criticism of the government is tolerated, the censors quickly shut down all calls for unofficial collective action of any kind.[10]

Yet censorship is not the key to the Chinese response to the networked age. The core of the strategy has been, by fair means and foul, to limit the access of the big American IT companies to the Chinese market and to encourage local entrepreneurs to build a Chinese answer to FANG. While Yahoo and Microsoft accepted government-mandated 'self-discipline',[11] Google pulled out of China in 2010 after repeated wrangles with the Chinese authorities over censorship and attacks on human rights activists' Gmail accounts. Ever since it registered the domain name www.facebook.cn in 2005, Facebook has tried to establish itself in China, but it was blocked in 2009, when Western social media companies were accused of fomenting unrest in mainly Muslim Xinjiang.[12] The result is that the Internet in China today is dominated by BAT: Baidu (the search engine, founded by Robin Li in 2000), Alibaba (Jack Ma's answer to Amazon, founded in 1999), and Tencent (created the year before by Ma Huateng, best known for its WeChat messaging app). These conglomerates are much more than clones of their US counterparts; each has shown itself to be innovative in its own right – and, with a combined market value in excess of $473bn and annual revenues of $20bn, they are almost as large in scale as their US counterparts. WeChat is used by 86 per cent of the Chinese Internet's users and is fast replacing the once mandatory Asian business card with easy-to-snap QR codes. Alibaba's revenue in China exceeded Amazon's in the United States in 2015; its share of total retail revenue in China (over 6 per cent) is twice that of Amazon's in the US.[13]

Needless to say, Silicon Valley gnashes its fangs at being shut out of the vast Chinese market. Zuckerberg has not yet given up hope, giving interviews in fluent Mandarin and even jogging through the smog of Tiananmen Square, but the recent experience of Uber cannot encourage him. Last year, after incurring losses in excess of $1bn a year, Uber ran up the white flag, accepting that it could not beat the home-grown ride-sharing business Didi Chuxing.[14] This outcome was a result partly of Didi's great agility and deeper pockets, but partly also of regulatory changes that seemed designed to put Uber at a disadvantage in the Chinese market.[15] The frustration of American companies with these and other setbacks is understandable. Yet it is hard not be impressed by the way China took on Silicon Valley and won. It was not only smart economically; it was smart politically and strategically, too. In Beijing, 'Big Brother' now has the big data he needs to keep very close tabs on Chinese netizens. Meanwhile, if it wants to collect metadata from the Middle Kingdom, the NSA has to get past the Great Firewall of China.

The conventional wisdom in the West remains that the Networked Age is as inimical to the rule of the Chinese Communist Party as it was to the Soviet Union. But there are those who beg to differ.[16] For one thing, the Party itself is a sophisticated network, in which nodes are interconnected by edges of patronage and peer or co-worker association. On the basis of betweenness centrality, for example, Xi Jinping is as powerful as any leader since Jiang Zemin, and much more powerful than Deng Xiaoping, with whom he is sometimes wrongly compared by Western commentators.[17] Network analysis is allowing students of Chinese government to move away from simplistic theories about factions and to realize the subtlety of modern *guanxi*. Cheng Li has emphasized the importance of mentor–protégé ties in Xi's ascent to power – those relationships between senior Party figures and their right-hand men (*mishu*). Those who distinguish between an elitist 'Jiang-Xi camp' and the populist 'Hu-Li camp' are exaggerating the rigidities of faction. Xi himself rose from being secretary to the then minister of defence, Geng Biao, to hold county-level and provincial positions in Hebei, Fujian, Zhejiang and Shanghai, where he built up his own network of protégés, including figures as different as the 'economic technocrat' Liu He and the 'conservative military hawk' Liu Yuan.[18] As Franziska Keller argues, China is better understood in terms of such networks of mentorship than in terms of factions. Other important networks include the one formed by

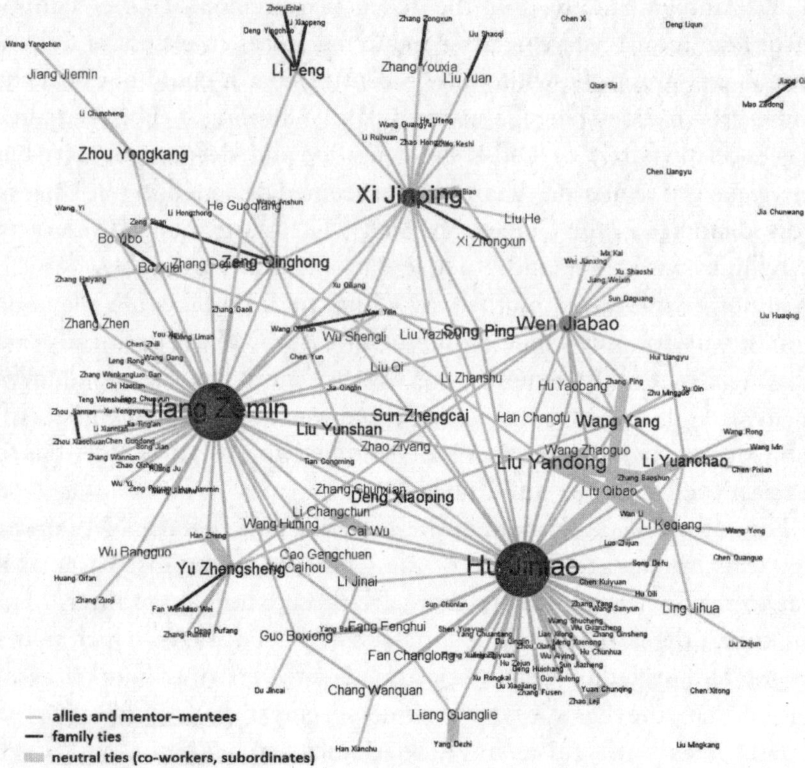

50. The Chinese Communist Party Central Committee members' network. The size of the node is proportional to the number of connections (degree), the size of the name proportional to betweenness centrality. Note how ties between mentors and mentees matter much more than family ties.

members of Xi's leading small groups[19] and the one connecting corporations to banks via the bond market.[20]

Far from wanting to nail Jell-O to the wall, the Chinese approach to social media is increasingly to take advantage of what microblogs reveal about citizens' concerns. When researchers from Hong Kong, Sweden and the United States mined a dataset of more than 13 billion blog posts on Sina Weibo between 2009 and 2013, they were surprised to find that 382,000 posts alluded to social conflicts and as many as 2.5 million mentioned mass protests such as strikes. The hypothesis is that the authorities are now using social media to monitor dissent, as well as to police corruption. Significantly, of 680 officials accused of corruption on Weibo, those eventually charged were mentioned nearly ten times more often than those not charged.[21] Another dataset – of 1,460 officials investigated for corruption between 2010 and 2015 – provides a further insight into the networks that run China, in this case the network of 'tigers and flies' (i.e. big and small offenders) whose misconduct has become a key target of Xi Jinping's government.[22] The possibility exists that information and computer technology could enable Beijing to build a system of 'social credit', analogous to financial credit in the West, that would (in official parlance) 'allow the trustworthy to roam everywhere under heaven while making it hard for the discredited to take a single step'.[23] China already has established systems of *hukou* (household registration) and *dang'an* (personal records), as well as schemes for rewarding outstanding workers and Party cadres. Integrating these with the data that the authorities can easily glean from the BAT companies would provide a system of social control beyond the dreams of the mid-twentieth-century totalitarian states.

At the same time, China's leaders seem much more adept at 'webcraft' than their American counterparts. While the Trans Pacific Partnership seems likely to expire due to the withdrawal of US support by the Trump administration, Chinese initiatives such as the Belt and Road initiative and the Asian Infrastructure Investment Bank are steadily attracting new participants. A fascinating test of the Chinese approach will be how far they are able to leapfrog ahead of the United States in the rapidly growing sector of financial technology. Since ancient times, states have exploited their ability to monopolize the issuance of currency, whether coins stamped with the king's likeness, banknotes depicting past presidents or electronic entries on a screen. However, blockchain-based digital currencies such as Bitcoin or Ethereum offer many advantages over a fiat currency like the US dollar or the Chinese yuan. As a means of payment – especially for online transactions – Bitcoin is faster and cheaper than a credit card or wire transfer. As a store of value, it has many of the key attributes of gold, notably finite supply. As a unit of account, to be sure, it is less than stable, but that is because it has become an attractive speculative object: digital gold. Worse, Bitcoin seems extraordinarily wasteful of computer resources because of the fact that it is 'mined' or 'hashed' and authenticated.[24] On the other hand, Bitcoin's distributed ledger technology appears to solve the problem of authentication and security so well that Bitcoin can also function as a fraud-proof messaging technology, while Ethereum can even automate the enforcement of contracts, without the need for the expensive bureaucratic monitoring that is an integral and expensive part of the existing system of national and international payments.[25] In short, 'trust is distributed, personalized, socialized . . . without the need for a central institution for verification'.[26] Of course, the Chinese authorities are no more ready to hand their payments system over to Bitcoin than they are to hand their taxi system over to Uber. Indeed, they are alarmed that 40 per cent of the global Bitcoin network is already accounted for by Chinese 'miners', while close to three quarters of Bitcoin trades are on the BTCC (Bitcoin China) exchange. However, Beijing clearly appreciates the potential of blockchain as a technology. That is why the People's Bank of China and a number of provincial governments are close to launching an 'official crypto-currency' – 'Bityuan', perhaps – in one or two provinces in the near future.[27] Singapore may beat Beijing in the race to introduce the first official cryptocurrency, but Beijing will surely beat Washington, DC.[28] If the Chinese experiments are successful, it would represent the beginning of a new epoch in monetary history, and a serious challenge to the dollar's future as the principal international currency.

60

The Square and the Tower Redux

At times, it seems as if we are condemned to try to understand our own time with conceptual frameworks more than half a century old. Since the financial crisis, many economists have been reduced to recycling the ideas of John Maynard Keynes, who died in 1946. Confronted with populism, writers on American and European politics repeatedly confuse it with fascism, as if the era of the world wars is the only history they have ever studied. Analysts of international relations seem to be stuck with terminology that dates from roughly the same period: realism or idealism, containment or appeasement, deterrence or disarmament. George Kennan's 'Long Telegram' was despatched just two months before Keynes's death; Hugh Trevor-Roper's *Last Days of Hitler* was published the following year. Yet all this was seventy years ago. Our own era is profoundly different from the mid-twentieth century. The near-autarkic, commanding and controlling states that emerged from the Depression, the Second World War and the early Cold War exist today, if at all, only as pale shadows of their former selves. The bureaucracies and party machines that ran them are defunct or in decay. The administrative state is their final incarnation. Today, the combination of technological innovation and international economic integration has created entirely new forms of network – ranging from the criminal underworld to the rarefied 'overworld' of Davos – that were scarcely dreamt of by Keynes, Kennan or Trevor-Roper.

Winston Churchill famously observed, 'The longer you can look back, the farther you can look forward.' We, too, must look back longer and ask ourselves the question: is our age likely to repeat the experience of the period after 1500, when the printing revolution unleashed wave after wave of revolution?[1] Will the new networks liberate us from the shackles of the administrative state as the revolutionary networks of the sixteenth, seventeenth and eighteenth centuries freed our ancestors from the shackles of spiritual and temporal hierarchy? Or will the established hierarchies of our time succeed more quickly than their imperial predecessors in co-opting the networks, and enlist them in their ancient vice of waging war?

A libertarian utopia of free and equal netizens – all interconnected, sharing all available data with maximum transparency and minimal privacy settings – has a certain appeal, especially to the young. It is romantic to imagine these netizens, like the workers in Lang's *Metropolis*, spontaneously rising up against the world's corrupt elites, then unleashing the might of artificial intelligence to liberate themselves from the drudgery of work, too. Those who try to look forward without looking back very easily fall into the trap of such wishful thinking. Since the mid-1990s, computer scientists and others have fantasized about the possibility of a 'global brain' – a self-organizing 'planetary superorganism'.[2] In 1997 Michael Dertouzos looked forward to an era of 'computer-aided peace'.[3] 'New information technologies open up new vistas of non-zero sumness,' wrote one enthusiast in 2000. Governments that did not react swiftly by decentralizing would be 'swiftly . . . punished'.[4] N. Katherine Hayles was almost euphoric. 'As inhabitants of globally interconnected networks,' she wrote in 2006, 'we are joined in a dynamic co-evolutionary spiral with intelligent machines as well as with the other biological species with whom we share the planet.' This virtuous upward spiral would ultimately produce a new 'cognisphere'.[5] Three years later, Ian Tomlin envisioned 'infinite forms of federations between people . . . that overlook . . . differences in religion and culture to deliver the global compassion and cooperation that is vital to the survival of the planet'.[6] 'The social instincts of humans to meet and share ideas,' he declared, 'might one day be the single thing that saves our race from its own self destruction.'[7] 'Informatization,' wrote another author, would be the third wave of globalization.[8] 'Web 3.0' would produce 'a contemporary version of a "Cambrian explosion"' and act as 'the power-steering for our collective intelligence'.[9]

The masters of Silicon Valley have every incentive to romanticize the future. Balaji Srinivasan conjures up heady visions of the millennial generation collaborating in computer 'clouds', freed from geography, and paying each other in digital tokens, emancipated from the state payment systems. Speaking at the 2017 Harvard Commencement, Mark Zuckerberg called on the new graduates to help 'create a world where everyone has a sense of purpose: by taking on big meaningful projects together, by redefining equality so everyone has the freedom to pursue purpose, and by building community across the world'. Yet Zuckerberg personifies the inequality of superstar economics. Most of the remedies he envisages for inequality – 'universal basic income, affordable childcare, healthcare that [isn't] tied to one company . . . continuous education' – cannot be achieved globally but are only viable as national policies delivered by the old twentieth-century welfare state. And when he says that 'the struggle of our time' is between 'the forces of freedom, openness and global community against the forces of authoritarianism, isolationism and nationalism,' he seems to have forgotten just how helpful his company has been to the latter.[10]

Histories of futurology give us little reason to expect much, if any, of the Silicon Valley vision of utopia to be realized. Certainly, if Moore's Law continues to hold, computers should be able to simulate the human brain by around 2030. But why would we expect this to have the sort of utopian outcomes imagined in the preceding paragraph? Moore's Law has been in operation at the earliest since Charles Babbage's 'Analytical Engine' was (partly) built before his death in 1871, and certainly since the Second World War. It cannot be said that there has been commensurate exponential improvement in our productivity, much less our moral conduct as a species. There is a powerful case to be made that the innovations of the earlier industrial revolutions were of more benefit to mankind than those of the most recent one.[11] And if the principal consequence of advanced robotics and artificial intelligence really is going to be large-scale unemployment,[12] the chances are surely quite low that a majority of mankind[13] will uncomplainingly devote themselves to harmless leisure pursuits in return for some modest but sufficient basic income. Only the sedative-based totalitarianism imagined by Aldous Huxley would make such a social arrangement viable.[14] A more likely outcome is a repeat of the violent upheavals that ultimately plunged the last great Networked Age into the chaos that was the French Revolution.[15]

Moreover, the suspicion cannot be dismissed that, despite all the utopian hype, less benign forces have already learned how to use and abuse the 'cognisphere' to their advantage. In practice, the Internet depends for its operation on submarine cables, fibre-optic wires, satellite links and enormous warehouses full of servers. There is nothing utopian about the ownership of that infrastructure, nor the oligopolistic arrangements that make ownership of major web platforms so profitable. Vast new networks have been made possible but, like the networks of the past, they are hierarchical in structure, with small numbers of super-connected hubs towering over the mass of sparsely connected nodes. And it is no longer a mere possibility that this network can be instrumentalized by corrupt oligarchs or religious fanatics to wage a new and unpredictable kind of war in cyberspace. That war has commenced. Indices of geopolitical risk suggest that conventional and even nuclear war may not be far behind.[16] Nor can it be ruled out that a 'planetary superorganism' created by the Dr Strangeloves of artificial intelligence may one day run amok, calculating – not incorrectly – that the human race is by far the biggest threat to the long-run survival of the planet itself and exterminating the lot of us.[17]

'I thought once everybody could speak freely and exchange information and ideas, the world is automatically going to be a better place,' said Evan Williams, one of the co-founders of Twitter in May 2017. 'I was wrong about that.'[18] The lesson of history is that trusting in networks to run the world is a recipe for anarchy: at best, power ends up in the hands of the Illuminati, but more likely it ends up in the hands of the Jacobins. Some today are tempted to give at least 'two cheers for anarchism'.[19] Those who lived through the wars of the 1790s and 1800s learned an important lesson that we would do well to re-learn: unless one wishes to reap one revolutionary whirlwind after another, it is better to impose some kind of hierarchical order on the world and to give it some legitimacy. At the Congress of Vienna, the five great powers agreed to establish such an order, and the pentarchy they formed provided a remarkable stability for the better part of the century that followed. Just over 200 years later, we confront the same choice they faced. Those who favour a world run by networks will end up not with the interconnected utopia of their dreams but with a world divided between FANG and BAT and prone to all the pathologies discussed above, in which malignant sub-networks exploit the opportunities of the World Wide Web to spread virus-like memes and mendacities.

The alternative is that another pentarchy of great powers recognizes their common interest in resisting the spread of jihadism, criminality and cyber-vandalism, to say nothing of climate change. In the wake of the 2017 WannaCry episode, even the Russian government must understand that no state can hope to rule Cyberia for long: that malware was developed by the American NSA as a cyber weapon called EternalBlue, but was stolen and leaked by a group calling themselves the Shadow Brokers. It took a British researcher to find its 'kill switch', but only after hundreds of thousands of computers had been infected, including American, British, Chinese, French and Russian machines. What could better illustrate the common interest of the great powers in combating Internet anarchy? Conveniently, the architects of the post-1945 order created the institutional basis for such a new pentarchy in the form of the permanent members of the UN Security Council, an institution that retains the all-important ingredient of legitimacy. Whether or not these five great powers can make common cause once again, as their predecessors did in the nineteenth century, is the great geopolitical question of our time.[20]

Six centuries ago, in Siena, the Torre del Mangia of the Palazzo Publico cast a long shadow over the Piazza del Campo, the fan-like space that was by turns a marketplace, a meeting place and, twice a year, a racetrack. The tower's height was to make a point: it reached exactly the same elevation as the city's cathedral, which stood on Siena's highest hill, symbolizing the parity of temporal and spiritual hierarchies.[21] A century ago, in Lang's *Metropolis*, hierarchical power was symbolized by the skyscrapers of Manhattan, which still keep the south and east of Central Park in shade for large portions of the day.[22] When the first great towers were built in New York, they seemed to be appropriately imposing accommodation for the hierarchical corporations that dominated the US economy.

By contrast, today's dominant technology companies eschew the vertical. Facebook's headquarters in Menlo Park, designed by Frank Gehry, is a sprawling campus of open-plan offices and play-areas – a 'single room that fits thousands of people', in Mark Zuckerberg's words, or (perhaps more accurately) an immense kindergarten for geeks. The main building at the new 'Apple Park' in Cupertino is a gigantic circular spaceship with only four storeys (above ground) – 'a centre for creativity and collaboration', designed by the late Steve Jobs, Norman Foster and Jonathan Ive as if to host a lattice-like network, each node an equal, with a uniform number of edges, but just one restaurant.[23] Google's new headquarters in Mountain View, set amid 'trees, landscaping, cafes, and bike paths', will be made of 'lightweight block-like structures which can be moved around easily', as if constructed from Lego and located in a nature reserve: an office without foundations or a floor-plan, mimicking the constantly evolving network it hosts.[24] Silicon Valley prefers to lie low, and not only for fear of earthquakes. Its horizontal architecture reflects the reality that it is the most important hub of a global network: the world's town square.

On the other side of the United States, however – on New York City's 5th Avenue – there looms a fifty-eight-storey building that represents an altogether different organizational tradition.* And no one individual in the world has a bigger say in the choice between networked anarchy and world order than the absent owner of that dark tower.

* The top floor is marked '68,' because the man whose name the building bears maintains, characteristically, that it is a sixty-eight-storey building. However, the sixth through to the thirteenth floors of Trump Tower simply do not exist.

Afterword

The Original Square and Tower: Networks and Hierarchies in *Trecento* Siena

To explain why this book is called *The Square and the Tower*, the reader must come with me to Siena. Walk across the shell-shaped Piazza del Campo to the Palazzo Pubblico, passing under the shadow of the campanile, the majestic Torre del Mangia. Nowhere in the world will you see so elegantly juxtaposed the two forms of human organization depicted in this book: around you, a public space purpose-built for all kinds of more or less informal human interaction; above you, an imposing tower intended to symbolize and project secular power. A central theme of this book is that the tension between distributed networks and hierarchical orders is as old as humanity itself. It exists regardless of the state of technology, though technology may affect which has the upper hand. Siena exemplifies this point, for the architecture of its square and its tower predates the advent of the printing press in Europe. The Torre del Mangia was built in the fourteenth century alongside the Palazzo Pubblico, which was itself completed in 1312. The brick-paved piazza also dates from the *Trecento*.[1]

Many people today make the mistake of thinking that the Internet has fundamentally changed the world. Yet, as a recent majority ruling of the United States Supreme Court noted, the Internet is merely 'the modern public square', in the words of Justice Anthony Kennedy.[2] The problems of 2017 are not nearly so novel as we would like to imagine. Does the president's predilection for authoritarian rule presage the end of the republic? Might social and political division

51. Lorenzetti's vision of a malign hierarchy, with the diabolical Tyrammides enthroned. Above the tyrant hover Avarice, Pride and Vainglory. Below lies Justice, bound and helpless.

escalate into civil strife? Might the challenge posed by a rising power to an incumbent power lead to war? Such questions would not have seemed unfamiliar to the men who erected the Torre del Mangia. If you doubt it, step inside the Palazzo Pubblico and ascend to its second storey. There, on the walls of the Sala dei Nove (Room of the Nine), you will find startling evidence that the dichotomy between network and hierarchy is an ancient idea.

The frescoes painted by Ambrogio Lorenzetti in the Sala dei Nove are among the greatest achievements of fourteenth-century Italian art. I first encountered them as an impecunious graduate student in the mid-1980s. So deeply did the frescoes impress me that, despite my straitened circumstances, I purchased reproductions of two of

Lorenzetti's scenes. I think they were the first pictures I ever bought, and I have faithfully hung them in a succession of studies – at Oxford, Harvard and Stanford – despite the fact that they are cheap and barely decipherable. Imperceptibly, almost by osmosis, they have influenced my thinking. Indeed, they are probably the reason Siena sprang to mind when I was trying to find a title for this book.

The frescoes were intended to inspire the nine elected officials who ruled the republic of Siena at that time. Each served for only two months at a time, but during that period the Nine lived in the Palazzo, apart from their families – in other words, separated from the dynastic networks that dominated Italian city-states in the time of the Renaissance. In a larger adjoining room, the Sala del Consiglio, the Sienese general council met (in effect, the legislature). However, according to the city's written constitution, the Nine were the executive and (in secular cases) the judicial branch. Painted between February 1338 and May 1339, the frescoes were designed to remind the Nine of just how much was at stake as they made their decisions.

The murals cover three of the four walls of the Sala dei Nove; only the south wall, which has the room's sole window, is not decorated.[3] Turn your back to the window and you see on the left (western) wall the fresco known to contemporaries as *War*. Facing you on the north wall is the fresco known to scholars as the *Allegory of Good Government* – clearly intended as the centrepiece, as it is the best lit of the three.[4] And, to your right, on the eastern wall, is *Peace*.

Scholars have long debated Lorenzetti's sources of inspiration. For many years, it was believed that the frescoes were intended to exemplify ideas about justice in the works of Aristotle (the *Nicomachaean Ethics*) and Saint Thomas Aquinas (his *Summa Theologica*). A more obvious debt is to the thirteenth-century Florentine writer Brunetto Latini, author of *Li Livres dou trésor* (c. 1260–65) and his abridged *Tesoretto*. More recent accounts have identified the astrological origins of much of the imagery as well as the veiled allusions to recent Tuscan history (in particular the rivalry between Siena and Pisa).

Early descriptions such as Lorenzo Ghiberti's from the early fifteenth century suggest that the original intent was simply to contrast 'the extortions made during war' with 'that which pertains to peace, [for example] how merchants' caravans travel . . . in utmost safety, how they leave their goods in the woods, and how they return for them'. In a sermon delivered nearly ninety years after the frescoes' completion, the Franciscan Saint Bernardino referred to them simply is 'la pace e la guerra':

> When I turn to peace, I see commercial activity; I see dances, I see houses being repaired; I see vineyards and fields being cultivated and sown, I see people going to the baths, on horses, I see girls going to marry, I see flocks of the sheep, etc. And I see a man being hanged in order to maintain holy justice. And for this [reason] everyone lives in holy peace and concord. On the other hand, when I turn to the other [fresco], I do not see commerce; I do not see dances, [I see] killing; no houses being repaired, [they are] damaged and burnt; the fields are not being cultivated; the vineyards are cut down; there is no sowing, the baths are not used nor [are there] other delights, I do not see anyone going out. Oh women! Oh men! The man is dead, the woman raped, the herds are prey [to predators]; men treacherously kill one another; Justice lies on the ground, her scales broken, she is bound, her hands and legs are bound. And everything is done with fear. But the Apocalypse, in the thirteenth chapter, presents war in the figure of a beast coming out of the sea with ten horns and seven heads, like a leopard, and with the feet of a bear. What do these ten horns signify, if not to be in opposition to the Ten Commandments? [The beast] with seven heads, for the seven mortal sins, appears as a leopard, for treachery; [with the] feet of a bear, that is full of revenge. Yet [by] forgiving, you end and eliminate the war.[5]

However, as this passage suggests, the terms 'peace' and 'war' need to be understood broadly – not in Tolstoy's sense of the relations between states, but in the more ancient contrast between civic harmony and the strife likely to arise from a tyrannical government. The *Allegory of Good Government* has been well summed up as 'a pictorial realization of the concept of *civitas* as the fundamental form of human association'.[6] The scenes of urban and rural peace on the eastern wall are intended to depict all the benefits of a well-governed city-state. The opposite wall is the antithesis, depicting all the costs of misrule.

Lorenzetti provided the central allegorical mural with a helpful explanatory inscription: 'This holy virtue [Justice], where she rules, induces to unity the many souls [of citizens], and they, gathered together for such a purpose, make the Common Good [*ben comune*] their Lord; and he, in order to govern his state, chooses never to turn his eyes from the resplendent faces of the Virtues who sit around him. Therefore to him in triumph are offered taxes, tributes, and lordship of towns; therefore, without war, every civic result duly follows – useful, necessary, and pleasurable.' On the left side of the wall sits Justice, with Heavenly Wisdom above her and, at her sides, a red angel and a white angel representing the Aristotelian categories of commutative and distributive justice. Looming even larger on the right side is a bearded patriarch clearly intended to personify the commonwealth of Siena itself (*ben comune*).[7] Sitting on his right (the viewer's left) is the reclining, almost erotic figure of Peace, olive branch in hand, and the more severe figures of Fortitude and Prudence.[8] On his other side are Magnanimity, Temperance and (another) Justice. Above them hover Faith, Charity and Hope.[9]

Of more interest to the modern eye, however, are the rather less imposing figures below this row of civic virtues. Seated at the feet of the larger personification of Justice, on the left, is Concord, and in a line next to her are twenty-four representatives of the *popolo grasso* – the prosperous citizenry from which the Nine were drawn. Strikingly, each of them is holding a rope, made up of two strands, one from each of Justice's scales, which Concordia winds into one. This rope is passed by them towards the figure of *ben comune*, whose right wrist it binds.[10] For Quentin Skinner, this clinches the case that the entire fresco was intended as a celebration of republican self-government, an illustration of Latini's claim that the 'good of the people' required that '*signorie* should be held by the commune itself'.[11] Yet it might also be said that Lorenzetti's image of a rope binding the urban elite together, and connecting them to the principles of justice and the commonwealth itself, was an anticipation of the modern conception of a social and indeed political network.[12]

Such interpretations are always in danger of being anachronistic. Lorenzetti makes it perfectly clear that effective military force is integral to good government: the knights in armour tower over not only the prosperous burghers but also their prisoners-of-war, who are bound together with a very different kind of rope. Nevertheless, the modern viewer cannot fail to be struck by the absence of soldiers from the eastern wall's two images of the peaceful city and its rural *contado*.

It has been argued persuasively that the cityscape on the east wall is 'literally a vision' of the allegorical figure of Peace on the north wall.[13] Clearly, the city is intended to be Siena: we see the *duomo* in the top left-hand corner, the Porta Romana in the centre and the nearby port of Telamon (Talamone).[14] However, this is an idealized Siena, exemplifying 'the cosmic harmony of communal life.' Again, the artist spells out what we are supposed to see:

> Turn your eyes to behold her, you who are governing, who is portrayed here [Justice], crowned on account of her excellence, who always renders to everyone his due. Look how many goods derive from her and how sweet and peaceful is that life of the city where is preserved this virtue who outshines any other. She guards and defends those who honour her, and nourishes and feeds them . . . requiting those who do good and giving due punishment to the wicked.

A casual glance might lead to the erroneous inference that economic prosperity is the sole benefit of just governance. However, as Saint Bernardino observed, not all the activities in the city are commercial. We also see a teacher instructing his pupils, for example, while the central group in the foreground are dancers, almost certainly (despite initial appearances) young men participating in a public dance – known as the *tripudium* – to express their joy at the state of peace. Likewise, the scene of peace in the countryside depicts not only trade and agriculture but also hunting. 'Without fear,' reads the inscription in the top left, 'every man may travel freely and each may till and sow, so long as this commune shall maintain this lady [Justice] sovereign, for she has stripped the wicked of all power.'

To all of this, the war-torn city depicted on the west wall stands in stark contrast. Just as allegorical figures dominate the north wall, so here we have Tyrammides, a diabolical cross-eyed monster with horns and fangs, a dagger in his right hand, his foot resting on a goat. Above the tyrant hover Avarice, Pride and Vainglory. To the left are Cruelty, Treason and Fraud; to the right, Fury, Division – immolating herself with a carpenter's saw – and War.[15] At the tyrant's feet lies Justice, bound and helpless. Though much of the lower part of this fresco has been damaged, we can discern scenes of murder, assault and destruction of property. 'Because each seeks only his own good,' we read, 'in this land Justice is subjected to Tyranny: wherefore along this road nobody passes without fearing for his life . . . since there are robberies outside and inside the city gates.'[16] It has been suggested that this unhappy city was intended to be Siena's rival, Pisa.[17] More likely, it was intended to exemplify all that Siena was not: a city under autocratic rule and therefore bereft of both peace and prosperity. Originally there were portraits of tyrannical emperors (Nero, Caracalla, Gaeta and Antiochus) in the lower border of the fresco.[18]

For its time, Lorenzetti's masterpiece was remarkably sympathetic to the self-governing city-state and hostile to both monarchy and empire. It would be too much to say that the artist was a prophet of the networked age that would dawn a century and half later; but certainly he was ahead of his time in so explicitly linking government based on the rule of law to economic prosperity and social cohesion. It must be remembered that not only Europe but most of Eurasia at this time was dominated by varieties of despotic rule. Siena's Golden Age from around 1260 until 1348 coincided with the rise and fall of the Mongol empire. It was a time when Sienese merchants travelled as far as Tabriz to buy silks from Central Asia, a time when the Pope received emissaries from the Yuan emperor Toghon Temür.[19] Though it is long lost, Lorenzetti's other contribution to the decoration of the Palazzo Pubblico was a rotatable *Mappamondo* that was sixteen feet in diameter and showed Siena at the centre of a commercial network extending across Eurasia.[20]

The tragedy was that precisely this trade network would provide the vectors along which the Black Death was transmitted. Bubonic plague struck Siena in 1348, less than a decade after the completion of *Peace and War*, and probably claimed Lorenzetti as one of its victims. That ended Siena's halcyon days.[21] Yet the frescoes in the Sala dei Nove have survived nearly 700 years, to provide us with a memorable reminder that the problems of war and peace – and of good and bad government – are nothing new. Technologies come and go. The world remains a world of squares and towers.

Appendix

GRAPHING SOCIAL NETWORKS IN THE NIXON–FORD ERA

In chapter 45, I use social network analysis (SNA) to examine Henry Kissinger's role in the Nixon and Ford administrations and, more generally, the relationships within those administrations, using as source material all the memoirs written and published by members of the two administrations. Readers interested in SNA will want to know more about figures 30–33, which are part of an ongoing research project on social networks in collaboration with Manny Rincon-Cruz, as well as my continuing work on the life of Henry Kissinger.

Most SNA projects map out relationships in a simple binary way – there either is or is not a connection between two actors – often captured in the form of a binary matrix. Most SNA computational methods are based only on such matrices, because, for a long time, most datasets from academia (e.g. those produced by sociologists and political scientists) were of this sort, and it is only recently that today's rapidly growing social media platforms have begun to provide more nuanced data. Even so, complicated datasets are still often simplified to allow researchers to use the binary approach. To the historian, this is problematic, as we are keenly interested in the different types of relationship that exist between individuals. Moreover, in medium-sized groups, a binary approach tends to reveal that more or less everyone is connected to everyone else, a close to worthless finding. SNA cannot easily distinguish between love and hate, least of all in the political realm, where friendship and enmity can be hard to distinguish. However, it is possible to identify the relative importance of relationships.

Slightly fewer than half of the individuals who served in significant roles in the Nixon and Ford administrations wrote memoirs that covered their time in government. To identify our sources, we first compiled a list of White House cabinet members, and then added a number of sub-cabinet-level individuals, sub-secretaries in key departments, anyone with sources and writings as listed in the Nixon Memorial Library, and any member of the administrations who had written a book on the Nixon and Ford years if found on Stanford's library system, Amazon and WorldCat. From this master list we again used Stanford, Amazon and WorldCat to identify all their writings. We then began a process of exclusion. Memoirs that were included were those that covered the entirety of an individual's tenure in the White House. Thus, for example, Kissinger's book on ending the Vietnam War was excluded. We also excluded books that were not memoirs or recollections, and books that were mainly or wholly compilations of primary sources.

We used these writings to approximate the extent to which actors remembered other individuals as having played a role in the politics of the age and in their own work for the administrations. The underlying phenomenon we were trying to capture in our analysis was the number of discrete events in which a writer remembered another historical actor. As a proxy, we relied on the careful labour already expended by authors, editors and publishers in indexing memoirs. Thus, the building block of our dataset was the number of pages in which an actor was mentioned in each memoir.

Obviously, there are significant variations in memoir length, memoir coverage, and how many words publishers put on the average page. Some of our writers covered their entire lives; others only their time in government. To allow for such variation, we avoided an absolute measure of how frequently an individual appeared in a memoir, because what we wanted to know was how important a given actor was in a writer's memoir relative to other Nixon and Ford administration actors in the social network. Thus we took the number of pages in which an individual was mentioned and divided it by the sum of the number of times all Nixon and Ford administration memoir writers were mentioned. Some memoirs span more than one volume, and some authors wrote more than one memoir. In both cases, we considered them to form one text, and so for each administration member we simply summed the number of mentions across volumes or books. This produced a number in the range [0,1], and we used this to calculate the strength of connection from the writer to the individual mentioned.

The area of the nodes in our graphs is scaled to the number of times an individual is mentioned. For our social network graph (figure 33), this corresponds to the inbound degree centrality of that individual, which is calculated by adding the weights of all inbound connections to that individual. In essence, this represents a frequency-normalized share of all mentions by all White House administration writers. Betweenness centrality has been calculated using directed, weighted edges rather than, as is done in most studies, merely by using the binary existence or non-existence of an edge connection.

Our visualizations use the D3 software package. The distance in the three ego graphs is proportional to the size of the nodes. The distance and arrangement of nodes on the social graph (figure 33) has no intrinsic meaning, and relies on D3's force-directed layout. The versions published here are screenshots of dynamic renderings from our web server.

One obvious defect of our approach is that not every member of the Nixon and Ford White House administrations wrote memoirs. One notable omission – notable because he is mentioned relatively frequently by others – is John N. Mitchell, Nixon's loyal Attorney General. Mitchell is the only Attorney General in US history to have served a prison term, a fate he suffered when he refused to cut any deals with those investigating the Watergate scandal. Mitchell also refused to write a memoir out of that same sense of loyalty. Yet the strikingly non-linear distribution of mentions means that even the addition of numerous other 'missing' memoirs would do little to change how influential an individual is in terms of degree or betweenness centrality. Like a number of other social networks discussed in this book, the Nixon–Ford social network seems to be governed, roughly speaking, by a power law.

Finally, it should be stressed that the Nixon–Ford graphs are not representations of the frequency or intensity of communication between individuals, which are the kind of measures sociologists and psychologists use to examine a social bond. Rather they seek to capture the importance that one individual had in the recollection of another – or, at least, the importance as the memoir writer wished to convey it to a reader. It is entirely possible that the distribution of values for frequency and intensity, if someone were to have detailed enough evidence and sources to construct these, would be different.

BOOKS USED IN NIXON–FORD NETWORK ANALYSIS

Agnew, Spiro T., *Go Quietly . . . Or Else* (New York: Morrow, 1980)

Bush, George H. W., *Looking Forward: An Autobiography* (Garden City, NY: Doubleday, 1987)

——— and Brent Scowcroft, *A World Transformed* (Garden City, NY: Alfred A. Knopf, 1998)

Cheney, Dick, *In My Time: A Personal and Political Memoir* (New York: Simon & Schuster, 2011)

Colby, William E., *Honorable Men: My Life in the CIA* (New York: Simon & Schuster, 1978)

Coleman, William T. with Donald T. Bliss, *Counsel for the Situation: Shaping the Law to Realize America's Promise* (Washington, DC: Brookings Institution, 2010)

Colson, Charles W., *Born Again* (Old Tappan, NJ: Chosen Books, 1976)

Connally, John B., *In History's Shadow: An American Odyssey* (New York: Hyperion, 1993)

Dean, John W., III, *Blind Ambition: The White House Years* (New York: Simon & Schuster, 1976)

Dent, Harry S., *The Prodigal South Returns to Power* (New York: John Wiley & Sons, 1978)

Ehrlichman, John D., *Witness to Power: The Nixon Years* (New York: Simon & Schuster, 1982)

Ford, Gerald R., *A Time to Heal: The Autobiography of Gerald R. Ford* (London: W. H. Allen, 1979)

Garment, Leonard, *Crazy Rhythm: My Journey from Brooklyn, Jazz, and Wall Street to Nixon, Watergate, and Beyond* (New York: Times Books, 1997)

Gergen, David R., *Eyewitness to Power: The Essence of Leadership, Nixon to Clinton* (New York: Touchstone, 2000)

Gulley, Bill and Mary Ellen Reese, *Breaking Cover* (New York: Simon & Schuster, 1980)

Haig, Alexander M., Jr., *Inner Circles: How America Changed the World: A Memoir* (New York: Warner Books, 1992)

Haldeman, H. R., *The Haldeman Diaries: Inside the Nixon White House* (New York: G. P. Putnam's, 1994)

Hartmann, Robert T., *Palace Politics: An Inside Account of the Ford Years* (London: McGraw Hill, 1980)

Helms, Richard M., *A Look Over My Shoulder: A Life in the Central Intelligence Agency* (New York: Presidio Press, 2004)

Hill, Clint and Lisa McCubbin, *Five Presidents: My Extraordinary Journey with Eisenhower, Kennedy, Johnson, Nixon, and Ford* (New York: Gallery Books, 2017)

Kissinger, Henry A., *White House Years* (Boston: Little, Brown, 1979)

———, *Years of Renewal* (New York: Simon & Schuster, 1999)

———, *Years of Upheaval* (Boston: Little, Brown, 1982)

Klein, Herbert G., *Making It Perfectly Clear* (Garden City, NY: Doubleday, 1980)

Kleindienst, Richard G., *Justice: The Memoirs of Attorney General Richard G. Kleindienst* (Ottawa, IL: Jameson Books, 1985)

Larzelere, Alex, *Witness to History: White House Diary of a Military Aide to President Richard Nixon* (Bloomington, IN: AuthorHouse, 2009)

Liddy, G. Gordon, *Will: The Autobiography of G. Gordon Liddy* (New York: St. Martin's Press, 1995)

Lungren, John C., *Healing Richard Nixon: A Doctor's Memoirs* (Lexington, KY: University Press of Kentucky, 2003)

Magruder, Jeb Stuart, *An American Life: One Man's Road to Watergate* (New York: Atheneum, 1974)

Mollenhoff, Clark, *Game Plan for Disaster: An Ombudsman's Report on the Nixon Years* (New York: Norton, 1976)

Moynihan, Daniel P., *A Dangerous Place* (New York: Little Brown & Company, 1978)

———, *A Portrait in Letters of an American Visionary* (New York: PublicAffairs, 2010)

Nessen, Ron H., *It Sure Looks Different from the Inside* (New York: Playboy Paperbacks, 1979)

Nixon, Richard M., *RN: The Memoirs of Richard Nixon* (New York: Simon & Schuster, 1990)

Peterson, Peter G., *The Education of an American Dreamer: How a Son of Greek Immigrants Learned His Way from a Nebraska Diner to Washington, Wall Street, and Beyond* (New York: Grand Central Publishing, 2009)

Price, Raymond Kissam, *With Nixon* (New York: Viking, 1977)

Richardson, Elliot L., *The Creative Balance: Government, Politics, and the Individual in America's Third Century* (New York: Holt, Rinehart, 1976)

———, *Reflections of a Radical Moderate* (Boulder, CO: Westview Press, 2000)

Rumsfeld, Donald H., *Known and Unknown: A Memoir* (London: Penguin Books, 2011)

Safire, William, *Before the Fall: An Inside View of the pre-Watergate White House* (New Brunswick, NJ, and London: Transaction Publishers, 2005)
Saxbe, William B., *I've Seen the Elephant: An Autobiography* (Kent, OH: Kent State University Press, 2000)
Seaborg, Glenn T. with Benjamin S. Loeb, *The Atomic Energy Commission under Nixon: Adjusting to Troubled Times* (London: Palgrave Macmillan, 1993)
Schlesinger, James R., *America at Century's End* (New York: Columbia University Press, 1989)
Shultz, George P., *Economic Policy beyond the Headlines* (Stanford, CA: Stanford Alumni Association, 1977)
———, *Learning from Experience* (Stanford, CA: Hoover Institution Press, 2016)
Simon, William E., *A Time for Action* (New York: Berkley Publishing Group, 1980)
———, *A Time for Truth* (New York: Reader's Digest Press, 1978)
Stans, Maurice H., *One of the Presidents' Men: Twenty Years with Eisenhower and Nixon* (Washington, DC: Brassey's Inc, 1995)
Ulasewicz, Tony, *The President's Private Eye: The Journey of Detective Tony U. from NYPD to the Nixon White House* (Westport, CT: MACSAM Publishing, 1990)
Usery, William J., Jr, *Laboring for America: Memoirs of Bill Usery* (Macon, GA: Stroud & Hall Publishers, 2015)
Walters, Vernon A., *Silent Missions* (Garden City, NY: Doubleday, 1978)
Weinberger, Caspar W., *In the Arena: A Memoir of the Twentieth Century* (Washington, DC: Regnery Publishers, 2001)
Yost, Charles W., *History and Memory: A Statesman's Perceptions of the Twentieth Century* (New York: W. W. Norton & Company, 1980)
Zumwalt, Elmo R., Jr, *On Watch: A Memoir* (New York: Quadrangle, 1976)

References

1. INTRODUCTION: NETWORKS AND HIERARCHIES

1. The Mystery of the Illuminati

1. Agethen, *Geheimbund und Utopie*, 72.
2. Markner, Neugebauer-Wölk and Schüttler (eds.), *Korrespondenz des Illuminatenordens*, xxi.
3. Van Dülmen, *Society of the Enlightenment*, 110f. Krueger, *Czech, German and Noble*, 65.
4. Markner, Neugebauer-Wölk and Schüttler (eds.), *Korrespondenz des Illuminatenordens*, xiv.
5. Over 2,000 according to some sources, e.g. Krueger, *Czech, German and Noble*, 65. In fact, only 1,343 names of Illuminati are known for sure: see the list at https://projekte.uni-erfurt.de/illuminaten/Mitglieder_des_Illuminatenordens and Schüttler, *Mitglieder des Illuminatenordens.*
6. Van Dülmen, *Society of the Enlightenment*, 105f.
7. More details of aristocratic membership in Melanson, *Perfectibilists.*
8. Agethen, *Geheimbund und Utopie*, 76.
9. Ibid., 234f.
10. Israel, *Democratic Enlightenment*, 748ff. On Bode's important contribution, not least as a record-keeper, see Simons and Meumann, '"Mein Amt ist geheime gewissens Correspondenz und unsere Brüder zu führen"'.
11. Israel, *Democratic Enlightenment*, 751.
12. Ibid., 300f.
13. Ibid., 842; Krueger, *Czech, German and Noble*, 66.
14. See Hofman, 'Opinion, Illusion and the Illusion of Opinion'.
15. See e.g. Payson, *Proofs of the Real Existence.*
16. Hofstadter, *Paranoid Style.*
17. McArthur, '"They're Out to Get Us"', 39.

18. Massimo Introvigne, '*Angels & Demons* from the Book to the Movie FAQ – Do the Illuminati Really Exist?', http://www.cesnur.org/2005/mi_illuminati_en.htm.
19. http://illuminati-order.com/; http://illuminati-order.org/newworldorder/.
20. Robert Howard, 'United States Presidents and The Illuminati/Masonic Power Structure', 28 September 2001: http://www.webcitation.org/5w4mwTZLG.
21. See e.g. http://theantichristidentity.com/barack-obama-illuminati.htm.
22. Wes Penre, 'The Secret Order of the Illuminati (A Brief History of the Shadow Government)', 12 November 1998 (updated 26 September 2009).
23. See e.g. Oliver and Wood, 'Conspiracy Theories'.
24. Ibid., 959.
25. Ibid., 956.
26. Ibid.
27. See e.g. https://www.infowars.com/george-soros-illuminati-behind-blm/.
28. Oliver and Wood, 'Conspiracy Theories', 964.
29. Knight, 'Outrageous Conspiracy Theories', 166.
30. Swami et al., 'Conspiracist Ideation in Britain and Austria'.
31. Livers, 'The Tower or the Labyrinth'.
32. Landes, 'The Jews as Contested Ground'.
33. Massimo Introvigne, '*Angels & Demons* from the Book to the Movie FAQ – Do the Illuminati Really Exist?' http://www.cesnur.org/2005/mi_illuminati_en.htm.
34. Markner, Neugebauer-Wölk and Schüttler (eds.), *Korrespondenz des Illuminatenordens*; Wäges and Markner (eds.), *Secret School of Wisdom*.
35. Roberts, *Mythology of the Secret Societies*, vii.

2. Our Networked Age

1. Margit Feher, 'Probe into Deaths of Migrants in Hungary Uncovers "Vast Network"', *Wall Street Journal*, 12 October 2016.
2. Herminia Ibarra and Mark Lee Hunter, 'How Leaders Create and Use Networks', *Harvard Business Review*, January 2007.
3. Athena Vongalis-Macrow, 'Assess the Value of Your Networks', *Harvard Business Review*, 29 June 2012.
4. Lauren H. Cohen and Christopher J. Malloy, 'The Power of Alumni Networks', *Harvard Business Review*, October 2010.
5. Andrew Ross Sorkin, 'Knowledge is Money, But the Peril is Obvious', *The New York Times*, 26 November 2012. See Enrich, *Spider Network*.

6. See Andrew Haldane, 'On Tackling the Credit Cycle and Too Big to Fail', January 2011: http://www.iiea.com/event/download_powerpoint?urlKey=andrew-haldane-on-fixingfinance.
7. Navidi, *Superhubs*, esp. xxiv, 83f., 84f., 95, 124f.
8. https://www.youtube.com/watch?v=vST61W4bGm8.
9. 'Assessing Russian Activities and Intentions in Recent US Elections', 6 January 2016: http://apps.washingtonpost.com/g/page/politics/the-intelligence-community-report-on-russian-activities-in-the-2016-election/2153/.
10. Donald J. Trump, speech on 15 August 2016: https://assets.donaldjtrump.com/Radical_Islam_Speech.pdf; speech at AIPAC, 21 March 2016: http://time.com/4267058/donald-trump-aipac-speech-transcript/.
11. Ito and Howe, *Whiplash*.
12. Ramo, *Seventh Sense*, 92.
13. Adrienne Lafrance, 'The Age of Entanglement', *The Atlantic*, 8 August 2016.
14. Khanna, *Connectography*.
15. Castells, *Rise of the Network Society*, 508.
16. Friedland, 'Electronic Democracy'. See also Boeder, 'Habermas's Heritage'.
17. Schmidt and Cohen, *New Digital Age*, 7.
18. Grewal, *Network Power*, 294.
19. Anne-Marie Slaughter, 'How to Succeed in the Networked World', *Foreign Affairs*, (November/December 2016), 76.
20. Slaughter, *Chessboard and the Web*, KL 2893–4.
21. Khanna, *Connectography*, 139.
22. See Kissinger, *World Order*, 347.
23. Martin Belam, 'We're Living Through the First World Cyberwar—But Just Haven't Called It That', *Guardian*, 30 December 2016.
24. Harari, *Homo Deus*, 344, 395.
25. Harari, *Sapiens*, KL 6475.
26. See e.g. Vinod Khosla, 'Is Majoring in Liberal Arts a Mistake for Students?' *Medium*, 10 February 2016: https://medium.com/@vkhosla/is-majoring-in-liberal-arts-a-mistake-for-students-fd9d20c8532e.

3. Networks, Networks Everywhere

1. West, *Scale*. See also Strogatz, 'Exploring Complex Networks'.
2. Watts, 'Networks, Dynamics, and the Small-World Phenomenon', 515.

3. West, 'Can There be a Quantitative Theory', 211f.
4. Caldarelli and Catanzaro, *Networks*, 23f.
5. Dittrich, *Patient H.M.*
6. Christakis and Fowler, *Connected*, 97.
7. Vera and Schupp, 'Network Analysis', 418f.
8. Jackson, 'Networks in the Understanding of Economic Behaviors', 8.
9. Liu, King and Bearman, 'Social Influence'.
10. Henrich, *Secret of Our Success*, 5.
11. Dunbar, 'Coevolution of Neocortical Size'.
12. Christakis and Fowler, *Connected*, 239.
13. Tomasello, 'Two Key Steps'.
14. Massey, 'Brief History', 3–6.
15. McNeill and McNeill, *Human Web*, 319–21.
16. Jackson, Rodriguez-Barraquer and Tan, 'Social Capital and Social Quilts'.
17. Banerjee et al., 'Gossip'.
18. https://www.youtube.com/watch?v=nLykrziXGyg.
19. See e.g. *Othello*, II, 3, and III, 4; *All's Well That Ends Well*, IV, 3.
20. *Oxford English Dictionary.*
21. See http://www.nggprojectucd.ie/phineas-finn/.

4. Why Hierarchies?

1. Massey, 'Brief History', 14.
2. Laura Spinney, 'Lethal Weapons and the Evolution of Civilisation', *New Scientist*, 2886 (2012), 46–9.
3. Dubreuil, *Human Evolution*, 178, 186, 202.
4. Turchin et al., 'War, Space, and the Evolution of old World Complex Societies'.
5. Gorky, *My Universities*, 69.
6. See most recently Acemoglu and Robinson, *Why Nations Fail.*
7. Boisot, *Information Space* and *Knowledge Assets.*
8. Powell, 'Neither Market nor Hierarchy', 271f.
9. Rhodes, 'New Governance'.
10. Thompson, *Between Hierarchies and Markets.*
11. Boisot and Lu, 'Competing and Collaborating in Networks'.

5. From Seven Bridges to Six Degrees

1. Caldarelli and Catanzaro, *Networks*, 9.
2. See Heidler et al., 'Relationship Patterns'.
3. Moreno, *Who Shall Survive?* xiii, lxvi.
4. Crane, 'Social Structure in a Group of Scientists'.
5. James E. Rauch, review of Jackson, *Social and Economic Networks*, in *Journal of Economic Literature*, 48, 4 (December 2010), 981.
6. Leskovec, Huttenlocher, and Kleinberg, 'Signed Networks in Social Media'.
7. McPherson et al., 'Birds of a Feather', 419.
8. Currarini et al., 'Identifying the Roles of Race-Based Choice and Chance'. See also Moody, 'Race, School Integration, and Friendship Segregation'.
9. Vera and Schupp, 'Network Analysis', 409.
10. Milgram, 'Small-World Problem'.
11. Watts, *Six Degrees*, 134. See also Schnettler, 'Structured Overview'.
12. Barabási, *Linked*, 29.
13. Jennifer Schuessler, 'How Six Degrees Became a Forever Meme', *The New York Times*, 19 April 2017.
14. Jackson, Rogers and Zenou, 'Connections in the Modern World'.
15. Davis, Yoo and Baker, 'The Small World of the American Corporate Elite'.
16. Lars Backstrom, Paolo Boldi, Marco Rosa, Johan Ugander, and Sebastiano Vigna, 'Four Degrees of Separation', 22 June 2012: https://research.fb.com/publications/four-degrees-of-separation/.
17. Smriti Bhagat, Moira Burke, Carlos Diuk, Ismail Onur Filiz, and Sergey Edunov, 'Three and a Half Degrees of Separation', 4 February 2016: https://research.fb.com/three-and-a-half-degrees-of-separation/.

6. Weak Ties and Viral Ideas

1. Granovetter, 'Strength of Weak Ties'.
2. Granovetter, 'Strength of Weak Ties Revisited', 202.
3. See also Tutic and Wiese, 'Reconstructing Granovetter's Network Theory'. Recent research using Facebook data largely confirms Granovetter's thesis: Laura K. Gee, Jason Jones and Moira Burke, 'Social Networks and Labor Markets: How Strong Ties Relate to Job Finding on Facebook's Social Network', 13 January 2016: https://research.

fb.com/publications/social-networks-and-labor-markets-how-strong-ties-relate-to-job-transmission-on-facebooks-social-network/.

4. Liu, King, and Bearman, 'Social Influence'.
5. Watts and Strogatz, 'Collective Dynamics of "Small-World" Networks'.
6. Watts, 'Networks, Dynamics, and the Small-World Phenomenon', 522.
7. Powell, 'Neither Market nor Hierarchy', 301, 304.
8. Calvó-Armengol and Jackson, 'The Effects of Social Networks on Employment and Inequality'.
9. Smith-Doerr and Powell, 'Networks and Economic Life'.
10. Bramoullé et al., 'Homophily and Long-Run Integration'; Jackson and Rogers, 'Meeting Strangers and Friends of Friends'.
11. Greif, 'Reputation and Coalitions in Medieval Trade' and 'Contract Enforceability and Economic Institutions'.
12. Coleman, 'Social Capital'.
13. Burt, *Structural Holes*, KL 46–9.
14. Burt, *Brokerage and Closure*, 7. See also Burt, *Neighbor Networks*.
15. Burt, 'Structural Holes and Good Ideas', 349f.
16. Carroll and Teo, 'On the Social Networks of Managers', 433.
17. Harrison and Carroll, 'Dynamics of Cultural Influence Networks', 18.
18. Goldberg et al., 'Fitting In or Standing Out?' 2f.
19. Berger, *Contagious*. See also Sampson, *Virality*.
20. For a good discussion see Collar, *Religious Networks*, 13f.
21. Katz and Lazarsfeld, *Personal Influence*.
22. Hill, 'Emotions as Infectious Diseases'.
23. Dolton, 'Identifying Social Network Effects'.
24. Christakis and Fowler, *Connected*, 22.
25. Kadushin, *Understanding Social Networks*, 209f.
26. Nahon and Hemsley, *Going Viral*.
27. Centola and Macy, 'Complex Contagions'.
28. Watts, *Six Degrees*, 249.

7. Varieties of Network

1. Rosen, 'The Economics of Superstars'.
2. Barabási and Albert, 'Emergence of Scaling in Random Networks'.
3. Barabási, *Linked*, 33–4, 66, 68f., 204.
4. Ibid., 221.
5. Ibid., 103, 221.
6. Dolton, 'Identifying Social Network Effects'.

7. Strogatz, 'Exploring Complex Networks'.
8. Cassill and Watkins, 'Evolution of Cooperative Hierarchies', 41.
9. Ferguson, 'Complexity and Collapse'.

8. When Networks Meet

1. Padgett and McLean, 'Organizational Invention and Elite Transformation'.
2. Padgett and Powell, *Emergence of Organizations and Markets*, KL 517f.
3. Loreto et al., 'Dynamics and Expanding Spaces'.
4. Barabási, *Linked*, 113–18.
5. Ibid., 135.
6. Castells, 'Information Technology, Globalization and Social Development', 6.
7. Mayer and Sinai, 'Network Effects, Congestion Externalities'.
8. Amy Zegart, 'Cyberwar', TEDxStanford: https://www.youtube.com/watch?v=JSWPoeBLFyQ.
9. Michael McFaul and Amy Zegart, 'America Needs to Play Both the Short and Long Game in Cybersecurity', *Washington Post*, 19 December 2016.
10. See e.g. Heylighen, 'From Human Computation to the Global Brain' and 'Global Superorganism'.
11. See e.g. Bostrom, *Superintelligence*.
12. Slaughter, 'How to Succeed in the Networked World', 84f.; Slaughter, *The Chessboard and the Web*, KL 2642–3, 2738.
13. Allison, 'Impact of Globalization'.
14. Ramo, *Seventh Sense*, 82, 118, 122.
15. See e.g. Tomlin, *Cloud Coffee House*.
16. Fukuyama, *Great Disruption*, 224. See also Fukuyama, *Origins of Political Order*, 13f., and *Political Order and Political Decay*, 35f.
17. Dominic Cummings, 'Complexity, "Fog and Moonlight", Prediction, and Politics II: Controlled Skids and Immune Systems', blog post, 10 September 2014: https://dominiccummings.wordpress.com/2014/09/10/complexity-fog-and-moonlight-prediction-and-politics-ii-controlled-skids-and-immune-systems/.

9. Seven Insights

1. On eigenvector centrality, see Cline and Cline, 'Text Messages, Tablets, and Social Networks', 30f.
2. Bennett, *History Boys*.

10. The Illuminati Illuminated

1. Agethen, *Geheimbund und Utopie*, 70f.; Israel, *Democratic Enlightenment*, 828f. Cf. Stauffer, *New England and the Bavarian Illuminati*, 142–228.
2. Wäges and Markner (eds.), *Secret School of Wisdom*, 14.
3. Ibid., 15.
4. Van Dülmen, *Society of the Enlightenment*, 55f.
5. See Schüttler, 'Zwei freimaurerische Geheimgesellschaften'. This ferment culminated in 1782 at the *Konvent* of German lodges held in Wilhelmsbad.
6. Hataley, 'In Search of the Illuminati'.
7. Israel, *Democratic Enlightenment*, 836.
8. Van Dülmen, *Society of the Enlightenment*, 106ff.
9. Markner, Neugebauer-Wölk and Schüttler (eds.), *Korrespondenz des Illuminatenordens*, xxiii.
10. Hataley, 'In Search of the Illuminati'. See also Markner, Neugebauer-Wölk and Schüttler (eds.), *Korrespondenz des Illuminatenordens*, xix.
11. Details of the 'New Plan for the Order' of Dec. 1782 are in Agethen, *Geheimbund und Utopie*, 75f. Cf. Wäges and Markner (eds.), *Secret School of Wisdom*, passim, and https://projekte.uni-erfurt.de/illuminaten/Grade_und_Instruktionen_des_Illuminatenordens.
12. Wäges and Markner (eds.), *Secret School of Wisdom*, 13.
13. Agethen, *Geheimbund und Utopie*, 112f.
14. Simons and Meumann, '"Mein Amt ist geheime gewissens Correspondenz und unsere Brüder zu führen"'.
15. Wäges and Markner (eds.), *Secret School of Wisdom*, 31ff.
16. Israel, *Democratic Enlightenment*, 831f.
17. Ibid., 841.
18. Agethen, *Geheimbund und Utopie*, 82.
19. Meumann and Simons, 'Illuminati', col. 881.
20. Melanson, *Perfectibilists*, KL 913.

21. Simons and Meumann, '"Mein Amt ist geheime gewissens Correspondenz und unsere Brüder zu führen"'.

II. EMPERORS AND EXPLORERS

11. A Brief History of Hierarchy

1. Cassill and Watkins, 'Evolution of Cooperative Hierarchies'.
2. Tomasello, 'Two Key Steps'.
3. Smail, *Deep History.*
4. McNeill and McNeill, *Human Web.*
5. Dubreuil, *Human Evolution*, 191.
6. Turchin at al., 'War, Space, and the Evolution of old World Complex Societies'.
7. Spinney, 'Lethal Weapons and the Evolution of Civilisation'.
8. Gellner, *Nations and Nationalism*, 10. See Ishiguro, *Buried Giant.*
9. Cline and Cline, 'Text Messages, Tablets, and Social Networks', 29.
10. Cline, 'Six Degrees of Alexander', 68f.
11. Tainter, 'Problem Solving', 12.
12. Allen and Heldring, 'Collapse of the World's Oldest Civilization'.
13. Malkin, *Small Greek World.*
14. Syme, *Roman Revolution*, 4, 7f.
15. Frankopan, *Silk Roads*, KL 118.
16. Christian, 'Silk Roads or Steppe Roads?'
17. Scheidel, 'From the "Great Convergence" to the "First Great Divergence"'.
18. Stark, 'Epidemics, Networks, and the Rise of Christianity'.
19. Harland, 'Connections with Elites in the World of the Early Christians', 391.
20. Collar, *Religious Networks.*
21. Fukuyama, *Origins of Political Order*, 273.
22. Ibid.
23. Ibid., 141–5.

12. The First Networked Age

1. Jackson, Rogers and Zenou, 'Connections in the Modern World'.
2. Barnett, (ed.), *Encyclopedia of Social Networks*, vol. I, 124.
3. For more on this subject, see Ferguson, *Civilization.*

4. Padgett and Ansell, 'Robust Action and the Rise of the Medici'.
5. Padgett, 'Marriage and Elite Structure in Renaissance Florence', 92f.
6. Padgett and McLean, 'Organizational Invention and Elite Transformation', 1463, 1467, 1545.
7. Ibid., 1545. See also Padgett and Powell, *Emergence of Organizations and Markets*, 810–14, 855–60, 861–7.

13. The Art of the Renaissance Deal

1. Cotrugli, *Book of the Art of Trade*, 3f.
2. Ibid., 24.
3. Ibid., 24.
4. Ibid., 5.
5. Ibid., 6.
6. Ibid., 57.
7. Ibid., 7.
8. Ibid., 7.

14. Discoverers

1. Rodrigues and Devezas, *Pioneers of Globalization.*
2. Chang, *Sino-Portuguese Trade*, 62.
3. Wills (ed.), *China and Maritime Europe*, 336.
4. Wade, 'Melaka in Ming Dynasty Texts', 34.
5. Sen, 'Formation of Chinese Maritime Networks'.
6. Wade, 'Melaka in Ming Dynasty Texts', 51.
7. Wills (ed.), *China and Maritime Europe*, 39

15. Pizarro and the Inca

1. Smith, 'Networks, Territories, and the Cartography of Ancient States', 839f., 845.
2. Garcia-Zamor, 'Administrative Practices', 152–64. See also Heady, *Public Administration*, 163f.
3. Fukuyama, *Political Order and Political Decay*, 249–51.
4. Burbank and Cooper, *Empires in World History*, 163–6.
5. Morrissey, 'Archives of Connection'.

6. Barnett (ed.), *Encyclopedia of Social Networks*, vol. II, 703f.
7. Katarzyna et al., 'Genome-Wide Patterns of Population Structure'.
8. Zuñiga, Jean-Paul, 'Visible Signs of Belonging'.

16. When Gutenberg Met Luther

1. Dittmar, 'Information Technology and Economic Change'.
2. Naughton, *From Gutenberg to Zuckerberg*, 15–21.
3. Pettegree, *Brand Luther*, 334.
4. Dittmar and Seabold, 'Media, Markets, and Radical Ideas'.
5. Elizabeth Eisenstein, quoted in Gleick, *The Information*, 399
6. Ahnert and Ahnert, 'Protestant Letter Networks in the Reign of Mary I', 6.
7. Ibid., 27f.
8. Ahnert and Ahnert 'Metadata, Surveillance, and the Tudor State'.
9. For a new and comprehensive account, see Eire, *Reformations*.
10. Adamson, *Noble Revolt*.
11. Namier, *Structure of Politics*.

III. LETTERS AND LODGES

17. The Economic Consequences of the Reformation

1. Owen, *Clash of Ideas in World Politics*, 34f.
2. Cantoni, Dittmat and Yuchtman, 'Reformation and Reallocation'.
3. Dittmar, 'Welfare Impact of a New Good'.
4. Dittmar, 'Ideas, Technology and Economic Change'.
5. Dittmar, 'Welfare Impact of a New Good'.
6. Schich et al., 'Network Framework of Cultural History'.

18. Trading Ideas

1. Taylor et al., 'Geohistorical Study of "the Rise of Modern Science"'.
2. Hatch, 'Between Erudition and Science', 51, 55.
3. Ibid., 55.
4. Edelstein et al., 'Historical Research in a Digital Age', 411–13.
5. Lux and Cook, 'Closed Circles or Open Networks?'

6. From the 1661 Royal Charter: http://royalsociety.org/uploadedFiles/Royal_Society_Content/about-us/history/Charter1_English.pdf.
7. Rusnock, 'Correspondence Networks', 164.
8. Lux and Cook, 'Closed Circles or Open Networks?' 196f.
9. Carneiro et al., 'Enlightenment Science in Portugal'.
10. Lamikiz, *Trade and Trust*, 152.
11. See Gestrich and Beerbühl (eds.), *Cosmopolitan Networks*, and Caracausi and Jeggle (eds.), *Commercial Networks*.
12. Hancock, 'Trouble with Networks', 486–8.
13. Ibid., 489.
14. Erikson and Bearman, 'Malfeasance and the Foundations for Global Trade'.
15. Erikson, *Between Monopoly and Free Trade,* figure 5.
16. Erikson and Bearman, 'Malfeasance and the Foundations for Global Trade', 219.
17. Erikson, *Between Monopoly and Free Trade,* 19.
18. Ibid., 26.
19. Erikson and Bearman, 'Malfeasance and the Foundations for Global Trade', 226f.
20. Rothschild, *Inner Life of Empires.*
21. Ibid. See also http://www.fas.harvard.edu/~histecon/innerlife/index.html.
22. http://www.fas.harvard.edu/~histecon/innerlife/geography.html.

19. Networks of Enlightenment

1. Edelstein et al., 'Historical Research in a Digital Age', 405.
2. Comsa et al., 'French Enlightenment Network', 498.
3. Ibid., 502.
4. Ibid., 507.
5. Ibid., 511.
6. Ibid., 513.
7. Goodman, 'Enlightenment Salons'. See also Goodman, *Republic of Letters* and (for a somewhat different view) Lilti, *World of the Salons.*
8. Comsa et al., 'French Enlightenment Network', 530.
9. Danskin, '"Hotbed of Genius"', 11.
10. Arcenas and Winterer, 'Correspondence Network of Benjamin Franklin'.
11. Winterer, 'Where is America in the Republic of Letters?'

20. Networks of Revolution

1. Starr, *Creation of the Media.*
2. Fischer, *Paul Revere's Ride*, KL 102–4.
3. Ibid., KL 128–33.
4. Gladwell, *Tipping Point*, 32, 35.
5. Ibid., 56f.
6. Ibid., 59f.
7. Wood, *American Revolution*, KL 568–9.
8. Middlekauff, *Glorious Cause*, KL 4437–45. See also Borneman, *American Spring*, KL 439–51.
9. Borneman, *American Spring*, KL 81–96.
10. Ibid., KL 1707–14.
11. Ibid., KL 1930–39.
12. Middlekauff, *Glorious Cause*, KL 4800–4824.
13. Ibid., KL 4825–31.
14. Borneman, *American Spring*, KL 2096–2138.
15. Ibid., KL 2175–81.
16. Han, 'Other Ride of Paul Revere'.
17. York, 'Freemasons', 315.
18. Morse, *Freemasonry and the American Revolution*, 23, 37, 41, 46, 50, 52, 62, 64f.
19. Bailyn, *Ideological Origins.*
20. York, 'Freemasons', 318.
21. Ibid., 325.
22. Clark, *Language of Liberty.*
23. York, 'Freemasons', 320.
24. Ibid., 320.
25. Ibid., 328.
26. Hackett, *That Religion*, 198f.
27. York, 'Freemasons', 323.
28. Hodapp, *Solomon's Builders*, 66f.
29. I am grateful to Joe Wäges for providing me with the relevant pages of the minute book for 30 November and 16 December 1773. The earlier meeting was adjourned 'on account of the few Brethren present (NB; Consignees of Tea took up the Brethren's Time)'. A contemporaneous drawing of the Green Dragon bears an inscription that reads: 'Where we met to Plan the Consignment of a few Shiploads of Tea. Dec. 16, 1773.' It is signed 'John Johnson, 4 Water Street, Boston'.

30. York, 'Freemasons', 326.
31. Hackett, *That Religion*, 198f.
32. Bullock, *Revolutionary Brotherhood*, 106f.
33. Ibid., 112f.
34. Ibid., 152f.
35. Ibid., 156.
36. Ibid., 301.
37. Alexander Immekus, 'Freemasonry', http://www.mountvernon.org/digital-encyclopedia/article/freemasonry/.
38. Patterson and Dougall, *Eagle and Shield*.
39. Hamilton, *Complete Works*, KL 84174–8.
40. Ibid., KL 35483–7.
41. Tocqueville, *Democracy in America*, Book I, chapter 2, Part I.
42. Ibid., Book I, chapter 12.
43. Ibid., Book II, chapter 5.

IV. THE RESTORATION OF HIERARCHY

21. The Red and the Black

1. Stendhal, *The Red and the Black*, KL 4034, 7742–3, 8343–5.

22. From Crowd to Tyranny

1. Tackett, 'La grande peur'.
2. Lefebvre, *Great Fear*, 207ff.
3. See in general Andress (ed.), *Oxford Handbook of the French Revolution*.
4. Roberts, *Napoleon*, KL 1586–91, 2060–65.
5. Ibid., KL 9658–84.
6. Ibid., KL 9645–8.
7. Ibid., KL 9651–7.
8. Ibid., KL 9505–10.
9. Ibid., KL 10215–19.
10. Ibid., KL 9658–84.
11. Ibid., KL 6981–7, 7015–21, 9239–48.
12. Shy, 'Jomini'.
13. Clausewitz, *On War*, Book 8, ch. 6B.

23. Order Restored

1. Ranke, 'Great Powers'.
2. Kissinger, *World Restored*, KL 102–19.
3. Ibid., KL 702–8. For a thorough discussion of Castlereagh's suicide, see Bew, *Castlereagh*, ch. 21.
4. Kissinger, *World Restored*, KL 1606–8.
5. Ibid., KL 5377–8, 5389.
6. Ibid., KL 5396–9.
7. Ibid., KL 6398–6400.
8. Ibid., 179.
9. Ibid., 80, 82.
10. Schroeder, *Transformation*, vii.
11. Slantchev, 'Territory and Commitment'.
12. Clark, *Hegemony in International Society.*
13. Holsti, 'Governance Without Government', 156.
14. Clark, *Hegemony in International Society*, 94–6.
15. Holsti, 'Governance Without Government', 152ff.
16. Ibid., 155f.
17. Ibid., 157.
18. Ibid., 164. See also Levy, *War in the Modern Great Power System*, table 4.1.
19. Hinsley, *Power and the Pursuit of Peace*, 214n.

24. The House of Saxe-Coburg-Gotha

1. Leopold to Victoria, 15 December 1843, in Benson and Esher (eds.), *Letters of Queen Victoria*, vol. I, 511.
2. *The Times*, 16 March 1863.
3. Nicholas, diary, 18 June 1893, in Maylunas and Mironenko, *Lifelong Passion.*
4. See Corti, *Alexander of Battenberg.*
5. Herbert von Bismarck, memorandum, 25 July 1888, in Dugdale (ed.) *German Diplomatic Documents*, vol. I, 365.
6. Nicholas, diary, 12 April 1894, in Maylunas and Mironenko, *Lifelong Passion.*
7. See Bernstein (ed.), *Willy–Nicky Correspondence.*
8. Royal Archives, Windsor, Geo. V., AA. 11, 2, Victoria to George [future George V], 26 June 1894.

25. The House of Rothschild

1. Dairnvaell, *Histoire édifiante et curieuse*, 8.
2. For details see Ferguson, *World's Banker*, 166f., 207, 294, 404, 409, 411, 530.
3. Anon., *Hebrew Talisman*, 28ff.
4. Iliowzi, *'In the Pale'*.
5. Prawer, *Heine's Jewish Comedy*, 331–5.
6. Rothschild Archive London (henceforth RAL), T20/34, XI/109/48/2/42, Nathan, Paris, to his brothers, 4 September, probably 1844.
7. RAL, XI/109/2/2/149, Salomon, Paris, to Nathan, London, 21 October 1815.
8. RAL, XI/109/2/2/153, Salomon and James, Paris, to Nathan, London, 25 October 1815.
9. RAL, T63 138/2, Salomon and James, Paris, to Nathan, London, 22 October 1817.
10. RAL, T29/181; XI/109/0/7/21, Carl, Frankfurt, to Salomon, 23 August 1814; RAL, T63/28/1, XI/109/8, Carl, Berlin, to his brothers, 4 November 1817.
11. RAL, T5/29, Braun, (James's clerk in) Paris, to James, London, 13 September 1813.
12. Rothschild, *Shadow of a Great Man*, 135–7.
13. Cathcart, *News from Waterloo.*
14. Gille, *Maison Rothschild*, vol. I, 187f.
15. Chateaubriand, *Correspondance générale*, vol. III, 663f.
16. Quennell (ed.), *Private Letters of Princess Lieven*, 237.
17. Davis, *English Rothschilds*, 132f.
18. RAL, T27/280, XI/109/7, James, Paris, to Salomon and Nathan, 18 June 1817.
19. Kynaston, *City*, vol. I, 54f.
20. Corti, *Rise*, 242.
21. Serre, *Correspondance du comte de Serre*, vol. IV, 249.
22. Aspinall (ed.), *Letters of King George IV*, vol. III, 175.
23. Corti, *Rise*, 424f., 427f.
24. Liedtke, *N. M. Rothschild & Sons.*
25. Fournier-Verneuil, *Paris: Tableau moral et philosophique*, 51–2, 64f.
26. Anon., *Annual Register, 1828*, 52.
27. Quoted in Glanz, 'Rothschild Legend in America', 20.
28. Kynaston, *City*, vol. I, p. 90f.

29. Cowles, *The Rothschilds*, 71.
30. Capefigue, *Grandes opérations*, vol. III, 103.
31. Pückler-Muskau, *Briefe*, 441.
32. Rubens, *Anglo-Jewish Portraits*, p. 299.
33. *The Times*, 15 January 1821.
34. Schwemer, *Geschichte*, vol. II, 149ff.
35. Balla, *Romance*, pp. 191ff.
36. Schwemer, *Geschichte*, vol. II, pp. 149ff.
37. RAL, XI/82/9/1/100, Amschel, Frankfurt, to James, Paris, 30 April 1817.
38. Byron, *Don Juan*, Canto XII, verses 4–10.
39. Reeves, *Rothschilds*, 101.
40. Gille, *Maison Rothschild*, vol. I, 487.

26. Industrial Networks

1. Buxton (ed.), *Memoirs*, 354.
2. RAL, I/218/I, Nathan to J. A. Matti, Frankfurt, 29 December 1802.
3. RAL, I/218/36, Nathan to Sichel & Hildesheimer, Frankfurt, 17 October 1802.
4. Moon, *Social Networks in the History of Innovation and Invention*, KL 492–4.
5. Pearson and Richardson, 'Business Networking in the Industrial Revolution', 659f.
6. Lamoreaux et al., 'Beyond Markets and Hierarchies', 16.
7. Moon, *Social Networks in the History of Innovation*, KL 498–504.
8. The idea comes from the economic historian Anton Howes: http://antonhowes.tumblr.com/post/143173119024/how-innovation-accelerated-in-britain-1651–1851.
9. Moon, *Social Networks in the History of Innovation*, KL 2128–37.
10. For a network study of 1848 that focuses on petition-signers in the city of Esslingen in Württemberg, see Lipp and Krempel, 'Petitions and the Social Context of Political Mobilization', 169.
11. Colley, *Britons*.
12. Davis, *Inhuman Bondage*, 235.
13. Drescher, 'Public Opinion and Parliament', 64.
14. Davis, *Inhuman Bondage*, 245.
15. See the seminal work of Williams, *Capitalism and Slavery*, which is now outdated. A more compelling recent account is Ryden, 'Does Decline Make Sense?'

16. Williams, *Capitalism and Slavery*, 150.
17. Loewe (ed.), *Montefiore Diaries*, vol. I, 97ff.
18. Buxton (ed.), *Memoirs*, 353ff.
19. Dimock, 'Queen Victoria, Africa and Slavery'.

27. From Pentarchy to Hegemony

1. The eleven were: Austria–Hungary, Belgium, France, Germany, Italy, Netherlands, Portugal, Spain, Russia, the United Kingdom and the United States. Author's calculations, based on data in the *Statesman's Yearbook*.
2. See in general Ferguson, *Empire*.

V. KNIGHTS OF THE ROUND TABLE

28. An Imperial Life

1. See in general Lownie, *John Buchan*.
2. Cannadine, 'John Buchan'.
3. Quigley, *Anglo-American Establishment*, 3.
4. Ibid., 49.
5. Ibid., 4f.

29. Empire

1. Cannadine, *Ornamentalism*, 124.
2. Ferguson, *Empire*, 230.
3. Ansell, 'Symbolic Networks'.
4. Standage, *Victorian Internet*, 97.
5. Gooch (ed.), *Diaries*, 26 July 1866, 143f.
6. Ibid., 147.
7. Spar, *Ruling the Waves*.
8. Jackson, *Thief at the End of the World*, 170. See also Dean, *Brazil and the Struggle for Rubber*.
9. Klaus, *Forging Capitalism*.
10. Lester, 'Imperial Circuits and Networks'.
11. Vera and Schupp, 'Bridges over the Atlantic'.
12. Ingram and Lifschitz, 'Kinship in the Shadow of the Corporation'.

13. Carnegie, 'Wealth'.
14. See Flandreau and Jobst, 'Ties That Divide'.
15. Tworek, 'Magic Connections'.
16. Taylor, Hoyler and Evans, 'Geohistorical Study',
17. Heidler et al., 'Relationship Patterns'.
18. Brudner and White, 'Class, Property and Structural Endogmany'.
19. Plakans and Wetherell, 'Kinship Domain in an East European Peasant Community', 371.
20. Fontane, *Stechlin*, 77.
21. See Lipp, 'Kinship Networks'.

30. Taiping

1. Campbell and Lee, 'Kin Networks'.
2. Keller, '"Yes, Emperor"'.
3. Kuhn, *Soulstealers*, 220.
4. Ter Haar, *White Lotus Teachings*, esp. 239f.
5. Kuhn, *Soulstealers*, 228f.
6. Duara, *Culture, Power and the State.*
7. Platt, *Autumn in the Heavenly Kingdom*, 43.
8. Taylor, *Five Years in China*. See also Cooke, *China*, 106–8.

31. 'The Chinese Must Go'

1. McKeown, 'Chinese Emigration', table 1, 156.
2. United States Congress, *Report of the Joint Special Committee*, iv–viii.
3. Gibson, *Chinese in America*, 281–373.
4. Bryce, 'Kearneyism', vol. II, pp. 385–406.
5. See Lee, *At America's Gates*, ch. 1.
6. Moretti, 'Social Networks and Migrations'.
7. Lee, *At America's Gates*, 25.

32. The Union of South Africa

1. Oxford and Asquith, *Memories and Reflections*, 213f.
2. Quigley, *Anglo-American Establishment*, 3.

3. Ferguson, *World's Banker*, ch. 27.
4. Quigley, *Anglo-American Establishment*, ch. 4.
5. May, 'Milner's Kindergarten'.
6. Ibid.
7. Nimocks, *Milner's Young Men*, 44.
8. Ibid., 18.
9. Ibid., 19.
10. Ibid., 20.
11. Magubane, *Making of a Racist State*, 300f.
12. Louw, *Rise, Fall, and Legacy of Apartheid*, 15.
13. Quigley, *Anglo-American Establishment*, ch. 4.
14. Louw, *Rise, Fall, and Legacy of Apartheid*, 10.
15. Darwin, *Empire Project*, 217–54.
16. Marks and Trapido, 'Lord Milner and the South African State', 73.
17. Ibid., 69–71.
18. Louw, *Rise, Fall, and Legacy of Apartheid*, 12.
19. Nimocks, *Milner's Young Men*, viii–ix.

33. Apostles

1. Levy, *Moore*, 65–122.
2. Allen, *Cambridge Apostles*, 86.
3. Levy, *Moore*, 22–5.
4. Skidelsky, *Keynes*, vol. I, 118.
5. Ibid., 240.
6. Lubenow, *Cambridge Apostles*, 69; Allen, *Cambridge Apostles*, 21.
7. Allen, *Cambridge Apostles*, 1.
8. Lubenow, *Cambridge Apostles*, 148. See table 3.1.
9. Ibid., 176.
10. Ibid., 190f.
11. Allen, *Cambridge Apostles*, 20.
12. Levy, *Moore*, 7.
13. Ibid., 296.
14. Skidelsky, *Keynes*, vol. I, 115.
15. Ibid., 127f., 235.
16. Hale (ed.), *Friends and Apostles*.
17. Skidelsky, *Keynes*, I, 116.
18. Ibid., 134f.
19. Ibid., vol. I, 181.

20. Ibid., vol. I, 142f.
21. Forster, *What I Believe*.
22. Skidelsky, *Keynes*, vol. I, 239f.
23. McGuinness, *Wittgenstein*, 95f., 118, 146–50.
24. Hale (ed.), *Friends and Apostles*, 284.
25. Skidelsky, *Keynes*, vol. I, 319.
26. Lubenow, *Cambridge Apostles*, 194.
27. Skidelsky, *Keynes*, vol. I, 324.
28. Ibid., 243f., 247.
29. Dolton, 'Identifying Social Network Effects'.
30. Ibid.
31. Forster, *Howard's End*, 214.

34. Armageddon

1. For more detail see Offer, *First World War*.
2. For a compelling recent account, see Clark, *Sleepwalkers*.
3. Schroeder, 'Economic Integration and the European International System'.
4. Kissinger, *World Order*, 78.
5. Ibid., 233.
6. Ibid., 80, 82.
7. Thompson, 'Streetcar Named Sarajevo', 470.
8. Antal, Krapivsky and Redner, 'Social Balance on Networks', 135.
9. Gartzke and Lupu, 'Trading on Preconceptions'.
10. Vasquez and Rundlett, 'Alliances as a Necessary Condition of Multiparty Wars', 15.
11. Maoz, *Networks of Nations*, 38f.
12. Lebow, 'Contingency, Catalysts and Non-Linear Change', 106f.
13. Trachtenberg, 'New Light on 1914?'
14. Schroeder, 'Necessary Conditions', 183., 191f.
15. Lichnowsky to Foreign Office, 29 July 1914, quoted in Trachtenberg, 'New Light on 1914?'
16. Grey to Goschen, 31 July 1914, quoted in Trachtenberg, 'New Light on 1914?'
17. Karl Kraus, *Die Fackel*, vol. 22 (1920), 23.
18. Buchan, *Greenmantle*, KL 118–37.

VI. PLAGUES AND PIPERS

35. Greenmantle

1. Chi et al., 'Spatial Diffusion of War', 64f.
2. See in general Hopkirk, *Like Hidden Fire.*
3. Al-Rawi, 'Buchan the Orientalist'.
4. Keller, 'How to Spot a Successful Revolution in Advance'.
5. McMeekin, *Berlin–Baghdad Express*, 15–16f.
6. Habermas, 'Debates in Islam', 234–5.
7. Berghahn, *Germany and the Approach of War*, 138ff.
8. McMurray, *Distant Ties*, KL 1808–21.
9. Landau, *Pan-Islam*, 94–8.
10. Geiss, *July 1914*, doc. 135.
11. Motadel, *Islam and Nazi Germany's War*, 19f.
12. McMurray, *Distant Ties*, KL 1826–38.
13. Ibid., KL 1850–56.
14. Rogan, *Fall of the Ottomans*, 40f.
15. Rogan, 'Rival Jihads', 3f.
16. McMeekin, *Berlin–Baghdad Express*, 87
17. Ibid., 376, n.8.
18. Ibid., 124.
19. 'The Ottoman Sultan's Fetva: Declaration of Holy War', 15 November 1914 in Charles F. Horne (ed.), *Source Records of the Great War*, vol. III (New York: National Alumni, 1923): http://www.firstworldwar.com/source/ottoman_fetva.htm.
20. Motadel, *Islam and Nazi Germany's War*, 19.
21. McMeekin, *Berlin–Baghdad Express*, 125.
22. Schwanitz, 'Bellicose Birth', 186–7.
23. Motadel, *Islam and Nazi Germany's War*, 21–5.
24. McMeekin, *Berlin–Baghdad Express*, 135. See also Morgenthau, *Secrets of the Bosphorus*, 110.
25. Landau, *Pan-Islam*, 98; Zürcher, *Jihad and Islam in World War I*, 83.
26. McKale, 'British Anxiety'.
27. Al-Rawi, 'John Buchan's British-Designed Jihad'.
28. McKale, 'British Anxiety'.
29. Motadel, *Islam and Nazi Germany's War*, 21–5.
30. Gussone, 'Die Moschee im Wünsdorfer "Halbmondlager"'.
31. Fogarty, 'Islam in the French Army', 25f.
32. Trumpener, *Germany and the Ottoman Empire*, 117f.

33. McMeekin, *Berlin–Baghdad Express*, 283.
34. Zürcher, 'Introduction', 24. See also Aksakal, '"Holy War Made in Germany?"' and 'Ottoman Proclamation of Jihad'.
35. Rutledge, *Enemy on the Euphrates*, 33–7.
36. McKale, 'Germany and the Arab Question', 249f., n.13.
37. Ibid., 238f.
38. Al-Rawi, 'John Buchan's British-Designed Jihad'.
39. Schwanitz, 'Bellicose Birth', 195f.
40. Fogarty, 'Islam in the French Army', 31–3.
41. Ahmad, 'Great War and Afghanistan's Neutrality', 203–12.
42. Rogan, 'Rival Jihads', 6–7.
43. Darwin, *Empire Project*, 295–7.
44. McKale, *War by Revolution*, 171.
45. McKale, 'British Anxiety'.
46. Rutledge, *Enemy on the Euphrates*, 33–7.
47. Cleveland and Bunton, *History of the Modern Middle East*, 132f.
48. Rogan, *Fall of the Ottomans*, 280f.
49. McKale, 'British Anxiety'.
50. McKale, 'Germany and the Arab Question', 246; Rogan, 'Rival Jihads', 14–16.
51. Rogan, *The Arabs*, 150f.
52. Ibid., 151f.
53. McKale, 'British Anxiety'.
54. McKale, 'Germany and the Arab Question', 244.

36. The Plague

1. McMeekin, *Russian Revolution*, 127–36.
2. Ibid., 206f.
3. Ibid., 155f.
4. Ibid., 163.
5. Ibid., 174.
6. Ibid., 195f.
7. Figes, *People's Tragedy*, 703.
8. McMeekin, *Russian Revolution*, 260ff.
9. Figes, *People's Tragedy*, 630.
10. Volkogonov, *Lenin*, 69f.
11. Figes, *People's Tragedy*, 631.
12. Leggett, *Cheka*, 108.

13. Ferguson, *War of the World*, 206.
14. Service, *Twentieth-Century Russia*, 108.
15. Kotkin, *Stalin*, vol. I, 433.
16. Ferguson, *War of the World*, 152.
17. Applebaum, *Gulag*.
18. Service, *Twentieth-Century Russia*, 117f.
19. Ferguson, *War of the World*, 210.
20. Ibid., 211–14.
21. Kotkin, *Stalin*, vol. II.

37. The Leader Principle

1. Calculated from the data in Laqueur, *Fascism* table 15, and Larsen, et al., *Who Were the Fascists?* table 1.
2. Herf, *Jewish Enemy*, KL 463–9.
3. The definitive work is Falter, *Hitlers Wähler.*
4. O'Loughlin, Flint and Anselin, 'Geography of the Nazi Vote'.
5. Ferguson, *War of the World*, 239.
6. Burleigh, *Third Reich*, 116.
7. Ibid., 194.
8. Ibid., 259.
9. Ibid., 5.
10. Satyanath, Voigtländer and Voth, 'Bowling for Fascism'.
11. Herf, *Jewish Enemy*, KL 347–65.

38. The Fall of the Golden International

1. Voigtländer and Voth, 'Persecution Perpetuated'.
2. Miller Lane and Rupp (eds.), *Nazi Ideology before 1933*, KL 168–77.
3. Ibid., KL 165–216.
4. Herf, *The Jewish Enemy*, KL 81–9. See also Cohn, *Warrant for Genocide.*
5. Friedländer, *Nazi Germany and the Jews*, 77f.
6. See in general Mosse, 'Die Juden in Wirtschaft und Gesellschaft', and *Jews in the German Economy.*
7. Windolf, 'German-Jewish Economic Elite', 137, 157.
8. Valentin, *Antisemitism*, 198f.
9. Windolf, 'German-Jewish Economic Elite', 158f. See also 152, 155.

10. Meiring, *Christlich-jüdische Mischehe*, table 1.
11. Jones, *In the Blood*, 158ff.
12. Ruppin, *Soziologie der Juden*, vol. I, 211f.; Hanauer, 'Jüdische-christliche Mischehe', table 2; Della Pergola, *Jewish and Mixed Marriages*, 122–7.
13. Ruppin, *Soziologie der Juden*, vol. I, 211f.
14. Burleigh and Wippermann, *Racial State*, 110.
15. Burgdörfer, 'Juden in Deutschland', 177.
16. Raab, 'More than just a Metaphor'.
17. Friedländer, *Nazi Germany and the Jews*, 19.
18. Ibid., 24.
19. Ibid., 234.
20. Ibid., 25–6.
21. Ibid., 259–60; Barkai, *From Boycott to Annihilation*, 75.
22. Barkai, *From Boycott to Annihilation*, 152f.
23. Ibid., 153.
24. Baynes (ed.) *Speeches of Adolf Hitler*, vol. I, 737–41.
25. Kopper, 'Rothschild family', 321ff.
26. Nicholas, *Rape*, 39.
27. Heimann-Jelinek, '"Aryanisation" of Rothschild Assets'.
28. Details are in Nicholas, *Rape*.
29. Ferguson, *Kissinger*, vol. I, 72, 80.
30. Düring, 'Dynamics of Helping Behaviour'.
31. Fallada, *Alone in Berlin*.

39. The Ring of Five

1. Cooper, *Diaries*, 274.
2. See in general Bloch, *Ribbentrop*.
3. Lord Lothian, 'Germany and France: The British Task, II: Basis of Ten Years' Peace', *The Times*, 1 February 1935.
4. Lownie, *Burgess*, 29.
5. Deacon, *Cambridge Apostles*, 103.
6. Lownie, *Burgess*, 34f.
7. Andrew and Gordievsky, *KGB*, 206, 209.
8. Ibid., 193ff.
9. Andrew, *Defence of the Realm*, 169ff.
10. Lownie, *Burgess*, 54.
11. Deacon, *Cambridge Apostles*, 107f.

12. Ibid., 115, 134.
13. Andrew and Gordievsky, *KGB*, 216.
14. Ibid., 221.
15. Macintyre, *Spy Among Friends*, 44ff.
16. Andrew and Gordievsky, *KGB*, 213.
17. Ibid., 184.
18. Ibid., 213.
19. Lownie, *Burgess*, 55.
20. Ibid., 136.
21. Ibid., 96.
22. Andrew, *Defence of the Realm*, 270; Andrew and Gordievsky, *KGB*, 300.
23. Andrew, *Defence of the Realm*, 270.
24. Lownie, *Burgess*, 130; Andrew, *Defence of the Realm*, 272.
25. Andrew, *Defence of the Realm*, 280, 289.
26. Andrew and Gordievsky, *KGB*, 296f.
27. Lownie, *Burgess*, 131, 147.
28. Ibid., 132, 160; Andrew, *Defence of the Realm*, 272, 280.
29. Andrew, *Defence of the Realm*, 219, 261.
30. Ibid., 268.
31. Ibid., 341; Andrew and Gordievsky, *KGB*, 297.
32. Andrew, *Defence of the Realm*, 281, 333.
33. Macintyre, *Spy Among Friends*, 144.
34. Andrew, *Defence of the Realm*, 339ff.
35. Ibid., 343.
36. Ibid., 422.
37. Andrew and Gordievsky, *KGB*, 399f.
38. Andrew, *Defence of the Realm*, 422f.
39. Ibid., 420–24.
40. Ibid., 424.
41. Ibid., 431.
42. Ibid., 432–5, rebuts Peter Wright's claims that there was a cover-up only explicable in terms of higher-level Soviet penetration of British intelligence.
43. Ibid., 436.
44. Macintyre, *Spy Among Friends*, 291.
45. Andrew and Gordievsky, *KGB*, 6.
46. Andrew, *Defence of the Realm*, 429.
47. Andrew and Gordievsky, *KGB*, 429, 436, 439ff., 707.

40. Brief Encounter

1. McSmith, *Fear and the Muse Kept Watch*, KL 5069–70.
2. Ibid., KL 5109–19.
3. Ibid., KL 5138.
4. Ibid., KL 5139–55.
5. Ibid., KL 5158–60.
6. Ibid., KL 5185–97.
7. Berlin, *Enlightening*, KL 2139–42.
8. Berlin, *Letters*, 599f.
9. For Berlin's detailed recollection of the encounter, written thirty-five years after the fact, see Berlin, *Personal Impressions*, KL 4628–4998.
10. Hausheer, 'It Didn't Happen'.
11. Ignatieff, *Berlin*, KL 3252–79.
12. She can be heard reading 'Cinque' in this recording from her visit to Oxford in June 1965, a year before her death: https://podcasts.ox.ac.uk/anna-akhmatova-reading-her-poems-about-isaiah-berlin-oxford-1965.
13. Dalos, *Guest from the Future*, 7, 86.
14. Akhmatova, *Word that Causes Death's Defeat*, 152.
15. McSmith, *Fear and the Muse Kept Watch*, KL 5271. Preposterously, Churchill wanted Berlin's help as a translator to help him obtain ice for some caviar he had acquired.
16. Dalos, *Guest from the Future*, 67.
17. Ignatieff, *Berlin*, KL 3252–79.
18. Dalos, *Guest from the Future*, 67f.
19. McSmith, *Fear and the Muse Kept Watch*, KL 5354–68.
20. Ibid., KL 5352.
21. Berlin, *Enlightening*, KL 2056–74. See also Dalos, *Guest from the Future*, 59–61.
22. Berlin, *Enlightening*, KL 1047–56, 1059–69.
23. Ignatieff, *Berlin*, KL 3284–3350; McSmith, *Fear and the Muse Kept Watch*, KL 5399–5414.
24. Berlin, *Enlightening*, KL 10773–4, 10783–10806, 10818–64, 10865–71.
25. Ibid., KL 16680–82; Dalos, *Guest from the Future*, 124–7, 133.
26. Dalos, *Guest from the Future*, 64f.

41. Ella in Reform School

1. MacDougall, 'Long Lines'.
2. See in general Wu, *Master Switch*.
3. MacDougall, 'Long Lines', 299, 308f., 318.
4. Wu, *Master Switch*, 8.
5. Ibid., 9.
6. Ibid., 113.
7. Christopher Wolf, 'The History of Electronic Surveillance, from Abraham Lincoln's Wiretaps to Operation Shamrock', Public Radio International, 7 November 2013.
8. Starr, *Creation of the Media*, 348.
9. Ibid., 363f.
10. Gambetta, *Sicilian Mafia*.
11. Jonathan Steinberg, 'Capos and Cardinals', *London Review of Books*, 17 August 1989.
12. Duggan, *Fascism and the Mafia*.
13. Scotten, 'Problem of the Mafia'. I am indebted to my student Frank Tamberino for this reference. See Tamberino, 'Criminal Renaissance'.
14. Lewis, 'The Honored Society', *New Yorker*, 8 February 1964, 42–105, and the longer *Honoured Society*. Also illuminating, the same author's *Naples '44*.
15. McAdam, *Political Process and the Development of Black Insurgency*, 90.
16. Ibid., 129
17. Jackson et al., 'Failure of an Incipient Social Movement', 36.
18. See Kurtz, *Not-God*; White and Kurtz, 'Twelve Defining Moments'; Makela et al., (eds.), *Alcoholics Anonymous*; Kelly and Yeterian, 'Mutual-Help Groups'.
19. Kurtz, *Not-God*, 64.
20. White and Kurtz, 'Twelve Defining Moments', 44f.
21. Ohler, *Blitzed*.

VII. OWN THE JUNGLE

42. The Long Peace

1. Jackson and Nei, 'Networks of Military Alliances', 15279. See also Levina and Hillmann, 'Wars of the World', Lupu and Traag, 'Trading Communities', and Maoz, 'Network Polarization'.

2. Dorussen and Ward, 'Trade Networks'.
3. Haim, 'Alliance Networks and Trade', 28.
4. Johnson and Jordan, 'Web of War'.
5. Keller, '(Why) Do Revolutions Spread?'

43. The General

1. Forester, *The General*, 222.
2. Samuels, *Command or Control*; Gudmundsson, *Stormtroop Tactics*.
3. Marston, 'Lost and Found in the Jungle', KL 2065.
4. Pocock, *Fighting General*, KL 1537–77.
5. Mumford, *Counter-Insurgency Myth*, 37f.
6. Beckett and Pimlott, *Counter-Insurgency*, 20.
7. Strachan, 'British Counter-Insurgency from Malaya to Iraq', 10.
8. Pocock, *Fighting General*, KL 2113–33.
9. Ibid., KL 2204–9.
10. Walker, 'How Borneo was Won', 11.
11. Ibid.
12. Tuck, 'Borneo 1963–66', 98f.
13. Walker, 'How Borneo War Won', 19.
14. Ibid., 9f.
15. Ibid., 10.
16. Ibid., 14.
17. Cross, *'Face Like a Chicken's Backside'*, 142f.
18. Ibid., 157.
19. Rosentall, '"Confrontation": Countering Indonesian Insurgency', 102.
20. Beckett and Pimlott, *Counter-Insurgency*, 110.
21. Walker, 'How Borneo Was Won', 12.
22. Ibid., 9.
23. Ibid., 17.

44. The Crisis of Complexity

1. 'General Sir Walter Walker', *Daily Telegraph*, 13 August 2001.
2. O'Hara, *From Dreams to Disillusionment*.
3. Scott, *Seeing Like a State*, 348.
4. Bar-Yam, 'Complexity Rising', 26.
5. See Bar-Yam, *Dynamics of Complex Systems*, 804–9.

6. Quoted in Thompson et al. (eds.), *Markets, Hierarchies and Networks*, 297.
7. Barabási, *Linked*, 201.
8. Lamoreaux et al., 'Beyond Markets and Hierarchies', 43f.
9. Ibid., 48f.
10. Chanda, *Bound Together*, 248.
11. Theodore Levitt, 'The Globalization of Markets', *Harvard Business Review* (May 1983).
12. Powell, 'Neither Market nor Hierarchy', quoted in Thompson et al. (eds.), *Markets, Hierarchies and Networks*, 270.
13. Ibid., 271f.
14. Ibid., 273f.
15. Rhodes, 'New Governance', 665.
16. Thompson, *Between Hierarchies and Markets*, 133.

45. Henry Kissinger's Network of Power

1. Ferguson, *Kissinger*, xiv.
2. Ibid., 310.
3. Ibid., 502.
4. Ibid., 728.
5. Ibid., 806.
6. Ibid., 807.
7. Ibid., 841.
8. Ibid., 849.
9. 'Principles, Structure and Activities of Pugwash for the Eleventh Quinquennium, 2007–2012': https://en.wikipedia.org/wiki/Pugwash_Conferences_on_Science_and_World_Affairs
10. Evangelista, *Unarmed Forces*, 32f.
11. Ibid., 33.
12. Staar, *Foreign Policies*, 86.
13. Ferguson, *Kissinger*, 505.
14. Ibid., 736.
15. Ibid., 740.
16. Ibid., 746f.
17. See Appendix.
18. 'Superstar Statecraft: How Henry Does It', *Time*, 1 April 1974.
19. Ibid.
20. Ibid.

21. Sargent, *Superpower Transformed*, 158.
22. Ibid., 159.
23. Ibid., 176.
24. Notably Cooper, *Economics of Interdependence*, and Keohane and Nye, *Power and Interdependence*.
25. 'Interdependence Day', *The New York Times*, 4 July 1976.
26. Brzezinski, *Between Two Ages*.
27. Bearman and Everett, 'Structure of Social Protest', 190f.
28. Henry A. Kissinger, 'The Need to Belong', *The New York Times*, 17 March 1968.
29. http://www.pbs.org/newshour/bb/white_house-july-dec11-nixontapes_11-25/.

46. Into the Valley

1. Barabási, *Linked*, 147.
2. Conway, 'How Do Committees Invent?'
3. Ibid.
4. Caldarelli and Catanzaro, *Networks*, 37.
5. Naughton, *From Gutenberg to Zuckerberg*, 45f.
6. Caldarelli and Catanzaro, *Networks*, 38.
7. Newman, *Networks*, 19f.
8. Brinton and Chiang, *Power of Networks*, 245.
9. Ibid., 297.
10. On the forerunners to the World Wide Web, see Hall, 'Ever Evolving Web'.
11. Castells, *Rise of the Network Society*, 63f. See also Newman, *Networks*, 5.
12. Caldarelli and Catanzaro, *Networks*, 39f., 43f.
13. Garton Ash, *Free Speech*, KL 494–496.
14. https://w2.eff.org/Censorship/Internet_censorship_bills/barlow_0296.declaration.
15. Goldsmith and Wu, *Who Controls the Internet?*, 21.
16. Ibid., 24.
17. Ibid., 15.
18. Ibid., ch. 3.

47. The Fall of the Soviet Empire

1. Benjamin Peters, 'The Soviet InterNyet', *Aeon*, 17 October 2016.
2. National Security Agency, 'Dealing with the Future: The Limits of Forecasting', 100: http://www.nsa.gov/public_info/_files/cryptologic_quarterly/limits_forecasting.pdf.
3. Osa, *Solidarity and Contention*, 117f.
4. Ibid., 165.
5. Malcolm Gladwell, 'Small Change: Why the Revolution Will Not Be Tweeted', *New Yorker*, 4 October 2010.
6. Grdesic, 'Television and Protest in East Germany's Revolution', 94.

48. The Triumph of Davos Man

1. Navidi, *Superhubs*, 95.
2. Nick Paumgarten, 'Magic Mountain: What Happens at Davos?' *New Yorker*, 5 March 2012.
3. https://www.weforum.org/agenda/2013/12/nelson-mandelas-address-to-davos-1992/.
4. Paul Nursey-Bray, 'The Solid Mandela', *Australian Left Review* (June 1992), 12–16.
5. Barnard and Popescu, 'Nelson Mandela', 241f.
6. Sampson, *Mandela*, 427.
7. Ibid., 429.
8. Jake Bright, 'Why the Left-Leaning Nelson Mandela was such a Champion of Free Markets', 6 December 2013: http://qz.com/155310/nelson-mandela-was-also-a-huge-champion-of-free-markets/.
9. Ronnie Kasrils, 'How the ANC's Faustian Pact Sold Out South Africa's Poorest', *Guardian*, 24 June 2013: https://www.theguardian.com/commentisfree/2013/jun/24/anc-faustian-pact-mandela-fatal-error.
10. Anthony Monteiro, 'Mandela and the Origins of the Current South African Crisis', 24 February 2015: https://africanamericanfutures.com/2015/02/24/mandela-and-the-origins-of-the-current-south-african-crisis/. See also Monteiro, 'Nelson Mandela: The Contradictions of His Life and Legacies', *Black Agenda Report*, 12 November 2013: http://www.blackagendareport.com/content/nelson-mandela-contradictions-his-life-and-legacies.
11. Sampson, *Mandela*, 428. See also Gumede, *Thabo Mbeki*, 81–4.

12. Ken Hanly, 'Mandela and Neo-Liberalism in South Africa', 18 December 2013: http://www.digitaljournal.com/news/politics/op-ed-mandela-and-neo-liberalism-in-south-african/article/364193. See also Danny Schechter, 'Blurring Mandela and Neo-Liberalism', 14 December 2013: http://www.truthdig.com/report/print/blurring_mandela_and_neoliberalism_20131214. Cf. Schechter, *Madiba A to Z*, KL 1619–61.
13. Klein, *Shock Doctrine*, 216f.
14. Landsberg, *Quiet Diplomacy of Liberation*, 107–10.
15. Andrew Ross Sorkin, 'How Mandela Shifted Views on Freedom of Markets', *The New York Times*, 9 December 2013. See also Barnard and Popescu, 'Nelson Mandela', 247.
16. Sampson, *Mandela*, 428f.

49. Breaking the Bank of England

1. This section draws on Ferguson and Schlefer, 'Who Broke the Bank of England?'
2. Stevenson, 'First World War and European Integration'.
3. For more details, see Ferguson, 'Siegmund Warburg, the City of London and the Financial Roots of European Integration'.
4. For an introduction, see Kerr, *History of the Eurobond Market*.
5. Milward, *European Rescue of the Nation-State*.
6. Schenk, 'Sterling, International Monetary Reform and Britain's Applications'.
7. Ferguson, *High Financier*, 229.
8. Granville, Cruz and Prevezer, 'Elites, Thickets and Institutions'.
9. Ferguson, *High Financier*, 230.
10. Lamont, *In Office*, 124.
11. Major, *Autobiography*, 271f.
12. Ibid., 275f.
13. Ibid., 284.
14. Ibid., 288.
15. Soros, *George Soros on Globalization*, 131.
16. Eichengreen and Wyplosz, 'Unstable EMS', 85.
17. Lamont, *In Office*, 201.
18. Major, *Autobiography*, 313. See also 'Nearer to No', *Economist*, 29 August 1992.
19. Major, *Autobiography*, 313–15, 325.
20. Lamont, *In Office*, 212f., 227.

21. Ivan Fallon, 'John Major's Days of Pain: The Sterling Fiasco', *Sunday Times*, 20 September 1992.
22. 'Sterling Knocked by EMU Worries', *The Times,* 10 June 1992.
23. Major, *Autobiography*, 316, 325.
24. Stephens, *Politics and the Pound*, 219.
25. Lamont, *In Office*, 216.
26. Ibid., 227f.
27. Peter Kellner, David Smith and John Cassidy, 'The Day the Pound Died', *Sunday Times*, 6 December 1992.
28. Lamont, *In Office*, 228.
29. Matthew Lynn and David Smith, 'Round One to Lamont – Norman Lamont', *Sunday Times,* 30 August 1992.
30. Lamont, *In Office*, 229.
31. 'Schlesinger's Schadenfreude – Diary', *The Times* , 18 September 1992.
32. Peter Kellner, David Smith and John Cassidy, 'The Day the Pound Died', *Sunday Times*, 6 December 1992.
33. Lamont, *In Office*, 236.
34. Ibid., 238.
35. Colin Narbrough and Wolfgang Munchau, 'Another Innocent Gaffe from the Bundesbank', *The Times*, 10 September 1992; David Smith, 'Lamont's Troubles in Triplicate', *Sunday Times,* 13 September 1992.
36. Philip Webster, 'Bundesbank Chief Raises Spectre of Devaluation', *The Times,* 16 September 1992; Christopher Huhne, 'Inside Story: The Breaking of the Pound', *Independent on Sunday*, 20 September 1992. Cf. Major, *Autobiography*, 329.
37. Lamont, *In Office*, 244f.
38. Peter Kellner, David Smith and John Cassidy, 'The Day the Pound Died', *Sunday Times*, 6 December 1992; Robert Chote and Nicholas Timmins, 'Pound Faces Toughest Test after EC Bows to Markets: German Interest Rate to Fall as Lira is Devalued in ERM Rescue', *Independent,* 13 September 1992.
39. Eichengreen and Wyplosz, 'Unstable EMS', 107.
40. 'Forever Falling?' *Economist,* 29 August 1992.
41. Christopher Huhne, 'Schlesinger: A Banker's Guilt', *Independent,* 1 October 1992.
42. Soros, 'Theory of Reflexivity', 7.
43. Soros, *Soros on Soros*, 12
44. Mallaby, *More Money Than God*, 435.
45. 'A Ghastly Game of Dominoes', *Economist,* 19 September 1992.
46. Mallaby, *More Money Than God*, 156f.

47. Abdelal, 'Politics of Monetary Leadership', 250.
48. Duncan Balsbaugh, 'The Pound, My Part in Its Downfall and Is It Time to Fight the Central Banks Again?' *IFR Review of the Year 2015*: http://www.ifre.com/the-pound-my-part-in-its-downfall-and-is-it-time-to-fight-the-central-banks-again/21223291.fullarticle. For other accounts with somewhat different figures, see Kaufman, *Soros*, 239; Mallaby, *More Money Than God*, 435. See also Drobny, *Inside the House of Money*, 274f.
49. Soros, *Soros on Soros*, 22. See also Soros and Schmitz, *Tragedy of the European Union*, 59f.
50. Kaufman, *Soros*, 239. Emphasis added.
51. Lamont, *In Office*, 249.
52. Anatole Kaletsky, 'How Mr Soros Made a Billion by Betting against the Pound', *The Times* , 26 October 1992.
53. Ibid.
54. Mallaby, *More Money Than God*, 160–66.
55. Eichengreen and Wyplosz, 'Unstable EMS', 60.
56. Engdahl, 'Secret Financial Network'.
57. Flavia Cymbalista with Desmond MacRae, 'George Soros: How He Knows What He Knows, Part 2: Combining Theory and Instinct', *Stocks, Futures and Options*, 9 March 2004.
58. James Blitz, 'How Central Banks Ran into the Hedge', *Financial Times*, 30 September 1992.
59. Balsbaugh, 'The Pound, My Part in Its Downfall'.
60. Thomas Jaffe and Dyan Machan, 'How the Market Overwhelmed the Central Banks', *Forbes*, 9 November 1992. See also Mallaby, *More Money Than God*, 435.
61. Kaletsky, 'How Mr Soros Made a Billion'.
62. Soros, *Soros on Soros*, 82.
63. Lamont, *In Office*, 259.
64. Slater, *Soros*, 180.
65. Ibid., 181.
66. Roxburgh, *Strained to Breaking Point*, 163; Matthew Tempest, 'Treasury Papers Reveal Cost of Black Wednesday', *Guardian*, 9 February 2005.
67. Johnson, 'UK and the Exchange Rate Mechanism', 97f.
68. Major, *Autobiography*, 312, Lamont, *In Office*, 285.
69. Kaletsky, 'How Mr Soros Made a Billion'.
70. 'Half-Maastricht', *Economist*, 26 September 1992.

VIII: THE LIBRARY OF BABEL

50. 9/11/2001

1. Borges, 'Library of Babel'.
2. On the powerful developmental effects of the international air transport network, Campante and Yanagizawa-Drott, 'Long-Range Growth'. On the tendency of the American system to produce delays even in normal conditions, see Mayer and Sinai, 'Network Effects'.
3. Calderelli and Catanzaro, *Networks* 40f.
4. Thomas A. Stewart, 'Six Degrees of Mohamed Atta', *Business 2.0*, December 2001.
5. Krebs, 'Mapping Networks of Terrorist Cells', 46–50.
6. Ibid., 51.
7. Jeff Jonas and Jim Harper, 'Effective Counterterrorism and the Limited Role of Predictive Data Mining', *Policy Analysis*, 11 December 2006.
8. Patrick Radden Keefe, 'Can Network Theory Thwart Terrorists?' *The New York Times*, 12 March 2006.
9. Valdis Krebs, 'Connecting the Dots: Tracking Two Identified Terrorists', Orgnet, 2002–8: http://www.orgnet.com/prevent.html.
10. Oliver, 'Covert Networks'.
11. Marion and Uhl-Bien, 'Complexity Theory and Al-Qaeda'.
12. Eilstrup-Sangiovanni and Jones, 'Assessing the Dangers of Illicit Networks', 34.
13. Minor, 'Attacking the Nodes', 6.
14. Morselli, Giguère and Petit, 'The Efficiency/Security Trade-off'. See also Kahler, Miles, 'Networked Politics.' See also Kenney, 'Turning to the "Dark Side"' and Kahler, 'Collective Action and Clandestine Networks'.
15. Sageman, *Understanding Terror Networks*, 96f. See also 135–71.
16. Berman, *Radical, Religious, and Violent*, 18.
17. Ibid., 17.
18. John Arquilla, 'It Takes a Network', *Los Angeles Times*, 25 August 2002.
19. National Consortium for the Study of Terrorism and Responses to Terrorism (START), 'Jihadist Plots in the United States, Jan. 1993–Feb. 2016: Interim Findings' (January 2017).
20. Nagl, *Learning to Eat Soup with a Knife*.
21. Army, *U.S. Army/Marine Corps Counterinsurgency Field Manual*.

22. Army, *Insurgencies and Countering Insurgencies*, section 4, paragraphs 6 and 7.
23. Ibid., section 4, paragraphs 20 and 21.
24. Army, *U.S. Army/Marine Corps Counterinsurgency Field Manual*, Appendix B.
25. Kilcullen, *Counterinsurgency*, 37.
26. Ibid., 183.
27. Ibid., 200.
28. Ibid., 4f., 10, 40, 197.
29. David Petraeus, 'The Big Ideas Emerging in the Wake of the Arab Spring', Belfer Center, Harvard Kennedy School of Government (2017).
30. McChrystal, *My Share of the Task*, 148. Details of how McChrystal and his team hunted down and killed Zarqawi, destroying his network in the process, are in chapters 11–15.
31. Simpson, *War from the Ground Up*, 106.

51. 9/15/2008

1. Neely, 'The Federal Reserve Responds'.
2. Ibid., 40.
3. Crawford, 'U.S. Costs of Wars'.
4. Watts, *Six Degrees*, 23.
5. Caldarelli and Catanzaro, *Networks*, 36f., 42, 95.
6. United States Government Accountability Office, 'Financial Crisis Losses'.
7. See Ferguson, *Ascent of Money*.
8. Financial Crisis Inquiry Commission, *Financial Crisis Inquiry Report*, KL 8518–21.
9. http://www.federalreserve.gov/monetarypolicy/fomchistorical2008.htm: FOMC meeting transcript, 16 September 2015, 20.
10. Ibid., 51.
11. Ibid., 28–29 October 2008, 118.
12. Ibid., 15–16 December 2008, 12.
13. Andrew Haldane, 'On Tackling the Credit Cycle and Too Big to Fail', Bank of England presentation, January 2011, slide 13.
14. Ramo, *Seventh Sense*, 136f. See also 42–4.
15. Jackson, Rogers and Zenou, 'Economic Consequences of Network Structure'. See also Elliott, Golub and Jackson, 'Financial Networks and Contagion'.

16. Louise Story and Eric Dash, 'Bankers Reaped Lavish Bonuses During Bailouts', *The New York Times*, 30 July 2009.
17. Davis et al., 'Small World', 303.
18. Ibid., 320.
19. Michelle Leder, 'Vernon Jordan Gets a Big Payday from Lazard', *The New York Times*, 15 March 2010.
20. Acemoglu et al., 'Value of Connections in Turbulent Times'. According to the authors' estimates, 'Over the next ten trading days, financial firms with a connection to Geithner experienced a cumulative abnormal return of about 12 percent (relative to other financial sector firms).'

52. The Administrative State

1. DeMuth, 'Can the Administrative State Be Tamed?' 125.
2. Patrick McLaughlin and Oliver Sherouse, 'The Accumulation of Regulatory Restrictions Across Presidential Administrations', Mercatus Center, 3 August 2015.
3. Patrick McLaughlin and Oliver Sherouse, 'The Dodd–Frank Wall Street Reform and Consumer Protection Act May be the Biggest Law Ever', Mercatus Center, 20 July 2015.
4. McLaughlin and Greene, 'Dodd–Frank's Regulatory Surge'.
5. Howard, *Life Without Lawyers*.
6. Scott, *Connectedness and Contagion*.
7. Fukuyama, *Political Order and Political Decay*, 208.
8. Ibid., 35f. See, however, Howard, *Rule of Nobody*, and White, Cass and Kosar, *Unleashing Opportunity*.
9. DeMuth, 'Can the Administrative State Be Tamed?' 151.
10. See e.g. McLaughlin and Sherouse, *Impact of Federal Regulation*; Patrick A. McLaughlin, 'Regulations Contribute to Poverty', Testimony to the House Committee on the Judiciary, Subcommittee on Regulatory Reform, Commercial and Antitrust Law, 24 February 2016.
11. Ferguson, *Great Degeneration*.

53. Web 2.0

1. Naughton, *From Gutenberg to Zuckerberg*, 224.
2. Ibid., 227.
3. Raymond, *The Cathedral and the Bazaar*, 21.

4. Ibid., 57f.
5. Ibid., 30.
6. Ibid., 125.
7. Ibid., 194.
8. Spar, *Ruling the Waves*, 369f.
9. Kirkpatrick, *Facebook Effect*, 74.
10. http://benbarry.com/project/facebooks-little-red-book. On the author of the Little Red Book, see http://www.typeroom.eu/article/ben-barry-used-be-called-facebook-s-minister-propaganda.
11. Kirkpatrick, *Facebook Effect*, 247.
12. Ibid., 109.
13. Ibid., 185, 274–7.
14. Ibid., 154–7, 180ff., 188.
15. Naughton, *From Gutenberg to Zuckerberg*, 106.
16. Kirkpatrick, *Facebook Effect*, 222–6.
17. Ibid., 251.
18. Ibid., 259.
19. García Martínez, *Chaos Monkeys*, 275–80, 298f.
20. Ibid., 482–6.
21. Alex Eule, 'Facebook Now Has 1.2 Billion Daily Users. Really', *Barron's*, 2 November 2016.
22. Smriti Bhagat, Moira Burke, Carlos Diuk, Ismail Onur Filiz, and Sergey Edunov, 'Three and a Half Degrees of Separation', 4 February 2016: https://research.fb.com/three-and-a-half-degrees-of-separation/.
23. Lars Backstrom, Paolo Boldi, Marco Rosa, Johan Ugander, and Sebastiano Vigna, 'Four Degrees of Separation', 22 June 2012: https://research.fb.com/publications/four-degrees-of-separation/.
24. Ugander et al., 'Structural Diversity in Social Contagion'.
25. Lillian Weng and Thomas Lenton, 'Topic-Based Clusters in Egocentric Networks on Facebook', 2 June 2014: https://research.fb.com/publications/topic-based-clusters-in-egocentric-networks-on-facebook/. See also Youyou et al., 'Birds of a Feather'.
26. Amaç Herdağdelen, Bogdan State, Lada Adamic and Winter Mason, 'The Social Ties of Immigrant Communities in the United States', 22 May 2016: https://research.fb.com/publications/the-social-ties-of-immigrant-communities-in-the-united-states/.
27. Jonathan Chang, Itamar Rosenn, Lars Backstrom and Cameron Marlow, 'Ethnicity on Social Networks', *Association for the Advancement of Artificial Intelligence* (2010).

28. Ismail Onur Filiz and Lada Adamic, 'Facebook Friendships in Europe', 8 November 2016: https://research.fb.com/facebook-friendships-in-europe/.
29. Eytan Bakshy, Itamar Rosenn, Cameron Marlow and Lada Adamic, 'The Role of Social Networks in Information Diffusion', 16 April 2012: https://research.fb.com/publications/the-role-of-social-networks-in-information-diffusion/; Lada A. Adamic, Thomas M. Lenton, Eytan Adar and Pauline C. Ng, 'Information Evolution in Social Networks', 22 May 2016: https://research.fb.com/wp-content/uploads/2016/11/information_evolution_in_social_networks.pdf; Adam D. I. Kramer, 'The Spread of Emotion via Facebook', 16 May 2012: https://research.fb.com/publications/the-spread-of-emotion-via-facebook/.
30. Jonathan Tepper, 'Friendships in the Age of Social Media', 14 January 2017: originally published on http://jonathan-tepper.com/blog/.
31. Naughton, *From Gutenberg to Zuckerberg*, 194f.
32. Data from http://whoownsfacebook.com/.
33. García Martínez, *Chaos Monkeys*, 229.
34. 'Who Are the 8 Richest People? All Men, Mostly Americans', *NBC News*, 16 January 2017.
35. Wu, *Master Switch*, 318
36. Shannon Bond, 'Google and Facebook Build Digital Ad Duopoly', *Financial Times*, 15 March 2017.
37. Farhad Manjoo, 'Why Facebook Keeps Beating Every Rival: It's the Network, of Course', *The New York Times*, 19 April 2017.
38. Robert Thomson, 'Digital Giants are Trampling on Truth', *The Times*, 10 April 2017.
39. Ramo, *Seventh Sense*, 240ff.
40. Kirkpatrick, *Facebook Effect*, 254.
41. http://benbarry.com/project/facebooks-little-red-book.
42. García Martínez, *Chaos Monkeys*, 355.
43. Kirkpatrick, *Facebook Effect*, 319.
44. Nick Bilton, 'Will Mark Zuckerberg be Our Next President?' *Vanity Fair*, 13 January 2017.
45. García Martínez, *Chaos Monkeys*, 263f.
46. Mark Zuckerberg, 'Building Global Community', 16 February 2017: https://www.facebook.com/notes/mark-zuckerberg/building-global-community/10154544292806634.
47. For a sceptical view, see Morozov, *Net Delusion*.

54. Coming Apart

1. Oxfam, 'An Economy for the 1%'.
2. Crédit Suisse Research Institute, *Global Wealth Databook 2015* (October 2015).
3. Piketty and Saez, 'Income Inequality', with figures updated to 2015.
4. U.S. Census Bureau, Current Population Survey, Annual Social and Economic Supplements: https://www.census.gov/data/tables/time-series/demo/income-poverty/historical-income-households.html.
5. Bricker et al., 'Measuring Income and Wealth'.
6. Agustino Fontevecchia, 'There Are More Self-Made Billionaires in the Forbes 400 Than Ever Before', *Forbes*, 3 October 2014.
7. Credit Suisse Research Institute, *Global Wealth Databook 2015* (October 2015). 'Middle class' is defined here as having wealth between \$50,000 and \$500,000. For a different definition, based on income, which arrives at a rather larger global middle class numbering 3.2 billion, see Kharas, 'Unprecedented Expansion'.
8. Hellebrandt and Mauro, 'Future of Worldwide Income Distribution'.
9. Sala-i-Martin and Pinkovskiy, 'Parametric Estimations'.
10. Milanovic and Lakner, 'Global Income Distribution'.
11. Corlett, 'Examining an Elephant'.
12. Rakesh Kochhar, 'Middle Class Fortunes in Western Europe', Pew Research Center, 24 April 2017.
13. Autor et al., 'Untangling Trade and Technology'.
14. Dobbs et al., *Poorer Than Their Parents*.
15. Chetty et al., 'Is the United States Still a Land of Opportunity?'
16. Case and Deaton, 'Rising Morbidity'.
17. Case and Deaton, 'Mortality and Morbidity'.
18. Nicholas Eberstadt, 'Our Miserable 21st Century', *Commentary*, 28 February 2017.
19. Gagnon and Goyal, 'Networks, Markets, and Inequality', 23.
20. Ibid., 3.
21. World Bank Group, *Digital Dividends*, 3.
22. Paik and Sanchargin, 'Social Isolation'.
23. Keith Hampton, Lauren Sessions, Eun Ja Her, and Lee Rainie, 'Social Isolation and New Technology', *Pew Internet & American Life Project* (November 2009), 1–89: http://www.pewinternet.org/2009/11/04/social-isolation-and-new-technology/.
24. Ibid., 70.
25. See in general Murray, *Coming Apart*.

55. Tweeting the Revolution

1. Wu, *Master Switch*, 250.
2. Pew Research Center, 'Global Publics Embrace Social Networking', 15 December 2010.
3. Malcolm Gladwell, 'Small Change: Why the Revolution Will Not Be Tweeted', *New Yorker*, 4 October 2010.
4. Schmidt and Cohen, 'Digital Disruption'.
5. Ibid.
6. Ibid. See also Shirky, 'Political Power of Social Media', 1. On the limits of digital social networks as agents of political change, see Shirky, *Here Comes Everybody* and Tufekci, *Twitter and Tear Gas.*
7. Hill, 'Emotions as Infectious Diseases'.
8. Hal Hodson, 'I Predict a Riot', *New Scientist*, 2931, 21 August 2013, 22.
9. Debora MacKenzie, 'Brazil Uprising Points to Rise of Leaderless Networks', *New Scientist*, 2923, 26 June 2013. See in general Barbera and Jackson, 'Model of Protests'.
10. Ramo, *Seventh Sense*, 105.
11. Sten Tamkivi, 'Lessons from the World's Most Tech-Savvy Government', *Atlantic*, 24 January 2014.
12. For the relevance of this insight to other conflicts, see Staniland, *Networks of Rebellion*.
13. Simcox, *Al-Qaeda's Global Footprint.*
14. Zimmerman, *Al-Qaeda Network*.
15. Wu, *Master Switch*, 250.
16. Glennon, 'National Security', 12.
17. Barton Gellman, 'NSA Broke Privacy Rules Thousands of Times per Year, Audit Finds', *Washington Post*, 15 August 2013.
18. https://www.facebook.com/zuck/posts/10101301165605491.
19. Lloyd Grove, 'Kathleen Sebelius's Daily Show Disaster: Jon Stewart Slams Obamacare Rules', *Daily Beast*, 8 October 2013.
20. Schmidt and Cohen, 'Digital Disruption'.
21. Cecilia Kang, 'Google, in Post-Obama Era, Aggressively Woos Republicans', *The New York Times*, 27 January 2017.
22. Gautham Nagesh, 'ICANN 101: Who Will Oversee the Internet?' *Wall Street Journal*, 17 March 2014.
23. Enders and Su, 'Rational Terrorists'.
24. Scott Atran and Nafees Hamid, 'Paris: The War ISIS Wants, *New York Review of Books*, 16 November 2015.

25. David Ignatius, 'How ISIS Spread in the Middle East: And How to Stop It', *Atlantic*, 29 October 2015.
26. Karl Vick, 'ISIS Militants Declare Islamist "Caliphate"', *Time*, 29 June 2014.
27. Graeme Wood, 'What ISIS Really Wants', *Atlantic*, March 2015.
28. Berger and Morgan, 'ISIS Twitter Census'. See also Joseph Rago, 'How Algorithms Can Help Beat Islamic State', *Wall Street Journal*, 11 March 2017.
29. Craig Whiteside, 'Lighting the Path: The Story of the Islamic State's Media Enterprise', *War on the Rocks*, 12 December 2016.
30. Wood, 'What ISIS Really Wants'.
31. UN Security Council, 'In Presidential Statement, Security Council Calls for Redoubling Efforts to Target Root Causes of Terrorism as Threat Expands, Intensifies', 19 November 2014: www.un.org/press/en/2014/sc11656.doc.htm. See also Spencer Ackerman, 'Foreign Jihadists Flocking to Syria on "Unprecedented Scale" – UN', *Guardian*, 30 October 2014.
32. Wood, 'What ISIS Really Wants'.
33. Bodine-Baron et al., *Examining ISIS Support*.
34. Fisher, 'Swarmcast'. See also Ali Fisher, 'ISIS Strategy and the Twitter Jihadiscape', CPD Blog, 24 April 2017: http://uscpublicdiplomacy.org/blog/isis-strategy-and-twitter-jihadiscape.
35. John Bohannon, 'Women Critical for Online Terrorist Networks', *Science*, 10 June 2016.
36. MacGill, 'Acephalous Groups'.
37. Even Obama's critics struggled to offer a coherent response to ISIS. For a conventional military/political counter-terrorism strategy, with no mention on cyberspace, see Habeck et al., *Global Strategy for Combating Al-Qaeda*.
38. Institute for Economics and Peace, *Global Terrorism Index 2016: Measuring and Understanding the Impact of Terrorism*, 4.
39. START, *Patterns of Islamic State-Related Terrorism, 2002–2015* (August 2016).
40. Institute for Economics and Peace, *Global Terrorism Index 2016*, 43.
41. Byrne, *Black Flag Down*, 18–20.
42. Stuart, *Islamist Terrorism*.
43. Rukmini Callimachi, Alissa J. Rubin and Laure Fourquet, 'A View of ISIS's Evolution in New Details of Paris Attacks', *The New York Times*, 19 March 2016.
44. Ali, *Challenge of Dawa*. See also Sookhdeo, *Dawa*.

45. Stuart, *Islamist Terrorism: Key Findings*, 2, 9, 11, 18.
46. Frampton et al., *Unsettled Belonging*.
47. Scott Atran and Nafees Hamid, 'Paris: The War ISIS Wants, *New York Review of Books*, 16 November 2015.
48. Berger and Morgan, 'ISIS Twitter Census'.
49. John Bohannon, 'How to Attack the Islamic State Online', *Science*, 17 June 2016. See also Berger and Perez, 'The Islamic State's Diminishing Returns on Twitter', and Wood, *Way of the Strangers*, 287.
50. http://www.bbc.com/news/uk-34568574.
51. Sutton, 'Myths and Misunderstandings'.
52. http://www.telegraph.co.uk/news/uknews/terrorism-in-the-uk/11546683/ Islamist-extremists-in-prison-revolving-door-as-numbers-soar.html.
53. Pew Research Center, *Future Global Muslim Population*.
54. Laurence and Vaisse, *Integrating Islam*, 40f. See also Khosrokhavar, *L'Islam dans les prisons*. See also Scott Atran and Nafees Hamid, 'Paris: The War ISIS Wants', *New York Review of Books*, 16 November 2015.
55. Antoine Krempf, '60% des détenus français sont musulmans?' Replay Radio, 26 January 2015.
56. Pew Research Center, *World's Muslims*.

56. 11/9/2016

1. For a defence of populism, see Roger Kimball, 'Populism, X: The Imperative of Freedom', *New Criterion* (June 2017).
2. Deena Shanker, 'Social Media are Driving Americans Insane', *Bloomberg*, 23 February 2017.
3. Deloitte, *No Place Like Phone*.
4. Hampton et al., 'Social Isolation and New Technology'.
5. Funke et al., 'Going to Extremes'.
6. Inglehart and Norris, 'Trump, Brexit, and the Rise of Populism'. See also Daniel Drezner, 'I Attended Three Conferences on Populism in Ten Days', *Washington Post*, 19 June 2017.
7. Renee DiResta, 'Crowds and Technology', RibbonFarm, 15 September 2016: http://www.ribbonfarm.com/2016/09/15/crowds-and-technology/.
8. Brinton and Chiang, *Power of Networks*, 207.
9. 'Mobilising Voters through Social Media in the U.S., Taiwan and Hong Kong', Bauhinia, 15 August 2016.

10. Pentland, *Social Physics*, 50f.
11. Bond et al., '61-Million-Person Experiment'.
12. Goodhart, *Road to Somewhere*.
13. Dominic Cummings, 'How the Brexit Referendum Was Won', *Spectator*, 9 January 2017.
14. Dominic Cummings, 'On the Referendum #20: The Campaign, Physics and Data Science', 29 October 2016: https://dominiccummings.wordpress.com/2016/10/29/on-the-referendum-20-the-campaign-physics-and-data-science-vote-leaves-voter-intention-collection-system-vics-now-available-for-all/.
15. Carole Cadwalladr, 'Revealed: How U.S. Billionaire Helped to Back Brexit', *Guardian*, 25 February 2017. Simon Kuper, 'Targeting Specific Voters is More Effective and Cheaper than Speaking to the Public on TV', *Financial Times*, 14 June 2017.
16. Salena Zito, 'Taking Trump Seriously, Not Literally', *Atlantic*, 23 September 2016.
17. Allen and Parnes, *Shattered*, KL 256–7, 566–9, 599–601, 804–6.
18. Ibid., KL 2902–4.
19. Ibid., KL 3261–73, 3281–5, 3291–3301.
20. Allcott and Gentzkow, 'Social Media and Fake News'.
21. Shannon Greenwood, Andrew Perrin and Maeve Duggan, 'Social Media Update 2016', Pew Research Center, 11 November 2016. See Mostafa M. El-Bermawy, 'Your Filter Bubble is Destroying Democracy', *Wired*, 18 November 2016.
22. Maeve Duggan and Aaron Smith, 'The Political Environment on Social Media', Pew Research Center, 25 October 2016.
23. 'Mobilising Voters through Social Media in the U.S., Taiwan and Hong Kong', Bauhinia, 15 August 2016.
24. Erin Pettigrew, 'How Facebook Saw Trump Coming When No One Else Did', *Medium*, 9 November 2016.
25. Pew Research Center, 'Election Campaign 2016: Campaigns as a Direct Source of News', 18 July 2016, 15.
26. https://www.youtube.com/watch?v=vST61W4bGm8.
27. https://www.wired.com/2016/11/facebook-won-trump-election-not-just-fake-news/.
28. Cecilia Kang, 'Google, in post-Obama Era, Aggressively Woos Republicans', *The New York Times*, 27 January 2017.
29. 'Facebook Employees Pushed to Remove Trump's Posts as Hate Speech', *Wall Street Journal*, 21 October 2016.

30. Farhad Manjoo, 'Algorithms with Agendas and the Sway of Facebook', *The New York Times*, 11 May 2016.
31. Issie Lapowsky, 'Here's How Facebook Actually Won Trump the Presidency', *Wired*, 15 November 2016.
32. Elizabeth Chan, 'Donald Trump, Pepe the Frog, and White Supremacists: An Explainer', Hillary for America, 12 September 2016.
33. Ben Schreckinger, 'World War Meme', *Politico*, March/April 2017.
34. Hannes Grassegger And Mikael Krogerus, 'The Data That Turned the World Upside Down', Motherboard, 28 January 2017.
35. Nicholas Confessore and Danny Hakim, 'Bold Promises Fade to Doubts for a Trump-Linked Data Firm', *The New York Times*, 6 March 2017.
36. Issie Lapowsky, 'The 2016 Election Exposes the Very, Very Dark Side of Tech', *Wired*, 7 November 2016.
37. Zeynep Tufekci, 'Mark Zuckerberg is in Denial', *The New York Times*, 15 November 2016.
38. Richard Waters, 'Google Admits Giving Top Spot to Inaccurate Claim on Trump Votes', *Financial Times*, 15 November 2016.
39. Allcott and Gentzkow, 'Social Media and Fake News'.
40. David Blood, 'Fake News is Shared as Widely as the Real Thing', *Financial Times*, 27 March 2017.
41. Boxell et al., 'Is the Internet Causing Political Polarization?'

IX: CONCLUSION: FACING CYBERIA

57. Metropolis

1. The original essay on this theme was Niall Ferguson and Moritz Schularick, 'Chimerical? Think Again', *Wall Street Journal*, 5 February 2007. We revisited it in ' "Chimerica" and the Rule of Central Bankers', ibid., 27 August 2015. The idea inspired Lucy Kirkwood's 2013 play of the same name.
2. So far as I am aware, this has never been done. Relevant data can be found at http://globe.cid.harvard.edu/.
3. See for example Barnett (ed.), *Encyclopedia of Social Networks*, vol. I, 297. The optimistic case is laid out by Slaughter, *The Chessboard and the Web*.

58. Network Outage

1. Kissinger, *World Order*, 93f.
2. Ibid., 371.
3. Steven Pinker and Andrew Mack, 'The World is Not Falling Apart', *Slate*, 22 December 2014. For a critique of Pinker's book, *Better Angels*, see Cirillo and Taleb, 'Statistical Properties'. See for a reply Steven Pinker, 'Fooled by Belligerence: Comments on Nassim Taleb's "The Long Peace is a Statistical Illusion"': http://stevenpinker.com/files/comments_on_taleb_by_s_pinker.pdf.
4. Kissinger, *World Order*, 340, 347, 368.
5. See Allison, *Destined for War.*
6. Jeffrey Goldberg, 'World Chaos and World Order: Conversations with Henry Kissinger', *Atlantic*, 10 November 2016.
7. Niall Ferguson, 'The Lying, Hating Hi-Tech Webs of Zuck and Trump are the New Superpowers', *Sunday Times*, 19 February 2017.
8. See e.g. Snyder, *On Tyranny.*
9. See e.g. (published on the same day) Jennifer Senior, '"Richard Nixon", Portrait of a Thin-Skinned, Media-Hating President', *The New York Times*, 29 March 2017; Jennifer Rubin, 'End the Nunes Charade, and Follow the Russian Money', *Washington Post*, 29 March 2017.
10. Dittmar, 'Information Technology and Economic Change'.
11. McKinsey Global Institute, *Playing to Win*, 11.
12. World Bank, *Digital Dividends*, 95.
13. Ibid., 207.
14. Ibid., xiii, 6.
15. Schiedel, *Great Leveler.*
16. World Bank, *Digital Dividends*, 217.
17. Alexis C. Madrigal, 'The Weird Thing About Today's Internet', *Atlantic*, 17 May 2017.
18. Thiel, *Zero to One.*
19. In the developing world, mobile-phone service costs vary from nearly $50 a month in Brazil to single digits in Sri Lanka. The price of Internet for a megabit per second is around 300 times higher in landlocked Chad than in Kenya: World Bank, *Digital Dividends*, 8, 71, 218.
20. Ibid., 13.
21. Charles Kadushin, 'Social Networks and Inequality: How Facebook Contributes to Economic (and Other) Inequality', *Psychology Today*, 7 March 2012: https://www.psychologytoday.com/blog/understanding-social-networks/201203/social-networks-and-inequality.

22. Sam Altman, 'I'm a Silicon Valley Liberal, and I Traveled across the Country to Interview 100 Trump Supporters – Here's What I Learned', *Business Insider*, 23 February 2017: http://www.businessinsider.com/sam-altman-interview-trump-supporters-2017-2.
23. 'As American as Apple Inc.: Corporate Ownership and the Fight for Tax Reform', Penn Wharton Public Policy Initiative, Issue Brief 4, 1: https://publicpolicy.wharton.upenn.edu/issue-brief/v4n1.php.
24. Sandra Navidi, 'How Trumpocracy Corrupts Democracy', Project Syndicate, 21 February 2017.
25. Cecilia Kang, 'Google, in post-Obama Era, Aggressively Woos Republicans', *The New York Times*, 27 January 2017; Jack Nicas and Tim Higgins, 'Silicon Valley Faces Balancing Act between White House Criticism and Engagement', *Wall Street Journal*, 31 January 2017.
26. Issie Lapowsky, 'The Women's March Defines Protest in the Facebook Age', *Wired*, 21 January 2017; Nick Bilton, 'Will Mark Zuckerberg be Our Next President?' *Vanity Fair*, 13 January 2017.
27. World Bank, *Digital Dividends*, 221–7.
28. Lada A. Adamic, Thomas M. Lenton, Eytan Adar and Pauline C. Ng, 'Information Evolution in Social Networks', 22–25 February 2016: https://research.fb.com/wp-content/uploads/2016/11/information_evolution_in_social_networks.pdf.
29. James Stavridis, 'The Ghosts of Religious Wars Past are Rattling in Iraq', *Foreign Policy*, 17 June 2014.
30. Turchin, *Ages of Discord*.
31. Maier, *Leviathan 2.0*.
32. Mark Galeotti, 'The "Trump Dossier," or How Russia Helped America Break Itself', *Tablet*, 13 June 2017.
33. Fareed Zakaria, 'America Must Defend Itself against the Real National Security Menace', *Washington Post*, 9 March 2017.
34. Nye, 'Deterrence and Dissuasion', 47.
35. Ramo, *Seventh Sense*, 217f.
36. Caldarelli and Catanzaro, *Networks*, 95–8, 104f.
37. Drew Fitzgerald and Robert McMillan, 'Cyberattack Knocks Out Access to Websites', *Wall Street Journal*, 21 October 2016; William Turton, 'Everything We Know about the Cyberattack That Crippled America's Internet', Gizmodo, 24 October 2016.
38. Fred Kaplan, '"WarGames" and Cybersecurity's Debt to a Hollywood Hack', *The New York Times*, 19 February 2016.
39. Nye, 'Deterrence and Dissuasion'.

40. Ken Dilanian, William M. Arkin and Cynthia Mcfadden, 'U.S. Govt. Hackers Ready to Hit Back If Russia Tries to Disrupt Election', NBC, 4 November 2016.
41. Nathan Hodge, James Marson and Paul Sonne, 'Behind Russia's Cyber Strategy', *Wall Street Journal*, 16 December 2017.
42. For the most recent WikiLeaks release, see Zeynep Tufekci, 'The Truth about the WikiLeaks C.I.A. Cache', *The New York Times*, 9 March 2017.
43. Bonnie Berkowitz, Denise Lu and Julie Vitkovskaya, 'Here's What We Know So Far about Team Trump's Ties to Russian Interests', *Washington Post*, 31 March 2017.
44. Nye, 'Deterrence and Dissuasion', 44–52, 63–7.
45. Mark Galeotti, 'Crimintern: How the Kremlin Uses Russia's Criminal Networks in Europe', European Council on Foreign Relations Policy Brief (April 2017).
46. Anne-Marie Slaughter, 'How to Succeed in the Networked World', *Foreign Affairs*, (November/December 2016), 80.
47. Slaughter, 'How to Succeed', 84f.; Slaughter, *The Chessboard and the Web*, KL 2738.
48. Slaughter, 'How to Succeed', 86.
49. Slaughter, *The Chessboard and the Web*, KL 2680–84.
50. Ian Klaus, 'For Cities of the Future, Three Paths to Power', *Atlantic*, 19 March 2017.
51. Ramo, *Seventh Sense*, 182.
52. Ibid., 233.
53. Ibid., 153. See also Clarke and Eddy, *Warnings*, 283–301.
54. Taleb, *Antifragile*.
55. Arbesman, *Overcomplicated*.
56. Caldarelli and Catanzaro, *Networks*, 97.

59. FANG, BAT and EU

1. Daniel Martin, 'Shaming of Web Giants', *Daily Mail*, 15 March 2017.
2. Guy Chazan, 'Germany Cracks Down on Social Media over Fake News', *Financial Times*, 14 March 2017.
3. GP Bullhound, *European Unicorns: Survival of the Fittest* (2016).
4. Adam Satariano and Aoife White, 'Silicon Valley's Miserable Euro Trip is Just Getting Started', *Bloomberg Business Week*, 20 October 2016; Mark Scott, 'The Stakes are Rising in Google's Antitrust Fight with

Europe', *The New York Times*, 30 October 2016; Philip Stephens, 'Europe Rewrites the Rules for Silicon Valley', *Financial Times*, 3 November 2016.

5. Goldsmith and Wu, *Who Controls the Internet?*, 5ff.
6. For a different view, see Hafner-Burton and Montgomery, 'Globalization and the Social Power Politics.'
7. Bethany Allen-Ebrahimian, 'The Man Who Nailed Jello to the Wall', *Foreign Policy*, 29 June 2016.
8. Spar, *Ruling the Waves*, 381.
9. Guobin Yang, 'China's Divided Netizens', Berggruen Insights, 6, 21 October 2017.
10. King et al., 'Randomized Experiment'.
11. Goldsmith and Wu, *Who Controls the Internet?*, 96.
12. Emily Parker, 'Mark Zuckerberg's Long March into China', *Bloomberg*, 18 October 2016; Alyssa Abkowitz, Deepa Seetharaman and Eva Dou, 'Facebook Is Trying Everything to Re-Enter China—and It's Not Working', *Wall Street Journal*, 30 January 2017.
13. Mary Meeker, 'Internet Trends 2016—Code Conference', Kleiner Perkins Caufield Byers, 1 June 2016, 170f.
14. Kirby et al., 'Uber in China', 12.
15. William Kirby, 'The Real Reason Uber is Giving Up in China', *Harvard Business Review*, 2 August 2016.
16. See e.g. Eric X. Li, 'Party of the Century: How China is Reorganizing for the Future', *Foreign Affairs*, 10 January 2017, and Bell, *China Model.*
17. Keller, 'Networks of Power', 32; Keller, 'Moving Beyond Factions', 22.
18. Li, *Chinese Politics*, 332, 347f.
19. Jessica Batke and Matthias Stepan, 'Party, State and Individual Leaders: The Who's Who of China's Leading Small Groups', Mercator Institute for China Studies (2017).
20. Lin and Milhaupt, 'Bonded to the State'.
21. 'Chinese Censors' Looser Social Media Grip "May Help Flag Threats"', *South China Morning Post*, 13 February 2017.
22. 'Visualizing China's Anti-Corruption Campaign', ChinaFile, 21 January 2016.
23. 'Big Data, Meet Big Brother: China Invents the Digital Totalitarian State', *Economist*, 17 December 2016.
24. Nick Szabo, 'Money, Blockchains and Social Scalability', Unenumerated, 9 February 2017.
25. Ibid.

26. Haldane, 'A Little More Conversation'. See also Bettina Warburg, How the Blockchain will Radically Transform the Economy', TED talk, November 2016.
27. David McGlauflin, 'How China's Plan to Launch Its Own Currency Might Affect Bitcoin', Cryptocoins News, 25 January 2016; 'China is Developing Its Own Digital Currency', Bloomberg News, 23 February 2017. Details of the PBOC plan at http://www.cnfinance.cn/magzi/2016-09/01-24313.html and http://www.cnfinance.cn/magzi/2016-09/01-24314.html.
28. Deloitte and Monetary Authority of Singapore, 'The Future is Here: Project Ubin: SGD on Distributed Ledger' (2017). See in general Bordo and Levin, 'Central Bank Digital Currency'.

60. The Square and the Tower Redux

1. For a suggestive comparison with the Renaissance, see Goldin and Kutarna, *Age of Discovery*.
2. Heylighen and Bollen, 'World-Wide Web as a Super-Brain'. See also Heylighen, 'Global Superorganism'.
3. Dertouzos, *What Will Be*.
4. Wright, *Nonzero*, 198.
5. Hayles, 'Unfinished Work', 164.
6. Tomlin, *Cloud Coffee House*, 55.
7. Ibid., 223.
8. Spier, *Big History and the Future of Humanity*, 138–83.
9. Naughton, *From Gutenberg to Zuckerberg*, 207, 236.
10. Mark Zuckerberg, 'Commencement Address at Harvard', *Harvard Gazette*, May 25, 2017.
11. Gordon, *Rise and Fall of American Growth*. For an optimistic view, see Schwab, *Fourth Industrial Revolution*.
12. Acemoglu and Restrepo, 'Robots and Jobs'.
13. World Bank, *Digital Dividends*, 23, 131.
14. Caplan, 'Totalitarian Threat'.
15. For a historically based prediction of an upsurge in violence in the United States, see Turchin, *Ages of Discord*.
16. Caldara and Iacoviello, 'Measuring Geopolitical Risk'.
17. Bostrom, *Superintelligence*. See also Clarke and Eddy, *Warnings*, esp. 199–216.

18. David Streitfeld, '"The Internet Is Broken': @ev Is Trying to Salvage It', *New York Times*, 20 May 2017.
19. Scott, *Two Cheers.*
20. Niall Ferguson, 'Donald Trump's New World Order', *The American Interest* (March/April 2017), 37–47.
21. Steinhof, 'Urban Images', 20.
22. https://www.nytimes.com/interactive/2016/12/21/upshot/Mapping-the-Shadows-of-New-York-City.html?_r=1.
23. Steven Levy, Inside Apple's Insanely Great (Or Just Insane) New Mothership', *Wired*, 16 May 2017.
24. Facebook:http://mashable.com/2015/03/31/facebook-new-headquarters-photos/#odtktL9aMgqH; Apple: http://www.fosterandpartners.com/news/archive/2017/02/apple-park-opens-to-employees-in-april/; Google: https://googleblog.blogspot.com/2015/02/rethinking-office-space.html.

Afterword

1. Joseph Polzer, 'Ambrogio Lorenzetti's "War and Peace" Murals Revisited: Contributions to the Meaning of the "Good Government Allegory"', *Artibus et Historiae*, 23, 45 (2002), 64. For background, see Timothy Hyman, *Sienese Painting: The Art of a City-Republic (1278–1477)* (New York: Thames & Hudson, 2003).
2. Charles Duan, '"Internet" or "internet"? The Supreme Court Weighs In', *Motherboard*, 22 June 2017.
3. Polzer, 'Ambrogio Lorenzetti's "War and Peace" Murals', 69.
4. Ibid., 70.
5. Nirit Ben-Aryeh Debby, 'War and Peace: The Description of Ambrogio Lorenzetti's Frescoes in Saint Bernardino's 1425 Siena Sermons', *Renaissance Studies*, 15, 3 (September 2001), 272–86.
6. Jack M. Greenstein, 'The Vision of Peace: Meaning and Representation in Ambrogio Lorenzetti's *Salla della Pace* Cityscapes', *Art History*, 11, 4 (December 1988), 504.
7. The black and white colours of his robe are those of the *Balzana*, Siena's standard; the she-wolf and her suckling twins at his feet allude to Siena's supposedly ancient Roman origin; the inscription on his shield is taken from Siena's official seal: Polzer, 'Ambrogio Lorenzetti's "War and Peace" Murals', 71.
8. Ibid., 86.

9. Quentin Skinner, 'Ambrogio Lorenzetti's Buon Governo Frescoes: Two Old Questions, Two New Answers', *Journal of the Warburg and Courtauld Institutes*, 62 (1999), 1–28.
10. Polzer, 'Ambrogio Lorenzetti's "War and Peace" Murals', 71. See also C. Jean Campbell, 'The City's New Clothes: Ambrogio Lorenzetti and the Poetics of Peace', *Art Bulletin*, 83, 2 (June 2001), 240–58.
11. Skinner, 'Ambrogio Lorenzetti's Buon Governo Frescoes', 14.
12. Polzer, 'Ambrogio Lorenzetti's "War and Peace" Murals', 82.
13. Greenstein, 'The Vision of Peace', 498.
14. Ibid., 494; Polzer, 'Ambrogio Lorenzetti's "War and Peace" Murals', 70.
15. Skinner, 'Ambrogio Lorenzetti's Buon Governo Frescoes'.
16. Diana Norman, 'Pisa, Siena, and the Maremma: A Neglected Aspect of Ambrogio Lorenzetti's Paintings in the Sala dei Nove', *Renaissance Studies*, 11, 4 (December 1997), 314.
17. Norman, 'Pisa, Siena, and the Maremma', 320.
18. Greenstein, 'The Vision of Peace', 503f.
19. Roxann Prazniak, 'Siena on the Silk Roads: Ambrogio Lorenzetti and the Mongol Global Century, 1250–1350', *Journal of World History*, 21, 2 (June 2010), 177–217.
20. Ibid., 180, 185, 188f.
21. Debby, 'War and Peace', 283.

Bibliography

I. INTRODUCTION: NETWORKS AND HIERARCHIES

Acemoglu, Daron and James A. Robinson, *Why Nations Fail: The Origins of Power, Prosperity, and Poverty* (New York and London: Crown/Profile, 2012)

Agethen, Manfred, *Geheimbund und Utopie: Illuminaten, Freimaurer und deutsche Spätaufklärung* (Munich: R. Oldenbourg, 1984)

Allison, Graham, 'The Impact of Globalization on National and International Security', in Joseph S. Nye, Jr, and John D. Donahue (eds.), *Governance in a Global World* (Washington, DC: Brookings Institution Press, 2000), 72–85

Banerjee, Abhijit, Arun G. Chandrasekhar, Esther Duflo and Matthew O. Jackson, 'Gossip: Identifying Central Individuals in a Social Network', working paper, 14 February 2016

Barabási, Albert-László, *Linked: How Everything is Connected to Everything Else and What It Means for Business, Science, and Everyday Life* (New York: Basic Books, 2014)

——— and Réka Albert, 'Emergence of Scaling in Random Networks', *Science*, 286, 5439 (15 October 1999), 509–12

Bennett, Alan, *The History Boys* (London: Faber & Faber, 2004)

Berger, Jonah, *Contagious: Why Things Catch On* (New York: Simon & Schuster, 2013)

Boeder, Pieter, 'Habermas' Heritage: The Future of the Public Sphere in the Network Society', *First Monday* (September 2005)

Boisot, Max, *Information Space: A Framework for Learning in Organizations, Institutions and Culture* (London: Routledge, 1995)

———, *Knowledge Assets: Securing Competitive Advantage in the Information Economy* (Oxford: Oxford University Press, 1998)

Boisot, Max and Xiaohui Lu, 'Competing and Collaborating in Networks: Is Organizing Just a Game?', in Michael Gibbert and Thomas Durand (eds.), *Strategic Networks: Learning to Compete* (Malden, MA: Wiley-Blackwell, 2006), 151–69

Bostrom, Nick, *Superintelligence: Paths, Dangers, Strategies* (Oxford: Oxford University Press, 2014)

Bramoullé, Yann, Sergio Currarini, Matthew O. Jackson, Paolo Pin and Brian W. Rogers, 'Homophily and Long-Run Integration in Social Networks', *Journal of Economic Theory*, 147, 5 (2012), 1754–86

Burt, Ronald S., *Brokerage and Closure: An Introduction to Social Capital* (Clarendon Lectures in Management Studies) (Oxford: Oxford University Press, 2007)

———, *Neighbor Networks: Competitive Advantage Local and Personal* (Oxford: Oxford University Press, 2010)

———, *Structural Holes: The Social Structure of Competition* (Cambridge, MA: Harvard University Press, 1992)

———, 'Structural Holes and Good Ideas', *American Journal of Sociology*, 110, 2 (September 2004), 349–99

Calvó-Armengol, Antoni and Matthew O. Jackson, 'The Effects of Social Networks on Employment and Inequality', *American Economic Review*, 94, 3 (2004), 426–54

Carroll, Glenn R. and Albert C. Teo, 'On the Social Networks of Managers', *Academy of Management Journal*, 39, 2 (1996), 421–40

Cassill, Deby and Alison Watkins, 'The Evolution of Cooperative Hierarchies through Natural Selection Processes', *Journal of Bioeconomics*, 12, (2010), 29–42

Castells, Manuel, 'Information Technology, Globalization and Social Development', United Nations Research Institute for Social Development Discussion Paper, no. 114 (September 1999), 1–15

Centola, Damon and Michael Macy, 'Complex contagions and the weakness of long ties', *American Journal of Sociology*, 113, 3 (2007), 702–34

Christakis, Nicholas A. and James H. Fowler, *Connected: The Surprising Power of Our Social Networks and How They Shape Our Lives* (New York: Little, Brown, 2009)

Cline, Diane H. and Eric H. Cline, 'Text Messages, Tablets, and Social Networks: The "Small World" of the Amarna Letters', in Jana Mynářová, Pavel Onderka and Peter Pavuk (eds.), *There and Back Again – The Crossroads II: Proceedings of an International Conference Held in Prague, September 15–18, 2014* (Prague: Charles University, 2015), 17–44

Coleman, James S., 'Social Capital in the Creation of Human Capital', *American Journal of Sociology*, 94 (188), S95–S120

Collar, Anna, *Religious Networks in the Roman Empire: The Spread of New Ideas* (New York: Cambridge University Press, 2013)

Crane, Diana, 'Social Structure in a Group of Scientists: A Test of the "Invisible College Hypothesis"', *American Sociological Review*, 34, 3 (June 1969), 335–52

Currarini, Sergio, Matthew O. Jackson and Paolo Pin, 'Identifying the Roles of Race-Based Choice and Chance in High School Friendship Network Formation', *Proceedings of the National Academy of Sciences*, 16 March 2010, 4857–61

Dittrich, Luke, *Patient H.M.: A Story of Memory, Madness and Family Secrets* (London: Chatto & Windus, 2016)

Dolton, Peter, 'Identifying Social Network Effects', *Economic Record*, 93, Supplement S1 (2017)

Dubreuil, Benoît, *Human Evolution and the Origins of Hierarchies: The State of Nature* (Cambridge: Cambridge University Press, 2010)

Dülmen, Richard van, *Der Geheimbund der Illuminaten: Darstellung, Analyse, Dokumentation* (Stuttgart: Frommann-Holzboog, 1975)

Dunbar, R. I. M., 'Coevolution of Neocortical Size, Group Size and Language in Humans', *Behavioral and Brain Sciences* 16, 4 (1993), 681–735

Enrich, David, *The Spider Network: The Wild Story of a Math Genius, a Gang of Backstabbing Bankers, and One of the Greatest Scams in Financial History* (New York: HarperCollins, 2017)

Ferguson, Niall, 'Complexity and Collapse: Empires on the Edge of Chaos', *Foreign Affairs*, 89, 2 (March/April 2010), 18–32

Forestier, René Le, *Les illuminés de Bavière et la franc-maçonnerie allemande* (Paris: Hachette, 1915)

Friedland, Lewis A., 'Electronic Democracy and the New Citizenship', *Media Culture & Society*, 18 (1996), 185–212

Fukuyama, Francis, *The Great Disruption: Human Nature and the Reconstitution of Social Order* (New York: The Free Press, 1999)

———, *The Origins of Political Order: From Prehuman Times to the French Revolution* (London: Profile Books, 2011)

———, *Political Order and Political Decay: From the Industrial Revolution to the Globalisation of Democracy* (London: Profile Books, 2014)

Goertzel, Ted, 'Belief in Conspiracy Theories', *Political Psychology*, 15, 4 (December 1994), 731–42

Goldberg, Amir, Sameer B. Srivastava, V. Govind Manian, William Monroe and Christopher Potts, 'Fitting In or Standing Out? The Tradeoffs of Structural and Cultural Embeddedness', *American Sociological Review*, 81, 6 (2016): 1190–1222

Gorky, Maxim, transl. Ronald Wilks, *My Universities* (London: Penguin Books, 1979 [1922])

Granovetter, Mark, 'The Strength of Weak Ties', *American Journal of Sociology*, 78, 6 (May 1973), 1360–80

———, 'The Strength of Weak Ties: A Network Theory Revisited', *Sociological Theory*, 1 (1983), 201–33

Greif, Avner, 'Contract Enforceability and Economic Institutions in Early Trade: The Maghribi Traders' Coalition', *American Economic Review*, 83, 3 (June 1993), 525–48

——, 'Reputation and Coalitions in Medieval Trade: Evidence on the Maghribi Traders', *Journal of Economic History*, 49, 4 (December 1989), 857–82

Grewal, David Singh, *Network Power: The Social Dynamics of Globalization* (New Haven: Yale University Press, 2008)

Harari, Yuval Noah, *Homo Deus: A Brief History of Tomorrow* (New York: HarperCollins, 2017)

———, *Sapiens: A Brief History of Humankind* (New York: HarperCollins, 2015)

Harrison, Richard J. and Glenn R. Carroll, 'The Dynamics of Cultural Influence Networks', *Computational & Mathematical Organization Theory*, 8 (2002), 5–30

Hataley, K. M., 'In Search of the Illuminati: A Light Amidst Darkness', *Journal of the Western Mystery Tradition*, 23, 3 (2012)

Henrich, Joseph, *The Secret of Our Success: How Culture is Driving Human Evolution, Domesticating Our Species, and Making Us Smarter* (Princeton: Princeton University Press, 2016)

Heylighen, Francis, 'From Human Computation to the Global Brain: The Self-Organization of Distributed Intelligence', in Pietro Michelucci (ed.), *Handbook of Human Computation* (New York: Springer, 2013), 897–909

———, 'The Global Superorganism: An Evolutionary-Cybernetic Model of the Emerging Network Society', *Social Evolution and History*, 1, 6 (2007), 57–117

Hofman, Amos, 'Opinion, Illusion, and the Illusion of Opinion: Barruel's Theory of Conspiracy', *Eighteenth-Century Studies*, 27, 1 (Autumn, 1993), 27–60

Hofstadter, Richard, *The Paranoid Style in American Politics and Other Essays* (New York: Alfred A. Knopf, 1965)

Israel, Jonathan, *Democratic Enlightenment: Philosophy, Revolution, and Human Rights, 1750–1790* (Oxford: Oxford University Press, 2011)

Ito, Joi and Jeff Howe, *Whiplash: How to Survive Our Faster Future* (New York: Grand Central Publishing, 2016)

Jackson, Matthew O., 'Networks in the Understanding of Economic Behaviors', *Journal of Economic Perspectives*, 28, 4 (2014), 3–22

———, *Social and Economic Networks* (Princeton: Princeton University Press, 2008)

Jackson, Matthew O. and Brian W. Rogers, 'Meeting Strangers and Friends of Friends: How Random are Social Networks?' *American Economic Review*, 97, 3 (2007), 890–915

Jackson, Matthew O., Tomas Rodriguez-Barraquer and Xu Tan, 'Social Capital and Social Quilts: Network Patterns of Favor Exchange', *American Economic Review* 102, 5 (2012), 1857–97

Jackson, Matthew O., Brian W. Rogers and Yves Zenou, 'Connections in the Modern World: Network-Based Insights', 6 March 2015

Jackson, Matthew O. and Brian W. Rogers, 'Meeting Strangers and Friends of Friends: How Random are Social Networks?', *American Economic Review*, 97, 3 (2007), 890–915

Kadushin, Charles, *Understanding Social Networks: Theories, Concepts, and Findings* (New York: Oxford University Press, 2012)

Katz, Elihu and Paul Felix Lazarsfeld, *Personal Influence: The Part Played by People in the Flow of Mass Communications* (New York: Free Press, 1955)

Khanna, Parag, *Connectography: Mapping the Global Network Revolution* (London: Weidenfeld & Nicolson, 2016)

Kleinbaum, Adam M., Toby E. Stuart and Michael L. Tushman, 'Discretion Within Constraint: Homophily and Structure in a Formal Organization', *Organization Science*, 24, 5 (2013), 1316–36

Knight, Peter, 'Outrageous Conspiracy Theories: Popular and Official Responses to 9/11 in Germany and the United States', *New German Critique*, 103: conference on *Dark Powers: Conspiracies and Conspiracy Theory in History and Literature* (Winter 2008), 165–93

Krueger, Rita, *Czech, German, and Noble: Status and National Identity in Habsburg Bohemia* (Oxford: Oxford University Press, 2009)

Landes, Richard, 'The Jews as Contested Ground in Postmodern Conspiracy Theory', *Jewish Political Studies Review*, 19, 3/4 (Fall 2007), 9–34

Leinesch, Michael, 'The Illusion of the Illuminati: The Counterconspiratorial Origins of Post-Revolutionary Conservatism', in W. M. Verhoeven (ed.), *Revolutionary Histories: Transatlantic Cultural Nationalism, 1775–1815* (New York: Palgrave Macmillan, 2002), 152–65

Leskovec, Jure, Daniel Huttenlocher and Jon Kleinberg, 'Signed Networks in Social Media', *CHI 2010* (10–15 April 2010)

Liu, Ka-Yuet, Marissa King and Peter S. Bearman, 'Social Influence and the Autism Epidemic', *American Journal of Sociology*, 115, 5 (2012), 1387–1434

Livers, Keith, 'The Tower or the Labyrinth: Conspiracy, Occult, and Empire-Nostalgia in the Work of Viktor Pelevin and Aleksandr Prokhanov', *Russian Review*, 69, 3 (July 2010), 477–503

Loreto, Vittorio, Vito D. P. Servedio, Steven H. Strogatz and Francesca Tria, 'Dynamics and Expanding Spaces: Modeling the Emergence of Novelties', in Mirko Degli Esposti, Eduardo G. Altmann and François Pachet (eds.), *Creativity and Universality in Language* (Berlin: Springer International Publishing, 2016), 59–83

McArthur, Benjamin, '"They're Out to Get Us": Another Look at Our Paranoid Tradition', *History Teacher*, 29, 1 (November 1995), 37–50

McNeill, J. R. and William McNeill, *The Human Web: A Bird's-Eye View of Human History* (New York and London: W. W. Norton, 2003)

McPherson, Miller, Lynn Smith-Lovin, and James M. Cook, 'Birds of a Feather: Homophily in Social Networks', *Annual Review of Sociology*, 27 (2001), 415–44

Markner, Reinhard, Monika Neugebauer-Wölk and Hermann Schüttler (eds.), *Die Korrespondenz des Illuminatenordens*, vol. I: *1776–1781* (Tübingen: Max Niemeyer Verlag, 2005)

Massey, Douglas S., 'A Brief History of Human Society: The Origin and Role of Emotion in Social Life', *American Sociological Review*, 67 (February 2002), 1–29

Melanson, Terry, *Perfectibilists: The 18th Century Bavarian Order of the Illuminati* (Walterville, OR: Trine Day, 2011)

Meumann, Markus and Olaf Simons, 'Illuminati', in *Encyclopedia of the Bible and Its Reception*, vol. 12: *Ho Tsun Shen – Insult* (Berlin and Boston, MA: De Gruyter, 2016), columns 880–83

Milgram, Stanley, 'Small-World Problem', *Psychology Today*, 1, 1 (May 1967), 61–7

Moody, James, 'Race, School Integration, and Friendship Segregation in America', *American Journal of Sociology*, 107, 3 (November 2001), 679–716

Moreno, J. L., *Who Shall Survive? Foundations of Sociometry, Group Psychotherapy and Sociodrama* (Beacon, NY: Beacon House Inc., 1953)

Moretti, Franco, 'Network Theory, Plot Analysis', *Literary Lab*, Pamphlet 2, 1 May 2011.

Nahon, Karine and Jeff Hemsley, *Going Viral* (Cambridge: Polity, 2013)

Oliver, Eric J. and Thomas J. Wood, 'Conspiracy Theories and the Paranoid Style(s) of Mass Opinion', *American Journal of Political Science*, 58, 4 (October 2014), 952–66

Padgett, John F. and Paul D. McLean, 'Organizational Invention and Elite Transformation: The Birth of Partnership Systems in Renaissance Florence', *American Journal of Sociology*, 111, 5 (March 2006), 1463–1568

Padgett, John F. and Walter W. Powell, *The Emergence of Organizations and Markets* (Princeton: Princeton University Press, 2012)

Payson, Seth, *Proofs of the Real Existence, and Dangerous Tendency, of Illuminism: Containing an Abstract of the Most Interesting Parts of what Dr. Robison and the Abbe Barruel Have Published on this Subject, with Collateral Proofs and General Observations* (Charlestown: Samuel Etheridge, 1802)

Pinker, Susan, *The Village Effect: Why Face-to-Face Contact Matters* (London: Atlantic Books, 2015)

Ramo, Joshua Cooper, *The Seventh Sense: Power, Fortune, and Survival in the Age of Networks* (New York: Little, Brown, 2016)

Roberts, J. M., *The Mythology of the Secret Societies* (London: Secker & Warburg, 1971)

Rogers, Everett M., *Diffusion of Innovations*, 5th edn (New York and London: Free Press, 2003)

Rosen, Sherwin, 'The Economics of Superstars', *American Economic Review*, 71, 5 (December 1981), 845–58

Sampson, Tony D., *Virality: Contagion Theory in the Age of Networks* (Minneapolis and London: University of Minnesota Press, 2012)

Schmidt, Eric and Jared Cohen, *The New Digital Age: Transforming Nations, Businesses, and Our Lives* (New York: Knopf Doubleday, 2013)

Schüttler, Hermann, *Die Mitglieder des Illuminatenordens, 1776–1787/93* (Munich: ars una, 1991)

———, 'Zwei freimaurerische Geheimgesellschaften des 18. Jahrhunderts im Vergleich: Strikte Observanz und Illuminatenorden', in Erich Donnert (ed.), *Europa in der Frühen Neuzeit: Festschrift für Günter Mühlpfordt*, vol. IV: *Deutsche Aufklärung* (Weimar, Cologne and Vienna: Böhlau, 1997), 521–44

Simons, Olaf and Markus Meumann, '"Mein Amt ist geheime gewissens Correspondenz und unsere Brüder zu führen". Bode als "Unbekannter Oberer" des Illuminatenordens', in Cord-Friedrich Berghahn, Gerd Biegel and Till Kinzel (eds.), *Johann Joachim Christoph Bode – Studien zu Leben und Werk* [*Germanisch-Romanische Monatsschrift*, *Beihefte*] (Heidelberg: Winter, 2017)

Slaughter, Anne-Marie, *The Chessboard and the Web: Strategies of Connection in a Networked World* (Henry L. Stimson Lectures) (New Haven: Yale University Press, 2017)

Smith-Doerr, Laurel and Walter W. Powell, 'Networks and Economic Life', in Neil Smelser and Richard Swedberg (eds.), *The Handbook of Economic Sociology* (Princeton: Princeton University Press, 2010), 379–402

Solé, Ricard V. and Sergi Valverde, 'Information Theory of Complex Networks: On Evolution and Architectural Constraints', *Lect. Notes Phys.*, 650 (2004), 189–207

Stauffer, Vernon L., *New England and the Bavarian Illuminati: Studies in History, Economics and Political Law*, vol. 82, no. 1, 191 (New York: Columbia University Press, 1918)

Strogatz, Steven H., 'Exploring Complex Networks', *Nature*, 410, 8 March 2001, 268–76.

Swami, Viren, Rebecca Coles, Stefan Stieger, Jakob Pietschnig, Adrian Furnham, Sherry Rehim and Martin Voracek, 'Conspiracist Ideation in Britain and Austria: Evidence of a Monological Belief System and Associations Between Individual Psychological Differences and Real-World and Fictitious Conspiracy Theories', *British Journal of Psychology*, 102 (2011), 443–63

Syme, Ronald, *The Roman Revolution* (Oxford: Oxford University Press, 1960 [1939])

Taleb, Nassim Nicholas, *Antifragile: Things That Gain from Disorder* (New York: Random House, 2012)

Turchin, Peter, Thomas E. Currie, Edward A. L. Turner and Sergey Gavrilets, 'War, Space, and the Evolution of Old World Complex Societies', *Proceedings of the National Academy of Sciences*, 23 September 2013, 1–6

Tutić, Andreas and Harald Wiese, 'Reconstructing Granovetter's Network Theory', *Social Networks*, 43 (2015), 136–48

Van Dülmen, Richard, *The Society of the Enlightenment* (Cambridge: Polity Press, 1992)

Vera, Eugenia Roldán and Thomas Schupp, 'Network Analysis in Comparative Social Sciences', *Comparative Education*, 42, 3, Special Issue (32): *Comparative Methodologies in the Social Sciences: Cross-Disciplinary Inspirations* (August 2006), 405–29

Wäges, Josef and Reinhard Markner (eds.), *The Secret School of Wisdom: The Authentic Rituals and Doctrines of the Illuminati*, transl. Jeva Singh-Anand (Addlestone: Lewis Masonic, 2015)

Waterman, Bryan, 'The Bavarian Illuminati, the Early American Novel, and Histories of the Public Sphere', *William and Mary Quarterly*, 3rd Ser., 62, 1 (January 2005), 9–30

Watts, Duncan J., 'Networks, Dynamics, and the Small-World Phenomenon', *American Journal of Sociology*, 105, 2 (1999), 493–527

———, *Six Degrees: The Science of a Connected Age* (London: Vintage, 2004)

Watts, Duncan J. and Steven H. Strogatz, 'Collective Dynamics of "Small-World" Networks', *Nature*, 393 (4 June 1998), 400–442

West, Geoffrey, 'Can There be a Quantitative Theory for the History of Life and Society?' *Cliodynamics*, 2, 1 (2011), 208–14

———, *Scale: The Universal Laws of Growth, Innovation, Sustainability, and the Pace of Life in Organisms, Cities, Economies, and Companies* (New York: Penguin Random House, 2017)

II. EMPERORS AND EXPLORERS

Adamson, John, *The Noble Revolt: The Overthrow of Charles I* (London: Weidenfeld & Nicolson, 2007)

Ahnert, Ruth and Sebastian E. Ahnert, 'Metadata, Surveillance, and the Tudor State', unpublished paper (2017)

———, 'Protestant Letter Networks in the Reign of Mary I: A Quantitative Approach', *ELH*, 82, 1 (Spring 2015), 1–33

Allen, Robert and Leander Heldring, 'The Collapse of the World's Oldest Civilization: The Political Economy of Hydraulic States and the Financial Crisis of the Abbasid Caliphate', working paper (2016)

Barnett, George A. (ed.), *Encyclopedia of Social Networks*, 2 vols. (Los Angeles and London: SAGE Publications, Inc., 2011)

Bryc, Katarzyna, et al., 'Genome-Wide Patterns of Population Structure and Admixture among Hispanic/Latino Populations', *Proceedings of the National Academy of Sciences*, 107, Supplement 2: *In the Light of Evolution*, IV: *The Human Condition* (11 May 2010), 8954–61

Burbank, Jane and Frederick Cooper, *Empires in World History: Power and the Politics of Difference* (Princeton and Oxford: Princeton University Press, 2011)

Chang, T'ien-Tse, *Sino-Portuguese Trade from 1514–1644: A Synthesis of Portuguese and Chinese Sources* (New York: AMS Press, 1978)

Christian, David, 'Silk Roads or Steppe Roads? The Silk Roads in World History', *Journal of World History*, 11, 1 (2000), 1–26

Cline, Diane Harris, 'Six Degrees of Alexander: Social Network Analysis as a Tool for Ancient History', *Ancient History Bulletin*, 26 (2012), 59–69

Coase, Ronald, 'The Problem of Social Cost', *Journal of Law and Economics*, 3 (October 1960), 1–44

Cotrugli, Benedetto, *The Book of the Art of Trade*, eds. Carlo Carraro and Giovanni Favero, transl. John Francis Phillimore (London: Palgrave Macmillan, 2016)

Dittmar, Jeremiah E., 'Information Technology and Economic Change: The Impact of The Printing Press', *Quarterly Journal of Economics*, 126, 3 (2011), 1133–72

——— and Skipper Seabold, 'Media, Markets, and Radical Ideas: Evidence from the Protestant Reformation', working paper (22 February 2016)

Ferguson, Niall, *Civilization: The West and the Rest* (London: Allen Lane, 2011)

Frankopan, Peter, *The Silk Roads: A New History of the World* (New York: Knopf Doubleday, 2016)

Garcia-Zamor, Jean-Clause, 'Administrative Practices of the Aztecs, Incas, and Mayas: Lessons for Modern Development Administration', *International Journal of Public Administration*, 21, 1 (1998), 145–71

Geiss, James, 'The Chang-te Reign, 1506–1521', in D. C. Twitchett and F. W. Mote (eds.), *The Cambridge History of China*, vol. VIII, *The Ming Dynasty, 1368–1644, Part* 2 (Cambridge: Cambridge University Press, 1998), 403–39

Gellner, Ernest, *Nations and Nationalism* (Oxford: Blackwell, 1983)

Gleick, James, *The Information: A History, a Theory, a Flood* (New York: Pantheon, 2011)

Harland, Philip A., 'Connections with Elites in the World of the Early Christians', in Anthony J. Blasi, Paul A. Turcotte and Jean Duhaime (eds.), *Handbook of Early Christianity: Social Science Approaches* (Walnut Creek, CA: Altamira Press, 2002), 385–408

Heady, Ferrel, *Public Administration: A Comparative Perspective* (New York: Marcel Dekker, Inc., 2001)

Ishiguro, Kazuo, *The Buried Giant* (New York: Knopf, 2015)

McNeill, William H., 'What If Pizarro Had Not Found Potatoes in Peru?', in Robert Cowley (ed.), *What If? 2: Eminent Historians Imagine What Might Have Been* (New York: G. P. Putnam's Sons, 2001), 413–29

Malkin, Irad, *A Small Greek World: Networks in the Ancient Mediterranean* (New York and Oxford: Oxford University Press, 2011)

Mann, Charles W., *1493: Uncovering the New World Columbus Created* (New York: Vintage, 2011)

Morrissey, Robert Michael, 'Archives of Connection: "Whole Network" Analysis and Social History', *Historical Methods: A Journal of Quantitative and Interdisciplinary History*, 48, 2 (2015), 67–79

Namier, Lewis, *The Structure of Politics at the Accession of George III*, 2nd edn (London: Macmillan, 1957 [1929])

Naughton, John, *From Gutenberg to Zuckerberg: What You Really Need to Know about the Internet* (London: Quercus, 2012)

Padgett, John F., 'Marriage and Elite Structure in Renaissance Florence, 1282–1500', *Redes, Revista Hispana para el Análisis de Redes Sociales*, 21, 1 (2011), 71–97

——— and Christopher K. Ansell, 'Robust Action and the Rise of the Medici, 1400–1434', *American Journal of Sociology*, 98, 6 (May 1993), 1259–1319

Pettegree, Andrew, *Brand Luther: 1517, Printing, and the Making of the Reformation* (New York: Penguin Books, 2015)

Rodrigues, Jorge and Tessaleno Devezas, *Pioneers of Globalization: Why the Portuguese Surprised the World* (Lisbon: Centro Atlântico, 2007)

Scheidel, Walter, 'From the "Great Convergence" to the "First Great Divergence": Roman and Qin-Han State Formation and Its Aftermath', Princeton/Stanford Working Papers in Classics (November 2007)

Sen, Tansen, 'The Formation of Chinese Maritime Networks to Southern Asia, 1200–1450', *Journal of the Economic and Social History of the Orient*, 49, 4 (2006), 421–53

Smail, Daniel Lord, *On Deep History and the Brain* (Berkeley: University of California Press, 2008)

Smith, Monica L., 'Networks, Territories, and the Cartography of Ancient States', *Annals of the Association of American Geographers*, 95, 4 (2005), 832–49

Stark, Rodney, 'Epidemics, Networks, and the Rise of Christianity', *Semeia*, 56 (1992), 159–75

Tainter, Joseph A., 'Problem Solving: Complexity, History, Sustainability', *Population and Environment*, 22, 1 (September 2000), 3–40.

Tocqueville, Alexis de, *Democracy in America*, transl. Harvey C. Mansfield and Delba Winthrop (Chicago: University of Chicago Press, 2000)

Turchin, Peter, Thomas E. Currie, Edward A. L. Turner and Sergey Gavrilets, 'War, Space, and the Evolution of Old World Complex Societies', *Proceedings of the National Academy of Sciences*, 23 September 2013, 1–6

Wade, G., 'Melaka in Ming Dynasty Texts', *Journal of the Malaysian Branch of the Royal Asiatic Society*, 70, 1, 272 (1997), 31–69

Wills, John E., Jr (ed.), *China and Maritime Europe, 1500–1800: Trade, Settlement, Diplomacy, and Missions* (Cambridge: Cambridge University Press, 2011), pp. 24–51

Yupanqui, Titu Cusi, *An Inca Account of the Conquest of Peru*, transl. Ralph Bauer (Boulder: University Press of Colorado, 2005)

Zuñiga, Jean-Paul, 'Visible Signs of Belonging', in Pedro Cardim, Tamar Herzog, José Javier Ruiz Ibáñez and Gaetano Sabatini (eds.), *Polycentric Monarchies: How Did Early Modern Spain and Portugal Achieve and Maintain a Global Hegemony?* (Eastbourne: Sussex University Press, 2013), 125–46

III. LETTERS AND LODGES

Arcenas, Claire and Caroline Winterer, 'The Correspondence Network of Benjamin Franklin: The London Decades, 1757–1775', unpublished paper.

Bailyn, Bernard, *The Ideological Origins of the American Revolution* (Cambridge: Harvard University Press, 1967)

Borneman, Walter R., *American Spring: Lexington, Concord, and the Road to Revolution* (New York: Little, Brown, 2014)

Bullock, Steven C., *Revolutionary Brotherhood: Freemasonry and the Transformation of the American Social Order, 1730–1840* (Chapel Hill, NC: University of North Carolina Press, 2011)

Cantoni, Davide, Jeremiah Dittmar and Noam Yuchtman, 'Reformation and Reallocation: Religious and Secular Economic Activity in Early Modern Germany', working paper (November 2016)

Caracausi, Andrea and Christof Jeggle (eds.), *Commercial Networks and European Cities, 1400–1800* (London and New York: Routledge, 2015)

Carneiro, A. et al., 'Enlightenment Science in Portugal: The Estrangeirados and Their Communication Networks', *Social Studies of Science*, 30, 4 (2000), 591–619

Clark, J. C. D., *The Language of Liberty, 1660–1832: Political Discourse and Social Dynamics in the Anglo-American World* (Cambridge: Cambridge University Press, 1994)

Comsa, Maria Teodora, Melanie Conroy, Dan Edelstein, Chloe Summers Edmondson and Claude Willan, 'The French Enlightenment Network', *Journal of Modern History*, 88 (September 2016), 495–534

Danskin, Julie, 'The "Hotbed of Genius": Edinburgh's Literati and the Community of the Scottish Enlightenment', *eSharp*, Special Issue 7: *Real and Imagined Communities* (2013), 1–16

Dittmar, Jeremiah E., 'Ideas, Technology, and Economic Change: The Impact of the Printing Press', draft paper (13 March 2009)

———, 'The Welfare Impact of a New Good: The Printed Book', working paper (27 February 2012)

Edelstein, Dan, Paula Findlen, Giovanna Ceserani, Caroline Winterer and Nicole Coleman, 'Historical Research in a Digital Age: Reflections from the Mapping the Republic of Letters Project', *American Historical Review* (April 2017), 400–424

Eire, Carlos M. N. *Reformations: The Early Modern World, 1450–1650* (New Haven, CT, and London: Yale University Press, 2016)

Erikson, Emily, *Between Monopoly and Free Trade: The English East India Company, 1600–1757* (Princeton and Oxford: Princeton University Press, 2014)

Erikson, Emily and Peter Shawn Bearman, 'Malfeasance and the Foundations for Global Trade: The Structure of English Trade in the East Indies, 1601–1833', *American Journal of Sociology*, 112 (2006), 195–230

Fischer, David Hackett, *Paul Revere's Ride* (Oxford: Oxford University Press, 1995)

Gestrich, Andreas and Margrit Schulte Beerbühl, *Cosmopolitan Networks in Commerce and Society, 1660–1914* (London: German Historical Institute, 2011)

Gladwell, Malcolm, *The Tipping Point: How Little Things Can Make a Big Difference* (New York: Hachette Book Group: 2006)

Goodman, Dena, 'Enlightenment Salons: The Convergence of Female and Philosophic Ambitions', *Eighteenth-Century Studies*, 22, 3 (1989), Special Issue: *The French Revolution in Culture*, 329–50

———, *The Republic of Letters* (Ithaca, NY: Cornell University Press, 1996)

Hackett, David G., *That Religion in Which All Men Agree: Freemasonry in American Culture* (Berkeley and Los Angeles: University of California Press, 2014)

Hamilton, Alexander, *The Complete Works of Alexander Hamilton*, ed. Henry Cabot Lodge (Amazon Digital Services for Kindle, 2011)

Han, Shin-Kap, 'The Other Ride of Paul Revere: The Brokerage Role in the Making of the American Revolution', *Mobilization: An International Quarterly* 14, 2 (2009), 143–62

Hancock, David, 'The Trouble with Networks: Managing the Scots' Early-Modern Madeira Trade', *Business History Review*, 79, 3 (2005), 467–91

Hatch, Robert A., 'Between Erudition and Science: The Archive and Correspondence Network of Ismaël Boulliau', in Michael Hunter (ed.), *Archives of the Scientific Revolution: The Formation and Exchange of*

Ideas in Seventeenth-Century Europe (Woodbridge: Boydell Press, 1998), 49–71

Hodapp, Christopher, *Solomon's Builders: Freemasons, Founding Fathers and the Secrets of Washington D.C.* (Berkeley: Ulysses Press, 2009)

Home, John, *Douglas: A Tragedy in Five Acts* (New York and London: S. French & Son, 1870)

Johnstone, Jeffrey M., 'Sir William Johnstone Pulteney and the Scottish Origins of Western New York', *Crooked Lake Review* (Summer 2004): http://www.crookedlakereview.com/articles/101_135/132summer2004/132johnstone.html

Lamikiz, Xabier, *Trade and Trust in the Eighteenth-Century Atlantic World: Spanish Merchants and Their Overseas Networks* (London and Woodbridge: The Royal Historical Society and Boydell Press, 2010)

Lilti, Antoine, *The World of the Salons* (Oxford: Oxford University Press, 2015)

Lux, David S. and Harold J. Cook, 'Closed Circles or Open Networks? Communication at a Distance during the Scientific Revolution', *History of Science*, 36 (1998), 179–211

Middlekauff, Robert, *The Glorious Cause: The American Revolution, 1763–1789* (Oxford: Oxford University Press, 2007)

Morse, Sidney, *Freemasonry in the American Revolution* (Washington, DC: Masonic Service Association, 1924)

Owen, John M., IV, *The Clash of Ideas in World Politics: Transnational Networks, States, and Regime Change, 1510–2010* (Princeton and Oxford: Princeton University Press, 2010)

Patterson, Richard S. and Richardson Dougall, *The Eagle and the Shield* (Washington, DC: US Government Printing Office, 1976)

Rothschild, Emma, *The Inner Life of Empires: An Eighteenth-Century History* (Princeton: Princeton University Press, 2011)

Rusnock, Andrea, 'Correspondence Networks and the Royal Society, 1700–1750', *British Journal for the History of Science*, 32, 2 (June 1999), 155–69

Schich, Maximilian, Chaoming Song, Yong-Yeol Ahn, Alexander Mirsky, Mauro Martino, Albert-László Barabási and Dirk Helbing, 'A Network Framework of Cultural History', *Science* 345, 6196 (2014), 558–62

Starr, Paul, *The Creation of the Media: Political Origins of Modern Communications* (New York: Basic Books, 2004)

Taylor, P. J., M. Hoyler and D. M. Evans, 'A Geohistorical Study of "the Rise of Modern Science": Mapping Scientific Practice through Urban Networks, 1500–1900', *Minerva*, 46, 4 (2008), 391–410

Winterer, Caroline, 'Where is America in the Republic of Letters?', *Modern Intellectual History*, 9, 3 (2012), 597–623

Wood, Gordon S., *The American Revolution: A History* (Modern Library Chronicles Series Book 9) (New York: Random House, 2002)

York, Neil L., 'Freemasons and the American Revolution', *The Historian*, 55, 2 (Winter 1993), 315–30

IV. THE RESTORATION OF HIERARCHY

Andress, David (ed.), *The Oxford Handbook of the French Revolution* (Oxford: Oxford University Press: 2015)

Anon., *The Hebrew Talisman* (London: W. Whaley, 1840)

Anon., *The Annual Register, Or, A View of the History, Politics, and Literature for the Year 1828* (London: Baldwin & Cradock, 1829)

Aspinall, A. (ed.), *The Letters of King George IV, 1812–30*, 3 vols. (Cambridge: Cambridge University Press, 1938)

Balla, Ignác, *The Romance of the Rothschilds* (London: E. Nash, 1913)

Benson, Arthur Christopher and Viscount Esher, *The Letters of Queen Victoria: A Selection from Her Majesty's Correspondence between the Years 1837 and 1861*, vol. I: *1837–1843* (London: John Murray, 1908)

Bernstein, Herman (ed.), *The Willy–Nicky Correspondence, Being the Secret and Intimate Telegrams Exchanged between the Kaiser and the Tsar* (New York: Alfred A. Knopf, 1918)

Bew, John, *Castlereagh: A Life* (Oxford: Oxford University Press, 2012)

Buxton, Charles (ed.), *Memoirs of Sir Thomas Fowell Buxton*, 5th edn (London: John Murray, 1866)

Capefigue, Jean Baptiste Honoré Raymond, *Histoire des grandes opérations financières: banques, bourses, emprunts, compagnies industrielles etc.*, vol. III: *Emprunts, bourses, crédit public. Grands capitalistes de l'Europe, 1814–1852* (Paris: Librairie d'Amyot, 1858)

Cathcart, Brian, *The News from Waterloo* (London: Faber & Faber, 2016)

Chateaubriand, François René, vicomte de, *Correspondance générale de Chateaubriand*, vol. III (Paris: H. et E. Champion, 1913)

Clark, Ian, *Hegemony in International Society* (Oxford: Oxford University Press, 2011)

Clausewitz, Carl von, *On War*, ed. Beatrice Hauser, transl. Michael Howard and Peter Paret, (Oxford: Oxford University Press, 2007)

Colley, Linda, *Britons: Forging the Nation* (New Haven, CT, and London: Yale University Press, 1992)

Corti, Egon Caesar Conte, *Alexander of Battenberg* (London: Cassell & Co., 1954)

———, *The Rise of the House of Rothschild* (New York: Cosmopolitan Book Corporation, 1928)

Cowles, Virginia, *The Rothschilds: A Family of Fortune* (New York: Alfred A. Knopf, 1973)

Dairnvaell, Georges ['Satan' (pseud.)], *Histoire édifiante et curieuse de Rothschild Ier, roi des Juifs* (Paris: n.p., 1846)

Davis, David Brion, *Inhuman Bondage: The Rise and Fall of Slavery in the New World* (New York: Oxford University Press, 2006)

Davis, Richard W., *The English Rothschilds* (London: Collins, 1983)

Dimock, Liz, 'Queen Victoria, Africa and Slavery: Some Personal Associations', paper presented to the AFSAAP Conference (2009)

Drescher, Seymour, 'Public Opinion and Parliament in the Abolition of the British Slave Trade', *Parliamentary History, 26, 1* (2007), 42–65

Dugdale, E. T. S. (ed.), *German Diplomatic Documents, 1871–1914*, 4 vols. (London: Harper, 1928)

Ferguson, Niall, *The World's Banker: The History of the House of Rothschild* (London: Weidenfeld & Nicolson, 1998)

Fournier-Verneuil, M., *Paris: Tableau moral et philosophique* (Paris : n.p., 1826)

Gille, Bertrand, *Histoire de la maison Rothschild*, vol. I: *Des origines à 1848* (Geneva: Librairie Droz, 1965)

Glanz, Rudolf, 'The Rothschild Legend in America', *Jewish Social Studies*, 19 (1957), 3–28

Gould, Roger V., 'Patron–Client Ties, States Centralization, and the Whiskey Rebellion', *American Journal of Sociology*, 102, 2 (September 1996), 400–429

Hinsley, F. H., *Power and the Pursuit of Peace: Theory and Practice in the History of the Relations between States* (Cambridge: Cambridge University Press, 1963)

Holsti, Kalevi, 'Governance Without Government: Polyarchy in Nineteenth-Century European International Politics', in Kalevi, *Kalevi Holsti: Major Texts on War, the State, Peace, and International Order* (New York: Springer, 2016), 149–71

Iliowzi, Henry, *'In the Pale': Stories and Legends of the Russian Jews* (Philadelphia: Jewish Publication Society of America, 1897)

Kissinger, Henry, *Diplomacy* (New York: Simon & Schuster, 2011)

———, *World Order* (London and New York: Penguin Press, 2014)

———, *A World Restored* (New York and London: Houghton Miflin/Weidenfeld and Nicolson, 1957)

Kynaston, David, *The City of London: A World of Its Own* (London: Chatto & Windus, 1994)

Lamoreaux, Naomi R., Daniel M. G. Raff and Peter Temin, 'Beyond Markets and Hierarchies: Toward a New Synthesis of American Business History', NBER Working Paper no. 9029 (July 2002), 1–63

Lefebvre, Georges, *The Great Fear of 1789: Rural Panic in Revolutionary France* (Princeton: Princeton University Press, 2014)

Levy, Jack S., *War in the Modern Great Power System* (Lexington, KY: University Press of Kentucky, 1983)

Liedtke, Rainer, *N. M. Rothschild & Sons: Kommunikationswege im europäischen Bankenwesen im 19. Jahrhundert* (Cologne, Weimar and Vienna: Böhlau, 2006)

Lipp, C. and L. Krempel, 'Petitions and the Social Context of Political Mobilization in the Revolution of 1848/49: A Microhistorical Actor-Centred Network Analysis', *International Review of Social History*, 46, Supplement 9, (December 2001), 151–69

Loewe, Louis (ed.), *Diaries of Sir Moses and Lady Montefiore*, 2 vols. (Oxford, 1983)

Maylunas, Andrei and Sergei Mironenko, *A Lifelong Passion: Nicholas and Alexandra, Their Own Story* (London: Weidenfeld & Nicolson,1996)

Moon, Francis C., *Social Networks in the History of Innovation and Invention* (Dordrecht: Springer, 2014)

Pearson, Robin and David Richardson, 'Business Networking in the Industrial Revolution', *Economic History Review*, 54, 4 (November 2001), 657–79

Prawer, S. S., *Heine's Jewish Comedy: A Study of His Portraits of Jews and Judaism* (Oxford: Clarendon Press, 1983)

Pückler-Muskau, Hermann Fürst von, *Briefe eines Verstorbenen: Vollständige Ausgabe*, ed. Heinz Ohff (Berlin: Kupfergraben Verlagsgesellschaft, 1986)

Quennell, Peter (ed.), *The Private Letters of Princess Lieven to Prince Metternich, 1820–1826* (London: John Murray, 1937)

Ranke, Leopold von, 'The Great Powers', in R. Wines (ed.), *The Secret of World History: Selected Writings on the Art and Science of History* (New York: Fordham University Press, 1981 [1833]), 122–55

Reeves, John, *The Rothschilds: The Financial Rulers of Nations* (London: Sampson Low, Marston, Searle and Rivington, 1887)

Roberts, Andrew, *Napoleon: A Life* (London: Viking, 2014)

Rothschild, Lord [Victor], *The Shadow of a Great Man* (London: privately published, 1982)

Rubens, Alfred, *Anglo-Jewish Portraits* (London: Jewish Museum, 1935)

Ryden, David Beck, 'Does Decline Make Sense? The West Indian Economy and the Abolition of the British Slave Trade', *Journal of Interdisciplinary History*, 31, 3 (2001), 347–74

Schroeder, Paul, *The Transformation of European Politics, 1763–1848* (Oxford: Oxford University Press, 1994)

Schwemer, Richard, *Geschichte der Freien Stadt Frankfurt a. M. (1814–1866)*, vol. II (Frankfurt am Main: J. Baer & Co., 1912)

Serre, comte Pierre François Hercule de, *Correspondance du comte de Serre 1796–1824, annotée et publiée par son fils*, vol. IV (Paris: Auguste Vaton, 1876)

Shy, John, 'Jomini', in Peter Paret (ed.), *Makers of Modern Strategy* (Princeton: Princeton University Press, 1986), 143–85

Slantchev, B., 'Territory and Commitment: The Concert of Europe as Self-Enforcing Equilibrium', *Security Studies*, 14, 4 (2005), 565–606

Stendhal, *The Red and the Black: A Chronicle of the Nineteenth Century*, transl. C. K. Scott Moncrieff (New York: Modern Library, 1926 [1830])

Tackett, Timothy, 'La grande peur et le complot aristocratique sous la Révolution francaise', *Annales historiques de la Révolution française*, 335 (January–March 2004), 1–17

Williams, Eric, *Capitalism and Slavery* (Chapel Hill, NC: University of North Carolina Press, 1944)

V. KNIGHTS OF THE ROUND TABLE

Allen, Peter, *The Cambridge Apostles: The Early Years* (Cambridge and New York: Cambridge University Press, 1978)

Andrew, Christopher, *The Defence of the Realm: The Authorized History of MI5* (London: Allen Lane, 2009)

——— and Oleg Gordievsky, *KGB: The Inside Story of Its Foreign Operations from Lenin to Gorbachev* (London: Hodder & Stoughton, 1990)

Ansell, Christopher K., 'Symbolic Networks: The Realignment of the French Working Class, 1887–1894', *American Journal of Sociology*, 103, 2 (September 1997), 359–90

Antal, Tibor, Paul Krapivsky and Sidney Redner, 'Social Balance on Networks: The Dynamics of Friendship and Enmity', *Physica D*, 224, 130 (2006), 130–36

Berlin, Isaiah, 'Meetings with Russian Writers in 1945 and 1956', in Berlin, *Personal Impressions* (New York: Random House, 2012)

Brudner, Lilyan A. and Douglas R. White, 'Class, Property and Structural Endogmany: Visualizing Networked Histories', *Theory and Society*, 26, 26 (1997)

Bryce, James, 'Kearneyism in California', in *The American Commonwealth*, vol. II, 2nd edn (London: Macmillan and Co., 1891)

Campbell, Cameron, and James Lee, 'Kin Networks, Marriage, and Social Mobility in Late Imperial China', *Social Science History*, 32 (2008), 174–214

Cannadine, David, *Ornamentalism: How the British Saw Their Empire* (London: Allen Lane, 2001)

Carnegie, Andrew, 'Wealth', *North American Review*, 391 (June 1889)

Chi, Sang-Hyun, Colin Flint, Paul Diehl, John Vasquez, Jürgen Scheffran, Steven M. Radil, and Toby J. Rider, 'The Spatial Diffusion of War: The Case of World War I', *대한지리학회지*, 49, 1 (2014), 57–76

Clark, Christopher, *The Sleepwalkers: How Europe Went to War in 1914* (New York: Harper, 2013)

Collins, Damian, *Charmed Life: The Phenomenal World of Philip Sassoon* (London: William Collins, 2016)

Cooke, George Wingrove, *China: Being 'The Times' Special Correspondence from China in the Years 1857–58* (London: Routledge & Co., 1858)

Darwin, John, *The Empire Project: The Rise and Fall of the British World System, 1830–1970* (Cambridge: Cambridge University Press, 2009)

Deacon, Richard, *The Cambridge Apostles: A History of Cambridge University's Elite Intellectual Secret Society* (London: R. Royce, 1985)

Dean, Warren, *Brazil and the Struggle for Rubber: A Study in Environmental History* (Cambridge: Cambridge University Press, 1987)

Dolton, Peter, 'Identifying Social Network Effects', *Economic Report*, 93, Supplement S1 (June 2017), 1–15

Duara, Prasenjit, *Culture, Power and the State: Rural North China, 1900–1942* (Stanford: Stanford University Press, 1998)

Ferguson, Niall, *Empire: How Britain Made the Modern World* (London: Allen Lane, 2003)

Flandreau, Marc and Clemens Jobst, 'The Ties That Divide: A Network Analysis of the International Monetary System, 1890–1910', *Journal of Economic History*, 65, 4 (December 2005), 977–1007

Fontane, Theodor, *Der Stechlin* (Stuttgart: Deutscher Bücherbund, 1978 [1899])

Forster, E. M., *Howard's End* (New York: A. A. Knopf, 1921)

———, *What I Believe* (London: Hogarth Press, 1939)

Garton Ash, Timothy, *Free Speech: Ten Principles for a Connected World* (New Haven, CT: Yale University Press, 2016)

Gartzke, Erik and Yonatan Lupu, 'Trading on Preconceptions: Why World War I was Not a Failure of Economic Interdependence', *International Security*, 36, 4 (2012), 115–50

Gibson, Otis, *The Chinese in America* (Cincinnati: Hitchcock and Walden, 1877)

Gooch, Lady Emily Burder (ed.), *Diaries of Sir Daniel Gooch, Baronet* (London: K. Paul, Trench Trübner & Co., 1892)

Hale, Keith (ed.), *Friends and Apostles: The Correspondence of Rupert Brooke and James Strachey, 1905–1914* (New Haven, CT, and London: Yale University Press, 1998)

Harvey, William Hope, *Coin's Financial School* (Chicago: Coin Publishing Company, 1894)

Heidler, Richard, Markus Gamper, Andreas Herz and Florian Esser, 'Relationship Patterns in the 19th century: The Friendship Network in a German Boys' School Class from 1880 to 1881 Revisited', *Social Networks*, 37 (2014), 1–13

Ingram, Paul and Adam Lifschitz, 'Kinship in the Shadow of the Corporation: The Interbuilder Network in Clyde River Shipbuilding, 1711–1990', *American Sociological Review*, 71 (2003), 334–52

Jackson, Joe, *The Thief at the End of the World: Rubber, Power, and the Seeds of Empire* (New York and London: Viking/Duckworth Overlook, 2008)

Jones, Charles, 'The Ottoman Front and British Propaganda: John Buchan's *Greenmantle*', in Maximilian Lakitsch, Susanne Reitmair and Katja Seidel (eds.), *Bellicose Entanglements 1914: The Great War as Global War* (Zurich: Lit-Verlag, 2015), 157–74

Keller, Franziska Barbara, 'How to Spot a Successful Revolution in Advance: Results from Simulations on Protest Spread along Social Networks in Heterogeneous Societies', unpublished paper (n.d.)

———, '"Yes, Emperor" – Controlling the Bureaucracy in an Authoritarian Regime: On the Appointment of Qing Dynasty Provincial Governors, 1644–1912', unpublished paper (March 2013)

Kissinger, Henry, *World Order* (London and New York: Viking, 2014)

Klaus, Ian, *Forging Capitalism: Rogues, Swindlers, Frauds, and the Rise of Modern Finance* (Yale Series in Economic and Financial History) (New Haven: Yale University Press, 2014)

Kuhn, Philip A., *Soulstealers: The Chinese Sorcery Scare of 1758* (Cambridge, MA: Harvard University Press, 1995)

Lebow, Richard Ned, 'Contingency, Catalysts and Non-Linear Change: The Origins of World War I', in Gary Goertz and Jack S. Levy (eds.), *Explaining War and Peace: Case Studies and Necessary Condition Counterfactuals* (Abingdon: Routledge, 2007), 85–112

Lee, Erika, *At America's Gates: Chinese Immigration during the Exclusion Era, 1882–1943* (Chapel Hill, NC: University of North Carolina Press, 2003)

Lester, Alan, 'Imperial Circuits and Networks: Geographies of the British Empire', *History Compass*, 4, 1 (2006), 124–41

Levy, Paul, *Moore: G. E. Moore and the Cambridge Apostles* (London: Weidenfeld & Nicolson, 1979)

Lipp, Carola, 'Kinship Networks, Local Government, and Elections in a Town in Southwest Germany, 1800–1850', *Journal of Family History*, 30, 4 (October 2005), 347–65

Louw, P. Eric, *The Rise, Fall, and Legacy of Apartheid* (Westport, CT, and London: Praeger, 2004)

Lownie, Andrew, *Stalin's Englishman: The Lives of Guy Burgess* (London: Hodder & Stoughton, 2015)

Lubenow, W. C., *The Cambridge Apostles, 1820–1914: Liberalism, Imagination, and Friendship in British Intellectual and Professional Life.* (Cambridge: Cambridge University Press, 1998)

McGuinness, Brian, *Wittgenstein: A Life*, vol. I: *Young Ludwig, 1889–1921* (London: Duckworth, 1988)

McIntyre, Ben, *A Spy among Friends: Kim Philby's Great Betrayal* (New York: Crown, 2014)

McKeown, Adam, 'Chinese Emigration in Global Context, 1850–1940', *Journal of Global History*, 5, 1 (March 2010), 95–124

Magubane, Bernard M., *The Making of a Racist State: British Imperialism and the Union of South Africa, 1875–1910* (Trenton, NJ, and Asmara, Eritrea: Africa World Press, Inc., 1996)

Maoz, Zeev, *Networks of Nations: The Evolution, Structure, and Impact of International Networks, 1816–2001* (Cambridge and New York: Cambridge University Press, 2011)

Marks, Shula and Stanley Trapido, 'Lord Milner and the South African State', *History Workshop*, 8 (Autumn 1979), 50–80

May, Alex, 'Milner's Kindergarten (act. 1902–1910)', *Oxford Dictionary of National Biography* (Oxford: Oxford University Press, 2005)

Moretti, Enrico, 'Social Networks and Migrations: Italy 1876–1913', *International Migration Review*, 33, 3 (1999), 640–58

Nimocks, Walter, *Milner's Young Men: The 'Kindergarten' in Edwardian Imperial Affairs* (Durham, NC: Duke University Press, 1968)

Offer, Avner, *The First World War: An Agrarian Interpretation* (Oxford: Oxford University Press, 1990)

Oxford and Asquith, Earl of, *Memories and Reflections, 1852–1927*, 2 vols. (London and Boston, MA: Cassell/Little, Brown, 1928)

Plakans, Andrejs and Charles Wetherell, 'The Kinship Domain in an East European Peasant Community: Pinkenhof, 1833–1850', *American Historical Review*, 93, 2 (April 1988), 359–86

Platt, Stephen, *Autumn in the Heavenly Kingdom: China, the West, and the Epic Story of the Taiping Civil War* (New York: Alfred A. Knopf, 2012)

Potter, Simon J., 'Webs, Networks, and Systems: Globalization and the Mass Media in the Nineteenth- and Twentieth-Century British Empire', *Journal of British Studies*, 46, 3 (July 2007), 621–46

Quigley, Carroll, *The Anglo-American Establishment: From Rhodes to Cliveden* (New York: Books in Focus, 1981)

Roldan Vera, E. and T. Schupp, 'Bridges over the Atlantic: A Network Analysis of the Introduction of the Monitorial System of Education in Early-Independent Spanish America', in J. Schriewer and M. Caruso (eds.), *Nationalerziehung und Universalmethode – frühe Formen schulorganizatorischer Globalisierung* (Leipzig: Leipziger Universitätsverlag, 2005), 58–93

Schroeder, Paul W., 'Economic Integration and the European International System in the Era of World War I', *American Historical Review*, 98, 4 (October 1993), 1130–37

———, 'Necessary Conditions and World War I as an Unavoidable War', in Gary Goertz and Jack S. Levy (eds.), *Explaining War and Peace: Case Studies and Necessary Condition Counterfactuals* (Abingdon, Oxon: Routledge, 2007), 147–93

———, 'Stealing Horses to Great Applause: Austria–Hungary's Decision in 1914 in Systemic Perspective', in Holger Afflerbach and David Stevenson (eds.), *An Improbable War? The Outbreak of World War I and European Political Culture before 1914* (New York: Berghahn Books, 2007)

Shirky, Clay, *Here Comes Everybody: The Power of Organizing without Organizations* (London: Penguin Books, 2009)

Skidelsky, Robert, *John Maynard Keynes*, vol. I: *Hopes Betrayed, 1883–1920* (London: Macmillan, 1983)

Spar, Debora L., *Ruling the Waves: Cycles of Discovery, Chaos, and Wealth from the Compass to the Internet* (Orlando, FL: Harcourt, 2003)

Standage, Tom, *The Victorian Internet: The Remarkable Story of the Telegraph and the Nineteenth Century's Online Pioneers* (London: Phoenix, 1999)

Taylor, Charles, *Five Years in China, with Some Account of the Great Rebellion* (New York: Derby & Jackson, 1860)

Ter Haar, B. J. *The White Lotus Teachings in Chinese Religious History* (Leiden: E. J. Brill, 1992)

Thompson, William R., 'A Streetcar Named Sarajevo: Catalysts, Multiple Causation Chains, and Rivalry Structures', *International Studies Quarterly*, 47, 3 (September 2003), 453–74

Trachtenberg, Marc, 'New Light on 1914?' Contribution to the H-Diplo/ISSF Forum on 1914 (forthcoming)

Tufekci, Zeynep, *Twitter and Tear Gas: The Power and Fragility of Networked Protest* (New Haven, CT, and London: Yale University Press, 2017)

Tworek, Heidi Jacqueline Sybil, 'Magic Connections: German News Agencies and Global News Networks, 1905–1945', unpublished Ph.D. dissertation, Harvard University (2012)

United States Congress, *Report of the Joint Special Committee to Investigate Chinese Immigration* (Washington, DC: Government Printing Office, 1877)

Vasquez, John A. and Ashlea Rundlett, 'Alliances as a Necessary Condition of Multiparty Wars', *Journal of Conflict Resolution*, (2015), 1–24

VI. PLAGUES AND PIPERS

Ahmad, Ali, 'The Great War and Afghanistan's Neutrality', in Maximilian Lakitsch, Susanne Reitmair and Katja Seidel (eds.), *Bellicose Entanglements: The Great War as a Global War* (Zurich: Lit Verlag, 2015), 197–214

Akhmatova, Anna, *The Word That Causes Death's Defeat: Poems of Memory*, transl. Nancy K. Anderson (New Haven, CT, and London: Yale University Press, 2004)

Aksakal, Mustafa, '"Holy War Made in Germany?" Ottoman Origins of the 1914 Jihad', *War in History*, 18, 2 (2011), 184–99

———, 'The Ottoman Proclamation of Jihad', in Erik-Jan Zürcher (ed.), *Jihad and Islam in World War I: Studies on the Ottoman Jihad on the Centenary of Snouck Hurgronje's 'Holy War Made in Germany'* (Leiden: Leiden University Press, 2016), 53–69

Al-Rawi, Ahmad, 'Buchan the Orientalist: *Greenmantle* and Western Views of the East', *Journal of Colonialism and Colonial History*, 10, 2 (Fall 2009), Project MUSE, doi: 10.1353/cch.0.0068

———, 'John Buchan's British-Designed Jihad in *Greenmantle*', in Erik-Jan Zürcher (ed.), *Jihad and Islam in World War I: Studies on the Ottoman Jihad on the Centenary of Snouck Hurgronje's 'Holy War Made in Germany'* (Leiden: Leiden University Press, 2016) 329–46

Applebaum, Anne, *Gulag: A History* (New York: Doubleday, 2003)

Barkai, Avraham, *From Boycott to Annihilation: The Economic Struggle of German Jews, 1933–1943*, transl. William Templer (Hanover, NH, and London: University Press of New England, 1989)

Baynes, N. H. (ed.), *The Speeches of Adolf Hitler*, vol. I (London: Oxford University Press, 1942)

Berghahn, Volker R., *Germany and the Approach of War in 1914* (London: Palgrave Macmillan, 1973)

Berlin, Isaiah, *Letters*, vol. I: *1928–1946*, ed. Henry Hardy (Cambridge: Cambridge University Press, 2004)

———, *Enlightening: Letters*, vol. II: *1946–1960*, ed. Henry Hardy (New York: Random House, 2012)

Bloch, Michael, *Ribbentrop* (London: Bantam, 1992)

Buchan, John, *Greenmantle* (London: Hodder & Stoughton, 1916)

Burgdörfer, Friedrich, 'Die Juden in Deutschland und in der Welt: Ein statistischer Beitrag zur biologischen, beruflichen und sozialen Struktur des Judentums in Deutschland', *Forschungen zur Judenfrage*, 3 (1938), 152–98

Burleigh, Michael, *The Third Reich: A New History* (London: Pan Books, 2001)

——— and Wolfgang Wippermann, *The Racial State: Germany 1933–1945* (Cambridge: Cambridge University Press, 1991)

Cannadine, David, 'John Buchan: A Life at the Margins', *The American Scholar*, 67, 3 (summer 1998), 85–93

Cleveland, William L. and Martin Bunton, *A History of the Modern Middle East* (Philadelphia: Westview Books, 2016)

Cohn, Norman, *Warrant for Genocide: The Myth of the Jewish World Conspiracy and the Protocols of the Elders of Zion* (New York: Harper and Row, 1965)

Cooper, Duff, ed. John Julius Norwich, *The Duff Cooper Diaries, 1915–1951* (London: Weidenfeld & Nicolson, 2005)

Dalos, György, *The Guest from the Future: Anna Akhmatova and Isaiah Berlin* (New York: Farrar, Straus and Giroux, 1999)

Della Pergola, Sergio, *Jewish Mixed Marriages in Milan 1901–1968, with an Appendix: Frequency of Mixed Marriage among Diaspora Jews* (Jerusalem: Hebrew University, 1972)

Duggan, Christopher, *Fascism and the Mafia* (New Haven, CT: Yale University Press, 1989)

Düring, Marten, 'The Dynamics of Helping Behaviour for Jewish Fugitives during the Second World War: The Importance of Brokerage: The Segal Family's Case', *Online Encyclopaedia of Mass Violence*, 29 March 2016, http://www.sciencespo.fr/mass-violence-war-massacre-resistance/en/document/dynamics-helping-behaviour-jewish-fugitives-during-second-world-war-importance-brokerage-se

Evangelista, Matthew, *Unarmed Forces: The Transnational Movement to End the Cold War* (Ithaca, NY, and London: Cornell University Press, 1999)

Fallada, Hans, *Alone in Berlin*, transl. Michael Hoffman (London: Penguin Books, 2010)

Falter, Jürgen W., *Hitlers Wähler* (Munich: C. H. Beck, 1991)

Ferguson, Niall, *Kissinger*, vol. I: *1923–1968 – The Idealist* (London and New York: Allen Lane/Penguin Press, 2015)

———, *The War of the World: History's Age of Hatred* (London: Allen Lane, 2006)

Figes, Orlando, *A People's Tragedy: The Russian Revolution, 1891–1924* (London: Weidenfeld & Nicolson, 1996)

Fogarty, Richard S., 'Islam in the French Army during the Great War: Between Accommodation and Suspicion', in Eric Storm and Ali Al Tuma (eds.), *Colonial Soldiers in Europe, 1914–1945: 'Aliens in Uniform' in Wartime Societies* (New York: Routledge, 2016), 23–40

Friedländer, Saul, *Nazi Germany and the Jews: The Years of Persecution, 1933–39* (London: Phoenix Giant, 1997)

Gambetta, Diego, *The Sicilian Mafia: The Business of Protection* (Cambridge, MA: Harvard University Press, 1993)

Garfinkle, Adam, *Jewcentricity: Why the Jews are Praised, Blamed, and Used to Explain Just About Everything* (Hoboken, NJ: John Wiley & Sons, Inc., 2009)

Geiss, Immanuel, *July 1914: The Outbreak of the First World War – Selected Documents* (London: Batsford, 1967)

Gussone, Martin, 'Die Moschee im Wünsdorfer "Halbmondlager" zwischen Gihad-Propaganda und Orientalismus', in Markus Ritter and Lorenz Korn (eds.), *Beiträge zur Islamischen Kunst und Archäologie* (Wiesbaden: Reichert, 2010), 204–32

Habermas, Rebekka, 'Debates on Islam in Imperial Germany', in David Motadel (ed.), *Islam and the European Empires* (Oxford: Oxford University Press, 2016), 231–53

Hanauer, Walter, 'Die jüdisch-christliche Mischehe', *Allgemeines Statistisches Archiv*, 17 (1928), 513–37

Hausheer, Roger, 'It Didn't Happen One Night in Leningrad', *Times Higher Education*, 26 May 2000: https://www.timeshighereducation.com/books/it-didnt-happen-one-night-in-leningrad-in-1945/156215.article

Heimann-Jelinek, Felicitas, 'The "Aryanisation" of Rothschild Assets in Vienna and the Problem of Restitution', in Georg Heuberger (ed.), *The Rothschilds: Essays on the History of a European Family* (Sigmaringen: D. S. Brewer, 1994), 351–64

Herf, Jeffrey, *The Jewish Enemy: Nazi Propaganda during the Second World War and the Holocaust* (Cambridge, MA: Harvard University Press, 2006)

Hopkirk, Peter, *Like Hidden Fire: The Plot to Bring Down the British Empire* (New York: Kodansha International, 1994)

Ignatieff, Michael, *Isaiah Berlin: A Life* (London: Vintage, 2000)

Jackson, Maurice, Eleanora Petersen, James Bull, Sverre Monsen and Patricia Redmond, 'The Failure of an Incipient Social Movement', *Pacific Sociological Review*, 3, 1 (1960), 35–40

Jones, Steve, *In the Blood: God, Genes and Destiny* (London: HarperCollins, 1996)

Kahler, Miles, 'Collective Action and Clandestine Networks: The Case of Al Qaeda', in Kahler (ed.), *Networked Politics: Agency, Power, and Governance* (Ithaca, NY, and London: Cornell University Press, 2009), 103–24

———, 'Networked Politics: Agency, Power, and Governance', in Kahler (ed.), *Networked Politics*, 1–22

Keddie, Nikki R., 'Pan-Islam as Proto-Nationalism', *Journal of Modern History*, 41, 1 (March 1969), 17–28

Kelly, John and Julie Yeterian, 'Mutual-Help Groups for Alcohol and Other Substance Use Disorders', in Barbara S. McCrady and Elizabeth E. Epstein (eds.), *Addictions: A Comprehensive Guidebook* (Oxford: Oxford University Press, 2013), 500–525

Kenney, Michael, 'Turning to the "Dark Side": Coordination, Exchange and Learning in Criminal Networks', in Kahler (ed.), *Networked Politics*, 79–102

Kharas, Homi, 'The Unprecedented Expansion of the Global Middle Class: An Update', *Brookings Working Papers in Global Economy and Development*, 100 (February 2017)

Kopper, Christopher, 'The Rothschild Family during the Third Reich', in Georg Heuberger (ed.), *The Rothschilds: Essays on the History of a European Family* (Sigmaringen: D. S. Brewer, 1994), 321–32

Kotkin, Stephen, *Stalin*, vol. I: *Paradoxes of Power, 1878–1928* (London and New York: Allen Lane/Penguin Press, 2014)

———, *Stalin*, vol. II: *Waiting for Hitler* (London and New York: Allen Lane/Penguin Press, 2017)

Kurtz, Ernest, *Not-God: A History of Alcoholics Anonymous* (Center City, MN: Hazelden, 1991)

Landau, Jacob M., *Pan-Islam: History and Politics* (Abingdon: Routledge, 2016)

Laqueur, Walter (ed.), *Fascism: A Reader's Guide: Analyses, Interpretations, Bibliography* (Aldershot: Scolar Press, 1991)

Larsen, Stein Ugelvik, Bernt Hagtvet and Jan Peter Myklebust, *Who were the Fascists? Social Roots of European Fascism* (Bergen: Universitetsforlaget, 1980)

Leggett, George, *The Cheka: Lenin's Political Police* (Oxford: Oxford University Press, 1981)

Lewis, Norman, *The Honoured Society: The Sicilian Mafia Observed* (London: Eland, 2003 [1973])

———, *Naples '44: A World War II Diary of Occupied Italy* (London: William Collins, 1978)

Lownie, Andrew, *John Buchan: Presbyterian Cavalier* (London: Constable, 1995)

Lüdke, Tilman, '(Not) Using Political Islam: The German Empire and Its Failed Propaganda Campaign in the Near and Middle East, 1914–1918 and Beyond', in Erik-Jan Zürcher (ed.), *Jihad and Islam in World War I: Studies on the Ottoman Jihad on the Centenary of Snouck Hurgronje's 'Holy War Made in Germany'* (Leiden: Leiden University Press, 2016), 71–94

MacDougall, Robert, 'Long Lines: AT&T's Long-Distance Network as an Organizational and Political Strategy', *Business History Review*, 80 (2006), 297–327

Macintyre, Ben, *A Spy among Friends: Kim Philby and the Great Betrayal* (London: Bloomsbury, 2014)

McKale, Donald M., 'British Anxiety about Jihad in the Middle East', *Orient XXI*, 24 June 2016: http://orientxxi.info/l-orient-dans-la-guerre-1914-1918/british-anxiety-about-jihad-in-the-middle-east,0940

———, 'Germany and the Arab Question in the First World War', *Middle Eastern Studies*, 29, 2 (April 1993), 236–53

———, *War by Revolution: Germany and Great Britain in the Middle East in the Era of World War I* (Kent, OH, and London: Kent State University Press, 1998)

McMeekin, Sean, *The Berlin–Baghdad Express: The Ottoman Empire and Germany's Bid for World Power 1898–1918* (London: Penguin Books, 2011)

———, *The Russian Revolution: A New History* (New York: Basic Books, 2017)

McMurray, Jonathan S., *Distant Ties: Germany, the Ottoman Empire, and the Construction of the Baghdad Railway* (Westport, CT, and London: Praeger, 2001)

McSmith, Andy, *Fear and the Muse Kept Watch: The Russian Masters – from Akhmatova and Pasternak to Shostakovich and Eisenstein – under Stalin* (New York and London: New Press, 2015)

Makela, Klaus et al. (eds.), *Alcoholics Anonymous as a Mutual-Help Movement: A Study in Eight Societies* (Madison, WI: University of Wisconsin Press, 1996)

Meiring, Kerstin, *Die christlich-jüdische Mischehe in Deutschland 1840–1933* (Hamburg: Dölling and Galitz, 1998)

Miller Lane, Barbara and Leila J. Rupp (eds.), *Nazi Ideology before 1933: A Documentation* (Austin: University of Texas Press, 1978)

Morgenthau, Henry, *Secrets of the Bosphorus* (London: Hutchinson & Co, 1918)

Mosse, Werner E., 'Die Juden in Wirtschaft und Gesellschaft', in Mosse (ed.), *Juden in Wilhelminischen Deutschland 1890–1914* (Tübingen: Mohr, 1976), 57–113

———, *Jews in the German Economy: The German-Jewish Economic Elite, 1820–1935* (Oxford: Oxford University Press, 1987)

Motadel, David, *Islam and Nazi Germany's War* (Cambridge, MA: Harvard University Press, 2014)

Nicholas, Lynn H., *The Rape of Europa: The Fate of Europe's Treasures in the Third Reich and the Second World War* (London: Macmillan, 1994)

Ohler, Norman, *Blitzed: Drugs in Nazi Germany*, transl. Shaun Whiteside (London: Allen Lane, 2017)

O'Loughlin, John, Colin Flint and Luc Anselin, 'The Geography of the Nazi Vote: Context, Confession, and Class in the Reichstag Election of 1930', *Annals of the Association of American Geographers*, 84 (1994), 351–80

Raab, Jörg, 'More Than Just a Metaphor: The Network Concept and Its Potential in Holocaust Research', in Gerald D. Feldman and Wolfgang Seibel (eds.), *Networks of Nazi Persecution: Bureaucracy, Business and the Organization of the Holocaust* (New York and Oxford: Berghahn Books, 2006), 321–40

Rogan, Eugene, *The Arabs: A History* (London: Allen Lane, 2009)

———, *The Fall of the Ottomans: The Great War in the Middle East, 1914–1920* (New York: Basic Books, 2015)

———, 'Rival Jihads: Islam and the Great War in the Middle East, 1914–1918', *Journal of the British Academy*, 4 (2014), 1–20

Rubinstein, W. D., *The Left, the Right, and the Jews* (London and Canberra: Croom Helm, 1982)

Ruble, Blair A., *Leningrad: Shaping a Soviet City* (Berkeley and Los Angeles: University of California Press, 1990)

Ruppin, Arthur, *Soziologie der Juden*, vol. I: *Die soziale Struktur der Juden* (Berlin: Jüdischer Verlag, 1930)

Rutledge, Ian, *Enemy on the Euphrates: The Battle for Iraq, 1914–1921* (London: Saqi Books, 2015)

Satyanath, Shanker, Nico Voigtländer and Hans-Joachim Voth, 'Bowling For Fascism: Social Capital and the Rise of the Nazi Party', *Journal of Political Economy* (forthcoming)

Schwanitz, Wolfgang G., 'The Bellicose Birth of Euro-Islam in Berlin', in Ala Al-Hamarneh and Jörn Thielmann (eds.), *Islam and Muslims in Germany* (Leiden: Brill, 2008), 183–212

Scotten, W. E., 'The Problem of the Mafia in Sicily', in Università Di Catania Facoltà Di Scienze Politiche, *Annali 80 del Dipartimento di Scienze Storiche* (Catania: Galatea Editrice, 1981), 622–9

Service, Robert, *A History of Twentieth-Century Russia* (London: Penguin Books, 1997)

Sperry, Earl E. and Willis M. West, *German Plots and Intrigues in the United States during the Period of Our Neutrality* (Washington, DC: Committee on Public Information, 1918)

Staar, Richard Felix, *Foreign Policies of the Soviet Union* (Stanford: Hoover Institution Press, 1991)

Starr, Paul, *The Creation of the Media: Political Origins of Modern Communications* (New York: Basic Books, 2004)

Tamberino, Frank, 'A Criminal Renaissance: The Postwar Revival of the Sicilian Mafia, 1943–1945', senior thesis, Harvard University (2017)

Trumpener, Ulrich, *Germany and the Ottoman Empire, 1914–1918* (Princeton: Princeton University Press, 2015)

Turchin, Peter, *Ages of Discord: A Structural-Demographic Analysis of American History* (Chaplin, CT: Beresta Books, 2016)

Valentin, Hugo, *Antisemitism Historically and Critically Examined* (London: Gollancz, 1936)

Voigtländer, Nico and Hans-Joachim Voth, 'Persecution Perpetuated: The Medieval Origins of Anti-Semitic Violence in Nazi Germany', *Quarterly Journal of Economics* (2012), 1339–92

Volkogonov, Dmitri, *Lenin: Life and Legacy* (London: HarperCollins, 1994)

White, William L. and Ernest Kurtz, 'Twelve Defining Moments in the History of Alcoholics Anonymous', in Marc Galanter and Lee Ann Kaskutas (eds.), *Recent Developments in Alcoholism: Research on Alcoholics Anonymous and Spirituality in Addiction Recovery*, vol. XVIII (New York: Springer, 2008), 37–57

Windolf, Paul, 'The German-Jewish Economic Elite, 1900–1930', *Journal of Business History*, 56, 2 (2011), 135–62

Zürcher, Erik-Jan, 'Introduction: The Ottoman Jihad, the German Jihad, and the Sacralization of War', in Zürcher (ed.), *Jihad and Islam in World War I: Studies on the Ottoman Jihad on the Centenary of Snouck Hurgronje's 'Holy War Made in Germany'* (Leiden: Leiden University Press, 2016), 13–29

VII. OWN THE JUNGLE

Abdelal, Rawi, 'The Politics of Monetary Leadership and Followership: Stability in the European Monetary System since the Currency Crisis of 1992', *Political Studies*, 46, 2 (June 1998), 246–7

Bar-Yam, Yaneer, 'Complexity Rising: From Human Beings to Human Civilization – A Complexity Profile', in *Encyclopaedia of Life Support Systems* (Oxford: United Nations, 2002), 1–33

———, *Dynamics of Complex Systems* (Reading, MA: Addison-Wesley, 1997)

Barnard, Rita and Monica Popescu, 'Nelson Mandela', in Steven Casey and Jonathan Wright (eds.), *Mental Maps in the Era of Détente and the End of the Cold War, 1968–91* (Basingstoke and New York: Palgrave Macmillan, 2015), 236–49

Bearman, Peter S. and Kevin D. Everett, 'The Structure of Social Protest, 1961–1983', *Social Networks* 15 (1993), 171–200

Beckett, Ian F. W. and John Pimlott, *Counter-Insurgency: Lessons from History* (Barnsley: Pen & Sword Military, 2011)

Bordo, Michael and Andrew Levin, 'Central Bank Digital Currency and the Future of Monetary Policy', working paper (May 2017)

Brinton, Christopher C., and Mung Chiang, *The Power of Networks: Six Principles That Connect Our Lives* (Princeton and Oxford: Princeton University Press, 2017)

Brzezinski, Zbigniew, *Between Two Ages: America's Role in the Technetronic Era* (New York: Penguin Books, 1970)

Caldaray, Dario and Matteo Iacoviello, 'Measuring Geopolitical Risk', working paper, 7 September 2016

Caldarelli, Guido and Michele Catanzaro, *Networks: A Very Short Introduction* (Oxford: Oxford University Press, 2012)

Castells, Manuel, *The Rise of the Network Society: The Information Age: Economy, Society, and Culture*, vol. I (Oxford: Oxford University Press, 2000)

Chanda, Nayan, *Bound Together: How Traders, Preachers, Adventurers, and Warriors Shaped Globalisation* (New Haven, CT, and London: Yale University Press, 2007)

Conway, Melvin, 'How Do Committees Invent?' *Datamation* (April 1968): http://www.melconway.com/research/committees.html

Cooper, Richard, *The Economics of Interdependence: Economic Policy in the Atlantic Community* (New York: Council on Foreign Relations, 1968)

Cross, J. P., *'A Face Like a Chicken's Backside': An Unconventional Soldier in South East Asia, 1948–1971* (Stroud: History Press, 2015)

Dorussen, Han and Hugh Ward, 'Trade Networks and the Kantian Peace', *Journal of Peace Research*, 47, 1 (2010), 29–42

Drobny, Steven, *Inside the House of Money: Top Hedge Fund Traders on Profiting in the Global Markets* (Hoboken, NJ: John Wiley & Sons, Inc., 2006)

Eichengreen, Barry and Charles Wyplosz, 'The Unstable EMS', *Brookings Papers on Economic Activity*, 24, 1 (1993), 51–144

Engdahl, William, 'The Secret Financial Network Behind "Wizard" George Soros', *Executive Intelligence Review*, 23, 44 (1 November 1996), 54–60

Evangelista, Matthew, *Unarmed Forces: The Transnational Movement to End the Cold War* (Ithaca, NY, and London: Cornell University Press, 1999)

Ferguson, Niall, *High Financier: The Lives and Time of Siegmund Warburg* (London: Penguin Allen Lane, 2010)

———, 'Siegmund Warburg, the City of London and the Financial Roots of European Integration', *Business History*, 51, 3 (May 2009), 364–82

——— and Jonathan Schlefer, 'Who Broke the Bank of England?' Harvard Business School Case N9-709-026 (8 January 2009)

Forester, C. S., *The General* (London: Michael Joseph, 1936)

Goldsmith, Jack and Tim Wu, *Who Controls the Internet? Illusions of a Borderless World* (Oxford and New York: Oxford University Press, 2008)

Granville, Brigitte, Jaume Martorell Cruz and Martha Prevezer, 'Elites, Thickets and Institutions: French Resistance versus German Adaptation to Economic Change, 1945–2015', CGR Working Paper 63 (n.d.)

Grdesic, Marko, 'Television and Protest in East Germany's Revolution, 1989–1990: A Mixed-Methods Analysis', *Communist and post-Communist Studies*, 47 (2014), 93–103

Gudmundsson, Bruce I., *Stormtroop Tactics: Innovation in the German Army, 1914–18* (Westport, CT: Praeger, 1995)

Gumede, William Mervin, *Thabo Mbeki and the Soul of the ANC* (Cape Town: Zebra Press, 2007)

Hafner-Burton, Emilie M. and Alexander H. Montgomery, 'Globalization and the Social Power Politics of International Economic Networks', in Miles Kahler (ed.), *Networked Politics: Agency, Power, and Governance* (Ithaca, NY, and London: Cornell University Press, 2009), 23–42

Haim, Dotan A., 'Alliance Networks and Trade: The Effect of Indirect Political Alliances on Bilateral Trade Flows', working paper, University of California, San Diego (2015)

Hall, Wendy, 'The Ever Evolving Web: The Power of Networks', *International Journal of Communications*, 5 (2011), 651–64

Hileman, Garrick and Michel Rauchs, 'Global Cryptocurrency Benchmarking Study' (Cambridge: Centre for Alternative Finance, 2017)

Jackson, Matthew O. and Stephen Nei, 'Networks of Military Alliances, Wars, and International Trade', *Proceedings of the National Academy of Sciences*, 112, 50 (15 December 2015), 15277–84

Johnson, Christopher, 'The UK and the Exchange Rate Mechanism', in Christopher Johnson and Stefan Collignon (eds.), *The Monetary Economics of Europe: Causes of the EMS Crisis* (London: Pinter, 1994), 85–102

Johnson, Dominic and Ferenc Jordan, 'The Web of War: A Network Analysis of the Spread of Civil Wars in Africa', *Annual Meeting of the Political Science Association*, 28, 02.09 (2007), 1–19

Jones, Matthew, *Conflict and Confrontation in South East Asia, 1961–65* (Cambridge: Cambridge University Press, 2002)

Kaufman, Michael T., *Soros: The Life and Times of a Messianic Billionaire* (New York: Alfred A. Knopf, 2002)

Kay, John, *Other People's Money: Masters of the Universe or Servants of the People* (London: Profile Books, 2016)

Keller, Franziska, '(Why) Do Revolutions Spread?' unpublished paper (2012)

Keohane, Robert and Joseph Nye, *Power and Interdependence: World Politics in Transition* (Boston, MA: Little, Brown, 1977)

Kerr, Ian M., *A History of the Eurobond Market* (London: Prentice-Hall, 1984)

Kilcullen, David, *Counterinsurgency* (London: C. Hurst & Co., 2010)

King, Gary, Jennifer Pan and Margaret E. Roberts, 'A Randomized Experimental Study of Censorship in China', working paper, 6 October 2013

Klein, Naomi, *Shock Doctrine: The Rise of Disaster Capitalism* (London: Penguin Books, 2014)

Lamont, Norman, *In Office* (London: Little, Brown, 1999)

Lamoreaux, Naomi R., Daniel M. G. Raff and Peter Temin, 'Beyond Markets and Hierarchies: Toward a New Synthesis of American Business History', NBER Working Paper no. 9029 (July 2002), 1–63

Landsberg, Christopher, *The Quiet Diplomacy of Liberation: International Politics and South Africa's Transition* (Johannesburg: Jacana Media, 2004)

Levina, Olga and Robert Hillmann, 'Wars of the World: Evaluating the Global Conflict Structure during the Years 1816–2001 Using Social Network Analysis', *Social and Behavioral Sciences*, 100 (2013), 68–79

Lupu, Yonatan and Vincent A. Traag, 'Trading Communities, the Networked Structure of International Relations, and the Kantian Peace', *Journal of Conflict Resolution*, 57, 6 (2013), 1011–42

Major, John, *The Autobiography* (London: HarperCollins, 1999)

Mallaby, Sebastian, *More Money Than God: Hedge Funds and the Making of a New Elite* (London: Bloomsbury, 2010)

Maoz, Zeev, 'Network Polarization, Network Interdependence, and International Conflict, 1816–2002', *Journal of Peace Research*, 43, 4 (2006), 391–411

Marston, Daniel, 'Lost and Found in the Jungle: The Indian and British Army Jungle Warfare Doctrines for Burma, 1943–5, and the Malayan Emergency, 1948–60', in Hew Strachan (ed.), *Big Wars and Small Wars: The British Army and the Lessons of War in the 20th Century* (Abingdon and New York: Taylor & Francis e-Library, 2006), Kindle Edition, KL 2045–2786

Milward, Alan S., *The European Rescue of the Nation-State*, 2nd edn (London: Routledge, 2000)

Mumford, Andrew, *The Counter-Insurgency Myth: The British Experience of Irregular Warfare* (London and New York: Routledge, 2012)

Naughton, John, *From Gutenberg to Zuckerberg: What You Really Need to Know about the Internet* (London: Quercus, 2012)

Navidi, Sandra, *Superhubs: How the Financial Elite and their Networks Rule Our World* (Boston, MA, and London: Nicholas Brealey, 2016)

Newman, Mark, *Networks: An Introduction* (Oxford: Oxford University Press, 2010)

O'Hara, Glen, *From Dreams to Disillusionment: Economic and Social Planning in 1960s Britain* (Basingstoke: Palgrave Macmillan, 2007)

Osa, Maryjane, *Solidarity and Contention: Networks of Polish Opposition* (Minneapolis and London: University of Minnesota Press, 2003)

Pocock, Tom, *Fighting General: The Public and Private Campaigns of General Sir Walter Walker* (London: Thistle Publishing, 2013)

Powell, Walter W., 'Neither Market Nor Hierarchy: Network Forms of Organization', *Research in Organizational Behavior*, 12 (1990), 295–336

Raymond, Eric S., *The Cathedral and the Bazaar: Musings on Linux and Open Source by an Accidental Revolutionary* (Sebastopol, CA: O'Reilly Media, 2001)

Rhodes, R. A. W., 'The New Governance: Governing without Government', *Political Studies*, 44 (1996), 652–67

Rosentall, Paul, '"Confrontation": Countering Indonesian Insurgency, 1963–66', in Gregory Fremont-Barnes (ed.), *A History of Counterinsurgency*, vol. II: *From Cyprus to Afghanistan, 1955 to the 21st Century* (Santa Barbara and Denver: Praeger, 2015), 95–125

Roxburgh, H. M. C. (ed.), *Strained to Breaking Point: A History of Britain's Relationship with Europe, 1945–2016* (Middlesex: CBY Publishing, 2016)

Sampson, Anthony, *Mandela: The Authorized Biography* (New York: Vintage Books, 2000)

Samuels, M., *Command or Control? Command, Training and Tactics in the British and German Armies, 1888–1918* (London: Routledge, 1995)

Sargent, Daniel J., *A Superpower Transformed: The Remaking of American Foreign Relations in the 1970s* (Oxford: Oxford University Press, 2015)

Schechter, Danny, *Madiba A to Z: The Many Faces of Nelson Mandela* (New York: Seven Stories Press, 2013)

Schenk, Catherine R., 'Sterling, International Monetary Reform and Britain's Applications to Join the European Economic Community in the 1960s', *Contemporary European History*, 11, 3 (2002), 345–69

Schroeder, Paul W., 'Economic Integration and the European International System in the Era of World War I', *American Historical Review*, 98, 4 (Oct. 1993), 1130–37

Scott, James C., *Seeing Like a State: How Certain Schemes to Improve the Human Condition Have Failed* (New Haven, CT, and London: Yale University Press, 1998)

Simpson, Emile, *War from the Ground Up: Twenty-First-Century Combat as Politics* (London: Hurst, 2012)

Slater, Robert, *Soros: The World's Most Influential Investor* (New York: McGraw-Hill, 2009)

Soros, George, 'Fallibility, Reflexivity, and the Human Uncertainty Principle', *Journal of Economic Methodology*, 20, 4 (2013), 309–29

———, *George Soros on Globalization* (New York: Public Affairs, 2002)

———, 'The Theory of Reflexivity', address to the MIT Department of Economics, 26 April 1994 (New York: Soros Fund Management, 1994)

———, with Bryon Wien and Krisztina Koenon, *Soros on Soros: Staying Ahead of the Curve* (New York: John Wiley & Sons, Inc., 1995)

——— and Gregor Peter Schmitz, *The Tragedy of the European Union: Disintegration or Revival?* (New York: PublicAffairs, 2014)

Staar, Richard Felix, *Foreign Policies of the Soviet Union* (Stanford: Hoover Institution Press, 1991)

Stark, David and Balazs Vedres, 'The Social Times of Network Spaces: Sequence Analysis of Network Formation and Foreign Investment in Hungary, 1987–2001', *American Journal of Sociology* 111, 5 (2006), 1367–1411

Stephens, Philip, *Politics and the Pound: The Conservatives' Struggle with Sterling* (London: Macmillan, 1996)

Stevenson, David, 'The First World War and European Integration', *International History Review*, 34, 4 (2012), 841–63

Strachan, Hew, 'British Counter-Insurgency from Malaya to Iraq', *Royal United Services Institute Journal*, 152, 6 (2007), 8–11

Stubbs, Richard, 'From Search and Destroy to Hearts and Minds: The Evolution of British Strategy in Malaya 1948–60', in Daniel Marston and Carter Malkasian (eds.), *Counterinsurgency in Modern Warfare* (Oxford and Long Island City, NY: Osprey Publishing, 2008), 101–19

Taylor, Ian, *Stuck in Middle GEAR: South Africa's post-Apartheid Foreign Relations* (Westport, CT, and London: Praeger, 2001)

Thompson, Grahame F., *Between Hierarchies and Markets: The Logic and Limits of Network Forms of Organization* (Oxford: Oxford University Press, 2003)

———, Jennifer Frances, Rosalind Levacic, and Jeremy Mitchell (eds.), *Markets, Hierarchies and Networks: The Coordination of Social Life* (London and Thousand Oaks, CA: SAGE Publications/The Open University, 1991)

Tuck, Christopher, 'Borneo 1963–66: Counter-insurgency Operations and War Termination', *Small Wars and Insurgencies*, 15, 3 (2004), 89–111

Walker, General Sir Walter, 'How Borneo was Won', *The Round Table*, 59, 233 (1969), 9–20

VIII. THE LIBRARY OF BABEL

Acemoglu, Daron, Simon Johnson, Amir Kermani, James Kwak and Todd Mitton, 'The Value of Connections in Turbulent Times: Evidence from the United States', NBER Working Paper no. 19701 (December 2013)

Allen, Jonathan and Amie Parnes, *Shattered: Inside Hillary Clinton's Doomed Campaign* (New York: Crown/Archetype, 2017)

Ali, Ayaan Hirsi, *The Challenge of Dawa: Political Islam as an Ideology and How to Counter It* (Stanford: Hoover Institution Press, 2017)

Allcott, Hunt and Matthew Gentzkow, 'Social Media and Fake News in the 2016 Election', NBER Working Paper no. 23089 (January 2017)

Army, Department of the, *Insurgencies and Countering Insurgencies*, FM 3-24/MCWP 3-33.5, 13 May 2014

———, *The U.S. Army/Marine Corps Counterinsurgency Field Manual: U.S. Army Field Manual No. 3-24: Marine Corps Warfighting Publication No. 3-33.5* (Chicago: University of Chicago Press, 2007)

Autor, David H., David Dorn and Gordon H. Hanson, 'Untangling Trade and Technology: Evidence from Local Labour Markets', *Economic Journal*, 125 (May), 621–46

Barbera, Salvador and Matthew O. Jackson, 'A Model of Protests, Revolution, and Information', working paper (February 2016)

Bell, Daniel, *The China Model: Political Meritocracy and the Limits of Democracy* (Princeton: Princeton University Press, 2015)

Berger, J. M. and Heather Perez, 'The Islamic State's Diminishing Returns on Twitter: How Suspensions are Limiting the Social Networks of English-Speaking ISIS Supporters', Program on Extremism Occasional Paper, George Washington University (February 2016)

Berger, J. M. and Jonathon Morgan, 'The ISIS Twitter Census: Defining and Describing the Population of ISIS Supporters on Twitter', The Brookings Project on U.S. Relations with the Islamic World Analysis Paper no. 20 (March 2015)

Berman, Eli, *Radical, Religious, and Violent: The New Economics of Terrorism* (Cambridge MA, and London: MIT Press, 2009)

Bodine-Baron, Elizabeth, Todd C. Helmus, Madeline Magnuson and Zev Winkelman, *Examining ISIS Support and Opposition Networks on Twitter* (Santa Monica: Rand Corporation, 2016)

Bond, Robert M., Christopher J. Fariss, Jason J. Jones, Adam D. I. Kramer, Cameron Marlow, Jaime E. Settle and James H. Fowler, 'A 61-Million-Person Experiment in Social Influence and Political Mobilization', *Nature*, 489 (September 2012), 295–8

Borges, Jorge Luis, 'The Library of Babel', in *Collected Fictions,* transl. Andrew Hurley (New York: Viking Penguin, 1998), 112–18

Boxell, Levi, Matthew Gentzkow, Jesse M. Shapiro, 'Is the Internet Causing Political Polarization? Evidence from Demographics', NBER Working Paper no. 23258 (March 2017)

Bricker, Jesse, Alice Henriques, Jacob Krimmel, John Sabelhaus, 'Measuring Income and Wealth at the Top Using Administrative and Survey Data', Brookings Papers on Economic Activity Conference Draft, 10–11 March 2016

Brinton, Christopher C., and Mung Chiang, *The Power of Networks: Six Principles That Connect Our Lives* (Princeton and Oxford: Princeton University Press, 2017)

Byrne, Liam, *Black Flag Down: Counter-Extremism, Defeating ISIS and Winning the Battle of Ideas* (London: Biteback Publishing, 2016)

Campante, Filipe and David Yanagizawa-Drott, 'Long-Range Growth: Economic Development in the Global Network of Air Links', NBER Working Paper no. 22653 (September 2016)

Case, Anne and Angus Deaton, 'Mortality and Morbidity in the 21st Century', Brookings Papers on Economic Activity Conference Drafts, 23–24 March 2017

———, 'Rising Morbidity and Mortality in Midlife among White Non-Hispanic Americans in the 21st Century', *Proceedings of the National Academy of Sciences*, 17 September 2015

Chetty, Raj, Nathaniel Hendren, Patrick Kline, Emmanuel Saez and Nicholas Turner, 'Is the United States Still a Land of Opportunity? Recent Trends in Intergenerational Mobility', NBER Working Paper no. 19844 (January 2014)

Corlett, Adam, 'Examining an Elephant: Globalisation and the Lower Middle Class of the Rich World', Resolution Foundation Report (September 2016)

Crawford, Neta C., 'U.S. Costs of Wars through 2014: $4.4 Trillion and Counting. Summary of Costs for the U.S. Wars in Iraq, Afghanistan and Pakistan', working paper 25 June 2014

Davis, Gerald F., Mina Yoo and Wayne E. Baker, 'The Small World of the American Corporate Elite, 1982–2001', *Strategic Organization* 1, 3 (2003), 301–26

Deloitte LLP, *There's No Place Like Phone: Consumer Usage Patterns in the Era of Peak Smartphone*, Global Mobile Consumer Survey 2016: UK Cut (London: Deloitte LLP, 2016)

DeMuth, Christopher, 'Can the Administrative State be Tamed?' *Journal of Legal Analysis*, 8, 1 (Spring 2016), 121–90

Dobbs, Richard, Anu Madgavkar, James Manyika, Jonathan Woetzel, Jacques Bughin, Eric Labaye, Liesbeth Huisman and Pranav Kashyap, *Poorer Than Their Parents? Flat or Falling Incomes in Advanced Economies* (McKinsey Global Institute, July 2016)

Eilstrup-Sangiovanni, M. and Calvert Jones, 'Assessing the Dangers of Illicit Networks: Why al-Qaida May be Less Threatening Than Many Think', *International Security*, 33, 2 (2008), 7–44

Elliott, Matthew, Benjamin Golub and Matthew O. Jackson, 'Financial Networks and Contagion', *American Economic Review*, 104, 10 (2014), 3115–53

Enders, Walter and Xuejuan Su, 'Rational Terrorists and Optimal Network Structure', *Journal of Conflict Resolution*, 51, 1 (February 2007), 33–57

Ferguson, Niall, *The Ascent of Money: A Financial History of the World* (London: Penguin Books, 2008)

———, *The Great Degeneration: How Institutions Decay and Economies Die* (London: Penguin Books, 2013)

———, *Kissinger*, vol. I: *1923–1968 – The Idealist* (London and New York: Allen Lane/Penguin Press, 2015)

Financial Crisis Inquiry Commission, *The Financial Crisis Inquiry Report, Authorized Edition: Final Report of the National Commission on the Causes of the Financial and Economic Crisis in the United States* (New York: PublicAffairs, 2011)

Fisher, Ali, 'Swarmcast: How Jihadist Networks Maintain a Persistent Online Presence', *Perspectives on Terrorism*, 9, 3 (June 2015), http://www.terrorismanalysts.com/pt/index.php/pot/article/view/426

Frampton, Martyn, David Goodhart and Khalid Mahmood, *Unsettled Belonging: A Survey of Britain's Muslim Communities* (London: Policy Exchange, 2016)

Funke, Manuel, Moritz Schularick and Christoph Trebesch, 'Going to Extremes: Politics after Financial Crises, 1870–2014', *European Economic Review*, 88 (2016) 227–60

Gagnon, Julien and Sanjeev Goyal, 'Networks, Markets, and Inequality', *American Economic Review*, 107, 1 (2017), 1–30

García Martínez, Antonio, *Chaos Monkeys: Inside the Silicon Valley Money Machine* (London: Ebury Press, 2016)

Glennon, Michael J., 'National Security and Double Government', *Harvard National Security Journal*, 5, 1 (2014), 1–114

Goodhart, David, *The Road to Somewhere: The Populist Revolt and the Future of Politics* (Oxford: Oxford University Press, 2017)

Habeck, Mary, with James Jay Carafano, Thomas Donnelly, Bruce Hoffman, Seth Jones, Frederick W. Kagan, Kimberly Kagan, Thomas Mahnken and Katherine Zimmerman, *A Global Strategy for Combating Al-Qaeda and the Islamic State* (Washington, DC: American Enterprise Institute, 2015)

Haldane, Andrew G., 'A Little More Conversation, a Little Less Action', speech given at the Federal Reserve Bank of San Francisco Macroeconomics and Monetary Policy Conference, 31 March 2017

Hellebrandt, Tomas and Paolo Mauro, 'The Future of Worldwide Income Distribution', Peterson Institute for International Economics Working Paper 15-7 (April 2015)

Hill, Alison L. et al., 'Emotions as Infectious Diseases in a Large Social Network: the SISa Model', *Proceedings of the Royal Society B: Biological Sciences* (2010), 1–9

Howard, Philip K., *Life Without Lawyers: Liberating Americans from Too Much Law* (New York: W. W. Norton, 2009)

———, *The Rule of Nobody: Saving America from Dead Laws and Broken Government* (New York: W. W. Norton, 2015)

Inglehart, Ronald F. and Pippa Norris, 'Trump, Brexit, and the Rise of Populism: Economic Have-Nots and Cultural Backlash', Harvard Kennedy School Working Paper RWP16-026 (August 2016)

Keller, Franziska Barbara, 'Moving Beyond Factions: Using Social Network Analysis to Uncover Patronage Networks among Chinese Elites', working paper, n.d.

———, 'Networks of Power: Using Social Network Analysis to Understand Who Will Rule and Who is Really in Charge in the Chinese Communist Party', working paper (November 2015)

Khosrokhavar, Farhad, *L'Islam dans les prisons* (Paris: Balland, 2004)

Kirkpatrick, David, *The Facebook Effect: And How It is Changing Our Lives* (London: Virgin, 2010)

Krebs, Valdis, 'Mapping Networks of Terrorist Cells', *Connections*, 24, 3 (2002), 43–52

Laurence, Jonathan, and Justin Vaisse, *Integrating Islam: Political and Religious Challenges in Contemporary France* (Washington, DC: Brookings Institution Press, 2006)

McChrystal, Stanley, *My Share of the Task* (New York: Penguin Books, 2013)

MacGill, V., 'Acephalous Groups and the Dynamics from a Complex Systems Perspective', *Proceedings of the 56th Annual Meeting of the ISSS – 2012* (San Jose, CA, 2013), 1–20

McLaughlin, Patrick A. and Robert Greene, 'Dodd–Frank's Regulatory Surge: Quantifying Its Regulatory Restrictions and Improving Its Economic Analyses', *Mercatus on Policy* (February 2014)

McLaughlin, Patrick A. and Oliver Sherouse, *The Impact of Federal Regulation on the 50 States* (Arlington, VA: Mercatus Center, George Washington University, 2016)

Marion, R. and M. Uhl-Bien, 'Complexity Theory and Al-Qaeda: Examining Complex Leadership', *Emergence: A Journal of Complexity Issues in Organizations and Management*, 5 (2003), 56–78

Mayer, Christopher and Todd Sinai, 'Network Effects, Congestion Externalities, and Air Traffic Delays: Or Why All Delays are Not Evil', NBER Working Paper no. 8701 (January 2002)

Milanovic, Branko and Christoph Lakner, 'Global Income Distribution: From the Fall of the Berlin Wall to the Great Recession', World Bank Policy Research Working Paper (December 2013)

Minor, T., 'Attacking the Nodes of Terrorist Networks', *Global Security Studies*, 3, 2 (2012), 1–12

Morozov, Evgeny V., *The Net Delusion: How Not to Liberate the World* (London: Allen Lane, 2011)

Morselli, Carlo, Cynthia Giguère and Katia Petit, 'The Efficiency/Security Trade-Off in Criminal Networks', *Social Networks*, 29, 1 (January 2007), 143–53

Murray, Charles, *Coming Apart: The State of White America, 1960–2010* (New York: Crown Forum, 2012)

Nagl, John A., *Learning to Eat Soup with a Knife: Counterinsurgency Lessons from Malaya and Vietnam* (Chicago: University of Chicago Press, 2002)

Neely, Christopher J., 'The Federal Reserve Responds to Crises: September 11th was Not the First', *Federal Reserve Bank of St. Louis Review*, 86, 2 (March/April 2004), 27–42

Oliver, Kathryn, 'Covert Networks, Structures, Process, and Types', Mitchell Centre Working Paper, 25 June 2014

Oxfam, 'An Economy for the 1%: How Privilege and Power in the Economy Drive Extreme Inequality and How This Can be Stopped', 210 Oxfam Briefing Paper, 18 January 2016

Paik, Anthony and Kenneth Sanchargin, 'Social Isolation in America: An Artifact', *American Sociological Review*, 78, 3 (2013), 339–60

Pentland, Alex, *Social Physics: How Good Ideas Spread – The Lessons from a New Science* (Melbourne and London: Scribe, 2014)

Pew Research Center Forum on Religion & Public Life, *The Future Global Muslim Population: Projections for 2010–2030* (Washington, DC: Pew Research Center, 2011)

———, *The World's Muslims: Religion, Politics and Society* (Washington, DC: Pew Research Center, 2013)

Piketty, Thomas and Emmanuel Saez, 'Income Inequality in the United States, 1913–1998', *Quarterly Journal of Economics*, 118, 1 (February 2003), 1–39

Raymond, Eric S., *The Cathedral and the Bazaar: Musings on Linux and Open Source by an Accidental Revolutionary* (Beijing and Cambridge: O'Reilly Media, 1999)

Sageman, Marc, *Understanding Terror Networks* (Philadelphia: University of Pennsylvania Press, 2004)

Sala-i-Martin, Xavier and Maxim Pinkovskiy, 'Parametric Estimations of the World Distribution of Income (1970–2006)', NBER Working Paper no. 15433 (2010)

Schmidt, Eric and Jared Cohen, 'The Digital Disruption: Connectivity and the Diffusion of Power', *Foreign Affairs*, 1 November 2010, 75–85

Scott, Hal, *Connectedness and Contagion: Protecting the Financial System from Panics* (Cambridge, MA: MIT Press, 2016)

Shirky, Clay, 'The Political Power of Social Media: Technology, the Public Sphere, and Political Change', *Foreign Affairs*, 90 (2011) 1–12

Simcox, Robin, *Al-Qaeda's Global Footprint: An Assessment of al-Qaeda's Strength Today* (London: Henry Jackson Society, 2013)

Simpson, Emile, *War from the Ground Up: Twenty-First-Century Combat as Politics* (Oxford: Oxford University Press, 2012)

Sookhdeo, Patrick, *Dawa: The Islamic Strategy for Reshaping the Modern World* (McLean, VA: Isaac Publishing, 2014)

Spar, Debora L., *Ruling the Waves: Cycles of Discovery, Chaos, and Wealth from the Compass to the Internet* (Orlando, FL: Harcourt, 2003)

Staniland, Paul, *Networks of Rebellion: Explaining Insurgent Cohesion and Collapse* (Ithaca, NY, and London: Cornell University Press, 2014)

Stuart, Hannah, *Islamist Terrorism: Analysis of Offences and Attacks in the UK (1998–2015)* (London: Henry Jackson Society, 2017)

———, *Islamist Terrorism: Key Findings and Analysis* (London: Henry Jackson Society, 2017)

Sutton, Rupert, 'Myths and Misunderstandings: Understanding Opposition to the Prevent Strategy', Henry Jackson Society Centre for the Response to Radicalisation and Terrorism, Policy Paper no. 7 (2016)

Tomlin, Ian, *Cloud Coffee House: The Birth of Cloud Social Networking and Death of the Old World Corporation* (Cirencester: Management Books, 2009)

Ugander, Johan, Lars Backstrom, Cameron Marlow and Jon Kleinberg, 'Structural Diversity in Social Contagion', *Proceedings of the National Academy of Sciences*, 109, 16 (17 April 2012), 5962–6

United States Government Accountability Office, 'Financial Crisis Losses and Potential Impacts of the Dodd-Frank Act', GAO-13-180 (January 2013)

Watts, Duncan, *Six Degrees: The Science of a Connected Age* (London: Vintage, 2004)

White, Adam J., Oren Cass and Kevin R. Kosar (eds.), *Unleashing Opportunity*, vol. II: *Policy Reforms for an Accountable Administrative State* (Washington, DC: National Affairs, 2017)

Wood, Graeme, *The Way of the Strangers: Encounters with the Islamic State* (London: Allen Lane, 2017)

World Bank Group, *Digital Dividends* (Washington, DC: International Bank for Reconstruction and Development/World Bank, 2016)

Wu, Tim, *The Master Switch: The Rise and Fall of Information Empires* (New York and London: Alfred A. Knopf/Atlantic, 2010)

Youyou, Wu, H. Andrew Schwartz, David Stillwell and Michal Kosinski, 'Birds of a Feather Do Flock Together: Behavior-Based Personality-Assessment Method Reveals Personality Similarity among Couples and Friends', *Psychological Science* (2017), 1–9

Zimmerman, Katherine, *The Al-Qaeda Network: A New Framework for Defining the Enemy* (Washington, DC: American Enterprise Institute, 2013)

IX. CONCLUSION: FACING CYBERIA

Acemoglu, Daron and Pascual Restrepo, 'Robots and Jobs: Evidence from US Labor Markets', NBER Working Paper no. 23285 (March 2017)

Allison, Graham, *Destined for War: America, China, and Thucydides's Trap* (Boston, MA, and New York: Houghton Mifflin Harcourt, 2017)

Arbesman, Samuel, *Overcomplicated: Technology at the Limits of Comprehension* (New York: Current, 2016)

Bostrom, Nicholas, *Superintelligence: Paths, Dangers, Strategies* (Oxford: Oxford University Press, 2014)

Brynjolfsson, Erik and Andrew McAfee, *The Second Machine Age: Work, Progress, and Prosperity in a Time of Brilliant Technologies* (New York: W. W. Norton, 2014)

Caplan, B. (2006), 'The Totalitarian Threat', in N. Bostrom and M. M. Cirkovic (eds.), *Global Catastrophic Risks* (Oxford: Oxford University Press, 2008), 504–18

Cirillo, Pasquale and Nassim Nicholas Taleb, 'On the Statistical Properties and Tail Risk of Violent Conflicts', Tail Risk Working Papers, 19 October 2015

Clarke, Richard A. and R. P. Eddy, *Warnings: Finding Cassandras to Stop Catastrophes* (New York: HarperCollins, 2017)

Dertouzos, Michael, *What Will Be: How the New World of Information Will Change Our Lives* (New York: HarperEdge, 1997)

Goldin, Ian and Chris Kutarna, *Age of Discovery: Navigating the Risks and Rewards of Our New Renaissance* (New York: St. Martin's Press, 2016)

Gordon, Robert J., *The Rise and Fall of American Growth: The U.S. Standard of Living since the Civil War* (Princeton: Princeton University Press, 2016)

Hayles, N. Katherine, 'Unfinished Work: From Cyborg to Cognisphere', *Theory Culture Society* 23, 159 (2006), 159–66

Heylighen, Francis and Johan Bollen, 'The World-Wide Web as a Super-Brain: From Metaphor to Model', in R. Trappl (ed.), *Cybernetics and Systems '96* (Vienna: Austrian Society for Cybernetics, 1996), 917–22

Keller, Franziska Barbara, 'Moving Beyond Factions: Using Social Network Analysis to Uncover Patronage Networks among Chinese Elites,' working paper, n.d.

———, 'Networks of Power: Using Social Network Analysis to Understand Who Will Rule and Who is Really in Charge in the Chinese Communist Party', working paper (November 2015)

Kirby, William C., Joycelyn W. Eby, Shuang L. Frost and Adam K. Frost, 'Uber in China: Driving in the Grey Zone', *Harvard Business School*, Case 9-316-135, 2 May 2016

Kissinger, Henry, *World Order* (London and New York: Allen Lane/Penguin Press, 2014)

Li, Cheng, *Chinese Politics in the Xi Jinping Era: Reassessing Collective Leadership* (Washington, DC: Brookings Institution, 2016)

Lin, Li-Wen and Curtis J. Milhaupt, 'Bonded to the State: A Network Perspective on China's Corporate Debt Market', working paper (2016)

McKinsey Global Institute, *Playing to Win: The New Global Competition for Corporate Profits* (San Francisco: McKinsey & Co., 2015)

Maier, Charles S., *Leviathan 2.0: Inventing Modern Statehood* (Cambridge, MA: Belknap Press, 2014)

Nye, Joseph, 'Deterrence and Dissuasion in Cyberspace', *International Security*, 41, 3 (Winter 2016/17), 44–71

Pinker, Steven, *The Better Angels of Our Nature: Why Violence Has Declined* (New York: Viking, 2011)

Schiedel, Walter, *The Great Leveler: Violence and the History of Inequality from the Stone Age to the Twenty-First Century* (Princeton: Princeton University Press, 2017)

Schwab, Klaus, *The Fourth Industrial Revolution* (Cologne and Geneva: World Economic Forum, 2016)

Scott, James C., *Two Cheers for Anarchism: Six Easy Pieces on Autonomy, Dignity, and Meaningful Work and Play* (Princeton and Oxford: Princeton University Press)

Slaughter, Anne-Marie, *The Chessboard and the Web: Strategies of Connection in a Networked World: The 2016 Henry L. Stimson Lectures* (New Haven, CT: Yale University Press, 2017)

Snyder, Timothy, *On Tyranny: Twenty Lessons from the Twentieth Century* (New York: Tim Duggan Books, 2017)

Spier, F., *Big History and the Future of Humanity* (Malden, MA, and Oxford: Wiley-Blackwell, 2011)

Steinhoff, Judith B., 'Urban Images and Civic Identity in Medieval Sienese Painting', in Timothy B. Smith and Judith B. Steinhoff (eds.), *Art as Politics in Late Medieval and Renaissance Siena* (Farnham, Surrey, and Burlington, VT: Ashgate, 2012), 15–38

Thiel, Peter with Blake Masters, *Zero to One: Notes on Startups, or How to Build the Future* (New York: Crown Business, 2014)

Turchin, Peter, *Ages of Discord: A Structural-Demographic Analysis of American History* (Chaplin, CT: Beresta Books, 2016)

Wright, Robert, *Nonzero: The Logic of Human Destiny* (New York: Vintage, 2001)

Index